CROATIA

Land, People, Culture

CROATIA
Land, People, Culture

VOLUME II

Editor
FRANCIS H. ETEROVICH
DE PAUL UNIVERSITY

Associate Editor
CHRISTOPHER SPALATIN
MARQUETTE UNIVERSITY

Published for the Editorial Board by
UNIVERSITY OF TORONTO PRESS

Printed in Canada by
University of Toronto Press,
Toronto and Buffalo
ISBN 0-8020-3226-5

Preface

We are pleased to present this second volume in a series which will eventually cover the entire cultural and political history of the Croatian people. In this volume, as in the first and indeed in the whole series, the major geographical area involved in the discussion is that of the two republics of Croatia and Bosnia-Hercegovina of present-day Yugoslavia, since the overwhelming majority of Croatians live there. However, the treatment is extended to the Croatian ethnic communities found in the other four Yugoslav republics and elsewhere in the world whenever the necessary data are available.

This second volume again comprises a collection of single contributions on various subjects by selected individuals. Generally the articles stand on their own, but there is naturally some overlapping of material from article to article in such areas as political and literary history because of their relevance to the development of numerous topics.

The first chapter, on Croatian political history from 1526 to 1918, is a continuation of the third chapter of volume I, and deals principally with the Croatian lands of Croatia Proper and Slavonia. The political history of the other Croatian lands of Dalmatia, Istria, Bosnia-Hercegovina, and the republic of Dubrovnik is not included here, because of the divergent course it took during the period in question, but will be taken up in subsequent volumes of the series. The history of all the lands inhabited by the Croatian people from 1918 to 1945 is also reserved for an article in a later volume.

Most of the other historical contributions in this and the preceding volume carry their accounts to the year 1945. Events in Croatian cultural and political life subsequent to that year have been excluded for the present because they are still too close to us to permit a proper historical perspective. The Communist experiment in postwar Yugoslavia has so often changed its basic policies, both economic and political, that only at some future time will we be able to ascertain the meaning of events and determine the success or failure of any aspect of that experiment. A description and brief assessment of the postwar period as it pertains to Croatian culture will, however, be offered in the final volume of the series.

Two specialized studies of Croatian history have been added to the three on the military, economic, and ethical aspects published in the first volume. The first is on maritime history, and the second on the history of book-printing to 1940. The omission from the latter of the period 1940–5, which was one of the most productive periods in book-printing in Croatia, will be remedied in a future volume. We would record here our regret at the death of Dr. Ivan Esih, who was able to complete his article for this volume to the year 1940.

A survey of Croatian literature for the years 1400 to 1835 is included. The period from 1835 to 1895 was covered in the first volume, and a study in a succeeding volume will deal with the remaining period up to 1945. This division of the treatment of literary history, as of political history, into several articles, rather than the single contribution allotted to most of the other aspects of Croatian culture, was felt to be necessary because of its great importance in the national life.

The brief study of the Croatian language offered here coincides in tenor and standpoint with those of Croatian linguistic scholars at home, as is evident from the recent "Declaration on the Name and Position of the Croatian Literary Language" issued in Zagreb on March 15, 1967, and signed by the nineteen Croatian cultural and scientific institutions. We are pleased to note this agreement between Croatian scholars at home and abroad.

The essays on the cultural achievements of the Bosnian and Hercegovinian Muslims, and on the ethnic and religious history of the population of Bosnia and Hercegovina, are the first of their kind in the English language. A transliteration table is included in the first of these to help the reader in the pronunciation of Arabic, Persian, and Turkish words and proper names.

The Croatian immigrants in North America, both in the United States and in Canada, are discussed in the two final essays, that on the United States naturally being considerably the longer because of the much greater size of the Croatian community there.

Finally, much informative material has been appended to this volume. The first appendix contains biographies of the authors with special emphasis on their academic and professional backgrounds. The second is a list of geographical names of places in Croatian lands and those historically connected with them, revised and extended from that appearing in volume I. Since Croatian words and proper names appear frequently throughout this volume, the third appendix is a table of pronunciation of Croatian letters designed to facilitate reading. Finally, for ease in locating names and topics, an extensive index has been included.

The authors represented in this volume, like those in the first, are specialists in the topics they discuss. Each author is responsible for the views expressed in his paper. We respect these views wherever there is no agreement on the interpretation of facts, feeling that a diversity of opinions on complex problems not yet solved definitively will enable the reader to appreciate them from more than one point of view. The articles of Dr. Balić and Dr. Mandić, which deal wholly or partially with Bosnian and Hercegovinian Muslims, should prove interesting in this respect, as should the essay on political history in which the author reassesses many views held by Croatian historians and, in particular, defends Austrian rule in Croatia. The approach to the Croatian language too, though common to Croatian linguists, differs from that widely accepted by linguists of other nations.

All contributions have been amply documented, and each concludes with a list of books and articles for further study and research. Bibliographical references in Croatian or oriental languages have been translated into English. The articles themselves generally exceed in length those of the first volume, but most of them cover four centuries of cultural development, a period far too long for treatment in the fifty-odd pages common to the essays in volume I. Considerable space has also been allotted to the economic and cultural contributions of Croatian immigrants to the United States. Finally, the articles were completed at the end of 1968, and the information and bibliographical data contained in them therefore end at that date.

A final comment on the structure of this series. It was our original intention to wait until all the contributions to the complete work were ready for printing and then to publish the entire series at one time. However, after due consideration, we felt that it would be preferable to offer completed essays without delay to the scholar and general reader, since much of the material is simply not otherwise available in English. Thus, in volume II as in volume I, we have included those contributions that were ready for publication. It is our hope that, when all the contributions to the series have been published, we may bring the work up to date and rearrange the articles logically and chronologically. Meanwhile, we have tried to serve the reader as best we can. We have exercised great care and concern to offer him the best available information and the most balanced interpretation of complex cultural phenomena. If this volume reaches the audience and achieves the use of volume I, we shall feel amply rewarded for our labor.

Francis H. Eterovich

Acknowledgments

Collective works are the result of combined efforts. We have been helped by many men and women – translators, librarians, typists, and proofreaders. It is our pleasant duty to mention the names of those who helped us most assiduously. The language editing has been the long and arduous task of Mrs. Zahava Dorinson of the English Department of De Paul University. We have no adequate words to express our heartfelt thanks to her for the work she has done. The magnitude of her task can perhaps be appreciated more fully if we point out that very few contributions came to us written in English. Mr. Ronald Lane of the Philosophy Department of the College of St. Benedict, St. Joseph, Minnesota, also contributed to the language editing. Our sincere thanks to him. Christopher Spalatin, our associate editor, and his lovely wife Helen deserve our special gratitude. They have indexed this volume as well as volume I.

We should like to note the names of the benefactors who have helped us to defray many expenses during the preparation of the manuscript of this volume. Our thanks in the first place go to Dr. Ivan Tuškan and his wife Dr. Maria Kroker-Tuškan, physicians in Cincinnati, and to Louis Chukman, Chicago; then to the Dominican Sisters, Sherbrooke, Quebec, Canada; Dr. Vlado Gračanin, Cincinnati; Osman Hatic, Milford, Ohio; Željko Keglević, Chicago; Dr. Živko Marčić, Milwaukee; John Prepolec, Detroit; Bogdan Raditsa, New York; and Peter Dicca, Lourenco Marques, Portuguese Africa.

The last, but not the least of our thanks go to our advisers: Kamil Avdich, head, Acquisitions Department, Northwestern Illinois State College, Chicago; Gerald Govorchin, University of Miami, Coral Gables, Florida; Josip Hamm, University of Vienna; Dominik Mandić, Croatian Historical Institute, Chicago; Vladimir Markotic, University of Calgary, Calgary, Canada; Petar Stanković, editor of *Hrvatski Glas* (Croatian Voice), Winnipeg, Canada; and Joseph Strmecki, University of Wisconsin, Madison, Wisconsin.

Contents

PREFACE, by Francis H. Eterovich, editor v

ACKNOWLEDGMENTS ix

LIST OF ILLUSTRATIONS xvi

LIST OF MAPS xvii

1 CROATIAN POLITICAL HISTORY 1526–1918, by Stanko Guldescu 3
The Cetin Election of January 1, 1527 3
The Struggle for Slavonia and Other Croatian Lands 6
The Founding of the Frontiers 8
The "Long War" and the Bocskay Rebellion 13
The Varaždin Border and the "Vlach" Statute of 1630 15
Seventeenth-Century Croatia 17
The Zrinski-Frankapan Conspiracy 19
The War of Liberation, 1682–99 23
Eighteenth-Century Croatia-Slavonia 24
The Croatian Pragmatic Sanction, 24; Maria Theresa and the Croatians, 29; The Josephine Era, 1780–90, 30; The Sabors of 1790–2, 31
Croatian Participation in the French Revolutionary and Napoleonic Wars 33
Croatia-Slavonia from 1815 to 1848 38
The Croatian Question 1849–68 40
The Schwarzenberg and Bach Eras 41
A Missed Opportunity, 1860–7 43
The Nagodba (1868) 47
The Great Croatian Program and the Croatian Serbs 50
The Origins of the Peasant Party 60
The Trialist Program on the Eve of Sarajevo 63

The Croatian Kingdom in 1914 64
The Sarajevo Murders and the Problem of Bosnia-Hercegovina 65
Croatian Participation in the War of 1914–18 70
The Yugoslav Committee 76
The Future of Croatia 82
Caporetto and Its Consequences 84
Austria Delenda Est! 86
The Croatian Dilemma in the Fall of 1918 89
The Last Round 91
Stjepan Radić and the Czechs 95
Bibliography 96
Croatian Political Chronology 1526–1918 105
Croatian and Bosnian Rulers 112

2 MARITIME HISTORY OF THE EASTERN ADRIATIC, by Willy A. Bachich 119
Prehistoric Times and Antiquity 119
The Middle Ages: 614–1420 122
The Early Modern Period: 1420–1815 128
The Areas under Venetian Rule, 129; The Flourishing Republic of Dubrovnik, 131; The Northern Coast and the Uskoks, 134
Austrian Rule: 1815–1918 137
The First World War: 1914–18 145
Between the World Wars: 1918–40 149
The Second World War: 1941–5 152
Bibliography 154

3 THE CROATIAN LANGUAGE, by Christopher Spalatin 157
Phonetics and Orthography 160
Accent 164
Morphology and Syntax 165
Bibliography 172

4 LITERATURE 1400–1835, by Franjo Trogrančić 175
The Fifteenth and Sixteenth Centuries: Humanism and Renaissance among the Croatians 175
The Beginnings of Croatian Literature in Dalmatia, 175; The First Poets, 180; The Theater in Dubrovnik, 186; The Literary Activity of the Protestants, 192; Kajkavian Literature, 194
The Seventeenth Century 195
The Dubrovnik Trio of the Golden Age: Gundulić, Palmotić, and Bunić, 195; The Imitators of Gundulić and Palmotić in Dubrovnik and Dalmatia, 201; Linguistic and Historical Literature, 205;

Literature in Bosnia, 207; The Counter-Reformation in Northern Croatia, 208; Literature in Upper Croatia, 210

The Eighteenth Century 214

Dalmatia and Dubrovnik, 215; Folklore Collectors, Latinists, Philologists, Historians, and Scientists, 219; Grabovac and Kačić, 223; Literary Activity in Slavonia, 228; Northern Croatia at the Dawn of the National Awakening, 233

Bibliography 240

5 THE DEVELOPMENT OF BOOK PRINTING 1483–1940, by Ivan Esih 251

The Beginnings in Venice 251

Istria and the Croatian Littoral 253

First Editions of Secular Literary Works 260

Croatian Protestant Literature 261

Printing in Other Lands 263

Zagreb 263

Dubrovnik 270

Zadar 272

Varaždin 273

Osijek 274

Karlovac 275

Sarajevo and Mostar 276

Some Smaller Cities 280

Lithography 281

Bookbinding 282

Deluxe Editions 284

Bookplating 288

Bibliography 289

6 CULTURAL ACHIEVEMENTS OF BOSNIAN AND HERCEGOVINIAN MUSLIMS, by Smail Balić 299

Transliteration of Arabic, Persian, and Ottoman Turkish Letters 299

Transliteration of Arabic Letters, 299; Transliteration of Persian and Ottoman Turkish, 300; Modern Turkish Spelling, 301

Prefatory Remarks 301

Foreign Words, 301; Personal Data on the Bosnian Writers, 302; Muslim and Christian (Gregorian) Calendars, 302

Introduction 302

Folk Culture 305

Poetry, 305; Epic Folk Poetry, 306; Lyric Folk Poetry, 312; Folk Music, 317; Folk Dramatic Art and Folk Tales, 319; Decorative Folk Art, 320; Dwellings, 321

Advanced Culture 323
Literary Activity of the Bosniaks in Oriental Languages, 323; Writers in Arabic, 324; Writers in Persian, 326; Writers in Turkish, 327; Poetry in Croatian, 328; Miniature Painting, Calligraphy, and Decorative Bookbinding, 330; Schools, Seminaries, and Other Institutions, 331; Architecture, 333

Appendix: Bosnian Authors Who Wrote in Oriental Languages 340
Prose Writers, 340; Poets, 348

Bibliography 354

7 THE ETHNIC AND RELIGIOUS HISTORY OF BOSNIA AND HERCEGOVINA, by Dominik J. Mandić 362

Croatians in Bosnia and Hercegovina 363
The Settlement of Slavs in the Balkans, 363; Bosnia and Hercegovina Were Croatian Lands in the Middle Ages, 364; The Conversion to Christianity of the Croatians in Bosnia, 366; The Bogomils in Bosnia and Their Conversion to Catholicism, 366

The Origin of the Muslims in Bosnia and Hercegovina 367
Were Muslim and Catholic Inhabitants of Bosnia and Hercegovina during Ottoman Rule Aware of Their Origin? 374; The Awakening of Croatian National Consciousness among Muslims in Bosnia and Hercegovina in the Nineteenth Century, 379

Origin and Colonization of the Present-Day Serbs in Bosnia and Hercegovina 381
Forcible Conversion of Croatian Catholics to the Orthodox Faith, 381; The Roman Colonization of Moors in the Balkans and in Other Regions of Europe, 383; The Role of the Bulgarians, Albanians, Greeks, and Armenians in Creating the Serbian Ethnic Group in Bosnia and Hercegovina, 386; Colonization of Bosnia and Hercegovina by the Ethnic Serbs, 386; Serbization of Vlachs, Orthodox Croatians, and Non-Slavs, 387

Summary and Statistical Data 388

Bibliography 390

8 THE CROATIAN IMMIGRANTS IN THE UNITED STATES OF AMERICA, by George J. Prpić 394

History 394
Croatian Immigration before 1880, 394; Croatian Immigration 1880–1900, 396; The High Point of Croatian Immigration, 398; The Number of Croatian Immigrants in the United States, 400

Life within Croatian Settlements 407
A Period of Development, 407; Religious Life, 408; Socioeconomic Activity, 410; Social and Political Activity, 412

The Croatian Contribution to the United States 423
Missionaries, 423; Early Pioneers, 425; Nikola Tesla, a Great

Inventor, 430; Captain Anthony Lucas, 432; Outstanding Cultural Contributions, 433; Other Contributions, 455; Sacrifice in Lives, 460
Conclusion 462
Selected Bibliography 464
Appendix: Croatian Papers and Periodicals in the United States 1884–1960 475

9 CROATIANS IN CANADA, by Nedo Pavešković 479
Immigration 479
Prior to the First World War, 479; Between the Two World Wars, 482; After the Second World War, 484
Life within Croatian Settlements 485
Prior to the First World War, 485; Between the Two World Wars, 486; After the Second World War, 489
Contribution to Canada 494
Folklore and Folk Music, 494; Music, 495; Education, 496; Arts, Literature, and Journalism, 496; Politics, 499; Sports, 499; Individual Contributions in Various Fields, 500; Economy, 501; Contribution in Wars, 503
Bibliography 504

APPENDIXES 507
A Biographies of the Authors 509
B Geographical Names 516
C Pronunciation of Croatian Letters 522

INDEX 523

Illustrations

Willy A. Bachich, "Maritime History of the Eastern Adriatic"
Between pp. 142 and 143
The harbor of Dubrovnik in the sixteenth century
Model of a large Ragusan carrack from about 1520
A large Ragusan sailing ship (*coca*), first half of the fifteenth century
Argosies returning in convoy home to Dubrovnik in 1520, saluting St. Blaise before arrival
Ships of the Uskoks in the harbor of Senj in the sixteenth century
Austro-Hungarian battleships, destroyers, and torpedo boats in 1913
Admiral Maksimilian Njegovan (1858–1930)

Smail Balić, "Cultural Achievements of Bosnian and Hercegovinian Muslims"
Between pp. 334 and 335
Mosque of Mehmed Pasha Ṣoqollu (Sokolović) at Istanbul, Turkey, facade
Pillar in the interior of the mosque of Rustam Pasha, the Croatian, at Istanbul, Turkey
The fortified city of Počitelj in Hercegovina, from the fifteenth century
Mosque of Farhād Pasha in Banjaluka
Model of the mosque of Ghāzī Khusrew Beg in Sarajevo
Courtyard of the Islamic Sheriat Theological School in Sarajevo
The Old Bridge on the Neretva River in Mostar, built in 1566
Mosque of Ḳara-Göz Beg at Mostar
The Old Bridge in Mostar at night
Ḥammām (public bath) at Mostar, from the sixteenth century

George J. Prpić, "The Croatian Immigrants in the United States of America"
Between pp. 430 and 431
Statue of Father Joseph Kundek, Jasper, Indiana

The new headquarters of the Croatian Fraternal Union at Kingston and Delaney Drives, Pittsburgh
Duquesne University Tamburitzans of Pittsburgh
A young Duquesne tamburitzan with his instrument
Maksimilian Vanka, painter, *Four Riders of the Apocalypse*, oil, 1957
Maksimilian Vanka, *Angelus in Croatia* (or *Faith in Croatia*)
Maksimilian Vanka, *The Morning Shift*
Paul Kufrin, sculptor, *David Lloyd George*
Paul Kufrin, *American Historical Indian*, looking intensely at approaching enemy from the top of a rock
Paul Kufrin, *After the Dream*
Joseph Turkalj, sculptor, detail of *Moses*, an 18-foot bronze statue standing in front of the Notre Dame University Library
Joseph Turkalj, *The Memories* (marble), 1961
Paul Draženović, "Alaskan pioneer gold miner"

Maps

facing page

Croatia and Bosnia-Hercegovina Today iii

HISTORICAL MAPS

"Croatian Political History 1526–1918"
The Triune Kingdom in 1526 before the Battle of Mohács 6
Reliquiae reliquiarum (Relics of the Relics) of the Croatian Kingdom in 1594 7
The Croatian Lands from the Treaty of Zsitva-Török 1606 to the Peace Treaty of Sistova 1791 24
Croatia and the Military Frontier 1785 25
Civil and Military Croatia after the Napoleonic Wars (1806–13) 34
Austrian Illyria 1814–22 35
Croatia in 1848 under Ban Jelačić 40

"Maritime History of the Eastern Adriatic"
Dalmatia (Illyria) before the Roman Period: From the Seventh to the First Century B.C. 124
Roman Illyricum from Augustus to the Sixth Century A.D. 124
Dalmatia and the Republic of Dubrovnik from the Fifteenth to the Beginning of the Nineteenth Century 125
The Eastern Adriatic Coast 1814–1918 140

CROATIA

Land, People, Culture

1

Croatian Political History 1526–1918

STANKO GULDESCU

THE CETIN ELECTION OF JANUARY 1, 1527

After the fall of the Croatian Kingdom of Bosnia in 1463, and the subjugation of the Croatian feudal lords in Hercegovina twenty years later, the next objective of the Turkish power was the conquest of the ancient Triune Kingdom of Croatia, Slavonia, and Dalmatia. Venice had amputated most of Dalmatia during the early part of the century,[1] and Ottoman possession of Bosnia imperiled the defense of what was left of this complex. Geographically the Croatian areas are tied together, and Turkish control of the valley of the Sana River, with the twin fortresses of Ključ and Kamengrad, thrust a Muslim wedge deep into the heart of the Croatian Kingdom proper. From these vantage points the Turks could strike quickly across the Livno and Livanjsko Polje into Croatia itself. Although the Jajce Banovina, founded by Croatian and Bosnian nobles during the reign of King Matthias Corvinus (1458–90), still held out, it could not protect the entire Croatian countryside against the plundering Turkish horse.

King Matthias's reign is a celebrated one in Hungarian historiography. However, his Croatian subjects received little help from him in containing the Ottoman menace. Matthias was more interested in aggrandizing his dominions at the expense of Austria and Bohemia than he was in protecting his Croatian possessions. Upon his death (1490), Hungary and Croatia-Slavonia passed again under the scepter of the Jagellon dynasty of Poland-Lithuania.[2] Owing to the indifference of the two

1/Between 1409 and 1420 the Venetians mastered the coastal areas of Dalmatia. Later in the century the Turks began to take over the inland districts.

2/Vladislav I Jagellon had been king of Hungary and Croatia-Slavonia from 1440 to 1444.

Jagellons who ruled between 1490 and 1526, the Croatians found themselves subjected to increasing Turkish pressure.

As far back as 1463, the Jagellons had concluded a treaty of mutual inheritance with the Austrian Hapsburg House. When, in 1493, the Ottomans inflicted a disastrous defeat upon the Croatians in the battle of Krbava Polje, Maximilian I Hapsburg at once directed his captains to render all possible assistance to the Croatians whenever they requested it.[3] Maximilian, the "last of the knights," enjoyed much popularity in Croatia. For a time he was in control of the northern part of the Triune Kingdom. His grandchildren, Ferdinand and Maria, married Anna and Louis Jagellon. Additional family inheritance pacts cleared the way for the Hapsburgs to succeed to the Hungarian and Croatian thrones when and if the Jagellon line became extinct.

But, in 1505, the Hungarian diet met on Rakos Field to adopt a resolution that was designed to exclude non-Magyars from the Hungarian throne in the future.[4] Vladislav II Jagellon did not enact this resolution into law, and in March of the following year he concluded still another family pact with Maximilian [5] who, for his part, let it be known publicly that he did not recognize the decision taken on Rakos Field. As a matter of fact, this resolution had been forced through the Magyar legislative body by a "pressure group" drawn from the baronial and lower nobility and headed by the jurist Stephen Verböczy[6] and the wealthy *vojvoda* (governor) of Transylvania, John Zápolya. The resolution had no real legal validity[7] even though the high dignitaries and prelates of the kingdom signed it. They soon repudiated this action, but the "national party" continued to invoke it against the claims of the Hapsburgs. As long as there were male Jagellons available, the question of the legality of the Rakos resolution was only of academic interest in any case.[8]

Maximilian died in 1519, and his oldest grandson, who, since 1516, had reigned over Spain and her possessions as King Charles I, succeeded him as Holy Roman or German Emperor. In 1521 Charles and Ferdinand

3/Dr. Stjepan Srkulj, *Hrvatska povijest u devetnaest karata*/Croatian History Illustrated in Nineteen Maps (Zagreb, 1937), 71.

4/The original Latin text of this resolution is given in Henrik Marczali (ed.), *Enchiridion fontium historiae Hungarorum* (A mágyar történet kútföinek kézikönyve) (Budapest, 1901), 317–20.

5/Text in *ibid.*, 336.

6/Author of the Tripartite Code which fastened serfdom "in perpetuity" upon the Magyar peasants.

7/However, it might be noted that neither did the Tripartitum. Nonetheless the latter remained the basis of Hungarian constitutional law until 1848.

8/See Ivan Kukuljević-Sakcinski (ed.), *Jura regni Croatiae, Dalmatiae et Slavoniae* (3 vols.; Zagreb, 1861–2), II, 254–9.

divided the Hapsburg lands between them. Ferdinand received the hereditary family holdings in Austria, while Charles kept Spain, the Netherlands, the Germanies, and the overseas possessions.

As archduke of Austria, Ferdinand ordered Nicholas Salm, high captain of the Austrian military forces, to aid the Croatians in defending the Triune Kingdom against Turkish attacks, particularly in the sector along the Una River. Many Croatians entered the Hapsburg service at this time. In 1522 Austrian soldiers were sent to help in the defense of Sinj, Klis, Krupa, Bihać, and Jajce.

Louis II Jagellon fell on the field of Mohács on August 29, 1526. He was the last male Jagellon, and many Croatians wished to have Ferdinand succeed him as their king.[9] Even before the death of Louis, Sabor, in correspondence with the archduke, had referred to him as "our natural ruler" and had alluded to Croatia-Slavonia as "Your Majesty's Kingdom."[10]

John Zápolya, however, had not involved the army that he commanded in the Mohács disaster. With his cohorts intact he was able to dominate, momentarily, the situation in central and eastern Hungary (Transylvania). He took possession of the Crown of St. Stephen and of the Hungarian royal symbols, and on November 10, part of the Hungarian estates elected and crowned him king.

Zápolya owned huge estates in Slavonia, and he was anxious to extend his rule over both Croatia and Slavonia. French diplomacy was active in his behalf,[11] and after some preliminary dealings with Ferdinand,[12] Krsto and Bernardin, of the Croatian House of Frankapan, espoused his cause. On January 7, 1527, the Slavonian Sabor recognized his accession.[13] Six days previously, however, the Croatian Sabor had met at Cetin, where it proclaimed Ferdinand king with the stipulation that he would provide for the defense of Croatia-Slavonia against the Turks and would respect the rights and privileges granted by former kings to the

9/L. Südland [Ivo Pilar], *Južno-slavensko pitanje*/The Southern Slav Problem (2nd ed.; Zagreb, 1943), 24–5.

10/Matija Mesić, "Hrvati nakon bana Berislavića do mohačke bitke"/The Croatians after [the Death of] Ban Berislavić up to the Battle of Mohács, *Rad* (Yugoslav Academy), XXII (1873), 100.

11/E. Laszowski-Szeliga (ed.), *Monumenta habsburgica regni Croatiae, Dalmatiae, Slavoniae* (3 vols.; Zagreb, 1914–17), I, 37–8. Vols. XXXV, XXXVIII, and XL of *Monumenta spectantia historiam Slavorum meridionalium* (43 vols.; Zagreb, 1869–1918).

12/On Krsto Frankapan's negotiations with Ferdinand, see F. Šišić (ed.), *Acta comitialia regni Croatiae, Dalmatiae et Slavoniae* (5 vols.; Zagreb, 1912–18), I, 11–12. (Vols. XXXIII, XXXVI, XXXIX, XLI, and XLIII of MSHSM referred to in footnote 11.)

13/*Ibid.*, I, 71–80.

Croatian nobility.[14] The latter at this time were, of course, the standard-bearers of the national interests of the Triune Kingdom.

It is unfortunate that the Croatians were divided among themselves as to who was the legitimate ruler of their country. Only the Magyar land-holding element in Slavonia felt any real attachment to Zápolya, however.[15] When Krsto Frankapan fell in battle against the Hapsburg forces on September 26, 1527, the Slavonian estates hastily assembled to pledge their loyalty to Ferdinand.[16]

THE STRUGGLE FOR SLAVONIA AND OTHER CROATIAN LANDS

On the same day that Frankapan fell at Varaždin, the Hapsburg forces defeated Zápolya's army at Tokay. "King John" had to flee to Poland. Among his advisers were numbered such Croatians as Bishops Simon Erdödi and Frano Jožefić, of Zagreb and Senj respectively, and the curious adventurer and diplomat Juraj (George) Utišenić, better known as Martinuzzi or "Friar George," and these persuaded the vojvoda to call in the Turks to enable him to hold his own against the Hapsburg power.[17]

14/On the Cetin election of January 1, 1527, and the recognition by the Croatians of the Hapsburg pretensions, see *ibid.*, I, 50–65; II, 459–61. See also J. Chmel (ed.) *Aktenstücke zur Geschichte Croatien und Slavonien in den Jahren 1526 und 1527* (Vienna, 1846), 35–38; *Jura regni*, II, 10–22; F. Šišić, *Pregled povjesti hrvatskoga naroda*/A Survey of the History of the Croatian People (3rd ed.; Zagreb, 1962), 268–70, and his *Die Wahl Ferdinands I von Österreich zum König von Kroatien* (Zagreb, 1917). The original documents dealing with the Cetin proceedings are preserved in the Wiener Staatsarchiv, Hungarica, in Vienna.

15/Krsto Frankapan acknowledged this fact himself in a letter written to the bishop of Senj on July 31, 1527. For the text of this communication see Ivan Kukuljević-Sakcinski, *Acta Croatica* (Zagreb, 1863), 230–2; see also Karl, Baron v. Czoernig, *Ethnographie der österr. Monarchie* (3 vols.; Vienna, 1857), II, 211; Pilar, *Južno-slavensko pitanje*, 24–8.

16/*Acta comitialia*, I, 134. On the collapse of the Zápolya faction in Slavonia, see also Pilar, *Južno-slavensko pitanje*, 25; Franjo Frankapan to Pope Paul III (no date), *Mon. habsburgica*, III, 47–9.

17/Erdödi's role in the Hapsburg-Zápolya contest was especially ambiguous. On January 7, 1528, he took an oath of loyalty to Ferdinand (*Acta comitialia*, I, 145). Later he repudiated this oath and again incited the Turks to invade Croatia. Only in 1530, after the Ottomans had twice refused to send additional help to him, did he espouse Ferdinand's cause permanently. See *Mon. habsburgica*, I, 293–5, 300–1, 309, 315, 318–22, 325–6, 329–30, 337, 346–7, 369–70, 375–6, 379–80, 400–1. Yet in 1537 his inability to provision the Hapsburg army caused the failure of the "Katzianer Expedition" of that year. The miscarriage of this carefully planned campaign resulted in the loss of Slavonia to the Turks for a century and a half, during which time it became a *pusto mjesto* (desert).

The result of Turkish intervention in the Hapsburg-Zápolya struggle was that Slavonia and parts of Croatia became battlegrounds. Despite the assistance he received from the Ottomans, who in 1529 advanced to the walls of Vienna itself, Zápolya had to make a number of rather grudging accommodations with his Hapsburg rival. By the first of these he abandoned his claim to the throne of Croatia-Slavonia, a fact which in itself demonstrates the separate identity of the Croatian kingdom at this epoch. On February 24, 1528, he agreed that if Ferdinand survived him, Hungary too would pass into Hapsburg hands.[18] Then, however, he married a young Magyar noblewoman who gave him an heir.

When the vojvoda died in 1540, "Friar George" counseled the widow to ask the Ottomans to defend the birthright of her son. Constantinople answered her plea willingly enough, but only to make central and southern Hungary Turkish pashaliks (provinces). Zápolya's widow and infant son had to abandon even Buda to the Turks, who soon made it a city of beggars. In the intermittent warfare that followed, Srijem and most of Slavonia were mastered by the Turks. The Croatians in these territories remained loyal to Ferdinand to the bitter end, despite the fact that the Ottomans promised to protect the property of anyone who declared for Zápolya's heir. Even the *kmets* (serfs) were offered their freedom if they would turn against those of their masters who supported the Hapsburgs. Nevertheless, the Slavonian Croatians offered such obstinate resistance to the tide of Ottoman conquest that the survivors did not dare to remain in Slavonia once their adversaries had conquered the greater part of the province but emigrated to more securely held Hapsburg territory. The final consequence of the struggle for Slavonia was that Srijem[19] was subordinated to the pashalik of Buda while the rest of Turkish-occupied Slavonia and the Lika and Krbava areas of Croatia proper were placed under the Bosnian Sanjak Beg. Only the combined diplomacy of France and Venice stopped the Ottomans from annexing all of Hungary including Transylvania.[20] Although the French and Venetians had incited the Porte to attack the Hapsburg power, they did not want to effect the total obliteration of the historic Hungarian state.

By 1548 "Friar George" realized that he had erred in facilitating the

18/On this peace see Šišić, *Pregled*, 275. For a Turkish judgment of the arrangement, see Matija Baronyay (Baronja) to Ban Nadásdy, June 7, 1538, *Mon. habsburgica*, II, 511–12.

19/The reports of Bans Thomas Nadásdy and Peter Keglević, written to Ferdinand in 1538, prove that Srijem at this time still was considered to be a part of the Croatian kingdom. For its status during the Middle Ages see S. Guldescu, *History of Medieval Croatia* (The Hague, 1964), index.

20/Šišić, *Pregled*, 272.

entrance of the Turks into Hungary. He entered into some rather devious negotiations with Ferdinand's field marshal, John Castaldo, who eventually had him murdered when he discovered that the Friar was dealing with the Turks as well.[21] Since Castaldo had to abandon Transylvania to the Ottomans anyway, the murder was pointless. The Porte made Zápolya's son its vassal ruler of Transylvania.

Now the high tide of Ottoman conquest had been reached. To be sure, Kostajnica fell in 1556, and Sisak and Bihać were lost as late as 1591–3. During these years 35,000 Croatians were borne away to the slave markets of the East. But the effect of the continuing Turkish pressure was to produce what some historians have referred to as a "masterpiece of Hapsburg improvisation," the Military Frontiers, the famed Krajina of Croatian song and story.

THE FOUNDING OF THE FRONTIERS

As early as 1518, the Croatian estates had effected an understanding with the diets of "Inner Austria" (Carinthia, Carniola, and Styria) which provided for mutual assistance against Turkish attacks. When this proved inadequate, the Austrians asked that an outer defense zone be established in Croatia between the Una and Kupa rivers. When so much of Slavonia, Croatia, and Hungary was lost to the Turks between 1526 and 1538, the Hapsburgs moved to meet the demands of the estates. They created a military defense zone which extended northwards from a point close to the junction of the Una and Sava through the valley of the Ilova and over Bilo Mountain to the Drava River. Essentially this first loosely organized border district was a security zone established to contain the Ottoman raids emanating from the newly established pashalik of Požega which Sultan Soliman II had formed from the Slavonian territory he had conquered.[22]

In the years that followed, the Muslims of the adjacent Turkish provinces organized a military border district of their own. It stretched from the Transylvanian frontier to the mouth of the Zrmanja River. Besides

21/On Utišenić see Ognjeslav Utješenović, "Izprave k životopisu kardinala br. Gjorgja Utiešenovica prozvanoga Martinusiem"/Documents on the Life of Cardinal Brother George Utiešenović called Martinuzzi (or Martinusi), *Starine* (Yugoslav Academy), XII (1880), 42–128.

22/On the early days of the Vojna Krajina see Karl Bernhard Edler v. Hietzinger, *Statistik der Militärgrenze des österr. Kaiserstaates* (3 vols.; Vienna, 1817–23), I, 15–28. Hietzinger's account should be compared with that given in Nicholas Istvanffy, *Historiarum de rebus Hungaricis libri XXXIV* (Köln, 1622); Šišić, *Pregled*, 284–5. See also the recent study of Dr. Gunther Rothenberg, *The Austrian Military Border in Croatia 1522–1747* (Urbana, 1960); Ignaz Fessler-Klein, *Geschichte von Ungarn* (5 vols.; Leipzig, 1867–83), VI, 185–93.

strong garrisons of horse and foot that they maintained in various towns and fortresses to meet the raids launched by the Zrinskis and other Croatian nobles into the new Ottoman holdings, the Turkish officials settled Orthodox settlers as military colonists in this territory. The Serbian historian Ćorović has acknowledged that the Ottoman adoption of this policy was a consequence of the antagonism that existed between the Catholic Croatians and the Orthodox Serbians in this era. As a rule, however, the Croatians failed to distinguish between Serbians and other Orthodox stocks (Albanians, Kutzo-Vlachs or Macedo-Rumanians, Bulgars, Greeks, etc.), considering all of these peoples as "Vlasi" (Vlachs, Vallachs). National songs dating from the sixteenth century mention the combats waged by the Banal and Border *četas*[22a] against enemy forces "half Turkish and half Vlach" fighting side by side and "springing together" against the Croatians. Obviously the Hapsburgs organized the Krajina on the model of the Ottoman border district and as a counterpoise to it.

Vienna also adopted the policy of settling military colonists in fortified villages in the border zones between the two empires. There grew up in front of these settlements the "Cordon," a line of blockhouses and watchtowers manned around the clock by detachments of *Graničari* (Frontiersmen). Always on the alert for the appearance of hostile forces the Frontiersmen could alarm the entire Border from Transylvania to the sea in an hour's time. Cannon shot, smoke signals, and the firing of poles smeared with pitch and surrounded by straw were as efficacious as the telegraph at a later date in conveying warnings of an attack in force.

The original establishment of 1538 comprised the Croatian Border, which ran from the Una to a point a little to the west of Zagreb, and the Slavonian Border, which extended southeastwards. In 1547 Ferdinand concluded another truce with the Ottomans. He intended to use the armistice period to prepare an all-out drive against the Muslims and hoped to expel them forever from the Hungarian and Croatian lands. However, his brother, Charles v, was more interested in the wars that he was carrying on with the French and the German Protestants than he was in Hungarian-Croatian affairs. Since Charles refused to help him, Ferdinand had to abandon his offensive plans and concentrate upon defense.

In 1548 the Hapsburg ruler entrusted to Captain Luka Székely the defense of Koprivnica, Djurdjevac, and Predavec. Thus arose the Border captaincy of Koprivnica. As captain of this district Székely had to arrange also for the defense of Virovitica and Grabrovnica. Five years later Ferdinand appointed as high captain of the Croatian and Slavonian

22a/Literally "companies," meaning "bands of warriors."

Borders the Styrian nobleman Hans Ungnad. To him was subordinated the captain of Senj, Ivan Lenković, who was responsible for the defense of the land between Senj and Bihać. In 1556 there arose in Vienna the first unified administrative organ for the conduct of military affairs in the Austrian Hapsburg countries. Besides the Austrian provinces proper (Upper and Lower Austria, Tyrol and Voralberg, Styria, Carinthia, and Carniola), Bohemia, Moravia, Silesia, "Royal" Hungary (the seven western counties), eastern Istria, and the remnant of the Triune Kingdom were included in this complex.

At this time the army of the House of Austria consisted of (1) levies raised by Ferdinand's vassals, (2) mercenary forces maintained by Ferdinand himself or by the various archdukes, (3) mercenary contingents hired by the estates (diets or legislatures) of the various Hapsburg provinces and kingdoms, (4) the *Landsturm* or levies raised by the provincial estates, and (5) in Hungary and Croatia-Slavonia, the *Ustanak* (mobilization). All of the various provincial estates continued to exercise the right of voting taxes and of conducting provincial and local administration and they were by no means prepared either to cooperate with one another or to allow the Hapsburgs to infringe upon their time-honored prerogatives.

In the Military Frontier organization that had come into being Ferdinand and his successors saw a means of raising a military force that would be independent of any authority but their own, and that could be maintained on a permanent basis and with less expense than was entailed in erratic hiring of mercenaries or levying of recruits by the various estates. When Ferdinand died in 1564 his eldest son, Maximilian II, besides succeeding him as Holy Roman Emperor, also received Upper and Lower Austria, Bohemia, Moravia, Silesia, "Royal" Hungary, and those parts of Croatia-Slavonia that remained outside of Turkish control and under Banal administration. Ferdinand's second son, Archduke Karl, got "Inner" Austria, that is Styria, Carinthia, and Carniola, along with Trieste and eastern Istria as well as Gorica. With regard to the Borders the interests of Maximilian and Karl coincided.

In 1566 the aged sultan, Soliman the Magnificent, invaded Hungary for the last time. He died before the walls of Sziget, which was defended almost to the last man by Nikola Zrinski and a Croatian-Hungarian garrison of 2500 men.[23] Dismayed by the losses they had suffered, the

23/On Zrinski's defense of Sziget, see Ferenac Črnko, *Povijest Sigeta grada*/History of the Town of Sziget (n.p., n.d.), 13–40. This eyewitness account probably was composed by Zrinski's secretary. See also Fr. Kidrič, "Oblega Sigeta v. sadobnem hrvatškem opisu"/The Siege of Sziget by a Contemporary Croatian Eyewitness, *Časopis za zgodovino in narodopisje*/Journal of History and Anthropology,

Ottomans abandoned their design of advancing to Vienna and in 1568 concluded the peace of Adrianople with the Austrians.

This peace was only a nominal one, for daily fighting continued along the Croatian and Slavonian Borders. The Inner Austrian estates decided that they would have to take over complete financial responsibility for the maintenance of these Border establishments. By this time the two Frontier districts had taken clear shape. Between the Kupa and the Adriatic lay the Croatian Border with its captaincies of Hrastovica and Ogulin. The "Windisch" Border now was being referred to as the Slavonian Border and contained the three captaincies of Križevci, Ivanić, and Koprivnica. The Ottomans were determined to win the line of the Kupa River, for, once across this stream, Zagreb and the Zagorje as well as the remainder of Hapsburg Slavonia would fall. In 1575 the famous Ferhat Pasha defeated General Count Auersperg at Radonja and one by one the great border fortresses began to crumble.[24]

Essentially the deterioration of the situation vis-à-vis the Turkish power was a consequence of financial exigency rather than military inferiority. Not only was the Hapsburg treasury in Vienna seriously embarrassed by the commitments that Austria had in France, Italy, and Germany, but also the Croatian estates were unable to bear the continued strain of the perennial fighting with the Muslims. Of course the situation of the Croatian masses had deteriorated alarmingly.[25] It was this circumstance more than any other that occasioned the peasant revolt led by Matija Gubec in 1573.[26] All Croatia was an armed camp, production of every kind was disrupted, and even great lords such as the Zrinskis and Frankapans had little liquid wealth.

Maximilian II was succeeded as German (Holy Roman) Emperor

II (1912), 42–97; Johann Valvasor, *Die Ehre des Herzogthums Krain* (4 vols.; Laybach, 1689), IV, 469–81.

24/Valvasor, *op. cit.*, IV, 489–98.

25/See letters of Ban Karlović to General Katzianer, Nov. 5, 1530, and March 29, 1531, *Mon. habsburgica*, I, 445–6; II, 15–16; Vuk Frankapan to Ferdinand, *ibid.*, II, 92–3, 131–3. See also Katzianer's letter to the Styrian estates describing conditions in Zagreb, *ibid.*, II, 406–7; the complaints submitted by Sabor on May 25, 1533, *Acta comitialia*, I, 308–10; and *Mon. habsburgica*, I, 447–50, 385–6, 389–90; II, 503–4.

26/On this uprising see F. Rački, "Gradja za povijest hrvatsko-slovenske seljačke bune god. 1573"/Materials for the History of the Croatian-Slovenian Peasant Revolt in the Year 1573, *Starine* (Yugoslav Academy), VII (1875), 164–322, and VIII (1876), 243–52; F. Šišić, *Hrvatska povijest*/Croatian History (3 vols.; Zagreb, 1908), II, 44–50; F. v. Krones, "Aktenmässige Beiträge zur Geschichte des windischen Bauernaufstandes v. J. 1573," *Beiträge zur Kunde steiermärkischen Geschäftsquellen*, V (1868), 3–34; Milan Durman, *Hrvatska seljačka buna 1573*/The Croatian Peasant Revolt (Zagreb, 1936); Josip Hartinger, *Hrvatsko-slovenska buna g. 1573*/The Croatian-Slovenian Uprising in the Year 1573 (Osijek, 1911).

and Bohemian, Hungarian, and Croatian king by the gifted but eccentric dilettante Rudolph II. The latter was glad to have his uncle, Karl, take over the responsibility of providing for the Military Frontiers. In 1578 the archduke negotiated a settlement with the estates of Styria, Carinthia, and Carniola whereby Styria assumed the permanent obligation of supporting the Slavonian Border establishment while Carinthia and Carniola agreed to do the same for the Croatian Border.

Later in the year the Croatian estates assented to this arrangement, which gave Archduke Karl control of the entire Krajina from the Sava to the Adriatic. Even the Ban of Croatia-Slavonia was subordinated to the archduke in military matters.[27] To be sure Rudolph II admonished Karl to be careful to observe the special rights of the Croatian Ban and Sabor, but in practice this was difficult to do. Owing to the flight from the land of so many of their serfs and the impoverishment of their estates, the Croatian aristocrats had to appeal to Karl again and again to send money and artisans to fortify or repair the fortifications of the various castles and other strongholds that constituted part of the Border system. Therefore they really were in no position to stand on their dignity, especially since they lacked the funds to pay the *haramije* or militia that for a time they had maintained at their own expense. All they could do in agreeing to the removal of the Military Borders from Banal control was to stipulate that the arrangement was a purely military one, and that it did not imply any permanent separation of Civil or Banal from Military Croatia (and Slavonia).[28] The fact remains, however, that the two areas stood apart from one another for three full centuries.

Croatian conflicts with the Hapsburg dynasty really date from this definitive separation of the Krajina from the kingdom proper. Initially Sabor did not object to the control placed in the hands of Archduke Karl so much as it did to the extension of the influence exerted by the Graz War Council which was established in the Styrian capital on the model of the existing institution in Vienna. With the chiefly Germanic generals who commanded the Frontier territories Sabor had incessant disputes also. For reasons of principle, apart from other considerations, few Croatians could bring themselves to agree that foreigners should have the power to regulate affairs in any part of the ancient Triune Kingdom. Therefore Sabor bitterly opposed the endeavors of the Council to levy war taxes independently of the approval of the Croatian

27/*Acta comitialia*, IV, 5–6.
28/Šišić, *Hrvatska povijest*, II, 53–5; Pilar, *Južno-slavensko pitanje*, 53.

estates. In 1594 the Croatians protested successfully against this presumption, and Rudolph II acknowledged the validity of Article 159, passed by the Sabor of 1578, which had stipulated that the archducal authorities were obligated to work in agreement with the Banal.

The fact is, however, that the acceptance of the sovereignty of the Hapsburg had placed the Croatians in a dilemma. It was only the Hapsburg connection that kept the remainder of the Croatian state from falling a prey to the Ottomans. From 1527 until the divorce of Military from Civil or Provincial Croatia-Slavonia the Croatians looked to Vienna rather than to the Hungarian capital of Pressburg or Pozsony (Buda, of course, was in Turkish hands for a century and a half). The tendency displayed in the time of Rudolph to curb the authority of the Ban and Sabor caused the Croatians to begin to pick up the Hungarian connection that had been severed in 1527. In 1593 Croatian delegates appeared at the meeting of the estates of "Royal" or Hapsburg Hungary.

THE "LONG WAR" AND THE BOCSKAY REBELLION

By this time the so-called Long War of 1593–1606 was in full swing. Beyond the Kupa lay "No Man's Land," *ničija zemlja*, the scene of daily fighting even in time of nominal peace. Here, between the Kupa and the Una, the Ban and Sabor were able to establish another militarily organized Border, but this one remained under their own jurisdiction rather than that of the Austrian military. On September 28, 1583, Rudolph II had confirmed the direct subordination of this territory to the Ban, who was designated commander of the Petrinja and Kupa *haramijas*. Nonetheless the Ban was dependent in some degree upon Archduke Ernst, who had functioned since 1576 as the *locum tenens* of the emperor-king in Upper and Lower Austria. Fortunately Ernst took a special interest in Croatian affairs and was not as hard for the Croatians to get along with as were the neighboring Border colonels and generals. Between 1591 and 1595 the Austro-Croatian forces won several important battles – the defeat inflicted upon the Ottomans at Sisak, at a time when peace was supposed to prevail between Vienna and Constantinople, was the event that really ushered in the "Long War."[29]

29/On the Sisak encounter and other Turkish-Croatian battles of this period see Šišić, *Pregled*, 286–7; Pavao Radić, "Isprave o bitci kod Siska dne 22 lipnja 1593 godine"/Documents Concerning the Battle at Sisak on June 22, 1593, *Starine* (Yugoslav Academy), XIX (1887), 172–92.

In 1597 military colonists were introduced into the Petrinja area from Bosnia and "Turkish Croatia," that part of Bosnia between the Vrbas and the Una. Croatian peasants from other parts of the ancient Triune Kingdom and Serbian refugees were included among the settlers. Later, towards the end of the seventeenth century, when the Ottomans were driven across the Una, these military colonies developed into the captaincies of Kostajnica, Glina, Dubica, and Zrin which came to form the Banal Border.

The "Long War" was complicated by an anti-Austrian uprising of Hungarian Protestants, led by a Transylvanian noble, Stephen Bocskay. Since the death of John Zápolya, if not earlier, Transylvania had functioned as a Turkish vassal state. Obliged to balance precariously between the Ottomans and the Hapsburgs, it usually was a source of trouble for the latter. Frequently the Transylvanians tried to stir up rebellion among the Croatians. Too many Magyars were Protestants and too willing to ally themselves with the Muslims for the Catholic Croatians to have any real community of feeling with them.[30] Bocskay, however, forced the Viennese court to concede religious liberty to the Protestants of royal Hungary,[31] and helped to arrange the Treaty of Zsitva-Török which restored peace between his Turkish allies and the Hapsburg state.[32]

In consequence of this peace, Bihać and the towns of the Bihać captaincy were lost to the Triune Kingdom. However, the jurisdiction of the Ban and Sabor still prevailed over Petrinja, Hrastovica, and the land below the Kupa. Topolovac, Moslavina, Čazma, Rovišće, and their vicinities were rewon, so that by virtue of the "Long War" some 1400 square kilometers of Croatian soil were regained from the Ottomans. However, the sultan's forces had won the Hungarian town of Kanisza from which they could strike easily from the north into the Medjumurje and the Zrinski properties, as well as into the Podravina. But Zsitva Török ended the dream that the Bosnian begs had cherished of conquering the entire Croatian kingdom. The borders of Banal Croatia now extended along the Drava below Bobovac southwest to the Sava downstream from Sisak, while from there the frontier line ran so as to leave Virovitica and a few other points to the Turks. Below the Sava the border ran from Blinja, which was Turkish, westward to the Korana at Barilović below Karlovac, the new Border center established by Archduke Karl. From Barilović on, the frontier was formed by the Korana in

30/For the relations of the Croatians with Bocskay see Šišić, *Pregled*, 288–9.
31/*Acta comitialia*, IV, 475–6.
32/The text of the Treaty of Zsitva Török appears in G. Noradounghian (ed.), *Recueil d'actes internationaux de l'empire Ottoman* (3 vols.; Paris, 1897–1903), I, 103–8.

such manner as to leave the Slunj sector to the Triune Kingdom. Beyond the Korana the watershed between the Gacka River and Plitvice Lakes constituted the border. West of present-day Donji Kosinj (old Bočać) the summits of the Velebit marked the occidental limits of the kingdom. The boundary in these mountains turned southeastward to the Zrmanja so that the Croatian Littoral with Karlobag, Jablanac, Starigrad, and other places remained in Croatian hands, while Obrovac was an Ottoman holding. Parenthetically, it should be noted that the fall of Klis[33] in 1537 had delivered all of present-day Dalmatia up to the Neretva into the hands of the Ottomans. The Venetians, who had fought twenty-one wars with the Croatians and Hungarians for the possession of this province during the Middle Ages, now held only a few coastal points on it.

After Zsitva-Török the remainder of the Croatian lands were not invaded by the Turks for more than half a century. However, the fighting along the Military Borders continued. The old Croatian Border now was referred to usually as the Karlovac (Karlstädter) Generality. It was divided into two parts. East of the Kupa lay the Generality proper with its two command posts of Karlovac and Žumberak (Sichelberg). It also included four independent captaincies and three lesser units. West of the Kapela Mountains lay that part of the Generality which bordered upon Turkish and Venetian Dalmatia and the Adriatic. The command post of Senj, the Otočac captaincy, and three subordinate units made up this part of the Karlovac Border. The Generality reached southward as far as Karlobag.

THE VARAŽDIN BORDER AND THE "VLACH" STATUTE OF 1630

In the seventeenth century the old "Windisch" Border came to be known as the Varaždin (Warasdiner) Generality. Stretching out along the Drava it was bounded on the east by Turkish-held Slavonia from the junction of the Strug and the Drava to the little Kutlina stream. Bilo Mountain barred it off from the old Virovitica *župa* (Comitat) which was under Ottoman control, while its frontier with the former Požega *župa* was the Ilova River. This stream separated it also from the

33/On this event see *Mon. habsburgica*, I, 174–6, 176–7, 180, 183, 189, 196–7, 204; II, 188–9, 273–4, 277–9, 283–6, 314–15, 333–5, 343, 344, 350, 356–9. See also Martin Perojević, *Petar Kružić, Kapetan i Knez Grada Klisa*/Peter Kružić, Captain and Count of the City of Klis (Zagreb, 1931).

narrow wedge of territory that later on was to form the domain of the Gradiška Border Regiment, but which during most of this century was an Ottoman possession also. Provincial or Banal Croatia adjoined the Generality on the south and west, and to the north lay Hungary.

In 1627 the Inner Austrian estates assumed full financial responsibility for the maintenance of the Karlovac Generality. The Varaždin Graničari took a leading role in suppressing Protestantism in Styria and, on October 5, 1630, received as their reward a special constitutional statute, the terms of which were extended later on to most of the other military districts. Every locality was granted the privilege of electing its own *knez* or village headman, together with two or three jurors from each village in the several captaincies. These officials then chose a chief magistrate (*supremus comes*) for the entire captaincy. This official had eight assessors (who were also elected officers) at his disposal. They formed a court of the first instance and had political and police as well as judicial powers. It is noteworthy that this Statuta Valachorum of 1630 provided for popular participation in local administration at a time that was marked by increasing absolutism of government, not only in Austria but almost everywhere else throughout Europe as well. The military authorities, however, had to confirm the elections.[34]

From the early part of the sixteenth century it had been Hapsburg policy to exempt the Borderers from the payment of feudal dues or seigneurial jurisdiction of any kind. They held lots of land in fief from the ruler in Vienna and in return for it they owed only military service. Every community had to supply a *haramija* detachment with a *vojvoda* (captain or leader) at the head and an ensign and several non-commissioned officers to assist. The village nominated these men, but the general colonel who commanded the Generality made the actual appointments.[35] Originally the ancient Croatian nobility had a hereditary right to the offices of vojvoda and ensign, but the extinction or emigration of many noble families allowed new blood to take over. Of course the majority of the higher Border officers were Austrian or German.

In effect the October Statute created along the Drava a tightly organized military state which could put between six and seven thousand men in the field in from two to three hours' time. All Graničari were

34/On the Statuta Valachorum see the recent treatment provided by Rothenberg, *The Austrian Military Border*, 72–5. The Latin text of the statute is given in F. Vaniček, *Specialgeschichte der Militärgrenze* (4 vols.; Vienna, 1875), I, 410–20.

35/J. Schwicker, *Geschichte der österr. Militärgrenze* (Vienna and Teschen, 1883), 19. See also J. C. Engel, *Staatskunde und Geschichte von Dalmatien, Croatien und Slavonien* (Halle, 1798), 181–2, 254–5, 258–68.

free men. Their exemption from feudal control of course exacerbated the perennial dispute between the Croatian estates and the authorities in Vienna and Graz with respect to the administration of the Borders. In 1635 the Karlovac and Varaždin generalities were united under the command of an officer of general rank who had his headquarters at Karlovac. From this time until the end of the century there was little change in the political and military condition of the Confines. Although the estates continued to press for the restoration of this historically Croatian territory to Banal control, the Krajina was effectually separated from the kingdom and became a special military administrative unit, in which the laws of the kingdom proper did not prevail.[36]

SEVENTEENTH-CENTURY CROATIA

The principal questions that occupied the attention of the Ban and Sabor between 1608 and 1680 were, apart from the status of the Borders, (1) constitutional relations with Austria and Hungary, (2) the wars waged by the House of Austria, and (3) the problems presented by the immigration of Serbs and other Orthodox stocks into Croatian territories.

In 1608 Sabor approved the adhesion of the remnants of the Triune Kingdom to the offensive and defensive alliance concluded between "Royal" Hungary and the hereditary Austrian estates. From this time on Sabor sent representatives to the meetings of the Hungarian diets. These delegates had specific instructions from Sabor on how to uphold the interests of their native land vis-à-vis the Hungarians. Laws passed in the Hungarian legislature were valid in Croatia only if and when accepted in the name of their nation by the Croatian representatives. Thus the delegates of 1608 signed the alliance agreement in the name of their nation, but with the stipulation that the Croatians expected assistance from the Austrians and "royal" Hungarians (those not living under Transylvanian or Turkish rule) in restoring the old Croatian freedoms which for some time had been curtailed.[37]

The eccentricities and absent-mindedness of Rudolph II had by this time become so marked that his brother, Archduke Matthias, took over the reins of government. Matthias was well disposed toward the Croatians, even to the extent of wishing to return the Border territories to Banal jurisdiction. He was willing also to curb the pretensions of the

36/On the continuing conflict between the estates and the Military Frontier authorities see Šišić, *Pregled*, 290–2, 296–7.

37/Kukuljević (ed.), *Jura regni*, II, 66.

great magnates and, especially in 1610, issued drastic warnings to the Erdödis, Draškovićis, and Oršićis to respect the rights of the villagers on their lands.[38] After a short reign, however, Matthias was succeeded in 1619 by Archduke Ferdinand of Styria. Ferdinand wanted to maintain the existing subordination of the Borders to Vienna and Graz. We have noted above that in 1630 he issued the special statute that fixed the status of the Confines definitively.

Meanwhile, in 1620, Croatia again had proposed the conclusion of closer ties with Inner Austria. Sabor's reference to the "mutual bonds of union and confederation" that obtained between the Triune Kingdom and Styria, Carinthia, and Carniola[39] was uttered at an inopportune moment. The Thirty Years War was now in progress, and the Austrians were divided among themselves, some being Catholics, others Protestants.

Under the leadership of Prince Gabriel Bethlen of Transylvania, the Hungarian Protestants attempted to woo the Croatians away from their Hapsburg allegiance.[40] Ferdinand II countered this move by appointing Nikola Frankapan high captain of the Petrinja Border. Aside from this territory, during this epoch, the Ban controlled only the *župa* of Varaždin, that of Zagreb to the Kupa, and western Croatia from Karlovac to the sea. His writ still prevailed, too, in the Medjumurje. But at some time between this date and the eighteenth century, and in a manner not revealed by existing records, the Hungarians succeeded in securing control of this area, which they have claimed ever since.

Throughout the Thirty Years War (1618–48) the Croatians fought loyally for the House of Hapsburg. Sabor proclaimed the Mobilization against all enemies of the dynasty. Any noble who failed to report for military service was threatened with the loss of his title and estates. It is hardly too much to say that save for the services rendered by the Croatian regiments led by the Zrinskis, the Isolanis, and other native commanders, the Austrian ruling house would have emerged with less strength than it did from the struggle against Denmark, Sweden, France, Holland, and the German, Czech, and Hungarian Protestants.

But the Croatians had little real interest in the wars in the west. Apart from loyalty to the ruler in Vienna, their only motivation in this greatest struggle of the century was that expressed on the wolf's head banner carried by some of the Croatian regiments: "Idem za plinom" (I march

38/*Acta comitialia*, V, 47–8.
39/*Jura regni*, II, 75.
40/*Acta comitialia*, V, 242–3.

for plunder). What the Croatians wanted was to drive the Turks out of the territories that once had belonged to the Triune Kingdom.

THE ZRINSKI-FRANKAPAN CONSPIRACY

The peace with the Ottomans concluded at Zsitva-Török in 1606 was extended in 1627.[41] After this date the Croatian estates carelessly entrusted to Hungarian hands several important powers hitherto reserved to Croatian competence. The financial jurisdiction and the authority of the Banal government suffered in consequence. Sabor stipulated that when the lands lost to the Turks and Venetians were rewon, the special authority conceded to the Hungarian diet during the period of Croatia's weakness would be returned to the Banal competence.[42] In 1655 the Croatian estates protested vigorously against Magyar references to *Hungaria et partes eius annexae*. The Croatians maintained sturdily that their kingdom was not included among the "annexed parts" of Hungary. Four years later an attempt was made to extend the authority of the Hungarian count palatine, the chief executive of "Royal" Hungary, over the Croatian countries. Sabor met at Varaždin in 1660 to adopt a resolution which affirmed that the Hungarian law passed to facilitate this control was invalid. It infringed the authority and jurisdiction of the Croatian Ban and ran counter to the laws of the Croatian kingdom itself.

But the Croatians of this era were living in the age of absolute monarchy, and if the Hapsburg Monarchy was less absolute than the contemporary French and Spanish regimes, it was not for want of trying. Throughout the seventeenth century, Croatian and Hungarian susceptibilities were aroused by the increasing weight of bureaucratic centralization emanating from Vienna. To be sure, the pressure of the seventeenth-century bureaucracy appears light indeed in comparison to the national, territorial, and local governmental burdens that people in the twentieth century have to contend with. Wars, in any age, facilitate the growth of absolutism. In the century of the Thirty Years War royal absolutism represented a more efficient and equitable form of government than any that the feudal regimes left over from the Middle Ages could provide. But the privileged classes were not inclined to sacrifice their long-established prerogatives for the sake of efficiency.

The Thirty Years War had left Austria in no condition to fight the

41/*Ibid.*, 407–9.

42/On this question see J. Pliverić, *Beiträge zum ungarisch-kroatischen Bundesrechte* (Zagreb, 1886), 152. See also his *Hrvatsko-ugarsko državno pravo*/Croatian-Hungarian Constitutional Law (Zagreb, 1900), 225.

still powerful Ottoman Empire. Vienna wished to prolong indefinitely the relative peace that had prevailed since 1606. But some of the great Hungarian and Croatian noble families had other plans, and along the frontiers fighting was endemic, for the Ottomans violated the armistice terms whenever it pleased them to do so. Nor were the Zrinskis and other Croatian noble families and their retainers disposed to turn the other cheek to the incessant Ottoman provocations, while the Frontiersmen were always ready for a fight on any excuse.

Between 1651 and 1663 Nikola and Petar Zrinski defeated the Ottomans and their Tatar and Mongol auxiliaries in several important but "unofficial" battles. The Zrinskis hoped to launch a "big war" against the Turks and to recover Slavonia, Srijem, Lika, Krbava, and possibly Dalmatia and Bosnia. In 1660 Nikola planned a surprise attack on the key Turkish position of Kanisza in Turkish Hungary, but the court sternly warned him not to break the nominal peace that prevailed between Vienna and Constantinople. Zrinski obeyed, but with very ill grace, and from this time on he seems to have flirted with the idea of divorcing both Hungary and Croatia from the Hapsburg complex.[43]

But Nikola and Petar continued their private war with the Ottomans, who became so enraged by the Croatian victories that in 1663 a great Turkish army marched westward for the first time since Zsitva-Török. The Austrian general, Count Raymond Montecucculi, defeated the Turkish masses at St. Gotthard. The Zrinskis had got their war and now they expected the Austrians to exploit the successes gained. Both of the Croatian noblemen, blissfully absorbed in the *Klein* or *Buschkrieg* that they had waged along the Frontiers for years past, appeared to be unaware of the menace to the Croatian as well as to the Austrian and "Royal" Hungarian countrysides presented by the Turkish cavalry.

The Ottoman horse was so numerous that it was impossible to prevent the ravaging of whatever countryside it wished and the slaughtering or enslaving of the inhabitants. Whoever might win the battles, the peoples and their property would pay a grim price. Austria was still recovering from the Thirty Years War and in no condition to risk a grapple to the death with the Turkish giant who, under the leadership of the able

43/The Magyar historian László Szalay says that Nikola received 10,000 Thalers from Paris in March 1664. See his *Magyarország története*/Hungarian Conspiracy (2nd ed.; Pest, 1866), v, 99–100. This account is based on contemporary sources and contains many verbatim citations from seventeenth and eighteenth century historians. See also Balthasar Bogišić (ed.), *Acta coniurationem Petri a Zrinio et Francisci de Frankopan nec non Francisci Nadasdy illustrantia (1663-1671). E tabulariis Gallicis desumpta redegit* (Zagreb, 1888), nos. III, V, CCLXIX, CCLXXIII, CCLXXXIV, CCLXXV, CCLXXVIII, CCLXXXI–II, CCLXXXIV–VII, CCXC, CCXCI–II.

Kuprili (or Köprülü) viziers, was experiencing one of his periodic revivals. Therefore, the reigning Hapsburg, Leopold I (1657–1705), decided to conclude peace while he could get it on relatively favorable terms. He calculated that in peacetime the Graničari and normal garrison forces could contain the Turkish border forays, so that Civil Croatia and the Austrian and "Royal" Hungarian countrysides would have a chance to flourish unmolested behind the protective wall provided by the Military Frontiers. Peace was arranged at Vasvár on the basis of the status quo. Austria even paid the sultan a sum of money to compensate him for "war damages." Constantinople contended that these last were the consequence of the raids launched by the Zrinskis into Turkish territory.

Neither the Hungarian nor the Croatian estates were at all satisfied with the Vasvár peace,[44] even though it contained, for the moment, the serious menace posed by the renascence of the Turkish offensive power. Nikola Zrinski stepped up the tempo of the negotiations that he had been carrying on with Sweden, Poland, Transylvania, Venice, and the German and "Royal" Hungarian Protestants. Also he initiated relations with the French. Before he could bring these various transactions to any kind of serious or successful conclusion, however, he lost his life in a hunt.

Nikola's brother, Petar, continued the negotations with France. He involved in them his brother-in-law, Fran, last of the great Croatian house of Frankapan which had given seven bans and innumerable leaders to the Triune Kingdom. The plotters did not realize that France cared nothing for either the Hungarians or the Croatians, although she was willing to use them for the purpose of embarrassing and tying the hands of Austria. Paris encouraged the conspirators for several years, then abandoned them as did all of the other powers with whom they had negotiated.[45] Zrinski and Frankapan could have escaped abroad,

44/For the reasons that made peace necessary, see Leopold's explanation to the Hungarian estates of August 10, 1664, cited in Bogišić, no. CCLXXIX. The text of the treaty appears on 233–5 of that volume. Hungarian historians usually attribute the inception of the Zrinski-Frankapan conspiracy to the disappointment engendered by this peace.

45/The complete story of these negotiations is presented in chapter IX of the writer's forthcoming work on Croatia-Slavonia during the period of 1526–1792. For the international ramifications of this anti-Hapsburg Fronde see also Gyula Pauler, *Wesselenyi Ferenc Nádor és társainak összeesküvése 1664-1671*/Francis Wesselenyi and the Conspiracy of 1664–71 (2 vols.; Budapest, 1876). This Hungarian account should be compared with a standard Croatian relation of the conspiracy such as that of the late Professor Oton Knezović, *Poviest Hrvata*/History of the Croats (Madrid, 1961), 184–95.

but they hoped to prevent the confiscation of their estates by proceeding to Vienna to answer the charges of treason that were brought against them after the details of the plot became known to the court. Leopold intended to pardon them, but his advisers, especially the vindictive Wenzel Lobkowitz and Count Montecucculi, who had an old feud with the Zrinskis, insisted that their treason would prove contagious unless they were punished as a commoner would be under similar circumstances.[46] Their execution at Wiener Neustadt on April 30 has been commemorated by Croatians as a day of mourning (and may be compared to the American tradition revolving around the Nathan Hale episode) since to all intents and purposes the two greatest Croatian families became extinct in their male lines within a few years of this tragic drama.[47]

In consequence of the plot,[48] the Croatian constitution was suspended

46/Minutes of council held by Lobkowitz, Montecucculi, Schwarzenberg, Lamberg, and Hocher on April 10, 1670, cited in F. Rački (ed.), *Acta coniurationem Bani Petri a Zrinio et Com. Fr. Frangepani illustrantia* (Zagreb, 1873), no. 262. See also Gremonville to Louis xiv, April 16, 1671, cited in Bogišić, *Acta coniurationem Bani Petri*, nos. ccxlvii and ccxlix (April 30, 1671). For the charges on which the counts were convicted see Rački, nos. 614, 618. Leopold intended to commute the death sentences imposed by the court to a term of imprisonment, but Lobkowitz and his other counselors harangued him so forcefully that he allowed the death penalty to stand. See Rački, nos. 619, 621, 622, 624.

47/Actually both Zrinskis were survived by sons. Adam, offspring of Nikola, fell as an Austrian lieutenant-colonel leading a charge against the Turks at Slankamen (1691). Petar's boy, Ivan Antun, distinguished himself in the wars against the French at the end of the century. Later he became involved in incriminating negotiations with the Turks and ended his days in prison (1703). Adam and Ivan Antun were the last scions of the Zrinski (Šubić) line. Fran Frankapan left no male heirs, but collateral branches of the Frankapan family remained in Italy.

48/Apart from the documents that tell the story of the plot in the volumes edited by Bogišić and Rački, see the following treatments of this great conspiracy, which Croatian historians usually have handled most uncritically: J. Mailath, *Geschichte des österr. Kaiserstaates* (4 vols.; Hamburg, 1848), iv, 58–90; *Posljednji Zrinski i Frankopani*/The Last Zrinskis and Frankapans (n.p., n.d.), F. Šišić, "Zrinsko-Frankopanska katastrofa," *Njiva* (1918), 271–80; Valvasor, *Die Ehre des Herzogthums Krain*, iv, 128–39; Em. Lilek, *Kritische Darstellung der ungarischen kroatischen Verschwörung und Rebellion (1663–1671)* (4 vols.; Celje, 1928); *Historia de las revoluciones de Hungaria* (Madrid, 1687). See also the works of Szalay and Pauler noted in footnotes 43 and 45 above. The altogether fallacious ideas about this episode in feudal particularism possessed by many Croatians of the last few generations are derived from such writings as those of the historical novelist Eugen Kumičić, e.g. *P. Zrinski i Fr. K. Frankopan i njihovi klevetnici*/P. Zrinski and Fran Frankapan and Their Accusers (Zagreb, 1899). The following works treat the question in a similar way: J. Kery [?], *Series banorum Dalmatiae, Croatiae, Slavoniae sub regibus Croatiae Hungariae et Ungariae-Austriae* (Tyrnau, 1737); Šišić, *Pregled*, 299–306; R. Lopašić, "Nekoliko priloga za poviest urote Petra Zrinskoga i Franje Frankopana"/Some Addenda to the History of the Conspiracy of P. Zrinski and F. Frankapan, *Starine* (Yugoslav Academy), xv (1883), 114–54; xvii (1885), 151-231; xxiv (1891), 41–112; Knezović, *Poviest Hrvata*, 184–95.

temporarily, the Primorje or coastal lands, which had been chiefly Zrinski or Frankapan property, were incorporated into a complex controlled directly by Austria, and bureaucratic pressure was increased at the expense of feudalism throughout the Hapsburg dominions. Both the Viennese and Graz war Councils wished to incorporate Banal Croatia outright into the Karlovac and Varaždin Military Frontiers. Indubitably the bulk of the Croatian lower nobility favored this plan, or at least the establishment of a direct connection of some kind with Austria rather than with Hungary.[49] They felt that in this way the defense of the remnants of the Triune Kingdom against Turkish attacks would be imposed upon the great magnates. In January 1672, the "Austrian party," which was very strong among the freeholders and in the towns, petitioned Leopold to separate Croatia from Hungary altogether and to attach it directly to the Austrian hereditary lands. Count Nikola Erdödi and other great nobles succeeded in preserving the historic individuality of the kingdom instead of allowing it to be absorbed by Austria or to become a part of the Krajina.[50]

THE WAR OF LIBERATION, 1682–99

Scarcely twenty years after the beginning of the Zrinski-Frankapan plot the Croatians achieved, in the "War of Liberation" of 1682–99, the partial satisfaction and realization of the Zrinskis' dreams of territorial restoration. The Treaty of Karlowitz in 1699 freed all of Slavonia, save for southeastern Srijem, all territory to the Una except for Novi, and the old Lika and Krbava *županas* from the Turkish yoke. However, for the moment most of these old Croatian lands remained outside the sphere of Banal jurisdiction. The Ottomans continued to rule "Turkish Croatia" (northwestern Bosnia). The Croatians resented the continued Ottoman possession of Kostajnica and the exclusion of Croatian representatives from the peace negotiations at Karlowitz.[51]

49/Rački, *Acta coniurationem Bani Petri*, nos. 599, 623.

50/The Karlovac general, Johann Herberstein, wanted to reorganize Croatia as a separate hereditary Hapsburg kingdom with a modernized (bureaucratic) administration. Since the Turks still held a great part of the old Croatian territory, there was some excuse for the Austrians to regard the areas of the Triune Kingdom that remained subject to Vienna as a province rather than as an autonomous legal entity. On Herberstein's ideas, see R. Lopašić (ed.), *Acta historiam confinii militaris Croatici illustrantia* [Spomenici hrvatske krajine] (3 vols.; Zagreb, 1884–9), II, 337–41, 342–55. (These are vols. XV, XVI, and XX of MSHSM.)

51/Count Alois Marsigli, one of the peace commissioners who was renowned for his exact knowledge of the areas adjacent to the Turkish frontiers, had as executive

Soon after the conclusion of hostilities with the Turks, Austria became involved in the War of the Spanish Succession (1701–13). Leopold intended to return to Croatian control the Varaždin Military Generality, which no longer was a Military Frontier properly speaking, since the territory recovered from the Ottomans in the war of Liberation now separated it from the Turkish border. The French war, which ensued from the dispute over the succession to the throne of Spain, was complicated by Bavarian intervention against Austria and by the formidable Raköczi uprising in Hungary and Transylvania. Faced with the necessity of waging war on several fronts, Leopold deemed it inadvisable to discard the reservoir of manpower provided by the Frontiers and to rely in his Croatian lands upon the erratic resources of the "mobilization." Therefore he rejected Sabor's demands that the Varaždin Generality, along with Slavonia and the Lika and Krbava areas, be returned to Banal authority.[52]

EIGHTEENTH-CENTURY CROATIA-SLAVONIA

During the eighteenth century the Hungarians gradually extended their control over the territory of the Triune Kingdom. From the death of Nikola Erdödi (1693) to 1790 the only Ban of Croatian blood was Ivan Drašković (1732–3). All other incumbents of this office during this span of a century were Magyars who had estates in Croatia-Slavonia. Many of the higher Croatian nobles, including the Erdödi family, considered Hungary to be their primary, and Croatia only their secondary, fatherland.

THE CROATIAN PRAGMATIC SANCTION

It was the lower nobility which opposed the closer identification of the Croatian kingdom with Hungary. In the Sabor of 1713 the protonotary, Juraj Plemić, proposed that delegates no longer be sent to take part in the deliberations of the Hungarian legislative body. He represented the element that wanted an Austro-Croatian *Anschluss* rather than a continuation of the old Hungarian-Croatian state relationship. Article 7

counselor Pavao Ritter Vitezović, a progenitor of the "Great Croatia" idea, who urged Austria to launch a new war to recover all of Bosnia–Hercegovina which should then be joined under the Hapsburg crown to the other Croatian lands. On the Karlowitz peace see *Acta historiam*, III, 144–9, 155–9, 164–8.

52/For the Austrian view of the state of the Croatian kingdom at this time, see *ibid.*, III, 171–2.

(the "Croatian Pragmatic Sanction") adopted by the Sabor of 1712 was the Croatians' direct answer to Article 13 passed by the Hungarian diet of 1708, which had stipulated that Croatian laws were valid only if they did not counteract Hungarian legislation. Although the Crown had not sanctioned the Hungarian law, the Croatians, to prevent future misunderstanding arising in connection with it, issued this article.

This statue declared that in default of male heirs to the Hapsburg possessions ("Which may God prevent") the Croatians would recognize as their lawful sovereign that princess of Hapsburg blood who also reigned over Styria, Carinthia, and Carniola.[53] Thus once again the Croatian desire for a permanent union with the Austrian provinces found expression as it had in the time of Maximilian I, in 1527, in 1535, and on many other occasions.

Thus, Article 7 implied quite plainly that the Hungarian-Croatian union was based entirely upon the dynastic tie as it had been since the conclusion of the original Hungarian-Croatian union at the beginning of the twelfth century. If there was no joint ruler, then there was no joint Hungarian-Croatian state either. Magyar inability to comprehend this Croatian viewpoint was to have disastrous consequences for Hungary in 1848–9 and in 1918. Actually the eighteenth-century Magyars were wiser than their descendants. In 1715 the Hungarian diet retreated from its former position and acknowledged the validity of all Croatian legal enactments, whether they were unilateral actions of Sabor or approved by the Hungarian diet, and without regard to whether or not they contradicted existing Hungarian laws. In an attempt to placate the Croatians the Hungarian diet also passed Article 118, which approved Sabor's demand for the reattachment to Civil or Banal Croatia of those parts of Slavonia that were rewon from the Turks in the War of Liberation. The Magyars even established a special commission to assist the Croatians in securing the reincorporation of the former Croatian territories.

Thus the Croatians demonstrated convincingly the autonomy of the Triune Kingdom vis-à-vis Hungary. Actually, throughout the early period of Hapsburg rule, Croatian autonomy was symbolized by the

53/The Croatian "Pragmatic Sanction" anticipated Charles VI's formal enactment which secured the accession to the undivided Hapsburg inheritance of his daughter, Maria Theresa. On this independently conceived Croatian action see F. Šišić, *Die kroatische Pragmatische Sanktion* (Zagreb, 1915), and his *Pregled*, 318–20; V. Klaić, "Hrvatska pragmatička sankcija"/The Croatian Pragmatic Sanction, *Rad* (Yugoslav Academy), CCVI (1915), 61–135; *Jura regni*, II, 101–9; T. Smičiklas, *Poviest hrvatska*/History of Croatia (2 vols.; Zagreb, 1879, 1882), II, 295; Pilar, *Južno-slavensko pitanje*, 35–6; Bogoslav Šulek, *Naše pravice*/Our Rights (Zagreb, 1868), part 1, p. 16, part a, 409; Knezović, *Poviest Hrvata*, 201–3.

Iura Municipalia or laws peculiar to the Croatian kingdom.[54] These laws provided that the Ban was the supreme Croatian executive. He convened and presided over Sabor, commanded the military forces of the kingdom, and, in effect, exercised regal powers. Furthermore, the Iura Municipalia put under the authority of Sabor the discussion and decision of all matters relating to the public life of the kingdom including the election of all high officials except the Ban and podban (the latter had to be the high count of either Zagreb or Križevci counties). The Iura Municipalia guaranteed to the Croatians some rights that the Magyars themselves did not possess. Taxes decreed by the Hungarian diet had to be approved by Sabor before they could be collected. Sabor had the right to conclude alliances independently of Hungary (as noted above, in 1620 it had effected an agreement for mutual defense with Styria, Carinthia, and Carniola). When Sabor's enactments were approved by the king, they had the force of law. Obviously, however, the existence of the Military Frontiers constituted a violation of the operation of the Iura Municipalia since the confines were outside the control of the Ban and Sabor.

Karl III (VI of Austria and the Holy Roman Empire) appreciated the proved devotion of the Croatians to his house. Naturally he approved an act passed by Sabor which stipulated that any inhabitant of Croatia-Slavonia who refused to recognize the new Hapsburg rule of succession automatically would forfeit his rights of citizenship as defined by the Iura Municipalia.[55] In 1723 he confirmed Croatian judicial independence of Hungary by establishing the Banal Bench. This body functioned as the supreme court of the Croatian kingdom and exercised jurisdiction throughout the Banal-ruled territories.[56] Karl also sanctioned Article 5 of the resolutions (laws) adopted by the Sabor of 1725. This important protocol was intended to preserve Sabor's independence of action vis-à-vis the Hungarian Council of Lieutenancy which had become the executive organ for the lands of the Crown of St. Stephen. Karl, too, must be given credit for stimulating the economic recovery of the Croatian territories, the condition of which during the period of Turkish ascendancy had been anything but flourishing. Particularly was this true of the Turkish-occupied sections such as Slavonia.[57] The

54/On these municipal rights enjoyed by the Croatians, see especially B. Šulek, *Hrvatski ustav ili konstitucija godine 1882*/The Croatian Constitution or the Constitution of the Year 1882 (Zagreb, 1883), 80–3.

55/*Jura regni*, II, 102, 104, 108–11, 111–12; Šišić, *Pregled*, 352.

56/*Jura regni*, II, 379–99; Šišić, *Pregled*, 352.

57/Tadija Smičiklas, *Spomenici o Slavoniji u* XVII *vijeku (1650–1702)*/Documents about Slavonia in the 17th Century, and *Dvjestogodišnjica oslobodjenja Slavonije*/

Hapsburg ruler ordered the construction of the great "Carolina" highway to run through western Croatia. The building of this route stimulated the exchange of goods throughout the Croatian lands. Karl also promoted the development of the ports of the Croatian Littoral and enacted legislation in behalf of the Croatian serfs.[58]

The Croatians had to fight two more wars with the Turks during his reign. Although the Graničari made an unwontedly poor showing in the conflict of 1716–18,[59] Prince Eugene of Savoy carried the Hapsburg banners far into Serbia and Bosnia. In 1718 the Treaty of Passarowitz returned to Croatia southeastern Srijem, Novi, Furjan and its vicinity, and that part of Bosnia between the Drina and the Glinica. Some 2450 square kilometers of territory were recovered in all.[60] Nonetheless, it is unfortunate that Vienna decided to conclude peace at this juncture. Austria now was at the zenith of her power and might have swept the Turks out of the northern Balkans altogether. The financial condition of the Hapsburg state did not correspond to its military strength, however, and Karl was preoccupied with Spain's designs on Italy and with securing the consent of the other European powers to the Pragmatic Sanction by which he sought to assure to his daughter, Maria Theresa, succession to his undivided inheritance.

Austria's involvement in the War of the Polish Succession (1733–6) was a consequence of the Hapsburg's efforts to buy foreign support for the Pragmatic Sanction. Sabor met at Glina in 1737 to sanction the representation of the Triune Kingdom in the peace negotiations that were to take place at Nemirov.[61]

Article 12 enacted by the Glina Sabor mentioned the historic right of the Croatian kingdom to Bosnia. This article pointed out that in the days of the national kings the Croatian boundaries had reached to the banks of the Vrbas and to the ancient fortress of Novi on the Una.

The Croatians hoped to recover all of Bosnia and Hercegovina when a new war broke out with the Ottomans in 1737. To secure Russian support for the Pragmatic Sanction, Karl allied himself with Moscow when the latter attacked the faltering Turkish Collossus. But now the

Bicentennial Anniversary of the Liberation of Slavonia (Zagreb, 1891). See also Josip Bösendorfer, *Crtice iz Slavonske povijesti*/Excerpts from Slavonian History (Osijek, 1910); *Acta historiam*, III, XCII; Schwicker, *Geschichte der österr. Militärgrenze*, 48–9.

58/Šišić, *Pregled*, 357–8.

59/Vaniček, *Specialgeschichte der Militärgrenze*, I, 342–50; Rothenberg, *The Austrian Military Border*, 104–5.

60/*Acta historiam*, III, CLXXXI, CLXXXIII–IV.

61/*Jura regni*, II, 119.

Ottomans rallied again as they had in the brave days of the Kuprilis. They allowed the Muscovites to sweep forward into the Crimea, but concentrated their forces against the Austrians and Croatians along the Danube and Sava. Karl's generals made the same mistake that their successors in the Serbian campaign of 1914 were destined to make. They divided their forces into five parts and allowed the Turks to establish local superiorities of more than four to one at all important points.[62] Still, it was less his own armies' failure that the fears engendered by the Russian advance into Moldavia that induced Karl to break off the war. Prince Eugene had warned him to beware of Russia. Once again Karl concluded peace too hastily to serve the best interests of his state. At Belgrade in 1739 the Austrians agreed to return to Turkish rule all of the territory along the right bank of the Sava, the Una, and the Danube, together with "Little Wallachia" up to the Aluta River.

Upon the occasion of Karl's death in 1740, Sabor made the egregious error of referring to the "Croatian Pragmatic Sanction" of 1712 as a "mere expression of loyalty." Magyars now had infiltrated heavily into the Croatian estates and these recognized as the binding enactment in the matter of the Hapsburg House Law the Hungarian acceptance of this statute.[63] Thus the Sabor of 1740 seriously weakened the Croatian claim to the right of independence of action vis-à-vis Hungary, an independence demonstrated convincingly in 1300–1, 1527, 1620, 1707, and 1712.[64]

Between 1740 and 1748 the Croatians distinguished themselves in defending Hapsburg territory against the attacks of the French, Bavarians, and Prussians. As a reward to the nation for the services rendered to her by its sons on the battlefield, in 1745 Maria Theresa returned to the authority of the ban the three old Slavonian counties of Virovitica, Požega (Bjelovar), and Srijem,[65] which had remained subject to the central administration in Vienna since their recovery from the Turks.

62/On the war of 1737–9 see Schwicker, *Geschichte der österr. Militärgrenze*, 62–5; C. Fraser, translation from the Turkish of Omar Bosnavi's *History of the War in Bosnia during the Years 1737–8 and 9* (London, 1830); Aleksije Olesnicki, "Bosanska vojska pod zapovjedništvom Bećir-paše Čengića u rusko-turskom ratu god. 1737"/The Bosnian Army under the Command of Bećir-Čengić Pasha in the Russo-Turkish War of 1737, *Rad* (Yugoslav Academy), CCLXIX (1940), 111–50. The Croatians in the Austrian service fought against their Bosnian Muslim brethren in this conflict.

63/*Jura regni*, II, 125.

64/In 1301 the Croatians acknowledged as their king Charles of Anjou-Naples, whereas the Hungarians opted for other candidates until the year 1307. On the several expressions of Croatian independence of Hungary see Eugen Kvaternik, *Das historische-diplomatische Verhältnis des Königreich Kroatien zu der ungarischen St. Stephans-Krone* (Zagreb, 1860), 129–34.

65/*Jura regni*, II, 402–3, 425–9; Šišić, *Pregled*, 324–6.

Austrian military men insisted that for reasons of security the Posavina or "Sava land" would have to remain part of the Krajina, however, so that the restoration was not complete.

MARIA THERESA AND THE CROATIANS

Maria Theresa's reign was one of reform and centralization of authority. She issued ordinances to lighten the load of serfdom borne by the peasants throughout her dominions, and it is significant that her legislation in favor of serfs began in the Croatian parts of her state. Here they continued along the lines indicated in the reign of her predecessors, Leopold I and Karl III.[66] However, the military reorganization of the Austrian army that was carried out during and after the French, Bavarian, and Prussian wars reduced the control exercised heretofore by the Ban and Sabor over the Croatian troops. No longer was the Ban their supreme commander, nor was the permission of Sabor necessary, as in past times, for their employment outside of the boundaries of the Triune Kingdom.

Likewise the administrative reforms undertaken by the queen included a reorganization of local government which affected adversely the autonomy of the Croatian county regimes. It must be acknowledged that these were not remarkable for their efficiency.[67] In 1776 the Primorje or coastal area was organized as the new county of Severin and placed under the authority of the Ban, who now exercised jurisdiction over seven counties in all.[68]

Maria Theresa always had a soft spot in her heart for the Croatians because of their military record in 1740–8 and 1756–63. Rather than suppress Sabor, as she did the legislative bodies of other parts of her dominions, she endeavoured to get along with the Croatian estates. Her legislation on behalf of the peasantry irritated the Croatian lords, how-

66/Josip Bösendorfer, "Kako je došlo do slavonskog urbara 1756. godine? Na osnovi arhivalne gradje iz arhiva županije virovitičke"/How Did the Slavonian Urbarium of 1756 Originate? Based on Archival Materials from the Archives of the County of Virovitica, *Rad* (Yugoslav Academy), CCXL (1931), 220–56, and CCXLII (1931), 1–92; M. Nežić, *Urbar hrvatsko-slavonski*/The Croat-Slavonian Urbarium (Zagreb, 1882), 163–83.

67/Josip Bösendorfer, "Prvi dani u životu županije virovitičke poslije reinkorporacije (1745–1749)"/The First Days in the Life of the County of Virovitica after the Reincorporation, *Rad* (Yugoslav Academy), CCVI (1915), 148–67. See also Šišić, *Pregled*, 350, and the royal rescript of regulations for the Croatian counties, *Jura regni*, II, 442–5.

68/Only insofar as political jurisdiction was concerned, however. In regard to commercial matters the Croatian counties were subordinated to Graz and Vienna.

ever. Furthermore, Sabor was offended by the establishment of a Croatian Council of Lieutenancy (*Consilium locumtenentiale croaticum*) in 1767 to handle political, economic, and, especially, military affairs. This institution was modeled on the Hungarian Council of Lieutenancy or Dicasterium with which it had equal rank.[69] The Croatian estates registered a solemn protest against its creation since it was not responsible to them. They agreed finally to its operation, however, on the condition that it be composed entirely of Croatians and that the Ban preside over it. Of the five other members of this body, one was a prelate, another a magnate, and the remaining three lesser nobles. From 1767 to 1779 the Consilium governed the Croatian lands from its seat at Varaždin. Sabor continued to meet until 1777 but did little except to note in its minutes the receipt and content of royal rescripts and commands transmitted to the Consilium. Finally, however, the estates offered resolute opposition to the separation from Civil or Banal Croatia of the land between the Kupa, Una, and Korana rivers. For reasons of military expediency the queen wished to place this region under the control of the Military Border. Sabor's recalcitrance over this issue caused Maria Theresa to refrain from convening the estates during the last three years of her reign.[70]

Also, in 1779, she abolished the Consilium which had incurred much unpopularity among the Croatians. Its demise, however, subjected the Triune Kingdom to the Hungarian Lieutenancy-Council. There was always to be a Croatian in this body and the Ban, too, had a seat and vote in it. The fact remains that for the first time in history the Croatian kingdom was subordinated legally to a Hungarian institution other than the crown itself.[71]

THE JOSEPHINE ERA, 1780–90

Maria Theresa was succeeded on the throne by her son, Joseph II (1780–90), who was the greatest of the eighteenth-century "enlightened despots." Along with a zeal for reform he possessed a mania for centralization. He broke up the Hungarian and Croatian county organizations and divided his state into ten new districts or "circles." The Zagreb "circle" took in the former counties of Zagreb, Varaždin, Križevci, Požega, and Severin, and included the Hungarian Zaladska county. Virovitica and Srijem counties were combined with the Hungarian counties of Baranja,

69/*Jura regni*, II, 234, 236. See also the decree of August 1, 1767, *ibid.*, II, 450–1; Šišić, *Pregled*, 329.

70/On the final years of Maria Theresa's reign over the Croatian lands see Šišić, *Pregled*, 330–2; Knezović, *Poviest Hrvata*, 212–14.

71/Rescript of August 29, 1779, *Jura regni*, II, 457–8.

Tolna, and Somod to form the Pest "circle." This administrative reorganization was in part a consequence of the difficulties that Joseph had experienced with the old county authorities.[72] Parenthetically it might be noted that Joseph pointed out in an official document that the Hungarian counties of Raab, Sopron, Moson, Komárno, Esztergom, Veszprem, and Eisenstadt (Železno) were inhabited chiefly by Croatians.

Croatian autonomy during Joseph's reign suffered from the circumstance that the Hapsburg, entirely apart from his zest for modernization and uniformity, had little use for the clergy and none for the nobility. But, save for a few representatives of freemen of the towns, Sabor's membership was drawn exclusively from the clergy or the nobility. Although Joseph allowed Sabor to meet often during his reign, he restricted its competence and activity. His legislation in behalf of the serfs freed them from feudal jurisdiction, while the commutation of the feudal dues that he proposed frightened the privileged orders thoroughly. They declared that they could not exist alongside a completely free peasantry.

Joseph also attempted to impose the use of the German language in administrative matters throughout his dominions. Most literate Croatians of that day had a working knowledge of German[73] and many peasants learned it, too, during their military service. Although there was no nationalistic purpose, in the nineteenth and twentieth century meaning of this term, in Joseph's Germanizing measures – he himself disliked Prussians and Saxons cordially and had little use for Bavarians – the Croatians, like other non-Germanic peoples, expressed resentment against the use of German in official parlance on the territory of the Triune Kingdom. Since the Magyars also were aroused by the pressure of Germanization, a rapprochement between the two old "brother peoples" obviously was in the offing.

THE SABORS OF 1790–2

When Joseph died in 1790, the Croatian estates decided to make common cause with their more numerous and affluent Magyar peers. Two months after the demise of the reforming monarch a distinguished Croatian proposed to Sabor that a "permanent union" be concluded between

72/Šišić, *Pregled*, 351–2. On the general implications for the Croatians of Joseph's reign see *ibid.*, 332–7. See also the valuable work of Joseph Kerezturi, *Collectio ordinationum Josephi II et repraesentationum diversorum regni Hungariae comitatuum* (Diószeg, 1790); Knezović, *Poviest Hrvata*, 214–17.

73/It must be admitted, however, that the Croatian estates were attached more genuinely, perhaps, to the use of Latin as their official language of communication than were their contemporaries in other countries.

the Triune Kingdom and Hungary.[74] Far from being a precursor of the nineteenth-century "Magyarone" element in Croatia-Slavonia, the author of this fateful suggestion, Nikola Skerlecz (Škrlec) was the real founder of the idea of Croatian state right as it has descended to modern times. Like other members of his class, he was willing to establish closer relations with the Hungarian kingdom until such time as "Turkish Croatia" (the western part of Bosnia up to the Vrbas and including the old fortress of Jajce), western Hercegovina, and Dalmatia were reunited with Croatia-Slavonia. With the addition of these territories to the parent kingdom, the Croatian aristocrats probably calculated that they would be able to stand on their own feet vis-à-vis either Vienna or the Hungarians.

But the Hungarian diet, despite the protests of the three Croatian delegates accredited to it by Sabor, added Article 58 to the Magyar constitution. This statute required the Croatian counties to accept the regulations imposed by the Hungarian Council of Lieutenancy. Sabor demanded that this council be abolished, even though a proportional number of Croatians were included in it. The Magyars also adopted a resolution that from this time on the taxes for Croatia-Slavonia should no longer be voted by Sabor. Henceforth they were to be levied by the "joint" Hungarian-Croatian diet which met usually at Pressburg. Sabor agreed to this stipulation on the condition that the Croatian taxes be approved separately "forever" from Hungarian taxes.

The fatal flaw in the Croatian position was that Sabor had agreed to abide by the decisions reached in a majority vote of the Hungarian parliament. Thus the Croatian estates abandoned the veto right which up to this time they had been able to exercise over matters relating to Croatia-Slavonia that were brought up in the "joint" diet. Since there were only three Croatian representatives in this body, they could always be outvoted. Thus the way was open for the Hungarians to extend their control over the Croatian territories. On the other hand the Croatians successfully resisted the efforts of the Magyars to substitute the Magyar language for Latin as the official idiom in the Triune Kingdom. Magyar was allowed to enter the Croatian school curriculum, but only as an elective subject.[75]

74/*Allocutio Nicolai Skerlecz de Lomnica supremi comitis comitatus zagrebiensis* (Zagreb, 1790). For the position of the Croatians vis-à-vis Hungary at this time see also *Declaratio ex parte nunciorum regni Croatiae quoad inducendam hungaricam linguam* (n.p., n.d.); Šišić, *Pregled*, 373–7; St. Srkulj, *Izvori za hrvatsku povijest*/Sources for Croatian History (Zagreb, 1910), 141–4.

75/On the language issue see Šišić, *Pregled*, 375–7; Knezović, *Poviest Hrvata*, 219–22; F. Fancev, "Dokumenti za naše podrijetlo hrvatskoga preporoda"/Docu-

The dependence of the Croatians upon the decisions reached by a Hungarian parliamentary majority concerning "joint" Hungarian-Croatian affairs, and particularly the control over Croatian taxes given to this majority, meant that from the constitutional point of view the Triune Kingdom had ceased to be a state in its own right. During the next fifty years, and especially after the period of the French wars of 1792–1814, the Hungarian authorities gradually were able to usurp the authority of Ban and Sabor. The Sabor of 1792 took official cognizance of the new relationship established with Hungary, that is that the military and financial autonomy of the Triune Kingdom had ceased to exist. At the same time it should be recognized that Croatian domestic affairs, apart from taxes and military matters, remained reserved to the authority of Sabor.

CROATIAN PARTICIPATION IN THE FRENCH REVOLUTIONARY AND NAPOLEONIC WARS

The Sabor of 1792 approved the four million florin army bill asked for by Leopold's successor, Francis, when the French republicans forced through a declaration of war against the Hapsburg state. In the spring and summer of that year Croatian units fought successfully against the French on the Rhine and in the Netherlands. When King Louis XVI of France was executed by the Jacobin element in the following year, the old veteran of the Seven Years War, General Quosdanovich (Gvozdanović), turned his Croatian horse loose on the French countryside. (Still in the early part of the twentieth century mothers in northern France were apt to warn misbehaving offspring that "the Croats would come to get them" if they did not mend their ways!)

In the fall of 1793 the Croatian general, Baron Jelačić, narrowly missed annihilating the chief army of the French Republic at Lauterbourg. In Napoleon Bonaparte's Italian campaign of 1796 the Croatians particularly distinguished themselves, and the future dictator and emperor of France himself missed falling into their hands by a hair.[76]

ments on the Indigenous Origin of the Croatian National Awakening, *Gradja*, XII (1933), 33–7.

76/Bonaparte and his staff rushed out upon a bridge spanning the Alpons River to rally the French troops who had been repulsed by two Croatian battalions holding the bridgehead. The Croatians also dashed onto the bridge, overwhelmed the French on the causeway, killed most of Bonaparte's staff, and knocked the little Corsican himself into the water. He was rescued by the future Marshal Marmont,

Sabor convened in May 1797 to discuss the terms of the Armistice of Leoben concluded between Bonaparte and his greatest opponent, Archduke Karl.[77] France and Austria had agreed to the obliteration of the ancient Venetian Republic and the Croatians hoped to recover Dalmatia in consequence.

As noted in *Croatia*, volume I, this province, theoretically at least, had belonged to Venice since 1409 when the legally crowned Croatian king, Ladislas of Naples, had sold his rights to Dalmatia to the Republic. From 1521 to 1644, however, most of this maritime province was in the hands of the Turks. Between 1635 and 1648 the soldiers of St. Mark rewon much of the coastal territory and extended their control into the hinterland. During the "War of Liberation" of 1682–99 a number of Dalmatian localities fell into Venetian hands also, and by the Peace of Karlowitz the Serenissima finally secured definitive possession of the entire region that she had purchased from Ladislas in 1409. By the Peace of Passarowitz of 1718 Venice added the territory along the left bank of the Cetina and upper arms of the Krka. For the remainder of the eighteenth century Dalmatia stagnated under the oppressive rule of Venice.

The Peace of Campo Formio of 1797 executed the provisions agreed upon in the Leoben armistice, and the Austrians sent Croatian troops under Baron Petar Rukavina to take possession of Dalmatia. The Dalmatians welcomed the change in sovereignty, except in the Boka Kotorska region. Here, too, the Croatian inhabitants brought out black and yellow Hapsburg flags to greet Rukavina's forces, but the Orthodox elements in this region preferred union with Montenegro. The old Venetian officials intrigued in favor of the Slavic power also.

Rukavina recommended to Vienna that Dalmatia be reunited with Croatia and Slavonia. However, at this time, Count Thugut, son of a Danube River boatman, had worked his way up to the top of the administrative ladder in Vienna, imposing his influence even upon Em-

but both of them had to hide to escape capture. There is much mention of Croatian participation in the Italian campaigns of 1794–7 in *Bonaparte in Italy. Campaign of General B. in Italy 1796–97*, by a General Officer, trans. from the French by T. E. Ritchie (Edinburgh, 1800); Raoul Chélard, *Les armées Françaises jugées par les habitants de l'Autriche 1797–1800–1809* (Paris, 1893); X. Desjardins, *Campagnes des Français en Italie* (Paris, 1803); *Études sur la campagne de 1796–1797 en Italie*, by J. C. (Captain of Artillery (Paris, 1897); *Examen de la campagne de Buonaparte en Italie dans les années 1796 et 1797* (Paris, 1814); G. Fabry, *Histoire de l'armée d'Italie* (1796–1797) (Paris, 1900); *Mémoires sur la campagne de 1796 en Italie* (Paris, 1905); Max Ritter v. Thielen, *Erinnerungen aus dem Kriegsleben eines 82 jährigen Veteranes des österr. Armee* (Vienna, 1863).

77/One of the few authentic exposés of the reasons for this peace is provided in Guglielmo Ferrero's *The Gamble. Bonaparte in Italy 1796–1797* (Toronto, 1939).

peror-King Francis, and he advised the sovereign against reuniting Dalmatia with the other Croatian lands. Although the Dalmatian nobility continued to agitate actively for reunion, Thugut's influence prevailed.

Indubitably, the recent Magyar-Croatian reconciliation affected official opinion in Vienna at this epoch. Viennese officialdom looked askance at the idea of turning over the Dalmatian coast to Hungary, which now seemed to be in a position to dominate the Hungarian-Croatian state relationship. The Austrians failed to see that a reunion of the Croatian lands would strengthen the Croatians vis-à-vis the Magyars and would not be in any way a menace to Austria. On the contrary, ties of gratitude might have bound the united Croatian kingdom more closely to Vienna than heretofore. But Thugut was determined to keep the coastal region under direct Austrian control and set up a special political administration for the province, while Francis II advised the Croatians that he could not consent to the merger of Dalmatia with the other parts of the ancient Triune Kingdom.[78] This was probably the greatest mistake Austria made in her relations with the Croatians.

The Austrians effected a number of changes and reforms in Dalmatia between 1797 and 1805;[79] however, by the terms of the Peace of Pressburg of 1805, Vienna had to surrender her recent acquisition to the French Kingdom of Italy, and the French remained in control of the province until 1809 when Croatian troops from the Civil and Military Provinces drove them out.

Archduke John had created in Banal Croatia a volunteer military formation that received the name of *domobranska vojska* or Home Defense Force. The Dalmatian Croatians rose against the French, whose regime was less popular with the people who had to endure it than with some of those who have chosen to write about it in retrospect.[80] The Banal regime exerted itself, too, to promote anti-French revolts.[81] Also, many

78/T. Smičiklas, *Poviest hrvatska*, II, 402–3; Grga Novak, "Pokret za sjedinjenje Dalmacije s Hrvatskom (1797–1814)"/Movement for the Union of Dalmatia and Croatia, *Rad* (Yugoslav Academy), CCLXIX (1940), 1–110; Knezović, *Poviest Hrvata*, 226–9.

79/On the Austrian administration during this period see Paul Pisani, *La Dalmatie de 1795 à 1815* (Paris, 1893), 33–50, 73–113. See also A. Paton, *Highlands and Islands of the Adriatic* (2 vols.; London, 1849), I, 262. This subject is treated fully in the author's forthcoming work dealing with Croatian history between 1814 and 1945.

80/L. Stavrianos recently has reiterated the several historical clichés concerning the period of French domination of Dalmatia in his *The Balkans since 1453* (New York, 1958), 213. Less naïve but still definitely too francophile is Dr. Jure Prpić's "French Rule in Croatia 1806–1813," *Balkan Studies*, v (1964), 221–76. See also Knezović, *Poviest Hrvata*, 229–33.

81/*Jura regni*, II, 276; V. Deželić, *Maksimilijan Vrhovac* (Zagreb, 1904), 147–63.

Croatian nobles contributed generously to the establishment of a military academy at Buda, an institution founded for the express purpose of training officers for service against the French; a number of young Croatians frequented it.

Croatian units fought brilliantly at Aspern and at Wagram in the war of 1809.[82] But, as usual, Austria did not choose to fight a war through to a successful conclusion in the manner of the British. The defeat at Wagram induced Vienna to negotiate the Peace of Schönbrunn, in which she surrendered to France all of Military and Civil Croatia on the right bank of the Sava. Through the loss of this territory, Croatia was exposed to great economic hardships. Count Adam Oršić remarked in his *Notebook* or diary that only Serbs and Jews, both of whom were "used to living poorly," were able to prosper in the Croatian lands during the next few years.

Austria also had to return Dalmatia and Istria to French control. The Dalmatians did not welcome this denouement to the war in which they had participated so enthusiastically, and asked the Hapsburg commander, General Knezović, to continue the struggle. As a soldier, Knezović could not disobey orders issued by his superiors. Many Croatians thereupon emigrated to the Hapsburg territories or to Bosnia to escape French rule.[83] Other veterans of Aspern and Wagram, and of the conflicts in Dalmatia and Italy, joined Andreas Hofer in his losing fight against the French and Bavarians in the Tyrol.[84]

Bonaparte added the parts of southern Croatia that he had acquired

82/Pisani, *La Dalmatie de 1795 à 1815*, 325. Croatian participation in the wars of 1805 and 1809 is mentioned prominently in Giuseppe Ferrer, *Mémoires d'un ancien capitain Italien sur les guerres et les intrigues d'Italie de 1806 à 1821* (Paris, 1845); A. v. Einsiedel, *Die Feldzüge der Österr. in Italien im Jahre 05* (Weimar, 1912); *Guerre de l'an 1809 entre l'Autriche et la France par un officier autrichien* [Gen. M. Stutterheim] (2 vols.; Vienna, 1811); Abbé Aimé Guillou, *Histoire de la campagne de S.A.I. le prince Eugène Beauharnais de France en 1809* (Milan, 1809); and the *Memoirs* of Marshal Marmont, vol. III (Paris, 1857).

83/See Pisani, *La Dalmatie de 1795 à 1815*, 364. In Dalmatia the Church was so hard hit by the French occupation that it was no longer able to take care of the poor as it had done in former times, even during the worst days of Venetian rule. Certainly Dalmatia did not prosper under the Venetian administration, but it was the ruinous effects of the French possession of this land that initiated the real economic decay of the once prosperous Croatian coastland. See André Blanc, *La Croatie occidentale* (Paris, 1937), 338–9 (footnote); Pisani, *La Dalmatie de 1795 à 1815*, 264–73, 309–10. All of the Croatian lands suffered severely from their inclusion within the French economic system. See M. Pivec-Stelè, *La vie économique des Provinces Illyriennes* (Paris, 1930), 355, see also 26–263 *passim*; R. Lopašić, *Karlovac* (Zagreb, 1879), 58–67, 81–2, 91, 311–16.

84/Czoernig, *Ethnographie der österr. Monarchie*, III, 111–13.

by the Peace of Schönbrunn to Carniola, Istria, Dalmatia, and Carinthia to form the "Kingdom of Illyria." Since Serbians as well as Slovenes and Croatians were included in this complex, the first effective impulse was given to what was to become the "Yugoslav" idea.

Although the French regime does not appear to have been unpopular among the Serbians and Slovenes, it is altogether erroneous to hold that the Croatians ever welcomed or were satisfied with the change in sovereignty. Especially bitter were the Croatians of Dubrovnik when they found that their old republic was to be incorporated in the French satellite state, and a number of Dubrovčani emigrated also.[85]

Sixteen thousand Croatians, Serbs, and Slovenes were drafted into the Napoleonic legions. Two Croatian regiments marched into Russia with the "Grand Army" in 1812. But when Austria again entered the lists against France in 1813, almost all Croatian formations serving under the tricolor defected to the Hapsburgs. Wild enthusiasm for war and reconquest of the lost lands prevailed throughout Hapsburg Croatia-Slavonia. Field Marshal Radivojević invaded French Illyria with only 9000 Croatian troops, but his ranks were swelled by volunteers from every quarter. All of the land between the Sava and the sea fell to him while Captain Lazarić drove the French out of Istria. Zagreb County resumed control of the districts that it had ceded in the peace of 1809. So many French prisoners passed through the Croatian capital at this time that a severe strain was placed upon its housing facilities and a large number of the captives had to be sent on to Osijek. Even the populations of the Adriatic islands and the inhabitants of Rijeka rose against the French and helped to augment the Gallic disaster. By the middle of October 1813 only Zadar, of all Dalmatian localities, remained in French hands. Napoleon's generals tried to induce the Bosnians to come to their assistance, but although the Croatian Muslims did try to relieve Zadar they attacked and massacred French garrisons at other points.

Trouble between Croatian and Serbian elements broke out in Boka Kotorska, where on November 20 the Croatian population petitioned General Tomašić to annex the whole district to Austria.[86] Russian agents stirred up the Serbian and Montenegrin residents of this area in the hope that its cession to Montenegro would facilitate the establishment of a

85/On Dubrovnik's relations with France and Austria up to the time of her annexation by the French see Pisani, *La Dalmatie de 1795 à 1815*, 125–42.

86/Pavao Butorac, "Boka Kotorska nakon pada mletačke republike do bečkoga kongresa (1797–1815)"/The Gulf of Kotor after the Fall of the Venetian Republic until the Congress of Vienna, *Rad* (Yugoslav Academy), CCLXIV (1938), 161–236; CCLXV (1938), 1–154.

Russian naval base there. To avoid an armed conflict that would have anticipated the one that came just a century later, Czar Alexander I of Russia finally yielded Boka Kotorska to the Hapsburgs. At this time also, the Croatian inhabitants of Kotor wanted Austria to take Albania from the Turks.

CROATIA-SLAVONIA FROM 1815 TO 1848

Following the defeat of France, Vienna restored to the Military Frontier system those parts of Military Croatia that she had ceded to Bonaparte in 1809. The other Croatian-inhabited lands were divided between the kingdoms of Illyria and Dalmatia. Sabor protested against the incorporation of Banal (Civil) Croatia in the Illyrian Kingdom on the ground that it was a violation of the Croatian constitution. On October 4, 1814, the estates refused to take the loyalty oath demanded of them. Vienna warned Sabor that its members would have to take the oath individually if Sabor as a corporate body declined to do so. They had to appear before the vice-governor, Gjurković, within a month's time or go into exile abroad. This threat broke, for the moment at least, the stubborn resistance of the Croatians to the division of the territories of the old Triune Kingdom. But it also drove them closer to Hungary.

In 1814–15 the Congress of Vienna met to reconstruct a Europe whose foundations had been shattered by the French Revolutionary and Napoleonic Wars. There were influential Magyars in the Austrian capital who enjoyed social intercourse with prominent German, French, and Russian, as well as Austrian personalities. Through these social connections the Hungarians were able to exert an influence in favor of the old Hungarian-Croatian state relationship. Their agitation in this direction bore fruit in 1822 when the Croatian lands to the right of the Sava, including the so-called "Hungarian Littoral" (coastland), were again incorporated with the lands of St. Stephen's Crown. The "gubernium" of Rijeka was restored as it had existed in 1809.

In 1825 Sabor sent delegates to attend the meetings of the Hungarian diet at Pressburg. From this time on the Magyars endeavored to impose the use of their language upon the Croatians. Especially as the rising star of the chauvinistic Louis Kossuth, a Magyarized Slovak, eclipsed those of the great trio of moderate Magyars, Count Stephen Széchenyi, Francis Déak, and Joseph Eötvös, the pressure was augmented for the replacement of Latin by Magyar as the language of government, courts, and schools in Croatia-Slavonia.

Although the language issue was the chief source of Hungarian-Croatian difficulties, there were other points of controversy too. Most of the Hungarian leaders stood for the emancipation of all serfs, whether in Hungary or in Croatia-Slavonia. The Croatian estates opposed full emancipation on the ground that it would deliver noble and peasant alike into the hands of Serbian and Jewish usurers. Sabor also defended the Croatian claim to Slavonia against pretensions to this territory advanced by the Kossuthist element in Hungary. Also, the estates offered serious opposition to the Hungarian demand that Protestants be granted full rights of citizenship in the Triune Kingdom.

Political parties now began to appear in the Croatian lands. The complex ramifications of the Illyrian movement and of the accompanying Croatian literary renaissance lie outside the scope of this survey. Suffice it to say that the "Illyrian" Party, which based its program upon the replacement of the older Kajkavian and Čakavian idioms by the Štokavian dialect as the Croatian literary language, confronted a pro-Magyar faction. Though numerous enough, the pro-Magyars were poorly organized.[87] In the county assemblies, however, they were able to exert much influence, and at this time these bodies were more important that Sabor itself. The estates now had little to do except to formulate officially and execute the desires of the local assemblies.

The "Illyrians" were so named because they originally espoused the idea that the Croatians, along with the Serbs and Slovenes, were descended from the ancient Illyrians of Roman times. When they outgrew this fantasy, they began to call themselves the "National Party." Their political activity vacillated between attachment to Austria, a sentimental wish for union with the Slavonic peoples, and an occasional flirtation with the idea of Pan-Slavism or of Russian mentorship. There were many "Illyrians" or "Nationalists," however, who wanted to defend the Hungarian and Croatian "constitutions" against the centralizing tendencies emanating from Vienna.[88]

In the long run, instability of the "Illyrian" or "National" program did a great disservice to the Croatian nation. In Austria the opinion took

87/On the Magyarone element among the Croatians at this time see Šišić, *Hrvatska povijest*, III, 240–6, *passim*; *Pregled*, 408–11; *Slaven und Magyaren* (Leipzig, 1844).

88/Šišić, *Hrvatska povijest*, III, 247–8. On the several currents of opinion among the "Illyrians" or "Nationalists" see also *ibid.*, III, 250, 275, 348–9, 382ff.; T. Smičiklas, "Obrana i razvitak hrvatske narodne ideje od 1790 do 1835 godine"/The Defense and Development of the Croatian National Idea from 1790 to 1835, *Rad* (Yugoslav Academy), LXXX (1885), 11–72; Bogoslav Šulek, *Šta namjeravaju Iliri?* / What Are the Intentions of the Illyrians? (Zagreb, 1844); D. Rakovac, *Mali katekizam za velike ljude*/A Little Catechism for Great Men (Zagreb, 1842), 25–7.

hold that the Croatians were opportunists, and not above a bit of political blackmail on occasion, but that when the *Vergatterung*[89] sounded they would hasten to form up around the Imperial banners.

Kossuth's hour now had come in Hungary. He refused flatly to acknowledge the historic individuality of the Croatian kingdom as expressed in its time-honored record of association with the Hungarian Crown. Thus he gave a fateful turn to the fortunes of his own people and of the Croatians as well, for his dictatorial disposition and powers enabled him to graft his own opinions onto a part of the Magyar nation. When, in 1848–9, he committed the Magyars to the hazards of revolution and civil war against their Austrian associates, he found the Croatians lined up against him. In the war Croatian forces contributed significantly to the defeat of the Hungarian armies, a result which could have been obtained without the Russian assistance that was proferred in 1849.[90] Regiments from the Banovina, and Graničari contingents as well, distinguished themselves also in the suppression of the revolution in Vienna in October 1848 and in the Italian fighting of 1848–9.[91]

THE CROATIAN QUESTION 1849–68

There is a long-standing historical cliché to the effect that after 1849 the Croatians received from Vienna as a reward what the Magyars got by way of punishment. Prince Felix Schwarzenberg, who was in charge of the Austrian government in 1849, wanted to return to the fundamental ideas of Joseph II who had visualized a blending of the Hapsburg

89/"To the Standard!" The bugle rallying call of the Hapsburg regiments on the battlefield. This opinion was expressed quite commonly throughout Austria until the end of the Monarchy in 1918.

90/Although the Russian intervention was inspired by the principle of monarchical solidarity vis-à-vis revolutionary and republican movements, it was motivated also by the presence in Kossuth's armies of thousands of Polish veterans of the revolt of 1830–3 against Russia. The Russians feared that if the Hungarian revolt was not suppressed speedily it would spread to their own Polish holdings. Croatian participation in the Hungarian fighting is detailed in *Rat Hrvata s Magjarima godine 1848–9*/The War of the Croatians with the Magyars in the Years 1848–9 (Zagreb, 1902); Josip Matasović, *Do ozore 1848. Bojni pohod brodskih graničara*/The Call to Battle of the Brod Military Frontiersmen (Zagreb, 1919); J. W. Warre, *Adventures and Anecdotes of the South Army of the Emperor of Austria during the Late Hungarian Campaign* (London, 1850); F. Bach, *Ottočaner Regiments-Geschichte vom Ursprung dieser Gegend, ihrer Bevölkerung und ihrer Geschichte* (Karlovac, 1853).

91/Bach, *op. cit.*

peoples in a strongly centralized military monarchy and unitary state. Schwarzenberg realized that the several nationalities would be disillusioned by such a program, but he thought that they could be satisfied with far-reaching concessions in legislation and administration. He returned to Banal jurisdiction Slavonia and the Medjumurje, which Kossuth had annexed to Hungary, and he returned Rijeka to Croatian control. A modern British authority on Hungary remarked of Schwarzenberg's dispositions that the "bias in favor of the Slavs was unmistakable."[92] Croatian municipal rights remained uninfringed, taxes were much lower than those in Hungary (though of course it must be borne in mind that Croatia was less wealthy than Hungary and therefore felt the "tax bite" more), and Croatia-Slavonia was exempted from military quartering and requisitioning. While the old Hungarian feudal functionaries, such as the Count Palatine, ceased to exist, the dignity and power of the Croatian Ban remained unimpaired. For some years Ban Jelačić ranked as one of the highest officers and most influential persons in the Monarchy. Jelačić hoped to realize the "Illyrian" ideal under Hapsburg auspices through the union of Croatia, Dalmatia, and Slavonia in a constitutional and autonomous state. Also the Croatian language became the official idiom of Croatia-Slavonia for administrative purposes. Furthermore the Croatian Baron Kulmer, in his capacity as minister without portfolio, really functioned as a special minister for Croatia-Slavonia in the Schwarzenberg cabinet. At first the Croatians were not at all dissatisfied with the rewards that their role in 1848–9 had brought them.

THE SCHWARZENBERG AND BACH ERAS

The Austrian problem after 1848 has been understood neither by the Croatians nor by any other people, not even by the Austrians themselves. Francis Joseph, who had acceded to the Hapsburg throne in 1848, had to devise a constitution that would be acceptable to a mosaic of peoples at different stages of cultural and political development and possessing

92/C. A. Macartney, *Hungary and Her Successors* (Oxford, 1937), 16. On Croatia during and after 1848, see also *Die kroatische Frage und Oesterreich* (Vienna, 1848); Josip Neustädter, *Le ban Jellacic et les événements en Croatie depuis l'an 1848* (Zagreb, 1939); J. Hinterfeld, *Ban Jellacic* (Vienna, 1871); Vaso Bogdanov, *Društvene i političke borbe u Hrvatskoj 1948/49*/The Social and Political Conflict in Croatia in 1848–9 (Zagreb, 1949); Knezović, *Poviest Hrvata*, 258–66; Šulek, *Naše pravice*, 237–92, *passim*.

distinct and often contradictory historic, traditional, and national rights and aspirations. There was no one political recipe that would satisfy all the divergent desires of the conglomeration of Hapsburg lands and peoples. Much has been said about the abortive Kremsier diet which proposed to reconstitute the Monarchy on a federalistic basis. The fact remains that the ideas projected at Kremsier would have been entirely unacceptable to the Croatians among other Hapsburg peoples.

Croatia stood apart from the great basic issues that Austria had to contend with between 1848 and 1868. These basic issues were: (1) the conflict between the principles of absolutistic and representative government, (2) the issue of conservatism versus liberalism, and (3) the question of whether the Monarchy ought to be organized on a centralistic or federalistic basis.

The March constitution of 1849 was replaced by the Sylvester Patent of December 31, 1851. This substitution was unfortunate, for the Patent was not based upon a sound interpretation of existing circumstances in the Imperial Austrian state nor was it executable in the terms in which it was expressed. Nonetheless it did recognize the full independence of Croatia-Slavonia from Hungary. Deputations from the Croatian and Dalmatian Sabors were charged with the task of determining the conditions under which the reunion of Dalmatia with the rest of the Triune Kingdom was to take place. The Croatians were displeased with the Patent, however, because it degraded their thousand-year-old kingdom to the status of a mere crown land of the Monarchy. Yet it should be understood that it was only the intellectual elements who were dissatisfied with the existing state of affairs. Ivan Kukuljević-Sakcinski acknowledged this in a letter to Ban Jelačić in which he referred with contempt to the "ignorant mass of the people" because they were content to vegetate under Austrian rule.

Schwarzenberg's death in 1852 removed the one man who might have made absolutism work. Dr. Alexander Bach endeavored to continue the system, not without achieving some success. Technically the Bach administration of 1852–60 was superior to anything known in most countries before this date. It remedied many abuses peculiar to the old provincial governments, including the county assemblies of Croatia-Slavonia. It was efficient, honest, and socially progressive. It carried out salutary reforms in agriculture and finance. Eminent Croatian lawyers participated in the elaboration of a new territorial organization of justice. The judicial laws of 1853 replaced the dead feudal system by modern judicial procedure and prepared the way for the later reforms carried out in 1860 and 1874. Courts of the first instance were established in local and district centers, the court of the higher instance remaining in Zagreb. The Bach regime did not infringe upon Croatian municipal rights, furthered educational development, and imposed lighter taxes upon the Croatians than upon most other peoples of the Monarchy. Nonetheless the "Bach Hussars" were resented by the Croatians because most of them were Czechs, Slovenes, or Austrians.[93] Since the landowners were deprived of their old police powers and patrimonial jurisdiction by the emancipation of the serfs, new authorities had to be set up by the regime to discharge these functions, and the new police were resented more than their predecessors had been.

A MISSED OPPORTUNITY, 1860–7

It took the world depression of 1857, which completed the financial bankruptcy of the Hapsburg state, and the war of 1859 to effect the downfall of the often unjustly maligned Bach regime. In 1860 the high nobility of Austria and Hungary prevailed upon Francis Joseph to issue the October Diploma. This federalistic instrument divided the duties of legislation between a central *Reichsrat* (Federal Council) in Vienna and the provincial diets. The kingdoms of the Hungarian Crown were included in the new constitutional complex "in the sense of their earlier constitutions." Once again Sabor and the county assemblies began to function. A Croatian-Slavonian Dicasterium for internal affairs, justice, religion, and education operated in the Austrian capital alongside the Hungarian Court Chancellery. This circumstance emphasized the direct connection of the Triune Kingdom with Austria, rather than with Hungary.

This first experiment in the restoration of constitutional government foundered upon the rock of resistance offered by the Germanic liberal bourgeoisie of Austria. In February 1861 Anton Schmerling took office with a new cabinet that leaned towards the old centralistic Austrian tradition. He changed the Federal Council set up by the Diploma into a full-fledged parliament which had entire competence over matters common to the whole Monarchy. Since the Diploma had confided to the

93/See J. Trdina, *Bahovi huzari in iliri. Spomini iz moje profesorske službe na Hrvaškem (1853–1863)*/The Bach Hussars and the Illyrians: Recollections of My Professorial Service in Croatia (Ljubljana, 1903). See also Knezović, *Poviest Hrvata*, 266.

Council jurisdiction over the affairs of Cisleithanian Austria (that part of the Hapsburg state west of the Leitha River), except for matters of local importance that could be delegated to the provincial diets, the Magyars viewed the new parliament as simply an extension of the former exclusively Cisleithanian (Austrian) body. They would have nothing to do with it. Only Transylvania of all the lands of Transleithanian Austria (the Hapsburg state east of the Leitha River) sent representatives to attend its sessions.

The Croatians followed the Magyar lead in refusing to send delegates to the central parliament. At the same time that he had issued the February Patent, Francis Joseph had directed the governments at Zagreb and Zadar respectively to arrange for the reunion of Dalmatia with Croatia-Slovonia. A delegation of Italian and Italianized Dalmatians[94] protested against the union project but met with a sharp rebuff at the hands of Metternich's pupil, Count Rechberg, who was consistently pro-Croatian. Francis Joseph himself told a Croatian delegation that came to Vienna to petition him on the matter that it was his wish that the union be accomplished, but that the Croatians and Dalmatians themselves would have to work out the terms upon which it was to be effected. But on September 29, 1861, the representatives of Sabor delivered an address to the monarch in which they stressed the closeness of the Croatian political association with Hungary.

The Croatians now had reached a fateful turning point in their history. In Sabor the pro-Magyar Unionist Party was formed from the aristocracy, the small nobility, and a section of the intelligentsia. The National Party continued to promote under the banner of Hapsburg South Slavism what Gaj had begun under the auspices of "Illyrism." It wanted to negotiate with Austria on an equal basis the *Anschluss* of Dalmatia to Croatia-Slavonia. Bishop Strossmayer of Djakovo (whose mentor was Franjo Rački, the distinguished historian)[95] was the leader of this group. Both Strossmayer and Rački lacked political training. Anti-Magyar themselves, they nonetheless were influenced deeply by Magyar methods and policies. They demanded that Budapest give to the Croatians not only a binding declaration respecting the Triune Kingdom's independence of Hungary, but also recognition of the Croatian character of the Medjumurje, the Krajina, Rijeka, and Dalmatia. If the

94/On the activity of the Italian element in Dalmatia see Ivan Milčetić, "Dr. Julije Bajamonti i njegova djela"/Dr. Julius Bajamonti and His Works, *Rad* (Yugoslav Academy), CXCII (1912), 97–250; Knezović, *Poviest Hrvata*, 268–71.

95/On Rački see V. F. Zagorski, *Rački et la renaissance scientifique et politique de la Croatie* (Paris, 1909), especially 178–81.

Hungarians agreed to the incorporation of these territories in the Croatian kingdom, they were willing to resume the old constitutional relationship with Hungary.

Unfortunately, without securing any kind of agreement with the Magyars concerning these matters, the leaders of the National Party commenced to follow blindly the Hungarian lead vis-à-vis Vienna. Since the Hungarian diet never had recognized the accession of Francis Joseph, the Magyars demanded that the documents relative to the abdication of Ferdinand v in 1848 be submitted to them for examination. Although the Croatians had helped Francis Joseph to gain and keep his throne, they echoed the Hungarian claim. Similarly the Croatian National Party, like the Unionists, supported the Magyar contention that the Hungarian lands, including Croatia-Slavonia, were joined to Austria in nothing but a personal union. The Croatian spokesmen ignored the fact that in 1848–9 their nation had sacrificed, with complete willingness, the lives of many of its sons for the sake of establishing a "real" union with the hereditary Austrian lands.

Thus Unionists and Nationalists both agreed upon a policy of collaboration with Budapest rather than with Vienna. However, in Sabor there was a third group led by Ante Starčević. His Party of Right viewed the old Croatian constitution as the foundation of its political program. Starčević, a radical Croatian nationalist, took the Rakóczi cult in Hungary as his model. He held the view that the only power with which the Croatians should treat was the king of Croatia-Slavonia and Dalmatia. That this ruler also happened to be the Austrian emperor and Hungarian king was a matter of incidental importance insofar as the Croatians were concerned. Starčević aimed to bring into being a Great Croatia that would extend from Istria to Kotor and from the Adriatic to the Drina.

All of the Croatian parties imitated the Magyars in pursuing a policy of "watchful waiting." The Unionists and Nationalists were waiting for the Magyars to accept their program. The Party of Right was waiting for the king to meet their demands. For their part the Magyars were waiting for a more favorable moment to press their claims. The political naïveté of the Croatians prevented them from comprehending that a nation entitled to send eighty-five members to the central parliament in Vienna was situated differently than a nation with a quota of nine representatives in this body.

Vienna believed devoutly in the *Kaisertreue* attitude of the Croatians, but failed completely to understand the advantage that could accrue to

Austria from the unification of Dalmatia with Croatia-Slavonia. Since Sabor would not send representatives to the central parliament in the Austrian capital, it was dissolved. Although Francis Joseph was conciliatory in other respects, this action made the Croatians more recalcitrant and they flatly refused to send a delegation to Vienna to discuss the reorganization of the Monarchy. This abstention played into the hands of the Hungarians, who were looking for an opportunity to reassert their control over Croatia-Slavonia. Budapest promised Zagreb that all of the "rightful" desires of the Croatians would be conceded on the condition that they refuse to cooperate with the Austrians in transforming the Monarchy into a federal state. The Croatians themselves considered that Francis Joseph's invitation to all of his peoples to participate in the work of political reorganization was designed to facilitate further centralization. In reality, the ruler at this time was not committed to a centralistic policy, and, even if he had been, Croatian neglect of the opportunity to state the opposition of their nation to centralism was inexcusable from a tactical point of view. Furthermore, the Croatians committed the egregious error of allowing the Magyars to negotiate for them in Vienna. Naturally, the Magyars did nothing to ingratiate their "brother people" with Francis Joseph and his advisers.

A fourth Croatian political party had now appeared upon the scene. It was led by the noted poet Ivan Mažuranić. He was not only a poet, but a capable high official of the Austrian government. His political career had sharpened his outlook and understanding of the real objectives of Austrian policy. He realized that it was imperative that the Croatians reach an understanding with Vienna in order that they might not have to pay the price of the conclusion of the Austrian-Magyar compromise that now was plainly in the offing. His group coalesced into the Independent National Party which had as its goal the conclusion of a "real" union with Austria. In the elections of 1865 Mažuranić's party won barely a third of the mandates in Sabor. Thus the last opportunity to secure Croatian participation in the central parliament in Vienna was lost.

On November 19, 1866, the Hungarian parliament had the satisfaction of listening to the reading of the rescript issued by Francis Joseph in which he indicated acceptance of the Déak program of Austro-Hungarian union. Too late the Croatians came suddenly to their senses. On December 18 Sabor decided to disregard completely the wishes and actions of Hungary and to initiate direct negotiations with the Court. But on June 12, 1867, the Austro-Hungarian Ausgleich or Compromise received the imperial and royal sanction. Francis Joseph thus had committed himself to the Magyars and was no longer free to negotiate with the Croatians.

Hungary had concluded the Ausgleich in the name of the Croatians without asking the permission of the latter to do so. Such was the natural consequence of the Magyarone line followed by the Unionists and the ostrichlike policies adopted by the Nationalists, although both groups were equally patriotic in intent.

THE NAGODBA (1868)

Déak and other wiser heads among the Magyars realized that they would have to make an accommodation with the Croatians. They could not ride roughshod over their old "brother people" as Kossuth and his followers had wanted to do. These moderate Magyars were willing to grant to Croatia-Slavonia full independence with respect to domestic legislation, the details of internal administration, and justice, religion, and education.[96] However, they desired to reserve finance to the competence of the joint Hungarian-Croatian diet. In this body the Croatian representatives, twenty-nine in number, would be a powerless minority. Further, the Magyars wanted to keep the Banal nomination in their own hands.

The result of the Hungarian-Croatian negotiations was the Nagodba or Compromise of 1868. In effect this was a state treaty concluded between Hungary and Croatia on the model of the presumed content of the original Pacta Conventa of 1102.[97] It established the political community of Croatia-Slavonia with Hungary and permitted the Hungarian laws of 1867 to regulate joint Hungarian-Croatian affairs. A clause in the Nagodba stipulated, however, that future fundamental laws should be elaborated only with the participation of the representatives of the Triune Kingdom.

96/For the views of the Magyar moderates see Francis Déak, *Denkschrift über das Verhältnis zwischen Ungarn und Kroatien* (Vienna, 1861); Baron Joseph Eötvös, *Die Garantien der Macht und Einheit Österreich* (Leipzig, 1859); see also Eötvös, *Über die Gleichberechtigung der Nationalitäten in Oesterreich* (Pest, 1871).

97/On this probably apochryphal agreement of 1102 see the discussion and footnotes offered in S. Guldescu, *History of Medieval Croatia*, chapter IX. See also M. Barada, "Postanak hrvatskog plemstva"/The Origin of the Croatian Nobility, *Časopis za hrvatsku povijest*/Journal of Croatian History, III (1943), 203–5.

Forty Croatian delegates were allotted to the lower table or house of the Hungarian parliament, while three sat in the upper house or Table of Magnates. Five Croatians were included in the sixty-man delegation that represented the Hungarian half of the Monarchy in negotiations with the Austrian delegation. The actual participation of the Croatians in the deliberations of the Hungarian parliament was confined to matters that concerned Croatia-Slavonia. Croatia-Slavonia formed a joint kingdom with Hungary with which it shared the burden of a common establishment for national defense, finance, commerce, and transportation. Ultimately, however, the Hungarian parliament had control over joint affairs.[98]

But since under the Nagodba Croatia ostensibly enjoyed full autonomy, it was assumed that Dalmatia would be joined to this Croatian complex. However, the Austrians were afraid to allow the seacoast to pass under the control of the Hungarian part of the Monarchy. The naval victory of Lissa (Vis) in 1866 had stimulated the idea of the development of Austrian sea power, and Vienna wanted the control of the navy and the coast to be in its own hands rather than in those of Buda. It is possible that had the Austrians seen fit to permit the unification of Dalmatia with Croatia-Slavonia, the hand of the Croatians, vis-à-vis the Magyars, would have been strengthened. It is also conceivable that the coast would have become Hungarian. In any case, the joker in the situation was that the Ban now was appointed by the king on the basis of nominations made by the Hungarian minister-president. Ostensibly the Ban was responsible to Sabor, but the Magyar Banal appointees usually contrived to muzzle Sabor fairly effectively for the remainder of the century. The conclusion of the Nagodba extinguished the Independent National Party, which fundamentally was pro-Hapsburg. Its role was taken over by the Starčevićs or "Pravaši," the party of Croatian rights. The Unionists supported the Hungarian Banal nominee, Baron Rauch. Since the electorate numbered something under fifty thousand, it was not difficult for the Ban to secure a majority through astute manipulation.

Section 59 of the Nagodba recognized that the Croatian kingdom was a political nation possessing a special territory of its own. Section 29 of

98/The volume of literature on the Nagodba is quite considerable, especially from the Hungarian side. Perhaps the most complete account offered in a language familiar to western readers is G. Horn, *Le Compromis de 1868 entre la Hongrie et la Croatie et celui de 1867 entre l'Autriche et la Hongrie* (Paris, 1907). See also *Die legitimen und historischen Rechte Croatiens und der Ausgleich mit Ungarn* (Vienna, 1871); Knezović, *Poviest Hrvata*, 279–84.

the Hungarian Nationalities Law also recognized that Croatia-Slavonia was a separate nation from the political point of view. Thus the Nagodba actually re-established the old Triune Kingdom as a sovereign state which of its own free will made over one of its departments, that of foreign affairs, to the central government in Budapest. But the minister for Croatia in the Hungarian cabinet, who functioned as the only channel of communication between the Ban and the king, was responsible not to Zagreb but to the joint parliament in the Magyar capital.

Croatia-Slavonia had its own cabinet which consisted of the chiefs of the administrative and justice departments with the Ban presiding over them. Autonomous provincial and municipal governing bodies continued to exist, but they derived their authority from Sabor, which was a unicameral legislature of ninety members. Originally the Nagodba had provided for 108 members of Sabor. Ban Khuen-Hederváry, however, introduced a "reform" whereby the number was reduced to eighty-eight. The system of local government was based upon the commune as the unit of administration. All males over twenty who paid state taxes had electoral rights within their commune. Each of the Croatian and Slavonian counties had its assembly as in former times. Croatian autonomy in domestic affairs, public instruction, and justice was assured by these administrative units.

After Déak and his closest collaborators passed from the political scene in Hungary, the Magyars endeavoured to limit the special rights granted to the Croatians by the Nagodba. In particular they worked to impose the Magyar language upon their fellow citizens. The process of Magyarization, however, was handled clumsily, and was irritating rather than efficient.[99] There were some advantages to be gained by knowing Magyar, and if the Hungarians had come up with a better-executed scheme of introducing it into Croatian life, the Croatians might not have resisted learning it as bitterly as they did.

During the latter part of the century Croatian youth began to frequent the University of Prague. This development was most unfortunate from the standpoint of the national interest since in the Czech capital they were exposed to the subtly subversive influence of the teachings of Pro-

99/Among other treatments of this issue, see Anonymous, *Die magyarisierung in Ungarn. Nach den Debatten des ungarischen Reichstages über den Unterricht der magyarischen Sprache an Volksschulen* (Munich, 1879); Jean Povolin (Baron Živković), *Zur Sanierung der Verletzungen des kroatisch-ungarischen Ausgleiches* (Vienna, 1886); *Magjarizacija u Hrvatskoj*/Magyarization in Croatia (Zagreb, 1908); Mirko Bogović, *Ursachen und Wirkungen – Tumulten in Kroatien* (Zagreb, 1883); Knezović, *Poviest Hrvata*, 287–8ff.

fessor Thomas Masaryk. Masaryk himself probably did not appreciate the full impact of his philosophy upon the minds of his Croatian students, many of whom returned from Prague full-fledged revolutionaries.[100]

THE GREAT CROATIAN PROGRAM AND THE CROATIAN SERBS

In the 1870s many Croatians dreamed of making Zagreb capital of a "Great Croatia" which would include Croatia, Slavonia, Dalmatia, Istria, and Bosnia-Hercegovina. Some extremists even proposed to add Serbia and Montenegro and the Slovene lands to this complex. This political chimera prevented the Croatian nation from taking advantage of the several real concessions and opportunities offered to it by the Nagodba.

The Serbs of southern Hungary energetically opposed the "Great Croatian" program. Many of the Serbian residents in Croatia-Slavonia also attacked Croatian aspirations with unrelenting zeal. They denied that there was any such thing as an independent Croatian culture or that the Croatians had a right to a separate statehood. For their part the Magyars considered that the formation of a "Great Serbian" state extending from the Adriatic to the Danube, and including Bosnia and Hercegovina, would constitute an effective check upon Croatian territorial and political aspirations. It was only later on, when they began to perceive the possible implications of the Yugoslav movement, that the Magyars turned against the Serbs.

There was a Croatian group which numbered among its members many military and naval officers, and which enjoyed the patronage of Archduke Albert, hero of the war of 1866. Frontier officers were especially prominent in this faction, which pressed for the annexation of Bosnia-Hercegovina. Many civilian Croatians also saw in the acquisition of Bosnia-Hercegovina the cement that would tie together the parts of the old Triune Kingdom. When elements in these provinces revolted against Turkish rule in 1875 Croatian annexationist aspirations were raised to fever heat. Archduke Albert's inspection of garrisons in Croatia-Slavonia in May 1877 was made the occasion for huge popular demonstrations. Veterans of the Italian campaigns of 1859 and 1866

100/On the influence of Czech "realism" upon Croatian university youth, see Dr. Jurišić, *Svetski rat i Hrvati*/The World War and the Croatians (Zagreb, 1917), 56.

crowded around him to express their willingness to follow once more wherever he led – meaning to Bosnia.

The Congress of Berlin of 1878 liquidated the "Near Eastern Question" for the moment by giving Austria-Hungary a mandate to occupy and administer Bosnia-Hercegovina. In its address to the king on the opening of Sabor in October 1878, the Croatian legislative body demanded that the provinces be incorporated in a "Great Croatian" kingdom which would include Dalmatia and the Military Confines. Thus there was launched the program of trialism as a substitute for the Austro-Hungarian dualism established in 1867. The new state was to have the same rights, autonomy, and political organization as the Austrian and Hungarian state organisms established by the Ausgleich. This Croatian exposition evoked vigorous protest from the Jewish-dominated journals of Vienna and Budapest, which vied with one another in ridiculing Croatian political pretensions.[101] The Croatian demands exercised an important influence in determining the decision of the Hungarian premier, Count Andrassy, to forego the outright annexation of the provinces. There were few Magyars who could view with equanimity even the vague prospect of a Croatian-Bosnian union.

The specific grievances that the Croatians cherished against the Magyars in general and the Nagodba in particular came to a head in the years following the occupation of Bosnia-Hercegovina, which, incidentally, was carried out chiefly by Croatian troops. These grievances included the complicated system of suffrage which was based upon the amount of taxes paid, the restrictive press laws, and the overt Magyar Macchiavellianism in connection with the Banal office. In 1883 mass disorders ensued in consequence of Hungarian insistence upon placing the Hungarian ensign alongside the Croatian flag that floated over the Tax Office. Budapest took advantage of the riots to dissolve Sabor and to suspend the Croatian constitution. More disorders resulted.[102]

To deal with this rather artificially produced crisis the Hungarian minister-president, Koloman Tisza, appointed as Ban a Magyar, Khuen-Hedervåry, who had estates in Slavonia. The twenty-year tenure of office of this individual (1883–1903) earned for him the grim appellation "the Iron Ban." His intention (in which he was successful) was to control political life in Croatia-Slavonia. To gain his ends he saw that he would have to rely upon the support of the Serbian minority resident in the

101/France, Ministère des affaires étrangères, *Documents diplomatiques français (1871–1914)*, 1re série (1871–1900), vol. II (Paris, 1929), 388–9 (M. de Vogüé to M. Waddington, October 18, 1878).

102/Bogović, *Ursachen und Wirkungen – Tumulten in Kroatien.*

Croatian lands. Accordingly he secured for the Croatian Serbs valuable privileges in regard to education and religion as well as participation in political and economic affairs.

Khuen's league with the Serbs affected the internal political life of Croatia-Slavonia most profoundly. Mažuranić's old Independent National Party, which had desired union with Austria instead of with Hungary, had not survived the conclusion of the Nagodba. Strossmayer's National Party had developed a type of cultural Yugoslavism which did not compromise its loyalty to the Hapsburg connection. The real basis of this "Yugoslavism" was Strossmayer's hope that the Slavic-speaking elements in Bulgaria, Bosnia, Hercegovina, Dalmatia, and Serbia would enter into a single Catholic community that would include both Croatia-Slavonia and Serbia. In other words he expected to revive the old idea of a Croatian Uniate Church through bringing the Orthodox congregations into communion with Rome.

Strossmayer really was much more interested in the Bulgarians than he was in the Serbs. His exchange of letters with the British statesman Gladstone, which partisans of the Yugoslav idea have harped upon so much, revolves around this idea of a Croatian-Bulgarian community. Although Strossmayer's political activity ceased in 1888, his tinkering with the Yugoslav idea had momentous consequences. Yugoslavists thereafter were to make frequent inaccurate and unauthorized use of his name and ideas to provide sponsorship for their individually conceived programs.[103]

Meanwhile the Military Frontiers, which had existed for three centuries, had been liquidated between 1869 and 1884. Once again these parts of the venerable Triune Kingdom were joined to their motherland, thus satisfying one Croatian aspiration of long standing. On the other hand, they added to the population of the Croatian kingdom a larger Serbian element. The sentiments of these people have been expressed adequately by the eminent physicist Dr. Michael Pupin, himself a Serb from the Military Frontiers, who bitterly resented their incorporation in Civil Croatia-Slavonia.

In the final decade of the nineteenth century the Independence Party or the "48ers" led by Louis Kossuth's incompetent and irresponsible son, Francis, gained ground in Hungary. After 1897 this fraction endeavored to transform the arrangement effected by the Ausgleich of 1867. They

103/On Strossmayer see Tade Smičiklas, "Misli i djela biskupa Strossmayera"/The Thought and Works of Bishop Strossmayer, *Rad* (Yugoslav Academy), LXXXIX (1888), 210–24; F. Šišić, *Dokumenti i korespondencija*/Documents and Correspondence (Zagreb, 1933); *Djela* (3 vols.; Zagreb, 1896).

wanted, at most, a mere personal union with Austria. Kossuth and his inner circle of followers actually wanted complete independence, and were too myopic to realize that if Hungary were divorced from Austria, the Croatians, the Rumanians of Transylvania, and the Hungarian Serbs – if not the Slovaks and Ruthenes or Carpatho-Russians – would demand separation from Hungary.

During the 1880s and the early part of the 1890s internal political life in Croatia centered on the sterile conflict between Starčević's Party of Right or the "Pravaši," and the "Obzoraši," or Independent National Party. Starčević's program, insofar as he had one, was based upon a denial of the validity of the Nagodba. His party blamed the Obzoraši for the continued existence of this agreement with Hungary, and whether the Pravaši were more interested in disavowing the Nagodba or in breaking up the Obzoraši is a moot question.

Eventually, however, the Hungarian-Serbian alliance forced Starčević to realize what Mažuranić had perceived thirty years earlier – that the natural interests of the Croatian nation were bound up with those of Austria rather than with Hungarian destinies. While he continued to aim at the creation of a "Great Croatia," a more pro-Austrian orientation became the foundation of his policy. Article IV of the Starčevist program of 1894 demanded only that the Croatian lands should deal equally with the "Kingdom of Hungary and the other lands of His Majesty" in regard to affairs of common interest. Thus Trialism set the basis of the Starčevist program, which seemed to have outlived the irresponsible stages of its development. The feud between the Pravaši and Obzoraši was patched up by a sort of compromise, the main feature of which was the latter's acceptance of Article IV of the 1894 program. Virtually all other Croatian political factions subscribed to the essential points of this program also. In Sabor the Trialist idea found expression in a three-point resolution adopted by all the Croatian parties represented in the legislature. This resolution provided for (1) the integrity of Hungarian territory, (2) a separate Croatian state with a parliamentary form of government that would operate within the framework of the Austro-Hungarian Monarchy, and (3) parity with Hungary and the other parts of the Monarchy in relation to all matters of common interest.[104]

104/J. Horvat, *Politička povijest Hrvatske*/Political History of Croatia (Zagreb, 1936), 306–7. On the ideas of Starčević and the Pravaši see also his *Nekoliko uspomena*/Some Recollections (Zagreb, 1872); Fr. Kerubin Šegvić, *Dr. Ante Starčević* (Zagreb, 1911); Jurišić, *Svetski rat i Hrvati*, 17; J. Jareb, *Pola stoljeća hrvatske politike*/Half a Century of Croatian Politics (Buenos Aires, 1960), 14ff.; Dr. Julius Makanec, *Entwicklung des croatischen Nationalismus* (Zagreb, 1943), 33ff.

Although Starčević and his followers were anti-Serbian, neither they nor the Obzoraši were able to elaborate a policy of systematic opposition to the Khuen-Hedervåry administration with its program based upon an alliance with the Croatian Serbs. Khuen encouraged political corruption and imposed severe limitations upon the press; nor had he any scruples about destroying the reputations of people who opposed him openly. Yet it must be acknowledged that the "Iron Ban" encouraged Croatian agricultural development, and that he improved and extended transportation facilities through a public works program that provided many new highways, bridges, and railroads, and repaired and improved existing ones. He augmented educational facilities, too, though more with an eye to the requirements of the Croatian Serbs than to those of the Croatians themselves.[105]

Whatever benefits Khuen may have conferred upon the Croatians they were outweighed by the malevolent effects of his encouragement of the growth of Serbian political power in Croatia-Slavonia. The younger Croatian Serbs formed an organization to promote the interests of their people. They published a daily newspaper, *Srbobran*, which lost no opportunity to attack the Croatians as well as Austria. *Srbobran* contended that most Croatians actually were Serbs – their ancestors had just happened to become Catholics rather than Orthodox. Furthermore, the historic Croatian kingdom was for the most part an original Serbian settlement area. *Srbobran* was willing to concede to the Croatians as their authentic national territory only a small enclave around Zagreb. It clamoured for the "reunion" of "Serbian" regions such as Slavonia, southern Croatia, Dalmatia, and the Vojvodina, presumably so that when the time was ripe they could all be joined to the territory possessed by independent Serbia. A prominent publicist and politician, Svetozar Pribićević, organized the Serbian Independent Party which assumed leadership of the Serbian elements living in Croatia.[106]

Starčević died in 1896, and his death hurt the Trialist movement. His followers split into two groups, each of which claimed to be executor of his political legacy. Dr. Josip Frank formed the Party of Pure Right whose program demanded complete separation from Hungary, just as the Hungarian Independence or Kossuthist Party wanted the total

105/Martin Polić, *Banus Graf Karl Khuen-Hederváry und seine Zeit* (Osijek, 1901); Jurišić, *Svetski rat i Hrvati*, 54–6.

106/On the views of the Pribićević group (the Hungarian and Croatian Serbs) towards the ideas of Croatian statehood and nationality, see A. Radonić, *Politički i kulturni razvoj moderne Hrvatske*/The Political and Cultural Development of Modern Croatia (Novi Sad, 1914). See also J. Bogdanov, *Spor izmegju Srba i Hrvata*/The Quarrel between the Serbs and the Croats (Zadar, 1895); Knezović, *Poviest Hrvata*, 433–4, 441–57, *passim*; Jurišić, *Svetski rat i Hrvati*, 57ff.

estrangement of Hungary, including Croatia-Slavonia, from Austria. The Frankists also campaigned for a speedy realization of the Trialist program. However, their conception of Trialism differed from Starčević's, as well as from Strossmayer's Yugoslavist ideas, in that they proposed to include only Croatians and Slovenes in the "Great Croatia" they dreamed of. What they were going to do specifically with the Serbian minority in the Croatian lands does not seem to have claimed their attention, but most of them indubitably hoped that the domestic Serbs would go to Serbia, Hungary, or overseas.

The real weakness of the Party of Pure Right was that it had no roots among the peasantry, which constituted between eighty and ninety percent of the Croatian people. Frank's followers were drawn from the clergy, students, small urban and professional classes, and included a sprinkling of the gentry. This group did improve upon the Starčević record in that it offered a more systematic opposition to the Khuen regime. It assailed the undemocratic suffrage law, the inequitable system of taxation, and the restrictions imposed upon freedom and civil liberties. As far as the Croatian Serbs were concerned, the Frankists believed in ruling the street. They aggravated earlier Croatian-Serbian clashes by wrecking the *Srbobran* offices, smashing up Serbian business concerns and banks, and repeatedly assaulting Serbian groups and individuals. That there was provocation for these tactics is evidenced by the statement of Pribićević, publicized in the pages of *Srbobran*: "A Great Serbia will arise on the ruins of Croatia" (a truly prophetic utterance).

In 1903 Count Pejačević replaced Khuen as Ban. A non-political personage, Pejačević was conciliatory and endeavored to restore normality to the political life of Croatia-Slavonia and to undo some of the damage done by his predecessor. Following his appointment the Progressive Party was organized. Its program was based upon preservation of the existing relationship with Austria and Hungary, economic and commercial improvement, and the introduction of more democratic institutions.

These favorable developments in the Croatian situation were offset by the marked deterioration of the national leadership. The role of the nobility in this connection had ended in 1848. During the following decades writers, priests, and intellectuals of various kinds, many of them of non-Croatian origin, took over the position vacated by the aristocracy. Towards the end of the century professional politicians, lawyers, and journalists were all scrambling for power and influence. It is an adequate commentary upon the decline of political ability among the Croatians of the Banovina that Serbs and Dalmatians now were professing to speak in the name of the Triune Kingdom as a whole.

In Rijeka freedom of the press prevailed. Here Frano Supilo founded

Novi List, a paper which propagated the fiction of Croatian-Serbian identity. In 1903 a Croatian deputation from Istria and Dalmatia had wished to present to the emperor-king a statement of grievances concerning the condition of their co-nationals in Croatia-Slavonia. Since the Ausgleich prohibited the interference of the ruler in Hungarian internal affairs, and since the Magyars protested strenuously against his receiving the deputation, Francis Joseph declined to discuss the situation of the Croatians of the Banovina with the Istrians and Dalmatians. This decision was probably a mistake, although it is difficult to see how the ruler could have acted otherwise without stirring up a real hornet's nest in Hungary. By the Army Order of Chlopy issued in this year, he had already administered one serious slap on the wrist to Magyar chauvinists, and to go over their heads now to talk with people who belonged to the Austrian half about conditions prevailing in the Hungarian half of the Monarchy would be to ask for trouble. However, Supilo and the Croatian Serbs took advantage of this incident to try to persuade the Croatians that the Hapsburgs were indifferent to them. Already the death of Crown Prince Rudolf at Mayerling had dealt a severe blow to the status of the dynasty in Croatia-Slavonia and Dalmatia-Istria. The new heir to the throne, Francis Ferdinand, while well disposed towards the Croatians, never achieved among them the popularity enjoyed by his predecessor.[107]

In 1905 the Hungarian Independence Party or "48ers" triumphed in the Hungarian parliamentary elections. Francis Joseph saw that this unwelcome event was a result of the restricted suffrage prevailing in the land of the Magyars. For the first time in the thirty-seven years since he had become the constitutional ruler of the Hungarian kingdom, he threatened to interfere in the administrative machinery of Hungary. He fully intended to introduce into the lands of St. Stephen's Crown the modern phenomenon of universal suffrage, just as he was on the point of introducing it into Austrian (Cisleithanian) political life. Apart from Croatia-Slavonia, the non-Magyar inhabitants of Hungary had a total of only nine representatives in the parliament in Budapest. But general male suffrage would destroy the power of the Magyar oligarchy overnight. Now, however, the oligarchy received unexpected help from an unexpected source – the Croatians.

The difficulties that the "48ers" were having with the crown inspired Supilo and people who shared his ideas to effect a reconciliation with the Serbs. Supilo's newspaper in Rijeka already had been propagating

107/However, on the occasion of the arrival of the archduke in Bosnia in 1914, *Hrvatski Dnevnik* (Sarajevo) declared "the Heir to the Throne is our hope."

the thesis of Croatian-Serbian identity; in doing so it enjoyed the protection of the Hungarian authorities. The latter considered that Supilo was a fool and that his anti-Austrian activities would be to the advantage of Hungary. Largely at Supilo's instigation, forty delegates from Croatia-Slavonia, Dalmatia, and Istria met at Rijeka on October 2, 1905. Here they drew up the celebrated Rijeka Resolution. This document congratulated the Independence Party of Hungary upon its victory in the recent elections. Two weeks later twenty-six Hapsburg Serbian representatives convened at Zadar, where they agreed to the propositions set forth in the Resolution. On November 14, some Dalmatian Croatians and Serbians got together at Zadar to declare that the Croatians and Serbians were one people and one nation. From these three meetings, accounts of which have often been considerably garbled, there emerged the so-called Serbo-Croatian Coalition.

The Rijeka Resolution[108] was largely the product of the able pen of Supilo, who, with Ante Trumbić, was chiefly responsible for bringing the Coalition to life. This group sought a working alliance with the Kossuthist faction in Hungary. Faced by combined Magyar-Croatian-Serbian opposition, the crown gave way, and in April 1906 allowed the Independence Party to take office in Hungary; as soon as the "48ers" were in power, they began to renege on the agreement concluded with the Coalition.

Now the Croatians were in a predicament, thanks to Supilo, Trumbić, and their associates. In effect, the Coalition had broken down the bridges that up to this time the Croatians had maintained to Vienna, only to find themselves repulsed and betrayed by Budapest. Because of the obvious bankruptcy of their policies, the leaders of the Coalition turned to Belgrade in sheer self-defense. They asserted and accepted the identity of Croatians and Serbs and thereby dug the grave of the Croatian people and nation. The Croatian Serbs, of course, were quite willing to accept the idea of Croatian-Serbian identity – on condition that the Serbs of Serbia proper were included in the new "brotherhood." By propagating the idea of Croatian and Serbian identity in Croatia-Slavonia and Dalmatia, Supilo, Trumbić, and their colleagues neces-

108/On the Rijeka Resolution, see Milan Hodža, *Federation in Central Europe* (London, 1942), 30–1, 35; Vicko Milić, *Postanak Riečke Resolucije i njezine posljedice*/The Origin of the Fiume (Rijeka) Resolutions and Their Consequences (n.p., n.d.); Knezović, *Poviest Hrvata*, 435–8, and the text of the Resolutions, 439–40; Jurišić, *Svetski rat i Hrvati*, 57. Note Jurišić's telling remark: "These Fiume [Rijeka] resolutions raised a lot of dust and it must be acknowledged that they inaugurated a new period in Croatian political history. Today [1917] we can say that the Fiume Resolutions were a serious mistake from the point of view of Croatia's political interests."

sarily were sponsoring the concept that the Croatians and Serbs of these territories and the Serbs of Serbia were one nation. Thus the Coalition willy-nilly embarked upon the road that led to the Zagreb treason trials of 1908–9.[109]

Hungarian sources have alleged that in 1908 Supilo had dealings with a Serbian general concerning the uniting of Rijeka, Croatia-Slavonia, and Dalmatia with Serbia. The Hungarians say that Supilo asked for a 100,000-dollar subsidy from Belgrade to enable his paper to continue its propaganda in favor of Croatian-Serbian unity. Also it is said that he repeated his offer of Croatian territory to Serbia in a memorandum addressed to the Russian Ambassador in Paris (Alexander Isvolsky), an inveterate Austrian-hater and the man who in August 1914 said exultingly: "This is my war!" (meaning that he had done his best to bring it on). The Hungarian sources say that to the original bid made to the Serbian general Supilo added all of southern Hungary as far as the line Pécs-Mohács and Szabadka-Zenta. There is a curious similarity between these reputed territorial offers made by Supilo and the actual dispositions effected in 1918–19.

In the elections of 1906 the Coalition triumphed at the polls. This success spelled the ruin of the Unionist Party, which perhaps does not deserve all of the opprobrium that has been heaped upon it. Its members felt that the Croatians were closer to the Magyars culturally, politically, and economically than to any other people.

The program of the Coalition relied upon cooperation with the Hungarian Independence Party on the basis of the Nagodba. But in May 1907 the Kossuthists enacted the Railway Officials Bill and thereby broke completely with their would-be collaborators. This statute at once raised the question of the precise nature of the Hungarian-Croatian constitutional relationship, an issue that had lain more or less dormant since 1868.

Section 9 of the Nagodba declared that the railways were a "joint enterprise" of the two associated kingdoms. Section 57 stipulated that

109/Anglo-American and French historians and publicists have completely garbled this episode. The best account in English is that provided by Professor Joseph W. Swain, *Beginning the Twentieth Century* (New York, 1930), 154–6. Thomas Masaryk's *Der Agramer Hochverratsprozess* (Vienna, 1909) should be compared critically with George Nastich's *Finale* (Sarajevo, 1908), and his *Wo ist die Wahrheit* (Sarajevo, 1908). See also (Veridicus), *Kroatien im Jahre 1907–1908* (Budapest, 1909); Alfred Rappaport, v. Arbengau, "Rund um den Friedjungsprozess," *Berliner Monatschrifte*, IX (1931), 339–57. Masaryk and R. W. Seton-Watson are the people chiefly responsible (along with the flamboyant London *Times* correspondent, H. W. Wickham-Steed) for perpetuating the usually accepted version of this affair. See, *especially*, Knezović, *Poviest Hrvata*, 443–5.

Croatian was the official language for all "joint government" organs within the boundaries of Croatia-Slavonia. The Railway Officials Bill specified that all rail personnel, whether in Hungary proper or in Croatia-Slavonia, had to know Magyar. The excuse for the enactment was that the railways were essential to the safety of both countries in time of war. Therefore railway employees had to be able to understand orders issued by the Magyar military officers. Also the Hungarians argued that the joint Hungarian-Croatian railways were subject to the Ministry of Commerce and Communications in Budapest. Therefore they were not a department of the joint government of Hungary and Croatia-Slavonia within the meaning of Section 57 of the Nagodba.

Whatever the military justification for the act may have been, the permanent deputation sent by Sabor to the Hungarian parliament devoted its energies to obstructing parliamentary business in Hungary for a full six months. Although all Croatian political parties fought the law bitterly, an executive order put it into effect and nullified the usual Croatian tactic of obstruction.

Budapest then effected the dissolution of Sabor in the hope that the Coalition would be crushed at the polls in a new election. But the restricted franchise in vogue in the Banovina played into the hands of the exponents of Serbo-Croatian unity. Many Croatian Serbs were well to do and hence could vote, while their poorer Croatian neighbours could not. Since the Serbs constituted the real backbone of the Coalition, this organization, whose program was a curious mixture of West European liberalism, socialism, and Czech "realism," was able to capitalize upon the Railway Bill by posing as its principal opponent, although the Frankists were equally antagonistic towards it. Again the Coalition won a majority of seats in the new elections. Conscious of their parliamentary predominance, and confident that they possessed more popular backing than they actually did, the Coalition flatly declined to work with the new Ban, Baron Paul Rauch, who was appointed in 1908 by the Wekerle administration in Hungary.

Rauch was the son of the man who had brought acceptance of the Nagodba thirty years before. Personally Rauch was a liberal, but he found that in Croatia-Slavonia he would have to govern despotically, without and in defiance of Sabor, because of the strength of the anti-Hungarian opposition. Crowds welcomed his arrival in the Triune Kingdom with stones and hisses. He dissolved Sabor and ordered new elections when the Coalition, which for the first time had an absolute majority in this body, boycotted his administration.[110]

110/Anonymous, *Die "Ritterliche" Affaire des Baron Paul Rauch* (Zagreb, 1908).

At this time the franchise law in Croatia-Slavonia was most undemocratic; thus not one candidate was elected who was willing to cooperate with Rauch, a result that probably would not have obtained had universal suffrage prevailed. The Coalition won fifty-seven seats in the new elections and the Frankists twenty-four. A single Unionist candidate was returned. The newly formed Peasant Party elected seven representatives.

This last-named group came into existence through the work of two peasant boys from the Sisak area. Stjepan and Ante Radić attended a gymnasium in Zagreb. When the king visited the city in 1895 Serbian elements in the Croatian capital hoisted the Serbian national flag on the Serbian cathedral as a way of insulting the dynasty with a degree of subtlety. Dynastically loyal Croatian groups attacked the Serbian population of the capital and tore down the Serbian flag. Students then burned a Hungarian flag. Stjepan Radić was involved in these disorders and was expelled for his part in them. He continued his studies in Prague, where he was influenced to some extent by Masaryk. Later he went to Paris and to Russia. Upon his return to Croatia he secured a seat in Sabor largely on the strength of his vitriolic attacks upon the Magyars and their Magyarone allies in Croatia-Slavonia, and against landlordism.

THE ORIGINS OF THE PEASANT PARTY

Meanwhile Ante Radić had come to understand that the weakness of the Frankists, which more than any other group stood for the genuine interests of the Croatian nation, lay in its lack of roots among the peasantry. Ante conducted a village-to-village campaign to awaken the political consciousness of the peasants and to organize them into an articulate political group. After five years of preliminary effort the Peasant Party made its official debut in December 1904.

Two years before, Stjepan Radić had advanced a plan for the federalization of the Hapsburg Monarchy in the pages of *Hrvatska Misao*. In its broad outlines Radić's scheme resembled the centralistic plan of a "Great Austria" visualized by Prince Schwarzenberg a half century earlier. Radić revived Schwarzenberg's idea of dividing the Monarchy along roughly ethnographic lines. He envisioned a Germanic Austrian state, a largely Magyar Hungary in which Ruthenians, Slovaks, Rumanians, and Hungarian Serbs would have guaranteed minority rights, a Czech kingdom that would include the three historic crown lands of Bohemia, Moravia, and Silesia, and a Polish kingdom formed from the Galician holdings of the Monarchy. Croatia, Slavonia, and Dalmatia would constitute an autonomous kingdom. Bosnia-Hercegovina, too, would receive autonomy and it would decide by vote of its population whether it wanted to be reunited with the Triune Kingdom or not. Rijeka was to receive independent status. The capital of the federal entity projected by Radić would be Vienna and the Hapsburg dynasty would reign over the entire complex.[111]

During 1905 Stjepan Radić wrote a series of truly great articles that dealt with the nationalities question in Austria. He made an open confession of his faith in the realization of the idea of a Great Austrian federal state. Ante seconded his efforts in this direction in the pages of the *Dom* which was written primarily for literate peasants. Angry Coalitionists at this time were accustomed to refer contemptuously to the Radić brothers as "Cesarevci" (Hapsburg Imperialists). Vienna always had a rare talent for ignoring the existence of elements favorable to its administration, however, and the efforts of the Radićs in its behalf received no support from that quarter. Despite the lack of official help vouchsafed to them, the Radićs held fast to the Great Austrian idea until after the initial defeats sustained by the Austro-Hungarian army in 1914. Actually, right up to the outbreak of war, their chief interest was in economic and social rather than in political reform of the Monarchy. Both of the brothers approved the annexation of Bosnia-Hercegovina which was carried through in 1908 – thirty years too late. Stjepan took it upon himself to explain to the Russians, who supported the Serbian claim to the provinces, that their annexation by the Hapsburg state would facilitate the creation of a "Great Croatia." Therefore he urged everyone in St. Petersburg with whom he could get an audience to advocate Russian acceptance of the inclusion of Bosnia-Hercegovina in a Danubian complex. He was too naïve to realize that the last thing the Russians wanted was the aggrandizement of Catholic Croatia.

During this epoch, the trialistic and federalistic ideas conceived by many Croatians were working at cross purposes with the "United States of Great Austria" idea which was being propagated by Francis Ferdinand's confidant, the Rumanian Aurel Popovici. Popovici argued for the creation of an all-people's union within the existing framework of the Monarchy. Few Croatians could see eye to eye with him on the changes that he proposed to make in the organization of the Austro-

111/A. Fischel, *Der Panslavismus bis zum Weltkrieg* (Stuttgart, 1919), 452–3.

Hungarian state. Although they complained of oppression, the Croatians were proud of the fact that the Triune Kingdom had enjoyed a privileged and special status for a very long time. The fact is that, as in 1849–66, there was not one people in the Monarchy, the Croatians least of all, willing to make the sacrifices that the peoples of the Thirteen Colonies in English North America had made to establish the American Union. This was unfortunate; for a fusion of the Croatian concept of Trialism, in its narrower sense, with the Popovici and Radić plans for the creation of a "Great Austria," could have produced fortunate consequences. After all, none of the Hapsburg peoples, save for a minority of Serbs and Italians, wanted to see the Monarchy break up.

When the Sabor of 1908 initiated its sessions after the February elections, the Coalitionist president of this body committed the egregious folly of indulging himself in a public eulogy of Garibaldi and the Italian Risorgimento movement. Anywhere in the Dual Monarchy, but especially in Croatia-Slavona, such a public pronouncement was tantamount to high treason. It is not inconceivable, however, that the speaker was unaware of the role played by the Croatians vis-à-vis Garibaldi and the Risorgimento. Serbian elements were getting hold of the Croatian educational system in increasing measure and were manufacturing their own version of history.

In any case, the king replied to this speech by dissolving Sabor. The Frankists had warned their parliamentary colleagues that this was what would happen if the Coalition did not remain rooted in the solid ground of the national claims of the Croatian nation.

From this moment until 1910, Rauch governed arbitrarily. He curbed the right of assembly and censored the right of the press. Yet he had some good ideas and promoted Croatian agricultural prosperity. His sound agricultural program was impeded by the uncompromising hostility of both Coalitionists and Frankists. His political tactics alarmed Austrian military men such as Chief of Staff Conrad v. Hötzendorff and General Moritz v. Auffenberg. These high-ranking officers urged Francis Joseph to support the Starčević-Frankist line in Croatia-Slavonia and the other Croatian lands. They warned the ruler that Croatians would have to be appointed to the Banal dignity as well as to the governorship of Dalmatia. They warmly advocated the adoption of Trialism too. The chief of staff, with typical bluntness, declared that to ignore the justifiable wishes of the Croatians would be to drive this "Kaisertreue" people into opposition to the dynasty.[112]

112/Conrad v. Hötzendorff, *Aus meiner Dienstzeit* (5 vols.; Vienna, 1925), I, 74–7.

THE TRIALIST PROGRAM ON THE EVE OF SARAJEVO

In 1910, Rauch was replaced by the old Croatian Unionist Dr. Nikola Tomašić. Tomašić ignored the Frankists, but cultivated the Coalition.[113] A new suffrage bill lowered property voting qualifications, thus quintupling the electorate. Sabor now was a quite unworkable body, however. Magyar interference with Croatian internal affairs on the one hand, and the intransigence and recalcitrance of both the Frankists and the Coalition on the other, were responsible for this state of affairs. Matters went from bad to worse. The deteriorating political conditions produced a reunion of right-wing elements. The several remnants of the Starčević, Unionist, Frankist, and Mažuranić groups consolidated their forces. Fifty-five delegates from Croatia, Slavonia, Bosnia-Hercegovina, Istria, and Dalmatia met and agreed that the hour had struck for the introduction of the program of Trialism.

They knew that they had the backing of the heir to the throne and of the Austrian military men, and that the emperor-king himself was not unfavorably disposed towards them. On January 12, 1912, they delivered to the ruler a memorandum which requested him to summon representatives from all the Croatian lands to meet in Zagreb. The purpose of the meting would be to effect an agreement "with our legitimate king" for the regulation of the internal affairs of the Triune Kingdom and its relations with the rest of the Monarchy.

In 1912, however, Francis Joseph could not of his own free will dispose of Bosnia, Istria, and Dalmatia as he might have done more conveniently in the earlier part of his reign. Nor was he in a position to give Croatia-Slavonia, with or without these regions, equal status with Austria and Hungary. Anti-Hapsburg writers often have cited the lack of real democracy in the Hapsburg state. The fact remains that the parliamentary and constitutional system adopted in 1867 tied the hands of the ruler. It was out of the question that he should employ in the issue of Croatian unification the famous Paragraph 14 of the Austrian Constitution. (This clause permitted direct assertion of authority on the part of the monarch whenever parliamentary machinery broke down; as it often did in the Austrian part of the Dual Monarchy, where the artifices employed in the Hungarian half of the joint complex to assure the functioning of the parliamentary system were not employed.)

113/For the ideas that inspired Tomašić, see his *Temelji državnoga prava Hrvatskoga Kraljevstva*/The Foundations of the State (Constitutional) Law of the Croatian Kingdom (Zagreb, 1910).

In any case the Austrians, from the emperor-king on down to the shop-girls of Linz, Vienna, and Innsbruck, always tended to view the Croatian question as *nicht aktuell.*

Finally, in 1913, constitutional rule was restored in Croatia-Slavonia. Baron Ivan Skerlecz took office as Ban with the firm intention of ending authoritarian rule. Despite acts of terrorism, some of them perpetrated by Croatian-Americans, Skerlecz (Škrlec) persevered in his policies. He effected a compromise in regard to the Railway Officials Act which settled this red-hot issue to the partial satisfaction of all concerned. Office workers were to have a knowledge of Magyar, while road employees and officials would continue to use Croatian in dealing with the public. Henceforth the railways language issue lost its importance as a disruptive element in Croatian life.

THE CROATIAN KINGDOM IN 1914

In point of actual fact the spring of 1914 witnessed a remarkable simmering down of antagonisms in the Croatian lands. Many of the more clear-headed Coalitionists were beginning to perceive that the irresponsible antics of their leaders, and of the Pribićević faction among the Croatian Serbs in particular, were ruining the country. A coalescence of the Starčević-Frank-Mažuranić and Unionist groups with the rising strength of the Peasant Party was in the offing. Had this combination come into existence it could have spelled the doom of the Coalition.

In a final summing up of Croatian political experience prior to 1914 it must be acknowledged that, despite the recurrent complaints about Hungarian oppression, from 1867 to 1914 the Croatians enjoyed a far greater degree of home rule than they ever were to have during the period 1919–41[114] or than they have possessed since 1945. During this period, and in fact until 1918, not a single Croatian received a death sentence for political reasons, even though attempts were made, some of them successful, to assassinate the most prominent Croatian government personalities, including Bans Škrlec and Cuvaj.[115] Croatia's well-defined political autonomy indubitably was infringed, especially in regard to financial affairs.[116] Nonetheless she retained enough of this

114/See Milan Vladisavljević, *Hrvatska autonomija pod Austrougarskom*/Croatian Autonomy under Austria-Hungary (Belgrade, 1939).

115/*Croatia* (Pittsburgh, Dec. 15, 1933).

116/The best account of Hungarian-Croatian financial relationships is that provided in B. Karlović, *Das kroatisch-ungarische finanzielle Überinkommen* (Zagreb, 1904). Also available in Croatian, *Financijska nagodba*/The Financial Agreement (Zagreb, 1904).

autonomy to protect with absolute success the national character and the national language in all of the more important domains of public life including public education, religion, justice, and internal administration. Her cultural development and educational progress were outstanding. Even in regard to the thorny question of finances, while the taxes were voted and collected by the Hungarian parliament and finance minister, forty-five per cent of the net receipts were allocated to the domestic government of Croatia-Slavonia. This certainly was a fair percentage, especially in view of the defensive requirements of the Hungarian state complex, surrounded as it was by hostile neighbors, all of them engaged in a feverish armament program. Hungary, too, had commitments to her Austrian partner who was in an even more precarious situation. In the final analysis the judgment of a contemporary observer of the Croatian scene still rings true today after a lapse of half a century.

> The Croats were on the point of securing economic independence, and a separate budget. Their claims were strongly supported by Archduke Franz Ferdinand, who was a determined supporter of the "triarchy" system in the Habsburg empire, but his recommendations were looked upon suspiciously by the other Slavic nationalities of Austria, especially by Bohemia. They feared that once the Croatians were granted full political independence they would lose interest in the struggle between Slavism and Germanism.[117]

THE SARAJEVO MURDERS AND THE PROBLEM OF BOSNIA-HERCEGOVINA

In October 1908 Austria-Hungary annexed the ancient Croatian territories of Bosnia and Hercegovina which she had occupied and administered since 1878.[118] Serbia claimed these provinces because the Turks,

117/Aurelio R. Palmieri, "Growth of Croatian Nationalism," *Catholic World*, CIX (June 1919), 344–59. Note also *Hrvatski Radnik*/The Croatian Worker, March 7, 1943: "Through the 839 years of her history Croatia was a kingdom and governed herself independently. Even during the Hapsburg regime, that is from 1868 to 1918 ... it was considered a distinct political entity within the great framework of the Austro-Hungarian Monarchy."

118/A great deal of nonsense has been written about the Austro-Hungarian occupation, administration, and annexation of Bosnia-Hercegovina. On the occupation itself see Austria, General Staff, *Die Okkupation Bosniens und Hercegovina* (Vienna, 1878–80); Franz Milobar, *Der Berliner Kongress und die bosnische Frage* (n.p., n.d.); Sir Arthur Evans, *Through Bosnia and Hercegovina on Foot* (London, 1876); Dr. Ivan Musić, *Hrvati i Hercegovački ustanak 1875–1878*/The Croatians and the Hercegovinian Insurrection (Sarajevo, 1955), and *Ustanak u Bosni*/The Insurrection in Bosnia (Sarajevo, 1960); M. Mandić, *Povijest okupacije Bosne i Hercegovine*/History of the Occupation of Bosnia and Hercegovina (Zagreb, 1910); F. Šišić, *Kako je došlo do okupacije, a onda do aneksije Bosne i Hercegovine 1878 odnosno 1908*/How Did the Occupation and Then the Annexation of Bosnia and

during their period of rule over them (1463–1878), had imported many Orthodox stocks into these lands. These elements were subjected to Serbian ecclesiastical influences with the result that by the nineteenth century forty percent of the Bosnians and Hercegovinians considered themselves Serbians whether they were ethnically so or not.[119]

Towards the end of 1908 a paramilitary organization, the Narodna Odbrana or National Defense Society, was formed in Serbia. Its membership was composed of high-ranking Serbian civil servants and senior military officers. Serbia wished to fight Austria-Hungary during the winter of 1908–9 because she thought that Russia would back her up in such a conflict. The intention of the Narodna Odbrana was to carry on a guerilla or partisan-type warfare against the Dual Monarchy such as Serbian irregulars for years past had waged against the Turks, Greeks, and Bulgars in Macedonia.[120]

Russia was not ready, however, to support the Serbian claims by military action. She advised Belgrade to wait a few years to settle accounts with the Monarchy.[121] In March 1909, Vienna, tired of Serbian provocations, presented her Balkan neighbor with an ultimatum that demanded (1) demobilization of the Serbian Army whose officers were howling for war, (2) official acknowledgment of the fact that Serbia had no legitimate claim to Bosnia-Hercegovina, (3) a promise that in the

Hercegovina in 1878 and 1908 Respectively Come About? (Zagreb, 1938); W. J. Stillman, *Hercegovina and the Late Uprising* (London, 1877); Knezović, *Poviest Hrvata*, 371–87.

119/On the ethnic question in Bosnia-Hercegovina, see Dr. Krunoslav Draganović, *Massenübertritte vom Katholiken zur Orthodoxie im Croatischen Sprachgebiet zur Zeit der Türkenherrschaft* (Rome, 1937). See also Joseph Baernreither, *Bosnien und die Hercegovina in der vorottomanischen Zeit* (Vienna, 1911); K. Draganović, *Poviest hrvatskih zemalja Bosne i Hercegovine*/History of the Croatian Lands of Bosnia and Hercegovina (Zagreb, 1942); Ami Boué, *La Turquie d'Europe* (4 vols.; Paris, 1840), II, 85–137; A. Malbaša, *Hrvatski i srpski nacionalni problem za vrijeme regima Benjamin Kallay (1882–1896)*/The Croatian and Serbian National Problem during the Time of the Regime of Benjamin Kallay (Osijek, 1940); Knezović, *Poviest Hrvata*, 296–370, *passim.*

120/On the Narodna Odbrana, see Z. A. B. Zeman, *The Break-up of the Habsburg Empire 1914–1918* (London, New York, Toronto, 1961), 26–30; Stanoje Stanojević, trans. Hermann Wendel, *Die Ermordung des Erzherzogs Franz Ferdinand* (Frankfurt, 1923); Joachim Remak, *Sarajevo* (New York, 1960), 43–4, 48, 153–4; S. B. Fay, *The Origins of the World War* (2nd ed.; New York, 1930), II, 76–85; "Nationalism in Action," in *Europe in the Nineteenth Century. A Documentary Analysis of Change and Conflict*, ed. E. N. Anderson, S. J. Pinceti, Jr., and D. J. Ziegler, I (New York, 1962), 304–35. This last contains a complete exposé of the objectives and methods endorsed by the Narodna Odbrana. See also E. C. Helmreich, *The Diplomacy of the Balkan Wars 1912–1913* (Cambridge and London, 1938), 40–3.

121/M. Bogitschewitsch, *Die auswärtige Politik Serbiens 1903–1914*, vol. I, *Geheimakten aus serbischen Archives* (Berlin, 1928), 150–6 (document no. 27).

future the Serbs would cultivate "good neighborly relations" with the Dual Monarchy.[122] Convinced that the Russians were unready to march at this time, Serbia finally backed down and met the Austrian demands. The Narodna Odbrana transformed itself into a "cultural" organization. It remained violently anti-Austrian, but concentrated on propagandistic rather than terroristic tactics in the congenial work of undermining Hapsburg authority in Bosnia-Hercegovina. In 1911, however, the Central Committee of the Society issued a pamphlet which called for war against Austria.[123]

A smoke screen of gymnastic, anti-alcoholic, and "literary" societies was created to promote the "Great Serbia" idea in the southern lands of the Hapsburgs. In addition to Dalmatia and the Banat of Temesvár (southern Hungary), Serbian nationalists wanted to annex Bosnia and Hercegovina. Historically, the last-named provinces were Croatian settlement areas.[124] Therefore, when dealing with Croatians, the Serb chauvinists took pains to speak of "Serbo-Croatian" unity rather than of the "Great Serbia" idea. Some Croatians were just ingenuous enough to be taken in by this tactic.

Austria-Hungary advanced greatly the material prosperity of Bosnia-Hercegovina,[125] which, under the Turks, had become a beggars' land. Only the Muslim Croatian third of the population appreciated Austrian rule, however. Catholic Croatians in these provinces felt that the administration favored the numerically larger Orthodox and Muslim groups. Not all Bosnian Serbs were anti-Austrian, but teen-age students were attracted by anarchistic and Marxist ideas and by the cult of romantic nationalism propagated by the Narodna Odbrana. In 1910, a Bosnian student, Bogdan Žerajić, tried to kill the Croatian General Varešanin, military governor of Bosnia. Serbian officers trained him in

122/Germany, Foreign Office, *Die Grosse Politik der europäischen Kabinette, 1871–1914. Sammlung der diplomatischen Akten des auswärtigen Amtes*, vol. XXVI, part 1, 731. See also *Austro-Hungarian Red Book* (English translation, Vienna, 1915) (document no. 7).

123/Zeman, *The Break-up of the Habsburg Empire*, 26.

124/See especially in this connection *Kroatien und dessen Bezeihungen zu Bosnien*, Von einem kroatischen Abgeordneten (Vienna, 1909); Dr. Petrinjensis, *Bosnien und das kroatische Staatsrecht* (n.p., n.d.); Dr. O. Dominik Mandić, *Bosna i Hercegovina* (Chicago, 1960), and his *Bogomilska Crkva Bosanskih Krstjana*/The Bogomil Church of the Bosnian Christians (Chicago, 1962), *passim*; Knezović, *Poviest Hrvata*, 299–457, *passim*.

125/The details are given in Ferdinand Schmid, *Bosnia und die Hercegovina unter der Verwaltung Oesterreich-Ungarns* (Leipzig, 1914). See also Dr. Arthur May, *The Habsburg Monarchy 1867–1914* (Cambridge, 1960), 406–7; Joseph Baernreither, *Fragmente eines politischen Tagebuches* (Berlin, 1928). Dr. Peter Sugar's *The Industrialization of Bosnia-Hercegovina* (Seattle, 1963) is based upon Austrian and Serbian source materials to the complete exclusion of Croatian ones.

Belgrade to carry out this act. Instead of identifying him as the juvenile delinquent that he was, the Serbian press hailed him as a martyr of Serbian nationalism. Thousands of copies of a bombastic little pamphlet that described him as a hero were printed in Serbia and smuggled into Bosnia.

From 1911 on, Serbian extremists stepped up the tempo of terrorism. They were afraid that the Frankists were going to effect a coalition with the Peasant Party and other right-wing elements. Such a combination would end the parliamentary ascendancy of the Coalition and could give a new turn to Croatian political development. Vienna was fumbling her way toward reforms that would go far to satisfy some of the Croatian demands. As a matter of fact, it was not Austria, but the ruling Magyar oligarchy in Hungary that was obstructing Croatian national aims. In any case, Serbian nationalists were willing to commit any crimes that might incite Austria-Hungary to acts of suppression that would drive the Bosnian Serbs into opposition to the Hapsburg regime.[126]

There had now come onto the scene a new group, the Crna Ruka (Black Hand), known also as the "Union or Death" Society. Its members had murdered the Serbian king and queen in 1903, and some of them belonged to the Narodna Odbrana; Major Milan Vasić, a member of the Central Committee of the Black Hand, also was acting secretary of the Narodna Odbrana. The Union or Death group sponsored an attempt upon the life of the Croatian Ban, Baron Cuvaj, an act calculated to provoke the Hapsburg authorities into adopting repressive measures that would alienate all Austro-Hungarian Slavs. Behind this Serbian policy of deliberate and calculated terrorism stood Russia, which to all intents and purposes had made Pan-Slavism its official policy.[127] At that, it was less the Czarist government than a section of Russian public opinion that endorsed the Serbian tactic of provocation towards its neighbor.

From 1911 to 1914, Bosnian Serb terrorists, inspired and equipped by Belgrade agencies, conducted a sporadic, if unsuccessful, target practice at the expense of Croatian officials in the Hapsburg state. They hoped to pressure the Croatians into abandoning their claim to Bosnia-Hercegovina. Finally, on June 28, 1914, the Black Hand scored its first real

126/Zeman, *The Break-up of the Habsburg Empire*, 31.

127/Hans Uebersperger, *Österreich zwischen Russland und Serbien* (Köln-Graz, 1958), 297–8. Note also the statement made by Count Witte, Russia's outstanding financier and economic genius, to the French ambassador, M. Maurice Paléologue, quoted in the latter's *An Ambassador's Memoirs* (3 vols., 6th ed.; New York, n.d.), trans. F. A. Holt, O.B.E.

bull's-eye when it engineered the murder of the heir to the throne of Austria-Hungary and his wife at Sarajevo.[128]

Archduke Francis Ferdinand was anything but a likeable personality. However, he was a friend of the Croatians because he appreciated their staunch Catholicism as well as the past services they had rendered to his dynasty. Right wing and Peasant Party groups among the Croatians expected him to realize the Trialist program when he ascended the throne. Therefore, his murder was a severe blow to Croatian national aspirations. On the evening of June 28, Croatian mobs stormed through the streets of many Bosnian and Croatian towns to wreck Serbian newspaper offices and printing plants. Sometimes they attacked Serbians and smashed their establishments.[129] Sabor, on June 30, held a special in memoriam assembly to honor Francis Ferdinand's memory. At this gathering, Frankist spokesmen assailed the policies of the Coalition and accused Svetozar Pribićević of preparing the ground for the murders.[130] Since Serbians dominated Sabor at this time, the Frankist leaders were barred from attending further legislative sessions. Nonetheless, the killing of the archduke and his wife, and the war provoked by this act, changed the attitude of the Coalition. Its Croatian members

128/The latest study of the ramifications of the Sarajevo murder plot is that of Remak, *Sarajevo*. He gives a complete list of other works on this affair, from those of R. W. Seton-Watson and A. J. P. Taylor, who have tried to whitewash the Serbs, to such violently anti-Serbian accounts as those of Father Puntigam and Miss M. E. Durham. See also Ljuba Jovanović, *The Murders of Sarajevo* (London, 1924), trans. from *Krv Slovenstva*/The Blood of Slavdom (Belgrade, 1924). Vladimir Dedijer's *The Road to Sarajevo* (Cambridge, 1964), although it supplies much valuable detail, is misleading in its general conclusions. It is deliberately designed to obscure Serbian responsibility for bringing on the war of 1914. On the Black Hand see Remak, *Sarajevo*, 44–60, and the sources cited on 272–3. See also Helmreich, *Diplomacy of the Balkan Wars*, 41–4. Note especially Helmreich's statement: "To distinguish between the two groups [Black Hand and Narodna Odbrana] would be to maintain a distinction without a difference, especially after the Black Hand virtually took over the leadership of the Narodna Odbrana, and from that time on until the Balkan war, the work of the revolutionary organizations outside Serbia was made one." It should be noted, however, that the Central Committee of the Black Hand knew nothing about the scheme to kill Francis Ferdinand until Dimitriyevitch and his colleagues already had got the assassins safely across the border.

129/Letter of General v. Appel to Colonel Brosch, cited in Leopold v. Chlumecky, *Erzherzog Franz Ferdinands Wirken und Wollen* (Berlin, 1929), 364–5. See also the reports of Bilinski, the Austro-Hungarian joint finance minister who was responsible for the civil administration of Bosnia and Hercegovina, cited in *Österreich-Ungarns Aussenpolitik von der bosnischen Krise 1908 bis zum Kriegsausbruch 1914* (9 vols.; Vienna, 1930), VIII; Remak, *Sarajevo*, 146–9; Z. A. B. Zeman, *The Break-up of the Habsburg Empire 1914–1918* (London, 1961), 57.

130/Zeman, 57.

were for the most part loyal to the Monarchy and were beginning to realize the artificial character of the thesis of Croatian-Serbian identity that they had been preaching since 1905. They now separated themselves from the politically suspect Serbian minority.[131]

CROATIAN PARTICIPATION IN THE WAR OF 1914–18

Except for a few politicians, intellectuals, and teachers and students, the Croatians in 1914 answered the call to arms willingly. Stjepan Radić wrote odes in honor of Francis Joseph and the war effort. Of the sixty-odd divisions that Austria-Hungary put into the field at the beginning of the war, no less than fourteen were Croatian; some Croatian Serbs were included in these formations, of course.

The nucleus of the Croatian part of the Hapsburg Army was formed by the Thirteenth Army Corps which had its staff headquarters and recruiting offices in Zagreb. Included in this corps were the 36th and 7th Infantry Divisions and the 42nd Honved or Domobran Division. Dalmatia contributed one infantry and one cavalry division; also, the Dalmatian Croatians and those of Istria supplied the bulk of the enlisted personnel and a high proportion of officers to the Navy. Especially heavy contributions to the war effort were made by the Croatians of Bosnia-Hercegovina. Muslim and Catholic Croatians formed the bulk of the eight Bosnian-Hercegovinian regiments and eight Jäger battalions. Several artillery formations were predominantly Croatian also, as were many airmen and technical specialists. All in all, during the course of the war, 1,200,000 Croatians out of a total population of 5,800,000 rendered military service, chiefly in the form of front-line duty. No other nationality in the Monarchy had such a high proportion of front-line fighters.

Most of the Croatian troops were designated for service on the Balkan Front against Serbia and Montenegro. Conrad v. Hötzendorff, Austro-Hungarian chief of staff, bungled his strategic dispositions at the start of the conflict, apparently because he indulged in wishful thinking and persuaded himself that Russia would not come to the assistance of the Serbs. When she did just this, her ally, France, automatically was involved. Conrad, though he disliked the Reich Germans, believed that it was the duty of the Dual Monarchy to invade Russia in order to give the German Army a free hand against France. An Austro-Hungarian

131/Jurišić, *Svetski rat i Hrvati*, 65–70; Zeman, 23, 60–2.

offensive into Russia had no place to go unless the Germans advanced from the west simultaneously, which they did not do. German ineptitude at the Marne made the Austro-Hungarian sacrifice a costly and useless gesture. The Dual Monarchy was not strong enough to fight a two-front offensive war, but Conrad wished to gratify the ambitions of his old classmate, Oskar Potiorek, the Czech military commander of Bosnia-Hercegovina and the man whose faulty security measures at Sarajevo had facilitated the successful execution of one of the most farcically conceived murder plots in history.

Potiorek wanted to make a reputation for himself as a military strategist by forcing the passage of the Drina River, the boundary between Bosnia and Serbia, instead of invading, if he was going to do so at all, by way of Belgrade. An invasion force striking out of Bosnia had great difficulties of terrain to contend with; it was sheer madness to initiate a move of this kind with only twelve divisions (less than 200,000 troops), none of whom had ever heard a shot fired in earnest, against 350,000 veteran Serbian and Montenegrin soldiers. Conrad made matters worse by encouraging Potiorek to undertake this dangerous offensive through sending the Second Austro-Hungarian Army southwards. Then, just when Potiorek needed it most, the chief of staff recalled the Second Army to the Russian Front where it arrived too late to save Lemberg (Lvov). Both Conrad and Potiorek had expected the Bulgarians to attack Serbia from the east. Had the Bulgars struck in August 1914, along the line Zaječar-Pirot-Kragujevac-Arandjelovac, Potiorek indubitably would have gone down in history as a great strategist. But Sofia could not make up her mind to repay the Serbians for past injuries until the fall of 1915.

Austria-Hungary's South Army fought a series of battles of indecisive character and finally withdrew from Serbian soil. Large Serbian forces penetrated into Srijem and the Banat. Although they were driven back across the Sava with heavy loss, the Serbian Timok Division being virtually destroyed, this episode had important consequences. Local Serbian elements gave signals from the towers of churches and other vantage points to direct the fire of the Serbian artillery. They rang bells to betray the presence of Austro-Hungarian troop concentrations and executed other acts of sabotage. In Srijem the Hapsburg troops and military authorities were chiefly Croatian and not inclined to stand for any nonsense from the Serbian population. They hanged 120 Srijemian Serbs and deported 516 others. These incidents touched off a sharp conflict between the military and civil authorities in the Croatian lands.

Primarily this conflict was the consequence of mistakes that were made by the ruling elements in both Austria and Hungary. Count Stürghk, prime minister of the Austrian half of the Monarchy, did not convene the Reichsrat (Parliament) because he knew that some of its members would take a stand against the war and promote disunity in the war effort. He did not realize that attacks that might be launched in the Reichsrat were less dangerous than the radical agitation of the Pribićević-led Serbian minority in Croatia-Slavonia, Dalmatia, and Bosnia-Hercegovina. Furthermore, censorship policies played into the hands of anti-Hapsburg politicians. Owing to the paucity of reliable news from the official agencies, public opinion gave credence to all sorts of fantastic lies disseminated by Russian and Serbian agents. The authorities made a mistake, too, when they dissolved the Croatian Sokols, an athletic organization. Though these groups were manipulated sometimes by politicians, they were loyal to the Monarchy. More justified an action than any of the above, however, was the arrest on July 26 of the Dalmatian deputies to the Reichsrat, Oskar Tartaglia and Josip Smodlaka.

From the beginning of the war, too, some Germanic elements in the Austrian half of the Dual Monarchy had the idea of restoring the Germanic hegemony lost in the preceding century.[132] Some German military men and a good many of their Magyar fellows were convinced that the Croatians had to be coerced into being loyal to the Monarchy. The fact is that most of these people accepted literally the synthetic concept of Croatian-Serbian unity propagated by the Coalition before the war; they did not know much about the difference between Croatians and Serbians and cared less.

Then, too, the curse of the old Austrian state was the network of police and military spies who, since the day of Metternich, had sought to emphasize their importance by submitting overdrawn reports relative to allegedly subversive activities. In 1914, the tenor of such reports was well calculated to persuade the military bureaucracy that the civil officials in Dalmatia, Bosnia, and Croatia-Slavonia were not as forceful and efficient as they should be. Therefore, the soldiers endeavored to abolish the Croatian civil administration altogether in the interests of the successful prosecution of the war. They enjoyed the support of the Frankist Party and other Croatian elements who realized that victory was the all

132/In 1915 the German Nationalist Party in Austria advanced a program which was designed to make the Germanic minority in Austria as powerful as was the Magyar element in Hungary. The so-called "Easter Demands" of 1916 went even further in demanding the creation of a Germanic hegemony in the Austrian part of the Monarchy. See Robert A. Kann, *The Multinational Empire. Nationalism and National Reform in the Habsburg Monarchy, 1848–1918* (2 vols.; New York, 1950), II. 242.

important consideration at this time, whether from the *Gesamtstaat* standpoint or from that of the Croatian nation per se.

In retrospect, however, it appears that the military men were less wise than their civilian associates. So long as their authority was not questioned, the Hapsburg civil authorities – even the Magyar bureaucrats – had a considerable fund of tolerant forbearance which they were willing to expend upon individuals of all nationalities. Unlike the soldiers, they realized that there were few Hapsburg Serbs and fewer still Croatians who were committed to the "Great Serbia" or "Yugoslav" ideas. For every Pribićević there were a hundred or a thousand Konstantin Maglićs.[133] But the military men insisted on condemning, or at least suspecting, whole nationalities because a few individuals showed sympathy for the enemy.[134] War always gives the military the power to deal with treason, whether real or suspected. The military bureaucracy used this power with what probably was unnecessary and mistaken severity. By so doing they managed, in the long run, to convince some elements among the Slavic and Latin nationalities that they were underprivileged and that it would be to their advantage to seek an accommodation with the enemy. A new type of radical anti-Hapsburg agitation made its appearance. There were many Croatians who failed to realize that the government in Vienna was endeavoring to resist Pan-German intransigence on the one hand and military intolerance on the other. More important than the Croatian displeasure with some of the procedures in force in the Monarchy was the fact that the alliance of the Pan-Germanic forces in Austria with the most benighted part of the military convinced France and England, as well as America, that the Hapsburgs were content to be tools of Berlin and of the Pan-Germanic element in the Monarchy itself. In the final analysis it was this misconception of the role of Austria-Hungary in the war that sealed its doom and that of Croatian national aspirations as well.

In point of actual fact, even the most bigoted Pan-Germans and the most distrustful of military administrators had no reason to complain of Croatian loyalty. The Croatian regiments distinguished themselves on

133/Hungarian-Serb airman and author of *The Dandy Hun*, trans. Arthur Mayne (London, 1932).

134/American treatment of the Nisei (Japanese-Americans) during the war of 1939–45 shows that the policies advocated by Austro-Hungarian military men were by no means peculiar to their mentality. Neither Conrad nor Auffenberg were affected by this military trend. They remained sincere friends of the Croatians and advocates of the Trialist program. As chief of staff, Conrad had too many other things on his mind to pay much attention to Croatian affairs, however, and Auffenberg was relieved of his command after Rawa Ruska. Sidelined and subjected to petty bureaucratic persecution for the rest of the war, Auffenberg could do nothing for the Croatians.

the Russian, Serbian, and Montenegrin fronts.[135] Serbians complained bitterly that it was their "Croatian brothers" who fought them most relentlessly.[136] But the entrance of Russia into the struggle necessitated the diversion of the bulk of the Croatian troops to the Russian theatre of war where Infantry Regiment No. 16, the "Warasdiner," was the first unit in the Hapsburg Army to receive official commendation. After offering strong resistance to the Russian "steamroller" in the Galician and Bukovinian campaigns of 1914, the Croatians stood on the Carpathian crests throughout the winter of that year and hurled back the repeated Russian offensives with stupendous losses.[137] In the spring of 1915, Croatian regiments were in the forefront of the great breakthrough at Gorlice-Tarnow which won back Galicia and sent the armies of the Stavka reeling deeply back into their own territory with the loss of 2,000,000 men.[138]

When Italy attacked the Dual Monarchy in the spring of 1915, other Croatian contingents appeared on the Trentino and Isonzo fronts, as well as in Albania. Here they battled successfully for three full years against great odds.[139] In October 1915, Croatian regiments spearheaded the invasion that swept the Serbians out of their own country into Albania from which land the Italian fleet succeeded in evacuating the remnants by sea.[140]

135/Hungarian minister-president Count Stephen Tisza, no friend of Croatian political aspirations, acknowledged in his New Year's Address of 1915 that they had fought with unexampled valor in Galicia and on the Serbian front, as well as in the Carpathian battles. See also Rifat Gvozdović Pasha, *Im blutigen Karst. Erinnerungen eines österreichishchen Offiziers aus dem Jahre 1914* (Stuttgart, 1915); Dr. Slavko Pavičić, *Hrvatska vojna i ratna povijest i prvi svjetski rat*/Croatian Military and War History and the First World War (Zagreb, 1943), 260–1ff.; Jurišić, *Svetski rat i Hrvati*, 68–9.

136/Serbia, General Staff, *Der grosse Krieg Serbiens für die Befreiung und Vereinigung der Serben, Kroaten, und Slowenen* (translated from Serbian; Berlin, 1929). The English novelist, Rebecca West also was advised of this fact by the Serbian veterans of the war as she reported in her controversial *Black Lamb and Gray Falcon* (2 vols.; London, 1942). See also Pavičić, *Hrvatska vojna*, 260–310; Rifat Gvozdović Pasha, *Unsere Helden im Süden* (Weimar, 1915).

137/Ivan Babić, "Military History," in *Croatia: Land, People, Culture* (Toronto, 1964), I, 149; Pavičić, *Hrvatska vojna*, 376–82, 391–412, 413–26.

138/Pavičić, *op cit.*, 460–77 *passim.*

139/Since the war some Croatian publicists have endeavoured to popularize the idea that in 1915–18 Croatian soldiers fought the Italians less in behalf of the Hapsburg state as such than because of opposition to the territorial designs of Italy upon Istria and Dalmatia. As late as June 1918, however, Italian airmen and prisoners noted the enthusiasm aroused in the Croatian regiments whenever the emperor-king (Karl III of Croatia-Slavonia) appeared among them. See also *Saturday Review*, December 2, 1916; Rifat Gvozdović Pasha, *Am Col di Lana* (Stuttgart, 1916).

140/On Croatian participation in the Serbian campaign of 1915 see Pavičić, *Hrvatska vojna*, 496–504 *passim.*

The victories of 1915 elicited great enthusiasm in Croatia-Slavonia and Dalmatia, as well as in Istria and Bosnia-Hercegovina. Sabor met on June 14, and the leader of the Coalition, the Croatian Dr. Lorković, declared that the diet should press now for the union of all of the Croatian lands. If the Monarchy survived the war, the sacrifices made on its behalf by the Croatians entitled them to demand this solution to the Croatian problem. If the Hapsburgs fell, a united Croatian kingdom would be in a better position to negotiate with the victors than would the separated Croatian territories.

Sabor adopted Lorković's declaration as an official expression of Croatian policy and aspirations. Both the disloyal elements among the Hapsburg Serbs, and the Magyar oligarchy in Budapest, were affected unpleasantly by this act. Serbs and Magyars alike realized that the Lorković program represented a concrete manifestation of the decline of Serbian influence in Croatian political life. The Hungarian prime minister Count Stephen Tisza tried to suppress the *Narodne Novine* because it printed Lorković's declaration and Sabor's acceptance of it. He also endeavored to prevent the official press agency of the Monarchy from bringing the Croatian actions to the attention of the Austro-Hungarian public as a whole.

Most Coalitionists now had repudiated the fictitious thesis of Serbo-Croatian identity that Pribićević, Supilo, Smodlaka, and part of the intelligentsia had propagated before the war. It is significant that the Lorković declaration said nothing about "Serbo-Croatian" cooperation, let alone unity.

Sabor's sessions effected a relaxation in political life in Croatia-Slavonia. A unanimous expression of loyalty to the Monarchy was passed, although open criticism of the internal administration was expressed in the legislative sessions. Croatian public opinion was impressed unpleasantly also by the obviously increasing dependence of the Austrian upon the Hungarian half of the Monarchy. Military considerations, and the inability of many Austrian areas to supply their food requirements, combined with the process of war industrialization, and the immigration into Vienna and other Austrian localities of people forced to flee from invaded provinces such as Galicia and the Bukovina, gave predominantly agricultural Hungary the upper hand in bargaining with her partner. The absence of a constitutional remedy for this situation provided a field day for the Magyar oligarchy whose political activity caused increasing apprehension among the Croatians.

Under the restricted system of suffrage that prevailed in Croatia-Slavonia, the Frankists were the second largest political faction. An ultra-patriotic group with strong branches in Istria, Dalmatia, and

Bosnia-Hercegovina, the Frankists should have enjoyed the favor of both Austrian and Hungarian authorities. Before the war, however, Tisza and most other Magyar political chiefs had protected and supported the Coalition and the Bosnian Serbs vis-à-vis the Frankists. These myopic Magyars believed that the Coalition thesis of Serbo-Croatian unity was less dangerous than the Frankist "Great Croatian" or Trialist program. Indeed, the Frankists were anti-Magyar, though pro-Hapsburg and pro-Austrian. Somewhat illogically, they resented the favor shown by Tisza to the Coalition. Actually, Budapest would have done better before 1914 to woo the Frankists rather than the Coalition. But the Coalition had never really recovered from the Hungarian infatuation that brought it into being, and many of its Serbian, and some of its Croatian members were determined to make it the "government party" at any cost. The Magyars never seemed able to perceive clearly the dangerous implications of the "Yugoslav" movement and spent their energies fighting the Frankist and Peasant Parties, although the anti-Hungarian attitudes of these groups could have been modified by wise concessions.

During the first years of the war the Frankists shared the belief of the military men that the civilian administrators in the Croatian lands either were tainted with Yugoslav sympathies or else were simply too benevolent to "stamp on the snakes that hissed at Sarajevo."[141] Therefore, this right-wing group was willing to see the soldiers take over the civil administration. Actually it was Tisza, no friend of the Croatians, who blocked the military and preserved the Croatian civil administration.

THE YUGOSLAV COMMITTEE

While political ranks were closing in the homeland and hundreds of thousands of Croatia's best men were fighting and dying on the several fronts, a group of expatriates was pursuing policies abroad that were bound to effect the ruin of Croatia if they succeeded.[142] Ivan Meštrović, one of the most noted sculptors of the twentieth century, but a very naïve politician, as he acknowledged himself in his memoirs,[143] was in

141/Statement that appeared in the *Armee Zeitung* after the Sarajevo murders.

142/See Jurišić, *Svetski rat i Hrvati*, 40–3.

143/Like Supilo, Meštrović was committed to the Serbian cause before the war. In 1913 the Serbian premier, Nikola Pašić, told him that a war between Austria-Hungary and Serbia was "inevitable." See Meštrović, *Uspomene na političke ljude i dogadjaje*/Recollections of Political People and Events (Buenos Aires, 1961), 9–132.

Italy when war broke out. Soon the congenital Dalmatian malcontents, Ante Trumbić and Frano Supilo, joined him there. These three men constituted the nucleus of the self-appointed exile South Slav or Yugoslav Committee which acquired its formal organization in 1915. Chairman of this expatriate group was Trumbić, one-time mayor of Split and a deputy in the Austrian Reichsrat.

These exiles were out of touch with the Croatians at home,[144] but they received support from Croatian-Americans. Ante Biankini, a Dalmatian who enjoyed influence in Croatian circles in Chicago; Niko Gršković, the shifty and slippery chairman of the Croatian organizations in Cleveland; and a number of Croatian language newspaper editors, lawyers, and innkeepers all were anxious to have their hands in the affairs of the old country. At the beginning of 1915, Smodlaka and Franko Potočnjak arrived in New York. They issued a plea for all "South Slav patriots" to support Russia and Serbia and cited forged or genuine Russian proclamations that were calculated to stir up unrest among the Hapsburg nationalities. Some of the more naïve Croatian-Americans became convinced of the benevolence of Russian and Serbian intentions towards Croatian national aspirations.[145]

Initially, however, Smodlaka and Potočnjak were unable to recruit volunteers for the Serbian Army. Father Nicholas Velimirović was sent by the Serbian government to overcome the hostility that existed between Croatian and Serbian groups in America. He induced twenty-eight editors of Croatian, Serbian, and Slovene language newspapers in the United States to subscribe to a resolution that committed them to work for the liberation and unification of all of the Yugoslavs. Velimirović exerted himself to secure the cooperation of Catholic and Orthodox priests in the hope that they would take the lead in effecting a rapprochement between Croatians and Serbians in the Americas where each group tended to disassociate itself from the other.

In May 1915, the Committee established its headquarters in London. It released a statement of its aims to the English nation and parliament. Also, it established an information bureau, and published a propaganda organ, the *Jugoslav Bulletin*, which appeared occasionally in a French

144/Dr. Fran Barac, rector of the University of Zagreb, visited Switzerland several times during the early war years. He was the only contact that the exiles had with people at home. In the last analysis it may be said that Barac represented no one but himself and a few other professors and students who had escaped military service. See Milada Paulova, *Jugoslavenski Odbor. Povijest jugoslavenske emigracije za svjetskog rata od 1914–1918*/History of the Yugoslav Emigration during the World War of 1914–18 (Zagreb, 1924), 104ff., 351ff.

145/On the activities of the "Yugoslav National Council" formed by Gršković in America see Paulova, *op. cit.*, 70. This is the standard source on the work of the Croatian exiles and emigrants.

edition. English propagandists and publicists such as R. W. Seton-Watson[146] and Henry Wickham-Steed took the exiles under their wing. They introduced them to Lord Crewe and other directors of English wartime propaganda as authentic representatives of the still unborn Yugoslav nation and as spokesmen of the Croatian people in particular. The expatriates tried to convince English and French politicians and public opinion that the Hapsburg Monarchy was an artificial and moribund state hated by the peoples who composed it.[147] They echoed Steed's *idée fixe* that Vienna was altogether subservient to Berlin, although the fact is that Vienna and Berlin were at odds with one another throughout the war (Budapest, however, often sought German support vis-à-vis the Austrians).[148]

The emigrés had no mandate from anyone. Nonetheless, they were able to pass themselves off as the political representatives of their nation, which they defined not as Croatian but as Yugoslav, an entirely mythical entity at this time. The Committee manufactured reports of happenings in the Croatian lands in the hope that they could convince the French and English that all Slavic peoples were ready to betray the Monarchy.

Early in 1915, however, Supilo discovered that Great Britain, France, and Russia had concluded the so-called London Pact, with Italy.[149] To bring Rome into the war against her old partner in the pre-1914 Triple Alliance, the three Entente powers promised to give her "Italia Irredenta," or those areas of the Dual Monarchy which the Italians claimed on the basis of national or historic right. Among these territories were the Croatian-inhabited sections of Istria and Dalmatia. When Supilo communicated the terms of this secret agreement to Croatians abroad, the split already manifest in Croatian-American circles became more pronounced. Large-scale police action was necessary to break up a mass melee between the "Yugoslav" and "Austriaki" factions in Pittsburgh,

146/For Seton-Watson's lack of competence as an authority on Croatian affairs see Knezović, *Poviest Hrvata*, 443–5.

147/The story of the several anti-Hapsburg groups in England is told in Harry Hanak, *Great Britain and Austria-Hungary during the First World War* (London, 1962). This work should be compared carefully with A. F. Pribram, *Austria-Hungary and Great Britain 1908–1914* (London, 1951).

148/Rudolf Bartulić, *Ungarns Rolle in Weltkrieg* (Lausanne, 1917).

149/F. Šišić, *Predratna politika Italije i postanak Londonskog Pakta 1870–1915/* Italian Policy before the War and the Origin of the London Pact (Split, 1933), 130ff. The London Pact prevented the conclusion of a separate peace between Austria-Hungary and France and England in 1917–18. See A. Demblin, *Czernin und die Sixtus Affaire* (Vienna, 1920); G. Manteyer, *Austria's Peace Offer 1916–1917* (London, 1921); L. Bittner *et al.* (eds.), *Österreich-Ungarns letzter Krieg* (8 vols.; Vienna, 1930), VII, 499–500, 552.

in December 1915. *Narodni List*, a leading Croatian-American newspaper, which was published in both Pittsburgh and New York, opposed the activities of the Committee, which, it declared, was completely under the thumb of Serbian elements who were pursuing chauvinistic "Great Serbian ambitions."

Other Croatian-American spokesmen attacked the "Serbo-Croat fallacy" and called upon Croatians in the Americas to support Austria-Hungary or at least to remain neutral vis-à-vis the war.[150] Had the Austro-Hungarian Embassy in Washington been able to support the "Austriaki" effectively, much could have been done to short-circuit the program of the anti-Hapsburg elements. Many Croatian-Americans were well disposed towards the Monarchy. But the Embassy had neither the men nor the funds to organize the Austrophiles, and, as the Czech-American Austrophobe society has disclosed, the Austro-Hungarian diplomatic and consular representatives in the United States allowed themselves to be separated or alienated from their own supporters there.[151]

On the other hand financial support for the activities of the Committee and its American representatives gradually was found in Latin America. By the end of 1915 several thousand volunteers were serving in the "Adriatic Legion" which was attached to the Serbian Army.

Up to this time Trumbić had tried to secure approval of the actions undertaken abroad by the Committee from the home politicians. He had no success in doing so and he never made the attempt again. The fact is that the Yugoslav Committee was more the agent of Belgrade than of Zagreb or the Hapsburg Croatians. There was no contact at any level between the expatriates and the people at home until the very end of the war. And until that time the Committee altogether disregarded authentically Croatian issues and developments. Nonetheless the special agent of the United States on Corfu, the Greek island where the battered and bedraggled Serbian military remnants were undergoing rehabilitation, reported to the secretary of state that the "Serbs, Croats, and Slovenes have shown far greater efforts and sacrifices than have the peoples of the Trentino and Transylvania" (H. Percival Dodge to Robt. Lansing, Aug. 17, 1917; State Department Files, National Archives, Washington, D.C.). This remark was a propos only of the Serbians.

The fall of Serbia and of Montenegro, and the disastrous defeats sus-

150/R. M. Krmpotić, *On Great Serbia* (Kansas City, 1915). See also his *Bosnia-Hercegovina and the Serbian Claims* (Kansas City, 1916).

151/E. Voska, *Spy and Counterspy* (New York, 1940). See also Konstantin Maglić's account of his experiences as an escaped prisoner in New York City during the war in *The Dandy Hun*.

tained by the Russians, had so discouraged the Croatian members of the Committee that they were ready to give up. Trumbić declared that there was no future for him in politics and that he was going to emigrate to Buenos Aires where he hoped to earn a living as a taxi driver. Then, however, Conrad launched his partially successful (but wholly unwise) Trentino offensive against the Italians. Now came the turning point of the war. The Germans had blundered more seriously than had Conrad; they had thrown away half a million men at Verdun. In answer to frantic Italian pleas for a diversionary offensive that would relieve the Austrian pressure on Italy, Czarist Russia, oblivious to the portents of doom that menaced her own existence, found the strength to give the Dual Monarchy a final thrust towards the abyss of destruction.

On June 4 the great Brussilov offensive against the Austro-Hungarian lines in Volhynia and the easternmost sector of the front got under way. From June 4 to 10 the Croatian divisions held like a rock and counter-attacked successfully against the Russians when all around them units of other nationalities were giving way.[152] But during the first hours of the Russian attack on June 4 Löffler's Hungarian Honved Brigade had disintegrated. This local disaster enabled the advancing Russians to envelop and eventually overwhelm the right wing of the 25th Croatian Regiment which held the line next to Löffler. As the 25th fell back towards the village of Valave they encountered General Jeszer, commander of a Ruthenian-Polish reserve division that had been thrown in to the line in an attempt to restore the situation.

"What outfit are you?" Jeszer asked.

"Zagreb Domobrans No. 25."

Jeszer turned to his staff and said: "These are those heroes who held out so marvelously around the Trigonometer." He congratulated Colonel Delić, commander of the 25th, who had with difficulty been persuaded

152/Ivan Babić in *Croatia: Land, People, Culture*, I, 149, says that the 36th and 42nd Croatian Domobran divisions collapsed in the sector between the Pruth and the Dniester. He attributes their defeat to the dissatisfaction caused by the refusal of the Hungarian Government to sanction the establishment of a "Great Croatian" state (i.e., the union of Dalmatia, Bosnia-Hercegovina, and Istria with Croatia-Slavonia). The Croatians wanted this projected complex to have the status already possessed by Hungary in the Dual Monarchy. It is evident from the first-hand accounts of the fighting presented in Pavičić, *Hrvatska vojna*, 532–62, that the Croatian soldiers were not preoccupied with political considerations at this time. Politics had nothing to do with the collapse of the 36th and 42nd. They just were holding too broad a sector of the front and they lacked the artillery support that had enabled them to throw back Brussilov's masses in previous offenses that he had launched in the same sector at the end of 1915 and in January and February 1916. Conrad had shifted too much artillery and manpower to the Italian front in order to gratify his lust for a mountain offensive against Italy.

by his staff to join the retreat; he had intended to die fighting in the trenches held by his men at the beginning of the attack.

All Croatian formations save the 25th fought successfully until June 10–12. But when the Russians achieved their major breakthrough at Luck other sectors of the Austro-Hungarian lines, including that held by the Croatians, were imperiled, and reserves available were inadequate either to relieve the front line troops or to counterattack with sufficient force to prevent the breakthrough from widening. Hence Croatian and other units that managed to hold their ground had to fight for more than a week without rest and without food save for the "iron rations" that they carried on their persons. These "iron rations" soon were exhausted. The Russians kept throwing in fresh troops to spell off their original front line fighters.[153] Finally on June 11–12 the Croatians, worn out by lack of sleep and food, had to beat a fighting retreat to avoid encirclement. Many units did not have a single unwounded officer or man. Emperor-King Karl himself expressed to the 25th and other Croatian commands his personal appreciation for the brilliant stand they had made against Brussilov's "steam roller."

But the Russian success encouraged the Rumanians to invade Transylvania. The entire harvest of 1916 in this "bread basket" of the Monarchy was lost. From this time on both the military and civilians in Austria-Hungary were faced with starvation. In Croatia-Slavonia food rationing was felt less severely than in some other parts of the Hapsburg state. On the Italian front the Croatian troops continued to fight with undiminished élan and the formations involved in the Luck disaster took a bloody revenge upon the Russians in June 1917, when the so-called Kerensky Offensive collapsed ignominiously.[154]

With the Brussilov offensive Russia had expended the last of her strength. The abortive Kerensky thrust was followed by her withdrawal from the war. Austro-Hungarian, German, Bulgarian, and Turkish forces descended like an avalanche upon the heads of the befuddled Rumanians who were left in the lurch by the Russians upon whom they had counted for aid. Thus, despite the German failure before Verdun, the situation of the Central Powers did not appear too precarious, on

153/Brussilov's tactics were the same as those employed by Suvarov in the War of the Second Coalition against Napoleon and the French, and by the Soviet commanders in the Russo-Finnish campaign of 1939–40. Relying on numerical superiority the Russians attacked without regard to losses, calculating that sooner or later the numerically weaker enemy would give way.

154/The details of Croatian participation in this last fight against the Russians are given in Pavičić, *Hrvatska vojna*, 601–7. The Croatians particularly distinguished themselves at the battle of Sniatyn during this offensive.

paper at least, at the end of 1917. However, the United States had declared war upon Germany in April 1917, and at the end of the year she decided to conduct hostilities against the Dual Monarchy also. Still, it was not yet clear that she was committed to the destruction of the Hapsburg state.[155]

Some months before his death in September 1917, Supilo resigned from the Committee. But in July of that year Trumbić, encouraged by the entrance of the United States into the war, and anticipating that sooner or later she would break with the Dual Monarchy, signed with the Serbian premier, Nicholas Pašić, the so-called Corfu Agreement. Trumbić now had stronger cards to play than heretofore because the American partisans of Serbo-Croatian unity had the upper hand, thanks to the war declaration, over the "Austriaki" who had to move circumspectly to avoid indictment for treason, and popular resentment. Trumbić got the Serbian statesman to consent to the display of the Croatian flag and coat of arms on the banner of the prospective Serb-Croatian-Slovene state of the future. The Croatian was naïve enough to interpret Pašić's amenability in this rather insignificant respect as a guarantee that after the war the Serbians would agree to a federative organization of the Yugoslav state, which the Corfu Declaration affirmed would "include all territory compactly inhabited by 'our' people."[156]

THE FUTURE OF CROATIA

Most Croatians were still loyal to the Hapsburg state. But in the spring of 1917 the Austrian Reichsrat convened for the first time since the outbreak of the war. Two Dalmatian Croatian members of this body, Andjelinović and Bartulović, both Frankists, openly propagated the thesis of South Slavic unity.[157] Emperor-King Karl IV (VII of Austria) favored rather than opposed this concept. Croatian, Serbian, and Slovenian deputies in the Reichsrat concluded a working agreement with

155/Charles Seymour (ed.), *The Intimate Papers of Colonel House* (Boston and New York, 1925), II, 448–551. When the Americans got into the war, however, they made a moral rather than a territorial issue out of it and outdid every other people in fanaticism. The ruling classes in particular were susceptible to English, French, and Czech exile or Czech-American propaganda. Wilson himself remarked, of the entry of the United States into the war: "It means that we shall lose our heads like the rest and stop weighing right and wrong."

156/F. Šišić (ed.), *Dokumenti o postanku Kraljevine Srba, Hrvata, i Slovenaca 1914–1919*/Documents Concerning the Origins of the Serb-Croat-Slovene Kingdom (Zagreb, 1920), document no. 56; Paulova, *Jugoslavenski Odbor*, 356ff.

157/*Hrvatska Država*, Sept. 1, 1917, and subsequent issues.

the Czech politicians in that body.[158] Msgr. Korošec, a Slovene prelate, was the first individual residing in the Dual Monarchy during the war to question publicly the right of the Hapsburgs to rule the Southern Slavs.[159] In December, Count Clam-Martinitz, military governor of Montenegro, which the Austrians had occupied at the beginning of 1916, proposed to Count Ottokar Czernin, foreign minister of the Monarchy, the unification of the Hapsburg, Serbian, Croatian, and Slovenian territories in a new subdualist Austro-Hungarian-Polish-South Slavic state. Czernin, although personally friendly to the Croatians and the idea of Trialism, repudiated this suggestion because he comprehended that German policies had forced the Poles to turn against the Dual Monarchy. Nor did he feel that the Hapsburg Serbs, and perhaps not even the Slovenes, would accept a subdualist solution at this date. He knew that the Czechs would offer resolute opposition to such a reorganization for the Monarchy unless Bohemia, Moravia, and Silesia received full parity with the Germanic, Hungarian, Polish, and Southern Slav lands. And the Germans, whether of the Reich or of Austria proper, let alone the Sudetens of Bohemia, were adamantly opposed to making any concessions of the kind indicated to the Czechs. It is an unfortunate fact that the German-speaking Austrians, until the 1938–45 epoch, usually felt closer to the Reichsdeutsche than to their fellow citizens of non-Germanic blood in the Hapsburg Monarchy. (Of course there is no more mixed ethnic group than the Austrians, as a casual inspection of the telephone directory of Vienna or of any other Austrian locality will demonstrate.)

Finding that Czernin rejected his first proposal for the solution of the nationalities problem in the Monarchy, Clam-Martinitz came up with another one. He now suggested that Montenegro and Serbia be united with Dalmatia and Bosnia-Hercegovina under the rule of Vienna, while Croatia and Slavonia be allowed to remain with Hungary. This project is worth noting as an instance of how completely even well-meaning Austrians could misunderstand the Croatian problem. In May 1918, Clam-Martinitz actually met with the military governors of Serbia and Bosnia-Hercegovina at Sarajevo to discuss this fantastic scheme. Even the Frankists were indignant because of the outright negation of their long-cherished plans of Trialism.

158/Croatian deputies in the Reichsrat were either from Dalmatia or Istria. Since Croatia-Slavonia was a constituent part of the Hungarian half of the Monarchy, her representatives did not sit in the Reichsrat, which represented the Austrian part of the Hapsburg state.

159/In the debate over the budget that took place in the Reichsrat during November 1917.

CAPORETTO AND ITS CONSEQUENCES

Meawhile the Russian Revolution of 1917 and the breakup of the old Czarist Army had relaxed some of the military pressure on Austria-Hungary. At the end of October 1917 the Hapsburg High Command was able to carry out the successful offensive of Caporetto which gave the Army enough to eat for the first time in months. Croatian units contributed in significant measure to this victory, the ultimate consequences of which have not been fully appreciated.[160]

Caporetto was one of the decisive battles of history, if only in a negative sense. Its political implications were enormous. Despite the fact that the German divisions who participated in it received a major share of the credit for the Italian debacle (because they took prisoner 60,000 unarmed members of Italian labor battalions), the Caporetto episode proved that the Austro-Hungarian Army, which had done most of the actual fighting, was a force that had to be reckoned with. But by pursuing the same tactic that the French had adopted to "restore morale" after the Chemin des Dames disaster earlier in the year, that is by shooting retreating soldiers quite indiscriminately, the Italians succeeded in stabilizing their line along the Piave. As always, the Germans did not know how to exploit a victory, and the Austro-Hungarian forces, still tied up in Russia and the Balkans, were unable to prosecute a vigorous winter campaign. Furthermore, England and France rushed ten crack divisions to Italy, and the Americans and even the Japanese sent air and naval squadrons along with special units to the Italian theater of war. The partial collapse of the Italian Army also did something to stimulate Italian national pride in that it created a demand for the rehabilitation of Italy's military prestige.

Entente propaganda organizations also gained a point because, after Caporetto, military and political authorities in London, Paris, Rome, and Washington were more easily persuaded that to win the war it was necessary to disintegrate the Dual Monarchy, a course that had appealed to few people of importance up to this time. The Czech "Mafia" organization exerted itself to acquaint the Croatians at home with the existence of the Committee abroad. Naturally the Czechs magnified the importance of the contacts maintained in enemy countries

160/On Caporetto and the Croatians see Amedeo Tosti, *Come ci vede l'Austria Imperiale, dall' ultimatum alla Serbia a Villa Giusti* (Milan, 1930), 205ff.; *Österreich-Ungarns letzter Krieg*, VI, 557; General Alfred Krauss, *Das Wunder von Karfreit* (Munich, 1924).

by the voluntary exiles and self-proclaimed spokesmen of the Croatian nation. They worked consciously to create among the Croatians a state of mind which would see in desertion to the Entente a means of escape from the consequences that normally could be expected from having fought on the losing side.

Hitherto, despite the casualties suffered by the Croatian troops in the field, the war had not been unpopular in the Croatian territories.[161] Indeed, the Croatians were probably the last of the Hapsburg nationalities to comprehend that, militarily speaking, the entrance of the United States into the conflict meant that the game was up. The food situation was better in Croatia-Slavonia than in neighboring Carniola (Slovenia), and it took reports in Croatian and Dalmatian newspapers that dog meat was being sold openly in the butcher shops of Berlin to impress the Croatians with the seriousness of the situation as the summer and the fall of 1918 arrived. Although few Croatians had any positive affection for Germans, they did consider Teutonic civilization to be of a high order. That such a cultured people could descend to the level of eating pets was a devastating revelation of the efficacy of the Entente blockade.

Both at the time and after the war many Croatians voiced the opinion that members of the reigning family should have shown themselves in Croatia-Slavonia, Dalmatia, Istria, and Bosnia-Hercegovina, as well as to the Croatian front-line troops and reserve formations. It was necessary to make sure that, whatever happened, the Croatians after the end of the fighting would elect to remain united with the Austrian hereditary lands as they had done in the days of Turkish power. But the Hapsburgs, though well intentioned and reasonably capable rulers, have not had the slightest flair for dramatic performance since the days of Maria Theresa. Nor could they ever grasp the potentialities of a united Croatian complex, either for the orderly development of the whole Monarchy, or for the survival, even in the face of defeat, of a nucleus of it.[162] The fact is that by the fall of 1918 many of the Hapsburgs themselves

161/On the general conditions and war psychology prevailing among the Croatians in 1917–18 see R. Herceg, *Die Ideologie des kroatischen Bauernbewegung* (Zagreb, 1923); J. Horvat, "Hrvatska politika u svjetskom ratu"/Croatian Politics in the World War, *Obzor spomen-knjiga* (Zagreb, 1936); Jurišić, *Svetski rat i Hrvati, passim*; Pavičić, *Hrvatska vojna, passim*. The last-named author is concerned only with the morale of the troops at the front and does not discuss conditions at home.

162/It is perhaps significant that there is less mention of the Croatians than of any other Hapsburg nationality in the popular compendium of direct Hapsburg participation in the war effort compiled by Dr. Artur Gaspar, *Unsere Dynastie im Felde* (Vienna, 1915). Though this work possesses literary merit, it illustrates the chronic Austrian inability to master propaganda techniques insofar as the nationalities in the Empire were concerned.

no longer believed in their inalienable right to rule. This loss of faith in their mission expressed itself in a manifest tendency to let events take their course, and this attitude was highly contagious among the Croatians as it was among the other Danubian peoples.

During the spring and summer of 1918 it was Starčevist rather than Coalition elements who began to pursue the Yugoslav idea openly. On March 3, these elements issued a declaration which called for a united Croatian, Serbian, and Slovenian state. No reference was made to Hapsburg sovereignty over such a complex. Korošec was agitating among the Croatians as well as the Slovenes against the continued existence of Austria-Hungary; in effect he was one of the most efficacious of Italian agents in furthering the prospects of Italian aggrandizement. As the food situation worsened, "a friend of the Hapsburgs" came to be regarded as an enemy of his own people. It took great moral and physical toughness at this time even for Frankists to continue to maintain that, whether for better or for worse, the national interests of the Croatian lands and people were tied to Austria rather than to any Balkan complex or to Hungary, if the latter chose to commit political suicide by divorcing herself from her Austrian partner.

AUSTRIA DELENDA EST!

Decisive for the fate of the Croatians and of the whole Monarchy was the final German offensive that began in March 1918. This undertaking provides another convincing evidence of the incompetence of German military leadership. In 1916 Conrad had tried to dissuade the Germans from attacking Verdun. Had Berlin at that time placed at his disposal the troops whose lives were thrown away uselessly at Verdun, Italy could have been knocked out of the war without endangering the Austrian lines in Volhynia. Again, before his removal as chief of staff, he tried to convince the Germans that it was necessary to force the Salonika Army of the Entente into the sea. Austria-Hungary's troops were tied down in Italy, Russia, Albania, Rumania, and occupied Serbia and Montenegro, which left only the war-weary Bulgarians to contain the Salonika Army. As usual, the Germans were unwilling to cooperate loyally with their allies, although they expected the ultimate in sacrifices from them. The entrance into the war of the United States made the result inevitable anyway, but the repudiation of Conrad's suggestions and the commitment to the West Front Offensive of 1918 greatly facilitated the ease of the Entente triumph in that year.

However, the initial success of this offensive caused France, England, and the United States to decide (upon military rather than political grounds) that it was necessary to encourage resistance to Vienna on the part of the nationalities, even though the stepped-up tempo of such endeavors after Caporetto had as yet produced little result. Henri Moysett, private secretary to the French Ministry of the Navy, and a keen student of Central European affairs, played an important role in seconding the efforts of Steed and Seton-Watson to convince the British government that Entente propaganda must concentrate its efforts against the Dual Monarchy rather than Germany. Steed drafted a memorandum for Lord Northcliffe, British propaganda minister, which was accepted as a basis for the policy to be followed by the Allied and Associated (Entente) Powers towards Austria-Hungary. Simply stated, the Powers at long last were won over to Steed's dictum of breaking up the Monarchy. Steed, long-time correspondent of the London *Times*, and a prime example of the type of "old-school-tie" Anglo-Saxon endowed with a racial superiority complex, hated Austria because, during his residence in Vienna, aristocratic society there had denied him an entrée into its closed circle. So anxious was he to consign this milieu to the outer political darkness, that he anticipated Hitler and the Nazis in demanding *Anschluss*, the absorption of Germanic Austria by Germany.

Although sound military strategy dictated purely defensive action by the Hapsburg Army in 1918, the desperate scarcity of food motivated the Austro-Hungarian commanders to risk another offensive on the Piave in June.[163] This desperation attack was called the "Bread Offensive" because the Austro-Hungarian Command hoped to capture provisions from the Italians and their allies as they had done in the Caporetto thrust. Had General Borojević's plan of attack been accepted, the Hapsburg forces probably would have scored at least a local success. But Conrad, now in charge of the Trentino front, was set on repeating his partially successful mountain offensive of 1916. His replacement as chief of staff, Arz v. Straussenberg, allowed his subordinates (Borojević, Conrad, and Waldstätten) to put their individual projects into operation in their respective sectors of the front. Thus the army was committed to a general offensive all the way from the Swiss frontier to the sea. It did not have the manpower or equipment to sustain an attack of this magnitude. Conrad's mountain thrust failed completely and Borojević had no reserves with which to exploit the initial successes scored by his troops in driving back the English, Italians, and the Czech legionnaires who were holding the Piave front. When heavy rains

163/*Österreich-Ungarns letzter Krieg*, VII, 177–365.

caused the Piave to rise behind the backs of his troops after they had gained the Italian shore, his advance was brought to a standstill.

Since April, Crew House, the Creel Committee (CPI) in the United States, and the French Maison Blanche had mounted a vigorous propaganda offensive against both military and civilian elements in Austria-Hungary. The "Yugoslav," Czech, and Polish exile Committees did what they could to help. It was Marxist propaganda, disseminated by war prisoners returning from Russia, however, rather than the Entente propaganda blasts, that weakend the will to fight of the Hapsburg army.[164] More important than either of these verbal barrages in lowering military and civilian morale was hunger which was no longer a mere specter but a grim reality, even in the predominantly Croatian agricultural lands.[165]

In the Reichsrat, deputies of all nationalities were allowed uncommon latitude in making speeches, some of which were treasonable by any standard. Karl hoped that his long-cherished plan of federalizing the Austrian half of the Monarchy would satisfy the desires of at least some of the nationalities on the one hand, and the much publicized demands of national self-determination advanced by President Wilson on the other. But Karl was bound by his Coronation Oath as king of Hungary to refrain from altering the constitutional structure of the Hungarian half of the Monarchy. Therefore he was in no position to satisfy the Croatian aspiration for national unity though he did appeal to the Magyar oligarchy to proclaim the federalization of Hungary too. Instead, Budapest announced the complete separation of the Hungarian Kingdom from Austria, even though for the moment the rule of the dynasty was not repudiated.

Hungary's divorce from Austria opened wide the floodgates of destruction, and the waters released sufficed, in the long run, to drown all of the Central European peoples. Even now the Magyars failed to realize that by deserting Austria they were decreeing the doom of historic Hungary. Conceivably the Slovaks and Ruthenians, or Carpatho-Russians, might

164/Leon Trotsky took advantage of the protracted peace negotiations carried on at Brest-Litovsk in the winter of 1918 to disseminate Marxist propaganda among the Austro-Hungarian formations standing deep in Russian territory, as well as among war prisoners. Many of the latter, when released from captivity in 1918, returned to the Dual Monarchy as full-fledged revolutionaries. See *Österreich-Ungarns letzter Krieg*, VII, 11, 13, 43–5; Gustav Krist, *Pascholl plenny* (Vienna, 1931). An English edition of this last-named work is available in the Library of Congress, *Prisoner in the Forbidden Land*, trans. E. O. Lorimer (London, 1938).

165/*Österreich-Ungarns letzter Krieg*, VII, 45.

have elected to remain with Hungary if the self-determination doctrine had been given a chance to operate. But Wilson had enunciated this doctrine, as a tactical political move rather than as a practical policy. In any case, the Croatians, Hungarian Serbs, and Transylvanian Rumanians promptly took advantage of the Hungarian declaration of complete independence of Austria to proclaim their own independence of Hungary.

THE CROATIAN DILEMMA IN THE FALL OF 1918

At this juncture the Croatians had a choice of three clear-cut alternatives. They could follow the line demanded by most Frankists, that is, evidence their iron determination to remain with Austria, even if they had to coerce the Austrian Social Democrats and Pan-Germans by sending Croatian regiments to Vienna to support the Court and the dynastically loyal Christian Social Party. But now there was neither a Jelačić on the scene as in 1848, nor a Croatian Mustapha Kemal or Baron Mannerheim. There was not even an Austro-Hungarian Benjamin Franklin to warn the several Danubian peoples that now, more than ever before in their history, they had to hang together or they would all hang separately.

The second alternative for the Croatians was to proclaim the national unification and independence of the Croatian state complex, that is the resurrection of the ancient Triune Kingdom of Croatia, Slavonia, and Dalmatia together with Istria and Bosnia-Hercegovina. While some bargaining with the Serbs and a partition of Bosnia and Hercegovina indubitably would have been necessary, the doctrine of national self-determination could have been invoked to justify the creation of such an entity. Again, however, a Croatian Mustapha Kemal or Mannerheim was needed to bring a national state of this kind into being. And it was a moot question whether a revived Triune Kingdom would have been a viable economic entity.

Carniola or Slovenia would have had to go along with Croatia-Slavonia and the other Croatian lands whether they remained united with the Austrian Hapsburg provinces or formed a separate state. But a part of the Slovenian clergy was campaigning in behalf of the Yugoslav idea despite the fact that the Slovenes had more in common with the Austrians than with the Serbians. Among the Croatian Serbs the radical element had raised its head once again after the failure of the "Bread Offensive."

They were able to persuade many Croatians that the Monarchy had no chance of surviving the war even in a diminished form.

This Serbian generation and those that followed it have continued to propagate this idea as a kind of Gospel truth. By doing so they have helped to obscure what really happened in the Croatian lands in the fall of 1918, as well as what the interests of the Croatian nation and people demanded.

Actually, of course, the actions of politicians and propagandists of whatever category were not the decisive factors in the autumn of 1918. At this juncture the fate of Central Europe depended upon whether Vienna could find someone who would accept her surrender before the anticipated Entente offensive on the Southwest Front got under way. If the offensive did precede the peace, then the question was whether the Hapsburg Army could repel it or not. If it could do so, the Monarchy, as such, had a good chance of surviving the war and even of being intrinsically stronger than it had been in 1914. The Germans were palpably finished in the west, and there was no danger that the Hapsburg state, if it could survive, would sink to the position of a mere German satellite as almost inevitably would have been the case had Germany triumphed in the war. The *raison d'etre* of the alliance with Germany was to secure protection against the manifest determination of Russia to destroy the Dual Monarchy, or at least to vivisect it. But the Russian collapse had removed this danger for the time being. Although Austria had discharged her obligations to her German partner with complete loyalty – and the attempts she had made to secure a separate peace were as much in the interests of the Germans as her own – she was not obliged to immolate herself upon the altar of German territorial greed and persistent military and political miscalculations. Vienna could afford to lose Galicia to the Poles and the south Trentino to the Italians if she could get rid of the German millstone that she had been obliged to wear tied around her neck as a kind of charm to ward off danger from the north. For a brief time it seemed that, despite the surrender of Bulgaria (September 30) and Turkey (October 4), which exposed the Austro-Hungarian southern flank in the Balkans, the Dual Monarchy might actually outlast her German partner as a military factor in the situation. If the Army could be withdrawn from Italy intact, especially if flushed with a last success, it would make short work of the Socialists in Vienna and the Slovene National Committee in Ljubljana, and could cut Czech aspirations down to size as well.

Inherent in this situation were great possibilities for the Croatian people and nation. Inevitably, after the war the Monarchy's center of gravity would shift southwards if an Austrian Slovenian-Croatian (Carniola, Croatia-Slavonia, Dalmatia, and Istria) nucleus survived intact.[166]

Since the beginning of September, Vienna had been trying to find someone who would accept her surrender. The Entente ignored her acceptance of Wilson's propaganda masterpiece, the Fourteen Point program. Wilson himself was willing to see half of Europe killed rather than to sacrifice his *idée fixe* of setting up republics wherever possible. Only on October 18, and then in a negative sense, did his secretary of state, Robert Lansing, a convinced hater of Austria, answer a second Viennese peace proposal.[167] Thus Wilson and his allies signed the political death warrant of the Monarchy and doomed its army to fight a last needless battle. The dove of peace had failed to bring succor to the Danubian peoples, so their fate was now in the bloodstained hands of the God of Battles. But to almost everyone it was apparent that the victors in the war had sanctioned the dissolution of Austria-Hungary in advance of its actual occurrence.[168] Even a successful resistance on the Piave might not deliver the Austrians, Croatians, and Slovenians from the shambles of a dictated peace. The possibilities inherent in the temporary destruction of Germany as a great power were not appreciated by many people, either in the Entente camp or in the Dual Monarchy.

THE LAST ROUND

On October 24 the Entente opened its offensive in upper Italy. Until October 28 the multinational army fought with some success against the Italian, English, French, Czech legionnaire and American forces sent against them. Two divisions, the Hungarian-Bosnian 7th Division and the Hungarian 12th Honved, a dismounted cavalry division, failed to do their duty. Croatian front-line troops fought with their usual élan, but the reserves refused to go up.

Emperor-King Karl endeavored to secure an armistice from the Italian

166/The apprehension of this fact is expressed clearly in Jurišić, *Svetski rat i Hrvati*, and was felt by Stjepan Radić among other Croatians. See footnote 176 below. Both the Frankist and Peasant Parties, as a whole, continued to stand for a federated Austria or Austria-Hungary. See Jareb, *Pola stoljeća hrvatske politike*, 19.

167/Lansing informed Count Julius Andrassy, Austro-Hungarian foreign minister, that Point 10, which postulated the continued existence of the Dual Monarchy after the war, had been invalidated by the course of events (meaning the ascendancy gained over Wilson by Masaryk and the Czecho-Americans). See Stephen Bonsal, *Unfinished Business* (New York, 1944), 81–2.

168/Bonsal, *ibid.*

command and appealed directly to Wilson to whom he offered a separate peace.[169] He accepted the demand expressed in the Lansing note for the independence of the several nationalities, if that was what they wanted. Thus there was no reason to continue hostilities. The war was over, the Entente had won. Austria-Hungary was breaking up into pseudo-national compartments; yet her army was still largely intact. Actually, its position at this time (the end of October) compared favorably with that of the German military machine on November 11.[170] Only on November 2, however, could the victorious powers get around to signing the armistice conditions with the Austrian representatives. By that time several things had happened.

Local committees in Dalmatia and Bosnia had rejected the emperor's federalization manifesto. But they acted in its spirit in proclaiming the allegiance of Dalmatia and Bosnia-Hercegovina to the so-called National Council which had set itself up in Zagreb under Czech inspiration.[171] On October 27, this body asked the Military Command in Zagreb to provide arms and ammunition for a civic guard. The Croatian generals in the Command should have known better than to place arms in the hands of the Croatian Serbs whose unreliability for service at the front had left them the foremost candidates for civic guard duty. On the following day the National Council declared independence from Austria and Hungary of the Croatians, Slovenians, and Hungarian Serbs.[172] Troops of all these nationalities were still fighting in Italy, Albania, and other parts of the Balkans, but the Croatians had now cut

169/Since his accession Karl had endeavored to end the war, through the conclusion of either a general or a separate peace. In the spring of 1918 Premier Clemenceau of France had publicized the separate peace negotiations between Austria-Hungary and France. By so doing he fatally weakened the position of the Hapsburgs vis-à-vis Berlin as well as the Germanic Austrians. It was only the direct threat of a German invasion of the Dual Monarchy that kept Austria-Hungary in the war in 1918. On the separate peace negotiations, see A. Demblin, *Czernin und die Sixtus Affaire*; G. Manteyer, *Austria's Peace Offer, 1916–1917*; *Österreich-Ungarns letzter Krieg*, VII, 499–500, 552.

170/Ludendorff's official report of August 8, 1918, and of subsequent days, discloses the hopelessness of the German military situation. Through his liaison officer, Lersner, he warned the German Chancellor: "The troops hold today but no one can forsee what will happen tomorrow. The break-through may occur at any moment, and upon a vital point. A division may fail to do its duty." Crown Prince Rupprecht of Bavaria on October 4 wired Berlin: "I do not think we can hold out through the coming winter. It is even possible that disaster will overtake us before then." Two weeks later he advised his cousin, Prince Max of Baden, the new chancellor, "resistance is diminishing hourly. Disaster can be expected at any moment. Ludendorff doesn't realize the gravity of the situation."

171/On the occasion of the visit to the Croatian capital of forty-two of the more radical Czech deputies in the Austrian Reichsrat.

172/Šišić, *Dokumenti*, no. 118.

their choice of alternatives to two. King Karl transferred his executive power to the Croatian Ban and conferred full military authority upon Croatian generals who had no idea how to exercise it. Also, the largely Croatian manned fleet was placed at the disposal of the National Council, which proceeded to disorganize it at the same time that the Ban was defaulting his newly acquired authority to this Serbian-dominated body.

On October 29, Sabor passed a law drafted by Svetozar Pribićević, whom the Austrians, with curious leniency, had failed to hang during the war. This law ended the constitutional relationships that had existed between the Croatians and Hungary for eight centuries past and for the last four centuries between Zagreb and Vienna. The National Council then turned its back upon the second alternative that had presented itself to the Croatians – that of independence. Under Serb inspiration it declared the partially resurrected Triune Kingdom to be part of a still non-existent Serbian-Croatian-Slovenian state. On November 1, even so staunch a Frankist as General Sarkotić, military commander of Bosnia-Hercegovina, handed over his authority to the National Council. Thus he missed a golden opportunity to make himself a Croatian Queipo de Llano,[173] if not a Mustapha Kemal. In this way the National Council was able to take over power piecemeal from the Hapsburg authorities. Everyone was so bewildered by the tempo of events and so worn out by the strain of war and the privations imposed by the Entente blockade that there was little disposition to resist the mandates of this political scarecrow.[174] The net result of the activity of the National Council and of the exile committee abroad was that the Italians were able to launch torpedo attacks upon the Croatian manned fleet which had become altogether disorganized owing to the separation of non-Croatian officers and men from their ships. Hundreds of Croatians lost their lives needlessly, and Rome was able to celebrate a naval triumph that matched the land victory that was being achieved in the battle of Vittorio Veneto.

Although most of the reserve formations were defecting by this time, the Austro-Hungarian front-line troops were effecting a rather orderly withdrawal after abandoning or blowing up their artillery and stores. The Entente troops were pursuing them very cautiously. British planes,

173/A Spanish royalist general who in 1936 took the republican stronghold of Seville with less than a hundred men. He put them in automobiles which roamed the streets shooting down all republican partisans. Sarkotić (or any other Croatian general) certainly would have experienced less difficulty in disposing of the National Council than de Llano had in mastering Seville. See Baron S. Sarkotić, "Meine letzten Audienzen beim Kaiser. Die Südslawische Frage," *Erinnerungen an Franz Joseph* I *Kaiser v. Österreich, Apostolische König v. Ungarn* (Berlin, 1930).

174/Dr. Julius Makanec, *Entwicklung des kroatischen Nationalismus* (Zagreb, 1943), 46, 81.

however, made great sport of slaughtering horses and mules in the retreating columns. Despite the lack of air cover, general dissolution set in only when the newly formed Karoyli government in Hungary ordered home the Hungarian regiments, which included Slovak, Transylvanian Rumanian, Ruthenian, Hungarian Serb, and Croatian formations. As the jubilant Magyars marched off with gypsy musicians playing wildly at the heads of their columns, a general *Sauve qui peut* set in. First in the race to the rear were the Czechs. Since they usually preferred *Etappendienst* (non-combative services) to front-line duty, it was largely they who staffed the military offices and communications agencies. Now army, divisional, corps, regimental, and battalion headquarters were left denuded of personnel, telephones and telegraph instruments remained unmanned, and even doctors in the field hospitals deserted their patients.

Austro-Hungarian GHQ had asked for an immediate cease-fire as early as October 30, but it was granted only on November 2. At 3 A.M. on November 3, all Austro-Hungarian units received orders to cease hostilities on land and sea, and in the air. Karl attempted to countermand this order because he realized (what his generals did not) that the Italians had not set a precise hour for the cessation of hostilities. Czech abandonment of the communications agencies prevented his counter-order from reaching many troops. These, regardless of their nationality, thought the war was over and desired only to reach their homes as quickly as possible.

The Italians and their allies could have rested on their laurels at this point. The only reason to begin with for the decision to launch the final offensive on the Southwest Front was that Rome badly needed a victory to strengthen her hand at the coming peace conference. The Italian Supreme Command was unused to success and could not forego the opportunity to exploit it. Hence it decided that the armistice would go into effect only at 3 P.M. on November 4. During the thirty-six hours that intervened between the issuance of the Austrian command to cease fire and the moment when the Italians and their allies chose to do so, many Croatian formations proceeding homewards were overtaken by Entente cavalry, planes, or armored cars and summoned to surrender. Usually the Croatians, like their former comrades in arms of other nationalities, complied. They thought that at worst they would suffer no more than a few days of confinement before being sent on to their homes, and there seemed to be no reason to risk death now when the war was over. Some units refused to surrender and shot their way through their would-be captors. Thus they avoided sharing the fate of the prisoners, many of whom were released only in the spring of 1919. Italy was totally unprepared to care for the 400,000 captives who fell into her hands, most of them after 3 A.M., November 3. Hundreds of Croatians, among other nationalities, died in the Italian prison camps in the winter of 1918–19 owing to cold, hunger, disease, or general privation.[175]

While they were undergoing these experiences, on December 1, the National Council accepted Serbian sovereignty over the Croatian lands. The Peasant Party had misgivings about this union, but allowed itself to be stampeded by Croatian Serbs and Czech pressure. Frankist representatives issued a last formal protest against this act of national suicide to which the long-time guardians of Croatian sovereignty and individuality, the Ban and Sabor, tamely acquiesced.[176]

STJEPAN RADIĆ AND THE CZECHS

Stjepan Radić made a final attempt to save both the Danubian Monarchy and the Croatian nation, which he felt had no future outside of whatever could be salvaged from the Hapsburg shipwreck. A few days after the National Council had opted for the union of the Croatian lands with Serbia (November 24, 1918), Radić hastened to Prague. By this time it had become apparent that the victorious powers understood that if Germanic Austria had been allowed to join the Reich, Germany would have won the war. Emperor-King Karl had not abdicated and was living quietly in one of the Hapsburg castles in Austria. Radić saw that there was still a chance to maintain the identity of the Croatian kingdom as a Central European rather than a Balkan entity and to prevent the formation of a vacuum in the area that had been united under Hapsburg control.[177]

In Prague Radić conferred with Masaryk, Beneš, and other Czech leaders. He asked them not to break up Central Europe and said very bluntly: "In the interest of all of us, and you Czechs first of all, do not carry through your project of smashing up that structure which it took

175/The complete story of the battle of Vittorio Veneto is told in *Österreich-Ungarns letzter Krieg*, VII, 565–806.

176/The leading Croatian historian, Ferdo Šišić, deliberately omitted mention of the Frankist protests in his *Dokumenti o postanku Kraljevine Srba, Hrvata, i Slovenaca, 1914–1919*. Šišić was a partisan of a Yugoslav union.

177/Radić was keeping in close touch with "black-yellow" (the Hapsburg colors) Croatian emigrants who had gone to Austria or Hungary after the end of the fighting. See Jareb, *Pola stoljeća hrvatske politike*, 19–20.

many centuries to create, nor alter it fundamentally. Never, perhaps, will there be a chance like this again. If a contrary policy is adopted the land of the Czechs will be the first victim of the attacks which surely will come."

Masaryk replied, "You, Mr. Radić, are pro-Austrian," and added some other unflattering words.

Radić rose, nodded coolly to Masaryk, and said: "Goodbye, Mr. Masaryk – listen to me and don't break up Austria-Hungary, because by doing so you will create a huge Germany which perhaps in twenty years will trample first upon you and then upon us. Think about that Mr. Masaryk and you other gentlemen."[178]

The record of this verbal exchange is important because many years later Radić's successor as leader of the Peasant Party, Vladko Maček, writing without the assistance of accurate notes to refresh his memory, and already himself far advanced in years, stated that by 1918 Radić had abandoned his ideal of a federal Austria which would include the "Great Croatia" of Trialist dreams.[179] Maček was in uniform throughout the war and was not familiar with Radić's activities and contacts in the fall of 1918. Hence, his statement in this connection is misleading; it has served only to fortify already existing misconceptions created by partisans of Serbo-Croatian-Slovenian unity.

Bibliography

DOCUMENTARY SOURCES

SIXTEENTH CENTURY

Chmel, Josef (ed.). *Aktenstücke zur Geschichte Croatien und Slavonien in den Jahren 1526 und 1527*. Wien, 1846. This is the first publication to concern itself with the Cetin Sabor and the election of December 31–January 1, 1526–7.

Gévay, Anton v. *Urkunden und Aktenstücke zur Geschichte der Verhältnisse zwischen Oesterreich, Ungarn, und der Pforte im* XVI. *und* XVII. *Jahrhunderte*. 9 vols. Wien, 1839–42.

Horvat, Karlo (ed.). *Monumenta historiam Uscocchorum illustrantia ex archivis romanis, praecipue e secreto vaticano desumpta*. 2 vols. Zagreb,

178/*Ibid.* Jareb's account is based upon Dr. I. Pernar, "Tragedija dr. Beneša"/The Tragedy of Dr. Beneš, *Hrvatski Glas* (Winnipeg), no. 40 (Sept. 28, 1948), and upon Marija Radić, "Uspomene i sjećanje na mog nezaboravnog supruga Stjepana Radića"/Memories of My Unforgettable Husband, Stjepan Radić, *Kalendar Hrvatski Glas za godinu 1957* (Winnipeg, 1957), 45.

179/Vladko Maček, *In the Struggle for Freedom* (New York, 1957).

1910, 1913. (Vols. XXXII and XXXIV of *Monumenta spectantia historiam Slavorum meridionalium* – quoted as MSHSM – published at Zagreb 1868–1918 by the Yugoslav Academy of Arts and Sciences.)

Ivić, Aleksa. "Prilozi za povijest Hrvatske i Slavonije u XVI i XVII vieku"/ Contributions to the History of Croatia and Slavonia in the 16th and 17th Centuries, *Starine* (Yugoslav Academy), XXXV (1916), 295–374.

Krones, Franz Xaver. "Aktenmässige Beiträge zur Geschichte des windischen Bauernaufstandes v. J. 1573," *Beiträge zur Kunde steiermärkischen Geschaftsquellen*, v (1868), 3–34. Contains copies of sixty-six original documents found in the Graz archives dealing with the Gubec revolt. All of these papers are dated between February 4 and February 25, 1573.

Kukuljević-Sakcinski, Ivan (ed.). *Jura regni Croatiae, Dalmatiae et Slavoniae*. Vol. II. Zagreb, 1862.

—— *Acta Croatica* (Listine hrvatske). Zagreb, 1863. Most of the documents reproduced in this volume are composed in the Croatian Glagolitic script. They cover the period 1100–1599. Some are written in Latin or in the Serbian Cyrillic script.

Laszowski-Szeliga, Emilij (ed.). *Monumenta habsburgica regni Croatiae, Dalmatiae et Slavoniae*. 3 vols. Zagreb, 1914–17. The documents in these volumes relate chiefly to the second quarter of the sixteenth century. They constitute vols. XXXV, XXXVIII, and XL of MSHSM.

Ljubić, Šime. *Commissiones et relationes Venetae*. Vols. II and III (MSHSM, vols. VIII, XI). Zagreb, 1877, 1880. Documents contained herein relate to Venetian-Croatian relationships between the years 1525 and 1571.

Lopašić, Radoslav (ed.). *Acta historiam confinii militaris Croatici illustrantia* (Spomenici hrvatske Krajine). 3 vols. Zagreb, 1884–9. (Vols. XV, XVI, and XX of MSHSM.) Vol. I covers the years 1479–1610; vol. II, 1610–93; vol. III, 1693–1780.

—— "Prilozi za poviest Hrvatske XVI i XVII vieka iz štajerskoga zemaljskoga arhiva u Gradcu"/Contributions to the History of Croatia in the 16th and 17th Centuries Drawn from the Styrian Provincial Archives in Graz, *Starine* (Yugoslav Academy), XVII (1885), 151–231; XIX (1887), 1–80. This is the main source for Croatian history during the period 1529–99, especially for the Varaždin territory.

Rački, Franjo. "Gradja za poviest hrvatsko-slovenske seljačke bune god. 1573"/Source-Materials for the History of the Croatian-Slovenian Peasant Rebellion 1573, *Starine* (Yugoslav Academy), VII (1875), 164–322; VIII (1876), 243–52.

Šišić, Ferdo (ed.). *Acta comitialia regni Croatiae, Dalmatiae et Slavoniae*. 5 vols. Zagreb, 1912–18. (Vols. XXXIII, XXXVI, XXXIX, XLI, and XLIIII of MSHSM.) Documents in vol. I relate to the years 1526–36, vol. II to 1537–56, vol. III to 1557–77, vol. IV to 1578–1608, and vol. V to 1609–30.

Thallóczy, Lajos, and Hodinka, Antal (eds.). *Codex diplomaticus partium regni Hungariae adnexarum*. Vol. I: *A Horvát véghelyek oklevéltára. 1490–1527*. Budapest, 1903. (Archives of the Croatian Frontier Fortresses.)

SEVENTEENTH CENTURY

Bogišić, Balthasar (ed.). *Acta coniurationem Petri a Zrinio et Francisci de Frankopan nec non Francisci Nadasdy illustrantia (1663–1671)*. Zagreb,

1888. (Vol. XIX of MSHSM.) Contains the correspondence between King Louis XIV of France and his ambassador in Vienna, the Chevalier de Grémonville, as well as other French diplomatic representatives abroad and the personnel of the French Foreign Ministry. The originals of the documents contained in this volume are to be found in the Archives of the Ministry of Foreign Affairs in Paris. The appendix includes reports submitted from various quarters to Louis' Minister, Hugues de Lionne.

Horvat, Karlo (ed.). *Monumenta historiam Uscocchorum illustrantia ex archivis romanis, praecipue e secreto vaticano desumpta.* Vol. II (vol. XXXIV of MSHSM). Zagreb, 1913. Documents contained herein relate to Uskok activities until after the Peace of Madrid of 1617.

Kukuljević-Sakcinski, Ivan (ed.). *Jura regni Croatiae, Dalmatiae et Slavoniae.* Vol. II. Zagreb, 1862.

Rački, Franjo (ed.). *Acta coniurationem bani Petri a Zrinio et com. Fr. Frangepani illustrantia.* Zagreb, 1873. Contains materials relating to the great conspiracy extracted from the Venetian, Roman, and Styrian archives, as well as those of the Haus-, Hof-, and Staatsarchiv in Vienna.

Šišić, Ferdo (ed.). *Acta comitialia regni Croatiae, Dalmatiae et Slavoniae.* Vol. V (vol. XLIII of MSHSM). Zagreb, 1918. The documents in this volume relate to the years 1609–30.

EIGHTEENTH TO TWENTIETH CENTURIES

Austria-Hungary, Ministry for Foreign Affairs. *Österreich-ungarns Aussenpolitik von der bosnischen Krise bis zum Kriegsausbruch 1914.* D. A. des österr.-ungar. Ministerium des Aussern. 8 vols. Wien, 1930.

Croatia-Slavonia, Sabor (Diet). *Saborski dnevnik Kraljevina Hrvatske, Slavonije i Dalmacije 1861–1887* (Stenografički zapisnici)/Minutes of Diet Sessions of the Kingdoms of Croatia, Slavonia, and Dalmatia 1861–1887 (Shorthand Minutes). 13 vols. Zagreb, 1887.

—— *Die vollständigen Landtags-verhändlungen des vereinigten Königreiche Kroatien, Slavonien, Dalmatien im Jahre 1845.* Leipzig, 1846.

France. Ministère des Affaires étrangères. *Documents diplomatiques français* (1871–1914). 1re série (1871–1900). Vol. I (May 10, 1871 to June 30, 1875): Paris, 1929. Vol. II: Paris, 1930.

Germany, Foreign Office. *Die grosse Politik der europäischen Kabinette, 1871–1914 Sammlung der diplomatischen Akten des auswärtigen Amtes.* Eds. Johannes Lipsius, Albrecht Mendelssohn Bartholdy, Frederick Thimme. Vol. XXV, part 2; vol. XXVI, part 1. Berlin, 1939.

Gesetze des Königreiche Kroatien, Slavonien, und Dalmatien von den Jahren 1869ff. Zagreb, 1877.

Great Britain, Foreign Office. *Die britischen amtlichen Dokumente über den Ursprung des Weltkrieges 1898–1914* (German edition of *British Documents on the Origin of the War*). Vol. I. Berlin, 1925.

Hrvatski zakoni. Sbirke tumačenih zakona valjanih u kraljevinah Hrvatskoj i Slavoniji/Croatian Laws. Collections of Interpreted Laws in Force in the Kingdoms of Croatia and Slavonia. Zagreb, 1885.

Office of Statistics, Zagreb. *Viestnik Kr. Zemaljskoga statističkoga ureda u Zagrebu*/Bulletin of the Royal National Statistical Office in Zagreb. 2 vols. Zagreb, 1891, 1900.

Sabor, in Zagreb. *Dnevnik sabora trojedne Kraljevine Dalmacije, Hrvatske, i Slavonije držana u glavnom gradu Hrvatske god. 1861*/Daily Minutes of the Diet of the Triune Kingdom of Dalmatia, Croatia, and Slavonia Convened in the Capital City of Croatia in the Year 1861. Zagreb, 1862.

—— *Dnevnik sabora ... od g. 1865–7*. Zagreb, 1867.

OTHER WORKS CONSULTED

GENERAL HISTORIES

Antoljak, Stjepan. *Pregled hrvatske povijesti*/A Survey of Croatian History. Zagreb, 1942.

Engel, Johann Christian v. *Geschichte des ungrischen Reichs und seiner Nebenländer*. Vol. III: *Staatskunde und Geschichte von Dalmatien, Croatien, und Slawonien*. Halle, 1798.

Horvat, Rudolf. *Povjest Hrvatske*/History of Croatia. Petrinja, 1904. Revised edition, Zagreb, 1924. This work covers only the period up to 1657. See also his *Slike iz hrvatske povjesti*/Illustrations from Croatian History (Zagreb, 1910).

Šišić, Ferdo. *Hrvatska povijest od najstarijih dana do potkraj 1918*/Croatian History from the Earliest Beginnings to the End of 1918. Zagreb, 1928.

—— *Hrvatska povijest*/Croatian History. 3 vols. Zagreb, 1908–13. Covers Croatian history to 1848.

—— *Pregled povijesti hrvatskoga naroda*/A Survey of the History of the Croatian People. 3rd ed. Zagreb, 1962.

Smičiklas, Tadija. *Poviest Hrvatske*/History of Croatia. Vol. II. Zagreb, 1882. This work covers the years 1526–1848.

Srkulj, Stjepan. *Hrvatska povijest u devetnaest karata*/Croatian History. Illustrated on Nineteen Maps. Zagreb, 1937.

Šufflay, Milan. *Hrvatska u svijetlu svjetske historije i politike*/Croatia in the Light of World History and Politics. Zagreb, 1928.

WORKS RELATING PARTICULARLY TO THE SIXTEENTH CENTURY (GENERAL)

Amelot de la Houssay, Abraham-Nicolas. *Histoire du gouvernement de Venise*. Vol. 3: *Suite de l'histoire du gouvernement de Venise, ou l'histoire des Uscoques*. Lyon: P. B. Ponthus, 1678.

Charrière, Ernest. *Négotiations de la France dans le Levant*. 4 vols. Paris, 1848–60. Gives details concerning Franco-Turkish commercial and political relationships in this century.

Chmel, Josef (ed.). *Aktenstücke zur Geschichte Croatien und Slavonien in den Jahren 1526 und 1527*. Wien, 1846.

Črnko, Ferenac. *Povijest Sigeta grada*/History of the City of Szigetvar. N.P., N.D. 13–40.

Gruber, Dane. *Borba Hrvata s Turcima od pada Sigeta do mira Žitva-Dörözkoga*/The Struggle of Croatians with the Turks from the Fall of Szigetvar to the Peace of Zsitva Török. Zagreb, 1879.

Hartinger, Josip. *Hrvatsko-slovenska seljačka buna godine 1573*/The Croatian-Slovenian Peasant Rebellion in 1573. Osijek, 1911.

Istvanffy, Nicholas. *Historiarum de rebus Hungaricis libri XXXIV*. Köln, 1622.

Of value chiefly for the author's own time (the last years of the sixteenth and early part of the seventeenth century).

Ivić, Aleksa. *Migracije Srba u Hrvatsku tokom 16, 17. i 18. stoleća*/Migrations of Serbs into Croatia during the 16th, 17th, and 18th Centuries. Beograd, 1923.

Postel, Guillaume. *De la république des Turcs*. Poitiers, 1560.

Pray, Georg. *Epistolae procerum regni Hungariae*. 3 vols. Posonii (Bratislava), 1806. This is the best Hungarian source for sixteenth-century Croatian history.

Sanuto, Marino. *Diarii di Marino Sanuto*. Vol. XLIII. Venezia, 1895. Valuable for Croatian developments between 1527 and 1533.

Šišić, Ferdo. *Die Wahl Ferdinands I von Österreich zum König von Kroatien*. Zagreb, 1917.

—— *Hrvatska povijest*/Croatian History. Vol. II. Zagreb, 1908.

Wahrhaffter Auszug und Bericht, was sich in christlichen kayserlichen Veltzug wider den Turchen vom 22 Augusti an bis auff den 9 September des 1566 jars. zugetragen etc. ... bericht ... was ... an allerley orten in ober Ungarn und in Krawaten hin und wider ... gehandelt worden. Nürnberg, 1566.

WORKS RELATING PARTICULARLY TO THE SEVENTEENTH CENTURY

Ballagi, Aladar. *Wallensteins kroatische Arquebusiere. Aus unbenutzten Quellen*. Budapest, 1884. Covers the years 1623–6.

Bauer, Ernest. *Hrvati u Tridesetgodišnjem Ratu*/Croatians in the Thirty Years War. Zagreb, 1941.

Horvath, Mihaly. *Geschichte der Ungarn*. Vol. II. Pest, 1855.

Klaić, Vjekoslav. *Život i djela Pavla Rittera Vitezovića 1652–1713*/Life and work of Paul Ritter Vitezović. Zagreb, 1941.

Lilek, Emilian. *Kritische Darstellung der ungarisch-kroatischen Verschwörung und Rebellion (1663–1671)*. 4 vols. Celje, 1928.

Lopašić, Radoslav. *Dva hrvatska junaka. Marko Mesić i Luka Ibrišimović*/Two Croatian Heroes: Marko Mesić and Luka Ibrišimović. Zagreb, 1888.

—— *Oko Kupe i Korane*/Around the Kupa and Korana. Karlovac, 1879.

Posljednji Zrinski i Frankopani/The Last Zrinskis and Frankapans. N.P., N.D.

Rattkaj, Baron Juraj. *Memoria regum et banorum regnorum Dalmatiae, Croatiae et Slavoniae inchoata ab origine sua et usque ad praesentem annum 1652 deducta*. Vienna, 1652. This is the first systematic Croatian history to be composed. It is valuable only for the first half of the seventeenth century however.

Smičiklas, Tadija *Spomenici o Slavoniji u XVII vijeku (1650–1702) and Dvjestogodišnjica oslobodjenja Slavonije*/Documents about Slavonia in the 17th Century (1650–1702) and The Second Centenary of the Liberation of Slavonia. Zagreb, 1891.

WORKS RELATING PARTICULARLY TO THE EIGHTEENTH CENTURY

Cuvaj, Antun. *Nikola pl. Skerlecz-Lomnicki*. Zagreb, 1913.

Keresturi, Joseph. *Collectio ordinationum Josephi II et repraesentationum diversorum regni Hungariae comitatuum*. Diószeg, 1790.

Klaić, Vjekoslav. *Die kroatische Pragmatische Sanktion*. Zagreb, 1915.
Krčelić, Baltazar A. *Annuae sive historia ab anno inclusive 1748 et subsequis (1767) ad posteritatis notitiam*. Ed. Tadija Smičiklas. Zagreb, 1901.
Lichtenstein, J. *Grundbauen der Statistik*. Wien, 1817. Contains much data on the Triune Kingdom in the eighteenth century.
Matasović, Josip. *Die Briefe des Grafen Sermage aus dem siebenjährigen Kriege*. Zagreb, 1923.

THE MILITARY FRONTIERS

Demian, J. A. *Statistische Beschreibung der Militär-Gränze*. 2 vols. Wien, 1806–7.
Fras, Franz Julius. *Merkwürdigkeiten oder historisch-statistisch topographische Beschreibung der Karlstädter-Militär-Grenze*. Karlovac, 1830.
Hietzinger, Carl Freiherr v. *Statistik der Militärgrenze des österreichischen Kaiserthums*. 3 vols. Wien, 1817–23.
Hilleprandt, Anton Edlen v. *Die Feldzuge in Oberitalien im Jahre 1848*. Wien, 1867.
Hirtenfeld, J. *Ban Jellacic*. Wien, 1861.

NINETEENTH-CENTURY CROATIA

Bresnitz von Sydačoff, Philipp Franz. *Die panslavistische Agitation und die südslavische Bewegung in Oesterreich-Ungarn*. Berlin and Leipzig, 1899.
——— *Die Wahrheit über Ungarn*. Berlin and Leipzig, 1901.
Horvat, Josip. *Ante Starčević. Kulturno-povijesna slika*/Ante Starčević: A Cultural and Biographical Portrait. Zagreb, 1940.
Horvat, Rudolf. *Najnovije doba hrvatske povijesti*/The Contemporaneous Era of Croatian History. Zagreb, 1906.
——— *Prije Khuena bana*/Before Ban Khuen. Zagreb, 1933.
Ibler, Janko. *Hrvatska politika 1903–1913*/Croatian Politics. 2 vols. Zagreb, 1914, 1917.
Jakšić, Gjuro. "Rakovička buna"/The Rakovica Uprising, *Šišićev Zbornik*. Zagreb, 1929.
Jelačić, A. *Seljački pokret u Hrvatskoj i Slavoniji godine 1848/9 i ukidanje kmetske zavisnosti seljaka*/The Peasant Movement in Croatia and Slavonia in the Years 1848–9 and the Abolition of Serfdom. Zagreb, 1925.
Jelačić, Baron Josip. *Eine Stunde der Erinnerung*. Zagreb, 1855.
Maček, Vladko. *Bit hrvatskoga seljačkoga pokreta*/The Essence of the Croatian Peasant Movement. Zagreb, 1938.
Marjanović, Milan. *Hrvatski pokret*/The Croatian Movement. 2 vols. Dubrovnik, 1903.
——— *Savremena Hrvatska*/Contemporary Croatia. Beograd, 1913.
Milić, Vicko. *Postanak Riečke Resolucije i njezine posljedice*/The Origin of the Rijeka Resolutions and Their Consequences. N.P., N.D.
Nastić, Djordje. *Wo ist die Wahrheit?* Sarajevo, 1908.
——— *Finale*. Sarajevo, 1908.
Nehajev, Milutin. *Rakovica*. Zagreb, 1932.
Neustädter, J. *Ban Jelačić i dogadjaji u Hrvatskoj od godine 1848*/Ban Jelačić and Events in Croatia from the Year 1848. Zagreb, 1942.

Paton, Andrew Archibald. *Highlands and Islands of the Adriatic*. 2 vols. London, 1849.

Pavlinović, Milan. *Različiti spisi 1869–1879*/Various Writings. Zagreb, 1895.

Polić, Martin. *Ban Dragutin grof Khuen-Hedervary i njegovo doba*/Ban Dragutin Count Khuen-Hedervary and His Times. Zagreb, 1901.

—— *Parlamentarna povijest Kraljevina Hrvatske-Slavonije-Dalmacije 1860–1890*/Parliamentary History of the Kingdoms of Croatia, Slavonia, and Dalmatia 1860–1890. 2 vols. Zagreb, 1899, 1900.

Radić, Stjepan. *Moj politički životopis*/My Political Biography. Zagreb, 1926.

Radonić, Jovan. *Politički i kulturni razvoj moderne Hrvatske*/Political and Cultural Development of Modern Croatia. Novi Sad, 1914. Expresses the views of the Serbians of southern Hungary towards the Croatian state and nationality.

Rothenberg, Gunther. *The Austrian Military Border in Croatia*. Urbana, 1960.

Šarinić, J. "Die Ideologie der kr. Bauernbewegung," *Slavische Rundschau*, xc (1937), 147–56.

Schönhals, Karl v. *Erinnerungen eines österreichischen Veteranen*. 2 vols. Stuttgart and Tübingen, 1852. Vol. ii.

Schwicker, J. H. *Geschichte des österr. Militärgrenze*. Wien and Teschen, 1883.

Šišić, Ferdo. "Kako je Jelačić postao banom"/"How Did Jelačić Become Ban?" *Jugoslavenska Njiva*, vii (1923), 169–83.

—— *Korespondencija Rački-Strossmayer*/Letters between Rački and Strossmayer. 4 vols. Zagreb, 1928–31. These volumes cover the period 1860–94.

Starčević, Ante. *Djela*/Works. 3 vols. Zagreb, 1893–6.

—— *Nekoliko uspomena*/Some Memories. Zagreb, 1870.

Strossmayer, Josip. *Dokumenti i korespondencija*/Documents and Letters. Zagreb, 1933.

Šulek, Bogoslav. *Šta namjeravaju Iliri?*/What are the Aims of the Illyrians? Zagreb, 1844.

Supilo, Frano. *Politika u Hrvatskoj*/Politics in Croatia. Rijeka, 1911. This work reproduces various articles written by Supilo that appeared in *Novi List*.

—— *Otvoreno pismo F. Supila zastupnika delničko-čabarskog kotara svojim izbornicima*/Open Letter of Francis Supilo, the Representative of Delnice-Čabar County, to His Constituency. Zagreb, 1910.

Tomašić, Dinko. *Politički razvitak Hrvata*/Political Development of the Croatians. Zagreb, 1938.

Trdina, Janez. *Bahovi huzari in Iliri. Spomini iz moje profesorske službe na Hrvaškem (1853–1863)*/Bach's Hussars and Illyrians: Memories from the Days of My Teaching Career in Croatia. Ljubljana, 1903.

Turković, Milan. *Geschichte des ehemaligen croatisch-slavonischen Militär-Grenze*. Sušak, 1936.

Utješenović, Mathias Ognjeslav. *Die Militär-gränze und die Verfassung; eine Studie über den Ursprung und das Wesen des Militärgränz Institution und die Stellung derselben zur Landesverfassung*. Wien, 1861.

Vaniček, F. *Specialgeschichte der Militärgrenze*. 4 vols. Wien, 1875.

Vladisavljević, Milan. *Hrvatska autonomija pod Austro-ugarskom*/Croatian Autonomy under Austro-Hungary. Beograd, 1939.

Živković, M. *Politički pabirci iz nedavne prošlosti Hrvatske ili Kako je nastala hrv.-ug. nagodba*/Political Gleanings from the Recent Past of Croatia, or How the Croatian-Hungarian Agreement Originated. Zagreb, 1892.

DALMATIA AND THE FRENCH REVOLUTIONARY AND NAPOLEONIC ERA

Antoljak, Stjepan. *Dalmacija i Venecija na preliminarima u Leobenu i na miru u Campo-Formio*/Dalmatia and Venice at the Preliminaries in Leoben and at the Peace Conference in Campo Formio. Zagreb, 1936.

Appendini, Francesco Maria. *Notizie istorico-critiche sulle antichità, storia e letteratura de' Ragusei.* 2 vols. Ragusa: A. Martecchini, 1802–3.

Cattalinich, Giovanni. *Memorie degli avvenimenti successi in Dalmazia dopo la caduta della republica Veneta con un saggio sull' amministrazione publica veneta e del regno d'Italia.* Spalato, 1841.

Dernière campagne de l'armée franco-italienne sous les ordres d'Eugène Beauharnais en 1813 et 1814. N.P., 1817.

Einsiedel, Alexander August von. *Die Feldzüge der Österreicher in Italien im Jahre 1805.* Weimar, 1812.

Études sur la campagne de 1796–1797 en Italie, by J. C. (Captain of Artillery). Paris, 1814.

Examen de la campagne de Buonaparte en Italie dans les années 1796 et 1797. Paris, 1814.

Gruber, Dane. *Stogodišnjica Napoleonove Ilirije (1809–1909)*/A Centenary of Napoleon's Illyria (1809–1909). Zagreb, 1910. This is a general survey that is lacking in details.

Guerre de l'an 1809 entre l'Autriche et la France par un officier autrichien [Gen. Karl M. von Stutterheim]. 2 vols. Vienna, 1811.

Guillou, Abbé Aimé. *Histoire de la campagne de S.A.I. le prince Eugène Beauharnais de France en 1809.* Milan, 1809.

Latinska jeremiada iz dobe francuske Ilirije/Latin Lamentation from the Times of French Illyria. Maribor, 1925. Enumerates the complaints of the peasants against the French soldiery.

Löwenthal, J. *Geschichte der Stadt Triest.* 2 vols. Triest, 1859. Chapter IV, vol. II deals with the French occupation of Dalmatia and Istria.

Novak, Grga. *Split u svjetskom prometu*/Split's Role in World Commerce. Split, 1913. This work contains a large number of documents covering the period 1806–13 in Dalmatia.

Pisani, Paul. *La Dalmatie de 1797 à 1815.* Paris, 1893. Valuable for both the Austrian and French periods. This work is based upon materials drawn from the provincial and municipal archives of Dalmatia and Ljubljana, which was the French administrative center.

Šišić, Ferdo. *Neke stranice iz novije naše historije*/Selected Pages from our Recent History. Zagreb, 1909.

WORKS RELATING PRINCIPALLY TO THE PERIOD 1815–1914

Bogdanov, Vaso. *Društvene i političke borbe u Hrvatskoj 1848–49*/Social and Political Struggles in Croatia 1848–49. Zagreb, 1949.

—— *Historija političkih stranaka u Hrvatskoj*/History of Political Parties in Croatia. Zagreb, 1958.
Bojničić, Ivan. *Zakoni o ugarsko-hrvatskoj Nagodbi*/Laws about the Croatian-Hungarian Agreement. Zagreb, 1907.
Correspondence Relative to the Affairs of Hungary 1847–1849. London, 1850. (Reports of the English Ambassador to Vienna, Viscount Ponsonby.)
Deželić, Velimir. *Dr. Ljudevit Gaj*. Zagreb, 1910.
—— *Maksimilijan Vrhovac*. Zagreb, 1904.
Horvat, Josip. *Stranke kod Hrvata i njihove ideologije*/Political Parties among Croatians and Their Ideologies. Beograd, 1939.
—— *Politička povijest Hrvatske*/Political History of Croatia. Zagreb, 1936.

LEGAL, CONSTITUTIONAL, AND SPECIAL STUDIES RELATING TO THE HUNGARIAN-CROATIAN STATE RELATIONSHIP

Bidermann, Dr. H. J. "Legislation autonome de la Croatie et aperçus de l'histoire du droit croate," *Revue de droit international*, VIII (1876), 215–92.
Déak, Francis. *Denkschrift über das Verhältnis zwischen Ungarn und Kroatien*. Wien, 1861.
Kvaternik, Eugen. *Das historisch-diplomatische Verhältnis des Königreichs Kroatiens zu der ungarischen St. Stephans-Krone*. Zagreb, 1861.
Pliverić, J. *Die rechtliche Verhältnisse Kroatien zu Ungarn*. Zagreb, 1885.
—— *Beiträge zum ungarisch-kroatischen Bundesrechte*. Zagreb, 1886.
—— *Hrvatsko-ugarsko državno pravo*/Croatian-Hungarian Constitutional Law. Zagreb, 1900.
Pregled političkoga i sudbenoga razdieljenja kraljevinah Hrvatske i Slavonije i uredjenja upravnih občinah/Survey of the Political and Legal Divisions of the Kingdoms of Croatia and Slavonia and the Organization of Administrative Municipalities. Zagreb, 1877.
Šulek, Bogoslav. *Naše pravice*/Our Rights. Zagreb, 1868.
—— *Hrvatski ustav ili Konstitucija g. 1882*/The Croatian Constitution of 1882. Zagreb, 1883.
Szilay, Ladislas. *Zur ungarisch-kroatischen Frage*. Pest and Leipzig, 1863.
Tomašić, Nikola. *Fundamente des Staatsrechtes des Königreiches Kroatien*. Zagreb, 1918.

WORKS RELATING SPECIFICALLY TO BOSNIA

Austrian General Staff. *Die Occupation der Bosnien und Hercegovina*. Wien, 1879–80.
Baernreither, Joseph. *Fragments of a Political Diary*. Ed. Jos. Redlich. London, 1930. [*Fragmente eines politischen Tagebuches*. Berlin, 1928.]
Handžić, M. *Islamizacija Bosne i Hercegovine*/The Islamization of Bosnia and Hercegovina. Sarajevo, 1940.
Herkalović, Toma. *Vorgeschichte der Occupation Bosnia und der Hercegovina*. Zagreb, 1878.
Hötzendorff, Conrad v. *Mein Anfang. Kriegserinnerungen aus der Jugendzeit, 1878–1882*. Wien, 1925.
Mandić, Dominik. *Bosna i Hercegovina*/Bosnia and Hercegovina. Vol. I:

Državna i vjerska pripadnost sredovječne Bosne i Hercegovine/The State and Religious Affiliation of Medieval Bosnia and Hercegovina. Chicago, 1960.

—— Vol. II: *Bogomilska Crkva Bosanskih Krstjana*/The Bogomil Church of Bosnian Christians. Chicago, 1962. This and vol. I relate to medieval Bosnia.

—— Vol. III: *Etnička povijest Bosne i Hercegovine*/Ethnic History of Bosnia and Hercegovina. Rim, 1967.

Croatian Political Chronology 1526–1918

1526 Turks under Soliman II defeat the Hungarians at Mohács (August 29). King Louis II Jagellon killed, leaving Hungarian, Bohemian, and Croatian thrones vacant. Light Croatian participation in this battle. Counts Krsto Frankapan and Ivan Karlović organize defense of Croatia-Slavonia against the Turks and assist Hungarians. John Zápolya, vojvoda of Transylvania, asserts his claim to the Hungarian and Croatian thrones. Archduke Ferdinand of Austria elected king of Bohemia by the Bohemian estates and claims Hungarian and Croatian thrones on the basis of inheritance (his wife, Anna, was the sister of Louis II Jagellon and daughter of Vladislav II Jagellon) and treaty (four mutual inheritance pacts concluded between the Hapsburgs and the Jagellon families during 1461–1515). Count Krsto Frankapan becomes Ban of Slavonia. Makes alliance with Ferdinand, but is persuaded by Bishop Simon Erdödi of Zagreb to switch his support to Zápolya. The majority of Hungarian nobles elect Zápolya king, and he is crowned with the holy Crown of St. Stephen. Minority Hungarian element recognizes accession of Ferdinand.

1527 Croatian Sabor meeting at Cetin accepts Ferdinand as king. Slavonian Sabor convenes at Dubrava near Čazma to recognize the accession of Zápolya. Civil war between the partisans of Ferdinand and Zápolya in Hungary and Slavonia. Frankapan defeated and killed at Varaždin (September). Slavonian Sabor now repudiates Zápolya and recognizes Ferdinand as the legitimate king. Hungarian partisans of Zápolya defeated at Tokay and Zápolya flees to Poland. Juraj Utišenić (Martinuzzi) becomes his chief adviser.

1528 With French and Turkish support Zápolya reconquers Transylvania and part of central Hungary. Civil war in Slavonia, where Magyar landowners support Zápolya as does Bishop Erdödi and the bishop of Senj, Frano Jožefić. Zápolya asks for Turkish assistance against the Hapsburgs. Lika and Krbava lost to the Ottomans.

1529 Zápolya acknowledges himself and Transylvania to be Turkish vassals. Turks besiege Vienna but are repulsed.

1529–33 Three-cornered civil war in Hungary between partisans of Zápolya, who are aided by the Turks, and Ferdinand's adherents. Little fighting in Slavonia after 1530, and in 1533 Zápolya renounces his claim to this Croatian territory. Several temporary truces.

1533 In June the Croatian-Slavonian Sabor convenes in Zagreb.

1533–8 War between the Austrians and the Turks continues. Failure of "Katzianer" expedition in 1537 results in Turkish conquest of Slavonia. Osijek falls. Srijem overrun.

1537 The Croatian hero and feudal lord Petar Kružić falls fighting the Turks at Klis, which passes into the hands of the Ottomans for more than a century and a half.

1538 Treaty of Nagyvárad between Ferdinand and Zápolya. Latter to reign over Hungary and Transylvania during his lifetime. After his death Ferdinand to be king of all Hungary.

1540 Zápolya dies, but his widow invokes Turkish protection for the rights of her infant son. Turks again invade Hungary and complete their conquest of most of Slavonia. Varaždin and several military border captaincies remain in the hands of the Austrians and Croatians.

1540–52 Intermittent warfare punctuated by several truces which the Turks invariably violate. Turks master central and southern Hungary. Transylvania remains a Turkish vassal state under Zápolya's successors. Many Croatians flee from Slavonia into western Hungary, which remains under Hapsburg control.

1556 Ferdinand succeeds his brother Charles V (Charles I of Spain) as Holy Roman (German) Emperor. His eldest son, Maximilian, assumes charge of the defense of the Croatian lands and continues to strengthen the fortifications of Zagreb.

1558 First joint Croatian-Slavonian-Dalmatian Sabor convenes.

1564 Ferdinand I dies and is succeeded by Maximilian II in Croatia-Slavonia.

1566 Great Turkish invasion of Hungary stopped by Count Nikola Zrinski at Sziget. Soliman dies here and his army abandons its intention to march on to Vienna. Zrinski and a Croatian-Hungarian garrison of 2500 men inflict 20,000 casualties on Turks before falling, almost to a man, at Sziget.

1568 Treaty of Adrianople establishes twenty-five-year truce.

1569 Death of Ivan Lenković, Croatian general in Austrian service and defender of Croatia against the Turks.

1573 Peasant uprising led by Matija Gubec is cruelly suppressed by Bishop Drašković and Colonel Gašpar Alapić. (Legend of punishment of the rebels may be apocryphal.)

1575 Ferhat Pasha Sokolović, a Hercegovinian Croatian and outstanding Turkish military leader and statesmen, defeats General Auersperg at Radonja. Several Croatian border fortresses fall.

1576 Maximilian II dies and is succeeded by Rudolph II.

1578 Formal organization of the Croatian and Slavonian Military Borders (Vojna Krajina) by Archduke Karl of Styria.

1579 Ferhat Pasha dies at Constantinople. Archduke Karl founds fortress city of Karlovac.

1582 Croatian Ban proclaims the "Insurrection" (Mobilization) against the Turks. Stepped-up tempo of fighting.

1583 Paulist Fathers (Pavlins) found first Croatian Gymnasium at Lepoglava.

1586 Ban Tomo Erdödi defeats large Turkish army at the mouth of the Glogovnica River near Čazma.

1591–3 Hasan Pasha (a Muslim Bosnian Croatian) attacks Sisak but is defeated. Other conflicts follow. Hasan defeated and killed in a battle before Sisak in 1593.

1593–1606 The Long War between Croatians and Austrians on the one hand and Turks on the other. Hungarian Protestants support Turks. Bocskay uprising in Hungary and Transylvania.

1604 Peace of Vienna grants religious liberty to Magyar Protestants. Croatians refuse to allow such liberty in Croatia-Slavonia.

1606 Peace of Zsitva-Török with Turks gives countryside of Croatia proper respite from the incessant Ottoman invasions of the preceding century and a half. Military Frontiers continue to be involved in small-scale *Buschkrieg* with Muslims.

1614–17 "Uskok War." Baron Ivan Isolani and Croatian *četas* distinguish themselves in fighting the Venetians and Dutch.

1617 Treaty of Madrid ends "Uskok War" and stipulates removal of Uskoks from the Adriatic Coast.

1619–48 Croatians serve in armies of Tilly, Wallenstein, and other imperial generals in the Thirty Years War.

1651–63 Counts Nikola and Petar Zrinski defeat the Turks and their Tatar and Mongol auxiliaries in a number of "unofficial" battles along the frontiers.

1663–4 Turkish war. Count Raymond Montecucculi defeats Turks at St. Gotthard.

1664 Peace of Vasvár restores status quo and enrages the Zrinskis who wish to continue the war for the purpose of recovering Slavonia, Dalmatia, and Bosnia.

1663–71 Zrinski-Frankapan conspiracy results in temporary loss of Croatian constitutional autonomy.

1665 Count Petar Zrinski named Ban of Croatia to succeed his deceased brother, Count Nikola.

1667 Earthquake destroys large part of Dubrovnik.

1671 Execution of Counts Petar Zrinski and Fran Frankapan because of involvement with Turks and French.

1683 Turks repulsed from Vienna, which was saved by the Polish king, Jan Sobieski.

1683–99 War of Liberation by the Holy League. Turks driven from Slavonia, Lika, Krbava, and Dalmatia.

1689 Fra Luka Ibrišimović, a Franciscan friar, defeats Turks near Požega.

1699 Peace of Karlovci (Karlowitz) fails to reunite these Croatian territories with Banal Croatia. Slavonia, Lika, Krbava under Austrian military administration. Dalmatia goes to Venice.

1701–13 War of Spanish Succession. Croatians fight against the French, Bavarians, and Italians along the Rhine, in Italy, and in Spain.

1703 Ivan Zrinski, last of his line, dies at Graz.

1703–11 Rákóczi rebellion in Transylvania and Hungary. Croatians fight for the Hapsburgs against the half-Croatian Prince Francis Rákóczi II (son of Jelena Zrinski).

1712 Sabor adopts resolution, called "Pragmatic Sanction," that in default of male heirs ("Which may God prevent") the Croatians will accept as their ruler that Hapsburg princess who also has the allegiance of the hereditary Hapsburg lands including Styria, Carinthia, and Carniola (the latter, along with southern Styria and Carinthia, being the homeland of the Slovenes).

1713 Charles VI (III of Croatia) issues formal Pragmatic Sanction.

1717–18 Turkish war. Prince Eugene captures Belgrade and defeats Ottoman armies decisively. Ottomans prostrate.

1718 Peace of Passarowitz liberates Srijem and Banat of Temesvár along with northwestern Bosnia and northern Serbia from Turkish rule. Graničari (Frontiersmen) make unusually poor showing in this struggle.

1723 Hungarian diet accepts Pragmatic Sanction recognizing right of succession of Karl III's daughters.

1725 Karl III reorganizes Banal Bench as Supreme Court of Croatia.

1733–6 War of the Polish Succession.

1737–9 Turkish war. By peace of Belgrade Turks recover northwestern Bosnia and Serbia. Srijem remains in Austrian hands.

1737 "Carolina" urbarial patent issued to define and limit the legal exploitation of serfs.

1740 Accession of Maria Theresa precipitates War of the Austrian Succession, or the Silesian Wars. Croatians fight for Austria against the French, Prussians, Bavarians, and Italians.

1745 Maria Theresa returns to Croatian rule the three ancient Croatian counties of Požega, Virovitica, and Srijem. Peasant rebellion by Orthodox elements settled in the Croatian lands initiates urbarial reforms.

1756–63 Seven Years War with Prussia.

1767 "Concilium" established for Croatia-Slavonia with its seat at Varaždin.

1776 The Primorje (Littoral) and Rijeka united directly with Croatia-Slavonia.

1779 Concilium abolished and Rijeka declared to be a *corpus separatum* of the Hungarian Crown.

1780–90 Anticlerical and social reforms of Joseph II cause Croatian nobility to seek alliance with Magyar nobility in defense of their class interests against Vienna.

1787–91 Turkish war. Croatians fight successfully against Ottomans.

1791 Peace of Sistova brings small accretion of territory to Croatia-Slavonia.

1790–2 Sabor concedes to the Hungarian diet the right to determine tax and recruit levies for the Croatian lands. In effect this means that from a constitutional point of view Croatian autonomy is abrogated.

1792–7 War of the First Coalition. Croatians fight in France, along the Rhine, and in Italy against the French Republicans and Napoleon Bonaparte.

1797 Peace of Campo Formio. In return for cession of Belgium (Austrian Netherlands) and the old Hapsburg lands in southern Germany, Austria receives all the territory of the old Venetian Republic including Dalmatia and Venetian Istria. Croatian troops under Baron Mato Rukavina occupy Dalmatia. Strong demand for union of Dalmatia and Istria with Croatia-Slavonia opposed by Count Thugut (Tunichtsgut).

1798–1802 War of the Second Coalition. Croatians serve under Archdukes Karl and John and the Russian general Suvarov.

1797–1805 Austrians reform Venetian administration in Dalmatia but leave in office the old Venetian bureaucracy which sabotages the reforms. Nonetheless much progress is made in beginning a system of public education, road construction, and public health. Administration of Baron Gooss particularly beneficial for Dalmatia.

1804–5 Austrian and Croatian participation in the War of the Third Coalition. By Peace of Pressburg Austria cedes Dalmatia, Istria, and Venice to France.

1806 The Croatian newspaper *Kraļski Dalmatin* published in Zadar. French occupy Dalmatia. Russian fleet takes possession of Korčula and the Gulf of Kotor. French end independence of Ragusan Republic by occupying this city.

1808 Formal French annexation of Dubrovnik (Ragusan Republic) proclaimed. Archduke John organizes Domobran (Home Defense Force) among Croatians.

1809 Croatians drive French from parts of Dalmatia and Istria in the War of 1809. By the Treaty of Vienna Austria cedes to France Military Croatia and all Banal Croatia from the right bank of the Sava.

1806–13 French administration of "Illyria" highly unpopular with Croatians. More popular with Slovenes and Serbian element in Dalmatia. Marshal Marmont, Napoleon's administrator in "Illyria," personally well liked.

1813–14 French driven from Dalmatia and Istria as Croatian population of these areas revolts against them.

1815 Croatians participate in battle of Tolentino in which Marshal Murat, ruler of Naples (The Two Sicilies), is defeated and the Bourbons restored to power.

1816–22 Croatian lands divided into Kingdom of Illyria and Kingdom of Dalmatia.

1822 Civil districts of Croatia-Slavonia and the Littoral separated and united with Hungary. Military Frontiers (Vojna Krajina) placed under direct control of War Office in Vienna. Dalmatia and Istria ruled from Vienna but much latitude allowed to Italian minority in the local administration of these provinces.

1825 Sabor convenes for the first time since the Napoleonic Wars.

1830–47 Magyar attempts to substitute their language for Latin in Croatian courts, schools, and administration stimulate rise of Croatian national feeling.

1831 Husein Beg Gradašćević, the "Dragon of Bosnia" and leader of the Bosnian Muslims opposed to the westernizing reforms of Sultan Mahmud II, defeats Turkish army at Travnik.

1832 Husein Beg killed.

1835–48 The Illyrian movement (Ljudevit Gaj).

1838 Count Janko Drašković establishes "National Reading Room" (Čitaonica) in Zagreb.

1843 Ivan Kukuljević-Sakcinski delivers the first speech in the Croatian language in Sabor. (Heretofore Latin was always used.)

1846 Vjekoslav Babukić, a native of Požega, named first professor of Croatian language and literature in Zagreb Academy.

1847 Sabor introduces Croatian instead of Latin into schools and administration.

1848 Baron Josip Jelačić becomes Ban. Croatia-Slavonia severs constitutional relationship with Hungary after Louis Kossuth displaces the Magyar moderates (Széchenyi, Déak, Eötvös, Szémere) who took a conciliatory attitude towards the Croatians. Croatia-Slavonia secures an autonomous government within the Hapsburg Monarchy. Demands unification of Dalmatia, Istria, and the Military Frontiers with Croatia-Slavonia. Jelačić abolishes serfdom in Croatia-Slavonia. Battle of Custozza won chiefly by Croatian forces in Italy.

1848 In September, Ban Jelačić invades Hungary, crossing the Drava. Battle of Schwechat. In October, Croatian army effects junction with Imperial Austrian Army under Prince Windischgraetz and storms Vienna to suppress the radical revolutionary movement there.

1848–9 Croatians aid Austrians in suppressing the Kossuthist rebellion in Hungary. Ban Jelačić leads Croatian army into Buda. Croatian contingent plays leading role in victory of Novara won by Marshal Radetzsky over the Piedmontese and other Italian forces.

1849 Croatia-Slavonia officially separated from Hungary and constituted as an autonomous crown land. Some political concessions made to the Croatians.

1851 The Muslim Croatian, Omer Pasha Latas, defeats Ali Pasha Rizvanbegović, leader of the Hercegovinian rebellion against the Turks. Beginning of Bach regime in Croatia-Slavonia.

1851–60 Croatia-Slavonia loses autonomy granted in 1849 and while remaining separate from Hungary is governed directly from Vienna.

1859 Croatian regiments fight brilliantly at Magenta, Solferino, and other battles of the war of 1859 against the French and Italians.

1860 Croatians granted separate government but allow themselves to be persuaded by the Hungarians not to participate in the sessions of the central parliament in Vienna.

1862 Croatian Court Chancellery begins to function in Vienna as governing organ for Croatia-Slavonia. Royal Chancellor Ivan Mažuranić issues regulation requiring the "Illyrian language" to be referred to as the Croatian language. The Academy of Arts and Sciences is founded in Zagreb. Royal Septemviral Bench begins to function in Zagreb.

1866 Croatian regiments under Davidović and Vukasović defeat Italians at Custozza. Croatian sailors under Admiral Tegethoff defeat Italian fleet at Lissa (Vis).

1867 Conclusion of the Austro-Hungarian *Ausgleich* puts the Croatians in the position of having to make their peace with the Magyars. Frantic last-minute negotiations with Vienna fail because of the *Ausgleich* commitments made by Austria.

1868 Croatians conclude Nagodba (agreement) with Hungary, Croatia-Slavonia receives administrative, educational, and judicial autonomy. Financial clauses of the Nagodba make Croatians dependent in some degree upon Hungary, a dependency accentuated by the fact that the Ban becomes an appointee of the Hungarian minister-president.

1871 Abortive Rakovica uprising led by Eugen Kvaternik crushed by Croatian border troops.

1873 Ivan Mažuranić becomes Ban. Reorganization of administration and of school system.

1874 Formal opening of Zagreb University.

1878–9 Croatian regiments under Frano and Ivan Filipović occupy Bosnia-Hercegovina and suppress Muslim-Serbian resistance.

1879 Renewal of Nagodba with Hungary.

1881–4 Military Croatia incorporated with Civil Croatia.

1883 Count Dragutin Khuen-Hedervåry becomes Ban. Favors Serbian minority in Croatia-Slavonia. Anti-Serbian and Anti-Hungarian riots in Zagreb and other localities.

1895 More anti-Serbian and anti-Hungarian riots in Croatia-Slavonia. Influence of Starčević and Frankist parties.

1905 Rijeka and Zadar Resolutions lay basis for emergence of Yugoslav movement under aegis of Serbo-Croatian Coalition (Supilo, Trumbić). Coalition collaborates with Kossuthist Independence Party in Hungary without securing any kind of *quid pro quo* for so doing.

1907 Railway Servants Act violates spirit if not letter of Nagodba by attempting to prescribe knowledge of Magyar for all officials and employees of the Hungarian-Croatian state railways.

1908 Annexation of Bosnia-Hercegovina by Austria-Hungary stimulates Croatian hopes of realization of Trialist program (union of Croatia-Slavonia with Dalmatia, Istria, and Bosnia-Hercegovina to transform the dualist Austro-Hungarian state into a triune monarchy).

1908–9 Annexation crisis and Austrian bungling of the Zagreb treason trials and the Friedjung Process plays into the hands of the Coalition, particularly of its Serbian elements.

1910 Bosnian-Hercegovinian Sabor formally inaugurated at Sarajevo. King Francis Joseph proclaims constitution for Bosnia-Hercegovina.

1910–14 Wave of terrorism and breakdown of school discipline in Bosnia-Hercegovina culminates in assassination of Archduke Francis Ferdinand, heir to the throne of Austria-Hungary and regarded by nationally minded Croatians as their chief sponsor. Anti-Serbian violence in Zagreb and other places after the murder.

1914–18 Croatian regiments fight with customary élan on Russian, Serbian, Italian, Albanian, and Rumanian fronts.

1918 In October, Serbian elements in Sabor and Czech politicians induce Croatian political leaders to separate the Triune Kingdom from the dissolving Austro-Hungarian state and to join with the Slovenes and Serbs to form a new kingdom.

Croatian and Bosnian Rulers

CROATIAN NATIONAL RULERS

PRINCES

PANNONIAN CROATIA

796 / Vojnomir
ca. 818–22 / Ljudevit (Louis) Posavski
827–43 / Ratimir
870–(?)* / Mutimir
884–96 / Braslav

DALMATIAN CROATIA

626–*ca.* 635 / Klukas
ca. 635–*ca.* 660 / Porga
ca. 740–*ca.* 780 / Budimir
ca. 785–*ca.* 802 / Višeslav
ca. 802–21 / Borna
821–*ca.* 830 / Vladislav
ca. 830–45 / Mislav
ca. 845–63 / Trpimir I
863–76 / Domagoj
876–8 / Iljko (probably apocryphal)
878–9 / Zdeslav
879–92 / Branimir
892–*ca.* 910 / Mutimir
ca. 910–*ca.* 923 / Tomislav

*Question marks (?) indicate that there is doubt as to the actual existence of the individual rulers indicated or as to the dates of their rule. For a detailed discussion of the chronology of the Croatian national rulers up to the union of Croatia with Hungary in 1102, see the following studies: Ferdo Šišić, "Genealoški prilozi o hrvatskoj narodnoj dinastiji"/Genealogical Contributions Concerning the Croatian

CROATIAN NATIONAL KINGS

DALMATIAN CROATIA

923–*ca.* 929 / Tomislav
ca. 929–*ca.* 935 / Trpimir II (?) (may be apocryphal)
ca. 935–44 / Krešimir I
944–8 / Miroslav
948–969/Mihajlo Krešimir II (The Old)
969–95/ Stipan Držislav
995–7 / Svetoslav Suronja
997–1030 / Krešimir III
997–*ca.* 1020/ Gojislav (co-ruler)
1030–*ca.* 1056 / Stipan I
ca. 1056–73 / Petar Krešimir IV
1073–6 / Slavac
1076–89 / Zvonimir Dmitar
1089–90 / Stipan II
1091–7 / Petar III Snačić (?) (may be apocryphal)

RED CROATIA OR DIOCLEA

1074–81 / Mihajlo I
1081–1102 / Bodin
1102 / Dobroslav
1102–3 / Kočapar
1103–14 / Vladimir
1114–16 / Gjuro
1116–23 / Grubeša
1123–31 / Gjuro (rules for the second time)
1132–43 / Gradihna
1143–*ca.* 1152 / Radoslav ("Knesius")
ca. 1152–*ca.* 1172 / (?) Under Byzantine control during this period. The real ruler was Manuel Comnenus (1143–80)
ca. 1173–89 / Mihajlo II

CROATIAN-HUNGARIAN KINGS

HOUSE OF ARPAD

1091–95/Almoš (Slavonia or Pannonian Croatia only)
1102–16 / Koloman
1116–31 / Stephen II
1131–41 / Bela II
1141–62 / Geza
1162–72 / Stephen III (Ladislas II, 1162–3; Stephen IV, 1163)
1172–96 / Bela III
1196–1204 / Mirko (Emeric)
1204–5 / Ladislas III
1205–35 / Andreas II
1235–70 / Bela IV
1270–2 / Stephen V
1272–90 / Ladislas IV (The Cuman, "Kumanac")
1290–1301 / Andreas III (The Venetian, "Mlečanin")

HOUSE OF ANJOU

1301–42 / Charles Robert
1342–82 / Louis I
1382–5, 1386 / Maria
1385–6 / Charles of Durazzo

OTHER HOUSE LINES

1387–1437 / Sigismund of Luxemburg
1437–39 / Albrecht of Hapsburg
1440–4 / Vladislav I Jagellon
1445–57 / Ladislas V (The Posthumous)
1458–90 / Matthias Corvinus
1490–1516 / Vladislav II Jagellon
1516–26 / Louis II Jagellon

National Dynasty, *Vjesnik Hrvatskog Arheološkog Društva* (Zagreb), XIII (1913), 1–93; Miho Barada, "Dinastičko pitanje u Hrvatskoj XI. stoljeća"/The Dynastic Question in Croatia in the 11th Century, *Vjesnik za arheologiju i historju dalmatinsku*, 50 (Split, 1928–9), 157–99; Dominik Mandić, *Rasprave i prilozi*/Studies and Contributions, XIV, "Hrvatski narodni vladari: Rodoslovlje i redoslijed"/Croatian National Rulers: Genealogy and Order of Succession (Rome: Hrvatski Povijesni Institut, 1963), 324–67.

CROATIAN KINGS OF THE HAPSBURG DYNASTY

1526–64 / Ferdinand I
1564–76 / Maximilian II
1576–1608 / Rudolph (Rudolph I Hapsburg was not a king of Croatia; therefore Rudolph II Hapsburg (1576–1608) bears the title of Rudolph I in Croatian history)
1608–19/Matthias I
1619–37 / Ferdinand II
1637–57 / Ferdinand III
1657–1705 / Leopold I
1705–11 / Joseph I
1711–40 / Charles III (of Croatia, VI of Austria and the Holy Roman Empire)

CROATIAN KINGS AND QUEENS OF THE HAPSBURG-LORRAINE DYNASTY

1740–80 / Maria Theresa
1780–90 / Joseph II
1790–2 / Leopold II
1792–1835 / Francis II
1835–48 / Ferdinand V (Ferdinand IV died prematurely without having reigned)
1848–1916 / Francis Joseph I
1916–18 / Charles IV (of Croatia, VII of Austria)

CROATIAN BANS

DURING THE RULE OF CROATIAN NATIONAL KINGS

949–970 (?) / Pribina
ca. 970–95 / Godimir
ca. 995–1000 / Gvarda
ca. 1000–30 / Božeteh
ca. 1035–58 / Stjepan Praska
1059–69 / Gojko
1070–3 / Zvonimir Dmitar (he became Croatian king 1076–89)
1074 / Petar

DURING THE RULE OF CROATIAN-HUNGARIAN KINGS

House of Arpad (1102–1301)

1102–3 / Ugra
1105 / Sergije
1116 / Bezimeni (anonymous)
1141 / Aleksije
1144–58 / Bjeloš
1158 / Arpa
1163 / Bjeloš (rules second time)
1164–74 / Ampodin
1181 / Mavro
1181–4 / Dioniz (rules in Littoral)
1185 / Šuban
1190–3 / Kalan
1194, 1195 / Dominik
1198 / Andrija
1199, 1200 / Nikola and Benko
1202 / Martin
1204 / Hipolit
1205, 1206 / Merkurije
1206, 1207 / Stjepan Mihaljev
1208, 1209 / Banko
1209 / Tomo
1209–11 / Bertold
1212 / Mihajlo
1213 / Martin
1213 / Jula
1212–14 / Simon
1214 / Okić
1215 / Ivan (rules in Slavonia)
1216 / Poza
1217 / Poncije de Cruce
1217, 1218 / Banko
1219 / Jula
1220, 1221 / Ernej
1220–2 / Okić
1224 / Salamon
1225 / Aladar (Ban of all Croatia)
1225 / Vojnić (Ban of Dalmatian Croatia)

Bans of All Croatia (totius Sclavoniae)

1242–5 / Dionizije
1245–8 / Ladislav of Transylvania
1248–60 / Stjepan Gutkeled
1261–5 / Roland (probably up to 1269)
1269 / Henrik Gising (from Aug. 1)
1270–2 / Joakim Pektar
1272, 1273 / Matej Čak
1273, 1274 / Henrik Gising
1274–5 / Dioniz Babonić
1275–7 / Ivan Gising, son of Henrik
1275, 1276 / Toma
1278 / Stjepan, son of Haholt
1278–88 / Nikola, brother of Joakim Pektar
1288–90 / Radoslav, brother of Ban Dioniz
1290–4 / Nikola Gising
1295–9 / Ivan Gising
1299 / Stjepan Babonić

Bans of Croatia and Dalmatia

1243–9 / Stjepan Babonić
1259 / Butko and Aleksandar of Podgorje
1263–6 / Stjepan, *knez* of Klis
1275/Nikola of Gacka
1278–1312 / Pavao Šubić, *knez* of Bribir

House of Anjou (1301–87)

Bans of All Croatia (totius Sclavoniae)

1301–9 / Henrik Gising
1310–16 / Stjepan Babonić
1316–22 / Ivan Babonić
1322–4 / Nikola Omedejev
1324–43 / Mikac Prodavić
1343–6 / Nikola Banić (Banfi)
1346–9 / Nikola Seč
1350 / Pavao Ugal
1351–2 / Stjepan Lacković
1353–6 / Nikola Banić
1356–61 / Leustahije Ratot
1362–6 / Stjepan Kanižaj
1366–8 / Nikola Seč
1368–80 / Petar Cudar
1381–5 / Ivan Banić of Lendava
1385–7 / Stjepan Banić of Lendava

Special Bans of Croatia and Dalmatia

1274–1312 / Pavao Šubić
1312–22 / Mladen Šubić (Ban of all Bosnia at the same time)
1356–8 / Ivan Ćuz
1358–66 / Nikola Seč
1366–7 / Konja Tomin Secenj
1368 / Mirko Lacković of Simontornja
1360–71 / Simon Mauricijev
1371–6 / Karlo Dracki
1377–80 / Nikola Seč
1380–3 / Mirko Bubek
1383–4 / Stjepan Lacković
1384–5 / Toma of St. George
1387 / Ladislav Lacković

Other Dynasties (1387–1526)

Bans of All Croatia (totius Sclavoniae)

1387–9 / Ladislav of Lučenac
1389–92 / Detrik Bubek
1392 / Ladislav Petrov
1392–95 / Ivan Frankapan
1395–7 / Detrik Bubek
1397–1401 / Nikola Gorjanski
1402 / Mirko Bubek
1403, 1404 / Ladislav of Grdjevac
1404–6 / Pavao Bisen
1406, 1407 / Herman of Celje
1412–15 / Pavao Čupor of Moslavina
1416–18 / David Lacković
1419–21 / Dionizije Marcali
1423–35 / Herman of Celje
1435–44 / Matko Talovac
1445–54 / Fridrik of Celje

1454–6 / Ulrik of Celje
1457 / Ivan Marcali
1457–63 / Ivan Vitovec and Nikola of Ilok
1464, 1465 / Mirko Zápolya
1466–70 / Ivan Tuz of Lak
1470–2 / Blaž Podmanički
1472, 1473 / Damjan Horvat of Litva
1473–6 / Ivan Ernušt
1476 / Andrija Banić (Banfi)
1477–81 / Ladislav of Egervary
1482 / Blaž Podmanički
1483–9 / Matija Gereb
1489–92 / Ladislav of Egervary
1492, 1493 / Ivan Rot
1492, 1493 / Mirko Derenčin
1493–5 / Ladislav Kanižaj (Nov. 22 to Mar. 1)
1495–7 / Ivan Korvin (to Oct. 28)
1498 / Juraj Kanižaj
1499–1504 / Ivan Korvin (Jan. 5, 1499, to Nov. 12, 1504)
1504 / Andrija Bot of Bajna
1505 / Franjo Balaša
1506, 1507 / Marko Horvat Mišljenović
1508–10 / Ivan Ernust
1508–10 / Juraj Kanižaj
1510–11 / Andrija Bot of Bajna (to Sept. 13)
1512–13 / Mirko Perenj (Mar. 25, 1512, to spring 1513)
1513–20 / Petar Berislavić (to May 20)
1520–4 / Ivan Karlović (Nov. 1520 to Aug. 1524)
1524, 1525 / Ivan Tahi
1525–31 / Franjo Bačan (Batthyany) (Mar. 12, 1525, to Sept. 30, 1531)

Special Bans of Croatia and Dalmatia

1387–90 / Dionizije of Lučenac
1394 / Butko Kurjaković Krbavski
1395–7 / Nikola Gorjanski
1408, 1409 / Ivan and Pavao Kurjaković
1412, 1413 / Petar Alben of Medvedgrad
1414–19 / Ivan Alben of Medvedgrad
1419–26 / Albert Ung
1426–32 / Nikola Frankapan I
1434–6 / Ivan Frankapan
1434–7 / Stjepan Frankapan
1438–53 / Petar Talovac
1444–8 / Franko Talovac
1453 / Ladislav Hunyady
1459–63 / Pavao Horvat Špirančić
1463 / Stjepan Frankapan
1473–6 / Damjan Horvat of Litva

House of Hapsburg (1527–1918)

1526–7 / Knez Krsto Frankapan (Ban of Slavonia and appointed Ban of Croatia by John Zápolya)
1527–31 / Knez Ivan Karlović
1525–31 / Count Francis Batthyany
1537–9 / Count Thomas Nadásdy (Ban of Slavonia)
1537–42 / Baron Petar Keglević (Vice-Ban 1533–7)
1542–56 / Knez Nikola Zrinski the Elder
1556–67 / Count Petar Erdödi
1567–78 / Bishop Juraj Drašković
1567–72 / Knez Franjo Frankapan of Slunj
1572–8 / Knez Gašpar Alapić
1578–83 / Baron Christian Ungnad
1583–95 / Count Toma Erdödi
1596 / Bishop Gašpar Stankovački (from Jan. 11 to June 30; Vice-Ban 1595–6)
1596–1606 / Baron Ivan Drašković I (Vice-Ban 1595–6)
1608–14 / Count Toma Erdödi
1615–16 / Knez Benko Turoc
1617–22 / Knez Nikola Frankapan of Tržac (Tržački)
1622–6 / Knez Juraj Zrinski
1627–39 / Count Sigismund Erdödi
1640–6 / Count Ivan Drašković II
1647–64 / Knez Nikola Zrinski the Younger

1665–70 / Knez Petar Zrinski
1670–80 / In 1670–4 Bishop Martin Borković was Vice-Ban. Count Nikola Erdödi also functioned in this capacity from April 3, 1671, until April 10, 1680
1680–93 / Count Nikola Erdödi (from April 10)
1693–1703 / Count Adam Batthyany
1704–32 / Count John Palfy
1732–3 / Count Ivan Drašković II
1733–41 / Count Joseph Esterhazy

House of Hapsburg-Lorraine

1743–56 / Count Karlo Batthyany
1756–83/Count Francis Nadásdy
1783–5 / Count Francis Esterhazy
1785–90 / Count Francis Balassa
1790–1806 / Count Ivan Erdödi
1806–31 / Count John Gyulay
1832–40 / Baron Franjo Vlašić
1840–2 / Bishop Juraj Haulik was Vice-Ban
1842–5 / Count Francis Haller
1845–8 / Bishop Juraj Haulik was Vice-Ban
1848–59 / Baron (later Count) Josip Jelačić
1859–60 / Count John Coronini
1860–7 / Baron Josip Šokčević
1868–71 / Baron Levin Rauch (Vice-Ban 1867–8)
1871–2 / Koloman pl. Bedeković
1872–3/Antun pl. Vakanović was Vice-Ban
1873–80 / Ivan Mažuranić
1880–3 / Count Ladislas Pejačević
1883–1903 / Count Dragutin Khuen-Hedervåry
1903–7 / Count Teodor Pejačević
1907–8 / Dr. Aleksandar pl. Rakodczay
1908–10 / Baron Pavao Rauch
1910–12 / Dr. Nikola pl. Tomašić
1912 / Slavko pl. Cuvaj (Jan. 10 to April 5)
1913–17 / Dr. Ivan Baron Škrlec (Skerlecz) (Nov. 27, 1913, to June 29, 1917)
1917–19 / Anton pl. Mihalović
1919 / Dr. Ivan Paleček (Jan. 20 to Nov. 24)
1919–20 / Dr. Tomislav Tomljenović
1920 / Dr. Matko Laginja (Feb. 22 to Dec. 11)
1921 / Dr. Tomislav Tomljenović (March 2 to July 3). Dr. Teodor Bošnjak was Vice-Ban from Dec. 23, 1920, to March 2, 1921

Royal Commissars
1883 / Baron Herman Ramberg (Sept. 4 to Dec. 1)
1912–13/Slavko pl. Cuvaj (April 5, 1912, to Sept. 21, 1913)
1913 / Dr. Ivan pl. Škrlec (July 21 to Nov. 27)

BOSNIAN NATIONAL RULERS

BANS

ca. 1150–63 / Borić
1163–1204 / Kulin
1204–23 / Stipan
1223–32 / Status of Bosnia unclear during this period but apparently claimed by Hungary though virtually independent; period of great disorder
1223–50 / Matej Ninoslav
1250–88 / Prijezda
1288–1302 / Stipan Kotromanić
1302–12 / Mladen Šubić
1312–53 / Stipan Kotromanić (rules again)
1353–77 / Stipan Tvrdko I

KINGS

1377–91 / Stipan Tvrdko I
1391–5 / Stipan Dabiša
1395–8 / Queen Jelena ("Gruba")
1398–1404 / Stipan Ostoja
1404–8 / Stipan Tvrdko II
1408–18 / Stipan Ostoja (second reign)
1418–20 / Stipan Ostojić
1420–43 / Stipan Tvrdko II (second reign)
1444–61 / Stipan Toma
1461–63 / Stipan Tomašević

BOSNIA UNDER OTTOMAN SULTANS

Under Ottoman rule (1643–1878) Bosnia-Hercegovina enjoyed a considerable political freedom. It was made into an Autonomous Ottoman Province (*valiluk*) ruled by governors (*valijas*) and divided into captaincies.

1259–1326 / Othman (or Osman) I (founder of Ottoman Empire)
1326–60 / Orkhan
1360–89 / Murad I
1389–1402 / Bajazet (or Bayazid or Bayezid) I
1402–10/Soliman (or Sulayman) I
1410–13 / Musa
1413–21/Mahomet (or Muhammad) I
1421–51 / Murad II
Bosnia came under Ottoman sultans in 1463.
1451–81 / Mahomet II "The Conqueror" (in 1453 takes Constantinople, in 1459 he is the master of Balkans, in 1463 he takes Bosnia, and his successor takes Hercegovina in 1482)
1481–1512 / Bajazet II
1512–20 / Selim I
1520–66 / Soliman II "The Magnificent" (died during the siege of Sziget, the fortress in southern Hungary, defended by the Croatian Ban Nikola Šubić Zrinski)
1566–74 / Selim II
1574–95 / Murad III
1595–1603 / Mahomet III
1603–17 / Achmet (or Ahmed or Ahmad) I
1617–18 / Mustapha I
1618–22 / Othman II
1622–3 / Mustapha I (second reign)
1623–40 / Murad IV
1640–49 / Ibrahim
1649–87 / Mahomet IV
1687–91 / Soliman III
1691–5 / Achmet II
1695–1703 / Mustapha II
1703–30 / Achmet III
1730–54 / Mahmud I
1754–7 / Othman III
1757–74 / Mustapha III
1774–89 / Abdul-Hamid I
1789–1807 / Selim III
1807–8 / Mustapha IV
1808–39 / Mahmud II
1839–61 / Abdul-Medjid
1861–76 / Abdul-Aziz
1876 / Murad V
1876–1909 / Abdul-Hamid II
Austria-Hungary took over Bosnia-Hercegovina in 1878.

2

Maritime History of the Eastern Adriatic

WILLY A. BACHICH

PREHISTORIC TIMES AND ANTIQUITY

For some 1300 years, the Croatian people have occupied the larger part of the eastern shores of the Adriatic Sea, a gulf which extends for 420 nautical miles. The eastern Adriatic, with its 36 large (over seven square kilometers in area) and 511 small islands and about 300 rocky islets, offered navigators many sea routes and harbors in the channels between the islands and in the bays along the coast. Since the beginning of the twentieth century, historians have known that there was a highly developed maritime activity on the eastern Mediterranean as far back as prehistoric times. That navigational skills were highly developed on the Adriatic as well was proved by the discovery on the islands of traces of Neolithic cultures showing relations with the Aegean, Cretan, and Maltese civilizations; such is a cave drawing that looks like a sailing ship which was found on the island of Hvar.[1]

Maritime activity continued in the Bronze Age, when Indo-European peoples populated the Adriatic shore, and in the Iron Age, and became especially great in the following epochs when trade was more developed. Apparently the inhabitants of the eastern part of the Adriatic were more active on the sea during some periods than others, but the seafaring activities of the coastal people never ceased, even when new peoples replaced or mixed with the old inhabitants. Thus, it can be

1/Grga Novak, *Prethistorijski Hvar: Grapčeva špilja*/The Prehistoric Island of Hvar: The Cave of Grabac (Zagreb: Yugoslav Academy, 1955). Extensive summary in English.

assumed that seamanship has been a constant phenomenon during the entire history of this region, as a result, no doubt, of the geographical nature of the area. The French scholar Camille Vallaux shares this view, considering that the old inhabitants of the Croatian coast were always a genuinely maritime population, dependent on sea trade and fishing for their livelihood.[2]

Chiefly as a consequence of Illyrian seamanship, an Illyrian naval power arose after 1000 B.C., developed first by the Iapyges and shortly afterwards maintained by the Liburnians, both Illyrian tribes. These tribes were strong enough not only to control the waters off the Adriatic coast but also to occupy parts of the opposite coast, the Iapyges in Apulia and the Liburnians farther to the north in the region of Picenum (Piceno), south of Ancona.[3] Later, Greek merchants from Syracuse came to the Illyrian shores; at first they came only as traders, but between the years 397 and 384 B.C. the Greeks built fortified colonies on the Adriatic islands, the first of which were Issa on the island of Vis, and Pharos on the island of Hvar. In the course of time, these activities aroused Illyrian hostility against the Greeks, a hostility which erupted around 250 B.C. after the Ardiaei, an Illyrian tribe then inhabiting the region of the Neretva River, had become powerful on both land and sea under their king, Agron.

The Ardiaei began to extend their territory towards the southeast using small, handy, swift ships called *lemboi* or *lembi.*[4] Some Illyrian

2/Camille Vallaux, *Géographie générale des mers* (Paris: Librairie Alcan, 1933), 642.

3/Alfredo Schiaffini, *Italia e Croazia* (Rome: Reale Academia Italiana, 1942), 7.

4/*Lembi* were small Illyrian ships, which figured in Roman history as well. The historian Polybius relates that in 216 B.C., Philippos v of Macedonia, an ally of Hannibal, ordered the construction of 100 of these ships to transport his forces to Italy. "During the winter Philip took into consideration that for his enterprise he would require ships and crews to man them, not it is true, with the idea of fighting at sea – for he never thought he would be capable of offering battle to the Roman fleet – but to transport his troops, land where he wished, and take enemy by surprise. Therefore, as he thought the Illyrian shipwrights were the best, he decided to build a hundred galleys [Lembi], being almost the first king of Macedonia who had taken such a step." Polybius, *The Histories*, trans. by W. R. Paton (Cambridge: Harvard University Press, 1960), book v, 109, p. 261.

The conquests of King Agron are described in the following: "Agron was king of that part of Illyria which borders the Adriatic Sea, over which sea Pyrrhus, king of Epirus, and his successors held sway. Agron in turn captured a part of Epirus and also Corcyra, Epidamnus and Pharus in succession, and established garizons in them. When he threatened the rest of the Adriatic with his fleet, the isle of Issa implored the aid of the Romans. The latter sent ambassadors to accompany the Issii and to ascertain what offenses Agron imputed to them. The Illyrian light vessels [lembi] attacked the ambassadors as they sailed up, and slew Cleemporus, the envoy of Issa, and the Roman Coruncanius; the remainder escaped by flight. Thereupon

groups made their way into the Ionian Sea, attacking Greek ships and island settlements, while Agron conquered Epirus and the islands of Corcyra and Pharus. The Ardiaei later also attacked the fortified colony of Issa, the most important Greek colony in the Adriatic. At Agron's death, his widow, Queen Teuta, sent her fleet into the Ionian Sea and, having defeated a Greek fleet in 230 B.C., captured Corfu.

Meanwhile, Rome and Carthage had been waging war on one another for many years, in the so-called Punic Wars, although the wars had been temporarily suspended by the time of Queen Teuta's conquests. In the First Punic War, from 264 to 241 B.C., which ended eleven years before the Ardiaei established themselves on the islands of the Ionian Sea, the Romans had won many sea victories. However, with the display of Queen Teuta's sea power, Rome feared her intervention in the Mediterranean struggle as an ally of Carthage and therefore decided to attack the Ardiaei and wipe out their fleet and Ionian naval bases. Because of its superior fleet and because Teuta's ally, Admiral Demetrius of Pharos, changed sides and surrendered Corfu to the Romans in 229 B.C., Queen Teuta's navy was defeated, and she was forced to sign a peace treaty that included restrictions on the entry of the Ardiaei into the Ionian Sea. Instead of being able to sail a fleet, the Ardiaei would be allowed to sail only two unarmed ships into the Ionian Sea from the Adriatic. The Illyrians never again controlled the Ionian Sea although they did venture to attack the Roman forces there, and Rome had to continue its struggles against them in the so-called Illyrian wars, gradually transforming Illyria into a Roman province.

Although Rome dominated the Adriatic Sea, little is known of the Dalmatian coast for nearly two hundred years after Teuta's defeat, until the Roman Civil wars and the time of Augustus Caesar (27 B.C. to A.D. 14), the first Roman emperor, during whose reign Illyria, including Dalmatia, was definitively transformed into a Roman province called Illyricum. We do know, however, that ships built by Liburnians, perhaps partly manned by Illyrians, played an important part in the naval wars during the time of Augustus and thereafter. These "Liburnae" were swift and easily maneuverable and helped Augustus's fleet to defeat the heavy ships of Antonius at the battle of Actium in 31 B.C.[5]

the Romans invaded Illyria by land and by sea." Appianus, *Roman History*, vol. II, book X, "The Illyrian Wars," trans. by Horace White (New York: The Macmillan Company, 1912), V, pp. 63–4.

5/"Diversae autem provinciae quibusdam temporibus mari plurimum potuerunt, et ideo diversa eis genera navium fuerunt. Sed Augusto dimicante Actiaco proelio, cum Liburnorum auxiliis praecipue victus fuisset Antonius, experimento tanti certaminis patuit, [esse] Liburnorum naves ceteris aptiores. Ergo, similitudine et nomine

There is some evidence that the original *liburna* had only one line of oars and that later, Roman-built *liburnae* had two lines, though the rowers were not on two separate floors. The *liburnae* were probably the ancestors of the Byzantine *moneres* and *dromons* and the first medieval galleys. Thus it can be seen that in antiquity the people of the Dalmatian coast contributed an important innovation in warship design to the navies of the time and those that followed.

In the six centuries following the battle of Actium, the Dalmatian coast was under Roman and, after the fourth century A.D., Byzantine domination. During this period, there was considerable maritime activity on the Dalmatian and Istrian coasts and there were four important shipping centers: the three large towns of Dalmatia, Salona (Solin), Narona (Vid), and Epidaurum (Cavtat), and, in the north, the town of Pola (Pula). In addition, seamen from the eastern Adriatic served throughout the Mediterranean on merchant ships and in the Roman and Byzantine navies. This long period was abruptly ended, early in the seventh century A.D., by the invasions of the Avars and the Slavs.

THE MIDDLE AGES: 614–1420

The invasions of the Avars and Slavs changed the political and cultural life of the Dalmatian coast, but did not interrupt its maritime activity. The Dalmatian ports, Salona, Narona, and Epidaurum, were completely destroyed about A.D. 614, but smaller towns on the coast survived. Among these were Spalatum (Split), built by the refugees from Salona; Ragusium (Dubrovnik), built by survivors from Epidaurum; Tragurium (Trogir); and Diadora or Jadera (Zadar). All of these towns, along with the northern islands of Curicum (Krk), Arba (Rab), Crexa (Cres), and Apsorus (Osor), remained independent of the Avar and Slav invaders and continued under Byzantine rule. From the ninth century, these towns and islands formed the Dalmatian province (*thema*) under a special Byzantine governor (*strategos*).

In the succession of new settlers after the Slavic invasion, the Croatians predominated after their arrival around A.D. 626. Their occupancy of the Dalmatian coast did not disturb the continuity of maritime acti-

usurpato, ad earundem instar classem Romani principes texuerunt. Liburnia namque Dalmatiae pars est, Iadertinae subiacens civitati, cuius exemplo nunc naves bellicae fabricantur, et appellantur Liburnae." Flavius Vegetius Renatus, *Institutorum Rei Militaris*, book v, 3 (Lugduni Batavorum: Ex officina Joannis Maire, 1744).

vity; indeed, the Croatians quickly learned their maritime skills from the earlier inhabitants.

Little is known about the Dalmatian coast in the centuries from A.D. 614 to 800, except for some scant information about some of the towns, and a report of an attack made first by the Slavs and then by the Croatians on the western coast of the Adriatic in A.D. 642. This expedition against the Longobards, successful at first, ended in defeat and the attackers were forced to return to Dalmatia.

Early in this period, in addition to the main group of Croatians, an independent group of the same nation called the Narrantani or Mariani also inhabited the coast.[6] This group lived in the region between the Cetina and Neretva rivers and on the islands of Brač, Hvar, and Vis. They were excellent seamen, as were all Croatians on the coast, and became famous as sailors and for their attacks against Venetian shipping. Their neighbors recognized them as skilled seafarers and considered them dangerous foes on the sea.

For the period after A.D. 800, Venetian chronicles provide somewhat more information on the seafaring activities of the inhabitants of the Dalmatian coast than is available for the previous two centuries. Apparently, Venetian trade along the Adriatic coast was threatened in some way by the Croatians, and the Venetian doge, Pietro Tradonico (836–64), decided to give protection, even to the extent of conquering some of the Dalmatian islands. He therefore armed a fleet and sent it to the Dalmatian coast. Although a Croatian fleet was organized to resist the Venetians, no major battles ensued. This struggle for control of trade in the Adriatic ended in a peace treaty signed in 839 by the Croatian duke, Mislav (830–45), and the doge, at the hamlet of St. Martin in Poljica, and by another treaty signed immediately afterwards by Drosaicus (Družak), the duke of Narrantani, and the doge, on either the island of Hvar or of Brač.[7] The provisions of these treaties are not known, but apparently they guaranteed the security of free Venetian navigation along the eastern Adriatic. Yet, the very next year the Narrantani provoked a new conflict and defeated a Venetian squadron, and in the same

6/The names Narrantani and Mariani (for the Croatian *Neretljani and Morani*) come from the Latin words: the *Narenta* (Croatian: *Neretva*) River and the *mare* (sea; in Croatian, *more*). We use the names Narrantani and Mariani following John Deacon (Joannes Diaconus) who was secretary to the doge Peter II Orseolo (992–1009). Deacon's work, *Chronicon Venetum*, the best Venetian source on early Croatian maritime history, was published by G. Monticolo, *Cronache veneziane antichissime*, I (Rome, 1890), 113.

7/Franjo Rački, *Documenta historiae chroaticae periodum antiquam illustrantia* (Zagreb: Yugoslav Academy, 1877), 355. Diaconus, ed. Monticolo, *Cronache veneziane antichissime*, I, 118.

year they attacked Istria. Lothair (840–55), king of Germany and Holy Roman Emperor, who had no navy and feared a threat to his lands, allied himself with the Venetians and the Istrian cities against the Croatians and the Narrantani, whom they called Sclavi (Slavs). Similar conflicts between the Croatians and the Venetians and their allies continued for some sixty years. In 846, for example, Croatian ships attacked the town of Caorle, near Venice, and in 865 the doge of Venice, Ursus Participatius (864–81), undertook a strong expedition against the Croatian duke, Domagoj (*ca.* 864–76). This Venetian expedition once again resulted in a peace treaty.[8]

During the same period, the Saracens (Arabs) were also active in the Adriatic, attacking harbors and ships especially in the great assaults of 841 and 842. In 869, the same Duke Domagoj who had resisted Doge Ursus Participatius was called on by Louis II (855–75), emperor of the Franks, brought his ships and troops to Bari, and in 871 helped retake that city which had fallen to the Saracens. After 871, the conflicts between Domagoj and Venice resumed, and Croatian ships, or at least ships belonging to the territory of Duke Domagoj, frequently attacked Venetian ships, even as close to Venice as the western coast of Istria. Duke Domagoj, because of the warlike strength shown by these attacks, was a person of importance to his contemporaries: understandably: Venetian chronicles speak of him as "the worst duke of the Croatians,"[9] while Pope John VIII (872–82) addresses him as "the glorious Duke Domagoj"[10] and asks him to prevent his subjects' attacks on Venetian shipping.

Yet, once again, it was not long before the Narrantani began attacking Venetian ships. Doge Pietro Candiano retaliated by sending a naval squadron against the Dalmatian coast, but it returned unsuccessful to Venice in 887. The doge himself, in August of that year, took command of the Venetian fleet of twelve heavy ships and attacked the Narrantani. At the outset he seized five of their ships, but later that year he was defeated and killed on the shore near Makarska.[11]

For a short time after this Venetian defeat, during the time of the first Croatian king, Tomislav (910–29), relations between Croatia and Venice were apparently peaceful. Tomislav, with the authorization of Byzantium, controlled all of the towns on the Dalmatian coast and maintained a strong army and navy. One of his successors, Krešimir I

8/Rački, 364; Diaconus, I, 123.

9/Rački, 366.

10/*Ibid.*, 6; Ferdo Šišić, *Priručnik izvora hrvatske historije: Enchiridion fontium historiae Croatiae*, I (Zagreb, 1914), 201–2.

11/Rački, 374–5.

(*ca.* 935–44), had a navy which consisted of 180 ships, of which 80 were *sagenas*, ships with crews of 40 men, and 100 were *conduras*, smaller ships with crews of 10 to 20 men.[12] Since the sagenas and conduras had such small crews, it has been suggested that the numbers for the crews refer to those used in peacetime, while larger crews would have been used in warfare. Unfortunately, this question cannot be settled because, although we can reasonably suppose that these ships were comparable to other ships of the early medieval type, no detailed descriptions or drawings of them exist.

The naval force built by Tomislav continued under his successors but, after 945, under King Miroslav (944–8), the Croatian forces declined. The Croatian navy was then reported to include 30 sagenas and over 30 conduras.

After 945, the Narrantani were once more strong on the sea, and again began to attack Venetian ships. As a result, in 948 Doge Pietro Candiano III made a fruitless expedition to their territory with a fleet of 33 heavy ships. After a second expedition in the same year, the doge made peace with the Narrantani, who turned from warfare to peaceful sea trade. This peace treaty was probably similar to the treaty signed in 846 by the Croatian duke Trpimir and the Venetians, requiring Venice to pay an annual tribute or census, which must have been equivalent to duties on shipping and travel along the Dalmatian coast.

Again, a peaceful period followed the treaty, lasting almost until A.D. 1000. In 996, when Doge Pietro Orseolo II discontinued paying the Venetian tribute, the Croatians retaliated by attacking Venetian ships, and in answer to these attacks the doge conducted a well-prepared and successful campaign in Dalmatia. In part, his success in the north was due to the outbreak of civil war in Croatia amongst several aspirants to the crown. In the south, he struck his most important blow by capturing 40 Narrantani nobleman at sea, as they were returning from a commercial voyage to Apulia. After this action, for the first time, Venice controlled the Byzantine towns on the eastern side of the Adriatic, but only under the supreme authority of Byzantium, to whom both Venice and those towns were subject. The doge, therefore, had to get formal authorization from the Byzantine emperor in order to govern the towns on the Dalmatian coast.

After about fifty years of Venetian dominance on the sea, and Venetian control of the Dalmatian towns, Venice's navy began to decline, accompanied by a reintegration of Byzantine authority over these towns

12/Constantine VII Porphyrogenitus, *De administrando imperio*, 31. Ed. Moravcsik and Jenkins (Budapest, 1949), 71–82, 150.

and a strengthening of the Croatian kingdom. As a consequence, during the reign of King Petar Krešimir IV (*ca.* 1056–73), Croatia became powerful again, and after 1058 this Croatian king had full authority over all the Dalmatian towns and islands and over the eastern coast of Istria as well. Petar Krešimir IV took the title "King of Croatia and Dalmatia," declared in a document dated 1070 that "Almighty God increased our reign on land and on sea," and spoke of the waters off the Dalmatian coast as "our Dalmatian sea."[13] In spite of this expansion, after his reign, in 1075 Venice once again secured a foothold on the coast, occupying some of the Dalmatian towns. The Croatian struggle for full control of the coast and all towns resumed, however, and under King Zvonimir (1076–89), in 1076, the Croatian kingdom regained its former power.

Little is known about Croatian maritime life during this period; yet it seems likely that seafaring was as important as ever. Since the kingdom was stretched out along the coast, sea travel would probably have been the best way to reach different parts of the kingdom. That people did travel to different parts of the kingdom is known; indeed (the king had no single permanent, but several temporary capitals, among which were Šibenik, Biograd, and Solin, near Split, and moved from one to another. In addition, the Croatian kings most probably maintained a navy, for they seized towns on the shore and on the islands. In fact, in 1082 King Zvonimir was summoned by Pope Gregory VII to help Robert Guiscard, the first Norman ruler of Sicily, in his war on Byzantium and Venice. Zvonimir sent his navy, together with ships from Dubrovnik, to aid in the struggle on the Albanian coast. After Pope Gregory VII and Robert died, Zvonimir lost his allies, but Venice dared not attack Croatia. He continued to reign in strength, and his authority was unchallenged on the sea until his death in 1089. However, great struggles for the crown of Croatia followed his death, and in 1102 a special agreement was concluded between Croatia and Hungary establishing a personal union between the two countries. The Hungarian king, Koloman of the Arpad dynasty, became king of Croatia as well, and was crowned in Biograd, on the Adriatic coast.

Apparently, permanent navies did not exist in medieval Croatia. In fact, in the Middle Ages most of the Mediterranean countries did not have permanent armies or navies, as Rome had had in antiquity and Byzantium had during almost the whole Middle Ages. In these countries, some cities or princes might have kept a small permanent guard or a ship or two for security purposes, but in wartime, emergency fleets

13/Šišić, *Priručnik*, 253.

had to be recruited by commandeering private merchant vessels and arming them, reinforcing their crews, and organizing their command. The larger a merchant fleet that was available in a region, the greater the potential naval force available for wartime. Some princes or city governments had ships built for their own use in peacetime traffic, sometimes leasing them to merchants, as Venice often did, or keeping them in condition all ready to be commissioned in the event of war. For the purpose of building and maintaining these ships, permanent dockyards were established in the Mediterranean and Adriatic ports, the largest of these being the Arsenale in Venice, founded in 1104. Smaller establishments existed also in the towns on the Dalmatian coast. As the centuries passed, permanent navies developed from these beginnings, especially in Venice and Genoa.

Maritime life apparently was of little interest to the authors of the medieval chronicles. As a result, the existing documents record little about seafaring, not only along the Adriatic coast but also throughout the Mediterranean. It can be taken for granted that shipping and fishing continued along the Dalmatian coast, although the chronicles tell hardly anything about these. The center of the Croatian kingdom was shifted inland as a result of the centuries-long struggles with Hungary and Venice, but the Hungarian-Croatian kings still maintained their control over the Dalmatian coastal towns until 1409. It is known that the towns of Dalmatia helped transport troops over the sea for the Croatian kings. One instance of such aid occurred during the struggle against Venetian shipping by the citizens of Zadar in 1203, and another instance in the war against Venetian sea traffic by this same town in 1346.

During these centuries, the Dalmatian ports continued their trade and concluded commercial treaties with towns on the Italian coast. In addition, the peace treaties signed in 1358 at Zadar and 1381 at Turin between Venice and King Louis the Great of Croatia-Hungary contained clauses relating to the use of the seas, including provisions binding both parties not to tolerate piracy. The only Croatian ruler of this period whose naval policy is known to us is this King Louis the Great. For example, it is known that he ordered three ships to be constructed at Dubrovnik and it is probable that he ordered additional ones built at other places. Also, we know that in 1358 he appointed Jacob de Cesamis, a nobleman from Zadar who was governor of the islands of Brač, Hvar, and Korčula at that time, his "Admiral on the Sea."

During these centuries, the inhabitants of the former Narrantani region of the Dalmatian coast considered it their right to attack Venetian shipping and often that of other towns, including those of Dalmatia.

The clan of the Kačić, who lived in the region of the fortified town of Omiš (Almissa), were particularly active, and became the successors of the Narrantani. They took their name from the family Kačić, once the most powerful in the region. Their activity lasted intermittently from the twelfth century until 1420, when the Turks began their conquests and the region fell under Venetian rule.

Many expeditions were undertaken against the Kačićs, most of them by Venice, and all of them unsuccessful. About 1290, while the strong counts of Bribir ruled in Dalmatia, the activity of the Kačićs ceased, but they revived it after 1300 and posed a considerable problem for King Louis when he agreed to prevent piracy on his coasts in the Treaty of Zara (Zadar) in 1358.

At the beginning of the fifteenth century, in 1409, the rule of the Dalmatian coast passed from the king of Hungary-Croatia to Venice, which bought the rights to Dalmatia from King Ladislas of Naples, a pretender to the crown of Hungary and Croatia who did not yet possess it. Ladislas had been recognized by some people on the coast and was therefore able to transfer the claim of parts of the Littoral to Venice while Sigismund, the real and crowned king, was too occupied elsewhere to prevent it. Meanwhile, however, after conquering Bosnia and occasionally attacking parts of Dalmatia itself, the Turks had begun moving into the regions adjoining Dalmatia. Dalmatian towns and islands had no protection and knew they could not easily resist the Turkish troops. They therefore chose to cease their resistance against Venice in order to defend themselves better against the Turkish invasion. As a consequence, between 1412 and 1420, Venice was able to take possession of the Dalmatian towns and their surrounding areas, except for Dubrovnik, and later the islands.

THE EARLY MODERN PERIOD: 1420–1815

As a result of the Turkish conquests and the Venetian purchase of parts of Dalmatia, the coastal region was separated into three political divisions. The northern from Istria to the Zrmanja River, including Rijeka and Senj, belonged to the kingdom of Croatia. The central part, which included the towns of Zadar, Šibenik, Trogir, and Split and the islands from Krk to Korčula, was under Venetian rule. In the southern part of this area, Venice had partial control over the city and the Bay of Kotor. The third region, the Republic of Dubrovnik, extended from the peninsula of Pelješac to the town of Cavtat, the Konavli *polje*, and southward to the entrance of the Bay of Kotor (the cap of Oštra), including the islands of Mljet and Lastovo.

THE AREAS UNDER VENETIAN RULE

The chief result of Venetian domination in the central part of the Dalmatian coast was that the inhabitants were better able to hold the Turks at bay. Although they had once fought Venice, the Dalmatians now preferred Venetian to Turkish rule and sought Venetian aid against Turkish attacks. Venice sent money and arms and sometimes even troops and ships; she also helped build fortifications for the towns. These actions not only protected Venetian Dalmatia but, at the same time, were in the vital interests of Venice herself, helping to keep her Adriatic Sea routes free of adversaries and to prevent the Turks from gaining a firm hold on the Adriatic shores from which to attack Venice. In spite of these efforts, however, the Turks did reach the coast at a few points: at Boka Kotorska (Hercegnovi), at the estuary of the Neretva River, and at Skradin near Šibenik; however, at all these points Turkish access to the open sea was prevented by fortresses, artillery emplacements, or ships.

For the aid Venice sent them, the Croatian inhabitants of Venetian Dalmatia, especially of the islands, had to pay a high price, in men sent to serve as crew and fighting forces in the Venetian navy and lives lost in battles. The Croatians served chiefly in the Venetian fleet in the Adriatic, a force under the command of the Captain of the (Adriatic) Gulf (in Latin: *Capitaneus Gulfi*). The Venetians also maintained a naval force on Crete, the Guardia de Candia, but few Croatians served in it.

Largely by voluntary enlistments in peacetime and by conscription in wartime, Dalmatia sent Venice its *homines de facto* (in Italian: *Gente da Fatto*), men ready for naval service. Most of the volunteers came from the numerous Croatian refugees from adjacent Turkish territory, who entered the service to make a living. If there were not enough volunteers to man the galleys, crews would be recruited on the islands (because the coast, except for the cities, was almost completely occupied by the Turks) by holding a number drawing. A man whose number had been drawn could send a substitute if he did not want to serve himself. During a great naval war, however, when there would be a general mobilization of the Venetian fleet and even more men would be required in the navy, the fleet could expand to over one hundred ships, and all the available men were required for service.

Methods similar to a modern mobilization were then used to bring the extra men into the navy.

Records show that a large proportion of the population of Venetian Dalmatia served in the Venetian fleet. In the year 1528, approximately 2000 men (2 per cent of the population) from the islands and the region around Zadar served in what was at that time a permanent peacetime navy. In 1556, however, 3600 Dalmatians served as oarsmen and *scapoli*, that is, as soldiers and sailors on 22 Venetian ships. In 1561, ten times as many Croatians were serving in the navy. In this year the population of Venetian Dalmatia, that is, of the islands and those parts of the mainland that were still free of Turkish domination, was about 100,000 people, and 21,240 *homines de facto* were reported. In addition, in the same year a report says that the people of the island of Krk could provide enough men for the crews of four galleys without using more than half of its *homines de facto*.

The battle of Lepanto in 1571, in which the combined fleets of Spain, Genoa, Malta, Pope Pius v, and Venice defeated the Turkish fleet in the Straits of Lepanto near Corinth in Greece, was a decisive victory in the European struggle against the Turks. The Croatians played their part, about 1500 of them falling in battle, and a considerable number dying of contageous diseases in the first year of war (1570), on ships and in Zadar where the Venetian fleet was based. Some seven or eight thousand (7–8 per cent of the population of Venetian Dalmatia) served in the fleet. In addition, the Dalmatians provided seven galleys[14] of their own for this battle, manned by Dalmatian officers and crews and carrying fighting men drawn from the islands of Krk, Cres, and Rab, and from the towns of Šibenik, Trogir, Hvar, and Kotor. Three additional galleys were provided by the islands of Korčula and Brač, and the town of Split, but these were not present at the battle itself.

During this period, fishing and coastal trading continued to be very important. Unfortunately, there are no figures available from which to estimate the number of ships or of people engaged in these activities. It is known, however, that the ancient fishing rights off the islands and near the shore were exercised. In the regions under her control, Venice

14/The performance of one galley, *La Donna* of Trogir (also called the *Tragurina*), became famous under the command of *supra-comito* (captain) Louis Cipico; in a critical moment it fought alone against six Turkish galleys. Except for the stern, the deck of *La Donna* had already been taken by the Turks, when the ship was saved by the intervention of galleys from the reserve. Cipico and the officer who defended the quarterdeck were fatally wounded, and 150 other men, probably two-thirds of the crew, were killed. (The galleys were called after the towns where they were armed, e.g. the *Sibenzana* from Šibenik and the *Catarina* from Kotor.)

restricted both foreign trade and sailing to foreign ports. These restrictions were a hardship to many Croatian communities; for example, the people of the island of Rab were impoverished because they had depended for their livelihood on foreign trade, especially the export of firewood to Italy. However, Venice did need ships, and so she encouraged the Croatian shipbuilding industry. Merchant ships were built, owned, and manned by Croatians and were sailed under the Venetian flag. The island of Korčula, for instance, was allowed to continue its long tradition of shipbuilding, and in the sixteenth century it had ten ships of 100 to 400 tons engaged in foreign trade. The city of Korčula was never a real naval base, however, as Hvar was for centuries. Although sometimes there were one or two galleys stationed there ready for action, it had no real shore installations for the Venetian navy like the store-houses for the Adriatic force, situated in Hvar. In addition, Hvar had two ships of her own in 1498, one of 600 tons and the other of 700, and 16 caravels of about 200 tons each. On the mainland, the small town of Perast, in the Bay of Kotor, had 32 ships in 1528 and shipowners in the same bay were very active in the following centuries until the end of the eighteenth. Prčanj (Perzagno) and Dobrota, both near Kotor, also deserve mention. At the end of this period, in 1805, this bay had 28 full-rigged three-masters, 127 brigs, and 77 three-masted polacres, all ships for overseas trade, and some 163 smaller sailing vessels for trading along the coast. There was also an old brotherhood of seamen of all classes, tradition says 1000 years old, but the first document mentions them in 1453 as "Fraternitas Nautarum." Later they were called Marinarezza of the Boka (in Croatian: *Bokeška mornarica*). The members, all seamen, could be mobilized to man the galley Kotor had to send to the Venetian fleet in great wars. This organization controlled the shipyards and their workmen as well. In the eighteenth century some private schools for the instruction of future masters (captains) of the merchant ships existed in Perast. In one of these some future Russian naval officers were trained in the second half of the eighteenth century.[15]

THE FLOURISHING REPUBLIC OF DUBROVNIK

More is known about the maritime history of Dubrovnik than about that of Venetian Dalmatia during the Middle Ages. This independent republic maintained a policy of neutrality and good relations with all the neighboring powers, in some periods paying an annual tribute to the

15/*Pomorska Enciklopedija* (Zagreb, 1957), vol. 4, 509–510.

Turkish sultan in order to remain free and to develop its trade. Several factors contributed to the development of her merchant fleet and to the fame of her ships in the sixteenth century, the golden age of her shipping, among them the enterprising spirit of her people, the ability of her shipbuilders, and the skill of the crews on her ships. These qualities were found not only in the people living within the city limits of Dubrovnik, but in those living throughout the territory of the republic as well; the inhabitants of the towns of Cavtat and Slano, and of the islands of Lopud, Koločep, and Šipan, particularly are worthy of note. In her golden age, the republic had a population of about 50,000, of which about one-half lived in the city and its immmediate surroundings. Some 5000 inhabitants, or 10 per cent of the total population, were professional seamen, while many other people were part-time seamen or involved in related activities.

Merchant shipping in Dubrovnik grew slowly in the fourteenth century with the development of large sailing ships called *cocas*. The period of greatest shipping activity began in 1450, and reached its peak between 1480 and 1600. Contemporary sources remarked on the expansion of shipping, and the introduction to the *Liber Croceus*, Dubrovnik's code of laws, published in 1507, begins: "By the grace of God, our ships have multiplied and our shipping has increased ..."[16] Several sources report that there were 70 to 80 privately owned *navi da gabbia* (masthead ships, i.e., large ships with full-rigged masts). The richest shipowner in the republic, Miho Pracatović, was a commoner from the island of Lopud who owned ten ships. In 1553, a Venetian officer from Venetian Dalmatia visited Dubrovnik and wrote: "They are sailing in all regions of the world and altogether have one hundred ships with mastheads, so that one observes that there is money in an unlimited quantity in Dubrovnik."[17] About a century later, Sir Paul Rycaut (1628–1700), a secretary to the British Embassy in Constantinople, wrote: "The inhabitants of Dubrovnik have in the past carried on great shipping traffic in the western parts of Europe. It has been said that the big,

16/See *Liber Croceus 1507* in G. Gelcich, *Delle istituzioni marittime e sanitarie della Repubblica di Ragusa* (Dubrovnik, 1889), 20. The translation is the author's. Details on the Ragusan merchant navy can be found in the author's book *Dubrovački brodovi u doba procvata dubrovačkog pomorstva u* XVI. *vijeku*/Ships of Dubrovnik in the Golden Era of Ragusan Seamanship in the 16th Century (Zagreb: Vasić i Horvat, 1941).

17/The name of the Venetian official was Giovanni Battista Giustiniani and his official title was *sindaco in Dalmazia*. His report was edited by Šime Ljubić, *Commissiones et relationes Venetae*, vol. II, 249 ("Monumenta spectantia historiam Slavorum meridionalium," vol. VIII; Zagreb: Yugoslav Academy, 1877).

spacious carracks, which are called argosies, famous for the great cargo they transport, were so called by corrupting the word 'ragusies' which comes from Ragusa."[18] Indeed, it is a fact that the English word "argosy" is derived from "Ragusa,"[19] testifying to the eminence of that port at the beginning of the sixteenth century and of the Ragusan ships that brought precious cargo from the eastern Mediterranean to England.

Venice had one of the largest merchant fleets in the Mediterranean; yet in 1559, for example, it had only 36 large sailing ships,[20] while the Ragusan shipowners owned between 50 and 70 (the fluctuations reflect the loss of ships and the building of new ones). For those times this was an exceptionally large number of ships, and the Ragusans maintained it because of the favorable opportunities they had in trade. This merchant fleet was built only for trade, but the ships had to be well armed and strong enough to defend themselves against the North African corsairs.

Because the Ragusans were such an important factor in the Mediterranean, belligerents often tried to enlist their aid, they could be of great help in solving transport problems, and their artillery was excellent. However, the Republic of Ragusa had to maintain her neutrality in the eyes of the Ottoman Empire, for her very existence depended on doing so. Thus she officially forbade the servicing of ships flying St. Blaise's flag in the fleets of belligerent monarchs. The powerful Charles v, German emperor and King of Spain, however, applied the old right of angary, the requisition of Ragusan ships in their harbors, chartering the ships in this form, although they flew their own flag and their crews and captains remained on board, so that, for example, when he undertook an expedition against the Turkish fortress of Coron in Morea, in 1532, under the command of his admiral, Andrea Doria, seven large Ragusan carracks took part. Again, when the emperor himself led forces against Tunis in 1535, there were four, and seven took part in the campaigns of the Holy League in 1537 and 1538. The greatest number of carracks, thirteen, took part in Charles's unfortunate expedition against Algiers in 1542, when some of them were lost.

Later, when Ragusan trade had begun to diminish somewhat, Philip II of Spain chartered ships from Dubrovnik, and Ragusan shipbuilders in Slano near Dubrovnik and in Naples built a number of ships for his

18/Sir Paul Rycaut, *The Present State of the Ottoman Empire* (London, 1675), 21.

19/See the entry on "argosy" in *Encyclopedia Britannica*, II (1962), 336.

20/Frederic Chapin Lane, *Venetian Ships and Shipbuilders of the Renaissance* (Baltimore, 1934), Table F, p. 240.

service. Twelve of these, under the command of Peter Ivelja, took part as a special squadron in the Invincible Armada. Later, when Ragusan ships and crews continued in the service of Spain in the Atlantic, Ivelja attained the rank of Capitan General de Mar, i.e., Admiral of Spain.[21]

The merchant fleet of Dubrovnik declined during the seventeenth century, especially after an earthquake in 1667, but at the beginning of the century the fleet still enjoyed its fine reputation. Bartolomeo Crescenzio of Rome wrote in 1607: "Among craftsmen and shipwrights of galleons [the largest ships of the period] the most numerous and probably also the ablest on the sea [the Mediterranean] are the Ragusans, for they do not build other types of ships ..."[22] Pantero Pantera wrote in Rome in 1614 that the "*naves* from Ragusa are the biggest and the most appreciated of all."[23]

The eighteenth century saw a renewal of shipping in Dubrovnik, and one source reports that by 1797 the Republic had 363 ships of fifteen or more tons each. Many other ships were small coastwise trading ships and seagoing ships under fifteen tons.

In 1808, the republic of Dubrovnik was defeated by Napoleon's forces and finally abolished. In order to save their ships from falling to the French, the shipowners had them take refuge in foreign ports, but, nevertheless, the independence of the republic of Dubrovnik had come to an end.

THE NORTHERN COAST AND THE USKOKS

From the Middle Ages to the eighteenth century part of the Croatian coast belonged to the Croatian kingdom, independent of both Venetian and Turkish control. This area, the *Primorje* or "Littoral," extends from Istria to the Zrmanja River, and has always had an active maritime life. Through the centuries, whenever possible, its inhabitants have owned fishing boats and seafaring ships and have been occupied with coastal trade. Rijeka and Senj had armed ships capable of sailing the high seas, but these cities could not develop their maritime activity to any great extent in the early centuries when Venice treated the Adriatic as her own. Later, however, especially during the eighteenth century, there was considerable advancement in shipping on the northern Adria-

21/Details on the war service of the Ragusan ships can be found in the author's book, *Dubrovački brodovi*.

22/Bartolomeo Crescenzio, *Nautica Mediterranea* (Rome: Bartolomeo Bonfaldi, 1607), 4–5.

23/Pantero Pantera, *L'Armata navale* (Rome: Egidio Spada, 1614), 40–1.

tic coast which was part of the Hapsburg Empire. Hapsburg monarchs Charles VI (1711–40), and empress Maria Theresa (1740–80), encouraged shipping at Trieste and other ports, such as Rijeka, Bakar, and Kraljevica, where ships were also built.

An interesting aspect of maritime life in the Primorje during the early part of the modern era concerns the activities of the Uskoks of Senj, which were like those of present-day guerillas on land and corsairs on the sea. The Uskoks, a name derived from the Croatian word *uskok* meaning "the escaped" (fugitive), had been organized as an army unit of the Hapsburg Empire by Ferdinand I (1503–64), who took over the rule of Austria by an accord with his older brother, Charles V, and who became king of Hungary in 1526, was elected king of Croatia in 1527, king of Germany in 1531, and finally, Holy Roman Emperor in 1556. The Uskoks, along with many others, had fled to the Hapsburg-controlled areas from the neighboring inland regions under Turkish rule and were organized as frontier guards in the fortified harbor at Senj and at some of the nearby ports. There were six to seven hundred at Senj, who served under their own officers, were commanded by the general of all the forces along the Croatian frontiers, and fought under the Hapsburg flag. Like so many soldiers of that time, they did not receive regular salaries or supplies from the government and had to subsist on the spoils from raids they made in the Turkish regions; thus there was constant raiding on both sides of the border for many years. The Uskoks quickly added seafaring skills to their military ones, learning seamanship from the people of Senj and those along the coast. They began using fast sailing ships large enough to hold twenty to forty men to raid Turkish-controlled regions, passing through Venetian and even Ragusan waters to reach these areas. Turkey asked Venice to prevent piracy in the Adriatic, making her responsible for any act they considered as such. As time passed, the Uskoks began stopping Venetian and other ships to seize Turkish property even though Venice did her best to protect them.

Venice protested against the Uskok attacks to the Hapsburg emperors and kings and at Graz to the archduke in charge of the southern provinces, but to no avail since the Hapsburgs not only opposed the Turks but had long been in conflict with Venice over their boundary in Italy, at Marano in Friuli, and opposed Venice's attempts to dominate the Adriatic. For a brief time lasting from 1570 to 1573, during the war of the Holy League against the Turks, Venice and the Uskoks cooperated, although the Uskoks did attack Venetian shipping occasionally.

Once again, after 1573, the Uskoks resumed vigorous raiding, and

Venice, considering them pirates, took strong measures against them. In response, they intensified their raiding, assaulting the Turks and attacking Venetian shipping, sometimes even Venetian warships and harbors. Because they were excellent seamen, and knew the coast well, they could attack swiftly and escape, taking advantage of weather conditions as well. As a result, the Venetians had difficulty both in protecting their ships and harbors and in catching the raiders after such attacks.

Again, Venice protested. The Uskoks were famous all over Europe at that time, however, and both the Hapsburgs and Papal Rome and Spain, all opponents of Venice's power, silently approved of the attacks. Nevertheless, the Hapsburg archduke's government at Graz did attempt to restrain the Uskoks, sometimes forcing them to return their booty. In 1602, General Rabatta, charged with bringing order to Senj, tried to wipe them out, apparently as a result of a secret, personal agreement with Venice, but after he had beheaded some and deported the rest to the north, the Uskoks guessed that he had exceeded his orders from the archduke at Graz, returned south, killed him and resumed their attacks on Venetian shipping.

During this period, the people on the Dalmatian coast helped the Uskoks; and the Venturini, refugees from Venetian Dalmatia, immigrated to Senj and allied themselves with them, the Uskoks, in turn, often marrying women from the Dalmatian islands. To protect herself, Venice armed special squadrons of galleys with landing troops and appointed a special commander-in-chief, Provveditore Generale contra Scocchi. She also built forts on straits among the islands and tried, without success to organize a special signal service in Dalmatia. In addition, she attacked Uskok forts and blockaded Senj, which was an important stronghold of defense against the Turks, though never daring to attack it for fear of provoking swift reprisals from the Hapsburg Empire. Indeed, in 1614, when Venice did attack some Hapsburg controlled areas on the eastern Istrian coast, the archduke in Graz declared war, although, on previous provocations, such as when Venice had blockaded Trieste and Rijeka, the Hapsburg government had not acted directly against Venice, but had restricted itself to encouraging the Uskoks.

This war, which is called the Gradisca War after the town of Gradisca (in the province of Gorizia, now part of Italy) which was besieged by Venice for almost three years, was to a great extent fought on the sea. It threatened to spread to other areas as well and so, to avoid a larger conflict, France and Spain acted as mediators, and a peace treaty was signed by Emperor Mathias II, Archduke Ferdinand of Austria, and Venice in Madrid in 1617. The problem of the Uskoks was finally solved by moving them north to various parts of Croatia. So ended this long-drawn-out series of raids against the wealth and power of Turkey and Venice. It seems all the more remarkable an episode when we realize that the Uskoks themselves never had more than 1500 men or 30 ships.

The development of shipping along the Croatian coast and its increasing prosperity in the eighteenth century have already been mentioned. In 1797, Venice lost her independence and the power in this area. In 1808 with the lowering of the flag of the republic of Dubrovnik, the last surviving maritime city-republic in the Mediterranean perished. Except for Dubrovnik's territory, i.e., up to the Pelješac Peninsula, from 1798 to 1806, Austria ruled this section of the coast extending south from Trieste to Albania. This rule was favorable to the increased development of shipping; but expansion was checked during the second phase of the Napoleonic Wars, when the combination of French wartime restrictions and the existence of the Napoleonic Illyrian Provinces greatly limited Croatian shipping. One of the French restrictions was the requirement that the larger ships fly the flag of Napoleon's Italian kingdom; as a result, many were attacked by Napoleon's enemies, notably the British, or by corsairs flying the British flag, and others were seized in harbors. Few Croatians, however, were directly involved in the British and French naval battles in the Adriatic, but, of the few officers and seamen who had been recruited into the French navy, many were killed. Some of these recruits served in the sea battle of March 13, 1811, near Cape Smokova on the island of Vis (Lissa) called the "First battle of Lissa," between Commodore Dubourdieu's squadron of French and Italian ships and Captain Sir William Hoste's British frigates and light ships. Other Croatian recruits in the French navy were captured or killed on board the ship-of-the-line, *Rivoli*, in 1812, by crews of the British ships *Victorious* and *Weasel*.

The end of the Napoleonic Wars found the maritime strength of the Croatian coast greatly reduced, the merchant fleet for trading on the high seas and along the coast having been especially weakened. By 1815, the number of ships was only one-third those existing in 1806. But tradition and initiative as well as skills and personnel still existed as bases for the swift revival and expansion of shipping.

AUSTRIAN RULE: 1815–1918

A new historical period began on the Adriatic coast in 1815 when Venice, Trieste, Istria, and the Croatian sections of the coast were united under the Austrian government, and became part of an even larger and rich geographical area in Central Europe. Austrian rule lasted for over a century until 1918.

At the beginning of its rule, the Austrian government established a Port Authority, the *Seebehörde* (in Italian: *Governo marittimo*), with headquarters at Trieste. This Authority was responsible for administering and regulating fishing, merchant shipping, shipbuilding, and port activities, as well as such auxiliary activities as maritime health and sanitary conditions. In 1870, an additional "Royal Hungarian *Seebehörde*" was opened in Rijeka as a result of the Austro-Hungarian Agreement of 1867, which gave Hungary autonomy within the Austrian Empire. Included under the authority of these second headquarters were Rijeka and the Croatian Littoral south of Rijeka to a point south of the town of Karlobag and opposite the southern end of the island of Pag. (These headquarters did not, however, have authority over the larger islands off the coast.) Because the two headquarters had authority over two clearly distinguished areas, there was no conflict between them.

Rijeka benefited greatly by the establishment of this additional port authority. For those involved in shipping, the relations with the government were simplified. The giving of the Port Authority there served also as a formal recognition of the city's leadership in shipping and drew even more trade there. Finally, more financial aid for shipping and for harbor improvements, became available.

Maritime activity in the eastern Adriatic was prosperous throughout the nineteenth century and became even more so after steamships were introduced in 1885. Their traditional maritime initiative and skill sparked both shipowners and sailors to reorganize their overseas shipping, this time under the Austrian flag. In the north, the important areas of development were Trieste, Istria, and the islands of the Gulf of Kvarner and of the Croatian Littoral. Farther south, the centers were around Dubrovnik and Boka Kotorska, in the area extending from the island of Korčula and the Pelješac Peninsula to the south.

Bosnia and Hercegovina, and the inland regions near the Dalmatian coast, remained in the hands of Turkey until 1878; thus the coast from Split to Kotor had no real economic hinterland, and the Neretva estuary no developed trade.

Overseas shipping in the region between Rab, Zadar, and the Neretva River had been restricted in earlier times by the Venetian government, although the inhabitants had been able to develop some shipping. Before the 1870s, this region had developed primarily an active coastal trade using small sailing ships, especially the *trabaccoli* (called *traba-*

kuli in Croatian), two-masted ships of 40 to 80 tons especially suited to sailing conditions along the coast. After 1878, however, when Bosnia-Hercegovina came under Austrian control, the region was able to expand its shipping somewhat.

As a result of the interest of the Austrian government in developing its new possessions, it built a railroad to the mouth of the Neretva River, to Dubrovnik, and to Boka Kotorska and regulated the delta of the Neretva River making it navigable for small steamers, as far as Metković.

Local trade, coastal trade, and fishing suffered little during the Napoleonic Wars of 1806 to 1814. Advances in the shipping industry fluctuated, being more rapid in some periods than in others, but throughout the nineteenth century maritime activities were an important source of livelihood for many Croatians. Many people combined sailing or fishing with farming, according to the season and weather conditions, as they had done in earliest times and still continue to do. In addition, small fishing vessels and small ships for coastal trade were built all along the coast, *trabaccoli* for trade, the smaller, single-masted *brazzere* for local trade, and *gaete* and *leuti* for the local fishermen and seamen.

Good statistics are available on the number of ships and seamen on the Croatian coast for the second half of the nineteenth century. For 1855, however, only estimates can be made because the figures in the official yearbook edited at Trieste reported Croatian shipping with that of Trieste and the region of Venice and Friuli. With this reservation then, we may say that the estimates of 1400 fishing vessels and 4500 men seem reasonable. In 1875, after the separate maritime authority had been opened in Rijeka, the figures for the Croatian coast were accurately reported separately from other regions: there were 1300 small fishing vessels in Dalmatia, 77 in the Croatian Littoral, 200 on the east coast of Istria and the islands of Cres, Lošinj, and Krk, and there were 5700 fishermen. In addition to the figures for fishing, there were over 2000 other boats registered, with about 5000 men registered as their crews. Twenty years later, the statistics for 1895 show an increase of about 50 per cent in the number of fishing vessels for the whole Croatian coast; ten years later, a further increase of 33 per cent is reported. Thus we can legitimately assume that by 1905 the Croatian regions had some 2900 fishing and 5500 other boats. In contrast to the growth of fishing, coastal trade diminished. In 1875 a total of 1180 small trading ships is reported: 420 *trabaccoli*, about 340 *brazzeras*, and about 420 small sailing vessels. By 1905, the number of small trading ships had increased by about 30 per cent. These statistics indicate the existence of an exceptionally vigorous local maritime activity.

Overseas shipping and trade in larger ships along the coast developed anew during the period after 1820, growing gradually to its former importance; and, in 1850, entering a flourishing period that lasted thirty years. During this period, the Croatian trading vessels for overseas trade included large, heavy ships such as barks, brigs, and brigantines of 200 to over 1000 tons. These ships required crews of eight to eighteen men, a reduction in the sizes of crews required for such large ships having been made possible by advances in the design of ships and their rigging. All these ships involved in foreign trade were ordered, paid for, and outfitted by local shipowners, built in local shipyards, and manned by local officers and crews. Before 1867, these ships sailed under the Austrian flag; after the Austro-Hungarian Agreement of that year, they sailed under the new flag that added the Hungarian colors to those of Austria. In 1854, there were about 450 ships and nearly 5000 men in foreign trade. In that year, 48 sailing ships were built, of which thirteen were built at Rijeka, four at Sušak, thirteen at Pećine, and four at Martinšćica. Four more of these ships were built at Bakar, and one was built at Kraljevica. About three-quarters of the large sailing ships built in the Austro-Hungarian Empire were built in the Croatian region and, of these, about two-thirds were built on the short stretch of coast extending from Rijeka to Bakar. In the Austria-Hungary of 1858, three-quarters of the master mariners (captains of ships that sailed the high seas) were Croatians – of a roster of 450 master mariners, 340 were Croatian.

The Crimean war (1854–6), in which combined British, French, and Turkish forces fought the Russians, provided the Croatians with many profitable opportunities in the Black Sea trade. Although this trade was certainly somewhat dangerous (in 1854, for example, twenty Croatian ships were lost in the Black Sea and a half-dozen more were lost en route to the Black Sea), the profits were great in spite of the risks and many people grew prosperous; in fact, there is a suburb of Sušak named Krimeja where some of those who prospered in the Crimean trade built houses.

There were 516 sailing ships for overseas service in the Austro-Hungarian Empire in 1875, with a total of 5230 men and an aggregate total of 225,600 tons. About 180 of these ships belonged to coastal regions where most shipowners were probably not Croatian, although the crews of these ships, especially those registered at Trieste, were partly supplied by Croatians from Dalmatia. The remaining ships were definitely Croatian and, of these, 142 came from the Croatian Littoral, 75 from the Dubrovnik area, and 129 from Lošinj, which was a rapidly developing shipping center.

Ships were individually owned, owned by a special system of shared ownership, or owned by shipping companies. Some of the ships in the eastern Adriatic belonged to their captains, but usually they belonged to a group of owners according to a system of divided ownership, the "carat" system. According to this system, the value of a ship was divided into twenty-four shares or "carats," of which each owner would buy a certain number. In Croatia, the first companies organized for the purpose of owning and operating ships were formed in Dubrovnik, before the introduction of steamships. One such company was the Maritime Association of Ragusa, which had a dozen barks of 650 to 900 tons each. Half of these ships were built between 1870 and 1875 in Gruž and Dubrovnik. Rather than having names, the ships were assigned numbers from one to twelve and were known, for example, as *Prvi Dubrovački*, "First of Dubrovnik." A second company was the Maritime Association of Sabioncello, now called Pelješac, which owned thirty sailing ships, of which twenty were barks of 500 to 1000 tons and the remaining were smaller ships. The only other shipping company in the northern Adriatic was the steamship company, the Austrian Lloyd Steam Navigation Company (known in the eastern Mediterranean, Indian Ocean, and Far East as the Austrian Lloyd) whose headquarters were at Trieste and which employed many Croatians. This company was founded in 1836 by a group of men, most of whom came from Trieste, and had ten steamers by 1838. In ten years, the number of its steamships had doubled, and the company continued to grow rapidly, owning seventy steamships in 1875 and eighty-nine in 1906. In 1914, although the number fell to sixty-two, the tonnage of the ships was increased.

The number of Croatian sailing ships involved in foreign trade fell as steamships came increasingly into use. In 1895 there were 111 of these sailing ships, about one-fifth of the number reported for 1875. In that same year, there were 203 steamships, totaling 135,000 tons, under the Austro-Hungarian flag; the number increased to 358 with 364,500 tons, in 1905. By 1915, the Austro-Hungarian merchant fleet was seventh among the world's merchant navies, with an aggregate tonnage of one million gross tons.

The changes in the shipping industry resulting from the use of steam power caused a revolution in the maritime world, in ownership, shipbuilding, harbor management, and related areas. Shipowners adopted the steamships reluctantly, but in order to meet competition they were forced to give up their sailing ships. In 1854, the whole Austro-Hungarian coast had 614 sailing ships bound for foreign ports, a total of 302,709 tons. The number fell in 1860 to 572 ships totaling 218,715 tons, but rose very slightly in 1870 to 574 ships and 266,562 tons. After that, the numbers fell steadily to 314 ships, 154,828 tons in 1880; 214 ships, 124,266 tons five years later; and 109 ships, 62,453 tons in 1890. In 1896, there were sixty ships with a total of 31,666 tons; in 1900, twenty ships with 13,427 tons; in 1905 eight ships with 9546 tons; and, finally, in 1910 there was only one sailing ship still carrying cargo to foreign ports.

Shipping companies became more important after the adoption of the steamship than they had been in the days of sailing ships. The larger size of the steamships (they were usually 3000 to 7000 tons, while later ones were 8000 to 10,000 tons, in contrast to the sailing ships, the largest of which were 500 to 1000 tons) increased the amount of capital required for construction and operation to such an extent that no single person or small group of people could underwrite them. Some of the older shipowners grasped this necessity and formed companies, but most were forced out of business and left the shipping industry.

Croatian ownership of ships decreased during this period, and non-Croatian businessmen from Trieste, Vienna, and Budapest formed companies in Trieste and Rijeka. However, Croatians, particularly at Rijeka, did continue to own ships that serviced ports on the Croatian Littoral, Istria, Krk, Cres, and Dalmatia. The small owners of these steamships in Rijeka combined in 1891 to form the Società in Azioni Ungaro-Croata di Navigazione Maritima a Vapore (Hungarian-Croatian Steamship Sea Navigation Company), usually referred to briefly as the Ungaro-Croata. This corporation soon branched out into a company for trade in the Adriatic, with fifty-five coastal steamships servicing the Croatian Littoral between Rijeka and Senj, Istria and Dalmatia, and another company with six large ocean-going cargo boats engaged in foreign trade.

Croatians founded other steamship companies as well for local services. The Società di Navigazione a vapore "Ragusa," which was called in Croatian Dubrovačka Plovidba, was founded in 1909 in Dubrovnik, and the Società Anonima Austriaca di Navigazione a Vapore "Dalmatia," called Dalmacija in Croatian, was formed in 1905 by the union of several smaller companies, and operated 29 ships totaling 6137 tons. Other Croatian shipowners also attempted to regain the maritime leadership of their sailing days, and the industry began to expand. Its economic position was strengthened by competition within the industry, by cooperation from the shipping industry in Trieste, and by encourage-

The harbor of Dubrovnik in the sixteenth century. Reconstruction made from the painting of Nicolaus Ragusinus (died 1515) in the Dominican church in Dubrovnik by Joh. Seits following instructions of the author, particularly in regard to the ships

Model of a large Ragusan carrack from about 1520 (built following instructions and plans of the author)

A large Ragusan sailing ship (*coca*), first half of the fifteenth century. (Reconstruction made by Joh. Seits in 1940 following instructions of the author)

Argosies returning in convoy home to Dubrovnik in 1520, saluting St. Blaise before arrival. (Picture drawn by Joh. Seits following instructions of the author in regard to the type of ship and its rigging)

Ships of the Uskoks in the harbor of Senj in the sixteenth century

ustro-Hungarian battleships, destroyers, and torpedo boats in 1913

Admiral Maksimilian Njegovan (1858–1930)

ment from the government. These advances persisted until the First World War, which in itself and combined with the dissolution of the Austro-Hungarian Empire and the renewed economic unity of the area brought profound new changes in Croatian shipping.

The introduction of the steamship deeply affected shipbuilding, as well as patterns of shipownership. Simultaneous with the introduction of steam power came the introduction of new types of construction using metal, first iron and later steel. So radical were the innovations in shipbuilding that most of the old shipyards had to be closed. Only local boatbuilders could continue their work; these remained operative mainly on the island of Korčula, at Betina on the island of Murter, at Trogir, and on many of the smaller islands. Outside of the shipyards in Rijeka and Lošinj, there was only one shipyard in Croatia, a new one established at Kraljevica. The one shipyard that was left in Rijeka was taken over in 1906 by the Ganz-Danubius Shipyard Company of Budapest, and its installations were renovated. This company also took over and modernized an old abandoned shipyard at Kraljevica. The Croatian owners of the shipyard at Lošinj modernized it in 1850, specializing in building small steamships.

The changes in ship design, in tonnage, and in numbers of ships necessitated a great deal of work on harbors and navigation markings. Between 1860 and 1914, the central governments of Austria and Hungary built many new ports, even at small towns along the coast and on the islands. The lighthouse system was improved in accordance with the latest advances in lighthouse and lighting design and operation; this modern, well-organized lighthouse system made the Austro-Hungarian coast one of the best lit in the world.

The improvements in harbors and the lighthouse system were financed by the central government (just as it financed the most important highways in Dalmatia) to improve the economy of these relatively poor provinces of Istria, the Croatian Littoral, and Dalmatia, which could scarcely pay the expenses for their provincial administrations. The central government also gave large subsidies to shipping companies because it wanted to facilitate communications among the islands and ports of the coast. These subsidies enabled the companies to maintain a great number of coastal shipping routes running the entire length of the coast, ensuring a rapid long-distance and local service and contributing to economic development.

After 1814, shortly after the beginning of Austrian rule in Dalmatia, the Austrian navy began recruiting Croatian sailors; it continued to do so until the dissolution of the Austro-Hungarian Empire. The navy used Pula (Pola) in Istria as its central port, with secondary bases in Šibenik and Boka Kotorska. Its recruiting officers worked in Trieste, Rijeka, Zadar (Zara), Šibenik, and Budva, a town south of Boka Kotorska. During the first fifty years of Austrian rule, sailors were recruited from all parts of the coast of the Empire, including Venice and Friuli. The statistical reports do not tell how many sailors came from each province, so it is difficult to determine what proportion was Croatian. However, it is estimated that one-half to two-thirds of the naval personnel were Croatian at that time; after about 1850 Croatians made up nearly three-fourths of the navy. At the battle of Vis (Lissa) in 1866, in which the Austrians under Admiral Tegethoff defeated the Italian navy, probably three-quarters of the sailors in the Austrian fleet were Croatian. This battle, called in Croatian *Viški Boj*, left a deep impression in the memory of the people on the coast, and for decades "Lissa Veterans" were honored there.

In its last years, the Austro-Hungarian Empire achieved its aim of becoming a major sea power. Under the compulsory military service system, each man in the Empire was bound to serve in the army or navy, the time required for the latter being four years, and men from the coast regions had no option but to fulfill their military obligation in the navy. In 1900 the Empire's navy comprised only about 10,000 sailors, half of whom came from the Croatian coast, including Dalmatia and the Kvarner islands Cres and Krk. Later, when a far greater number of men was required, Croatian regions could supply only one-third of the total, even though all the full-time seamen and fishermen were drawn into the navy, and the remainder was recruited from other parts of the Empire.

Croatians seem to have been represented among the petty officers, who entered the navy as volunteers, in about the same proportions as among the sailors. However, few commissioned naval officers were Croatians, although in the years immediately preceding 1914, more Croatians than ever before entered the navy through the Naval Academy in Rijeka (these took part as junior naval officers in the First World War). Nevertheless, some naval officers of Croatian origin rose as high in rank as captain and rear-admiral. Among these the most distinguished was Admiral Maximilian Njegovan who achieved the highest position possible for an Austrian naval officer, becoming Admiral, Commander in Chief of the Fleet and Chief of the Navy, from February 1917 to February 1918. Njegovan, born in Zagreb in 1858 to a family from the Military Frontier, entered the Naval Academy at fifteen and, after thirty-four years of service with the fleet, including the command of torpedo boats as lieutenant, and battleships as captain, he became Rear-Admiral in 1911. During the Balkan war in 1913, when the Great Powers ordered the measure, he took part in the blockade of Montenegro, commanding the Austrian squadron of battleships, cruisers, and destroyers. From 1914 to 1917 he commanded the First battle squadron which consisted of the six, and later, the seven largest battleships of the fleet, of 20,000 and 14,500 tons.

In 1914 the Austro-Hungarian Monarchy, then seventh in sea power, commanded three battleships of 20,000 tons, three of 14,500 tons, and six of 8,000–10,000 tons, two armored cruisers, four modern, fast cruisers, three small cruisers, eighteen destroyers of 400–800 tons, and fifty deep sea torpedo boats. Three smaller battleships, one armored cruiser, two cruisers – one of them was sunk in the Far East – seven destroyers, and twelve torpedo boats, all about twenty or more years old, served as forces for local defense together with eighteen smaller torpedo boats of more up-to-date design. Seven submarines completed these forces, which were manned by some 19,400 men, and the total navy mobilization was nearly 34,000.

The port of Pula was strongly defended by coastal artillery and some 1300 mines in spacious mine-fields. The secondary bases of Šibenik and Boka Kotorska were also defended by mines, and the latter by coastal artillery as well. A developed system of signal and lookout stations allowed an almost exact control of every movement along the coast.

After 1913, the fleet – the two battle-squadrons, the modern cruisers, the deep sea torpedo boats, and destroyers – was prepared for eventual cooperation with the Italian fleet and the German cruisers in the Mediterranean, if the Triple Alliance should act together providing steamers to escort the fleet with coal and supplies, in accordance with the Naval Convention of June 23, 1913, between Austria, Italy, and Germany. But it seemed improbable to the officers of the Austrian navy that Italy would enter the war on the side of her allies.

THE FIRST WORLD WAR: 1914–18

In August 1914, when war broke out, it was clear that Italy would remain neutral; the Austrian navy knew, however, that one day its most important and most dangerous enemy would be the Italian fleet. With the outbreak of war the Austrian navy had to reckon with the strong French Armée Navale with the enterprising admiral, Boué de Lapeyrère, reinforced by British naval forces, which meant that a fleet action would be a dangerous adventure, probably leading to heavy losses that would seriously weaken it for a future encounter with Italy.

The French fleet could not do much harm to the Adriatic East coast as long as no large landing forces could be engaged in the Adriatic, but it did enter the southern Adriatic ten times during the first five months of war, for the sole purpose of protecting ships carrying supplies to Montenegro. During the first of these French forays, while it was blockading Montenegro, the Austrian cruiser, *Zenta*, was surprised, cut off, and sunk by the French squadrons. However, the commander-in-chief of the Austrian fleet, Admiral Haus, remained with his main force in the northern Adriatic. After the tenth foray, when an Austrian submarine attacked and seriously damaged the big flagship of the French commander-in-chief, the French curtailed the cruises of the fleet in the southern Adriatic.

Given the situation, with very strong adversaries in the Mediterranean where it had no base of its own, the Austro-Hungarian fleet pursued limited objectives: to defend the coast of the Empire together with the flank of the army in the northern Adriatic and the troops fighting near the southern frontier, and to undertake actions which would help the operations of its army or its allies. In addition to defending the coast, the navy had to protect the transports along the coast, especially in 1916–18, when the Austrian army in the south and in Albania received its supplies and men by sea. Insofar as it was necessary, the navy engaged in offensive action too. The base for the main fleet was at Pula, and a force of cruisers, destroyers, torpedo boats, and submarines was based in Boka Kotorska together with an armored cruiser and three second-class battleships for eventual support.

When Italy entered the war against the Austro-Hungarian Monarchy in May 1915, the activity in the Adriatic became more intensive. The Austrian fleet attacked the Italian coast several times in order to destroy the railways and bind Italian forces in defense of the coast. On May 24, 1915, just a few hours after Italy declared war, when the heaviest of the Austrian attacks was made against the entire length of the Italian coast with the purpose of destroying the railroad lines parallel to the coast, twelve battleships, one armored cruiser, five other cruisers, fourteen destroyers, thirty torpedo boats, three submarines, and six seaplanes were engaged in the actual attack, while other destroyers and torpedo boats safeguarded the approaches to the Austrian harbors. The objective, which was only partly achieved, was to trouble movements of Italian troops in their initial deployment. Later in the war, the Austrians attacked the coast using cruisers or destroyers, and later still, they attacked the flank of the Italian army in the northern Adriatic once with two second-class battleships.

The Italians themselves undertook to attack the coast of the Monarchy, with some small success; but in 1915, after losing two armored cruisers of 8000 and 10,000 tons by the action of submarines, they limited themselves to the deployment of ships in Venice and Brindisi. In the latter port they kept a vital force of cruisers and destroyers, reinforced by French and British ships of the same class, with some second-class battleships as support; this force was to protect communications with southern Albania, where the Italians occupied Valona to which ships from Brindisi were frequently dispatched. Later, the Brindisi-Valona force protected the drifters and patrol vessels of the antisubmarine barrage and nets in the Strait of Otranto where Allied submarine installations had been organized in 1916 to prevent the German submarines from using their base in the Adriatic. The Italian main force, consisting of five 20,000-ton battleships, was anchored during the war at Taranto, outside, although near, the Adriatic, while the French main force was at Malta, and later at Corfu.

The geographic situation of the Dalmatian coast, with its many islands and channels, was a certain advantage for its defenders, protecting their routes along the coast. Yet this same advantage could become a disadvantage if the islands were occupied by an enemy, since he, too, could defend himself easily and, furthermore, could use the islands as bases for a major offensive directed toward cutting the coast in two. The Allies evaluated this situation and planned a landing operation on the islands preparatory to attacking the coast and, later, the interior of the country. However, the risk of such an operation, the deficiency of troops, and the strength of the Austrian forces, which would operate near their bases, were threat enough to forestall larger projected Allied operations.

In the southern Adriatic Austrian forces launched some attacks against Allied movements and, later, against the afore-mentioned Otranto Barrage to facilitate the passage of submarines to the Mediterranean and back to the Adriatic. On December 29, 1915, there was action between cruisers and destroyers when an Austrian flotilla attacked the Albanian coast. There was minor destroyer action leading to Otranto in 1916; then, on May 15, 1917, a new attack was launched by three Austrian cruisers and four destroyers moving on the Otranto Strait and the region of Valona. In this action a convoy was attacked and partially destroyed, and in Otranto one cruiser sank a series of the drifters in the Barrage. On their way back to the Boka, the Austrian cruiser force engaged in combat with a superior force of British and Italian cruisers and Italian destroyers. One of the Austrian cruisers was seriously damaged, but the entire force escaped with all ships when two Austrian ships, an armoured cruiser and an old battleship, came to support them. About a year later, in June 1918, a far larger action of the Austrian fleet was planned, and the four 20,000-ton, and three 10,000-ton battleships, together with cruisers and destroyers, set off for the southern Adriatic to attack the Otranto Barrage and to destroy the Allied light force which they expected to meet coming out of Brindisi. However, the action was cancelled and the forces returned to their bases after the 20,000-ton battleship "*Szent Istvan*," on its way south, was sunk by two torpedos from an Italian motor torpedo boat it had casually encountered.

In 1917–18 transports along the coast to Albania were more and more frequent, escorted by Austrian torpedo boats or destroyers. Losses in these convoys were rare, although Allied submarines cruised in the Adriatic and there was danger of attack by surface forces.

The light forces moved about a great deal and sometimes saw action, while the bigger ships seldom left port. Nevertheless, the Austrian fleet fulfilled its mission almost completely, for no island was occupied, no serious action was undertaken against the coast or the flanks of the army, and the Empire had almost no army forces on its coast with the exception of the land-fronts at the north and south. The entire defense of the coast, except for the coast artillery and the garrisons in Pula and Boka, was conducted by the navy. Also, navigation on the coast went on as mentioned, successfully defended by the fleet.

We should note here also that although most of them were operating in the Adriatic, the Austrian fleet sent some submarines to the Mediterranean.

Like most of the other belligerents in the First World War, Austria had separate air forces for its army and navy. The naval air force was manned chiefly by naval officers and some petty officers, and the personnel of the naval air bases was furnished by petty officers and men of the navy. This force was very active during the whole of the war and was equipped in 1914–15 with the best seaplanes of that time for reconnaissance and for air protection of the fleet. (Not until later in the war were seaplanes of the Allied naval air forces superior to those of the Austrians.) These planes were used for bombing attacks on Italian ports and installations and on army units on the fronts near the sea.

The Austrian navy saw no heavy losses during the entire war. The heaviest losses in naval officers occurred, not surprisingly, in the naval air force and in the submarine service where petty officers and many men were lost. Large ships, cruisers, destroyers, and torpedo boats experienced relatively few casualties, so that most of the naval personnel, among them large numbers of Croatians, survived the war.

BETWEEN THE WORLD WARS: 1918–40

At the end of the First World War, the Austro-Hungarian Empire collapsed and several new countries were formed, based on the nationalities that had been component parts of the empire. The Austrian fleet was at first handed over to the provisional Serbo-Croatian-Slovenian government, but that was not recognized by the Allies, and with few exceptions the warships of this fleet were scrapped.

In 1920, the Austro-Hungarian merchant fleet was divided between Yugoslavia and Italy according to the terms of the Trumbić-Bertolini Agreement, named after the ministers who negotiated it. The place of residence of the owners of a shipping company, or, in the case of foreign ownership, the preferences of a majority of shareholders in a company, determined to which country the shipping companies and ships were assigned. Under this system Yugoslavia acquired a seventh of the former Austro-Hungarian fleet, i.e. 135 steamships totaling 140,000 gross tons. Because Italy acquired the ports of Trieste, Rijeka, and Lošinj, the large steamship companies registered in those ports were ceded to her. Among these large companies were the Austrian Lloyd Corporation, the Cosulich-Austro-Americana Company, the Navigazione Libera Triestina, the Tripkovich Company, and the Hungarian Adria Corporation. Some of the other large shipping companies were registered in Yugoslavian ports. Most of the companies under foreign ownership were transferred to Italy because most of the foreign shareholders either lived or chose to live there. Of the shareholders who were former members of the Austro-Hungarian Empire, most were from Vienna and from Budapest; these shareholders also preferred Italy. Thus, even though there were some Croatian shareholders in the larger shipping companies, they were outvoted by those who preferred the companies and their ships to be transferred to Italy.

Within Yugoslavia, Croatians retained their predominance in the shipping industry. Along the coast, Croatians owned almost all the ships and were active in the renewal of the shipping industry as shipowners and shareholders in shipping companies, as managers of such companies, and as officers and crews of the ships. The statistics for the shipping industry accurately reflect the extent of Croatian participation. Under Croatian leadership, the merchant fleet grew quickly in the years after the agreement of 1920. By 1938, the last year before the Second World War began to affect this industry in Yugoslavia, the merchant fleet had almost tripled and Yugoslavia had 232 ships totaling 418,000 gross tons.

The Yugoslavian government's administration of the shipping and fishing industries was similar to that of the Austro-Hungarian government. As under the former system, the government paid the shipping companies subsidies so that the sixty-six shipping lines along the coast and among the islands could be maintained as before. A new use had arisen for these shipping lines because, in addition to the needs of the local inhabitants, those of tourists, who had begun to visit the coast in ever increasing numbers, became increasingly important.

Shipbuilding expanded after the First World War, as has been mentioned, although at first most of the new ships were built for the navy rather than the merchant fleet. Later on, not only were new ships (built or bought in foreign countries) added to the merchant fleet, but also many of the original 135 ships were replaced so that more steamships were built or bought than is shown by the increase in the number of ships. There were two major commercial shipyards, one in Split and one in Kraljevica. In 1936, these two shipyards were reorganized into a single company, the Jugoslavenska Brodogradilišta (Yugoslav Shipyards, Inc.), linked with large French and British firms. Local boatbuilders continued to build small boats as before, and the building of larger fishing boats and ships for coastal trade continued at shipyards at Korčula, Trogir, and Betina (on the island of Murter).

The tripled tonnage of the merchant fleet between 1920 and 1938 and the other signs of increased activity partly resulted from the amalgamation of older shipping companies to form larger enterprises. For example, the Jadranska Plovidba Company was formed by the union of the Ungaro-Croata Corporation and the Dalmacija Company, the Jugoslavenski Lloyd came into being through the combination of the Račić Company with the Yugoslav-American Navigation Company which had been formed shortly before, and the Oceania Corporation resulted from the amalgamation of several small companies involved in the Mediterranean trade. One exception to this process was the Dubrovačka Plovidba, whose expansion resulted not from the combination of smaller companies but directly from increased capitalization by its shareholders.

The small trading ships operating along the coast and among the islands, so necessary to those areas, continued to be important between the two world wars. Many of these ships were furnished with motors, while retaining their sails; and some new coastal traders were built also, for navigation with Diesel motors only. For 1940, 758 such small coastal trading ships were reported. Some 12,000 additional small boats were also registered; of these, about half, that is 6700, were fishing boats and 20,000 fishermen were reported in the government statistics.

The new Yugoslavian navy was developed during the period between the wars. As was true of the Austro-Hungarian navy, the Croatians were again very active. Most of the former members of the Austro-Hungarian navy had come from areas that became parts of Yugoslavia, and they formed the basis for the new navy and its organization. Development of the navy began in 1919–20, using insofar as was possible the shore installations of the former Austrian navy in its secondary bases at Boka Kotorska and Šibenik. Some auxiliary vessels, most of them of small size, and twelve torpedo boats, without their torpedo armament, were all the Allied powers left to Yugoslavia, and the torpedo boats were in such a poor state of maintenance that it took years to repair them (indeed, four of them, of an older type of 200 tons, soon had to be disarmed and scrapped). Construction of a modest naval dockyard at Tivat had been started by the Austrian navy; this was continued by the new navy, although it took years and a considerable sum of money to complete it.

For training purposes, six 500-ton minelaying gunboats were acquired in 1920 and an old cruiser in 1925, and these were repaired in Germany where they had been purchased at a low price. These training ships were necessary, and new constructions were beyond the reach of the budget. A school training system was set up – a naval academy for future officers, a school for engineer-petty officers, another for petty officers of the maritime branches, and training centers for specialists in gunnery, torpedo, mines, wireless communications, etc. In addition to its numerous petty officers with long service terms to man the technical branches, the navy took men liable to military service for a two-year term and trained them as seamen, as gunners, for torpedo-mine service, and as stockers and signalmen, and so on.

With specialized personnel from the Austrian navy as instructors, a relatively skilled personnel could be trained, while the existing ships were fully armed, the torpedo boats with their torpedos, the gunboats with modern guns, and the old cruiser as an antiaircraft ship. The shore establishments and schools were slowly enlarged, mine defenses were prepared, and the system of signal and lookout stations along the coast and the wireless stations were reorganized and modernized. A modest naval air service with seaplanes was also set up, using the former naval air stations and enlarging them.

After this systematic preparation, and after it had overcome the opposition created by lack of official understanding in the kingdom, the Admiralty was able, in 1926, to begin the construction of its first units of real fighting value in England – two submarines and two small motor torpedo boats. Two additional submarines were built in France in 1928–9, and in 1931–2, the navy's first surface fighting ship, the destroyer *Dubrovnik*, was built in Scotland. A depot-ship (tender) for submarines and a depot-ship for seaplanes, five small minelayers, and a sailing ship with auxiliary motor as a training ship for long cruises were built or acquired in this period. In 1936, eight motor torpedo boats of an efficient type were built in Germany. Finally, in 1937 three modern destroyers were built; the hulls of two were built in the enlarged shipyard in Split, the hull of the other in France, and the engines in England.

THE SECOND WORLD WAR: 1941–5

A new program was initiated in 1938–9 when two submarines and a new series of motor torpedo boats were ordered in Germany, a big flotilla-leader begun in Split, and two destroyers in process of being ordered; but the Second World War brought this program to an abrupt conclusion.

When Yugoslav neutrality was suddenly violated in 1941, the existing flotilla – it would be an exaggeration to speak of a fleet – numbered one very large destroyer, two additional destroyers (a third was in process of repair), four submarines, ten motor torpedo boats, six older torpedo boats, and a relatively well developed naval air force. The war was so short that no real and serious actions were undertaken by the navy, and no enemy warship, i.e., Italian, came into sight of the Yugoslav coast. The surrender of the Yugoslav armed forces was signed by the High Command of the Kingdom, on April 17, 1941, the eleventh day of war, after an independent Croatian state had been proclaimed in Zagreb and in the northern ports of Šibenik and Split. Some units in the north were disarmed near Split in Divulje, while the ships in Boka Kotorska were disarmed after the capitulation. However, one submarine, three torpedo motor boats, and a number of seaplanes flew to the Mediterranean and joined the British forces. Despite the conditions of the surrender, which prohibited such an act, one of the two destroyers was blown up by two of its officers in order to prevent its use by the enemy. In the event, the Italians armed nearly all the warships they found disarmed in Yugoslav ports, including the oldest of them. Most of these were later lost while sailing under the Italian flag or, after the surrender of Italy, under the German ensign.

The new Independent State of Croatia had to cede important parts of the Croatian coast, together with some of the ports, to Italy and was forbidden to maintain warships on the rest of the coast, so that while a naval organization was formed with former personnel of the Yugoslav navy, and was maintained for the future, it had no practical employment. However, as a means of affirmation that the Croatian navy existed notwithstanding the Italian prohibition, a detachment of Croatian officers and men were sent, under the command of a naval captain, to the Black Sea, where they cooperated with the Germans, manning patrol boats and other small vessels.

The skill of Croatian seamen became manifest also after 1942 when Partisans, belonging to the "Council of National Liberation," organized operations on the sea. With merchant seamen, fishermen, and some personnel of the former Yugoslav navy, recruited in territory they held, an important number of improvised patrol boats or small vessels for transport were armed, often only with some rifles or machine guns, and these served in many small actions, taking advantage of their local knowledge which neither the Italians nor, later, the Germans could share. This improvised small flotilla did some damage to the enemy's traffic, and at the end of the war it carried commandos from one island to the other, helping to achieve the occupation of some of them. Only seamen as good as those the Croatian coast could offer were able to handle such an operation.

Although the navy disappeared in 1941, surviving only in the reduced forms we have noted, the coastal merchant fleet was compelled to continue some service along the coast, under Italian and other flags. The numerous ocean steamers continued in service under their own flag, however, outside the Mediterranean, and mostly in the Atlantic, during Yugoslav neutrality from 1939 to 1941; and these cooperated later with the Western allies. The steamers, generally between 3000 and 6000 BRT, were efficient in this traffic and forty-seven of them were lost in service, to German submarines or mines. Another eight were sold, in 1941 and later, and only twenty-five such ships survived the war and its destruction. Many of the crews were saved, but we do know that 400 Croatian merchant seamen lost their lives in the oceanic war, a number corresponding to the crews of about eleven ships.

We have seen that the maritime skill and seamanship of the Croatians have always survived critical periods and even heavy losses to burst forth again. We can feel certain that there will be a new revival. Indeed, a new fleet of ocean and coastal merchant ships can already be seen growing up on the Croatian coast and crossing the oceans. Also, some of the shipowners who have come from that coast and now live in Western countries have acquired or built ships and manned them mostly with Croatian seamen under the flags of America, Panama, or other Western countries. These ships too represent, in their owners and in their crews, a genuine continuity of Croatian seamanship.

Bibliography

Andreis, P. *Storia della città di Traù.* Spalato: M. Perjević, 1909.

Appendini, Francesco Maria. *Notizie istorico-critiche sulle antichità, storia e letteratura de' Ragusei.* 2 vols. Ragusa: A. Martecchini, 1802–3.

Bačić, Villi A. *Dubrovački brodovi u doba procvata dubrovačkog pomorstva u XVI. vijeku*/Ships of Dubrovnik in the Golden Era of Ragusan Seamanship in the 16th Century. Zagreb: Vasić i Horvat, 1941.

—— *Povijest prvog svjetskog rata na Jadranu*/A History of the First World War on the Adriatic Sea. Zagreb: Hrvatski Izdavalački Bibliografski Zavod/Croatian Publishing Bibliographical Institute (HIBZ below), 1944.

Brajković, Vladislav. *Étude historique sur le droit maritime privé du Littoral Yougoslave.* Marseille: S. A. du Sémaphore, 1933.

Caddeo, Rinaldo. *Roma sul mare.* ("*Storia Marittima dell' Italia,*" II) Milano: Garzanti, 1942.

Canale, Cristoforo. *Della Milizia Marittima: Libri* IV. Venezia, 1540. Re-edited by Mario Nani-Mocenigo. Roma: Libreria dello Stato, 1930.

Casoni, Giovanni. *Forze Militari, Venezia e le sue Lagune.* Venezia, 1847.

Cattalinich, Giovanni. *Storia della Dalmazia.* 3 vols. Zara, 1834–5.

Crescenzio, Bartolomeo. *Nautica Mediterranea.* Roma: Bartolomeo Bonfaldi, 1607.

Dandulo, Andrea. *Chronica,* ed. Muratori, XII, 13–416. 2nd ed. by E. Pastorello. Bologna, 1938–58. 1–684.

Diaconos, Joannes. *Chronicon Venetum.* ("Cronache veneziane antichissime," I.) Ed. G. Monticolo. Roma, 1890.

Fijo, Oliver. *Parobrodarstvo Dalmacije 1878–1918*/Dalmatian Seamanship 1878–1918. Zadar: Yugoslav Academy, 1962.

Gelcich, Giuseppe. *Delle istituzioni marittime e sanitarie della repubblica di Ragusa.* Trieste, 1882.

Jal, A. *Archéologie navale.* 2 vols. Paris, 1840.

—— *Glossaire nautique.* Répertoire polyglotte. Paris, 1848–50.

James, William. *Naval History of Great Britain.* London: Bently, 1837.

Jurien de la Gravière, J. P. E. *La Guerre de Chypre et la Bataille de Lepante.* Paris: Plon, 1888.

Kreglianovich-Albinovich, Giovanni. *Memorie per la storia della Dalmazia.* Zara, 1809.

Lane, Frederic Chaplin. *Venetian Ships and Shipbuilders of the Renaissance.* Baltimore: The Johns Hopkins Press, 1934.

Liburnicus. *Der Kampf um die Ostküste der Adria. Eine geschichtliche Studie.* Zagreb: HIBZ, 1944.

Lisičar, V. *Koločep nekoć i sad*/Koločep, Past and Present. Dubrovnik, 1932.

Ljubić, Šime. *Commissiones et Relationes Venetae.* ("Monumenta spectantia historiam Slavorum Meridionalium," VIII.) Zagreb: Yugoslav Academy, 1877–80.

Lloyd Austriaco. *Annuario Marittimo per l'Anno 1856.* Trieste, 1856.

Luetić, Josip. *Brodovlje Dubrovačke Republike 17. stoljeća*/Ships of the Ragusan Republic in the 17th Century. Dubrovnik: Maritime Museum of the Yugoslav Academy, 1964.

——— *O pomorstvu Dubrovačke Republike u 18. stoljeću*/Maritime History of the Ragusan Republic in the 18th Century. Dubrovnik, 1959.

Minucci, Minuccio. *Storia degli Uscocchi, continuata fino all'anno 1616 dal P.M. Paolo* [*Sarpi*]. Venezia: R. Meietti, 1676.

Monumenta historiam Uscocchorum illustrantia ex archivis romanis, praecipue e secreto vaticano desumpta. Collegit et redegit Dr. Carolus nob. Horvat. Vol. I, 1550–1601 (MSHSM, 32); Zagreb, 1910. Vol. II, 1602–20 (MSHSM, 34); Zagreb, 1913.

Monumenta Ragusina. Zagreb: Yugoslav Academy.
Vol. I (1306–47), 1879. Vol. II (1347–52, 1358–60), 1882. Vol. III (1359–64), 1895. Vol. IV (1364–96), 1896. Vol. V (1301–36), 1897.

Nani Mocenigo, Mario. *Storia della marina Veneta da Lepanto alla caduta della Repubblica.* Roma: Ministero della Marina, 1935.

Novak, Grga. *Prošlost Dalmacije*/The Dalmatian Past. Zagreb: HIBZ, 1944.

——— "Grapčeva špilja na otoku Hvaru"/Grabac Cave on the Island of Hvar, *Jugoslavenski historiski časopis*, III (Ljubljana, Zagreb, Beograd, 1936).

Pantera, Pantero. *L'Armata navale.* Roma: Egidio Spada, 1614.

Pomorska Enciklopedija/The Maritime Encyclopedia. 8 vols. Zagreb: Leksikografski Zavod FNRJ, 1954–61.

Poparić, Bare. *O pomorskoj sili Hrvata za dobe narodnih vladara*/Maritime Power during the Period of National Rulers. Zagreb, 1899.

——— *Povijest Senjskih Uskoka*/A History of the Uskoks of Senj. Zagreb: Matica Hrvatska, 1936.

Porphyrogenitus, Constantine VII. *De administrando imperio.* Ed. Moravcsik-Jenkins. Budapest, 1949.

Rački, Franjo. *Documenta historiae chroaticae periodum antiquam illustrantia.* Zagreb: Yugoslav Academy, 1877.

Randaccio, Carlo. *Storia navale universale antica e moderna ...* 2 vols. Roma: Forzani, 1891.

Razzi, Serafino. *La Storia di Raugia.* Lucca: V. Busdraghi, 1595. Re-edited Dubrovnik, 1903.

Romanin, Samuele. *Storia documentata di Venezia.* Venezia: P. Maratovich, 1853–61. Re-edited Venice, 1920.

Schiaffini, Alfredo. *Italia e Croazia.* Rome: Academia Reale d'Italia, 1942.

Šišić, Ferdo. *Priručnik izvora hrvatske historije: Enchiridion fontium historiae Croatiae*. Vol. I. Zagreb, 1914.

Stella, L. A. *L'Italia Antica sul Mare*. Milano: Hoepli, 1930.

Tadić, Jorjo. *Španija i Dubrovnik u* XVI. *stoljeću*/Spain and Dubrovnik in the 16th Century. ("Srpska kraljevska akademija," 93.) Beograd: Grafički zavod "Slavija," 1932.

Torr, Cecil. *Ancient Ships*. Cambridge: University Press, 1894.

Vučetić, A. *O dubrovačkoj pomorskoj sili*/The Maritime Power of Dubrovnik. Dubrovnik, 1882.

3

The Croatian Language

CHRISTOPHER SPALATIN

The Croatian language belongs to the Slavic family of languages, listed here in descending order according to the number of speakers: Russian, Ukrainian, Polish, White Russian, Czech, Bulgarian, Serbian, Croatian, Slovak, Slovenian, Macedonian, and Lusatian. These languages are spoken by more than 200 million people altogether, Russian being spoken by more than 100 million and Lusatian by only 200,000. All of them stem from a language called Common Slavonic, which was spoken many centuries ago within a comparatively small territory between the rivers Oder (west) and Dniester (east), and between the Baltic Sea (north) and the Carpathian Mountains (south). That territory was surrounded by Balts and Iranians to the east, and by Teutonic tribes to the west.

In spite of the fact that these Slavic tribes were closely united as far as language is concerned, we can suppose that they spoke three dialects, each characteristic of one of three different groups, eastern, western, and southern. That dialectal differentiation gave birth to what we call today the Eastern, Western, and Southern Slavic languages. Russian, Ukrainian, and White Russian belong to the Eastern group; Polish, Czech, Slovak, and Lusatian to the Western group; and Bulgarian, Serbian, Croatian, Slovenian, and Macedonian to the Southern group.

In the middle of the sixth century, the future Southern Slavs, i.e., the Slovenes, Croatians, Serbs, Macedonians, and Bulgarians, crossed the Carpathian Mountains, going south. They traveled over the territories south of the Carpathians, to the rivers Sava and Danube, and invaded the Balkan Peninsula down to the Peloponnesus and Constantinople. For about two centuries the territory of the Western Slavs (Czechs and Slovaks) was contiguous with that of the Southern Slavs (Slovenes,

Croatians, and Serbs), just as that of the Eastern Slavs (Ukrainians) was adjacent to the territory of the Southern Slavs (Bulgarians and Macedonians). There were no Austrians, Hungarians, and Rumanians living in the lands they occupy today: the Germans were farther west, the Hungarians were still in Asia, and the Rumanians were scattered all over the Balkans and perhaps concentrated in the triangle between Niš, Skopje, and Sofia. In the ninth century the eruption of Hungarians into European territory separated the Southern Slavs from the Eastern and Western Slavs, while the Slavs on Greek territory were absorbed by the natives. Later on the Austrians moved east, slowly assimilating some Slavs, while the Roman remnants in the Balkans split into two parts: one, called Macedo-Rumanian, stayed in the Balkan Mountains, and the other, called Daco-Rumanian, probably moved north, crossed the Danube, and settled in today's Rumania.

Today the Southern Slavs occupy the territory of the two countries Yugoslavia and Bulgaria, and speak two groups of South-Slavic languages: in the east, Bulgarian and Macedonian, and in the west, Slovenian, Croatian, and Serbian. It is possible that the Rumanian Niš-Skopje-Sofia triangle had some bearing on the division of the South-Slavic languages into two groups, although later, as has been pointed out, the larger group of Rumanians moved north beyond the Danube, while the minority remained under a strong Slavic linguistic influence. The latter exist today as scattered groups called Arumanians in Macedonia, Megleno-Rumanians in Greece (near Salonica), and Istro-Rumanians in Croatia (in Istria).[1]

In this essay, rather than employing the usual term Serbo-Croatian, we shall refer to Serbian and Croatian, because we are dealing with two distinct national entities and their two literary languages. Serbs and Croatians speak various dialects of a common language; from two separate subdialects of the Shtokavian dialect, one called Ekavian and the other Ijekavian, they have developed two standard languages, and each of the two nationalities is extremely sensitive to its own brand. In spite of this opposition, there are Serbs, for instance in Bosnia, whose native subdialect is Ijekavian, and Croatians, those of the Kajkavian dialect, who use Ekavian forms. Yet no Croatian writes Serbian, nor does any Serb write Croatian. Any such attempt on the part of either points to an artificial effort undertaken with specific political objectives. The term

1/For a more detailed exposition of this early and rather obscure period, see Kristian Sandfeld, *Linguistique balkanique; problème et résultat* (Paris: E. Champion, 1930); Ivan Popović, *Istorija srpskohrvatskog jezika*/History of the Serbo-Croatian Language (Novi Sad: Matica Srpska, 1955); and George Y. Shevelov, *A Prehistory of Slavic* (Heidelberg: Carl Winter, 1964).

Serbo-Croatian might be practical and adequately designate the native, vernacular, or so-called popular language (*narodni govor*), but, from the point of view of the standard language (*književni jezik*, which refers to both[2] standard and literary language), there is no such linguistic combination, half Serbian half Croatian, as the compound adjective suggests. As Professor Mate Hraste of Zagreb University says:

> It is well known that the Serbian literary language has had a completely different development from the Croatian literary language, be it due to the determination of Serbian writers, or, for a certain time, to the historical circumstances. From the first written monuments to the times of Vuk Karadžić, the middle of the nineteenth century, the language of Serbian literature has always been an artificial one (Serbian-Slavonic, Russian-Slavonic, Slavonic-Serbian) and has had very little to do with the speech of the Serbian peasant. That is why Vuk Karadžić fought so courageously and uncompromisingly for the introduction into literature of the language of the ignorant peasantry. That was not the case with Croatian literature. From the very first days of written Croatian in the twelfth century[3] (Baška Tabletts) to the Illyrian National Awakening in the nineteenth century, when the Croatians started writing their literary works in the Shtokavian dialect exclusively, the non-ecclesiastic Croatian literature was written in the vernacular and in all three dialects (Chakavian, Kajkavian and Shtokavian), in most cases according to the dialect spoken in the writers' province.[4]

In Yugoslavia today there are four literary languages: Serbian, Croatian, Slovenian, and Macedonian. Slovenian is the language of the northwesternmost corner, Macedonian of its southern corner, and the remaining area is divided between Serbian and Croatian. In the eastern part of this central area, the literary language is Serbian whereas in the western, it is Croatian. The two languages have two cultural and national foci, Belgrade and Zagreb. The Serbs, with Belgrade as their national center, speak and write Serbian; the Croatians, with Zagreb as their national center, speak and write Croatian. In order to stress the oneness of the Serbocroatian (*sic*) or Croatoserbian (*sic*) language, the official standpoint of the present Yugoslav regime holds that Croatians and Serbs have one, not only vernacular, but also standard or literary language, with two variants, eastern (Serbian) and western (Croatian).[5]

2/In recent years the expression *standardni jezik* is being used among linguists to distinguish between the two. See Dalibor Brozović, "Zašto baš 'standardni jezik'?"/ Is a Standard Language Necessary? *Telegram* (Zagreb), May 27, 1966.

3/The Croatian written language was used even before that century. There are charters and codices written in the vernacular as early as the tenth century.

4/Mate Hraste, "Strani elementi u hrvatskom ili srpskom narodnom i književnom jeziku"/Foreign Elements in the Croatian or Serbian Vernacular and Literary Language, *Radovi Slavenskog instituta* (Zagreb), II (1958), 43.

5/Ljudevit Jonke, *Književni jezik u teoriji i praksi*/Literary Language in Theory

PHONETICS AND ORTHOGRAPHY

The Croatian language comprises three dialect groups distinguished by their respective words for "what?": *što, ča,* and *kaj.* Hence the names of these dialects: Shtokavian, Chakavian, and Kajkavian. Another classification of Croatian dialects is made on the basis of the triple development of the Common Slavic sound "yat": *e, i, (i)je.* Hence the names Ekavian, Ikavian, and (I)jekavian for variants that occur, for example, in words such as 'child': *dete, dite, dijete.* Whereas the Serbian literary language is Shtokavian and Ekavian, the Croatian literary language is Shtokavian and (I)jekavian.

The Croatian language has thirty sounds: five vowels and twenty-five consonants. The five vowels are:

LETTER	CROATIAN WORD	EXPLANATION	ENGLISH WORD	IPA[6]
a	*da,* 'yes'	like the *a* in	father	[a]
e	*ne,* 'no'	like the *e* in	set	[e]
i	*vi,* 'you'	like the *ee* in	see	[i]
o	*oko,* 'eye'	like the *o* in	go (without the glide)	[o]
u	*tu,* 'there'	like the *oo* in	too	[u]

In both accented and unaccented syllables these vowels keep their full vocalic sonority and are never reduced to an obscure vowel sound like the *a* in the English 'idea,' *e* in 'Cicero,' *o* in 'nicotine,' and *u* in 'circus.' In their fullness they resemble the vocalic system of Romance languages, with a quality midway, let us say, between the French open and closed *a, e,* and *o.* The vowels *i* and *u* are more closed than the English accented *i* in 'live' and *u* in 'full.'

and Practice (2nd enl. ed.; Zagreb: Znanje, 1965), 189–91. The existence of two literary variants is contested today by those Serbian and Montenegrin linguists who are afraid that the political unity of Croatians and Serbs may be affected by their linguistic differences. Those linguists (mostly Croatians) who maintain today that there are two variants of one literary language (Croatoserbian or Serbocroatian) used to insist in 1954 on the oneness of the Serbo-Croatian literary language. This shift in emphasis reflects the prevailing extent of freedom of expression: in 1954 there was very little freedom of expression, in 1966 there is more. See the controversy on this subject between the Croatian Jonke and the Montenegrin Rašović in *Telegram* (Zagreb) of March 25 and April 1, 1966, and between Jonke and the Serb Jovan Vuković in *Jezik* (Zagreb), XIII (1965–6), 1 (8–15), and 4 (113–18).

6/Symbols of the International Phonetic Alphabet.

The consonants are approximately like their English equivalents:

LETTER	CROATIAN WORD	EXPLANATION	ENGLISH WORD	IPA
b	*Bog*, 'God'	like the *b* in	bee	[b]
c	*car*, 'emperor'	like the *ts* in	fits	[ts]
č	*čast*, 'honor'	like the *ch* in	church	[tʃ]
ć	*kuća*, 'house'	like the *t* + *y* in	get you	[tj]
d	*dan*, 'day'	like the *d* in	day	[d]
dž	*džep*, 'pocket'	like the *j* in	judge	[dʒ]
dj[7]	*Djuro*, 'George'	like the *d* + *y* in	did you	[dj]
f	*fakat*, 'fact'	like the *f* in	fact	[f]
g	*grad*, 'city'	like the *g* in	get	[g]
h	*heroj*, 'hero'	like the *h* in	here	[h]
j	*jak*, 'strong'	like the *y* in	you	[j]
k	*kuća*, 'house'	like the *k* in	kill	[k]
l	*lav*, 'lion'	like the *l* in	like	[l]
lj	*ljeto*, 'summer'	like the *lli* in	million	[λ]
m	*majka*, 'mother'	like the *m* in	mother	[m]
n	*noć*, 'night'	like the *n* in	night	[n]
nj	*njega*, 'care'	like the *ny* in	canyon	[ŋ]
p	*papa*, 'pope'	like the *p* in	pope	[p]
r	*rad*, 'work'	like the *r* in	three	[R]
s	*sin*, 'son'	like the *s* in	son	[s]
š	*škola*, 'school'	like the *sh* in	ship	[ʃ]
t	*top*, 'cannon'	like the *t* in	take	[t]
v	*velik*, 'large'	like the *v* in	vain	[v]
z	*zora*, 'dawn'	like the *z* in	zoo	[z]
ž	*živ*, 'alive'	like the *su* in or *j* in French *jour*	measure	[ʒ]

As we have seen, Croatian does not have "neutral vowels" like the English schwa, and thus it is rich in full vowels. On the other hand, it has consonantal nexi which present difficulties for foreign learners. Among these, the so-called vocalic or syllabic *r* in words like *smrt*, *prst*, *vrt*, *rdja* is most difficult. When initial (as in *rt*) or preceded by a vowel (as in *po'rvati se*) the *r* is uttered with a kind of initial schwa-sound, and it is not pronounced as [poʀvaᴛise] but something like [poəʀvaᴛise]. But such words are few. On the other hand, the syllabic *r* surrounded by consonants occurs more often, and is very characteristic of the Croatian phonic system. This is why the English words 'perfect' and 'hurts' may sometimes sound in a Croatian mouth like [prfekt] and [hrts]. Peasants around Dubrovnik, for instance, show the same vocalization of the *r*

7/Instead of *dj* we would like to use a barred *d*, as is common today in Croatian publications, but refrain for typographical reasons.

between consonants when changing the Italian *perchè* into Croatian *prke(kati)*. According to Maretić, the only difference between the *r* in *ruka* and *r* in *prst* is that, unlike other Croatian consonants, the *r* functions as a vowel in the latter, forming a syllable with the preceding *p* and the following *st*.[8]

Many Croatian words end in a vowel: all neuter and most feminine nouns. Many consonantal groups are "lightened" by the insertion of the vowel *a*, called the mobile *a*. Thus *lovc* becomes *lovac*, 'hunter'; *konc* becomes *konac*, 'thread, end'; *ognj* becomes *oganj*, 'fire'; *početk* becomes *početak*, 'beginning.' Even some borrowings may receive it: *akcent* becomes *akcenat*, 'accent,' and *psalm* becomes *psalam*, and there are many other examples. While an Italian cannot easily pronounce such words as *film* and *autobus* without adding a kind of *e* at the end, many final consonantal nexi have entered Croatian and are pronounced without any difficulty, like *gips*, *indeks*, *punč*, *puls*, *patrijarh*, *kirurg*, *golf*, and others. In some instances we find as many as four consecutive consonants within a word – *kraljevstvo*, *pokućstvo* – all of which are pronounced. It may indeed be a challenge for a foreigner to pronounce the word *čvrst*. Thus, because of its abundance of vowels the Croatian language seems just as "soft" as Italian[9] and "softer" than German, French, or Latin; at the same time, because of its consonantal nexi, it gives the contrary impression of harshness.

The twenty-five Croatian consonants are usually divided into fifteen non-palatalized or hard, and ten palatal and palatalized or soft consonants. The consonants *c*, *č*, *ć*, *dž*, *dj*, *j*, *lj*, *nj*, *š*, *ž* are soft and the others hard; some *r*'s are soft and some hard (cf. the Kajkavian dialect which still distinguishes the soft *rj* from the hard *r* and has *morje* for *more*). Stems ending in hard consonants call for *-o*, those ending in soft consonants *-e*. This phonetic bias pervades the language in various parts of speech and morphological changes, i.e., in verbs, common and proper nouns, pronouns, adjectives, in masculine and neuter genders, in nominative and instrumental cases, in singular and plural. Thus *treće*, *Bogom*, *more* would be inconceivable as **trećo*, **Bogem*, **moro*. The only major exceptions to this rule today are the hypocoristic forms in *-o* like *ujo*, *učo*, which end in *-o* even after a palatal consonant.

8/Tomo Maretić, *Gramatika hrvatskoga ili srpskoga književnog jezika*/Grammar of the Croatian or Serbian Literary Language (3rd ed.; Zagreb: Matica Hrvatska, 1963), 33. See also Asim Peco, "Sur la nature du r syllabique en serbocroate," *Bulletin de la Faculté des lettres de Strasbourg*, XXXVIII, no. 3 (1960), 23.

9/Maretić made the count of vowels in different languages and compared them with Croatian. See his *Gramatika*, 22–23.

HARD CONSONANTS	VOWEL *o*	VOWEL *e*	SOFT CONSONANTS
Neuter nouns, in nominative and instrumental			
b	*nebo -om*, 'sky, heaven'	*polje -em*, 'field'	lj
l	*djelo -om*, 'work'	*gondže*, 'rosebud'	dž
Verbs with the infix *-ova-* and *-eva-*			
d	*ludovati*, 'to be mad'	*sužnjevati*, 'to be a prisoner'	nj
Neuter adjectives			
h	*suho*, 'dry'	*treće*, 'third'	ć
p	*skupo*, 'expensive'	*smedje*, 'brown'	dj
Masculine nouns in the instrumental			
f	*rafovi*, 'shelves'		
m	*gromovi*, 'thunders'	*miševi*, 'mice'	š
n	*sinovi*, 'sons'		
Masculine nouns in the instrumental			
g	*Bogom*, 'with God'	*starcem*, 'with the old man'	c
r	*darom*, 'with a gift'		
s	*spisom*, 'with a document'	*nožem*, 'with a knife'	ž
z	*mrazom*, 'with the frost'		
Proper names, neuter pronouns			
k	*Željko*	*Hrvoje*	j
v	*ovo*, 'this'	*moje*, 'my, mine'	
Possessive adjectives			
t	*bratov*, 'brother's'	*očev*, 'father's'	č

Three of the English consonants are not found in Croatian: the two *th*'s ([θ] in 'thing' and [ð] in 'that') and the *w* ('watch').

Unlike Russians, Ukrainians, White Russians, Bulgarians, Serbs, and Macedonians, who use a Cyrillic alphabet, Croatians, like Poles, Czechs, Slovaks, and Slovenes, use a Latin alphabet, in which, as a rule, each letter represents one definite speech sound and each sound normally corresponds to one definite letter (seldom two letters). Such a phonetic alphabet is in complete contrast to the English etymologic alphabet. While English and French spellings usually do not reflect phonetic changes, and tend rather to preserve traditional forms, Croatian orthography is, on the contrary, phonetic. English keeps *k* in 'knee' and does not reduce *ow* to *o* in 'knowledge' to keep its spelling closer to 'know';

French does not change *b* into *p* in *subtilité* in spite of the fact that the word is prounced with a *p*, and it continues to write a considerable number of silent letters; but Croatian records in writing almost every phonetic change. Thus *vezem* is changed into *vesti* (*z* to *s*), *gladak* into *glatka* (*d* to *t*), *častan* into *časna* (*t* is dropped), *vrabac* into *vrapca* (*b* to *p*), *misliti* into *mišljenje* (*sl* to *šlj*). Most mutations are due to a regressive assimilation by sonority or palatalization. Serbian orthography is even more consistently phonetic, as can be seen from a comparison of the two futures, Serbian *videću* and *Croatian vidjet ću* (although it is written, *t* is not pronounced).

ACCENT

Like English, and unlike Spanish, Croatian lacks accent marks on words to show the special emphasis on a given syllable in comparison to other syllables of the same word. Thus in the English 'monarchy' and Croatian *monarhija*, we do not know that in the first case 'mo-' carries the stress and in the second '*-nar-*,' whereas in the Spanish *monarquía* the stressed vowel is marked by the acute accent. While English and Spanish have an expiratory stress, the Croatian stressed vowels, especially when they are long in duration, have a strong musical quality; during its emission the tone of the stressed vowel will be rising or falling. This is why it is said that Croatian has a pitch, a musical or chromatic accent. In the English 'monsignor' and the Croatian *monsinjor* all the sounds are more or less the same and the same syllable '-si-' will be stressed, but by comparison the tone in the English '-si-' will be falling, and the Croatian *-si-* rising. If we add to this the fact that the difference between long and short vowels is rather conspicuous in Croatian, we shall easily understand that Croatian has four different accents: a long rising in *lúka*, 'harbor'; a short falling accent in *Ona je gȍra*, 'She is worse'; a long falling accent in *Lûka*, 'Luke'; and a short rising accent in *To je gòra*, 'That is a mountain.' Unstressed vowels also can be long or short and even create morphological differences. *Ràzgledam* (perfective aspect) has one meaning, and *ràzglēdām* (imperfective aspect) has another; one case is *moje žène*, 'my wives' (nominative plural), another *moje žènē*, 'my wife's' (genitive singular), the long vowel being marked by a macron only in some dictionaries or for pedagogical purposes. This alternation of stressed and unstressed, falling and rising, long and short syllables creates a special rhythm, so that to an English ear, the Croatian speech seems to have a "singing" quality.

In complete contrast to French, a Croatian word of two or more syllables will never be stressed on its final syllable, but preferably, though not always, on the first syllable, as in English. Thus, the name Jupiter will have the stress on *Ju-* in English and Croatian, and on *-ter* in French.[10]

MORPHOLOGY AND SYNTAX

As a Slavic language, Croatian is, on the whole, characteristically Slavic in its morphology and syntax.

1/It has a system of cases for nouns, adjectives, pronouns, and numerals: nominative, genitive, dative, accusative, vocative, locative, and instrumental. To illustrate the richness of inflections we give here a paradigm of one kind of noun declension:

Singular: *jelen, jelena, jelenu, jelena, jelene,* (*o*) *jelenu, jelenom.*
Plural: *jeleni, jelena, jelenima, jelene, jeleni,* (*o*) *jelenima, jelenima.*

All nouns belong to one of the three genders, masculine, feminine, or neuter. As a rule, masculines end in a consonant, like *kruh,* 'bread'; feminines in *-a* like *kuća,* 'house'; neuters in *-o* or *-e* like *selo,* 'village,' and *polje,* 'field.' The feeling for grammatical gender is as strong as the one for inflection. For instance in *s Trumanovom vladom,* 'with Truman's cabinet,' *-ov-* corresponds to the possessive *s* in English and *-om* expresses accompaniment and the feminine gender of *vlada.*

There is a particular feature in the declension of masculine nouns. If they designate something animate, their accusative singular is identical with their genitive singular; if something inanimate, their accusative singular is identical with their nominative singular: *Vidim oca,* 'I see the father,' and *Vidim vrt,* 'I see the garden.' This difference appears not only in nouns but also in pronouns, adjectives, and numerals of masculine gender: *Vidio sam onog velikog slona,* 'I saw that large elephant,' in contrast to *Kupio sam onaj veliki stol,* 'I bought that large table.' Even with adjectives used without nouns: *Izaberi najljepšeg* (*kokota*), 'Choose the most beautiful one (rooster),' in contrast to *Uberi najljepši* (*cvijet*), 'Pick up the most beautiful one (flower).'

In Croatian the subject of a relative clause can only be *koji* (we are

10/This is why, in her Serbo-Croatian grammar, Monica Partridge adopted a practical system for the English-speaking learner, expressed in this note: "Where no stress is marked on a word, this word carries a short stress on the first syllable" (p. 17). See Bibliography.

disregarding the other relative *što*), whereas in English it can be either 'who' for persons or 'which' for things. However, in the objective case Croatian uses *kojega* for persons and *koji* for things. For relative pronouns too, the identity of accusative-genitive is reserved for animates, and of accusative-nominative for inanimates. Thus: *Cvijet koji je preda mnom* ..., 'The flower which is in front of me ...,' and *Čovjek koji je preda mnom* ..., 'The man who is in front of me ...,' but: *Cvijet koji vidiš* ..., 'The flower which you see ...,' and *Čovjek kojega vidiš* ..., 'The man whom you see ...'

Even some feminine nouns may be affected by this "animism." Those that are retain the same accent in the accusative case that they had in the nominative if they signify something animate, but alter the accent in the accusative if they signify something inanimate. For instance *žèna* and *vòda*: *Pozdravi žènu*, 'Greet the woman,' and *Donesi vȍdu*, 'Bring the water.' A different switch in stress may take place in some masculine nouns in the locative case depending upon the meaning of the noun, animate or inanimate. For instance *grâd* and *vûk*: *u grádu*, 'in the city,' and ȍ *vūku*, 'about the wolf.' Not only the nature of the accent is changed but its position too.

2/Croatian has two numbers, singular and plural; except for a few forms, the dual has disappeared.

3/Adjectives have three genders, just as do nouns, and three degrees, positive, comparative, and superlative. The distinction between the definite and indefinite form of many adjectives is peculiar to Croatian. An adjective is indefinite in the predicative position: *Moj prijatelj je dobar*, 'My friend is good.' An adjective is definite or indefinite in the attributive position: *dobar prijatelj*, 'a good friend,' and *dobri prijatelj*, 'the good friend.' This distinction between the two forms in the attributive position is somewhat fading out.

4/The Croatian language does not have any kind of articles, definite, indefinite, or partitive.

5/Like other Slavic languages, Croatian has in many cases two conjugations for each verb according to the verbal aspects, perfective and imperfective.

	PERFECTIVE	IMPERFECTIVE
	kupiti = to buy	*kupovati* = to be buying
Present	*kupim* = I buy (in dependent clauses only)	*kupujem* = I am buying
Past	*kupio sam* = I bought	*kupovao sam* = I was buying
Future	*kupit ću* = I shall buy etc.	*kupovat ću* = I shall be buying etc.

Sometimes there is a third aspect, iterative, *pokupovati* = to buy here and there.

As Milan Rešetar says,[11] with an imperfective verb the speaker visualizes the verbal action or state as continued, not having in mind its end, completion, or result. On the contrary, with the perfective verb the speaker visualizes its completion, end, or result. This does not imply that the completion will be achieved, but only that the moment of completion is present in the speaker's mind.

Croatian verbs have voices, tenses, moods, and persons. Unlike Italian, French, or German, Croatian has only one auxiliary verb, *biti*, 'to be,' for the formation of active compound tenses. The passive voice is formed with the same auxiliary as the active one, but with a different participle, Croatian having not only a passive (*hvaljen*) but also an active (*hvalio*) participle. Thus, *ja sam hvalio*, 'I have praised,' *ja sam hvaljen*, 'I am praised.' Croatian uses 'to be' for both the active and passive voice; however, the latter is not frequently used. The future tense is formed by combining the infinitive and an auxiliary, as it is in English, French, or German. Whereas English wavers between 'shall' and 'will,' Croatian has only 'will' (*hoću*) in its enclitic form *ću*, as do Modern Greek and Rumanian. In orthography Croatian never amalgamates the infinitive and the auxiliary (*hvalit ću*), whereas Serbian usually has a synthetic future tense in speech and writing (*hvaliću*). In speech, however, there is no difference between the Serbian *hvaliću* or *pašću* and the Croatian *hvalit ću* or *past ću*.

The imperfect and the aorist tenses have practically disappeared from today's speech and the pluperfect is used infrequently. Thus Croatian has only one past tense, as does English, more or less, unlike Romance languages which constantly distinguish between an imperfect and a perfect. The distinction between imperfective and perfective verbs makes up for that "deficiency." Croatian knows of a conditional, but not a subjunctive mood. As a rule Croatian, unlike English and French, expresses verbal persons in verbal endings and not by accompanying personal pronouns: *pjevam*, 'I sing,' is like the Latin *canto*, and not like the English 'I sing' or the French *je chante*. Therefore, as in Latin, the interrogative form of the verb will not be indicated by inversion, like the English or French 'Can we?' and *Pouvons-nous?*, but by adding an interrogative particle (an enclitic) to the verb, *Možemo li?*, or in Latin, *Possumusne?* Almost all the verbs end in *-ti* in their infinitives, *pjevati*, *govoriti*, and only a few end in *-ći* like *reći*. As a matter of fact, this *-ći* is derived from *k* + *ti* (*rekti*), i.e., a consonant + *ti*. Thus all the Croatian infinitives end

11/*Elementargrammatik der serbo-kroatischen Sprache* ("Slawistische Bibliotek." v; 4th ed., Halle, 1959), 145.

in *-ti*. An infix between the root base of the verb and the ending *-ti* determines the conjugation: *kaz-a-ti, vid-je-ti, pit-a-ti, stan-ova-ti.*

6/Pronouns are not particularly abundant except for demonstratives, among which Croatian distinguishes three cases: *ovaj* near the speaker, *taj* near the interlocutor, *onaj* far from both, like the Italian *questo-codesto-quello*. For relatives in the nominative case there is no distinction between animate and inanimate antecedents; i.e., masculine 'who' and 'which,' as we have said, are translated in the same way, *koji*. There are no special sets of possessives to make a distinction between adjectival and pronominal uses like the English ('my, mine') and the French (*mon, le mien*). Neither are there two sets for demonstratives like the French (*ce, celui-ci*); in other words, *ovaj* is used both as an adjective and as a pronoun. For personal pronouns there are stressed and unstressed forms – *njega-ga, njemu-mu, njoj-joj, nju-je(ju)* – as in French, but the use is different. The place of the object pronoun is not as rigid as it is in English (after the verb) or in French (before the verb); 'I see him' will be translated *vidim ga* or *ja ga vidim* according to the stress.

One of the peculiarities of Croatian is the use of the same reflexive pronoun, personal and possessive, for all persons in the singular and plural: *Hvalim se* (*ja se hvalim*), 'I praise myself,' *Volim svoju majku*, 'I love my mother'; *Hvališ se* (*ti se* ...), 'You praise yourself,' *Voliš svoju majku*, 'You love your ...'; *Hvalimo se* (*mi se* ...), 'We praise ourselves,' *Volimo svoju majku*, 'We love our ...'; *Hvale se* (*oni se* ...), 'They praise themselves,' *Vole svoju majku*, 'They love their ...'

Compared to English, Croatian has a considerable number of so-called reflexive verbs that today no longer have a reflexive meaning, just as do French and Italian: for example, *Sjećam se* for 'I remember' (French *Je me souviens*, Italian *Mi ricordo*).

7/Although a double negation logically makes for a strong affirmation, Croatian can accumulate a number of negative words in the same sentence and still preserve its negative meaning. For instance, the following sentence has four negatives: *Nikada nikamo ni s kim ne idem*, 'I never go any place with anybody.'

8/Croatian has an important number of unaccented words. They are called enclitics and form a phonetic unit with a preceding accented word, *Vȉdim ga*, 'I see him,' while others (proclitics) absorb the accent of the following word, *Idem pȍ vodu*, 'I'll fetch the water.' The need of the enclitics to lean against a stronger word upsets the usual grammatical word order. No sentence can start with an enclitic: *Mî smo umorni*, 'We are tired,' cannot be inverted in Croatian into 'Are we ...?' until the unaccented *smo* has been changed into accented *jèsmo*, *Jèsmo li umorni?*, and *mi* dropped as redundant.

An enclitic has a determined place in the sentence. Being an unstressed part of speech, it cannot occupy the first place in it. As a matter of fact, a Croatian enclitic should always be in the second place. While one normally says *Došla je*, 'She came,' one cannot say *Majka došla je*, but *Majka je došla*, 'Mother came.' *Je* is one of the most frequent enclitics, of which there are altogether about forty. The subject usually occupies the first position, but if it is accompanied by a series of modifiers, the second position in the utterance might become "too distant" for the enclitic. In that case the subject is usually separated from its modifiers, and the enclitic "comfortably" takes its place within the syntagmatic unit of the subject. For instance, *Ova se knjiga lako čita*, 'One reads this book easily.' The enclitic *se*, a part of the predicate, being inserted between *ova* and *knjiga*, breaks the subject syntagme. As a German verb in an independent clause occupies the second place, in Croatian an enclitic takes second position both in dependent and independent clauses, immediately after the first stressed word. This important rule, being more phonetic than syntactic, might be better formulated by saying that the enclitic follows the first stress. Thus, *U dobru je // lako dobar biti*, 'It is easy to be good, when everything around you is good,' or *U dobru, // lako je dobar biti*, and not *U dobru // je lako dobar biti.*

9/Thanks to a great abundance of inflections, Croatian has a very flexible word order (except for the enclitics), with words arranged according to the part of the sentence one wants to emphasize. The sentence 'I am reading a book' can be rendered in six ways: *Čitam knjigu*, *Ja čitam knjigu*, *Knjigu čitam*, *Knjigu ja čitam*, *Knjigu čitam ja*, and *Čitam ja knjigu*, with varying stylistic values.

10/In direct and indirect discourse the pattern of word order differs from that of any other great Western language. To illustrate, Croatian direct discourse agrees with Latin if the question does not contain an interrogative word, with Italian, if it does. There is no inversion like that in English or French: 'Is he coming?' *Vient-il?*, but an interrogative particle is used as in Latin (*-ne*) or the familiar French (*est-ce que*): Latin *Venitne?*, French *Est-ce qu'il vient?*, Croatian *Dolazi li?* The inversion of the subject indicates in English and French the difference between direct and indirect discourse. Direct: 'What time is it?,' French *Quelle heure est-il?*, Croatian *Koliko je sati?* Indirect: 'Tell me what time it is,' French *Dites-moi quelle heure il est*, Croatian *Recite mi koliko je sati.* In Croatian as in Italian the word order remains the same (*Che ora è?* and *Mi dica che ora è*).

11/The sequence of tenses also points to a mode of thought different from that of most great Western languages in which a past tense in the main clause regularly demands a past tense in the dependent clause. In English "He asked me: 'Where do you come from?' " will be changed into "He asked me where I came from"; present changes to past. In German *Er hat mich gefragt: "Woher sind Sie?"* will be changed into *Er hat mich gefragt, woher ich bin,* but the tense remains the same. In Croatian *Zapitao me: "Odakle si?"* will become *Zapitao me odakle sam*; the present indicative is used in both cases. French, Italian, and Spanish change as does English, whereas in German and Croatian the tense remains the same. (In German, only the word order is changed!)

12/In most Western languages verbs of immediate perception usually govern a specific construction. Thus the Latin *Scio canem currere* becomes *Video canem currentem,* whereas French returns to an infinitive *Je vois le chien courir* like the German *Ich sehe den Hund laufen.* While in these languages an infinitive or a participle is used regularly, in Croatian an explicit construction is required. Therefore, "I see the dog running" will be translated into *Vidim psa kako (gdje) trči*; an English gerund is replaced by a Croatian dependent clause.

13/Like other Slavic languages Croatian has a facility for forming possessive adjectives of nouns: *brat-bratov,* 'brother-brother's;' *sestra-sestrin,* 'sister-sister's'; *Petar-Petrov,* 'Peter-Peter's'; etc.

14/If one listens to a speaker of Croatian, he will frequently hear the words *da* and *koji. Da* is an adverb of affirmation, the English 'yes,' and it is also used as a conjunction in at least five different dependent clauses. Although it corresponds in some instances to the English conjunction 'that,' it can never be dropped as it is in English declarative clauses. In Serbian *da* is used even more frequently, owing to the fact that Serbs replace an infinitive by *da* + the present tense.[12] *Koji* is a relative pronoun for persons and things, and as such is used as frequently as both the English 'who' and 'which.' It should be noticed that in French, Italian, and Spanish the relative pronoun is monosyllabic, and in German the monosyllabic *der* is used far more frequently than the longer *welcher* (the same holds true for the French *lequel*). In Croatian, a good stylist will avoid this monotony and enliven his writing by using synonymous conjunctions for *da,* and by replacing the dissyllabic *koji* with the monosyllabic *što,* just as 'who-which' may be replaced in English by 'that.'

12/This overuse of *da* is sometimes called *dakanje*. See also L. Jonke, *Književni jezik,* 400.

15/Although in close contact with different linguistic worlds, Germanic (German) and Romance (Latin and Italian), and their great civilizations, Croatian has preserved its Slavic characteristics to a great extent. If we exclude a few minor points of phonetics and syntax, we can state that the Slavic patrimony of the Croatian language felt a Romance (French and Italian) and Germanic (German) influence only in its vocabulary. The vocabulary of the common people shows a strong German influence in the north and a strong Venetian influence in the south, while the language of the "intelligentsia" was especially affected by German. Although Russian is the language of the most numerous and important Slavic nationality, and there was lengthy Turkish domination of the eastern part of Croatia, neither languages left a noticeable mark on Croatian, whereas Serbian shows both of these influences to a greater extent. Noticeable English influence is being felt only since the Second World War.

The very facts that Croatians have Slavicized the eastern part of the Adriatic Sea and that Croatian fishermen have succeeded the Roman fishermen in the former Roman province of Dalmatia make it clear that Dalmatian Croatians are the most intimate link between the Slavic and Roman worlds. Numerous toponyms and a number of maritime expressions remain as witnesses of that encounter. On the Dalmatian coast the city of Dubrovnik is the most telling example of this unique symbiosis in architecture, literature, and language. The Croatian language, like Polish, Czech, Slovak, and Slovenian, forms a bridge between the European East and West inasmuch as it is a Slavic language in which we find expressed the ideas and trends of thought and attitude that characterize Western culture.

NOTE/In footnote 5 we observed that the leading Croatian linguists referred to a so-called Croatian variant of the Croatoserbian literary language. As explained at the beginning of this chapter, we simply call this the Croatian literary or standard language. On March 15, 1967, nineteen Croatian cultural and scientific institutions issued a "Declaration on the Name and Position of the Croatian Literary Language" which agrees with our viewpoint. The Declaration asked for an amendment to the Yugoslav Constitution whereby all federal documents should be published in four languages, Serbian, Croatian, Slovenian, and Macedonian, instead of three, Serbocroatian or Croatoserbian, Slovenian, and Macedonian. The amendment was rejected and about forty signers of the Declaration were either reprimanded or expelled from the Communist Party. In spite of this public political repression, Croatian linguists, writers, and philosophers kept insisting so much on the demands of the Declaration that it may be said now that the Declaration is completely vindicated.

Bibliography

GENERAL WORKS

Filipović, Rudolf. *The Phonetic Analysis of English Loan-Words in Croatian.* ("Institute of Phonetics, Faculty of Philosophy, University of Zagreb," VIII.) Zagreb, 1960.

Jonke, Ljudevit. *Književni jezik u teoriji i praksi*/Literary Language in Theory and Practice. 2nd ed. enl. Zagreb: Znanje, 1965.

Kadić, Ante. *Croatian Reader.* 's Gravenhage: Mouton and Co., 1960.

Popović, Ivan. *Istorija srpskohrvatskog jezika*/History of the Serbo-Croatian Language. Novi Sad: Matica Srpska, 1955. (Cyrillic)

—— *Geschichte der serbokroatischen Sprache.* Wiesbaden: O. Harrassowitz, 1960. This is an expanded version of the Serbian edition.

Ružić, Rajko Hariton. *The Aspects of the Verb in Serbo-Croatian.* Berkeley and Los Angeles: University of California Press, 1943.

Sandfeld, Kristian. *Linguistique balkanique; problèmes et résultats.* Paris: Champion, 1930.

Skok, Petar. *Naša pomorska i ribarska terminologija*/Our Maritime and Fishing Terminology. ("Pomorska biblioteka Jadranske straže.") Split, 1933.

—— *Dolazak Slavena na Mediteran*/The Slavs' Arrival at the Mediterranean. ("Pomorska biblioteka Jadranske straže.") Split, 1934.

GRAMMARS

Cronia, Arturo. *Grammatica della lingua serbo-croata.* Milano, 1959.

Hodge, Carlton T., and Janković, Janko. *Serbo-Croatian: Basic Course.* Vol. I (Units 1–25). Washington, D.C.: Foreign Service Institute, Department of State, 1965.

Leskien, August. *Grammatik der serbo-kroatischen Sprache.* Teil I. Heidelberg: C. Winter, 1914.

Lord, Albert Bates. *Beginning Serbocroatian.* 's Gravenhage: Mouton and Co., 1964.

Magner, Thomas F. *Introduction to the Serbo-Croatian Language.* 2nd ed. State College, Pa.: Singidunum Press, 1962.

Maretić, Tomo. *Gramatika hrvatskoga ili srpskoga književnoga jezika*/Grammar of the Croatian or Serbian Literary Language. 3rd ed. Zagreb: Matica Hrvatska, 1963.

Meillet, Antoine, and Vaillant, Antoine. *Grammaire de la langue serbo-croate.* 2nd ed. Paris: Champion, 1952.

Partridge, Monica. *Serbo-Croatian: Practical Grammar and Reader.* Belgrade: Jugoslavija, 1964.

Petrovich, Woislav. *Serbo-kroatische Konversations-Grammatik* (Methode Gaspey-Otto-Sauer). 4th ed. Heidelberg: Julius Groos, 1931.

Prince, John Dynely. *Practical Grammar of the Serbo-Croatian Language.* New York, 1960.

Rešetar, Milan. *Elementargrammatik der serbo-kroatischen Sprache.* ("Slawistische Bibliotek," v.) 4th ed. Halle, 1959.
Schmaus, Alois. *Lehrbuch der serbo-kroatischen Sprache.* 3rd rev. ed. München, 1964.

DICTIONARIES

Benešić, Julije. *Hrvatsko-poljski rječnik*/Croatian-Polish Dictionary. Zagreb, 1949.
Berneker, Erich Karl. *Slavisches etymologisches Worterbuch. Heidelberg*: C. Winter, 1908–14. Includes A–Mor.
Dayre, Jean, Deanović, Mirko, and Maixner, Rudolf. *Hrvatskosrpsko-francuski rječnik*/Dictionnaire croate ou serbe-français. 2nd ed. Zagreb: Novinarsko izadavačko poduzeće, 1960.
Deanović, Mirko and Jernej, Josip. *Hrvatskosrpsko-talijanski rječnik*/Croatoserbian-Italian Dictionary. Zagreb: Školska knjiga, 1956.
—— *Talijansko-hrvatskosrpski rječnik*/Italian-Croatoserbian Dictionary. 3rd ed. Zagreb: Školska knjiga, 1960.
Drvodelić, Milan. *Hrvatskosrpsko-engleski rječnik*/Croatoserbian-English Dictionary. Zagreb: Školska knjiga, 1961.
—— Englesko-hrvatsko-srpski rječnik/English-Croato-Serbian Dictionary. Zagreb: Školska knjiga, 1962.
Filipović, Rudolf, *et al. Englesko-hrvatski rječnik*/English-Croatian Dictionary. Zagreb: Zora, 1959.
Iveković, F., and Broz, Ivan. *Rječnik hrvatskoga jezika*/Dictionary of the Croatian Language. 2 vols. Zagreb: Albrecht, 1901.
Klaić, Bratoljub. *Rječnik stranih riječi, izraza i kratica*/Dictionary of Foreign Words, Expressions, and Abbreviations. Zagreb: Zora, 1958.
Miklošić, Franc. *Etymologisches Wörterbuch der slavischen Sprachen.* Wien: W. Braunmüller, 1886.
Ristić, Svetomir, and Kangrga, Jovan. *Enciklopediski nemačko-srpskohrvatski rečnik*/Enzyklopädisches deutsch-serbokroatisches Wörterbuch. Beograd, 1936. (Cyrillic)
—— *Enzyklopädisches deutsch-serbokroatisches Wörterbuch.* 2 vols. 2nd rev. ed. München, 1963.
Rječnik hrvatskoga ili srpskoga jezika/Dictionary of the Croatian or Serbian Language. 18 vols. Zagreb: Yugoslav Academy, 1880–1962. Includes A–Tustošija.
Rječnik hrvatskosrpskoga književnog jezika/Dictionary of the Croatoserbian Literary Language. 2 vols. Zagreb, Novi Sad: Matica Hrvatska, Matica Srpska, 1967. From A to K.
Šamšalović, Gustav. *Njemačko-hrvatski rječnik*/German-Croatian Dictionary. Zagreb: Zora, 1960.
Velikanović, Iso, and Andrić, Nikola. *Šta je šta: Stvarni hrvatski rječnik*/The Croatian Duden. Zagreb: Minerva, 1938.

ORTHOGRAPHIES

Up until 1960 Belić compiled the phonetic orthography for the Serbian literary language and Boranić for the Croatian literary language. In 1944, *Ured za hrvatski jezik* of Zagreb prepared the etymologic orthography for the Croatian literary language. In 1960 an official edition of a new phonetic orthography combined the Serbian and Croatian peculiarities on the assumption that there is only one Serbocroatian or Croatoserbian literary language with two variants, eastern and western. These are the latest editions of the four orthographies.

Belić, Aleksandar. *Pravopis srpskohrvatskog književnog jezika*/Orthography of the Serbocroatian Literary Language. 4th ed. Beograd: Prosveta, 1950–2. (Cyrillic)

Boranić, Dragutin. *Pravopis hrvatskoga ili srpskoga jezika*/Orthography of the Croatian or Serbian Language. 10th ed. Zagreb: Školska knjiga, 1951.

Hrvatski pravopis/Croatian Orthography. Compiled by Ured za hrvatski jezik. Zagreb: Hrvatska državna tiskara, 1944.

Pravopis hrvatskosrpskog književnog jezika/Orthography of the Croatoserbian Literary Language. Compiled by Pravopisna komisija. Zagreb: Matica Hrvatska, 1960. At the same time the same book was published in Cyrillic script under the title: *Pravopis srpskohrvatskog književnog jezika*/Orthography of the Serbocroatian Literary Language. Novi Sad: Matica Srpska, 1960.

4

Literature

1400–1835

FRANJO TROGRANČIĆ

THE FIFTEENTH AND SIXTEENTH CENTURIES: HUMANISM AND RENAISSANCE AMONG THE CROATIANS

THE BEGINNINGS OF CROATIAN LITERATURE IN DALMATIA

The fifteenth century was a turbulent epoch for all the Balkan peoples, especially for the people of Croatia, for it marked a decisive turning point in their national life. From a political point of view, it represents the decline of national independence, since even those territories which were spared Austrian and Hungarian domination came under Turkish rule. The northern regions (ancient Croatia and Slavonia) had had close ties with Hungary from the twelfth century, and by the fifteenth these regions were dominated by Austro-Hungarian influence politically and culturally. The Dalmatian coast, except for the little republic of Dubrovnik, lay under the domination of Venice. In the southeast, Bosnia became a Turkish province in 1463, and Hercegovina suffered the same fate only twenty years later.

The Turkish occupation of Bosnia and Hercegovina prevented the Christian population from normal development and an expression of their higher cultural life for centuries to come. In Dalmatia, however, there was no such obstacle since it remained in a Roman Catholic sphere of culture and, in the Middle Ages, belonging to a distinct religious group was the decisive factor in determining the type of culture a people developed. This characteristic was, indeed, shared by the northern regions, but the geographical position of Dalmatia favored the earlier development of Renaissance culture there. The commercial, cultural, and political connections between the two shores of the Adriatic are as old as the history of the peoples who inhabit them. Because of them, the Dalmatian cities of the coast were the natural link between the Balkan Peninsula and Italy; for centuries, even after the arrival of the Croatians, these cities gave shelter to many outstanding individuals from beyond the Adriatic, especially during the Venetian rule. These people, besides occupying the highest public positions as diplomatic, political, and administrative officials, were frequently the bearers and spreaders of the culture identified in the fifteenth century as humanistic.

Furthermore, there were numerous opportunities and occasions for the inhabitants of Dalmatia to cross the Adriatic and to become acquainted with diverse cultural and literary currents at their sources. First of all, the members of various religious orders went to Italy for higher studies. Then too, the children of well-to-do Dalmatian families were sent to Italian schools to come into direct contact with the ideas then in vogue. Thus we find from the middle of the fifteenth century a large group of outstanding Croatian humanists who perpetuated their fame and that of their scientific activity in various Italian centers, working as professors in the universities and in the other scientific institutions of Italy, and at the same time contributing to the development of the great humanistic culture in the Croatian coastal cities.

However, this cultural ferment was not yet sufficient to inaugurate a Croatian national literature in the cities of Dalmatia: another prerequisite had to be met, that is, the assimilation of the Roman and Slavic inhabitants of the cities.[1] The population which took refuge in the coastal cities of Dalmatia and on the islands of the Adriatic at the time of the invasion of the Slavs in the sixth and seventh centuries A.D. was composed almost entirely of descendants of Roman colonists and Romanized Illyrians who spoke a Romance language, or rather a group of Romance dialects. The ethnographic character of the old Dalmatian cities (Dubrovnik, Split, Trogir, Zadar, etc.) and of the islands (Rab, Osor, Hvar, Krk, etc.) at the middle of the tenth century is explicitly documented by Constantine Porphyrogenitus: "... the inhabitants of which [the cities] are called Romani to this day."[1a] But by the twelfth century

1/It is true that Dalmatia, or rather, ancient Croatia, from the end of the ninth to the end of the fifteenth centuries, had its Glagolitic literature. But the models of the new literature, the circumstances which gave rise to it, and the goals it sought were completely different. The Glagolitic literature, purely religious in character, could not serve as the source of these new impulses inasmuch as it was fossilized linguistically and not at all viable.

1a/*De administrando imperio*, edited by Moravcsik-Jenkins (Budapest, 1949), chap. 29, 125.

another chronicler (the archbishop of Tyre, William) who travelled through Dalmatia said of the language of the inhabitants that "except for the few who live on the seacoast and who differ from others in their way of life and in their language, which is Latin, the remaining population uses a Slavic language and dresses like barbarians."[2] The church historian Baronius (1538–1607) attests this also, saying that Pope Alexander III, on the occasion of his visit to Zadar in 1177, was saluted by clergy and citizens "with great hymns and canticles re-echoing in their Slavic language."[3]

These Romanized cities, with their Slavic background, situated in a territory surrounded by Slavic peoples, could not prevent the slow, but continuous, and irresistible Slavization within their walls, and became, more or less rapidly, Croatian. Dubrovnik seems to have become Slavic especially quickly, viz., in the twelfth century, although the old Romance dialect did not disappear until the second half of the fifteenth century. In the cities of Dalmatia, the process of Croatization was completed within the first half of the fifteenth century.[4]

However, the old Dalmatian literature,[5] prior to the first half of the fifteenth century, consisted primarily of chronicles and annals,[6] translations of texts necessary for divine service,[7] and important juridical works.[8] But that the Croatian language was already sufficiently de-

2/"... exceptis paucis, qui in oris maritimis habitant, qui ab aliis et moribus et lingua dissimiles latinum habent idioma, reliquis sclavonico sermone utentibus et habitu barbarorum." *Willermi Tyrensis Historiae*, edited by Bongars ("Gesta Dei per Francos," I; Hanoviae, 1611), II, chap. 17, 660. See also Ferdo Šišić, *Enchiridion fontium historiae croaticae*, I, pt. 2 (Zagreb, 1914), 403.

3/"Immensis laudibus et canticis altissime resonantibus in eorum sclavica lingua." Baronius' text has been commented on in detail by S. Strgačić in his study "Papa Aleksandar III u Zadru" (Pope Alexander III in Zadar), in the collective work *Radovi Instituta Historije Jugoslavenske Akademije u Zadru* (Studies of the Historical Institute of the Yugoslav Academy in Zadar), I (Zagreb, 1954), 153–87.

4/The fact that the Venetian dialect was conserved for a relatively long time in the Dalmatian cities, especially among the upper classes, is not a consequence of the prevalence of the old Dalmatian language, but rather the result of importation during the Venetian domination. This can be clearly seen by the fact that although this dialect was spread throughout Dalmatia, it did not survive in Dubrovnik, the only city which, after the first half of the fourteenth century, was never under Venetian rule. The other cities were under Venetian administration for several centuries and absorbed a number of immigrant Italian families.

5/See n. 1.

6/Especially worthy of mention is the *Ljetopis popa Dukljanina* (Chronicle of the Priest of Dioclea) which deals with Croatian history from the sixth to the twelfth centuries.

7/*Misal kneza Novaka* (Missal of Prince Novak; 1368); *Misal Hrvoja Vukčića Hrvatinića* (Missal of Hrvoje Vukčić Hrvatinić), beginning of the fifteenth century.

8/*Vinodolski Zakonik* iz godine 1288 (Statute of Vinodol in 1288), *Vrbnički Statut* iz godine 1388 (Statute of Vrbnik of 1388), etc.

veloped for purely literary uses seems clear from the fact that for some time prior to this period the people sang church hymns in the vernacular and folk poetry was already flourishing. Traces of attempts at composing poetry in Croatian are already evident in the first decades of the fifteenth century if not in the late fourteenth century.

The second half of the fifteenth century offers the first products of a truly national literature. Indeed, in this period we find native poets and literateurs writing in the vernacular though influenced by contemporary humanism.

Before the emergence of literary activity in the Croatian language, Croatian writers used Latin almost exclusively for their literary efforts, largely because Latin had for so long a time been the language of written documents of every kind. This was true especially during the period of humanism in Italy, and during the Croatian feudal period when Latin was the official language. The young men who attended the universities of Bologna, Padua, Mantua, etc., as a rule looked forward, if they had the necessary patronage and aptitude, to ecclesiastical careers, or, for the more fortunate, political careers; and everywhere at the courts persons able to display elegant classical Latin in diplomatic correspondence and on diplomatic missions were much in demand.

Among the older Croatian poets and humanists who became known in countries outside Croatia, the most noteworthy were the Dubrovnik diplomat Vuk Bobaljević (first half of the fifteenth century) and Ivan Česmički (1434–72), known by his humanistic pseudonym of Janus Pannonius. After a long stay in Italy at the study-centers of Ferrara and Padua, Česmički was named bishop of Pécs in Hungary when he was only twenty-six years old, and he fashioned a brilliant career at the court of Matthias Corvinus. He left elegies, panegyrics, epigrams, and epithalamia. His special lyrical talent was most evident in his elegies. While he is appreciated also for his religious poems, they are learned but rarely deeply moving, since Pannonius, a true humanist, seeks no comfort in religion and speaks of God like a Platonist rather than a Christian. From his epigrams, on the other hand, in which so many outstanding individuals of the time appear most vividly, one can find Česmički's vision of life and the world.

In the second half of the fifteenth century, the canon of Šibenik, Juraj Šižgorić (Georgius Sisgoreus), left a collection of Latin poems, *Elegiarum et carminum Libri III* (Venice, 1477), containing elegies, epithalamia, odes, love poems, occasional poems, all characterized by rich classical allusions. His *De situ Illyriae et civitate Sibenici* (1487), on the other hand, is a historical work in which he writes about "Some old customs in Šibenik" (*De moribus quibusdam Sibenici*), about "The pillaging of the Field of Šibenik" by the Turks (*De Sibenicensis agri vastatione*), and about Croatian folk poetry, Croatian proverbs (dicteria), etc.

Among the Croatians living outside the country who contributed to the religious and humanistic culture and literature of Europe was Juraj Dragišić or Georgius Benignus (1450–1520), a native of Srebrenica in eastern Bosnia, who became famous throughout Europe. He was a man of vast culture and great talent; his contemporaries classed him *in primos sui temporis theologos numerandus.* He lived the greater part of his life in Italy, where he wrote *De natura coelestium spirituum* and *Dialectica nova secundum mentem S. Thomae de Aquino* (Rome, 1489). He defended Savonarola in his *Propheticae solutionis pro Hieronymo Savonarola* (Florence, 1497), and the German humanist and Hebraist J. Reuchlin in his *Defensio praestantissimi viri Johannis Reuchlin* (Cologne, 1517). These essays provoked much hostility, so that he was forced to find temporary refuge in his native land.

Some Croatian humanists sought renown through their Latin verses and considered vernacular poetry to be of a lower order and Latin alone as the language of poetry and scholarship. Among these were two members of the noble family Crijević, one a poet, the other a historian. The poet, Ilija, was most typical of the better representatives of humanism in Dubrovnik. Born in 1463, he was sent at thirteen to Rome to the school of Pomponio Leto. At twenty-two, he was awarded the title of poet laureate, on that occasion changing his name to Aelius Lampridius Cerva and continuing to frequent the most exclusive Roman literary circles. Afterwards he lived in Dubrovnik, where he worked as a teacher, orator, and a directing member of the Republic. He died there, a priest, in 1520. He was more literateur than poet, and distinguished himself by his wide and deep humanistic-classical culture and his elegant latinity; nevertheless, in spite of the prevailing conventionality of contemporary love-poetry, he exhibited here and there in his verses some genuine spontaneity. His sincerity of feeling is revealed often, too, in his letters to the friends and colleagues of his happy Roman sojourn, and in his patriotic and religious poems. However, his thematic depth fell short of both his almost incredible metrical facility and his prolific literary achievement. His relative, the historian Abbot Alojzije (Aloysius de Cerva), called also Corrinus Tubero (1450–1527), studied in Paris where he acquired a solid cultural background. His principal work, *Commentaria de rebus quae temporibus suis gestae sunt,* was placed on the Index because its spirit was adjudged too liberal.

Another literary figure of the period is the aristocratic Jakov Bunić or Jacobus de Bona (1469–1534), who was called "Splendor Illyriae" because he wrote one of the better examples of religious poetry in Latin and was one of the greatest exponents of the Counter-Reformation in the humanist period. He left an allegorical composition, *De raptu Cerberi*, and a lengthy epic (10,000 verses), *De vita et gestis Christi* (Rome, 1526). The latter leans heavily on Virgil for its inspiration and has been overshadowed by the near-contemporary poem *Christias* of Girolamo Vida.

THE FIRST POETS

Contemporary with the two Crijevićs, or at most some decades younger, were the first Croatian poets of Dalmatia, some of whom used the national language exclusively, and some together with Latin. They belonged to two poetic schools: that of Split, with Marulić as its leader, and that of Dubrovnik, which was united around Šiško Menčetić (1457–1527) and Džore Držić (1461–1501), both members of the old Dubrovnik nobility.

The poems of the first two poets of Dubrovnik, Menčetić and Držić, are preserved in a collection made by Nikša Ranjina in 1507, and arranged in no particular order. These poems are by and large erotic, and frequently contain acrostics in which Držić limits himself to spelling out his own name and Menčetić memorialized the names of his many loves. It is questionable whether these poets wrote solely under the influence and example of contemporary Italian poets. The fact is that Croatian folk poetry was flourishing at this time, and that these poets must have been acquainted with it, since their poems exhibit many of the themes, rhymes, meters, and other characteristics of folk poetry. The greater part of their poetic output is, nonetheless, a faithful reflection of contemporary Italian poetry. Nor could it have been otherwise; for in the fifteenth century, if not earlier, Italian literature was enthusiastically read not only in Dubrovnik but along the entire Croatian littoral where the urban population understood Italian. Most popular were the Canzoniere of Petrarch; some of the poems of Menčetić and Držić are simply translations of the sonnets of Petrarch and other Italian poets such as S. Ciminelli, A. Poliziano, and L. Pulci. Another strong influence on the first poets of Dubrovnik was the poetry of the Venetian L. Giustiniani (1388–1446).

The influence of Italian poetry is especially evident in the use of acrostics, and in allusions to mythology, the classics, and the Bible. However, these first Croatian poets were less dependent on Italian meter, preferring their own adaptation of the twelve-syllable distich (rhyming in the middle and at the end), the meter of the most ancient Croatian folk poetry.

Petrarch and his followers exerted their greatest influence on the subject matter and theme. The Croatian poets express the same conceptions of love, embodied in a lady who is considered the most beautiful and perfect in the universe, and they suffer the indescribable grief of unrequited love. These form two of the basic motifs of poetry on both sides of the Adriatic, and they are repeated to satiety, with more or less sincerity of sentiment, more or less skill, with the same comparisons and hyperboles, all purely external ornamentation, all sterotyped and conventional. But this is not particularly surprising; these traditional models fashioned to accommodate the entire gamut of emotions had destroyed the individuality and personality of even the better Italian followers of Petrarch.

Despite the modest quality of their poetic production and their close imitation of contemporary Italian models, these poets of Dubrovnik and their annonymous predecessors are *prava svitlos našeg jezika* ("true lights of our language"). They had broken very early with Church Slavonic written in Glagolitic characters and introduced into literature the people's living language, simultaneously adapting the Latin alphabet to it. This was a most important contribution, for in doing so they not only created a literary vehicle for an entire people, but the way to a national language and literature. When one recalls that this process did not develop in Serbia and Russia until several centuries later, one can recognize these men as pioneers not simply of Croatian literature alone, but as the first poets of the Slavic world.

While Menčetić and Držić were writing in Dubrovnik, carrying on the work of their anonymous predecessors (called *začinjavci*), and drawing upon folk Croatian poetry and the poetry of Italy, in Split Marko Marulić or Marcus Marulus (1450–1524) was engaged in his extraordinarily varied literary activity in Latin and Croatian. Marulić was a Christian ascetic and a profoundly learned man; he was a philosopher and moralist, historian and classicist, and a poet and painter as well. Most of his writings make no pretense of being scientific or literary in any modern sense of these terms, and almost all of his words tend to be practically infused with a spirit of Christian didactics. He was a practical philosopher who preached in his books the just life that he himself led, and who proposed to himself as the aim of his life and literary activity the education and moral renewal of his people. Living in a century in which there was "weak faith and execrable morals" (*fides infirmissima et hujus saeculi mores deprecatissimi*) Marulić preferred "uprightness without learning rather than learning without uprightness" (*probitatem sine doctrina, quam sine probitate doctrinam*).

Marulić's Latin works are of primary importance in that they best reflect both his thought and purpose. Moreover, it is because of these that his reputation spread beyond the modest confines of his own country, and he became one of the most celebrated and widely read authors of his time. In fact he was considered "the strongest defender of the faith, the principal philosopher of his time, and second to none in the knowledge of Sacred Scripture" (*fidei propugnator acerrimus, princeps suae aetatis philosophus, sacrarum literarum scientia nemini secundus*) and "the glory of Dalmatia after Saint Jerome" (*post divum Hieronymum Dalmatiae secundam gloriam*).

His first Latin work, *De institutione bene beateque vivendi iuxta exempla sanctorum* (Venice, 1506), is a collection of anecdotes on the lives of the Church fathers proposed as models for our imitation. The work is divided into six books, subdivided into chapters, each of which treats a specific Christian thought, virtue, precept, and the like. It was enormously successful, going through ten editions and translations. St. Francis Xavier, on his long voyage to the Orient, carried with him only his breviary and this book.

The *Evangelistarium* (Venice, 1516) was a treatise on the theological virtues.

His other works, *De humilitate et gloria Christi* (Venice, 1519), *Quinquaginta parabolae* (Venice, 1510), *Dialogus de laudibus Herculis* (Venice, 1524), and others, speak of the perishability of earthly grandeur and the vanity of the things of this world; these too are pervaded by Marulić's religious conviction that only a virtuous life can bring true peace and happiness.

His historical works are inspired by earnest patriotism; for example, his translation of the Chronicle of the Priest of Dioclea, as well as the works *In eos qui beatum Hieronymum Italum esse contendunt, Epistola ad Hadrianum VI*, etc. Finally, in his little-known epic poem, *Davidias*, 14 cantos in Virgilian hexameters, the poet celebrates one of the many "*liberators*" dear to the Renaissance, for the consolation of his people subject to the Turks.

Important as his Latin works are for an evaluation of the richness and virtuosity of his literary career and for giving us an insight into his genius and his life, from a strictly literary point of view and in terms of his contribution to Croatian literature Marulić's works in the mother tongue are far more important. His religious poem, *Istorija svete udovice Judit u versih hrvacki složena,* written in 1501 and published in Venice in 1521, is the first printed work of Croatian literature. It is substantially the Book of Judith somewhat amplified and told in verse: the 2126 dodecasyllables show the influence of Italian classics, and the versification and diction of the medieval Croatian (*začinjavci*) and Latin (*stari poet*) poets. But in spite of the indubitable historical value and the obvious popular success of the work (three editions in three years), it must be pointed out that the pious Marulić made no pretensions to great poetic gifts; he had wished simply to offer an edifying book of encouragement to those who could read neither Latin nor Italian. The occasion was appropriate and the subject a burning one, for Holofernes could symbolize any of the Turkish tyrants who infested the land at the time. He followed the same course of fidelity to the Bible in his second religious poem, *Istorija od Suzane*, a paraphrase of the story of the chaste Suzanna (Dan. 13). The work is characterized by conspicuous moralizing, particularly with reference to the sixth and ninth commandments, and like his "Judith" it is interesting also for its local color.

Marulić's other minor works stressed the moral dimension: *Od začetja Isusova* (On the Incarnation of Jesus), *Od uzvišenja Gospina* (On the Assumption of Our Lady), *Svrhu muke Isukrstove* (On the Passion of Christ), *Urehe duhovne* (Spiritual Ornaments), *Dobri nauci* (Good Teachings), etc. In this group of didactic writings is his paraphrase of the so-called *Disticha moralia Catonis,* which went under the title of *Stumačenje Kata.* There were also minor works in the verse and dialogue form common in the Middle Ages under the name of *disputatio* or *conflictus*: *Govorenje duše osujene* (Discourse of a Condemned Soul), *Od muke Isusove* (On the Passion of Jesus), etc. Finally, Marulić also wrote moral and didactic compositions of humorous bent, a form which originated in the so-called liturgical dramas performed all over Europe and so popular in the Middle Ages. Among these were *Poklad i Korizma* (Shrovetide and Lent) and *Spovid koludric* (Confession of the Nuns).

Still contemporary with Marulić and the two poets of Dubrovnik but essentially of the next generation was Hanibal Lucić (about 1485–1553), the first poet of Hvar, a noble of vast humanistic and classical learning and translator of Ovid's *Heroides*. In spite of his perfect knowledge of Italian and the fact that he supported the interests of his own class in the Republic of Venice, he wrote exclusively in Croatian, a circumstance which offers significant evidence that in his time Croatian was the mother tongue of the nobility of Hvar.

The basic motifs of his first lyrics, *Scladanya izvarsnich pisan razlicich*

(Love Songs; Venice, 1556), repeat those of the Italian heirs of Petrarch, Bembo, Ariosto, etc., and the first Dubrovnik poets, Menčetić and Držić. Of these lyrics, written in fluent dodecasyllables with double rhyme and skillful octosyllables, the poem "Jur nijedna na svit vila" (No Such Fairy in All the World), which has much beauty and originality, is worthy of mention. Some of his lyrics are reminiscent of folk poetry in tone, an indication of the wide diffusion of Croatian folk poetry throughout the national territory at that time.

In addition to the epistle, a form much cultivated in the period of humanism, Lucić composed the first completely original drama of Croatian literature, his masterpiece, *Robinja* (The Slave Girl; Venice, 1585), written in dodecasyllables, on a subject drawn from folk poetry and from national legend with Croatians as protagonists. The play is set in the Dubrovnik of his day, whose urbane civilization contrasted with the hinterlands devastated by the Turks.

Mavro Vetranović Čavčić (about 1482–1576), of a noble family from Dubrovnik, was a Benedictine theologian and a poet, and wrote religious, satirical, and political songs. In spite of the dominant Christian-didactic note in his work – a characteristic he shares with Marulić – he is an autobiographical lyric poet who allows us to glimpse his extraordinarily sensitive soul, his own emotions, and vivid details of his own life. With the words *plač* ("a cry"), *suze* ("tears"), and *uzdasi* ("sighs"), he himself describes the tone and content of his poetry. He is a poet of universal suffering; a completely personal sorrow pervades his poems, one resulting from an analysis of the pleasures of the world viewed by the conscience of a Christian philosopher. He introduces nature into his poetry (Ballad of the Grasshopper), likes to make use of allegory, and is interested in events of the day: everything makes its impression on him. For one living apart from the world Vetranović took an unusually active part in the literary problems of his time and fought for liberty in literature, as in "Pjesanca u pomoć poetam" (A Poem to Help the Poets). He composed several allegorical songs for Shrovetide in strophes of four eight-syllable lines with alternating rhyme, but these were somewhat prolix; they imitate Tuscan verses, omitting, however, the morally objectionable elements of the latter. They seem almost to have been written to replace the dissolute and licentious songs of Nalješković.

However, Vetranović takes precedence over all the writers of Dubrovnik in the staging of religious poetic drama performances developed from liturgical plays; his *Uskrsnuće Isusovo* (The Resurrection of Jesus) and *Suzana čista* (The Chaste Suzanna) were written without literary pretense and simply to edify. Consequently, the scenic background is rather modest and primitive corresponding to the cultural level and mentality of the contemporary public. From a technical point of view, a better work is *Posvetilište Abramovo* (The Sacrifice of Abraham), a play in 2636 twelve-syllable lines. The play is especially interesting as a historical document because, as was customary at the time, it interprets the biblical account in contemporary terms. Thus it offers abundant examples of the national folklore and the customs and dress of Dubrovnik. And because it reflected their own lives so faithfully, it became very popular with contemporary audiences.

The last, greatest, and most original work of Vetranović is the unfinished philosophical-allegorical poem *Pelegrin* (The Pilgrim), composed in 7220 twelve-syllable lines. It consists of a description of humanity's Way of the Cross, in rising from sin to spiritual perfection under divine grace; basically, it is an allegory-fantasy explaining the two fundamental institutions of the Church, confession and communion.

The goldsmith of Dubrovnik, Andrija Čubranović (about 1480–1530), is responsible for some fifty of the poems in the songbook of N. Ranjina; his verses are modeled on the lyrics of the troubadours and Petrarch. In addition, he is credited with a type of Mardi Gras poem *Jedjupka* (The Gypsy Girl), which is a lyric composition in eight-syllable lines with alternating rhyme. Čubranović undoubtedly knew Italian literature, and the *canti carnascialeschi* could have served as distant models; but his "Gypsy" has been considered from the beginning one of the most original and beautiful works in the entire body of early Croatian literature. In fact, the imitation is no more than purely formal; there is none of the obscene, bawdy, and dissolute tone which characterizes Florentine songs of that kind. It is rather a true poetry of love: spontaneous and elegant in tone, lively and melodious in verse structure, the language natural in its gypsy tang. The poem was acclaimed by contemporary poets to such an extent that it soon had its plagiarizers and imitators.[9]

The second poet of central Dalmatia, and a native of Hvar, is Petar Hektorović (1487–1572), who maintained a friendly correspondence with the poets of Dubrovnik and Split. His Croatian translation of the *De remedio amoris* of Ovid attests to his rigorous background in the classics. His main work, however, is the fishermen's eclogue *Ribanje i ribarsko prigovaranje* (Fishing and Fishermen's Tales) written in 1556 and

9/Only recently, some literary historians have attempted to cast doubt on the authorship of the work and the very name of the author, but their arguments, based upon mere hypothesis, have proved insufficient to shake the faith in the authenticity of documents and traditions dating back five centuries. See Milivoj A. Petković, *Dubrovačke maskerate*/Dubrovnik Masquerades ("Posebna izdanja," 166; Beograd: Srpska Akademija Nauka, 1950).

made up of 1684 endecasyllables. Except for the moralizing digressions which tend to weigh down the realistic descriptions of an excursion in the boat of simple fishermen from Hvar to the nearby islands, *Ribanje* can be considered one of the most beautiful and original works of Croatian literature prior to Gundulić. Everything in it is natural, flowing, and plastic, from the rhyme to the construction of each sentence; every description is vivid and overflowing with life and reveals the poet's love of the healthy and peaceful life. We owe to Hektorović also the first written example of folk poetry in the two songs in the eclogue recited by fishermen. They are especially valuable since he recorded both the lyrics and the musical notation.

Another poet of the first half of the sixteenth century is Petar Zoranić (1508–69), descendant of an old and noble family of Zadar. His principal work, *Planine* (The Mountains; Venice, 1569), is a pastoral novel in which verse and prose are alternated, and contain the first example in prose of a profane character in Croatian literature. The work consists of a description of a five-day trip through the forests of the world and the underworld, and is enlivened by lyric poems and amorous episodes interwoven with personal comment and a medley of literary allusions (to Dante, Sannazzaro, Petrarch, etc.). If read without preconceived notions, *Planine* cannot be considered a didactic work of philosophical and moralistic character. It is not an allegorical representation of the struggle of man against himself and against the world in his effort to gain eternal life, as some have interpreted it; rather it is an idyllic description of pastoral life made up of amorous joys and sufferings, an idyllic vision of nature seen through mythology and the classics and veiled by a sense of melancholy which spreads over the landscapes and the characters. It is a vision profoundly sad and lonely, recalling the passing of time; it resembles the *Arcadia* of Sannazzaro.

THE THEATER IN DUBROVNIK

Around the middle of the fifteenth century Croatian literary activity in Dalmatia became increasingly concentrated in Dubrovnik, since the cultural orientation of the literary centers of central and northern Dalmatia (Hvar, Split, Zadar, etc.) began to change following the Venetian occupation. In this rich and free, though small republic, which was spared Venetian domination and any new Romanization, there was an ever increasing interest in literature, partly because Croatian was not only the everyday language of all social classes there, but also because it was the official language. Here, the Old Croatian literature would finally reach its greatest apogée during the first half of the seventeenth century.

During the sixteenth century there were two poets and playwrights who were able to discard the conventional erotic and moral-philosophical themes and, by seeking inspiration in the realities of everyday life, were able to create, through a simple but nonetheless expressive style, literary works which can be enjoyed even today after four centuries.

Nikola Nalješković (1510–*ca.* 1587), merchant by profession, poet by vocation, and a distinguished scholar,[10] wrote *Pjesni ljuvene* (Songs of Love), *Pjesni bogoljubne* (Religious Poems), and numerous poetic epistles. However, he achieved greater fame with his twelve carnival songs (*Pjesni od maskerate*) imitating the Florentine models. Two of these songs stand apart, in that they are really examples of so-called nuptial songs. Three of the ten carnival songs proper are sung by only one person, and an entire group of masked singers participate in the others. All of the songs, however, have a strong erotic tone and reflect the rather dissolute life of the Dubrovnik of that epoch. The verses are composed of dodecasyllabic quartets and sextets.

In an attempt to introduce a more idealistic spirit into the theater and into Italian literature, Sannazzaro, followed by others, had turned to the simple, idyllic pastoral life. At first, he created brief dramatic scenes in which mythological characters played side by side with the shepherds, and thus gave birth to the pastoral drama, which reached its apex with the *Aminta* of Tasso and the *Pastor fido* of Guarini.

The main characteristic of the pastoral dramas of Dubrovnik was the celebration of the peace and freedom enjoyed by that city. Nalješković wrote four pastoral dramas, all based on the life of the city. They stay clear of obscene and bawdy situations, as well as of equivocal language, but create an impression of hasty and mechanical effort, because in trying to produce the greatest possible effect through formal and scenic elements, he gave little emphasis to the action, the development of characters, the dialogue, or the style.

A growing emphasis on comic realism resulted in the production of the first comedies in the literature of Dubrovnik. It appears that Nalješković was the first to introduce scenes of city life in this new genre, and in so doing he reveals himself as a keen observer of the social conditions of his time; moreover, his comedies reflect even the material life of Dubrovnik,

10/His work *Dialogo sopra la sfera del mondo* (Venezia, 1579) procured him fame as a great mathematician and astronomer, so that Pope Gregory XIII and the Commission, when considering the reform of the calendar, asked his opinion on the matter.

that is, the manners and customs, as well as the spoken language interwoven with popular idiomatic expressions and very few italianisms. Only three of his comedies are extant, all three in dodecasyllables with a prologue summarizing the plot. The purpose of the author is simply to entertain the public, even though some of the scenes are rather rough. He arouses interest with the theme itself; the style is lively, poetic, and flexible and each character is faithfully mirrored in his actions. Every drama and comedy of Nalješković, as earlier literary critics have pointed out, clearly reflects his constant concern to keep his works within the guidelines of the Great Council of Dubrovnik of 1535, which had invited all writers to contribute to fostering a sense of morality among the youth; his achievement was to retain the comic element within a didactic framework.

Marin Držić (1508–67) was a priest without a genuine priestly vocation, and a typical Renaissance character, of hearty and dynamic temperament, witty and of wide cultural background. He produced some lyric poetry, replete with stereotyped sighs and panegyrics, which reflects his great lack of talent and temperament for this genre; he was obviously swept along in the literary fashion of his time. His religious dramas *Posvetilište Abramovo* and *Porod Jezusov* (Abraham's Sacrifice, Birth of Jesus) are poor plagiarisms and were the last sacred dramas to be presented in Dubrovnik, giving way to the mundane drama which became popular from the beginning of the second half of the sixteenth century in both Italy and Dalmatia.

Držić finally found his own form in the pastoral drama and in comedy. His two pastoral dramas, *Tirena* and *Venera i Adon*, are clearly superior to those of Nalješković; he divides the dramas into acts, pays particular attention to the development of the plot, avoids meaningless phrases, and uses song and dance for purely decorative purposes.

His realistic comedies, which reveal undeniable dramatic genius, are more appreciated, however. Composed with extreme ease and rapidity, they are meant to be performed on the stage rather than read. It is important to note that Držić had rebelled against the commonly held opinion that all literary works should be written in verse. Refusing to conform, he wrote *Plakir* (Cupid) and *Skup* (The Miser) in prose; nonetheless, he focused more attention on his works in verse. Following the style of the farces popular in contemporary Siena and attentive to the rustic poetry of Tuscany, Držić introduced into Croatian literature not only the ease and directness of the vernacular language, but also realistic descriptions of the manners and customs of the town and country people. A tendency to deal with the social life of Dubrovnik was already evident in his pastoral dramas, but his comedies take a decisive step in this direction. No longer do we find the usual mythological characters, the shepherds vapidly and foolishly in love; now his plays concern the real life of his time and are an occasion to criticize the vices of the society of his day according to the old adage *ridendo castigat mores* ("he lashes with scorn"). Držić achieves the transition from pastoral drama to comedy proper through his *Novela od Stanca* (The Mockery of Stanac), in which an old and superstitious farmer from Hercegovina comes to Dubrovnik to sell his wares, and is met by a group of carefree rakes, who through the use of fairy costumes and the promise of making the old man young again are able to cut off his beard and steal all his goods, leaving him alone and lost in the middle of the night, grieving and frustrated. Each character in this successful comedy is well developed, and the figure of Stanac is particularly incisive. This short dramatic work, rapid in pace, is composed of only 136 dodecasyllables, and is Držić's best comedy.

Tripče (Tryphon) is a comedy whose plot is based on the traditional rivalry between the citizens of Dubrovnik and Kotor, which had already been the subject of satirical poems by the earlier poets of Dubrovnik, examples of which appear early in Ranjina's Songbook of 1507. *Tripče* is a comedy full of intrigue modeled after those of Pietro Aretino (1492–1557), whose work Držić must have certainly known.

The comedy *Arkulin* (A Buffoon) contains an incredible number of amorous situations; the comic extremes succeed in evoking pity for the protagonist. The theme has probably been taken from an Italian farce, *Harlequin*, the false hero. However, the plot of Držić's play is rather poor, and the characters insufficiently developed.

The two plays which truly epitomize the best attributes of this literary genre are *Dundo Maroje* (Old Man Maroje) and *Skup* (The Miser); the theme of both is the stinginess of old people and the wastefulness of the young, and the action evolves from the conflict between the ideal love of the young and the materialistic calculations of the old. *Maroje* is one of Držić's best plays; the scene is Rome, and the plot involves an old miser and his spendthrift son who lavishes on a courtesan a considerable amount of money which his father has given him for the purchase of some fabrics. The action is natural and lively, the dialogue brisk, and the play does not lack for moments of superb comedy.

Skup, Držić's only play superior to *Maroje*, is a rearrangement of the *Aulularia* of Plautus; however, the main theme has been taken and the scene transplanted to his own Dubrovnik, giving it local color and creating a play meant to reflect the society of his day. In fact, only the subject and some of the characters have been taken from the *Aulularia,* the play being completely independent of Plautus in the details of the comedy, which are a genuine product of Dubrovnik.

These two comedies have assured a prominent place for Držić not only in Croatian literature but in the whole of Slavic literature as well, which up to the eighteenth century remained unaware of the existence of this literary genre.

By the second half of the sixteenth century Dubrovnik had changed completely: the patriarchal mode of life had disappeared, the prosperity consequent upon the brisk trade with the hinterland and the whole Balkan Peninsula had raised the culture of the city to a level comparable with that of the more advanced Italian city-states, the enriched middle class competed freely with the nobility in every sphere of life, and good education was available to many. Cultural progress could be noted especially in letters and in the sciences. Following Italian models, literary groups were formed in which even women, such as Cvijeta Zuzorić (Fiora Zuzzeri), took part.

One poet of that era, from the modern standpoint more prolific than creative, was Dinko Ranjina (1536–1607), a very capable merchant and descendant of a noble family of Dubrovnik. He lived in Italy for a long time and was later elected rector of the Republic of Dubrovnik seven times. During his stay in Italy he published, at his own expense, a small volume of poems in Italian (Venice, 1563) together with his *Pjesni razlike* (Miscellaneous Poems; Florence, 1563). The poems are for the most part idyllic-erotic lyrics, elegies, or satires, set against a background of philosophical moralizing. On the other hand, his *Pjesni od kola* (Poetry for Dances) is evidently a direct imitation of popular poetry.

Ranjina was a man of broad culture and extremely refined taste; besides the classic Greek and Latin literature, he also had an excellent knowledge of Italian literature, which, indeed, influenced him greatly. However, he did not allow himself to be dominated by any one poet, and it may be said, perhaps, that having been formed in the Italian literary school of the fifteenth century, his style recalls the composers of Strambotti popular at the end of that century. That he was subject to a great number of influences is understandable in view of his extremely impressionable temperament, although the very ease with which he absorbed them deprived him of greater individuality. Tedious repetitions, conventional mannerisms and epithets, originated by the Petrarchans and the "Strambottisti," render his poetry rather monotonous and make the reader doubt the sincerity of his inspiration, so that the value attributed to his poetry by his contemporaries has subsequently been largely and justly diminished; today, he is considered the forerunner of indigestible baroque poetry. Nevertheless, in justice, we should recognize that his poetry contains great purity and richness of language within its facile and varied prosody.

Ranjina is only one example of the generally fallow period upon which Croatian literature had now entered. Following the successes of Vetranović, Nalješković, and Držić, literature in Dubrovnik came to a standstill until the appearance of the great Gundulić at the turn of the seventeenth century. There were, of course, several poets during the second half of the sixteenth century, but none were outstanding; the literary production of the later years consisted for the most part of translations and epistles, although there were some verses, but the latter could hardly be called great poetry. Almost all the translations were of pastoral dramas and tragedies, but the comedies had been completely forgotten; it was as if, after the death of the two playwrights, the public of Dubrovnik had had its fill of "common representations," and looked to the theater for something more sophisticated and serious.

The second half of the sixteenth century is therefore characterized less by original works than by the activity of imitators and translators. Thus the learned commoner and the *rector artistarum* of Padua, Dominko Zlatarić (1558–1609), is better known for his interesting translations than for his poetry. His *Pjesni razlike* (Miscellaneous Poems), clearly Petrarchan in style, are totally shrouded in sadness and pessimism, and perhaps their only value lies in the seriousness of their subjects and their careful poetic form. Zlatarić translated the *Electra* of Sophocles, Ovid's *Love and Death of Pyramus and Thisbe* (Venice, 1597), and the *Aminta* of Tasso and Guarini's *Pastor fido*, two of the best Italian pastoral dramas. These translations display the richness and flexibility of the Croatian language during the sixteenth century, when it was still free and not yet bound by rules of versification. The translation of *Aminta*, under the title *Ljubmir*, which was published before the original (1580), reveals, moreover, the close literary ties between the Italian and Croatian writers.

Although throughout the sixteenth century there were many writers of lyric poetry and drama in Dubrovnik, epic poetry was completely neglected. It remained the proud privilege of northern Dalmatia to introduce into Croatian literature the first epic poem whose theme was taken from an event in the contemporary national history. *Vazetje Sigeta grada* (The Capture of the City of Sziget, 1584) was written by Brne Krnarutić (1515–73), a native of Zadar and a captain of Croatian troops in the Venetian army; the theme of this historic poem is the vigorous defense of the Hungarian city of Sziget against the overwhelming attack of the Turks, during which the Croatian Ban Nikola Zrinski died a heroic death in 1566. The account is simple, developed with a wealth of historical detail, and free from both fantasy and distorting personal reflection. The poem is thus a truly valuable historical document.

It is legitimate to remark that during the sixteenth century prose was virtually non-existent. The little that can be found is in no way a part of literature proper, although it is of linguistic importance in that it carefully documents the spoken language of the time. This absence of literary works in Croatian prose can be explained by the fact that the literary class of that time showed a marked preference for Latin, the universal language, or Italian, which then seemed to facilitate communication with the contemporary civilized world; moreover, the age had never granted to prose the same privileged position as that held by poetry. It follows, then, that anyone proposing to write or to translate some work into Croatian would be likely to limit himself to verse. The only writer to really defy the tradition was Držić. It is very interesting to observe how Zoranić, in his *Planine*, uses prose only in the less important passages, remaining, throughout the rest of the work, faithful to the literary fashion of his time; and even then, his prose is more poetic than the verse of many another poet. We may conclude, then, that up to the end of the sixteenth century Croatian literary prose can be found only in the prayer and devotional books of the period, which were written, of course, without any consideration of purely literary values.

THE LITERARY ACTIVITY OF THE PROTESTANTS

While humanism and Italian literature were echoing all along the Croatian coast, especially in Dubrovnik, effecting a literary activity of great intensity, the young Croatian literature was exposed to another strong impulse from the north, an impulse that could have easily carried it much beyond the limit actually achieved had it not been cut off and stifled almost in its very inception. This aborted influence was, in fact, the religious movement known as the Reformation.

Limited at first to Germany, the Reformation soon found followers in neighboring countries; first in Slovenia, from whence it passed to Croatia and to that portion of Istria belonging to the Hapsburg and, therefore, the German sphere of culture. But the Protestant movement was stillborn on Croatian soil.

In the South Slavic lands, Protestantism enjoyed a short-lived success only in Slovenia. In Istria it remained limited almost exclusively to the clergy and nobility because the German element was so small that the fight that State and Church were waging against the followers of the new doctrine was not difficult. This was especially true of the Venetian portion of Istria where the civil and ecclesiastical authorities put up a strong and rigid defense against the new phenomenon. The persecution was extremely severe; it suffices to recall the case of Ivan Vergerije, bishop of Pula, whose body was exhumed and cremated in public, merely because his brother, Petar Pavao, a known Protestant and bishop of Kopar, had once declared that his brother Ivan shared his opinion. A similar case was that of Marcus de Dominis (Gospodnetić), archbishop of Split. Although he had died before seeing the end of his own trial, the sentence was read before his cadaver, his picture, and his works, and then all were burned.

On the other hand, in Upper Croatia and in Prekomurje, the Reformation was spread by officers and soldiers of the Austrian Army, who were for the most part natives of Carniola and Styria. The Austrian garrisons were in fact centers of the Protestant movement, two of the best known being Karlovac in Croatia and Koprivnica in Podravina. In these lands the Reformation counted quite a number of followers even among the leaders of society, one such example being the Ban, Petar Erdödi, and his predecessor, the hero of Sziget, Nikola Zrinski. However, in 1556, the new governor of Croatia, Bishop Juraj Drašković, forced all Protestants to return to Catholicism or leave the country.

For the most part, the same sources of Protestant influence affected both Croatian literature and the cultural and literary history of Slovenia. In fact, the dependence of Croatian Protestant literature on the Slovenian is so evident that it is only fair to admit that without the great figures of Slovenian Protestantism, the development of such Croatian literature would have been extremely difficult even in its limited quantity and given its small importance.

The promoter of Slovenian Protestantism was the former Catholic priest Primož Trubar (1508–86), who was joined by Baron Ivan Ungnad. In Germany, where they had taken refuge, they translated into Slovenian the books considered most indispensable for the diffusion of the new doctrine: a catechism, the Bible, and the New Testament. Advised by Petar Pavao Vergerije, Trubar considered making a Croatian translation of the Protestant books and having them printed in Glagolitic and Cyrillic characters, so that they could be used in Istria, Croatia, and Dalmatia, but the plan was abandoned after Trubar broke off with Vergerije. Trubar had no luck with Matija Vlacić-Franković (M. Flatius Illyricus) either. Fate seemed to decree that all that would be done for

Croatian literature in the next fifty years would be the work of two or three Croatian writers, more modest in their aim than those mentioned above, but extraordinarily active. Antun Dalmatin, known as "The Patriarch," and Stjepan Konzul Istranin, both of whom labored tirelessly at the very center of all Protestant activity for Slovenia and Croatia, Urach in Bavaria, and continued their work until the death of Trubar. And with theirs are usually linked the names of Juraj Juričić of Vinodol and Juraj Cvečić of Pazin.

Protestant literary activity in Croatia limited itself, for the most part, to the translation of Genesis, the books of the Prophets, the New Testament, some evangelical works, and some catechisms; for the explanation of the Gospel an apostil was published: *Kratko istlmačenje vsih nedeljskih evangelijov i poglavitesih praznikov kroz sve leto* (A Short Explanation of the Gospel for All Sundays and Holidays). The most important of the apologetic works are *Artikuli ili deli stare prave vere krstjanske* (Fundamentals of the Old True Christian Faith) and *Bramba* (Apologetics). The models for these works were mainly the Slovenian translations of Trubar, rendered from the German, or else German Protestant books of this type.

The history of these pioneers of Protestant literature in Slovenia and Croatia is indeed very sad. Exposed in their own country to the most cruel persecution, and suffering the harshness of privation and humiliation in their exile, they consecrated themselves nonetheless to this national and religious cause and carried on a truly admirable literary activity. Their program was perforce religious in character, but it identified itself with and complemented their national program in the best sense of the word. In fact, the writing of the Gospel and the preaching of the divine word in the vernacular rather than in the already dead language of Latin or any other foreign language then used in the Church meant, for that age and those countries, the reawakening of national feelings and a love for the mother tongue; these men were then, at one and the same time, shepherds, patriots, and writers.

KAJKAVIAN LITERATURE

Toward the middle of the sixteenth century, when literary tradition south of the river Kupa could already boast a number of centuries of life and activity, the northern regions of Croatia, with Varaždin and Zagreb as their political and cultural centers, were just beginning to enter the literary agon. In fact, during this period the territory enjoyed a certain degree of political and cultural autonomy within the Hapsburg Empire, and it was at that time that the first poetic and prose works of a vernacular literature began to appear. Quite apart from the influence exercised by the poetry of southern Croatia, and apart from the Glagolitic activity so closely related to the literature of the north, there rapidly developed an original and autonomous poetry written in the Kajkavian dialect, and preserved in a number of collections, the oldest of which dates back to 1593. The major portion of this poetry is religious in character, although it does contain some didactic, lyrical, and epic poems as well.

This literary activity of northern Croatia received further impetus through the establishment of a publishing house at Nedelišće. It was here that the notary Ivan Pergošić published the *Decretum tripartitum* in 1574, a translation of the Common Law of the Hungarian jurist István Verböczy. Pergošić translated some portions of the codex into Shtokavian, a fact which points to the need that even the first Kajkavian writers felt to break free of the narrow limitations of their own dialect. Aside from this point, the work is of greater import to the history of jurisprudence than to literature. The *Decretum* is, however, the first attempt to use the Kajkavian dialect as a literary medium.

It is interesting and significant that writings in the Kajkavian dialect dealt almost exclusively with subjects of practical and current interest, that is, common law and national history, two themes almost totally absent in the literature of Dubrovnik written in the vernacular.

An interesting early historian was Antun Vramec (1531–87), pastor of Saint Mark's in Zagreb, who besides writing two volumes of "Explanations of the Gospels" (Varaždin, 1586) also wrote a *Chronicle* (Ljubljana, 1578), in which he relates in careful chronological order and with great objectivity the most important historical events of his time.

Another work of the period gives an account of the battle of Sziget; it is conserved for us in the Glagolitic script and was composed originally in the Kajkavian dialect by Ferenc Crnko, chamberlain of Nikola Zrinski. The author, a witness of that sad and glorious event of Croatian history, wrote so vivid a description that his work was translated into Latin and German.

THE SEVENTEENTH CENTURY

THE DUBROVNIK TRIO OF THE GOLDEN AGE: GUNDULIĆ, PALMOTIĆ, AND BUNIĆ

Three great poets emerged in Dubrovnik during the first half of the seventeenth century: Gundulić, Palmotić, and Bunić. Thus Dubrovnik became the literary center not only of Dalmatia, but of all the other

Croatian provinces, and for good reason acquired the title "the Croatian Athens." Its prominence as a center of culture was due in no small measure to its favorable political climate; for while some Croatian provinces (Bosnia, Hercegovina, a portion of Upper Croatia and of Slavonia) were still under Turkish domination, and others (Istria, Dalmatia, and the rest of Upper Croatia and Slavonia) were controlled by Venice or Hungary, Dubrovnik alone was able to preserve its independence in the face of constant Venetian and Turkish advances.

New names and models brought about a radical change in the literature of Dubrovnik during the period in question. Although it is true that literature in the time of Gundulić was characterized by a tendency to pious moralizing, it was also true that, notwithstanding the example of the pious writers of religious drama, Gundulić and Palmotić wrote deeply moving works free of false sentimentality, works which reveal them as genuine poets.

There was an important new literary tendency gaining momentum, one which concerned itself with politics and patriotism; although this interest had already been expressed in the fifteenth century, it did not assume the definite literary character which Gundulić, with *Osman* and *Dubravka*, and Palmotić, with *Pavlimir*, were to assign to it. The Italian literature of the seventeenth century, whose writers were spurred on to new political and patriotic consciousness as a result of the Spanish domination of their land, had an undeniable influence on the spread of this new literary theme. Another important factor in reawakening expressions of patriotism in Croatian literature was the energetic effort of the Church to convince both Austria and Venice to move against the Turks.

In the poetry of the seventeenth century we also find a more sophisticated diction and a parallel advance in prosody; the heavy dodecasyllable is replaced by the more flexible eight-syllable verse generally divided into two quatrains.

Among the various factors which helped bring about this flourishing of the literature and culture of Dubrovnik at this time, perhaps the single most important and decisive one was the settling of the Jesuits in that city. They came not only to educate and raise the level of morality among the youth, but, with a clear view of the Turkish threat, to awaken the dormant Croatian and Slavic patriotism, which was, in fact, easily indentifiable with the defense of Christian values. The Jesuits also gave new impetus and direction to the old gymnasium, which served to forge future generations of men of culture and letters.

In precisely this spiritual and cultural setting the best poet in the history of Dalmatia and Dubrovnik, Ivan (Dživo Franov) Gundulić (1589–

1638), was born. The first phase of his literary career produced erotic lyric poems which he called vain and frivolous (*tašte i isprazne*) and the rewriting of some ten Italian melodramas (*Arijadna* of Rinuccini, *Prozerpina ugrabljena* of Claudiano, *Armida* of Tasso, *Dijana*, etc.), which were presented on the stage with great success. Gundulić, however, often felt the urge to forswear these writings, considering them trivial and profane works, "products of the shadows," and not proper for a "Christian writer"; in line with his newly formulated principles, he therefore embarked on a new and more authentic literary career with a paraphrasing of the "Psalms of Penance" of David (1621).

A year later, he published the little poem *Suze sina razmetnoga* (The Tears of the Prodigal Son), a poetic rendition of the well-known parable of the Gospel. This is a group of extremely sensitive lyrics, made up of three songs (1332 lines), each corresponding to one of the three stages in the soul of a sinner: acknowledgment, confession, and repentance. The poem is a rich lyrical outburst which, because of its sincerity of feeling, the harmony of its elements, the suggestive beauty of the descriptions, and its brilliant style, has been judged by many to be one of the finest works in Old Croatian literature, a judgment supported by the fact that even today it is read with pleasure.

In contrast to the literary preference of the sixteenth century for non-moralistic pastoral dramas and comedies, Gundulić chose to write didactic mythological-romantic dramas. His *Dubravka* (staged in 1628), original in its theme and general treatment, is considered the best drama of its kind in Old Croatian literature. Apart from the fact that the work aims to entertain, it differs from other pastoral dramas in being patriotic allegory, didactic and moralistic in purpose; Gundulić explains to his audience that to attain a wise and free form of government, it is necessary to lead a healthy family and social life based upon love, mutual respect, and equality before the law. The lesson is woven around the yearly third of February celebration in honor of St. Blaise, patron of the city. The main event of every celebration is the marriage of the most handsome young man to the most beautiful girl of the republic. This simple theme offers Gundulić a perfect opportunity to sing the praises of his beloved city and its liberty, thus turning his pastoral drama into a hymn and a panegyric in honor of Dubrovnik.

Whereas in his first poem *Suze*, the poet is a pious Christian, and in his drama *Dubravka*, a proud local patriot, in his long heroic-romantic poem *Osman*, he becomes the generous Slav. In searching for a subject for his epic poem, Gundulić had for a time toyed with the idea of translating the *Gerusalemme liberata* of Tasso and dedicating his version to the Polish king, Sigismund III, who was at that time leading his nation in the defense of Christianity against the encroachments of the Ottoman Empire. But soon, influenced by the great Polish victory at Khotin near Chernovtsy (Ukraine) in 1621, and by the tragic death of the youthful and arrogant Sultan Osman, which was interpreted as the beginning of the end of the Ottoman Empire and, consequently, of Turkish domination in Europe, Gundulić abandoned his original project, substituting for it a more ambitious one: the creation of a modern epic, Christian and patriotic in theme and recounting the victory of the Polish prince Ladislas and the death of Osman. Throughout this long poem (twenty cantos, with cantos XIII and XIV incomplete and unedited until 1826), Gundulić faithfully follows the course of historical events, without, however, being a servile chronicler. His *Osman* is rather a romantic version of history, since he often deviates from historical detail and weaves in new sentimental subplots for esthetic reasons as well as to maintain the interest of the reader. After all, Gundulić is first of all a lyric poet. His personality permeates the poem, with a spirit which flows spontaneously from his sensitive lyrical soul; indeed, perhaps the best parts of the poem are precisely those in which the elements of lyricism and subjectivity are not bound by the recounting of the epic events. It should be noted that Gundulić makes exclusive use of the Ijekavian dialect as well as the spoken language of Dubrovnik, purified of the archaisms of the fifteenth and sixteenth centuries.

Gundulić occupies a privileged position in Croatian literature. Of the three masterpieces which earned him his reputation as the greatest poet of the Dalmatian cultural period, his *Suze* is by far the most beautiful and perfect of all his works. *Dubravka* was written with form as the primary consideration, that is, he was concerned with composing a drama, and *Osman*, too, seems to have stemmed from a determination to produce an epic for which the subject was especially appropriate, but his *Suze*, above all, flowed spontaneously from the depths of his soul. The fact that he is better known for his *Osman* is explained by the new subject matter of the poem, which was welcomed by a public already weary of the constant flow of religious works. However this may be, it can definitely be said that Gundulić skillfully and harmoniously fused in all three of his masterpieces deep Christian and patriotic sentiment together with a refined literary taste, resulting in examples of excellent composition and poetic form, lofty style, and a rich and pure language.

The dramatic work of Gundulić, while preserving many elements of the earlier tradition, retarded considerably the trend toward obscenity and bawdy humor. The fresh direction he gave to literature in Dubrovnik inspired an apt follower in the person of Junije (Džono) Palmotić (1607–57), a descendant of an old aristocratic family and a student of the Jesuits. Writing poetry became a passion with him at an early age; beginning at first in Latin (with poems of a religious nature for the most part), he soon wrote in Croatian, following the example of Gundulić. However, Palmotić is better known for his plays in the baroque and decadent manner fashionable at the time. He translated, adapted, and composed several dramas and tragicomedies ranging in content from themes of classical mythology or Italian poems to popular Slavic traditions, and thereby provided a repertory for the theatrical companies of Dubrovnik for a few years. Several of these dramas were staged in the main square (*prid dvorom*) and some were even accompanied by music, in imitation of the current Italian fashion of "dramas set to music." The tragicomedies *Došastje od Eneje k Ankizu* (The Coming of Aeneas to Anchises) and *Lavinija* are merely adaptations of the ninth and the eleventh and twelfth songs of Virgil's *Aeneid*; *Natjecanje Ajaksa i Uliksa* (Contest between Ajax and Ulysses), *Elena ugrabljena* (The Abduction of Helen), *Akil*, the drama *Atalanta* from the tenth book of Ovid's *Metamorphoses* (x,560), and others were also adaptations for the stage. The dramas of *Armida* and *Alčina* were based on themes from the Italian poems *Gerusalemme Liberata* of Tasso and *Orlando furioso* of Ariosto.

Palmotić draws on Italian poems even for the subject matter of his patriotic dramas, such as *Captislava* and *Bisernica* (which can be considered one and the same drama) and the more original *Danica* (a work of transition between the romantic and patriotic dramas). However, he uses Croatian names for his characters and localities, drawing for both upon the different Croatian provinces (Dalmatia, Bosnia, Hercegovina, northern Croatia) in order to stress their common ethnic origin and age-old friendly relations. The best of these melodramas is *Pavlimir*, in three acts, which deals with the origins of Dubrovnik according to the legend reported in the Chronicle of the Priest of Dioclea, a legend he may have encountered in the *Regno degli Slavi* (The Kingdom of the Slavic People) of Orbini (Pesaro, 1601) as well as in the chronicles of Dubrovnik.

Curiously enough, the analysis of human passions constitutes a major element in the dramas and tragicomedies of Palmotić, but even more curiously, these same passions figure hardly at all in the plot, which develops independent of psychological motivation; dramatic conflict emerges and is resolved apparently by the intervention of supernatural forces. It would seem that Palmotić tried to avoid exciting the emotions of his audience with intensely dramatic scenes. But his plays lack coherence, not only because of the changing attitudes of some of his characters, but also because of their basic lack of individual personality. His characterizations are inconsistent and awkward: instead of acting, his characters talk, and, even worse, in a baroque language completely inappropriate to the personalities they purport to represent. Finally, the dramatic effect of the characters is weakened as a result of the constant, almost obsessive, moralizing. While we can certainly derive some pleasure from the elegant poetic diction and the occasional richness of the language, it must be confessed that, on the whole, none of his numerous works can be considered great drama; indeed, all are witness to a seriously limited dramatic gift.

Although Palmotić seems to have preferred the drama to any other literary genre, his favorite work seems to have been his religious poem *Kristijada*, over which he labored for several decades, polishing and perfecting it until the time of his death. He wished, no doubt, to leave to posterity evidence of having been a *homo christianus et studiosus verae religionis cultor*. This poem was, then, a paraphrastic translation from the Latin of the monumental *Christias* of the sixteenth-century Italian poet Girolamo Vida. Palmotić thus entrusted his own fame as a man of letters to a work pious in purpose. He dedicated his version of the poem to Queen Christina of Sweden, on the occasion of her conversion to Catholicism.

None of the poets contemporary with Gundulić escaped his influence in the area of love poetry with the exception of Dživo Bunić Vučičević (1591–1658). Immediately following the death of Gundulić, Bunić enjoyed a great deal of authority with the city's literary groups. A prudent and honest merchant, an ardent patriot, a conscientious city official, he had the advantage over Gundulić of never having abandoned the lyric poetry in which he felt himself at greatest ease.

Bunić has left us *Plandovanje* (Leisure Time), a collection of some seventy love poems which rank among the most beautiful lyric compositions of the seventeenth century. In addition he wrote eclogues, such as *Razgovori pastijerski* (Pastoral Discourses), reminiscent of Virgil's, and some religious poems, *Pjesni duhovne* (Spiritual Poems) and a much praised poem clearly inspired by Gundulić, *Mandaljena pokornica* (The Penitent Magdalen; Ancona, 1530), which serve as transition to the religious poems of the seventeenth century. All of these, however, lack the freshness of *Suze*. The originality of Bunić does not consist so much in his ideals and feelings, expressed at times in contrived pathos, but rather in his having utilized with exquisite taste all the techniques and devices of poetry to compose graceful erotic poems. Bunić's lyrics certainly contributed to the revitalizing of Croatian poetry which was taking place during the seventeenth century under the influence of a newly discovered Italian appreciation for the classical lyric poets. In the works of Bunić anacreontic themes, the influence of Horace, and especially the preciosity of Marini and his literary school, are evident. But again, the distinguishing mark of Bunić's poetry is the form: instead of the dodecasyllable he uses the flowing, musical octosyllable; moreover, his poems are remarkably free from hyperbole, plays on words, and heavy baroque diction. Although lacking in original or profound thought, his lyrics are nonetheless engaging precisely because of their simple elegance of form and the warmth of their spontaneous and delicate expression.

THE IMITATORS OF GUNDULIĆ AND PALMOTIĆ IN DUBROVNIK AND DALMATIA

So great was the influence of Gundulić and especially of Palmotić on the drama that none of their contemporaries and immediate successors was able to defy the canons they established or, consequently, to write a single original work. The dramatic imagination of these two centered on romantic and patriotic themes, and exerted so strong an attraction that they dominated the theatre throughout the second half of the seventeenth century. The works of Paskoje Primović, Ivan Dživo Gučetić, Vice Pucić Soltanović, and Dživo Šiško Gundulić, for example, were merely derivative. Only Antun Gledjević (1659–1728) shows some independence. He does not direct his work exclusively to the service of moralizing as was then common, as can be seen in his dramas *Damira*, *Olimpija*, *Ermijona*, and *Zorislava*, but focuses on action resulting from human passions and omits the intervention of supernatural forces. His excellent characterizations portray men of flesh and blood; and, finally, he replaces the monotonous dodecasyllable with the lighter octosyllable.

Aside from poems of a religious-didactic character, the seventeenth century produced compositions dealing with those great (albeit sorrowful) political events of that period which concerned the small republic of Dubrovnik. For example, the *Trublja slovinska* of Vladislav Menčetić (1600–66) is a panegyric in honor of Petar Zrinski, author of *Adrianskog mora sirena* and grandnephew of the Ban Nikola, who had died heroically at Sziget in 1566. The poet looks to Petar for the liberation of his fellow countrymen from the Turkish yoke – a nice poetic and patriotic dream, inasmuch as in 1671, by order of the emperor Leopold, his hero was decapitated in Wiener Neustadt. The poem is impressive, dictated as it was spontaneously from a sincere enthusiasm for the hero on the part of a free citizen of Dubrovnik, who takes this opportunity to wish the same freedom to his less fortunate countrymen. The poem clearly sees the function of Croatia in the defense of Christianity and of Western culture, when it says:

> Italy would have drowned long ago
> in the sea of slavery,
> had the pounding waves of the Ottoman Empire
> not smashed against Croatian shores.[11]

The 1667 earthquake, which destroyed more than half of the city, coupled with the discovery of new water routes to the Orient, gravely damaged the economy of the republic and signaled its decline. These events were to leave a lasting impression on the literature of the city; they were treated in the works of such writers as Nikola Bunić, Baro Bettera, St. Gradić (*De Laudibus serenissimae reipublicae Venetae et cladibus patriae meae*; Venice, 1675), and especially Jaketa Palmotić Dionorić (1623–80), in his *Dubrovnik ponovljen* (Dubrovnik Reconstructed; Dubrovnik, 1678), a poem of 15,644 eight-foot lines dealing with the moral and material reconstruction of Dubrovnik following the disaster. A poorly organized work, this last poem is made up of a great number of varied elements which often have little or nothing to do with the main subject. The best part describes the panic, the destruction, and the deaths which occurred during the earthquake. While it cannot be said that the poem has any great literary value, it is, nevertheless, an important historical and cultural document.

Literature was to reflect yet another significant event, the Turkish defeat at Vienna in 1683. The first writer to record this victory for Christianity was Petar Kanavelović (1637–1719), who composed a small poem in honor of the victor, John Sobieski. Kanavelović is, however, even better known for his historical romance with religious overtones, *Ivan Biskup Trogirski* (Ivan, the Bishop of Trogir; Osijek, 1658), in which he describes the life, death, and miracles of the bishop of Trogir. His debt to Gundulić is evident, although the poem lacks organization and the psychological motivation of the characters is faulty.

Although there was relatively little written in this vein, the humorous poetry of this period is rich and interesting. The writers from Dubrovnik aimed much of their satire at their commercial rival, the city of Kotor, especially after Kotor was occupied by the Venetians. Šiško Menčetić

11/Od robstva bi davno u valih/potonula Italija,/o hrvatskieh da se žalih/more otmansko ne razbija.

had previously written in ironic poem attacking the corrupt language of that city.[12] The Benedictine Vetranović launched a bitter assault against the inhabitants of Perast (close neighbors of Kotor) who had sacked the island of Mljet, a property of the Benedictines. M. Držić ridiculed the citizens of Kotor in his comedy *Tripče*, and Paskoje Primović Latinčić joined in these attacks with his satires.

But apart from these satires directed against the people of Kotor and Korčula, there were other humorous works ridiculing the Petrarchan school of poetry. Representative of these are *Gorštak* (Mountaineer) by Ivan Bunić, *Radonja* by Vladislav Menčetić, and especially *Derviš* by Stjepo Djordjić or Djurdjević (1579–1632). In *Derviš*, a poem in fifty stanzas of six eight-foot lines, the protagonist, an exuberant peasant, is rendered sad and comical at the same time through the use of rough and elemental language studded with Turkish words.

The imitators of Gundulić and Palmotić from Dalmatia and the Croatian Littoral are numerous, but few of them are worth mentioning. Juraj Baraković (1548–1628) celebrated the city of Zadar in his poem of thirteen songs, *Vila Slovinska* (The Slavic Fairy), modeled after Zoranić's *Planine* (Mountains). He reduces the mythological themes to a minimum, preferring to linger over events of contemporary life, to emphasize the natural beauties of his country, and to express his love for it. His uncompleted poem *Draga rabska pastirica* (Draga, a shepherdess from Rab) is a panegyric to the city of Rab, a history in verse of the island of Rab from the times of Attila to its conquest by the Venetians. While in his first poem we can still find spontaneous and original passages, the same cannot be said of the second poem; *Draga* is rather a work done on commission and motivated by gratitude toward the nobles of that island. In spite of these shortcomings, Baraković, among all the Dalmatian writers of the seventeenth century, is distinguished by a genuine national sentiment, a superb versifying ability, and above all, by a preoccupation with life as it was lived, that is, a genuine realism. In this his work stands in marked contrast to that of his contemporaries, who wrote within a broad cosmopolitan convention that repeated fixed erotic, religious, or didactic themes regardless of their relevance to contemporary reality. Furthermore, it is thanks to Baraković's interest in and love of folk poetry that we still possess the beautiful *bugarštica* (folk poem) "Majka Margarita."

The learned, extremely active and prolific canon of Šibenik, Ivan Tomko Mrnavić (1580–1637), wrote several historical and religious works in both Latin and Italian, but unfortunately these have no merit

12/See *Stari Hrvatski Pisci* (Zagreb: Yugoslav Academy), II (1937), 336.

as poetry. His poem *Život Magdalene od knezov Zirova, plemena Budrišića* (Life of Magdalen Budrišić, Countess of Zirovo; Rome, 1626), a prosaic biography in verse, reveals the author's poor poetic gift despite its sincere patriotic sentiment; in it for the first time in literature the word *domovina,* meaning "fatherland," appears. Even less successful is his drama *Osmanšćica* (1631), a treatment of the same subject which inspired the *Osman* of Gundulić, that is the tragic death of Sultan Osman and the prelude to the coming liberation of Christians from the Turkish yoke. It is, however, a drama in form and title only; it contains words, but no action.

On the other hand, the priest from Bol on the island of Brač, Ivan Ivanišević (1608–65), left a work of greater value in *Kita cvitja razlikova* (Bouquet of Flowers; Venice, 1642), a short collection of poems whose theme is generally religious and which reveals the author's sublime conception of the poet's vocation. In spite of the fact that he lived in a period in which the baroque and the Italian euphuism were the literary fashion, he was not carried away by their empty formalism, but rather cultivated a style that was simple, natural, and classical. He resembles Gundulić in the sincerity of his sentiments, and some of his poems, because of their refreshing quality, are among the best religious compositions in Croatian literature.

The theater of this period is best represented by Marin Gazarović, a nobleman of Hvar, who wrote some sacred dramas (*Prikazanje Sv. Beatrice, Faustina i Simplicija*/Play of Saints Beatrice, Faustinus, and Simplicius, *Prikazanje života Svetih Ciprijana i Justine*/Play of Saints Cyprian and Justina, etc.) and pastoral dramas (*Ljubica, Murat*) composed in octosyllables and dialogue form. But rather than being original dramas, these are adapted translations from the Italian of pious, moralistic, medieval legends in verse.

The longest work in Croatian literature is the labor of a priest from Split, Jerolim Kavanjin (1643–1714), *Bogatstvo i ubožtvo* (Wealth and Poverty; Zagreb, 1661). A religious poem of 32,658 eight-foot lines written in the Shtokavian-Ijekavian dialect, and baroque in style, it fails in its attempt to blend a poetic religious motive with the patriotic. The work gives the impression of being a poetic diary, in which the author has noted all his diverse impressions in the order in which they occurred throughout his life.

Andrija Vitaljić (1642–1725), a priest from Vis, wrote few works but all of them are religious in character. He translated the Psalms in elegant verse form (*Iztumačenje pisnih Davidovih*/Interpretation of the

Psalms of David; Venice, 1703), using the Chakavian-Ikavian dialect. Taking the *Kristijada* of Palmotić as his model, he composed in the Shtokavian-Ijekavian dialect his *Ostan Božje ljubavi* (Spurring on the Love of God; Venice, 1712), a poem in ten cantos glorifying the infinite divine love which Jesus brought to fruition through his passion and death. In this poem the lyrical subjective element prevails over the narrative and objective. Though it lacks overall unity, it has the merit of elegance and musicality.

LINGUISTIC AND HISTORICAL LITERATURE

The Jesuit Bartol Kašic Bogdančić (Cassius), who was born in Pag in 1575 and died in Rome in 1650, wrote several pamphlets of Christian edification in his native dialect Chakavian-Ikavian, but it is his philological work which earned him greater renown. He wrote the first Croatian grammar, *Institutiones linguae illyricae* (Rome, 1604), and for the first time indicated with proper precision the accentuation of Croatian words. In the capacity of apostolic delegate he traveled through Bosnia and Hercegovina and mastered the Shtokavian dialect as is evidenced by his *Život Gospodina našega Isukrsta* (Life of Our Lord Jesus Christ; Rome, 1638), and especially by his *Ritual rimski* (Roman Ritual; Rome, 1640) where he calls the Shtokavian-Ikavian dialect the dialect of Bosnia, declares it "the most common, and that which everyone can easily understand," and for that reason proposes it as the common national language.

The activity of Kašić is similar to that of Šime Budinić of Zadar (died 1600) and Faust Vrančić of Šibenik (1551–1617) in the preceding century, and fits within the scope of the Counter-Reformation's program. In Budinić's *Pokorni psalmi Davidovi* (Penitential Psalms of David; Venice, 1582), we encounter the first effort to introduce diacritical marks into the Croatian alphabet, an effort which would finally succeed two and one half centuries later. The main work of Vrančić was *Dictionarium quinque nobilissimarum Europae linguarum: latinae, italicae, germanicae, dalmaticae et ungaricae* (Venice, 1595).

Two Jesuits were also involved in this vital work of lexicography, Jakov Micaglia (1600–54) and A. Della Bella (1655–1737), whose respective works were *Thesaurus linguae illyricae* (1649) and *Dizionario italiano-latino-illirico* (1728). The latter is important for the wealth of its quotations from the old literature of Dubrovnik and also because in it, for the first time, we see a differentiation between the two accents on the long vowels of the Shtokavian dialect. We should also mention here the immense *Lexicon latino-italico-illyricum* (Dubrovnik, 1801), by the tireless Franciscan lexicographer Joakim Stulli (1729–1817). *Grammatica della lingua illirica* (1808) by F. M. Appendini (1768–1837), considered one of the best of the old grammars of the Croatian language; *Vocabolario di tre nobilissimi linguaggi: italiano, illirico e latino* (1699) by Ivan Tanzlinger Zanotti (1651–1705); *Dictionar* (Graz, 1670) by Juraj Habdelić (1609–78); and *Gazophylacium* (1740) by Ivan Belostenec (1595–1675), who spent his life collecting, from native speakers, words used in the regions where the Shtokavian, Chakavian, and Kajkavian dialects were spoken.

In spite of the fact that all this activity was aimed primarily at facilitating the work of missionaries in the Croatian territory, which had such a variety of dialects, it rendered an invaluable service to the further development of Croatian literature, contributing, however unintentionally, to the dissemination of the Shtokavian dialect (at the expense of the Chakavian and Kajkavian dialects and thus to the preparation of a common language. This was, indeed, an outcome of the activity carried on by the Counter-Reformation, although this tendency toward a common literary language did not emerge fully until the nineteenth century.

The Counter-Reformation contributed both directly and indirectly to Croatian national history as well. The national ideas already fostered by humanism became more definite in the atmosphere of the Counter-Reformation, which used this nationalism to revive the pride of the Slavic people. Quite apart from *De origine successibusque Slavorum* (Venice, 1532), in which the learned Dominican from Hvar, Vicko Pribojević (Priboevus), sings the past and present glories of the Slavic people, we have *Il regno degli Slavi* (Pesaro, 1601) by the Benedictine of Dubrovnik, Mavro Orbini (died 1614), which certainly does enter into the plans of the Propagation of the Faith. This work, which was translated into Spanish and Russian, enjoyed a great if unmerited success in Slavic historiography; in fact, the imaginary and novelistic framework of this book, which often falls into the legendary and grotesque (except when dealing directly with contemporary events), makes it a mere exaltation and glorification of the Slavic people. Quite another matter is *De regno Dalmatiae et Croatiae* (Amsterdam, 1666), which is a carefully documented and thought out study written with great acumen by Ivan Lučić of Trogir (died in Rome, 1679). It is the first critical history of Dalmatia, old Croatia, and the neighboring countries, and extends up to the Venetian occupation of Dalmatia in the fifteenth century. During periods of political quarrels between Croatians and Hungarians, a period, consequently, of increased interest in their own national history, *De regno* would be quoted with great frequency and even reprinted in part.

LITERATURE IN BOSNIA

A significant factor in the destiny and cultural history of the Croatians of Bosnia, Hercegovina, and Slavonia was the activity of the Franciscan friars. Native Franciscans appeared in Bosnia during the first half of the fourteenth century; their first convent of Sutjeska near Vareš dates back to 1378, or shortly before that of Srebrenica ("Silver Mine") which would give its name to the entire Franciscan province, *Bosnia argentina* ("Silvery Bosnia"). They immediately gained the affection and trust of the people, sentiments rendered even more profound and mutual during the Turkish occupation and persecutions, when the Franciscans remained the only clergy to share with the people the pains of that heavy yoke. Although they labored to save souls under the most prohibitive conditions, they did not neglect to cultivate the sciences and letters. In fact they left modest works in theology, philosophy, jurisprudence, medicine, oratory, philology, etc., but more important were their catechisms, prayer books, and Christian inspirational works, almost all of them translations or adaptations in Croatian of Latin or Italian works. These works of the Franciscans are of great philological interest and value; they are written in the dialect which two centuries later would be adopted as the literary language by other Croatian regions. They are interesting also from the point of view of orthography since some of them are printed in the so-called *bosančica* or *bosanska ćirilica* or *hrvatsko pismo* (Bosnian Cyrillic script), that is an adaptation of the original Cyrillic alphabet.

The appearance of the Franciscans in Croatian literature during the seventeenth century stems from the Counter-Reformation, which caused their literary activity to take on an exclusively religious-didactic character. In contrast, few Croatian Muslims from Bosnia wrote in their native tongue, preferring to distinguish themselves as military leaders and scientists at the service of the Sublime Porte or as poets in Arabic. Among the Muslim writers from Bosnia who did contribute to the development of Croatian literature was Muḥammad Hawāʾī Uskūfī from Tuzla, who compiled the first Croatian-Turkish dictionary, *Maqbūlʾ-i*

ʿārif (1631), and also left some fine religious poems. The rich and generous Ḥasan Ḳāʾimī-Baba from Sarajevo, besides his poems in Turkish, wrote some patriotic ones in Croatian, known as "kaside" (*ḳaṣīda*).

The greatest representative of Croatian literature in Bosnia during the late sixteenth and early seventeenth centuries is the Franciscan Matija Divković, who was born in Jelaške near Vareš in 1563 and died in the nearby convent of Olovo in 1631. He is the only one to have left works of genuine poetic value. Despite their didactic intent, they are filled with beautiful tales, and have become with the passing of time a popular patrimony distinguished for their simple yet attractive style and their rich and pure language. He wrote *Nauk krstjanski* (Christian Doctrine, Venice, 1611); *Besjede svrhu evandjelja* (Sermons Based on the Gospel; Venice, 1616), which are basically adaptations of various Latin and Italian catechisms; *Sto čudesa blažene Divice Marije* (One-Hundred Miracles of the Virgin Mary; Venice, 1616), a compilation from the Latin version by the fifteenth-century German Dominican Johannes Herolt. From Divković's poems included in the *Nauk* ("Pjesanca na Božić"/Song for Christmas, "Pjesanca na dan mrtvijeh"/Song for All Souls Day, "Plač"/Weeping, etc.), we are led to believe that he must have been very familiar with the literary production of Dalmatia and Dubrovnik as well as the works in the Glagolitic script, since the *Nauk* comprises ancient ecclesiastical songs of the Croatian Littoral that only Divković reproduced in the Bosnian language (the Shtokavian-Ikavian dialect). His so-called sacred dramas in eight-foot lines were also written in that dialect: *Abramovi versi* (Abraham's verses) and *Život svete Katarine* (The Life of St. Catherine).

Many Franciscans followed the example of Divković and wrote religious pamphlets which were for the most part translations and compilations of foreign works or works of Croatian writers from Dalmatia and Dubrovnik. Among these were Pavao Posilović of Glamoč (died 1651), Stjepan Matijević of Tuzla, Pavao Papić of Sarajevo, Ivan Bendulović of Donji Vakuf, and Ivan Ančić of Duvno.

THE COUNTER-REFORMATION IN NORTHERN CROATIA

Although after the Turkish defeat at Vienna (1683) and the peace of Karlowitz (1699) northern Croatia could consider itself at peace, the seventeenth century witnessed an internal turmoil which tended to discourage the growth of literary activity, for Croatia's position within the Hungarian cultural sphere was not at all advantageous from the point of view of literary development. Latin was the official language of the state, the courts of law, and the schools, and was, in general, the language spoken by the nobility and most educated persons. The few works written in Croatian resulted from the propaganda of the Catholic Church, which, following the example of the Reformation, adopted the national tongue.

However, as is to be expected, these books were for the most part religious in nature: the prayer book (*Molitvene knjižice*, 1640) of the Jesuit Nikola Krajačević Sartorious (1582–1653) as well as his Gospel (*Sveti evangeliomi*; Graz, 1651), the latter published by the energetic bishop of Zagreb, Petar Petretić (1619–67); the practical catechism *Pervi otca našega Adama greh* (The First Sin of our Father Adam; Graz, 1674) and *Zercalo Mariansko* (Marian Mirror; Graz, 1662) of Juraj Habdelić (1609–78). The interest of these works lies largely in the fact that they contain some religious poems meant to substitute for the *nečiste pogane, latrene i popevke* (profane love poems). To facilitate the substitution, the poems are set to the music of folk songs. Thus, these religious poems are excellent original sources for tracing the flowering of folk poetry in the Kajkavian territory even prior to the Reformation.

Two other Kajkavian poets, Matijaš Magdalenić and Gabrijel Jurjević, belonged to this same group of religious writers. They treated philosophical, moral, and religious themes, the former in *Zvončac* (Meditations on the Four Final Things; Graz, 1670), the latter in *Listi heroov* (Stories of Great Men; Vienna, 1675). But these works are no more than adaptations and free translations of the religious works of now forgotten Hungarian writers.

An important development at this time was the re-editing and republishing of the Glagolitic books, a project conceived and carried out by the Congregation for the Propagation of the Faith. Ever since the fifteenth century a great need had been felt for these books in the regions where Mass was being celebrated in Church Slavonic.[13] This task was first assigned to two Franciscans: Franjo Glavinić (1586–1650), well known for his broad cultural background, and Rafael Levaković (1580–1648), a man of remarkable intelligence. Together, after many difficulties, they published a catechism, *Nauk krstjanski* (Christian Doctrine, 1628), and a breviary in Glagolitic (1648) which contain several features of the Russian variant of Church Slavonic. The successful publishing of the Croatian Glagolitic books owed much to the tireless work of two men: the conceiver and promoter of the revision of Glagolitic books,

13/V. Nicolao Šojat, *De privilegio linguae paleoslavicae in liturgia romana* (Roma, 1947).

the bishop of Zadar, Vicko Zmajević (died 1745); and the editor of *Missale romanum slavonico idiomate editum* (1741),[14] also a bishop of the same city, Matija Karaman (1700–71).

LITERATURE IN UPPER CROATIA

In spite of the disadvantageous political and social conditions existing in northern Croatia, some literary activity did develop there which reflected the state of mind of all levels of society, who shared a Christian and anti-Turkish feeling. This historic and patriotic literature foreshadowed the future role of this region in Croatian political life in general. This literary activity is of even greater import in view of the absence of literary models in the countries to the north, under whose cultural influence Croatia found itself.

Among the writers of the seventeenth century, Katarina Zrinski (1625–73), the wife of Ban Petar and one of the most interesting figures of Croatian history in that period, occupied a unique position. A descendant of the noble family of Frankapan, she was the spirit of the conspiracy against the Hapsburgs devised by her husband and her half-brother Frano Krsto Frankapan. That conspiracy ended in sorrow on the scaffolds of Wiener Neustadt in 1671 with the beheading of Zrinski and Frankapan, and Katarina died insane two years later in a convent in Graz. This tragedy marked the disappearance of the two best-known noble families which for some centuries had governed the fortunes of Croatia. However, while Katarina made a far greater contribution to politics than she did to literature, her manual of prayers, *Putni tovaruš* (Road Companion, 1661), written in the Chakavian-Ikavian dialect combined with elements of the Kajkavian dialect, was the first work in Croatian literature to be written by a woman.

Another writer of this period was her husband, Petar Zrinski (1621–71), who translated from Hungarian into Croatian the poem of his brother Nikola, *Adriai Tengernek Syrenaia* (Vienna, 1651), dealing with the deeds of his own ancestor Nikola, the hero of Sziget (1556), and published it in Venice (1660) under the title *Adrianszkoga mora syrena* (Siren of the Adriatic Sea), later changed to *Opsida sigetska* (Siege of *Sziget*). This intrepid leader and governor was a man of great culture, though he lacked marked poetic talent. Nevertheless, his rough language is remarkably attractive, especially when contrasted with the sugary and empty phrases which characterized the Dalmatian and Dubrovnik poets of that epoch. In addition, there is great philological interest in the

14/Cf. Japundžić Marko, T.O.R., *Matteo Karaman (1700–1771), Archbishop of Zadar* (Roma, 1961).

dialect he used and the archaisms with which his poem literally swarms. *Opsida sigetska* is a historical and sentimental poem which blends the ideal with reality and fantasy. In spite of his effort to eliminate some of the legendary elements, the poem is still closer to the original Hungarian text than is the *Kristijada* of Palmotić to the *Christias* of Marco Girolamo Vida.

The poet of truest lyric genius was Frano Krsto Frankapan (1643–71), whose poems remained undiscovered until two hundred years after his tragic death, when the Imperial Archives were opened and among the trial documents a bundle of papers entitled "Frangipani croatice conscripta" containing a number of poems written on loose sheets of paper and entitled *Gartlic za čas kratiti* (The Garden in Which to Cheat Time; Zagreb, 1871) was found. The poems form a collection, some lyric, some erotic, some thoughtful, each reflecting the state of mind experienced by the poet in the critical situation which soon was to lead him to the scaffold. Although the poems are neither totally original nor profound in thought, they do have a certain freshness, a lightness and variety in structure and prosody; above all, the tension of simultaneous overtones of sadness and joy expresses a moving sincerity and feeling. Of special interest are those poems which the poet calls *dijačke*, which are very close in content and form to the folk poems in Shtokavian, although Frankapan, like Zrinski, writes in a mixed Chakavian-Kajkavian dialect.

We have seen that the contribution of northern Croatia to literature proper was rather limited during the seventeenth century. A better showing was made in national history, through the efforts of two authentic historians: Ratkaj and Vitezović.

Juraj Ratkaj (1612–66), baron, ex-Jesuit, canon of Zagreb, and a deeply committed patriot, wrote in a language rich in Shtokavian-Ikavian elements from southern Croatia. A product of his great love for his country is the *Memoria regum et banorum regnorum Dalmatiae, Croatiae et Slavoniae* (Vienna, 1652), in which he demonstrates the sovereign equality of Croatia and Hungary in the Empire, underlining the continued Croatian sovereignty as seen in the person of the Ban.

Pavao Ritter Vitezović (1652–1713), who was primarily a scientist, was also active in letters, especially in Latin verse. He was one of the most interesting figures of the seventeenth century; he devoted his life to science and letters and to his homeland, gaining fame even abroad for his scientific works. He was born in Senj in 1652 of a recently ennobled family with a military past, and died in Vienna in 1713.[15]

As a poet, Vitezović is primarily known for *Odilenje sigetsko* (Separa-

15/V. Vj. Klaić, *Život i djela Pavla Rittera Vitezovića*/Life and Works of Pavao Ritter Vitezović (Zagreb, 1914).

tion at Sziget; Linz, 1648; complete ed., Vienna, 1685; 3rd ed., Zagreb, 1836). Whereas his other occasional poems, epistles, and anagrams, written in Latin, are of interest only insofar as they reveal the life of the poet and illuminate the events of his time, his *Odilenje* is more important, dealing as it does with the same theme as the *Opsida sigetska* of Zrinski. But it is made up of monologues, dialogues, epistles, and epitaphs, loosely held together and grouped in four parts, and they do not make for pleasurable reading in spite of the fact that the verses are more formally correct, and show greater metrical skill than do those of Zrinski and Krnarutić.

Among the other non-scientific works of Vitezović in Croatian are the *Priričnik* (Book of Proverbs; Zagreb, 1703), a collection of proverbs and old folk sayings, and moral and philosophical maxims; *Kalendarium* (1695); and especially *Lado horvacki iliti Sibila* (Sybil), which was a great success and similar to the Italian "books of fate" by means of which the reader could delude himself into believing he could foresee his fate.

Zrinski and Vitezović share certain characteristic qualities of diction, since they both freely mix the Chakavian and Kajkavian dialects; but while in Zrinski the mixture is casual, in Vitezović it is consciously aimed at blending three dialects for the purpose of creating a common Croatian literary language. Vitezović's efforts anticipated by more than one hundred years the Illyrian Awakening from which would finally emerge a unified Croatian literary language.

His conscious concern with Croatian language extended to orthography as well. Worthy of note is his effort to apply diacritic signs to the Croatian alphabet, an effort already begun by Budinić 120 years before with his *Penitential Psalms of David* (1582) and the translation of Peter Canisius' catechism under the title *Summa nauka hristianskoga* (An Epitome of Christian Doctrine; Rome, 1583).

Among Vitezović's historical works the best known is *Kronika* (Zagreb, 1696), a chronology of the most important world events beginning with the creation of the world and going up to 1690; in it he set forth his complete political and cultural program. His second historical work is *Croatia rediviva* (Zagreb, 1700), in which he speaks of great Croatia in the spirit of Orbini. His lamentations in *Plorantis Croatiae saecula duo* (Zagreb, 1703) and *Bosnia captiva* (Trnava, 1712), verse chronicles in elegant hexameters dealing with the national history of the sixteenth and seventeenth centuries, spring from a burning patriotism. Particularly well known is his great Croatian heraldic work, *Stemmatografia sive armorum Illyricorum delineatio, descriptio et restitutio* (1701).

With his political, literary, and linguistic program, Vitezović exercised so great an influence on Croatian national life as to be considered the father and precursor of the Croatian political, cultural, and literary revival which would only become effective some one hundred and fifty years later. Following his example, later generations would create a common literary language based on the Shtokovian dialect; Ljudevit Gaj would also follow his norms in orthographical reform, and the term "Croatian" would definitely replace the terms *slovinski*, *slavenski*, and *ilirski*, or, at the very least, these names become synonymous with it, embracing thus, under the one name, all the various ethnic provinces: northern Croatia, Dalmatia, Istria, Bosnia, Hercegovina, and Slavonia.

Juraj Križanić (1618–83), a Greek-Catholic priest and Pan-Slavist, became a philologist by pure accident. Even as a youth he cherished the idea of the union of Western and Eastern Christianity, and to this idea he devoted all his efforts as a theologian, historian, and philologist. At first he wanted to win back for the Catholic Church only the Serbian Orthodox people who had settled within the Croatian national territory; later, however, after he had come in contact with Russian religious thinkers in Rome, he enlarged his original plan to include bringing to Catholicism the most numerous Slavic people, the Russians. To this end he travelled to Rome, Constantinople, Poland, the Ukraine, and Russia, where he endured exile in Siberia, and finally he crowned a life of suffering and struggle for his faith in Christ by his death at the siege of Vienna in 1683. His life-long program had called for the Russians to lead the other Slavic people to unification under a common language, culture, and literature.

While no trace of his projected Croatian grammar is extant, we do have proof of his ability and the boldness of his plan in his reform of the Cyrillic orthography, which represents the first attempt of its kind and precedes that of Vuk S. Karadžić by almost two centuries. But his main philological work is *Principii grammaticali* (Moscow, 1848–9) in which he tried to create a language composed of equal parts of Church Slavonic, Russian, and Croatian; even though experience has shown that such artificial languages are not viable, the work has the distinction of being the first comparative Slavic grammar.

Although the greater part of the linguistic projects of Križanić inevitably fell short of their aim, not only because of their very nature but because they were premature, his political and social projects might have been extremely effective had they been advanced a few years later. Križanić delineated his own ideas on politics, economics, and society in his *Politika*, in which he speaks of the ideal government of a country, constantly mindful of the situation in Russia, for whose land and people he had a most sincere affection. It should be recognized, however, that underlying this attraction to Russia was his religious purpose of gaining for the Church of Rome the largest group of Slavic people, an ideal which he carried to his grave. Križanić was, then, sincere in his Pan-Slavism, but even more, he was an uncompromising Catholic. His failure to achieve the unification of the churches or even of the Slavic peoples cannot render less admirable his tireless activity, his great energy, the boldness of his proposals, and the breadth of his culture.

THE EIGHTEENTH CENTURY

In the history of Croatian literature, the eighteenth century marks the end of the provincial and the beginning of a national literature; moreover, it draws a clear dividing line between two literary periods: one, represented by an older generation, considered culture and literature a privilege reserved for the upper classes in their leisure time; the other, represented by younger men, saw the arts and sciences as means of fulfilling a sacred duty to improve the social, cultural, and political conditions of the nation. These new ideas did not originate in Croatia, but rather reached it through Italy and especially Germany.

The Italian influence was felt particularly through the many academies which were being established in Zadar, Split, Dubrovnik, etc., modeled after those in Italy, whose aim was to replace the degenerated literary taste of the Italian marinism with an older simplicity by directly imitating the classical Latin and Greek writers. But as a result of replacing the national tongue with Latin, Croatian literature suffered considerable impoverishment; naturally, other factors contributed to this literary decline, such as the political and economic dissolution of the little republic of Dubrovnik, whose greatest blow was the earthquake of 1667. No better were the conditions in the rest of Dalmatia, where the people lived under the rule of Venice, which did not seem interested either in improving the economy of the country or in stimulating a literature in the national language. And so the Croatian Adriatic coast, which for the past three centuries had been the center of Croatian literary activity, had to surrender this role to the less oppressed regions under Hapsburg rule, although these regions certainly could not boast of the same literary tradition.

Later, following the Germanization and centralization under Maria Theresa and Joseph II, a great national movement would be engendered and carried aloft on the wings of the French Revolution. The awakening of a national conscience and the impulse given to general education would effect a momentum which would create an interest in a literature in the Croatian language, a language which was to bloom rich and strong and was to contribute greatly to the unification of all the provinces of Croatia and to a political, cultural, and literary revival during the first half of the nineteenth century.

DALMATIA AND DUBROVNIK

Before passing to an analysis of the literature of northern Croatia, the new cultural center of the country, let us first examine the surviving literary activity in Dubrovnik. Academies were being founded everywhere with the aim of reviving an interest in letters and the sciences. Their ultimate achievement was rather mediocre, however. Despite the later introduction of French into the discussions of the academies, French literature never had any great influence on letters in Dubrovnik, with the exception of the theater, where the plays of Molière had a notable success. Therefore, it may be said that the Croatian literature of Dubrovnik marks a descending parabola during the eighteenth century, in both quality and quantity. Although there was no lack of literary genius at that time, most of the gifted men there preferred to enter the service of other countries, with the result that there were very few works of value written in the national tongue. Nevertheless, that literature might have taken a more favorable turn in Dubrovnik is demonstrated by the example of Ignjat Djurdjević, one of the best poets in the history of this city who appears as the last spark of a smothered fire.

Ignjat Djordjić or Djurdjević (1675–1737), of recent nobility, was at first a carefree and strange young man for whom satires and love poems had provided "serious bothers." He later became a Jesuit and then a Benedictine, completely dedicated to religious poetry and the sciences. Djurdjević is a *poeta natus*, an essentially lyric poet, who blended refined taste with almost perfect form in poems revealing his broad culture.

His lyric poems, *Pjesni razlike* (Miscellaneous Poems; Zagreb, 1855), are for the most part love poems, humorously light in tone; seldom does he treat love seriously, and he avoids the conventional theme of unrequited love and the trite descriptions of the loved one so common in the Dubrovnik imitators of Petrarch. The poet captures moments of happiness or sorrow, and paints small and complete pictures, rendered even more beautiful by lively imagery, vigorous diction, and formal elegance of style, but the sentiments expressed seem completely insincere. Nevertheless, some of the poems, with their undeniable charm, are among the best in all the literature of Dubrovnik; such are "Zgoda ljuvena" (Love Scene) or those modeled after the eclogues of Ovid, *Ekloge aliti razgovori pastierski* (Pastoral Conversations), or the poems in dialogue *Pjesni pirne iliti začinke* (Nuptial Songs) and obscene epithalamia. Despite the common themes, and the rather mechanical associations, his poems reveal something too of the poetic flight of Bunić and the immediateness of Frankapan.

His *Pjesni razlike* also contains poems in the epic style; his "Popievka više smrti Marka Kraljevića" (Song on Marko Kraljević's Death) is interesting since here he treats for the first time themes of folk poetry. But Djurdjević's gifts lay elsewhere, and, conscious of this fact, he preferred to limit himself simply to translations of the epic poems of Virgil and Ariosto. He also translated some of the fables of Aesop.

The works which were to achieve for him his fame in the history of literature belong to the next phase of his work: *Suze Marunkove*, *Uzdasi Mandaljene pokornice*, and *Saltijer*. *Suze Marunkove* (The Tears of Marunko; Zagreb, 1839), though an imitation of the *Derviš* of Stjepo Djurdjević, is as fine a work as its model because of the healthy humor which pervades it, the successful characterization of Marunko, the protagonist, who, with the gracefulness of a bear, exhibits the pangs of unrequited love, and, finally, because of its thoroughly delightful nonsense.

Uzdasi Mandaljene pokornice (The Sighs of the Penitent Magdalen; Venice, 1728) was inspired by the *Suze* of Gundulić; it is a lyric poem of more than 4000 octosyllables, divided into eight songs, each containing a lyric monologue of Magdalen and a conclusion in which the poet expresses appropriate philosophical and moral reflections. But, with the exception of the first two songs in which the sinful life of the beautiful protagonist is described with apparent pleasure, the rest of the poem seems to lack sincere feeling. How different from the lyricism of Gundulić: empty rhetoric in the one, deeply felt emotion in the other! Djurdjević never really moves the reader because he does not truly feel in these poems. And this lack of imagination and inspiration is not compensated by fascinating language and style; on the contrary, his technical virtuosity only heightens the obvious qualitative disproportion between form and content.

It is precisely because the poet's depth of commitment is equal to his form that his *Saltijer Slovinski* (Croatian Psalter; Venice, 1729) is in every way superior. This is a free translation of the Book of Psalms in which the poet has masterfully reproduced the spirit of the original through a majestic style which is at the same time beautifully simple. Almost all of his octosyllables are fluent, elegant, and marked by vigorous diction, proof of his profound knowledge of the poets of Dubrovnik, and especially of Gundulić and Palmotić.

Djurdjević's historical writings are also of some significance; his ardent patriotism acted as a constant spur to new research, so much so that he may be considered the first historian of Dubrovnik. His *Vitae et carmina nonnulorum illustrium civium Rhacusinorum* is a valuable source of information for the history of literature of Dubrovnik; it is a biographical index of the famous men of the Republic, listed in alphabetical order according to their baptismal names, as was the custom in that period. He was careful to report all that he could find on each one, from biographical data to lists of their works, basing his work, with scrupulous care, exclusively on original documents. The work is of especially great importance because it often contains the only known information about certain writers of Dubrovnik.

The Franciscan friar Sebastijan Slade or Dolci (1698–1777) continued in Dubrovnik the work of Djurdjević on the history of language and literature with his *De Illyricae linguae vetustate et amplitudine* (Venice, 1754), but he worked in the spirit of the pseudo-philological theories of Orbini, trying to demonstrate that the Slavic language is among the most ancient and the one from which all other European languages developed. His work *Fasti Ragusini* (Venice, 1767), a collection of short biographies of the most important men of Dubrovnik, is much more valuable.

In the pure lyric, Djurdjević had only one follower, Dživo Šiško Gundulić (1677–1721), nephew of the author of *Osman*. In addition to his short poems, mostly about love, he left a short lyric poem, *Suze i tužbe Radmilove* (The Tears of Radmil; Zagreb, 1702), but the idyllic aspects as well as the lyrical and earthy (which stop short of obscenity) leave the reader rather cold, with only an admiration for the elegant prosody, inferior though it is to the *Sospiri d'Ergasto* of G. B. Marino, Šiško's source of inspiration.

Ivan Franatica Sorkočević or Sorgo (1706–71), Marin Zlatarić (1753–1829), and Luka Bunić (1708–88) wrote humorous and occasional poems, but their main activity was the translation of Ovid, Virgil, Horace, and Tasso. It was Josip Betondić (died 1764) who did culture the invaluable service of preserving some of the folk poems in long meter, the so-called *bugarštice* which at that time were already beginning to disappear among the people. Then Nikola Marči (1718–1806) left the only epic poem of the eighteenth century, *Život i pokora Marije Egipkinje* (Life and Penance of Saint Mary of Egypt; Dubrovnik, 1791).

This is not strictly a poem, but a tale in verse; in fact, there are few lyric passages in it. The principal aim of the author seems to be to present in chronological order the events treated in the legend.

The dramatic literature of eighteenth-century Dubrovnik is abundant, but, unfortunately, with the exception of a few rare original plays, it is largely made up of translations from the Italian and French: Corneille, Goldoni, Maffei, Metastasio, and Molière, who became the most popular of all the foreign playwrights to be presented in Dubrovnik. Almost all of Molière's plays were translated, although too freely at times. In fact, most of the translators did not bother to reproduce faithfully the deep meaning and tragic character of so many of his plays, but simply adapted them so as to provoke laughter. Among the more or less qualified translators we should recall the names of Petar Bošković (1705–27), I. F. Sorkočević, Timotej Gledj (*ca.* 1696–1787), and Marin Tudišević (1707–88).

It is difficult to follow with precision the theater of Dubrovnik during the eighteenth century; we do know, however, that towards the end of the seventeenth century plays were staged *prid dvorom* (that is, in the main square) or in the houses of the local nobility. Later, in 1682, the great hall of the old dockyard, known as the *orsan*, which was to be destroyed by fire in 1786, was transformed into a theater. Only later on was a modern theater with boxes built. It is interesting to note that up to the year 1788 local artists performed on the Dubrovnik stage; after that year they were replaced by companies of Italian actors, and the Senate created a special fund to cover the expenses of such contracts. The city that at one time had promoted the staging of the dramas of its favorite sons (Držić, Gundulić, Palmotić, etc.) now saw itself forced to support foreign companies and to watch plays which not only were frequently mediocre and poorly interpreted, but were acted in a foreign tongue.

Nevertheless, the fact that the cultural atmosphere of the city was still interesting, its rich traditions still alive, and the spirit of its people still able to exert a strong attraction is attested by the Frenchman Marc Bruère Desrivaux who became its citizen and championed the spirit of his newly adopted country more than did most native writers, even to the point of changing his name to Marko Bruerović (before 1770–1823). Born in Lyons, France, he soon came to Dubrovnik, where in 1772 his father became "Chargé d'affaires et commissaire général des relations commerciales"; he had begun his studies in Marseilles and continued them in a Paulist college in Dubrovnik, where he learned Latin, Italian, and Croatian. He soon became a diplomat for the French Republic and in 1793 he received the post of consul in Travnik (Bosnia), then in Dubrovnik, and finally in Scutari, today's Albania, where he was to render great service to the people of Dubrovnik. From 1814 to 1816, he was consul of Dubrovnik under Austrian rule. He died on a trip to Tripoli, in Libya.

Bruerović is one of the last poets of stature in the eighteenth century, when Slavic letters in Dubrovnik were vanishing. He wrote Latin, Italian, and French verses, but most of all in the purest of vernacular Croatian; poems for festive occasions, epigrams modeled after the odes of Horace, masquerades, *Čupe* (Maids, 1805), and *Spravjenice* (Maids, 1805), a distant echo of the carnival poems; satires in which he reproaches Dubrovnik with neglecting its language, its national customs, and its traditions; epistles (to P. Aletić, A. Sorkočević, P. Gučetić, etc.), which are characterized by their originality, sincerity, and warmth; two plays whose setting is Dubrovnik, *Zvjezdoznanci* (Astronomers) and *Vjera nenadana* (Sudden Faith); and so on. He used a great variety of meters (among them the Italian endecasyllable) but especially the decasyllable of folk poetry (translating some of the latter into Italian). He composed smooth-flowing charming verses which are among the best written in Dubrovnik during the eighteenth century, a period, we must repeat, of the greatest decadence of Croatian letters there.

FOLKLORE COLLECTORS, LATINISTS, PHILOLOGISTS, HISTORIANS, AND SCIENTISTS

A salient feature of the derivative literature of Dubrovnik during the eighteenth century is the interest shown in folk literature, which began to be recorded directly from the people's mouths and collected systematically. Thus, the popular non-religious poetry may well be older than the Latin poetry of the first Croatian humanists, for towards the middle of the fifteenth century, the humanist from Šibenik, J. Šižgorić, in his work *De situ Illyriae et civitate Sibenici*, recalls the love songs, epithalamia, dirges, etc. of his own province and sings their praises. Although it is true that even as far back as Menčetić, several poets of Dubrovnik were familiar with the folk poetry of their time, considering that both the form and the language were very primitive, they merely imitated its tone and often reworked it to change material that did not suit their taste. Only a very few of them preserved some poems in complete and unadulterated form: in the *Ribanje* of P. Hektorović there are two popular epic poems and one lyric (complete with musical notation); in the *Vila slovinka* (The Slavic Fairy) of J. Baraković, we have the beautiful *bugarštica* (a long-verse poem) "Majka Margarita"; and, finally, among the popular poems of F. K. Frankapan, there is an authentic folk epic. A collection of manuscripts entitled *Popijevke slovinske skupljene g. 1758 u Dubrovniku* (Croatian Songs Collected in Dubrovnik in 1758), containing some eighty popular songs, eleven lyric and the remainder epic in character, was discovered in the Franciscan library in Dubrovnik. Thus, there were people of taste and discernment even before Kačić and Fortis (see below), but especially before Vuk Karadžić who, in the second half of the nineteenth century, fully realizing the artistic value of the genre, began annotating and collecting folk songs before they should disappear from among the people. Among the many men who undertook this task of preservation, we should make special mention of the priest and literary critic Djuro Matijašević (1670–1728), member and guiding spirit of the Academy of Idlers and occasional poet, who left a *Dictionarium Latino-Illyricum* of about 13,000 terms and an essay on grammar, *Meditationes Grammaticae*.

For the most part these folk poems, which at that time were still sung by the people, were made up of lines of fifteen or sixteen syllables. The subsequent collections contained songs written in decasyllables which would gradually replace the long-meter. However, despite the undeniable interest which this folk literature inspired throughout all of Dalmatia and especially in Dubrovnik, beginning in the seventeenth and growing even greater in the eighteenth century, it never exerted as much influence on literature as might have been expected; rather it remained an isolated phenomenon and was for all practical purposes an object of curiosity.

The first man to cultivate the national folklore was the canon of Dubrovnik, Djuro Ferić Gvozdenica (1739–1820), who was known primarily as a writer and poet in Latin. His classical and humanistic background certainly enabled him to appreciate the popular works, but he seized on the rather poor notion of explaining, in Latin, some one hundred popular proverbs, entitling his work *Fabulae ab Illyricis adagiis desumptae* (Dubrovnik, 1794). Croatian folk poetry had already become known in other countries through German (1775) and French (1778) translations of the beautiful ballad *Hasan Aginica*[16] (The Wife of Hasan-Aga), which the abbot Alberto Fortis included in his book *Viaggio in Dalmazia* (Venice, 1774), in both its original language and

16/See the English translation of the ballad on pp. 314–15.

an Italian version. The poem seems to have interested Goethe too, and his German translation was published by Herder in his *Volkslieder* (1778), a collection which later on was to bear the more famous title of *Stimmen der Völker in Liedern.* It also inspired the noted German historian Johannes Mueller to address to Ferić a Latin epistle asking him for additional material on Croatian folklore. Ferić replied with the *Ad clarissimum virum Joannem Müler epistola* (Dubrovnik, 1798), in which he speaks of folk poetry, of costumes, of the *kolo* (a type of square dance), of the *gusle* (a rudimentary violin, usually with only one string made of horsehair, which was the accompanying instrument for folk singers), etc., finally adding at the end of the letter Latin translations of thirty-seven poems; he failed, however, to reproduce their original beauty, inasmuch as he sought to prove himself a good Latinist by a needless affectation in words and phrases. He took up folk poetry in his *Ad clarissimum virum Julium Bajamontium epistola,* in which he translated some folk songs into Latin in the manner of no less a one than Virgil – at least according to the opinion of an admirer of his.[17] Ferić's attitude was inspired by the love and pride he felt for his country, which are particularly evident in his *Periegesis orae Rhacusinae* (Dubrovnik, 1803), in which he speaks of the republican institutions, the history, the folklore, and the geography of his motherland. Only his *Paraphrasis psalmorum poetica* (Dubrovnik, 1791) is in no way harmonious with his patriotic ideals; nevertheless, it serves, together with his other works in Latin, as a bridge between himself and the other great Croatian Latinists of the eighteenth century who made the small republic so well known in the world.

The greatest of these Latinists was certainly the Jesuit Rudjer Josip Bošković (1711–87), the famous mathematician, physicist, astronomer, and philosopher, who wrote numerous essays in Latin, Italian, and French which were very much valued in European scientific circles. He spent most of his life abroad (in London, Paris, Rome, Vienna) and kept up a correspondence with the most famous personalities of his time. Besides his poems for festive occasions, which he composed as a member

17/The most complete collection of folk poetry, which constitutes a proud chapter of Croatian literature, is the ten-volume *Hrvatske narodne pjesme* edited by Matica Hrvatska, which was begun in 1897 and is not as yet completed. Many other Croatian folk poems are to be found in the collection of Vuk Stefanović Karadžić, *Srpske narodne pjesme* (Beograd, 1891ff.). Although Vuk extended his search for folk songs not only to the Serbian linguistic and ethnic territory but also to that of Croatia, it is interesting that he still chose to entitle his collection *Srpske narodne pjesme* (Serbian Folk Songs).

of the Academy of Arcadia, he wrote a long poem on astronomy, *De solis ac lunae defectibus* (London, 1760). His philosophical system was atomic dynamism, of which he was the originator and which he set forth in a large volume entitled *Philosophiae naturalis theoria* (Vienna, 1758). In his shorter works he explained his theories on matter (*De materiae divisibilitate et principiis corporum*; Lucca, 1755), on motion (*De continuitatis lege et consectariis pertinentibus ad prima materiae elementa eorumque vires*; Rome, 1754), on space and time (*De spatio ac tempore ut a nobis cognoscuntur*; Vienna, 1758), on the pre-established harmony of Leibnitz, on the principle of sufficient reason, on superior and inferior beings, on the principle of induction, and so on.

Following the example of Lucretius in the *De rerum natura*, Benedikt Stay or Stojković (1714–1801) celebrated the philosophy of Descartes in hexameters in his *Philosophiae recentioris versibus traditae libri sex* (Venice, 1744); but he is most renowned for his poetic representation of Newton's natural philosophy in *Philosophiae recentioris versibus traditae libri decem* (Rome, 1755, 1760, 1792).

Unlike Bošković, who traveled so much throughout Europe, Rajmund Kunić (1719–94) spent almost all his life in Rome, where he was elected a member of the Arcadia and of the Academia occultorum. He became famous for his Latin translation of the *Iliad, Homeri Ilias latinis versibus expressa* (Rome, 1776). In his *Anthologica sive epigramata anthologiae selecta latinis versibus reddita* (Rome, 1771), almost all Greek classics are represented. Besides these works he also composed some original Latin poems dedicated to his Croatian and Italian friends, which reveal a profound knowledge of Latin and Latin prosody.

Another outstanding figure among the great Latinists of this period was Brno Džamanjić (1735–1820), a member of the Academy of Arcadia, who left a translation of the *Odyssey* (1777); he also translated some of the works of Hesiod and Theocritus, which were printed together with his own original epic and didactic poem *Echo* (1764). Džono Rastić or Junije Resti (1755–1815), the last scion of this noble family of Dubrovnik, was a cultured man of broad knowledge in the classics and in Italian, French, Spanish, and English literature. He left accurate translations of Homer, Theocritus, Pindar, and Sappho, but of greater importance are his original poems in Latin, published posthumously by Appendini under the title *Junii Antonii comitis de Restiis patricii Ragusini Carmina* (Padua, 1816); the volume consists of odes, elegies, epigrams, epistles, and especially satires, in which, as a true aristocrat, he attacks the new ideas, *vitia aetatis*, proclaimed by Voltaire, Rousseau, and the encyclopedists.

GRABOVAC AND KAČIĆ

In the first half of the nineteenth century, after having completed with some dignity its manifold cultural mission of several centuries, Dubrovnik would emerge from lofty isolation and contribute anew to the political, cultural, and literary rebirth which would encompass all the Croatian provinces in a movement dedicated to coordinating the national energies for the unification of lands which had long been separate spheres of political and cultural influence by virtue of historical circumstances. Meanwhile, as the other Croatian provinces were reawakening to a new political and cultural life in the eighteenth century, the literature of Dubrovnik was living out its own agony.

It is hard to see why Dalmatia, which was still ruled by Venetian aristocracy in the century of enlightenment, nurtured so poor a literary growth. Very few writers composed in their native tongue, and those who did dealt largely with pious themes. There were two important exceptions, however, the Franciscans Kačić and Grabovac. The latter, though the less known of the two, deserves serious attention and genuine esteem, not only because he opened the way to Kačić, but also because he became the first writer to give his life for the patriotic ideals he professed in his writings. Grabovac was born in Vrlika in 1697; after having taught philosophy and theology for a few years, he was named chaplain to Croatian troops in the Venetian army, a position which enabled him to live in Venice, Verona, and Brescia. In 1747, he published in Venice his *Cvit razgovora naroda i jezika Iliričkoga aliti rvackoga* (Flowers of Conversation on the People and the Illyric or Croatian Language). Although the book had already been approved by both the ecclesiastic and political authorities, Grabovac was accused of high treason and taken first to the jails Sotto i Piombi, in Venice, and later, already dying, to the island of Holy Spirit, where he died the following year as a result of maltreatment and a disease contracted during his stay in prison.

Grabovac, who had lived among his fellow Croatians far from his country, and witnessed how they had shed so much blood in the Venetian wars against the Turks, had written his book to help conserve and keep alive in his countrymen their national spirit and their love for their homeland and for the old traditions. The first part of his work contains religious poems, very similar to the religious poetry of his fellow Franciscans in Bosnia. Some of the poems expressing patriotic sentiments make up the incriminating part of the book. At times these emerge in his preoccupation with the moral education of the men placed under his guidance. Sometimes he disapproves of and regrets, as did Vitezović, the eagerness with which some of his countrymen follow the fashion of denaturalization; at other times he bitterly points out the exploitation of his people, and affirms sarcastically:

> When the king wants to conquer someone
> he first calls on the Croatians
> but when the spoils are divided,
> then everyone asks: where have you been?[18]

This was the only book Grabovac ever published and was not as widely read as he would have wished; nor did it have the effects he had hoped for, since it was suppressed as soon as some of the copies had been distributed. Although artistically deficient, it is nevertheless a valuable sign of the changing times and of a matured national consciousness; it served as an example of the type of writing needed to reawaken national pride and patriotism.

Grabovac had a genuine disciple in Andrija Kačić Miošić (1704–60), who was born in Brist near Makarska. He too entered the order of Minor Friars, and was sent to Budapest, where he remained for seven years, the time required to complete the courses in philosophy (three years) and theology (four years). For the next twenty years he taught in the theological schools of Dalmatia, and in 1750 he withdrew to the peaceful atmosphere of the convent of Zaostrog, where he died ten years later. His literary activity was confined to this last decade. His first work was on a type of logic or a manual of philosophical propaedeutic (*Elementa peripathetica iuxta mentem subtilissimi doctoris Joannis Duns Scoti*; Venice, 1752) and promised no contribution to literature. A few years later he published his *Razgovor ugodni naroda slovinskoga* (Pleasant Conversation of the Slavic People; Venice, 1756), which by 1759 already boasted a second edition. It is very probable that the *Cvit* of Grabovac induced him to make use of historical material already collected in order to write a book which would educate his people in their faith as well as familiarize them with their own history and the heroic wars they had fought against the Turks.

Taught by the tragic experience of Grabovac that in order to be able to publish a work of admittedly patriotic sentiment he must prove himself beyond all doubt a loyal citizen, Kačić dedicated a few poems in his first edition to the Turkish-Venetian wars, making an opportunity to sing the praises of the Doge and the ruling class of the Republic. Probably for the same reason he wrote the dedication in Latin, and in it he cites the *Anfiteatro di Europa* by I. N. Doglioni (Venice, 1623) as the main

18/Kad kralj oće da kog srve/tad Rvate meće prve,/a dobitak kad se dili/tad pitaju: gdi ste bili?

source for his book, although he generally follows the Pan-Slavist Orbini, a name which could not have been very welcome in Venetian politics. The *Razgovor* is a work which relates, sometimes in prose but more often in verse, the history of the southern Slavic people, especially the history of the Croatians from the times of Alexander the Great to 1756. The work is divided into two parts: the first, for the most part in prose, contains the history of the Croatian kings; the second, much longer and written almost entirely in verse, gives an account of the wars against the Turks.

As noted earlier, Kačić wrote *Razgovor* in order to reawaken in his people an interest in and love for their glorious history, and above all to point out their valuable contribution in the wars against the Turks so as to offer examples worthy of imitation. In so doing he provided the historical basis for the already existing folk songs which dealt with the same themes that he brought up to date and reworked in the light of history. He was fully convinced that the people, who had written their own history in the epic folk poetry, would welcome a work written in verse. Therefore, instead of succumbing to the passion of the systematic historian and writing a dry chronicle in the style of the *Cvit* of Grabovac, with remarkable intuition, he did not concentrate on the ancient history of the country, but rather stressed the recent wars fought against the Turks, the same wars in which many of his readers had taken part or which had left in their families unforgettable memories to be passed on from generation to generation. Although Kačić never pretended to be a professional historian, he was nonetheless acutely conscious of the question of the veracity of the events he was celebrating, and at times found it difficult to make his way through the maze of contradictory theses proposed by historians of the Slavic Middle Ages. The care with which he pursued historical truth can be seen even in the introduction to the *Razgovor*, in which he declares he has taken everything "with great attention from Latin, Italian, and Croatian books, from letters, diplomas, certificates and depositions by the elderly and the religious" and cites a great variety of sources (G. Sagredo, Doglioni, Baronio, Vitezović, etc.).

It is interesting to compare the *Razgovor* with folk poetry. Doubtless Kačić knew this poetry well; this is clear from the very tone and form of his work. In fact, Kačić's poems generally seem so much like genuine folk poetry that Abbot Fortis mistook the *Razgovor* for a collection of folk songs, and indeed many lines and a number of passages do seem to have been taken verbatim from popular folk poetry. The purity of his language draws him especially close to the folk speech and far from the poetic diction characteristic of the Dubrovnik poets of the preceding centuries. It might be said, then, that the only difference between folk poetry and Kačić's is that while the anonymous poet abandons his creations to the people to be altered in time by the collective imagination, Kačić ensures, by means of the press, that his poetry will remain as he wrote it.

However, a more careful analysis reveals significant differences between the poems of Kačić and folk poetry, especially in composition. While any one folk poem as a rule treats only one theme and is a complete poetic embodiment of it, Kačić strives to unite various themes, so much so that at times his poetry functions as a chronicle in verse. Moreover, with the exception of anadiplosis, his poetry lacks the frequency and variety of imagery which is so important an element of folk poetry. Kačić's poems differ from the popular ones in form as well; in fact, not only are some of his poems written quatrains of eight-foot lines rhyming *abab*, following the Dubrovnik model, but even his decasyllabic poems seem modern because they employ rhyme, a device seldom found in folk poetry.

In spite of these technical and thematic differences, Kačić's poems often sound like the most genuine of the folk songs, a fact which suggests that Kačić was a poet who developed his natural gift by breathing the air of the folk poetry which could still be heard among the people. Kačić is the first Croatian poet to have addressed the common people in a manner both comprehensible and effective; his works prove that literature in general and poetry in particular need not be the delight of privileged classes alone, but may appeal to all people. At the same time he is the best and most authentic representative of the Franciscan friars in Dalmatia, Bosnia, Hercegovina, and Slavonia whose activity had the main purpose of keeping alive in the simple people the Christian faith of their ancestors and a pride in their national traditions. Consequently, in spite of the clearly regional character of Croatian literature prior to the National Awakening of the 1830s, Kačić had already combined in his *Razgovor* all the elements found in the history of the entire Croatian ethnic territory. His was the first work truly popular with all Croatians, and has appeared in no fewer than fifty editions.

In comparison with the *Razgovor*, his second work, *Korabljica* (The Little Ark; 1760) in prose, is only of slight importance; it is a pious chronicle from the creation of the world up to the author's own times, and is analogous in spirit and tenor to the many similar works written by his religious brothers in Dalmatia and Bosnia. Clearly the *Korabljica* could not attain the popularity of the *Razgovor*, since religious history was far less interesting to the people than the history of their national rulers and the Turkish wars celebrated in the first work.

Mateša Antun Kuhačević of Senj (1697–1772) spent the best years of his life in Austrian prisons, which were no less inhuman than the Venetian ones occupied by Grabovac. Like Grabovac, he felt a sincere patriotism which was clearly reflected in his poetic epistles and poems dealing with current events. Kuhačević studied at the Military Academy of Vienna, fought in the wars of succession of Poland and Austria, and finally retired from the army in 1745. He did not enjoy the pleasures of peace, however; he was sent to Vienna as a delegate from Senj, and in order to defend the ancient privileges of this free city, he presented for the occasion a *Synoptica informatio*. Unfortunately, at that very time, a riot broke out in Lika against the reorganization of the Vojna Krajina, and he was accused of having been its instigator. Arrested in Vienna in 1747, he was transferred in chains to the prison of Karlovac; after three years of terrible suffering, he was condemned to life imprisonment and sent to Moravia to the same prison of Spielberg which Silvio Pellico was to render infamous with his book *Le mie prigioni*. He was transferred later to the prison in Graz, and when finally freed at the age of 75, he did not survive the return trip to his native land (1772).

Like Grabovac, having lost his freedom for love of his country, Kuhačević began to write poetry much as Frankapan had done, in order to alleviate the long years of painful separation from the outside world. The entire tragedy of this noble patriot was recorded in his Latin autobiography, which is no longer extant, and in *Osam prijateljskih poslanica* (Eight Friendly Letters) addressed to his uncle, his nephew, his sister, and the judge who had unjustly condemned him. In spite of some metrical imperfections, his rough rhyming dodecasyllabic lines can be read with greater pleasure than can many poems from Dubrovnik which are chiseled with great formal perfection, but lack truly moving experience. Kuhačević took the material for his songs at times from pleasant memories of his uncle, and at times from his tender love for his sister and nephew, from the hard and sad life of a convict, from his generous forgiveness of the judge, from a sincere and burning patriotism, and finally from a profound sense of Christianity raised to a truly inspiring plane in the solitude of his prison.

Whereas in the eighteenth century Dubrovnik and Dalmatia produced I. Djurdjević and Grabovac and Kačić, Bosnia, which was to remain under Turkish domination until 1878, could not boast of any worthy follower of the seventeenth-century Divković. The pioneers in literature were still the Franciscans, but their works were predominantly didactic and moralizing in character. The works were no longer written in *bosančica*, but rather almost exclusively in Latin characters. All the literary and cultural activity of the Franciscan fathers of that century (Stjepan Markovac-Margitić, Lovro Sitović Ljubuški, Filip Laštrić, etc.) was directed toward effecting the cultural, national, and economic emancipation of the people.

LITERARY ACTIVITY IN SLAVONIA

With the arrival of the eighteenth century Slavonia enters the world of letters. This Croatian province, which is bounded by the Drava, Sava, and Kupa rivers, remained under Turkish domination from the time of the battle of Mohács (1526) up to the peace of Karlowitz (1699), sharing the fate of Bosnia, its sister to the south. Actually, in one respect its situation was even worse, since during the Austrian-Turkish wars all the armies marched across it. Thus, the material and cultural conditions of these northeastern Croatian lands, which were later to retain their medieval name of Slavonia, were indeed wretched. The feudal property of the Croatian nobility, sacrificed almost entirely in the struggles for liberation, fell into the hands of foreigners without ties to the land and alien to Croatian traditions. Moreover, a great number of Serbians immigrated to the peripheral areas of Slavonia whose Croatian population had dispersed as a result of the constant wars.

Just as Divković and his followers had tried to preserve and keep alive in the people their ancestral faith during the worst crisis in the history of Bosnia, so also did the Franciscans in Slavonia. During the Turkish domination, they were the only clergy in the province, and, up to 1757, belonged to the same Franciscan province of Bosnia argentina. They bore witness to the same ideal and duty by composing prayer books in the vernacular, as well as devotional books and patriotic poems.

But after the liberation, the literary and cultural activity of the region grew until it surpassed in quantity as well as quality all the works of eighteenth-century Croatian literature, except for those of Djurdjević in Dubrovnik and Kačić in Dalmatia. The Jesuits contributed their share, immediately after the liberation, to this wholehearted effort to raise the cultural and moral level of the people. In the vicinity of Požega their work was especially effective. Later, the secular clergy and laymen joined their efforts to those of the religious orders. Cultural and civic improvements were effectively advanced also by the wave of rationalism spreading from Germany, which had found in Maria Theresa and Joseph II two fervent propagandists.

In addition to those who cultivated religious and moral literature, there were also those who celebrated the war exploits of their countrymen, and certainly there was no lack of material since the Slavonians had also participated in the Seven Years War. Then, too, Kačić was already popular in their lands, having been widely circulated by the Franciscans. But the surge of literary activity in Slavonia was by no means limited to efforts to raise cultural standards. Books were also written on economic and social reforms. Some plays were written, modeled for the most part on the religious dramas of Dubrovnik; indeed, Croatian writers of all regions felt great admiration for the literary products of Dalmatia and Dubrovnik. Finally, every poet and writer of Slavonia wrote in the Shtokavian-Ikavian dialect and called his own language *jezik slavonski, jezik ilirički,* or *jezik rvacki.*

The most important religious poet in Slavonia was the Jesuit Antun Kanižlić (1699–1777) from Požega. He was educated in Jesuit schools and soon joined the order, serving at various times as preacher, teacher, *prafectus scholarum,* etc. He wrote catechisms, *Obilato mliko duhovno* (Abundant Spiritual Food; Zagreb, 1752) and *Mala i svakomu potrebna bogoslovica* (A Small Catechism for Everybody; Venice, 1763); devotional books, *Utočište blaženoj divici Mariji* (Blessed Virgin Mary Our Refuge; Venice, 1759), *Primogući i srdce nadvladajući uzroci za ljubiti Gospodina Isukrsta* (Powerful and Heart-Compelling Reasons for the Love of Lord Jesus Christ; Zagreb, 1760); and prayer books, *Bogoljubnost molitvena* (Devotional Prayer; Trnava, 1756).

Kanižlić had an excellent command of the language, which he had gained not only from studying the works of the writers from Dalmatia and Dubrovnik but also from his contact with the people. With the purpose of aiding in the government program of uniting with Rome the Serbian and Rumanian Orthodox of the Austrian Monarchy, he composed in Croatian the monumental (about 1000 pages) dogmatic and polemical work *Kamen pravi smutnje velike* (The True Stumbling Block of the Great Scandal; Osijek, 1780). It is the first scholarly work written in the national tongue and, as such, demonstrated the suitability of Croatian for the treatment of scholarly matters dealt with heretofore only in Latin or Italian.

Kanižlić's masterpiece, however, is the religious poem *Sveta Rožalija Panormitanska Divica* (St. Rosalia, Virgin of Palermo; Vienna, 1780), which is similar in theme to the religious works of the seventeenth century such as the *Suze* of Gundulić and the *Uzdasi* of Djurdjević. Indeed the poem is somewhat derivative, expecially in its baroque style so characteristic of the poetry of Dubrovnik. It is written in doubly rhymed dodecasyllables, in the form of an epistle sent by a young convert to her parents from a cave in the mountain where she devotes herself to prayer and penance. The lyric sections and the descriptions of nature are particularly beautiful; the poem is marred, however, by the derivative imagery of its allegorical figures and personifications.

Among the writers of Slavonia, the influence of Kačić is especially pervasive in Emerik Pavić (1715–80), who was one of the most zealous, if not very fortunate, imitators of old "Milovan."[19] He wrote several theological works in Latin, but is best known for his Latin translation of the prose sections and some of the poems of the Razgovor, a translation entitled *Descriptio soluta et rhytmica regum, banorum, caeterorumque Slavinorum seu Illyricorum* (Budapest, 1764). Moreover, in his *Nadodanje glavnih dogadjaja Razgovoru ugodnom naroda Slovinskoga* (Main Events Added to the Pleasant Conversation of the Slavic People; Budapest, 1768) Pavić extended the *Razgovor* by adding to it some ten poems which celebrate the cultural and patriotic activity of the Franciscans in Slavonia as well as the heroic exploits of the Slavic people under Turkish domination.

Kačić had a host of followers in Slavonia (many of whom were anonymous), and among these was Josip Pavišević of Požega (1734–1803), one of the most learned Franciscans there, who wrote in Latin and translated from French, Italian, and German. He was closest of all to Kačić, at least in form, with his *Kratkopis poglavitijih dogadjaja* (Epitome of Main Events; Budapest, 1762) and his *Polaženje na vojsku* (Recruitment of Soldiers; Osijek, 1779), patriotic works enlivened here and there by poems and by a light sense of humor.

One of the best poets in Slavonian literature, who wrote in the manner of folk poetry, was the priest Antun Ivanošić (1748–1800), whose popular humorous poems are among the finest in pre-nineteenth-century Croatian literature; his poem *Svemogući neba i zemlje stvoritelj* (The Omniponent Creator of Heaven and Earth; Zagreb, 1788) places him on the same level as Kanižlić.

Another follower of Kačić was Blaž Bošnjak, whose reputation rests on his long poem of eighteen songs, *Izpisanje rata* (Description of War; Osijek, 1792), a dry chronicle in verse, rich in the kind of detail that might be of interest to a historian.

The champion of nationalism in Slavonia was Matija Antun Reljković. He was born in 1732 in Svinjar and received his early education from the Franciscans; later he decided to take up a military career, and as a lieutenant he saw action in the Seven Years War, during which he was captured by the Prussians. After he was released he left the army and retired to Vinkovci, where he died in 1798.

His confinement as a war prisoner became a turning point in the life of this twenty-five-year-old officer; his stay in the ancient city of Frankfurt on the Oder enabled him to encounter first-hand both French and

19/This is a kind of pseudonym which Kačić gave to himself in his *Razgovor*.

German culture and literature, and he saw the contrast between the cultures of these more advanced countries and that of his own Slavonia. Thus he conceived the desire to raise the cultural and economic standards of his country.

In his *Satir iliti divji čovik* (Satyr or Savage Man; Dresden, 1762), Reljković describes his valiant, but primitive compatriots, their way of life, their character, their lax morals, their prejudices, and their superstitions, and then attempts to teach them better ways. Fortunately, he realized that his purpose could never be achieved by means of a solemn moralistic essay. He followed the example of Kačić (although he did not intend to be a poet), and wrote his work in decasyllabic verse, "for my compatriots are singers and poets by nature."[20]

In the first part of the work the satyr sings of the natural beauty and wealth of Slavonia, where people ought surely to be able to live happily. Then, the poet gives way to the preacher, who reproaches the Slavonians for their moral, cultural, and economic decadence, and for the vices which have brought it about, vices bred under the long Turkish domination. He then invites them to avoid idleness, dissipation, and obscene language.

A true rationalist, Reljković has only one ideal: to bring the people to school; for him, widespread education is the condition for any moral and economic progress. The work was received with great enthusiasm and became the most popular book in Slavonia; even today, the purity of its language, its humor, and its wit make it pleasurable reading.

Encouraged by the success of his *Satir*, and always with the aim of enlightening his people, Reljković translated Aesop's Fables, *Esopove fabule za slavonsku u skulu hodeću dicu* (Aesop's Fables for Slavonian Youths Going to School; 1804), and compiled a Slavic-German grammar, *Nova Slavonska i nimačka gramatika* (New Slavonian and German Grammar; Zagreb, 1767), with the intention of purifying the language of its many Turkish expressions and of establishing rules of orthography. But of all his works only the *Satir* has remained alive among the people; the many editions of this work (one of the greatest publishing successes in all Croatian literature prior to the nineteenth century) clearly indicate the enthusiastic response accorded the book.

The *Satir* did provoke bitter enmity as well, however, especially among the clergy and the military, for these were the classes Reljković reproached for having tolerated the deplorable conditions of Slavonia. Typical of his enemies was the Franciscan Djuro Rapić of Gradiška (1715–77), who in his own *Satir* attempts to instruct the people in the

20/"Jerbo su i onako domoroci moji svi pivači i od naravi pisnici."

spirit of Christian doctrine, convinced that the work of Reljković and his followers could offer only a pseudo-education. To Rapić and other critics, the followers of Reljković replied: Vid Došen (1720–1778) with the *Aždaja sedmoglava* (The Dragon with Seven Heads; Zagreb, 1768) and especially Adam Tadija Blagojević (1746–*ca.* 1797) with a collection of poems, *Pjesnik-putnik* (The Traveling Poet; Vienna, 1771), in which he criticizes in general the Franciscans' fear of progressive ideas and exalts the principal champion of new ideas, the emperor Joseph II. Moreover, with some of his translations from the German on class equality and religious tolerance, Blagojević exposes vividly the conflict between the new generation and the old world of the conservatives – that is, the transition between a fading feudalism and the beginnings of an emerging concern with social reform.

Always with the purpose of enlightening the people, but also to attract and entertain them, during the second half of the century the Franciscans in Slavonia followed the example of the Jesuits in Croatia: they restored the old school spectacles and revived the theater, casting off the old forms of religious drama so that it might gain acceptance by a new public. Among the many adaptations and more or less free translations of Ivan Velikanović (1723–1807) were plays about St. Margaret of Cortona (*Prikazanje svete Margarete iz Kortone*), St. Susan (*Sveta Suzana*), and St. Theresa (*Sveta Terezija divica*). Grga Cevapović (1786–1829) wrote *Josip sin Jakoba patriarke* (Joseph, Son of the Patriarch Jacob) and Aleksandar Tomiković (1743–1829), *Josip poznan od svoje braće* (Joseph Recognized by His Brothers), which is no more than a liberal translation of the oratorio of Metastasio *Giuseppe riconosciuto.*

Poetry occupies a very modest place in the literature of Slavonia. Indeed, during the eighteenth century poetry was in retreat, so to speak, over the entire Croatian national territory. Probably the most important poet of the era was the Franciscan Matija Petar Katančić (1750–1825), who was well known as a scholar even abroad. He was a man of great intelligence and culture; besides Croatian he knew Latin, Greek, German, French, Italian, and Hungarian. *Totus vixit litteris,* and he left works valued even today in such varied fields as philology, archaeology, history, geography, epigraphy, and numismatics. These works were written in Latin, and only the volumes concerned with national history were published: *Orbis antiquus* (Budapest, 1824–5), *Istri adcolarum geographia vetus* (Budapest, 1826–7), and *Specimen philologiae Pannoniorum* (Zagreb, 1795). These three works aim especially at establishing the ethnic character of these Croatian lands.

As a youth, Katančić tried his hand at poetry; he wrote the collection *Fructus Auctumnales* (Zagreb, 1794), containing poems in Latin and Croatian. Among the most beautiful for their simplicity, their liveliness, grace, and freshness, are those which obviously imitate the folk songs, the so-called *popivke narodne*. In general, these are lyrics, elegies, ballads, epigrams, and occasional poems. They are based on persons and events of the period, but contemporary personalities are lost in conventional situations and inflexible linguistic forms. In his Croatian poems Katančić generally adopted the classical prosody. That is, for him the fundamental law of Croatian metrics lay in the quantity of syllables, a thesis which he defended in *Brevis in prosodiam illyricae linguae animadversio*, a difficult task since it went counter to the nature of the Croatian language; fortunately it did not have many adherents. Besides this, he wrote three *Razgovori pastirski* (Pastoral Discourses) in distichs and hexameters, and a satire of the *Satir* of Reljković, *Satir od kola sudi* (Satyr's Judgment of the Kolo), in which he defends some popular customs denying that they are of Turkish origin (the square dance, *kolo*, for instance).

The poetic activity of Katančić is rather secondary; nevertheless, his modest work is of some interest and significance, since he was the only pseudo-classicist in Slavonian literature, as well as the only Slavonian lyric poet.

NORTHERN CROATIA AT THE DAWN OF THE NATIONAL AWAKENING

Whereas in the seventeenth century literature in northern Croatia had been the monopoly of the nobility, in the eighteenth it became a special vocation of the clergy, both because the nobility had drawn away from the people and adopted German and because Latin was the official language. Thus literature in both the national language and in the Kajkavian dialect of that province took the same direction; it is made up mostly of prayer manuals, legends of the saints, sermons, and didactic and religious pamphlets. A parallel development is evident in the works of science, theology, history, geography, linguistics, and physics, written mostly in Latin. Literature was confined to the clergy almost until the end of the century; only in the last decades did a regenerating spirit begin to intrude from the west.

The religious orders were particularly active, the Paulists above all; but even their literary activity remained rather one-sidedly devoted to history. It is pleasing mostly for the patriotic spirit which pervades all of it and which is quite apparent in their most important writer, Hilarion

Gasparotti (1714–62). The Paulists showed great concern with the history of their own order, as exemplified in the writings of Ivan Kristolovec, Nikola Benger, Josip Bedeković, and others.

The literary activity of the Jesuits was also scholarly and therefore written in Latin. The best-known and most prolific of the Jesuit writers who were aware of social problems was Juraj Mulih (1753), who wrote some twenty works, religious and didactic in character. While the Jesuits did their best work in theology rather than history, they did produce historians, and these wrote almost exclusively in Latin. The most authoritative historian among the Latinists was without doubt Josip Mikoci (1734–1800) of Zagreb, author of the much-read book *Otiorum Croatiae liber unus* (Budapest, 1806), which deals with the history of Croatia from its beginnings up to its unification with Hungary (1102). The ex-Jesuit Kazimir Bedeković (1728–82) was, on the other hand, more theologian than historian, and his sacred dramas, although written in Latin, are of greater interest to literary history.

Similar in tone and direction was the literary activity of the secular clergy. Beside some of the mediocre writers of the time, Adam Baltazar Krčelić (1715–78) seems a writer of some stature and a serious scholar. He was one of the few who understood the positive aspects of the so-called enlightened absolutism; he defended and followed Reljković, trying especially to raise the general cultural level of the country. A favorite subject of his was the history of Croatia in general and of Zagreb in particular. The most important of his historical works, written in Latin, are the two following, published in Zagreb in 1770: *De regnis Dalmatiae, Croatiae, Slavoniae notitiae praeliminares* and especially *Historiarum cathedris ecclesiae Zagrabiensis.* The first takes up the history of Croatia, Slavonia, and Dalmatia from their origins to the seventeenth century, the principal aim being to show, in the face of Venetian claims and at the moment of the general Turkish retreat, the Croatian right over Croatia, Slavonia, Bosnia, and Hercegovina, countries which Vitezović had already called *tota Croatia.* The second work deals with the history of the bishopric of Zagreb from its founding (1091) up to the year 1603. Both works are notorious for their barbaric Latin style. Krčelić also published *Scriptorum ex regno Slavoniae a saeculo XIV usque ad XVII inclusive collectio* (Varaždin, 1774), which is the first manual of the literary history of the northern Croatian regions.

The Kajkavian Croatian poetry of the eighteenth century is richer than that of the preceding centuries, and is more varied, in both form and content. Nevertheless, like all other Croatian provinces, northern Croatia produced very little in poetry during the century. For this part of Croatia, the century of enlightenment, and the cult of exact sciences, particularly mathematics and history, is at one and the same time the century of mass education and the century which cried out for a cultural, social, and political liberation of the territories which were gradually being freed from Turkish domination. These compelling needs absorbed all men of culture who loved their country. Thus, during this period, lyric poetry was a most neglected literary genre. In order to remedy this neglect and to satisfy a genuine need for lyric expression the so-called *pjesmarice*, collections of poems, generally anonymous, began circulating throughout the country and especially in the castles of the nobility; this poetry closely resembles that of the romantic period with its predominantly amorous and patriotic themes.

The greatest devotees of drama in northern Croatia were the Jesuits; all of their plays were, of course, clearly didactic and moralistic. Although they wrote in Latin on the whole, they did produce some plays in Croatian, but their plays were, more than anything else, translations from German.

One of the few original dramas written in Croatian during that period is *Matijaš Grabancijaš Dijak* (Matthias the Necromantic Scholar) by the ex-Paulist priest Tito Brezovački of Zagreb (1757–1805). This is a play based on the popular belief in necromancy, which the playwright obviously does not share. The protagonist is an intelligent young man who makes fun of the ignorance and incredulity of the others in order to bring them to their senses. The play is, in fact, a satire on the contemporary life of Zagreb, written in the manner of the current Viennese farces. It is still appealing, even today, especially for its colloquial tone and lively humor. *Diogeneš ili sluga dveh zgubleneh bratov* (Diogenes or the Servant of Two Lost Brothers; Zagreb, 1823), on the other hand, is not nearly as good a play. Diogeneš, the central character, is the initiator of the action. He is both talkative like Figaro and quite direct in his speech and teaches the others the lesson they deserve. He is, in short, another Matijaš, through whom the author would *castigare mores* by means of laughter.

With his didactic plays and his patriotic poetry in obvious imitation of folk poetry, Brezovački stands above all the contemporary Kajkavian writers. However, although the writings of these Kajkavian authors were truly modest achievements, we owe to them the popularization of some novels, dramas, and short stories of world renown. Among such writers were the parish priest Antun Vranić (died 1824), who translated Defoe's *Robinson Crusoe*; Matija Jandrić (1776–1828), who Croatized and produced a liberal translation of Goldoni's comedy *Il vero amico*; and learned abbot Ivan Krizmanić (1776–1852), who translated into Croatian Milton's *Paradise Lost.*

On the eve of the appearance of Ljudevit Gaj, Jakob Lovrenčić (1797–

1842) wrote the first original novels in Kajkavian. He became especially famous for his *Petrica Kerempuh* (Shock-Headed Peter or The Boy with the Wild Hair; Varaždin, 1834), a book which is modeled on Croatian and German folk tales and is still read today.

Some of these writers of northern Croatia, as well as many others not mentioned here, at the time of the National Awakening, willingly sacrificed the Kajkavian dialect of their native province and adopted the Shtokavian, which was to become the standard literary language of all Croatian provinces. However, Ignjat Kristijanović (1796–1884) remained faithful to his native dialect in his devotional books and in his grammatical studies. So also did his uncle, the parish priest and professor, Tomo Mikloušić (1767–1833), an ardent patriot and follower of Reljković in his effort to educate the masses, who edited calendars and collected folk literature.

Our analysis thus far should make clear the great difference between the literature of the eighteenth century and that of the preceding century. Writers from the southern provinces dominate Croatian literature up to the time of Djurdjević; moreover, from the Middle Ages on, the major southern literary centers were under considerable Italian influence, so that the literature of the seventeenth century is an organic development from that of the sixteenth. With the exception of religious literature, its principal exponents were the small and exclusive aristocracy and the educated upper middle class, which constituted its public as well. This literature is homogeneous, uniform, as are, in fact, the literatures of contemporary Italy and the Catholic countries of south-central Europe, supervised as they were by ecclesiastical authorities.

But with the coming of the eighteenth century literary activity expands, especially in the second half of the century when a great many writers from the territories recently freed from Turkish domination begin to write extensively. With the ever increasing participation of the northern provinces in the cultural life of the country, we witness a gradual weakening of the traditionally predominant orientation towards Italian culture and a systematic replacement by the culture of the northern countries, mainly Germany and Austria, which, in turn, pass on to the Croatians the ideas of western Europe in general. With the slow, but inevitable, wane of an aristocracy, which at one time had served as its main support, literary activity becomes a legitimate preoccupation of writers born of the common people. The period is characterized by a paucity of lyric poetry; writers are concerned with practical goals, rather than art, and intellectual works now take precedence over works of the imagination. An interest in national history grows very rapidly also; although this interest had already been bearing fruit in previous centuries, it is only in the eighteenth and nineteenth centuries that new editions of the old works of history, especially those of J. Mikoci and M. P. Katančić, begin to appear.

The eighteenth century produced other factors favoring the further cultural and political unification of the thus far divided Croatian provinces. During the sixteenth and seventeenth centuries, the provinces of the Croatian national territory had each been exposed to different spheres of political and cultural influence, and as a result had developed rather unequal levels of culture; however, following the liberation of the northern provinces from Turkish domination in the eighteenth century, the culture was equalized and generally rose to a higher level than that of the previous centuries, a fact which was to facilitate final unification.

A rather significant place in the cultural life of Croatia was occupied by the schools of theology, philosophy, and law, all grouped in 1776 under the name of the Academy of Sciences of Zagreb, which, up to the time of the National Awakening, would be the central educational institution for all Croatian provinces, facilitating the equal education of Croatian youth while at the same time bringing together future exponents of the national culture. Although opportunities to engage in the common cultural enterprise had not been altogether wanting before, the Academy of Zagreb made them more frequent and more significant. Granted, therefore, that Croatian literature of this period had lost much of the artistic excellence of its aristocratic past in exchange for a more popular character, it is undeniable that the more uniform level of the actual culture had allowed literature to spread among the masses throughout the entire national territory, so that gradually it shed the limitations of its regional character.

While it is true, then, that Kačić cannot be compared with Gundulić, it is also true that the popularity of his *Razgovor ugodni* belongs to an entirely new phenomenon. The new spirit fostered by the change from an aristocratic to a popular literature can be further seen in the interest shown by each province in the literary works of the others and by all of them in the older literature, especially that of Dubrovnik. It is no wonder, then, that the Jesuit writers of Slavonia should continue the traditions of Bosnia and the coastal areas, an activity which is admirably represented by Kanižlić; and when Katančić calls him a rival of the writers of Dubrovnik, this means not only that the poetry of Dubrovnik is the measure of Croatian literary values in general, but that it is considered a common glory of the Croatian past even in the cultural centers of the north.

At the time of Appendini, the interest in the literature of Dubrovnik was especially strong; this is the period of collections, transcriptions, and classifications of the manuscripts intended for publication. An equal interest in literary history was apparent in northern Croatia, where Krčelić, following the example of Vitezović, wrote the monumental *Scriptorum ex regno Slavoniae collectio*, which is the first manual of literary history in northern Croatia; also there is Adam Alojzij Baričević (1756–1806) with his *Historia litteraria Croatiae*, in which he attempts to include all of literature through the centuries, regardless of region of origin, and present it as the common literature of all the people.

With the newly acquired knowledge of a common cultural patrimony, the national sentiments are reawakened and strengthened; the desire to unite all Croatians in one state had already been expressed by Vitezović in his *Croatia rediviva* (1700) making it the ideal of all patriots. With regard to the political aspect of the Croatian awakening, it must be pointed out that alongside the official policy represented by Croatian statesmen, which resulted at times in dangerous compromises and a corresponding disregard of the national interest, there also existed a semiofficial policy, often expressed by writers and men of culture in general, and it was precisely this semiofficial policy which preserved the national pride. This policy, more than anything else, served to maintain, alive and effective, patriotism and its ideals, insisting that the Croatian people alone had the right to determine the future of the nation. And until 1832, when the cry *Još Hrvatska nij propala* (Croatia Is Still Alive) of Lj. Gaj became the motto of the awakening, the political ideal of unity and freedom was nurtured in works such as the *Libera regna sumus* of Brezovački, the *Regina Croatia* of Miklošić, and the *Hrvatska zemlja stara kraljica* (Croatian Land Old Queen) of Štoos.

But the program and preparation for the national revival may be found not so much in political acts themselves, but rather in literature, where all the problems that would be solved only by future generations are raised and necessarily impressed on the minds of educated men preoccupied with their country's future. While the political program plans the constitution for a Croatia which includes her ethnic and historic territory, the cultural program aims at the creation of a literary language with a common orthography. In fact, the latter problem dates back to the time when the nation was still divided.

There is no doubt that the need for a common literary language had been felt before. Proof of this are the several efforts made both in the north and the south of Croatia. In the Kajkavian literature, before and after Vitezović, there had been a clear tendency to draw closer to the Bosnian and Slavonian dialects. We have also seen how, modeled after the Italian Academy of Arcadia, linguistic centers had been founded on the Croatian coast whose principal aim was to preserve the purity of the language and to collect material for the publication of grammars and dictionaries; these academies kept in close communication with similar institutions of northern Croatia and with individual scholars who shared the same interest. Thus, we can already see in Djurdjević, the last important writer of Dubrovnik, how, coupled with his literary creativity, he maintains a scholarly interest in questions of language and orthography. In northern Croatia we witness the bold project of Vitezović, the effort of Jambrešić for new diacritical signs, the Mandić-Lanosović-Krmpotić-Stulli Commission which deserves great credit for its efforts in bringing the Kajkavian dialect and the Shtokavian language closer together. From Kašić in the south to Vitezović in the north, the importance of the question of a common literary language is underlined by the welcoming of the Shtokavian dialect. In reality this was the best and the only possible solution, not only in view of the inheritance of the rich literature of Dubrovnik, but also because of the already widespread literature in that dialect which brought together authors from different regions such as Gundulić, Djurdjević, Kačić, Kanižlić, Divković, Reljković, and Katančić.

Finally, simultaneous with the tendency to create a common literary language, there is the tendency to unify the orthography, which continues to draw ever closer to the principle of phonetics formulated by Mihanović: "One should use the letter which is suggested by the true pronunciation of the syllable," or in short: "Write as you enunciate."[21]

Clearly, toward the end of the eighteenth century much had been accomplished to lead Croatians of all regions to recognize one another as members of the same nation and to unite them in one common literary language. Those people are mistaken, therefore, who link the political, cultural, and literary revival of Croatia exclusively to Lj. Gaj; and they are even more mistaken in attributing it to suggestions received from abroad. The Revival or the Croatian Illyrian Movement in its many aspects is not a result of foreign fecundation, but is rather an indigenous development. It is mostly an autochthonous product, and its roots must be sought in the eighteenth century and even beyond.

21/"Quam litteram vera sillabae pronuntiatio insinuat, illa littera debet scribi. Sic scribe sicut enuntias."

Bibliography

COLLECTED AND SELECTED WORKS OF THE OLD WRITERS

Baraković, Juraj. *Djela Jurja Barakovića*/Juraj Baraković's Works. P. Budmani and M. Valjavac. ("Stari pisci hrvatski," 17.) Zagreb: Yugoslav Academy, 1889.

Brezovački, Tito. *Djela Tituša Brezovačkoga*/Tito Brezovački's Works. Ed. M. Ratković ("Stari pisci hrvatski," 29.) Zagreb: Yugoslav Academy, 1951.

Česmički, Ivan. *Pjesme i epigrami*/Poems and Epigrams. Introduction by M. Kombol. Trans. N. Šob. Zagreb: Yugoslav Academy, 1951.

Čubranović, Andrija. *Pjesme*. *See* Nalješković, Nikola.

Dimitrović, Nikola. *Pjesme Nikole Dimitrovića i Nikole Nalješkovića*/The Poems of Nikola Dimitrović and Nikola Nalješković. Ed. V. Jagić and Gj. Daničić. ("Stari pisci hrvatski," 5.) Zagreb: Yugoslav Academy, 1873.

Držić, Gjore. *Pjesme*. *See* Menčetic Vlahović, Šiško.

Držić, Marin. *Djela Marina Držića*/Marin Držić's Works. 2nd ed. by M. Rešetar. ("Stari pisci hrvatski," 7.) Zagreb: Yugoslav Academy, 1930. 1st ed. by F. Petračić, 1875.

Gjorgjić or Gjurgjević [Djurdjević], Ignat. *Djela Injacija Gjorgji*/Injacije Gjorgji's Works. Ed. M. Rešetar. ("Stari pisci hrvatski," 24, 25.) Zagreb: Yugoslav Academy, 1918–26.

Gjurgjević, Ignjat. *See* Gjorgjić.

Glegjević, Antun. *Djela Antuna Glegjevića*/Antun Glegjević's Works. Ed. P. Budmani. ("Stari pisci hrvatski," 15.) Zagreb: Yugoslav Academy, 1886.

Grabovac, Filip. *Cvit razgovora naroda i jezika iliričkoga aliti rvackoga*/The People's Finest Edifying Discourse in the Illyrian or Croatian Language. Ed. T. Matić. ("Stari pisci hrvatski," 30.) Zagreb: Yugoslav Academy, 1951.

Gučetić-Bendešević, Savko. *Djela*. *See* Zoranić, Petar.

Gundulić, Gjivo (Ivan) Frano. *Djela Gjiva Frana Gundulića*/Gjivo Frano Gundulić's Works. 3rd ed. by Gj. Körbler. ("Stari pisci hrvatski," 9.) Zagreb: Yugoslav Academy, 1938. 1st ed. by A. Pavić, 1877; 2nd by Gj. Körbler, 1919.

Gundulić, Ivan. *Osman*. Ed. M. Ratković. ("Pet stoljeća hrvatske književnosti," 13.) Zagreb: Zora and Matica Hrvatska, 1962.

Hektorović, Petar. *Pjesme Petra Hektorovića i Hanibala Lucića*/The Poems of Petar Hektorović and Hanibal Lucić. Ed. S. Žepić. ("Stari pisci hrvatski," 6.) Zagreb: Yugoslav Academy, 1874.

Ivanošić, Antun. *See* Kanižlić, Antun.

Jegjupka. *See* Nalješković, Nikola.

Kačić Miošić, Andrija. *Djela Andrije Kačića Miošića*/Andrija Kačić-Miošić's Works. Ed. T. Matić. ("Stari pisci hrvatski," 27, 28.) Zagreb: Yugoslav Academy, 1942.

Kanižlić, Antun. *Pjesme Antuna Kanižlića, Antuna Ivanošića i Matije Petra Katančića*/The Poems of Antun Kanižlić, Antun Ivanošić, and Matija Petar Katančić. Ed. T. Matić. ("Stari pisci hrvatski," 26.) Zagreb: Yugoslav Academy, 1940.

Katančić, Matija Petar. *See* Kanižlić, Antun.

Kavanjin, Jerolim. *Povist vangjeoska bogatoga a nesrećna Epuluna i uboga a čestita Lazara*/Gospel Story of the Rich but Unfortunate Man and the Poor but Happy Lazarus. Ed. J. Aranza. ("Stari pisci hrvatski, 22.) Zagreb: Yugoslav Academy, 1913.

Lucić, Hanibal. *Pjesme*. *See* Hektorović, Petar.

Marulić, Marko. *Pjesme Marka Marulića*/The Poems of Marko Marulić. Ed. I. Kukuljević-Sakcinski and V. Jagić. ("Stari pisci hrvatski," 1.) Zagreb: Yugoslav Academy, 1869.

—— *Davidias*. Ed. J. Badalić. ("Stari pisci hrvatski," 31.) Zagreb: Yugoslav Academy, 1954.

Menčetić, Šiško. *Pjesme Šiška Menčetića i Gjore Držića, i ostale pjesme Ranjinina zbornika*/The Poems of Šiško Menčetić and Gjore Držić and the Remaining Poems Found in the Ranjina Collection. ("Stari pisci hrvatski," 2.) 2nd ed. Ed. Milan Rešetar. Zagreb: Yugoslav Academy, 1937.

Menčetić Vlahović, Šiško. *Pjesme Šiška Menčetića Vlahovića i Gjore Držića*/ The Poems of Šiško Menčetić Vlahović and Gjore Držić. Ed. V. Jagić. ("Stari pisci hrvatski," 2.) Zagreb: Yugoslav Academy, 1870.

Mišetić Bobaljević, Sabo. *See* Nalješković, Nikola.

Nalješković, Nikola. *Pjesme*. *See* Dimitrović, Nikola.

—— *Pjesme Nikole Nalješkovića, Andrije Čubranovića, Miše Pelegrinovića i Saba Mišetića Bobaljevića i Jegjupka neznana pjesnika*/The Poems of Nikola Nalješković, Andrija Čubranović, Mišo Pelegrinović and Sabo Mišetić Bobaljević, and *Jegjupka* by an unknown author. Ed. S. Žepić. ("Stari pisci hrvatski," 8.) Zagreb: Yugoslav Academy, 1876.

Palmotić, Junije Djordje. *Djela Gjona Gjora Palmotića*/Gjono Gjoro Palmotić's Works. Ed. A. Pavić and I. Broz. ("Stari pisci hrvatski," 12, 13, 14, 19 in 4 vols.) Zagreb: Yugoslav Academy, 1882–92.

Pelegrinović, Mišo. *Pjesme*. *See* Nalješković, Nikola.

Ranjina, Dinko. *Pjesni razlike*/Miscellaneous Verse. Ed. M. Valjavac. ("Stari pisci hrvatski," 18.) Zagreb: Yugoslav Academy, 1891.

Reljković, Matija Antun. *Djela Matije Antuna Reljkovića*/Matija Antun Reljković's Works. ("Stari pisci hrvatski," 23.) Zagreb: Yugoslav Academy, 1916.

Sasin, Antun. *Djela*. *See* Zoranić, Petar.

Vetranić. *See* Vetranović Čavčić.

Vetranović Čavčić, Mavro. *Pjesme Mavra Vetranovića Čavčića*/The Poems of Mavro Vetranović Čavčić. Ed. V. Jagić, I. A. Kaznačić, and Gj. Daničić. ("Stari pisci hrvatski," 3, 4.) Zagreb: Yugoslav Academy, 1871–72.

Zlatarić, D(om)inko. *Djela Dominka Zlatarića*/Dominko Zlatarić's Works. Ed. P. Budmani. ("Stari pisci hrvatski," 21.) Zagreb: Yugoslav Academy, 1899.

Zoranić, Petar. *Djela Petra Zoranića, Antuna Sasina, Savka Gučetića Bendeševića*/Works of Petar Zoranić, Antun Sasin, Savko Gučetić-Bendešević. Ed. P. Budmani. ("Stari pisci hrvatski," 16.) Zagreb: Yugoslav Academy, 1888.

Zrinski, Petar. *Adrijanskoga mora sirena*/Siren of the Adriatic Sea. Ed. J. Matić. ("Stari pisci hrvatski," 32.) Zagreb: Yugoslav Academy, 1954.

HISTORIES OF LITERATURE

Adamović, Vice. *Dubrovčani izvan zavičaja*/Dubrovnik People outside their Native City. Dubrovnik, 1914.

Andjelić, Djordje. *Istorija jugoslovenske književnosti*/History of Yugoslav Literature. 3rd ed. Beograd: Geca Kon, 1933.

Appendini, Francesco Maria. *Notizie istorico-critiche sulle antichità, storia e letteratura de' Ragusei*. Ragusa, 1802–3.

Barac, Antun. *Jugoslavenska književnost*/Yugoslav Literature. Zagreb: Matica Hrvatska, 1959.

Bogdanović, David. *Pregled književnosti hrvatske i srpske*/Survey of Croatian and Serbian Literature. 3 vols. Zagreb: St. Kugli, 1914–16.

Bošković, Jovan. *Pismo o književnosti srpskoj hrvatskoj*/A Letter on Serbian and Croatian Literature. Novi Sad, 1892.

Broz, Ivan. *Crtice iz hrvatske književnosti*/Sketches from Croatian Literature. 2 vols. Zagreb, 1886–8.

Bućar, Franjo. *Povijest hrvatske protestantske književnosti za reformacije*/ History of Croatian Protestant Literature during the Reformation. Zagreb: Matica Hrvatska, 1910.

Ciampoli, Domenico. *Letterature slave*. Milano, 1889.

Cronia, Arturo. *Storia della letteratura serbo-croata*. Milano: Nuova accademia editrice, 1956.

Dolci (*Lat.* Dulcius, *Cr.* Slade), Sebastiano. *Fasti Letterario-Ragusini*. Venetiis, 1767.

Filipović, Ivan. *Kratka povijest književnosti hrvatske i srpske*/A Short History of Croatian and Serbian Literature. Zagreb, 1875.

Forko, Josip. *Crtice iz slavonske književnosti u* XVIII. *stoljeću*/Sketches from the Literature of 18th-Century Slavonia. Osijek, 1888.

Gavrilović, Andra. *Istorija srpske i hrvatske književnosti*/History of Serbian and Croatian Literature. 3 vols. Beograd, 1910–13.

Gesemann, Gerhard. *Die serbokroatische Literatur*. Wildpark-Potsdam: Athenaion, 1930.

—— *Srpskohrvatska književnost*/Serbocroatian Literature. Translation from German. Beograd: Geca Kon, 1934.

Gudel, Vladimir. *Stare kajkavske drame*/Old Kajkavian Plays. Zagreb, 1900.

Hadžijahić, Muhamed. *Hrvatska muslimanska književnost prije 1878*/Croatian Muslim Literature Before 1878. Sarajevo, 1938.

Haler, Albert. *Novija dubrovačka književnost*/Recent Literature of Dubrovnik. Zagreb, 1944.

Ilešić, Fran. *Zgodovina hrvatske književnosti*/History of Croatian Literature. Ljubljana, 1915.

Jagić, Vatroslav. *Historija književnosti naroda hrvatskoga i srpskoga*/History of the Literature of the Croatian and Serbian Peoples. Zagreb, 1867.

Jakošić, Josip. "Scriptores Interamniae vel Pannoniae Sauiae, nunc Slavoniae dictae anno 1795 conscripti (cum continuatione a. 1830)," *Gradja*, II (Zagreb: Yugoslav Academy, 1899).

Janez, Stanko. *Pregled zgodovine jugoslavenskih književnosti*/Survey of the History of Yugoslav Literatures. Maribor, 1953.

Jedrlinić, Tomo. *Kratki pregled hrvatske i srpske književnosti do Preporoda*/ A Short Survey of Croatian and Serbian Literature up to the National Awakening. Ljubljana, 1927.

Ježić, Slavko. *Hrvatska književnost od početka do danas, 1100–1941*/Croatian Literature from Its Beginning to the Present Day, 1100–1941. Zagreb: A. Velzek, 1944.

——— *Hrvatski preporod*/The Croatian Awakening. Zagreb: Društvo hrvatskih srednjoškolskih profesora, 1944.

Jireček, Josef Konstantin. *Beiträge zur ragusanischen Literaturgeschichte*. Berlin, 1899.

Jotić, A. St. *Istorija književnosti SHS*/History of the Literature of the Serbs, Croatians, and Slovenes. 3 vols. Beograd, 1921–4.

Kadić, Ante. *Contemporary Croatian Literature*. 'S Gravenhage: Mouton and Co., 1960.

Kombol, Mihovil. *Poviest hrvatske književnosti do narodnog preporoda*/History of Croatian Literature up to the National Awakening. Zagreb: Matica Hrvatska, 1945.

Kostrenčić, Ivan. *Urkundliche Beiträge zur Geschichte der protestantischen Literatur der Südslawen in den Jahren 1559–1665*. Wien, 1874.

Krčelić, Adam Baltazar. *Scriptorum ex regno Sclavoniae a saeculo XIV usque ad XVII inclusive collectio*. Varaždin, 1774.

Krek, Gregor. *Einleitung in die slavische Literaturgeschichte und Darstellung ihrer älteren Perioden*. Graz, 1874.

Kreševljaković, Hamdija. *Kratak pregled hrvatske knjige u Herceg-Bosni od najstarijih vremena do danas*/A Short Survey of Croatian Letters in Bosnia-Hercegovina from the Oldest Times till Today. Sarajevo, 1912.

Kukuljević-Sakcinski, Ivan. *Glasoviti Hrvati prošlih vjekova*/Famous Croatians from Past Centuries. Zagreb, 1886.

Lapčević, Dragiša. *Istorija srpske i hrvatske književnosti*/History of Serbian and Croatian Literature. Beograd: Geca Kon, 1931.

Laszowski, Emilijan (ed.). *Znameniti i zaslužni Hrvati ... 925–1925*/Croatians of Fame and Merit ... from 925 to 1925. Zagreb, 1925.

Leskien, August. *Altkroatische geistliche Schauspiele*. Leipzig, 1884.

Ljubić, Šime. *Ogledalo književne povijesti jugoslavjanske*/A Survey of the Literary History of the South Slavs. 2 vols. Rijeka, 1864–9.

Lozovina, Vinko. *Dalmacija u hrvatskoj književnosti*/Dalmatia in Croatian Literature. Zagreb: Matica Hrvatska, 1936.

Lucianović, Melchiorre. *Storia della letteratura Slava (Serba e Croata) dalle origini fino ai giorni nostri*. Spalato, 1880.

Majaron, Paulina. *Povijest hrvatske književnosti*/History of Croatian Literature. Zagreb, 1894.

Malin, Franjo. *Kratki pregled istorije jugoslovenske književnosti*/A Short Survey of the History of Yugoslav Literature. Novi Sad, 1930.

Matić, Tomo. *Hrvatska književnost mletačke Dalmacije i život njihova doba*/ The Croatian Literature of Venetian Dalmatia and the Life of the Epoch. Zagreb, 1926.

——— *Prosvjetni i književni rad u Slavoniji prije preporoda*/Cultural and Literary Activity in Slavonia before the National Awakening. Zagreb: Yugoslav Academy, 1945.

Maver, Giovanni. "Letteratura serbo-croata," *Storia delle letterature moderne d'Europa e d'America*. Milano, 1960.

Medini, Milorad. *Povjest hrvatske književnosti u Dalmaciji i Dubrovniku/*

History of Croatian Literature in Dalmatia and Dubrovnik. Zagreb: Matica Hrvatska, 1902.

Miklošić, Tomo. *Izbor dugovanj vsakovrstneh*/A Selection of Different Subjects. 2nd ed. Zagreb, 1839.

Miler, Ferdo Ž. *Povijest hrvatske književnosti*/History of Croatian Literature. Zagreb, 1894.

Missoni, Attilio. *Compendio di storia della letteratura serbo-croata*. Napoli, 1945.

Mitrović, Bartolomeo. *La letteratura serbo-croata*. Firenze, 1902.

——— *Studi sulla letteratura serbo-croata*. Firenze: B. Seeber, 1903.

Murko, Matthias. *Geschichte der südslawischen Literaturen*. Leipzig: C. F. Amelang, 1908.

Pantić, Miroslav. *Dubrovačka književnost*/Literature of Dubrovnik. Beograd, 1960.

Pavić, Armin. *Historija dubrovačke drame*/History of the Drama of Dubrovnik. Zagreb: Yugoslav Academy, 1871.

Pechan, Antun. *Poviest hrvatske književnosti*/History of Croatian Literature. 2nd ed. rev. Zagreb, 1883.

Petrović, Nikola. *Jugoslovenska književnost*/Yugoslav Literature. 3 vols. Beograd, 1938.

Poljanec, Franjo. *Historija stare i srednje jugoslovenske književnosti*/History of Old and Middle Yugoslav Literature. 2nd ed. rev. Zagreb, 1937.

Popović, Pavle. *Littérature jugoslave*. A lecture. Roma: Tip. dell'Unione, 1915.

——— "The Literature of the Southern Slavs," reprinted from *The Englishwoman*. London: Strangeways, [1917].

——— *Jugoslovenska književnost*/Yugoslav Literature. 5th ed. Beograd: Geca Kon, 1930.

——— *La littérature yougoslave*. Suivie d'un essai de bibliographie française de la littérature yougoslave par P. Popović, Miodrag Ibrovac. Paris, 1931.

Prohaska, Dragutin. *Das kroatisch-serbische Schrifttum in Bosnien und der Herzegowina*. Zagreb: M. Breyer, 1911.

——— *Pregled hrvatske i srpske književnosti*/A Survey of Croatian and Serbian Literature. Zagreb, 1919.

——— *Pregled savremene hrvatsko-srpske književnosti*/A Survey of Contemporary Croato-Serbian Literature. Zagreb: Matica Hrvatska, 1921.

Safařik, Pavel Josef. *Geschichte der südslawischen Literatur*. Ed. J. Jireček. 3 vols. Prag: F. Tempsky, 1864–5.

——— *Geschichte der slawischen Sprache und Literatur nach allen Mundarten*. 2nd ed. Prag: F. Tempsky, 1869.

Savković, Miloš. *L'Influence du réalisme français dans le roman serbo-croate*. ("Bibliothèque de la Revue de littérature comparée," 107.) Paris: H. Champion, 1935.

——— *La littérature yougoslave moderne*. Belgrade: Bureau central de presse, 1936.

——— *Jugoslovenska književnost*/Yugoslave Literature. 2 vols. Beograd: Znanje, 1954.

Šegvić, Kerubin. *Kratka povijest hrvatske (srpske) književnosti od prvih poče-*

taka do god. 1900/A Short History of Croatian (Serbian) Literature from the Beginning to the Year 1900. Zagreb, 1911.
Špoljar, Krsto, and Vaupotić, Miroslav. *Književni godišnjak*/Literary Yearbook. Zagreb: Lykos, 1961.
Stanojević, Milivoj St. *Early Yugoslav Literature, 1000–1800*. ("Columbia University Slavonic Studies," 1.) New York, 1922.
Stefanović, Dragutin, and Stanisavljević, Vukašin. *Pregled jugoslovenske književnosti*/A Survey of Yugoslav Literature. 2nd ed. Beograd: Zavod za izdavanje udžbenika Narodne Republike Srbije, 1960.
Stojanović, J. *Dubrovačka književnost*/Literature of Dubrovnik. Dubrovnik, 1900.
Strohal, Rudolf. *Kratak osvrt na hrvatsku glagolsku književnost*/A Rapid View of Croatian Glagolitic Literature. Zagreb, 1913.
—— *Hrvatska glagolska knjiga*/Croatian Glagolitic Letters. Zagreb: Tiskara "Merkur," 1915.
Šurmin, Gjuro. *Povijest književnosti hrvatske i srpske*/History of Croatian and Serbian Literature. Zagreb: L. Hartmann, 1898.
—— *Iz zajedničke književne prošlosti Bosne i Hercegovine*/From the Common Literary Heritage of Bosnia and Hercegovina. Zagreb, 1901.
—— *Hrvatski Preporod*/The Croatian National Awakening. 2 vols. Zagreb, 1903–4.
Trogrančić, Franjo. *Letteratura medioevale degli Slavi meridionali*. Roma, 1950.
—— *Storia della letteratura croata dall'Umanesimo alla rinascita nazionale*. Roma, 1953.
Ujević, Mate. *Hrvatska književnost*/Croatian Literature. Zagreb, 1932.
Urbani, Umberto. *Scrittori jugoslavi*. Trieste, 1930.
—— *Serbo-croata (letteratura e lingua)*. Torino, 1938.
Veljković, Momir. *Istorija jugoslovenske književnosti*/History of Yugoslav Literature. Beograd, 1939.
Vodnik (Drechsler), Branko. *Prvi hrvatski pjesnici*/The First Croatian Poets. Prag, 1901.
—— *Slavonska književnost u* XVIII. *vijeku*/The Literature of Slavonia in the 18th Century. Zagreb, 1907.
—— *Povijest hrvatske književnosti*/History of Croatian Literature. With a survey of Croatian Glagolitic Literature by V. Jagić. Zagreb: Matica Hrvatska, 1913.
—— *Pregled hrvatsko-srpske književnosti u ogledima*/A Survey of Croato-Serbian Literature by Texts. Zagreb, 1923.
Warnier, Raymond. *Littérature yougoslave*. Paris, 1937.
Zore, Luka. *Kratki pregled razvitka naše književnosti u Dubrovniku*/A Short Survey of the Development of Our Literature in Dubrovnik. Zadar, 1869.
Županić, Niko. *Aperçu général de la littérature yougoslave*. Paris, 1919.

ANTHOLOGIES OF POETRY AND PROSE

Badalić, Hugo. *Hrvatska antologija*/A Croatian Anthology. Zagreb, 1892.
Barac, Antun. *Ilirska knjiga*/Illyrian Book. Beograd, 1931.

Bartulović, Niko. *Jadranska antologija*/An Adriatic Anthology. Split, 1934.

Bogdanović, David. *Antologija hrvatske lirike*/Anthology of Croatian Lyric Poetry. Zagreb, 1924.

Crnković-Tomić. *Scrittori jugoslavi*. Rijeka, 1956.

Cronia, Arturo. *Antologia serbo-croata*. Milano: Trevisini, [1934].

—— *Le più belle pagine della letteratura serbo-croata*. Milano, 1963.

Dukat, Vladoje. *Sladki naš kaj: Ogledi iz stare kajkavske književnosti*/Our Sweet Kaj: Selections from Old Kajkavian Literature. ("Tekstovi i pregledi," 7.) Zagreb, 1944.

Frangeš, Ivo. *Antologija hrvatskog eseja*/Anthology of Croatian Essays. ("Biblioteka Antologija jugoslavenske književnosti.") Geograd: Nolit, 1957.

Grgec, Petar. *Stare slave djedovina*/Old and Glorious Land of Ancestors. Zagreb, 1924.

Kadić, Ante. *Croatian Reader with Vocabulary*. 's Gravenhage: Mouton and Co., 1960.

Kaznačić, Ivan August. *Vienac gorskog i pitomog cvieća*/A Wreath Made of Mountain and Garden Flowers. Dubrovnik, 1872.

Kukuljević-Sakcinski, Ivan. *Pjesnici hrvatski* XV *vijeka*/Croatian Poets of the 15th Century. Zagreb, 1856.

—— *Književnici u Hrvata iz prve polovine* XVII *vijeka s ove strane Velebita*/ Northern Croatian Writers from the First Half of the 17th Century. Zagreb, 1869.

—— *Pjesnici hrvatski* XVI *vijeka*/Croatian Poets of the 16th Century. 2 vols. Zagreb, 1856, 1867.

Magjer, R. F. *U pjesmi i priči*/In Verse and Story (An anthology for youth). Osijek, 1906.

Mamuzić, Ilija. *Antologija ilirskog pokreta*/Anthology of the Illyrian Movement. ("Školska biblioteka," 37–38.) Beograd: Nolit, 1958.

Maraković, Ljubomir. *Hrvatska književna kritika*/Croatian Literary Criticism. ("Sto godina hrvatske književnosti, 1830–1930," 5.) Zagreb, 1935.

Matić, Svetozar R. *Izbor dubrovačkog pjesništva*/A Selection of Poems from Dubrovnik Literature. Beograd, 1923.

Matić, Tomo. *Iz hrvatske književnosti u Slavoniji prije Preporoda*/Selections from Croatian Literature in Slavonia before the National Awakening. ("Tekstovi i pregledi," 4.) Zagreb, 1942.

Matković, Marijan. *Antologija hrvatske drame od Marina Držića do Miroslava Krleže*/Anthology of Croatian Drama from Marin Držić to Miroslav Krleža. ("Biblioteka Antologija jugoslovenske književnosti.") Beograd: Nolit, 1958.

Milaković, Josip. *Naša pjesma: antologija hrvatskoj mladeži*/Our Poetry: An Anthology for Croatian Youth. Vol. I, Donja Tuzla, 1903. Vol. II, Sarajevo, 1905.

—— *Hrvatska pjesma*/Croatian Poems. Zagreb, 1907.

Milković, Zlatko. *Hrvatske balade*/Croatian Ballads. Zagreb, 1941.

Pavlović, Dragoljub. *Dubrovačka poezija*/Poetry from Dubrovnik Literature. ("Jugoslovenski stariji pisci. Odabrana dela.") Beograd, 1950. (Cyrillic)

—— *Dubrovačke poeme*/Dubrovnik Poems. Beograd, 1953.

—— *Iz naše književnosti feudalnog doba*/Selections from Our Literature of the Feudal Epoch. Sarajevo, 1954.

—— *Antologija dubrovačke lirike*/Anthology of Dubrovnik Poetry. Beograd: Nolit, 1960.

Pucić (or Pocić, *It.* Pozze), Medo (Orsat). *Slavjanska Antologija iz rukopisah Dubrovačkieh pjesnikah*/A Slavic Anthology from the Manuscripts of Dubrovnik Poets. Beč (Vienna), 1844.

Rakovac, Dragutin, and Vukotinović, Ljudevit. *Pjesmarica*/A Collection of Poems. 2nd ed. Zagreb, 1842.

Rešetar, Milan. *Antologija Dubrovačke lirike*/A Lyric Anthology of Dubrovnik Literature. Beograd: Srpska Književna Zadruga, 1894. (Cyrillic)

—— *Libro od mnozijeh razloga*/A Book of Many Examples. ("Zbornik za istoriju, jezik i književnost srpskog naroda," 15.) Beograd, 1926. (Cyrillic)

Šenoa, August. *Antologija pjesničtva hrvatskoga i srbskoga narodnoga i umjetnoga*/Anthology of Croatian and Serbian Folk and Artistic Poetry. Zagreb: Matica Hrvatska, 1876.

Slamnig, Ivan. *Antologija hrvatske poezije od najstarijih zapisa do kraja* XIX *stoljeća*/Anthology of Croatian Verse from the Oldest Records to the 19th Century. Zagreb: Lykos, 1959.

Špoljar, Krsto. *Ljubav pjesnika: Mala antologija hrvatske ljubavne poezije*/ Poet's Love: A Small Anthology of Croatian Love Poetry. Zagreb: Lykos, 1956.

Strohal, Rudolf. *Zbirka starih hrvatskih crkvenih pjesama*/A Collection of Old Croatian Church Hymns. Zagreb, 1916.

—— *Čitanka iz književnih djela starih bugarskih, hrvatskih, srpskih i slovenačkih*/A Reader of Literary Selections from Old Bulgarian, Croatian, Serbian, and Slovenian Works. Zagreb, 1921.

Šurmin, Gjuro, and Bosanac, Stjepan. *Čitanka iz književnih starina staroslavenskih, hrvatskih i srpskih*/A Reader of Old Slavonic, Croatian, and Serbian Literary Selections. Zagreb, 1901.

Trogrančić, Franjo. *Antologija hrvatske lirike*/Anthology of Croatian Poetry. Roma, 1953.

—— *Poeti croati moderni.* Milano, 1965.

Wiesner, Ljubo. *42: Hrvatska pjesma kroz stoljeća*/Forty-Two Croatian Poems through the Centuries. Zagreb, 1942.

SPECIAL TREATISES

Bašagić, Safvet. *Bošnjaci i Hercegovci u islamskoj književnosti*/Bosnians and Hercegovinians in Islamic Literature. Sarajevo: Zemaljski Muzej u Bosni i Hercegovini, 1912.

—— *Znameniti Hrvati Bošnjaci i Hercegovci u Turskoj carevini*/Famous Croatians from Bosnia and Hercegovina in the Turkish Empire. Zagreb: Matica Hrvatska, 1931.

Batinić, Mijo Vjenceslav. *Djelovanje franjevaca u Bosni i Hercegovini za prvih šest viekova njihova boravka*/The First Six Centuries of Franciscan Activity in Bosnia and Hercegovina. 3 vols. Zagreb: Dionička tiskara, 1881–7.

Berić, Dušan. *Iz književne prošlosti Dalmacije*/From the Dalmatian Literary Heritage ("Biblioteka suvremenih pisaca.") Split: Matica Hrvatska, 1956.

Cronia, Arturo. *Il canzoniere raguseo del 1507*. Zara, 1927.

——— *Aspetti caratteristici dell'Umanesimo in Dalmazia.* Venezia, 1955.

Dayre, Jean. *Dubrovačke studije*/Studies in Dubrovnik Literature. Zagreb, 1938.

Deanović, Mirko. "Odrazi talijanske akademije 'Degli Arcadi' preko Jadrana"/ Imitations of the Italian Academy "Degli Arcadi" on the Other Side of the Adriatic, *Rad*, 248, 250 (Zagreb: Yugoslav Academy, 1934).

Eterović, Karlo. *Fra Andrija Kačić-Miošić na temelju novih istraživanja*/New Findings on Fr. Andrija Kačić-Miošić. Dubrovnik, 1922.

——— "Hrvatska crkvena prikazivanja"/Croatian Religious Plays, *Narodna Starina*, xi (Zagreb, 1932).

Fancev, Franjo. "Jezik hrvatskih protestantskih pisaca 16. vijeka"/The Language of the Croatian Protestant Writers in the 16th Century, *Rad*, 212 (Zagreb: Yugoslav Academy, 1916).

——— "Bibliografija hrvatske protestantske književnosti za reformacije"/Bibliography of Croatian Protestant Literature during the Reformation, *Starine* (Yugoslav Academy), xxxix (Zagreb, 1938).

——— "Koliko ima istine u prepričavanju o 'Hrvatskom protestantizmu'"/ What is True about "Croatian Protestantism," *Savremenik*, xxvi (Zagreb, 1938).

——— "Dubrovnik u razvitku hrvatske književnosti"/Dubrovnik in the Development of Croatian Literature, *Ljetopis*, lii, 113 (Zagreb: Yugoslav Academy, 1940).

Fermendžin, Eusebius. *Acta Bosnae potissimum ecclesiastica* ... ("Monumenta spectantia historiam Slavorum meridionalium," 23.) Zagreb: Yugoslav Academy, 1892.

Handžić, M. *Književni rad bosansko-hercegovačkih muslimana*/The Literary Activity of Bosnian and Hercegovinian Muslims. Sarajevo, 1934.

Herceg, J. *Ilirizam*/The Illyrian Awakening. Beograd, 1935.

Jagić, Vatroslav. *Život i rad Jurja Križanića*/The Life and Work of Juraj Križanić. ("Djela JAZU," 28.) Zagreb: Yugoslav Academy, 1917.

Javarek, Vera. "Three 16th Century Dalmatian Poets," *Slavonic and East European Review*, xli (1962).

Jelenić, Julijan. *Kultura i bosanski franjevci*/Culture and the Bosnian Franciscans. 2 vols. Zagreb, 1912–15.

——— *Bio-bibliografija Franjevaca Bosne Srebreničke*/Bio-bibliography of the Franciscans of the Bosnian Franciscan Province of Srebrenica. Zagreb, 1925.

Jensen, Alfred. *Gundulić und sein "Osman."* Göteborg, 1900.

Ježić, Slavko. *Život i rad Frana Krste Frankopana*/The Life and Work of Frano Krsto Frankapan (with an anthology of his works). Zagreb: Matica Hrvatska, 1921.

Karaman, Ljubo. *La Dalmatie à travers les âges: Son histoire et ses monuments.* Split, 1933.

Klaić, Vjekoslav. *Život i djela Pavla Rittera Vitezovića*/The Life and Works of Pavao Ritter Vitezović. Zagreb: Matica Hrvatska, 1914.

Kombol, Mihovil. *O Marku Maruliću*/About Marko Marulić. Zagreb, 1950.

Košuta, Leo. "Siena nella vita e nell'opera di Marino Darsa," *Ricerche slavistiche*, ix (Roma, 1961).

Krčelić, Baltazar Adam. *Annuae ili historija.* Ed. N. Majnarić. Trans. V. Gortan. ("Hrvatski latinisti," 3.) Zagreb: Yugoslav Academy, 1952.

Kukuljević-Sakcinski, Ivan. "Život Jerolima Kavanjina"/Jerolim Kavanjin's Life. A biographical sketch in *Dra J. Kavanjina Bogatstvo i Ubožtvo.* Zagreb, 1861.

——— "Marko Marulić i njegovo doba"/Marko Marulić and His Epoch, *Pjesme Marka Marulića,* ed. I. Kukuljević Sakcinski. ("Stari pisci hrvatski," 1.) Zagreb: Yugoslav Academy, 1869.

Magdić, Mila (ed.) *Život i djela Senjanina Mateše Ant. pl. Kuhačevića*/The Life and Works of Mateša Antun Kuhačević of Senj. Senj, 1878.

Matković, J. *Bibliografija bosanskih Franjevaca*/Bibliography of Bosnian Franciscans, Sarajevo, 1896.

Murko, Matthias. *Die Bedeutung der Reformation und Gegenreformation für das geistige Leben der Südslaven.* Separate reprint from *Slavia.* Prag and Heidelberg, 1927.

Novak, Grga. *Prošlost Dalmacije*/The Dalmatian Past. ("Zemlje i narodi," 4, 5.) Zagreb, 1944.

Pavlović, Dragoljub. *Iz književne i kulturne istorije Dubrovnika*/From Dubrovnik's Literary and Cultural Past. ("Jugoslovenski pisci.") Sarajevo: Svjetlost, 1955.

Petravić, Ante. *Jedan hrvatski Silvio Pellico*/A Croatian Silvio Pellico. Split, 1917.

Praga, Giuseppe. *Storia di Dalmazia.* Padova, 1954.

Prpić, T. *Književni regionalizam u Hrvata*/Literary Regionalism among Croatians. Zagreb, 1936.

Radonić, Jovan. *Rimska kurija i južnoslavenske zemlje od* XVI *do* XIX *veka*/The Roman Curia and South-Slavic Lands from the 16th to the 19th Century. ("Posebna izdanja," 155.) Beograd: Srpska akademija nauka, 1950. (Cyrillic)

Ratković, M. *Ivan Gundulić* (with a complete bibliography of Osman). Zagreb, 1955.

Rojnić, M. *Kulturne i književne veze Istre i Hrvatske u prošlosti*/Past Cultural and Literary Ties between Istria and Croatia. Zagreb, 1931.

Ruvarac, Kosta. *Značajnost dubrovačke književnosti*/The Significance of Dubrovnik Literature. Novi Sad, 1866.

Šimrak, Janko. *De relationibus Slavorum meridionalium cum S. Romana Sede Apostolica saec.* XVII *et* XVIII. Zagreb, 1925.

Škavić, Josip. "Književnost u Slavoniji u XVIII stoljeću"/Literature in 18th Century Slavonia, *Republika,* 1954 (Zagreb).

Smičiklas, Tade. *O postanku Gundulićeva Osmana*/On the Origin of Gundulić's Osman. Zagreb, 1887.

Šrepel, Milivoj. "Marulićeve latinske pjesme"/Marulić's Latin Poems, *Gradja,* II (Zagreb: Yugoslav Academy, 1899).

Stojković, Marijan. "Rimska papinska protivureformacija u južnoslavenskim zemljama"/The Roman Papal Counter-Reformation in South-Slavic Lands, *Nastavni vjesnik* (Zagreb, 1938).

Tamaro, Attilio. *La Vénétie Julienne et la Dalmatie.* 3 vols. Roma: Società Nazionale "Dante Alighieri," 1918–19.

Torbarina, Josip. *Italian Influence on the Poets of the Ragusan Republic*. London: Williams and Norgate, 1931.

Voinovitch (Vojnović), Louis (Lujo). *Histoire de Dalmatie*. 2 vols. Paris: Hachette, [1934].

Warnier, Raymond. "Illyrisme et nationalisme croate," *Zbornik ... Marka Marulića*, ed. Josip Badalić and Nikola Majnarić. ("Djela JAZU," 40.) Zagreb: Yugoslav Academy, 1950.

5

The Development of Book-Printing

1483–1940

IVAN ESIH

THE BEGINNINGS IN VENICE

Within a few years after the German Giovanni da Spira (Johannes von Speyer) founded the first printing house in Venice in 1469, Croatians were working in the printing shops there, some of whom were later to become noted master craftsmen and even eventually to own their own printing shops, a success facilitated by the close cultural relations between the Venetians and the nearby South Slavic peoples. An especially large number of these craftsmen came from Dubrovnik, a city that maintained a brisk trade and close political contacts with the Venetian Republic.

Soon after the invention of printing, Venice had become the major center of the new art. Between 1470 and 1500 approximately 10,000 books or more were printed in Europe, 2885 of which were printed in Venice, 925 in Rome, 751 in Paris, 526 in Strasbourg, 530 in Cologne, 382 in Nuremberg, 351 in Leipzig, and 134 in Mainz. However, Venice contributed more than simply the greatest number of books, for by the end of the century da Spira had assisted and taught printing to more than two hundred diligent and enterprising craftsmen, among them many whose accomplishments raised printing to the level of a genuine art. Several Croatians belonged to that group of pioneer printers: Dobruško Dobričević from Lastovo, better known as "Boninus de Boninis de Ragusia, natione Dalmata," who worked as a printer from 1478 to 1503; Andrija Paltašić of Kotor, from 1467 to 1492; Juraj Dalmatin (Georgius Dalmata), 1482; and Grgur Dalmatin (Gregorius Dalmata), 1483.

The first Croatian books were printed in Venice, either in Latin script or in Glagolitic, a distinct script developed for Church Slavonic and used for divine worship and even more extensively for devotional reading by individuals or monastic groups. At one time, Glagolitic, or Church Slavonic, was very close to spoken Croatian, but, like Church Latin, it became "fixed" centuries ago and is now quite remote from the secular language. Nevertheless, to this day Glagolitic plays a definite role in the national life. The first Croatian book, printed in Glagolitic, was a beautifully adorned folio missal, used in divine worship in Dalmatia, Istria, and the Kvarner Islands, where the national language was preserved in churches. It was called *Misal po zakonu rimskoga dvora/* Missale Romanum, croatice-glagolitice, and was published on February 12, 1483. Although it contains no indication of either the place of publication or the name of the printing house, it is definitely Venetian in origin. It is unfortunate that modesty led Gutenberg and the first printers to omit the names of their establishments, the places, and the dates of publication from their books, for this practice has created great difficulties in identifying the printers and their presses, so that only by a study of the design of the letters can the time and place of production of the oldest printed books be determined.

The same Glagolitic missal appeared later in a number of other editions, but the first edition, because of both the quality of the type and the appearance of the initials, surpassed all later ones. Only six copies of the first edition have been preserved – in Zagreb, Vienna, Rome, and the Library of Congress in Washington – the last being especially well preserved in its original binding. Mirko Breyer, a Croatian bibliographer and bibliophile (1863–1946), has proved[1] that the letters in the *editio princeps* were cast after older handwritten codices. From the appearance of these letters, he concludes that the closest prototype is a famous missal written on parchment in 1368, the Missal of the Novak family, nobility attendant on the Royal Household of the Hungarian-Croatian king, Louis I the Great (1326–82).

A Glagolitic edition of the *Breviarium Romanum Croatice* was issued at Venice in 1493, by the publishing house of the master Andrea Thoresani de Asola; the most complete copy of this work is preserved in the Bavarian National Library in Munich. In 1495 the *Lectionarium*, the first Croatian book using Gothic letters, was issued at Venice by the printing house of Damianus de Gorgonzola Mediolanensis, who states at the end of the book: "This is the happy ending of the Gospels and the Epistles together with introductions and blessings for the whole

1/Mirko Breyer, *O starim i rijetkim jugoslavenskim knjigama*/Old and Rare Yugoslavian Books (Zagreb: Yugoslav Academy, 1952), 8.

year written in the Illyrian [Croatian] language diligently revised by Brother Bernardin of Split."[2] Of four extant copies of this publication, one is at the Jesuit Library in Dubrovnik.

Bernardin's *Lectionarium* was edited in Zagreb, 1885, by the linguist Tomo Maretić, and published as the fifth book in a series of Works of the Yugoslav Academy of Sciences and Arts. There are two more Venetian editions of this *Lectionarium.* The second edition, edited by Canon Benedict Zborovčić in 1543, was printed in Gothic script, and richly illustrated at the Venetian press of the Nicolini de Sabio Brothers. In 1586, a third, more modest edition, with vignettes in the text, was printed at G. A. Rampazetti in Venice.

During the sixteenth century, we know that at least three Glagolitic books were published in Venice. The first, a *bukvar* (primer), the *Introductorium Croatice*, appeared in 1527; it is a small book, interesting not only for its finely illustrated sections, but also for its contents – including an alphabet and a section on grammar. In 1528, a new edition of the Missal was printed through the efforts of the Franciscan Pavao Modruški (Paul of Modruš) at the Venetian house of Bindoni and Pasini. A second edition of the *Breviarium* was prepared by Mikula Brozić, a pastor of Omišalj (on the island of Krk), at the house of the sons of Thoresani in 1561.

ISTRIA AND THE CROATIAN LITTORAL

Despite the political boundaries separating Istria from Croatia, the two were ethnically and culturally united, their unity manifest in language, folk songs, legends, and all aspects of popular national life.

From the ninth through the fifteenth centuries, Glagolitic literature was the strongest link between Istria and Croatia. Broadly, this Glagolitic area included the territories of northern Dalmatia, coastal Croatia, the Kvarner Islands and Istria, though it is impossible to place any strict boundaries. The Istrian Glagolitic priests realized that they were a part of a larger group and labeled their own language Croatian. The *Razvod istarski* (Istrian Land-Registry) of 1375 was written for the Istrian municipalities by Father Mikula *jezikom hrvatskim* (in the Croatian language).[3] In 1463, Father Fraščić from Lindar near Pazin wrote the

2/"Euangelia et epistole cum prephationibus et benedictionibus per anni circulum in lingua ylliricha feliciter expliciunt; emendata et diligenter correcta per fratrem Bernardinum Spalatensem."

3/Ivan Milčetić, "Hrvatska glagoljska bibliografija. Dio I. Opisi rukopisa"/ Croatian Glagolitic Bibliography, Part I, Descriptions of Manuscripts, *Starine* (Yugoslav Academy), XXXIII (Zagreb, 1911), 466; and Dr. Milko Kos, "Studija o

Tumačenje psaltira hrvackoga (Commentary on the Croatian Psalter), and later copied his psalter including a commentary known from some Cyrillic manuscript.[4] Professor Matko Rojnić has established the continuity of the literary and cultural ties between Istria and Croatia from the earliest beginnings to the period of the National Awakening,[5] and in recent times, more substantial evidence of the mutual ties has been uncovered, which is at present being studied and critically evaluated.

The Croatian Littoral together with Rijeka, Istria, and the Kvarner Islands played an important role in the development of Croatian culture soon after the arrival of the Croatian people in these parts – that is, from the tenth to the beginning of the eighteenth century. For centuries this area was the cradle and hearth of Croatian literacy, both of the written and the printed word.

Despite their limited resources, the Glagolitic priests did not simply encourage the printing of Glagolitic books in Venice, but tried to transplant the new art of printing to their native soil. We have very little information concerning the technical organization of the first Croatian printing shops; we can see that the type styles of the first texts in Croatian were not, strictly, a Croatian contribution, despite the fact that they were cast in domestic workshops.

In 1493, a canon from Senj, Blaž Baromić (born in Vrbnik), sojourned in Venice and worked as proofreader for the Glagolitic breviary, in the publishing house of Andrea Thoresani de Asola. In the same year, Baromić returned to Senj, bringing with him a printing press and other equipment necessary for the establishment of a shop. Thus, the fledgling art was brought to Croatia by a native son who transmitted faith in the significance and value of the printed word, and displayed great diligence and enterprise as well as technical skill. Silvestar Bedričić is mentioned with Blaž Baromić as co-founder of this first Croatian press in Senj;[6] assisting them was Deacon Gašpar Turčić from Senj, who also learned his craft in Venice.

Istarskom razvodu"/Study of Istrian Land Boundaries, *Rad* (Yugoslav Academy), CCXL (1931), 105–203.

4/Dr. Josef Vajs, "Žaltař Fraščičův," *Slavia* (Praha), I (1922), 269–84.

5/Matko Rojnić, "Nacionalno pitanje u Istri 1848–49"/The National Question in Istria 1848–9, *Historijski zbornik* (Zagreb), II (1949), 77–114. An English summary is found on pp. 113–14.

6/Recent discussions among Croatian scholars about the location of the first Croatian printing house have pointed to places in the Croatian Littoral, such as Senj, Modruš, or Kosinj, instead of Venice. For Kosinj see Josip Badalić, *Jugoslavica – usque ad annum MDC. Bibliographie der südslawischen Frühdrucke* (2nd ed.; Baden-Baden: Librairie Heitz, 1966), 23ff. For Modruš see Valentin Putanec, *Prva Tiskara u Hrvatskoj i Jugoslaviji – Modruš 1482-1484*/The First Printing Shop in Croatia and Yugoslavia: Modruš 1482–4 (Zagreb, 1959). Dr. Putanec attempts to prove that the first printing plant in Croatia was located in Modruš, not in Senj.

The Glagolitic missal, *Missale Glagoliticum*, which Baromić and Bedričić produced in 1494, was the first book printed in Croatia. In typography this Senj missal is not at all comparable to its Venetian predecessors. It was a small octavo, the letter impressions were not very distinct, and the quality of the paper was poor. However, these shortcomings were inevitable since the missal was the first work of its kind and was produced under primitive circumstances. The only existing copy of this missal of 1494 is now preserved in the Library of the National Museum in Budapest.

Although in the year 1496 a small book, *Spovid općena* (Confessio generalis), was printed in Senj, the following decade was not productive as far as we know. However, in 1507, Grgur of Senj, who had been living in Venice, returned and with the assistance of native clerics completed the *Naručnik Plebanušev*, a Croatian translation of the widely circulated Latin original *Manipulum curatorum* by Guido dè Monte Rocherii (or Rotherii). *Transit Svetoga Jerolima* (The Death of St. Jerome) was printed in 1508 in Senj, as was *Kvarežimal*, a translation of the Latin *Quadragesimale*, by Roberto Caracciolo, a Franciscan friar (died 1495).

The second printing house on Croatian soil, which also printed in Glagolitic, was founded in Rijeka in 1530. It was established by another Croatian printer, and a distinguished promoter of culture, Šimun Begna-Kožičić of Zadar, the Roman Catholic bishop of Modruš. With the assistance of two Italian printers, Kožičić printed four books in the years 1530 and 1531. The first was the *Oficii blaženie devi Marie* (The Office of the Blessed Virgin Mary) printed in black and red; this prayer book is preserved in the National Library in Weimar. In the year 1531, the *Misal Hrvacki po rimski običai* (Croatian Missal According to the Roman Rite) was printed, with an interesting mixture of semi-Gothic and Glagolitic initial letters. The missal has 232 leaves, two woodcuts by Matija Trevižanin (Matteo Trevizano), "The Annunciation" and "The Crucifixion," and a picture of St. Jerome above the title. A small ritual, *Knižica Krsta* (Book of Christ), followed in the same year.[7] The last book preserved from the Rijeka press was issued in 1531, and is entitled *Šimuna Kožičića Zadranina Biskupa Modruškoga knižice od' žitie rimskih' arhierěov' i cesarov'* ... (Simon Kožičić of Zadar, Bishop of Modruš, a Book about Church and State Life in Rome ...).

Croatian printing had begun under extraordinarily adverse circumstances. At the end of the fifteenth century, the island of Krk fell under Venetian rule, while Turkish forces conquered Bosnia and Hercegovina,

7/It was first described by Dr. Petar Kolendić in his monograph "Zadranin Šimun Kožičić i njegova štamparija na Rijeci"/Šimun Kožičić of Zadar and His Printing Shop in Rijeka, *Magazin Sjeverne Dalmacije* (Split), 1935, 95–107.

pressing in on other Croatian lands and especially on those areas where the Glagolitic script was used. The last decades of the fifteenth and the entire sixteenth century were the most difficult period in the history of the Croatian people; during this time, several of the old Croatian tribal *župas* were devastated in combat with the Turks. In 1495, the priest Martinac wrote from the Paulist cloister in the town of Novi on the Croatian Littoral and, depicting the new misfortunes brought about by the Croatian defeat at Udbina in 1493, he begged his readers to forgive any errors, as the book was written during difficult times:

> And saddened by mourning, I reflect constantly upon the great war and the turbulence which has occurred in our times and which was instigated against all inhabited lands by the Turks, descendants of Ismael, son of Agar, the servant of Abram. They conquered the whole of Greece, Bulgaria, Bosnia and Albania and assaulted the Croatian people sending forth great hordes ... Then they pillaged all Croatian and Slavonic lands to the Sava and Drava, as far as the region of Moslavina; they plundered and devastated all Slovenian lands to the sea ... And then began the lamentation of families and widows and many others. There was great sorrow in all those who lived in these parts, such as has not been heard since the onslaughts of the Tartars, Goths and the damned Attila ... In the year of our Lord, 1493.[8]

Because of the hardships of the times, Croatians who continued to produce written works published them in other lands where more favorable conditions prevailed.

The first books printed in Bosnian script (*bosančica*) appeared at the beginning of the sixteenth century. The oldest extant examples of these are the *Molitvenik* (Prayer Book) and *Molitve sv. Brigite pred Križem* (Prayers of Saint Bridget before the Crucifix), published in Venice in 1512 with the assistance of Franjo Ratković from Dubrovnik. The only copies we have of both books are in the Bibliothèque nationale in Paris.

At the beginning of the eighteenth century, with altered economic-political conditions, the literary heartland was transferred first to the northwest, the territory of developing Protestantism, and later, to the north and northeast, to the area between the Sava and Drava rivers, and more specifically the area around Zagreb, the new cultural center.

During the seventeenth century, yet another attempt had been made

8/Stjepan Ivšić, "Sredovječna hrvatska glagoljska književnost"/Croatian Glagolitic Literature in the Middle Ages, *Sveslavenski zbornik* (Zagreb, 1930), 138–9. "I priobižden misliju vsagda za rati velike i nemirija, jaže prikljućiše se v vrimena naša, juže dvigoše Turci sući od išćedija Zmaila, sina Agari rabinje Avramlje, proti vsej vseljenej zemalj. I obujamši vsu Grčiju i Bulgariju, Bosnu i Rabaniju, nalegoše na *jazik hrvatski*, posilajući zastupi velike; ... Tagda že robljahu vse zemlje hrvatske i slovinske do Save i Drave daže do Gore Zaprte, vse že dežele Kranjske daže do mora, robeće i harajuće ... I tagda načeše cviliti rodivšije i vdovi mnoge i proči ini. I bisi skrb velija na vseh živućih v stranah sih, jakaže nest bila od vremene Tatarov i Gotov i Atele nečistivih. Let Gospodnjih 1493."

to establish Croatian printing in Rijeka. In 1621, Fran Glavinić, a Franciscan historian and writer born in Kanfanar in Istria, a guardian of the Franciscan monastery in Trsat, obtained permission from Viennese authorities to bring the former Ungnad press from Urach to Rijeka. The printing press arrived in Rijeka, but Glavinić, under orders from the Vatican, had to send it to Rome, where it was used to print church books in Croatian, either in Glagolitic or Latin script.

Available texts mention no other printing press in this area until the year 1790, when we hear of Croatian publications in Rijeka coming from the press of Lovrenc Karlecki. This establishment remained the property of the Karlecki family until 1854. Between 1860 and 1880 Croatian books and pamphlets were printed at presses in Rijeka. Included were works by Andrija Torkvat Brlić, Mirko Bogović, and Erazmo Barčić. At the same time, the sizable press of E. Mohović in Rijeka printed Italian newspapers as well as works in Croatian.

During the latter part of the nineteenth century, Croatian printing flourished in Kraljevica; there the magazine *Primorac*, edited by Martin Polić, was printed in the "Primorska Tiskara" from 1873 to 1880, appearing first once, then later three times a week. The same establishment printed light, entertaining books for a small library. Exactly when this press ceased operation is uncertain, but the early 1880s seems likely. Also during the eighties the printing press resumed operation in Senj, where books, periodicals, and other publications were printed;[9] to this day there is still a printing establishment there.

At the end of the nineteenth century, a group of Croatians from Rijeka founded the "Dionička Tiskara" where Supilo's *Riječki Novi List* (The Rijeka New Paper, 1907–15) was printed. There books and pamphlets were printed in editions of the G. Trbojević bookshop, the People's Reading Room, and others. Supilo's paper was suspended in 1915 and the firm transferred to Sušak, where it operated until the Second World War, and then continued operations sporadically during the war while one section of the press was transferred to the interior of the country. After the war, it was incorporated with other small printing shops in Sušak and Rijeka in the United Press of Rijeka.

The "Narodna Tiskara" of G. Kraljeta also operated in the eighties in Sušak. Besides books, it published reviews and newspapers, among them the daily *Sloboda* (Freedom) and the literary magazine *Hrvatska Vila* (Croatian Fairy). The Narodna Tiskara was later renovated and

9/Among other publications are two works by Ivan Radetić, 1879, 1896; one by Josip Draženović, 1893; *Bugarkinje* (Laments) by Kranjčević, 1885; and a second edition of Parčić's *Rječnik talijansko-slovinski* (Italian-Croatian Dictionary), 1908 (although the third edition, the Croatian-Italian section, was printed in Zadar in 1901 at the Narodni List Press).

today is a part of the United Press of Rijeka. The Slovenian press of Gabrščček in Gorica was also, for a time, under the direction of Kraljeta.

In addition to these presses in Sušak and Rijeka, the latter was the home of a large Capuchin press, the "Myriam" press, which published Croatian newspapers and brochures with religious themes until the annexation of Rijeka by the Italians in 1924 forced the Croatian Capuchins to leave the city.

Early literary works from Istria were also printed in Trieste. A larger number of Istrian books, however, were published in Vienna at a house publishing school texts, and in Graz, at the Kurzbeck Publishing House and at the Publishing and Printing House of Leykam and Widmanstad. At the end of the eighteenth and the beginning of the nineteenth centuries in Trieste, the presses of Gašpar Weiss, Ivan Marenigh, and Trattner-Vinković were functioning, publishing the works of Croatian authors. Gašpar Weiss's press, later transferred into the hands of a native son, Ivan Marenigh, published two works of Šime Starčević, a parish priest in Karlobag (died 1858). These were *Nova ričoslovnica ilirska, vojničkoj mladosti krajičnoj poklonjena* (New Illyrian Grammar Presented to the Youth of the Military Frontier) and *Nova ričoslovnica ilirsko-francuska iz njemačkog prenesena za potrebovanje mladosti ilirskih daržavah* (New Illyrian-French Grammar, Translated from the German, for the Use of the Youth of the Illyrian Provinces), both published in 1812.[10]

Diocesan records of Kopar, Poreč, and Novigrad reveal that also in the western part of Istria Slavic liturgy was used in the churches and that church books were written in Glagolitic script. A look at the map of Istria indicating places where Slavic liturgy in Glagolitic script was in customary use shows that they extended all the way to Trieste. It prevailed in those districts for centuries. As for Slovenian Istria, Glagolitic divine worship was used throughout the diocese of Kopar, except for two churches in the city of Kopar itself. In Šmarje, for example, Glagolitic liturgy prevailed until 1833, and in Krkavce until 1889. Istrian Croatians and Slovenes fought keenly against the Italian imposition of Latin in order to preserve the Glagolitic liturgy as their religious and cultural heritage.[11]

A great contribution to the strengthening of love for the national lan-

10/Nikola Žic, "Bibliografijske bilješke o hrvatskim knjigama iz Istre"/Bibliographical Notes on Croatian Books from Istria, *Hrvatska prosvjeta* (Zagreb), nos. 6, 7, 8 (1937); and Nikola Žic, "Prve štamparije u Trstu"/The First Printing Presses in Trieste, *Grafička revija* (Zagreb), no. 2 (1938).

11/Dr. Vladimir Orel, "Glagolica u Istri"/Glagolism in Istria, *Primorski dnevnik* (Trieste), May 1950.

guage and to the resistance to Italianization was the prayer book of Bishop Juraj Dobrila, *Oče, budi volja Tvoja* (Father, Thy Will be Done), first printed in Trieste in 1854, and frequently reprinted. It was a kind of primer of the national language for the people of Istria in the first decades of their national awakening.

Other presses that can be noted are the ones in Pazin, where *Pučki Prijatelj* (The People's Friend) was printed, the diocesan press "Kurykta" in Krk, and smaller shops in Opatija and Volosko. The Staroslavenska Akademija in Krk printed more than twenty church and religious books.[12]

The first popular author and propagator of culture in the new Istria was Josip Volarić (1805–77), a school superintendent from Vrbnik whose writings ranged from grammars and educational articles to poetry. During his time, many Croatian school texts were printed in Trieste. One circular from January 1852 advertises 20 "Illyrian school texts" obtainable at the "Trieste City Hall."[13]

A newspaper for Croatians, *Naša Sloga*, began publication at the press of Viktor Dolenc in Trieste in 1870; at the time *Balkan*, another Croatian daily paper, was also appearing. During that epoch the *Tršćanski Lloyd* was published as were other papers – weeklies, semi-monthlies, and monthlies – for instruction, entertainment, and humor. There were also women's magazines and technical and scientific journals. At that time in Trieste, journalism, printing, publishing, and bookselling were just as important among the Slovenes and Croatians as the Italian publishing activity.

During the fascist era, Croatian and Slovenian newspapers were gradually banned so that in 1929 even *Edinost*, the oldest Slovenian daily in Trieste, ceased publication. Ten other smaller papers, weeklies and monthlies, continued for a time despite the arduous conditions imposed by the Italian domination. Eventually, however, the Croatians and Slovenes, who had had a strongly developed press, were left without any publication in their national languages.[14]

Josip Krmpotić, born in Stupnik near Brod in January 1884, left Upper Croatia for Trieste, where he set type for *Edinost* and *Naša Sloga*. Later, he was in charge of the first Croatian printing press in Pula, with the founding of which the Slovenian cultural leader Andrej Gabršček from Gorica was connected. Gabršček was responsible for the fact that Pula

12/Viktor Novak and Fran Zwitter (eds.), *Oko Trsta*/About Trieste (Beograd: Državni izdavački zavod Jugoslavije, 1945), 298.
13/*Ibid.*
14/Ivo Mihovilović, *Trst* (Zagreb, 1945).

had two printing establishments which were of special importance to the Croatian national cause. When Martinolić, the proprietor of the largest press, had become insolvent as a result of certain breaches of law, Pula was without a printing press. Through the Viennese firm of the Brothers Geel who controlled the auction, Gabrščeck was successful in obtaining this press, which he renamed the "Narodna Tiskara A. Gabrščeck" (The National Press, owned by A. Gabrščeck). As its manager (according to his memoirs) he hired the above-mentioned Croatian Josip Krmpotić, who was an "extremely capable and completely trustworthy man."[15] This press published materials for various Istrian towns, especially Volosko, Pazin, Kastav, and Buzet. The Narodna Tiskara A. Gabrščeck was later taken over by an Istrian concern headed by Dr. Matko Laginja. Krmpotić left it to work elsewhere, but both establishments with which he was associated were of great assistance to the Croatians and Slovenes of Istria.

FIRST EDITIONS OF SECULAR LITERARY WORKS

The first decade of the sixteenth century saw the appearance in Venice of the first secular books. In the year 1501, the poet and scholar Marko Marulić was finishing his *Istorija svete udovice Judit* (The Story of the Holy Widow Judith), which was printed in Venice in 1521; the only extant copy of this edition is found in the Library of the Franciscan Monastery in Dubrovnik. In 1556 Hanibal Lucić, from the island of Hvar, published his love poems together with his dramatic composition *Robinja* (The Slave Girl), under the collective title of *Skladanja* (Compositions). Petar Hektorović published his *Ribanje i ribarsko prigovaranje* (Fishing and Fishermen's Tales) in 1568. A year later, *Planine* (Mountains) by Petar Zoranić appeared, and in 1584, Brno Karnarutić of Zadar published his epic composition *Vazetje Sigeta grada* (The Capture of Sziget).

In 1595, also in Venice, Faust Vrančić of Šibenik published the first dictionary of the Croatian language under the title *Dictionarium quinque nobilissimarum Europae linguarum Latinae, Italicae, Germanicae, Dalmaticae et Ungaricae* (a second printing was issued in Prague in 1606). In Rome two of his works were published: in 1605, *Machinae Novae* in Latin, and in 1606, *Život nikoliko izabranih divic* (The Lives of a Number of Chosen Virgins) in Croatian.

15/Andrej Gabrščeck, *Goriški Slovenci 1830–1900*/Slovenes in the Gorica Region from 1830 to 1900 (Ljubljana, 1932), I, 591.

Jegjupka (Gypsy) by Andrija Čubranović was published in Venice in 1599, eighty years after the poet's death. The posthumous play *Tirena*, a pastoral by Marin Držić, had been published in 1551, and Dinko Ranjina's *Pjesni razlike* (Diverse Poems) was issued in Florence in the year 1563, in large size with a beautifully illustrated cover and a portrait of the poet. A splendid publication from the Venetian Aldo's press in 1597 combined the works of Dominko Zlatarić in a deluxe edition: the translation of Sophocles' tragedy *Elektra*, the paraphrase of Ovid's poem *Ljubav i Smrt Pirama i Tizbe* (The Love and Death of Pyramus and Thisbe), and *Ljubmir*, a translation of Tasso's pastoral narrative *Aminta*. During Ivan Gundulić's lifetime, only the following works were published: *Suze sina razmetnoga* (The Tears of the Prodigal Son), in Venice in 1622; *Pjesni pokorne kralja Davida* (Penitent Songs of King David), in Rome in 1621 and in 1630; and in Ancona, *Pjesanca o veličanstvu Božjem* (Song of God's Majesty) in 1622 and *Arijadna* in 1633.[16]

In 1532, the patriotically Pan-Slavist historical work of the Dominican Vinko Pribojević, *Oratio de origine successibusque Slavorum*, was printed in Venice by Nicolini de Sabio; this same work was published at Aldo's in Venice in 1595, and in an Italian translation by Belisari Malaspalli of Split. A celebrated historical work, in Italian, is *Il Regno degli Slavi hoggi corrottamente detti Schiavoni* by Don Mavro Orbini, abbot of the Benedictine monastery situated on the islet in the lake within the island of Mljet near Dubrovnik, published in Pesaro in 1601.

CROATIAN PROTESTANT LITERATURE

In Urach, near Tübingen in Württemberg, a Croatian Protestant press was established to propagate Protestant literature in Croatian and other southern Slavic lands. In addition to the contributions of Christoph, fourth Duke of Württemberg (1515–68), and some other German nobles, means for this enterprise were procured by a Styrian Protestant emigrant, Baron Hans Ungnad. From 1561 to 1565, up to twenty-five different Croatian Protestant books in Glagolitic, Cyrillic, and Latin scripts were produced in this printing house, in editions of 25,000 copies each – an enormous quantity for those times. Only about 300 copies are now extant, most of them preserved in German libraries. It is worth noting that the first Croatian Protestant publication, in 1560, called in German *Crabatische Probzettel* (Croatian Specimen), was printed not in Urach,

16/Ivan Gundulić's published works include *Osman* and *Dubravka* issued approximately 200 years after the author's death, in 1826 and 1837 respectively.

but in Nuremberg, where Glagolitic letters were cast for the Urach printing press.[17]

In Nedelišće, a market town (District of Čakovec) of Medjumurje, Juraj Zrinski, the son of the Ban and count Nikola Zrinski, the hero of Sziget, founded a printing office in 1570, where two Croatian Protestant books were printed: Mihajlo Bučić's *Novi Zavjet* (The New Testament) and *Katekizam* (Cathechism). Zrinski also printed the translation of István Verböczy's book *Decretum Tripartitum*, in the old Croatian Kajkavian dialect. Verböczy (1460–1542) was a distinguished Hungarian jurist whose code was for centuries the principal textbook for law students and a valuable manual for judges. Verböczy's *Decretum* was first published in Latin in Vienna in 1517,[18] and translated into Hungarian by Blasius Veress, a Debrecen notary, in 1565. A Croatian translation into the Kajkavian dialect was prepared in 1574 by Ivan Pergošić, a town notary in Varaždin, royal butler, counsellor, and captain, and dedicated to the proprietor of the Protestant printing press in Nedelišće, Count Juraj Zrinski. The printer's seal at the end indicates that the work was printed by Rudolph Hoffhalter, evidently of the Hoffhalter family of printers, one of whom, Raphael, printed Veress's translation of Debrecen. Only five copies of the Pergošić translation remain, one each in the Zagreb and Budapest university libraries, and the other three in the Hungarian National Museum in Budapest. Some three centuries later, Karlo Kadlec prepared a critical edition of the Pergošić translation, which was published by the Serbian Academy of Sciences in Belgrade in 1909.[19]

In 1578, Hans Mannel, the first printer in Ljubljana, who operated from 1575 to 1582, printed a world chronicle in Croatian, *Kronika vezda znovih spravlena* (Chronicle Brought up to Date), written by the Zagreb canon Antun Vramec. Of the two known extant copies, one is in Ljubljana and the other in Zagreb.

17/Franjo Bučar, *Povijest hrvatske protestantske književnosti za reformacije*/A History of Croatian Protestant Literature during the Reformation (Zagreb: Matica Hrvatska, 1910), 80; F. Bučar and F. Fancev, "Bibliografija hrvatske protestantske književnosti za reformacije"/A Bibliography of Croatian Protestant Literature in the Time of the Reformation, *Starine* (Yugoslav Academy), XXXIX (1938).

18/Hitherto, through the four centuries since its appearance, Verböczy's *Decretum* has been published in no less than fifty-one editions, in the Latin original or in various translations: ten in the sixteenth, nine in the seventeenth, sixteen in the eighteenth, fourteen in the nineteenth, and two in the twentieth century. The Croatian translation by Ivan Pergošić reads as follows: *Dekretum, koteroga je Verbewci Ištvan dijački popisal, a potverdil ga je László, koteri je za Matijašem kralj bil* ... Nedelišće, 1574.

19/Dr. Mihajlo Lanović, "Stjepan pl. Verböczy, veliki učitelj staroga našega prava"/S. Verböczy, the Famous Teacher of Our Old Civil Law, *Rad* (Yugoslav Academy), 277 (1943), 65–102.

PRINTING IN OTHER LANDS

Although printing establishments had been opened in southern Croatia during the sixteenth century, their presses operated sporadically, and by the beginning of the seventeenth century none was still in operation. Thus, on the whole, during the sixteenth and seventeenth centuries, Croatian authors who wrote in Latin or Croatian had to have their books printed in Venice, Vienna, Graz, Ljubljana, or Trnava, Slovakia.

In the seventeenth century, the father of critical Croatian historiography Ivan Lučić (Joannes Lucius) of Trogir wrote *De regno Dalmatiae et Croatiae* (six volumes, folio format), which was printed in Amsterdam in 1666 by the printer Johannes Blaeu. It is a remarkable work which shows careful attention to the critical accumulation of material. According to Franjo Rački, this work, which was reprinted four times and translated into Italian as well, remained the definitive work of its kind for two centuries. Because of Lučić's successful methods, the Italians regard him as the forerunner of their great historian Lodovico Antonio Muratori (1672–1750).[20]

Many books by Croatian authors were issued at Trnava, which has been regarded as the cultural center of Slovak Catholicism since the Middle Ages. In residence at Trnava were the Croatian professors Juraj Žigmond Lakić (1739–1814), Dr. Miho Soretić (1740–87), and others. Among other books, Frano Zdelar's *Series banorum Dalmatiae et Sclavoniae sub regibus Croatiae, Ungariae* ... (1737) was printed there. An extensive bibliography of books printed in Trnava over many centuries was compiled by Alojz Zellinger in 1931.[21]

ZAGREB

In Zagreb itself, where secondary schools and institutions of higher learning were established from the beginning of the seventeenth century, there was great need for a domestic printing press. Croatians had to send even their calendars to foreign countries for publication! Only in the mid-seventeenth century, however, was a benefactor found to assist in organizing one, Petar Bošnjak, born in the county of Križevci. He

20/Franjo Rački, "Povjesnik Ivan Lučić, Trogiranin. Na uspomenu 200. godišnjice njegove smrti"/The Historian Ivan Lučić of Trogir, on the Bicentennial of His Death, *Rad* (Yugoslav Academy), XLIX (1879), 65–102.

21/*Pantheon tyrnaviense, bibliographicam continens recensionem operum typis tyrnaviensibus ab anno 1578-1930 editorum* (Tyrnaviae: typis Soc. S. Adalberti, 1931). Alojz Zellinger published this bibliography to celebrate the fiftieth anniversary of his scholarly activity, 1881–1931. Born in Slovakia in 1863, he died during the Second World War.

went to Hungary, where he was employed as secretary to the Hungarian palatine, Ferenc Wesselenyi, from 1654 to 1667. On the 11th of October 1656, Bošnjak (Bosnyak) wrote from Bratislava (then Pozsony) to a friend in Croatia that he had just married through the mediation of the palatine and his wife; and he promised that he would bequeath his estate to his people. After his death, around 1660, his last will revealed his wish that a portion of his estate be used to set up a printing shop. The royal personal advisor, Ivan Zakmardi (Szakmardy) Dianovečki (1600–70), turned over to the Zagreb Jesuits a sum of 1900 florins in the deceased's name, for the founding of a public press (*pro erigendo typo publico*). With this money, three years later, probably in 1664, the Jesuits purchased a printing press from the Jesuit College in Ljubljana and brought it to Zagreb. The amount of work produced by this press, if any, was evidently small, for we know of nothing which it published. The press was neglected and later transferred to the Bishop's Palace where it lay forgotten.

Several years later, the distinguished Croatian and Latin author Pavao Ritter Vitezović (1652–1713), who was born in Senj but lived in Zagreb, cherishing the ideal of Zagreb as a center for Croatian book publishing, uncovered the forgotten Jesuit press at the Palace of Bishop Aleksander Ignjat Mikulić, repaired it, and began to use it himself. Vitezović had learned the printing trade in Carniola from a friend, the Slovenian historian Johann Weikhard Freiherr von Valvasor (1641–93), and in 1694 he bought new machinery in Vienna, and together with friends sought management of a National Printing Press. The Croatian diet in Varaždin decreed on November 11, 1694, that the bishop of Zagreb turn over the press which had been deposited in his palace to Vitezović, who would assume the task of publishing books in Zagreb.

Immediately after the diet's decision, Vitezović transferred the National Press (*tipographia regni*) from Vlaška Street (at the time under the jurisdiction of the bishop of Zagreb) to a house in "the free royal city of Gradac Hill," which is today Zagreb's upper town. Here he also lived, naming the place "my museum," following his friend Valvasor's example. Vitezović managed the press from 1695 until the great Zagreb Fire on June 14, 1706. In the years 1695 to 1697 he issued Croatian religious works written by the Zagreb canon Mihajlo Šimunić, and in 1703 he printed a poem by Baron Ivan Čikulin from Susjedgrad entitled *Žalost i javkanje turskih, a radost i veselje kršćanskih duš koje se leto 1697 na Ivanje pod Bihaćem s teli razlučiše* (Sorrow and weeping for the Turkish, but joy and happiness for the Christian souls, which in the summer of 1697, on June 24, died during the siege of Bihać). The same press published Vitezović's *Kronika aliti szpomen vszega szvieta vikov* (Chronicle or a History of the Whole World) in 1696. This work was dedicated to the canon Ivan Znika, a patron of literature and art. At about the same time Znika had printed, at his own expense, the musical work *Cithara octochorda*, a collection of Croatian church songs. This was published in Vienna, by the university printer Leopold Voigt, because there was no available type in Zagreb for printing musical notation.

Vitezović's press also printed the Latin chronicles entitled *Plorantis Croatiae saecula duo* (1703) and *Croatia rediviva regnante Leopoldo Magno Caesare* (1700) and a series of school textbooks, many prayer books, Croatian almanacs for various years, *Priričnik aliti razliko mudrosti cvitje* (The Manual of Proverbs and Wisdom; 1702), *Articuli regni Sclavoniae*, Šimunić's *Propoviedi* (Sermons), a work about heraldry, *Stemmatographia, sive armorum Illyricorum delineatio, descriptio et restitutio* (Zagreb, 1700; Vienna, 1701; 2nd ed., Zagreb, 1702), and other works. By writing, printing, and selling, Vitezović, with his manifold talents, made Zagreb a true center of Croatian literature and book publishing.

After the Great Fire, when, despite his efforts, one section of the printing shop was destroyed, Vitezović could not compensate for his losses and was no longer able to continue operations. In addition, he quarreled with influential persons on the Kaptol (canon's territory) so that, angered, he abandoned Zagreb and emigrated to Vienna, where he died on January 20, 1713.

Ivan Ignatius Straka became the manager of the National Press after Vitezović, but it is not known whether he issued even a single book. After Straka, Jakob Vjenceslav Heyvl or Heivel was named director of the Press. Heivel, *regni Croatiae typographus*, as he called himself, came from Carinthia and set up the Press in a Franciscan monastery in Zagreb. Throughout the remainder of the eighteenth century printing presses were in operation in Zagreb.

After Heivel, Ivan Bartolemej Pallas is mentioned as a Zagreb printer, 1723–7; during these few years he printed a great number of Croatian and Latin books. The Croatian historian Vjekoslav Klaić believes that possibly the Zagreb Jesuits also founded a printing shop which functioned in 1727–8. If so, it was probably poorly equipped and printed only smaller publications for use by the members of the order.

After Pallas' death, his widow assumed control until she was replaced by Ivan Krstitelj Weitz, who managed the Press from 1729 to 1751. Weitz always called and signed himself *horvatskoga orsaga štampar* or *inclyti regni Croatiae typographus*. Under his management many Croatian,

Latin, and German texts were printed in this shop, including the works of Ivan Belostenec, Stjepan Fuček, Juraj Mulih, and Adam Baltazar Krčelić. Weitz began to issue, apparently at his own expense, a remarkable calendar, in Latin, under the title *Calendarium Zagrabiense*, a significant item in the history of Croatia in the eighteenth and the first half of the nineteenth century. He began the calendar in 1745 and continued to publish it until his death. In the calendar of 1750, we find an inventory of books with the note "Apud typographum in domo regnicolari habitantem inveniuntur impressa sequentia" ("The following printed works are found at the Royal Printer's bookstore").

Weitz was not only a printer, but also an artist in woodcut. In 1743, he printed in his shop a work of Marino Barleti, a priest from Scutari, *Vita et res praeclarae gestae Christi athletae Georgii Castrioti Epirotarum principis ... a Turcis Scander-beg id est Alexander magnus cognominatus – reimpressa.* Zagrebiae, typis Joannis Baptistae Weitz, inclyti regni Croatiae typographi anno 1743. The woodcut portrait of Skenderbeg on the title page, which is a faithful copy of a similar one by Ammann which appeared in the German edition of Barleti's book in Frankfurt in 1577, was made by Ivan Weitz.

Contemporary with the operation of Weitz's establishment was the Jesuit Press managed by Adalbert Wilhelm Veszeli (Wesely, Wesseli). In 1742 it printed a dictionary of some 1200 pages: *Lexicon latinum interpretatione illyrica, germanica, et hungarica locuples*, compiled by Andrija Jambrešić. The title page states that it was printed "typis academicis Societatis Jesu per Adalbertum Wihl. Weszeli." It is noted that the book was printed "cum privilegio sacrae regiae maiestatis et superiorum permissu," indicating that besides Church authorities, the state also, with its own powers of censure, was beginning to influence books and the periodical press.

After the death of Weitz, the National Press was managed by his widow, Maria Anna, from 1751 to 1753 and, subsequently, by their children. Shortly thereafter it was taken over by Antun Reiner, an accomplished sculptor and copper-engraver who managed it from 1753 to 1758. In 1754 he was granted an imperial patent by Maria Theresa, with printing privileges in Zagreb, under the stipulation that he print the Croatian history of Canon Krčelić. Reiner further equipped and expanded the shop, but despite assistance from state authorities, the establishment met with little success. He continued with the publication of *Calendarium Zagrabiense*; an inscription of the time reads: "typis Antonii Reiner, inclyti regni Croatiae typographi privilegiati." Each calendar contained an inventory of books which he sold in the king's residence (*in domo regnicolari*). Also worth noting is the third edition of the *Cithara octochorda*, published in 1757 and containing all the texts and musical notation of Croatian and Latin church melodies sung throughout the year. The work comprised 360 pages in folio.

Reiner's successor was Kajetan Franjo Harl from Graz, who worked from 1759 to 1763, when he sold his press to Josip Ivan Schotter. The latter managed his affairs so inefficiently that the press had to be sold by auction; it was purchased by the bookbinder and bookseller Franjo Žaverije Zerauscheg (Cerauschegg or Cerauscheg, who probably was referred to as Cerovšek in Croatian) who operated the shop for two years, during 1764–5.

In 1767 Maria Theresa made provision for the first Cabinet to the Royal Council in Croatia (*consilium regium*). This council began functioning under the presidency of the Ban Nadažd (Nadasdy) in August 1767, with its seat in Varaždin, then the national center of political and cultural life. The Zagreb Kaptol began to consider establishing its own printing press, for fear the National Press might be transferred to Varaždin. The Kaptol Press was opened at the end of 1768 or the beginning of 1769, in Nova Ves, with Anton Jandera as manager. At that time the National Press was purchased by Andrija Besse (Wesse) and managed by the Czech-born Jandera, who had previously worked for Zerauscheg.

In the *Calendarium Zagrabiense* of 1769 we read that it was printed "typis Antonii Jandera venerabilis typographi in Nova Villa." Under Jandera's direction the Press issued the Croatian historical books of Canon Adam Baltazar Krčelić. Jandera also attempted to publish a newspaper in Latin, *Ephemerides Zagrabienses*, pointing up his resistance to the influence of the German language, which had begun to penetrate Zagreb and, indeed, the whole of Croatia. When he died in 1772, twenty-seven different titles and 10,515 copies of books were found in his estate. His widow hired Joseph Karl Kotsche, a Czech, to manage the Press. In 1773 a calendar was produced with the inscription "typis Julianae viduae Jandieranae per Josephum Carolum Kotsche p.t. factorem."

When Jandera's widow, nee Maglić, tried to continue the Press's operations, she faced a formidable competitor in the person of the well-known Viennese printer and bookseller, Johann Thomas Trattner (1717–98). In addition to his main interests in Vienna, Trattner had founded and managed subsidiary printing houses and bookshops in all larger cities of the Monarchy. In 1773, he opened a printing press in Varaždin, and for twenty years produced school texts for use throughout Croatia.

In 1774 Trattner founded the Trattner Press in Zagreb, and waged a bitter battle for existence with the Kotsche Press. Seeking to eliminate his competitor, he and his manager, Franjo Hörner, began to issue a German paper in Zagreb, entitled *Kroatischer Korrespondent*, the first newspaper in Zagreb.

Upon Hörner's advice, Bishop Maksimilijan Vrhovac (1752–1827) purchased Trattner's press in 1794, together with the bookshop. As early as 1794 the "Biskupska Tiskara" (*Typi episcopales*) printed two contemporary works by the Zagreb professor Matija Petar Katančić: *Fructus autumnales* and *De Columna Milliaria.* Two German works and a study by the archeologist and historian Andrija Blašković, *Historia universalis Illyrici*, were also published there. Vrhovac operated his press during the reign of Emperor and King Francis II (1792–1835). Because of the French Revolution, this was a period of general reaction against the Monarchy in all its lands, and the state authorities exercised strict censorship. Consequently, Francis II looked with suspicion upon a bishop who dabbled in printing.

In 1795, Bishop Vrhovac transferred the management of his press to his brother-in-law, Antun Novosel, who was at the same time the curial *župan* (*comes curialis*) in the Bishop's Palace. When Novosel died in 1818, his widow, Francisca, took charge of the press and operated it until 1825 when the bishop of Zagreb sold it to Josip Rossi who was its manager at the time. According to Dr. Velimir Deželić,[22] this press published approximately 200 books and 100 calendars during the years 1794–1824, most of them in Latin but some in Croatian and a few in German.

Josip Rossi did not manage the Press for long, and in 1826 sold it to Franjo Župan (Suppan), who had been proprietor of his own bookstore as far back as 1808. Župan (born in Bjelovar in 1784 and died in Zagreb, 1847) was the only printer in Zagreb for twelve years until the father of the Croatian National Awakening, Dr. Ljudevit Gaj, founded his printing house.

Gaj's press was established in 1838, after he had become familiar with existing techniques at Hasse's press in Prague. Gaj's press was called the "Kraljevska povlastjena ilirska narodna tiskara dra. Ljudevita Gaja" (The King's Privileged Illyrian National Press of Dr. Ljudevit Gaj), and published *Narodne ilirske novine* (The National Illyrian Press News) and *Danica ilirska* (The Illyrian Morning Star). Later, the historian and academician Dr. Bogoslav Šulek, an honorary doctor of Karl Uni-

22/Dr. Velimir Deželić (1864–1941), writer, historian, and director of the University Library in Zagreb (1910–20), has published a number of bibliographical studies among which is the following: "Biskupska, a zatim Novoselova tiskara u Zagrebu"/First Bishop's, then Novosel's Press in Zagreb, *Narodna Starina* (Zagreb), 1926.

versity in Prague, joined Gaj's staff. In 1856 Gaj purchased the former Župan Press and amalgamated it with his own, so that again, until 1858, there was only one printing press in Zagreb.

In 1858, another press was opened by Karl Albrecht, a Croatian of German descent. He came to Zagreb from Varaždin, where he had worked in the lithographing and printing shop of Josip Platzer. Albrecht married Platzer's daughter, acquired the lithographic machinery, and transferred it to Zagreb in 1853; later, he added a printing press. Albrecht secured his honorable place in Croatian cultural history with the publication of the beautifully adorned and popular calendar *Dragoljub*.

In 1861, Antun Jakić opened a third press in Zagreb, which achieved significant success, and a fourth press appeared in 1867, when Karl Bokau moved there from Karlovac.

In 1871 an organization called the Press, Inc., was established by the partisans of the bishop Josip Juraj Strossmayer, founder of the University of Zagreb and the Yugoslav Academy. It issued the daily *Obzor* (Horizon) as the continuation of former *Pozor*, *Zatočnik*, and *Branik*. Strossmayer patronized the Press liberally so that it later expanded, adding a bookstore and preparing its own editions. Many of these latter were issued in deluxe form. This press also issued the Croatian periodical *Vijenac* (Wreath), a fine example of the printing art. In 1919, the Croatian Printers' Establishment took over the Press, Inc., merging the two houses into one enterprise.

In 1869, Miloš Zec, former principal assistant to Dr. Ljudevit Gaj, inherited the post of editor-in-chief of *Narodne novine*. This newspaper was printed at Dr. Gaj's press until 1873. Ivan Hörer, who had been the page setter at the Press in 1864 and had become proofreader for *Narodne novine* in 1865, was made manager in 1870. In 1873, however, the press was taken over by Dragutin Albrecht in partnership with Velimir Gaj. At this time the printing of *Narodne novine* was transferred first to the press of L. Hartmann and Company, and then to the I. Granitz Press, where the paper was published until July 31, 1874. After August 1, 1874, *Narodne novine* was printed in its own shop, a new press founded by Miloš Zec and Ivan Hörer with the formation of endowment funds. In 1897 it was renamed the "Zemaljska tiskara u Zagrebu" (The National Press in Zagreb). It was the first press in Zagreb to use mechanized typesetting (in 1898), and later it installed larger and more practical machines such as Linotype and Intertype. With the addition of lithography in 1912, photoengraving in 1913, and somewhat later, the bookbindery, the press had at last succeeded in organizing all accessory business departments in the field of graphics. Offset type was added in 1930, and later the lithography and photoengraving departments were reorganized.

In the first half of the twentieth century, many presses were founded in Zagreb, the more important ones being those of Ignac Granitz, Antun Scholz, Stjepan Boranić, Stjepan Kugli, the Jugonovinsko Inc., Kuzma Rožmanić, the Merkantile, Gaj, the Linotype Co., the Archbishopric Press, and the Croatian Press. Also, in 1919, the "Hrvatska Tiskara" changed its name to the "Jugoslavenska Štampa" (Yugoslav Press) and acquired the most modern equipment available for newspaper publishing.

In 1920, the "Typografija" was established by the merger of the presses of Jan Novak and Dragutin Stjepan Schulhof and the I. Granitz Press; it is still in operation using all the modern techniques. Between the two world wars, the Typografija was the strongest Croatian newspaper enterprise. It issued and printed three dailies – *Obzor* (Horizon), *Jutarnji List* (The Morning Paper), and *Večer* (Evening) – and later the illustrated weekly *Svijet* (The World).

DUBROVNIK

Although there were a few unsuccessful attempts to introduce printing into Dubrovnik earlier, it took root only in the last quarter of the eighteenth century. We know of the last will of Father Luka Radovinović, who bequeathed his printing equipment to Father Pavao Vukašinović in 1502, but nothing seems to have come of this early attempt. We learn of another abortive effort in the second half of the sixteenth century, on the part of the book-printer Guillelmus Teutonicus, probably one of the many students or followers of Gutenberg, all of whom seemed to be flooding Venice at this time. Teutonicus was a contemporary of the printer Dobruško Dobričević, who published over forty books, and it is to Croatia's honor (as Mirko Breyer tells us) that he published the first artistic edition of Dante's *La Divina Commedia.*[23]

Traces of the efforts to establish printing in Dubrovnik after the catastrophic earthquake of 1667 are found in the petition (May 25, 1753) of Ivan Garmogliosi, who wished "because of love for my home-

23/Dante Alighieri, *Canto, overo Comedia del Divino* (coi Comment di Cristophoro Landino). Bressa: per Boninum de Boninis de Ragusio, 1487. Mirko Breyer (1863–1946), a well-known Croatian authority on rare books, wrote two articles about Dubruško Dobrić in his book *Prilozi k starijoj književnoj i kulturnoj povjesti hrvatskoj*/Contributions to Older Croatian Literary and Cultural History (Zagreb, 1904), 1–20.

land and because of a sincere desire for her every moral and material good and fame, to introduce the art of printing books." The petitioner was the uncle and foster father of the Ragusan writer Stjepan Šuljaga, who, in addition to being in the Dubrovnik diplomatic service, was for many years the director of the Baglioni Press in Venice, but whether or not he supported the petition we do not know. In any case, while the Dubrovnik Senate was unanimous in granting the petition, the press never materialized.

In 1777, the Venetian Carlo Antonio Occhi came to Dubrovnik primarily as a bookseller. On November 25, 1783, he became the first authorized printer in Dubrovnik and specialized in the publishing of books in Croatian. Altogether, we know of fifty different works printed by him in Dubrovnik. He also published a catalogue in 1784 that listed the publications of others as well as his own. The excellence of his work is widely acknowledged.

Occhi's assistant and fellow Venetian Andrea Trevisano took over the press in 1789, having secured financial assistance from the Senate and an authorization to supply the state offices. In a petition, Trevisano noted how he was eventually left without any means and how his return to Venice was frustrated by the current political situation. He worked until his death in 1801 and printed, among others, new editions of the historical works *Annali di Ragusa* by Jakov Lukarević and *Commentaria de temporibus suis* by Ludovik Crijević Tuberon.

Trevisano was succeeded by Antun Martecchini (1802–37), who came with the first Kotor printer, Andreolo, and settled in Dubrovnik. The Senate transferred the press to him with various privileges, stipulating that no one else would be permitted to open another printing house in Dubrovnik. Martecchini was the last Dubrovnik printer and bookseller during the time of the Republic. His printing career, and that of his son and successor Petar Fran, were contemporaneous with its fall, the period of French occupation, and a good part of the Austrian rule up to the middle of the nineteenth century. Father and son worked assiduously, improving what had been a somewhat neglected enterprise. Special mention should be made of the fine edition of Appendini's work *Notizie istorico-critiche sulle antichità, storia e letteratura de' Ragusei* (1803), a book still considered significant in the study and understanding of the culture of old Dubrovnik. The first edition of Gundulić's *Osman* was printed there in 1826, as well as the last two of the three parts of Joakim Stulli's six-volume Croatian-Italian-Latin Dictionary (the first part, *Lexicon latino-italico-illyricum*, was published in Budapest in 1801): *Rječosložje iliričko-italijansko-latinsko* in 1806 and

Vocabolario italiano-illirico-latino in 1810. The last part of this monumental and voluminous work was dedicated to Marshal Marmont, who made it possible for the eighty-year-old author to complete and publish the great work of his lifetime. After Antun's death in 1837, Petar carried on and followed Occhi's and later his father's plan in publishing collections (1832–64) of the works of Dubrovnik's old poets and authors. In 1841, he published a beautifully bound work, the *Galleria di Ragusei illustri*, complete with decorative illustrations.

An able draftsman and woodcutter, the young Martecchini reproduced many a memorable object or artifact in Dubrovnik by history or tradition, such as monuments, national costumes, coins, medals, arms, and portraits, and from this material he arranged an album of 120 plates. A young man widely known for his great industry, he collected books, manuscripts, and antiques for his private library and made plastic reproductions of various monuments, and in his twentieth year, began work on the biography of the writer Petar Kanavelić (or Kanavelović) from Korčula (1637–1719).

In about 1870, Dragutin Prettner took over Petar Martecchini's press. However, in these late decades of the nineteenth century, another press also flourished in Dubrovnik, the "Tipografia di Giuseppe Flori" (in Croatian: Tiskarnica Joza Flori), which had been publishing a series called "Biblioteca storica della Dalmazia," edited by Josip Gelčić. In 1906 a new Croatian press, "Štamparija de Giulli i dr." (Printing Press of de Giulli and Co.), was founded in Dubrovnik, which was taken over by Milan Gösl in 1920 and renamed "Štamparija Jadran" (Adriatic Printing Press).

ZADAR

In Zadar printing was begun in the seventeenth century. Some sources mention the printer Pietro Baba, of whose work unfortunately no example remains. Later came the Battara brothers, who issued in 1789 the first Croatian book known to have been printed in Zadar, *Vrime sfeto uloxeno prid prisfetim Sakramentom, olli bogogliubne poxude prema istom sakramentu, koje mogu sluxiti za pripravu, i zafagliegne na Pricescjegnje* – Prikazane od jednoga Misnika Kupuczina Darxave od Bresce (The sacred time spent before the Blessed Sacrament, or devout prayers toward the same Sacrament, which can serve for preparation before and thanksgiving after Communion – as written by a Capuchin priest of Brescia Province). Vjekoslav Maštrović believes that this thirty-two-page booklet was published by Anton Luigi Battara, a bookseller of Zadar, and Maštrović adds that because of this, the Battara bookshop and printing house advertised this work as its own publication.[24] Then, beginning in 1791, mention is made of Antonio Bubalini, the bookseller and printer who came from Trieste and who printed and sold various books in Zadar.

In 1797, a more important printer, Dominik Fracasso, began to work in Zadar, but he sold his press to Anton Luigi Battara in 1803. At first Battara signed his editions "Anton Luigi Battara" and later, from 1829, only "Battara," the name associated with the most productive period of this well-known Zadar press, 1829 to 1876. After 1876, books appeared with the inscription "Tisk. Vitaliani-Janković nasljednici Battara" (The Vitaliani-Janković Press, successors to Battara). Vitaliani and Janković worked together until about 1887, when each formed his own firm. Beginning in 1893, Vitaliani was associated with the press which was then known as the "Tiskarski i Litografični Zavod" (the Printing and Lithographic Establishment).

The Governor's press under the name "Utišteonica od Vladanja" (Stamparia Governiale, Utisctenje Vladagna) operated in Zadar in 1817, 1819, and 1823. It was later known as the "Tiskarnica Vlade" (The Government Press) in 1851, "Vladna Tiskarnica" in 1858, and the "Tiskara namjesnička" in 1860.

Maštrović lists other older printing houses in Zadar: the presses of Ivan Demarchi and Rougier, later combined to Demarchi-Rougier; the press of *Narodni List* (Juraj Biankini); the press of Ivan Woditzka and of Spiro Artaleo; the "Katolička hrvatska tiskarna" (Catholic Croatian Press) of Ivo Prodan; the "Obrtnička trgovačka tiskarna" (Industrial Trade Press) of A. Armanini; the presses of Enrik Schönfeld, of Josip Ferrari, and of Petar Bilan; the "Vjesti" Press; and the "Tiskarsko poduzeće" (Printing Enterprise) of Mani and Mlinar, later called the "Gradsko tiskarsko poduzeće" (City Printing Enterprise).[25]

VARAŽDIN

Count Juraj Zrinski brought his press from Nedelišće to Varaždin in 1586, where it was operated by Hans Mandelc (Manlius, Mannel), who

24/Vjekoslav Maštrović, *Jadertina croatica*, "Bibliografija knjiga, časopisa i novina izdanih na hrvatskom ili srpskom jeziku u Zadru," I, ed. Josip Badalić (Zagreb: Yugoslav Academy, 1949), 5.

25/Vjekoslav Maštrović, *Jadertina croatica*, II (Zagreb: Yugoslav Academy, 1954), 1–2.

had also been a printer of Protestant books in Ljubljana. In Varaždin, Mandelc printed one Croatian and two Latin books by Vramec, Pergošić, and Škrinjarić. A little later he left for Hungary, and the press was abandoned.

On January 29, 1773, Johann Thomas Trattner obtained the right to establish a press in Varaždin. He worked there from 1773 until the Great Fire of April 25, 1776. After this, there was no press in Varaždin until 1821, when Ivan Sanf Sangilla von Freundsberg (Frundsberg) opened his. Between 1821 and 1823, he issued three school texts by Antun Rožić, followed by a history of Hungary by Josip Sever and *Razlaganje sv. evangeliuma* (A Guide to the Holy Gospel) by Josip Vračan. Still later, he produced books by Josip Risman, Jakov Lovrenčić, and others. Beginning in 1821, Sangilla issued the *Horvatski kolendar* (The Croatian Calendar) edited by T. Mikloušić. He sold all his books to Burgenland Croatians in Austria and Hungary. Josip Platzer, Sangilla's brother-in-law, bought the press at auction price in 1833, and managed it successfully until 1876.

OSIJEK

As Professor Ivan Medved says,[26] it is certain that in 1748 the Franciscan Antun Papušlić published his *Sacer mons Alverniae*, held to be the first book printed in Osijek. In the same year, another work by the same author – *Praelectiones thelogicae* – was also published there. The first Osijek press was operated for the needs of the Franciscan province, and the first printer was Josip Antun (Fortunat) Hueber. In the year 1795, mention is made at the Osijek monastery of two bookbinders: Father Melchior Bracher and Jacobus Schreyer. In 1775 the first lay printer in Osijek, Ivan Martin Divald, placed a petition to Maria Theresa before the Osijek authorities: in this he asked for permission to take over the Franciscan Press since he felt there was a need in Osijek for a press independent of the monastery's authority. This petition of Divald's was registered in the record book of the Osijek *županija*, on the 27th of September 1775, and today is to be found in the Osijek archives. This date marks the true beginning of printing in Osijek. Divald (Divalt) worked there from 1770 to 1806, and became known in Osijek as the first printer to

26/Ivan Medved, "Prvi osječki tipografi i knjigoveže"/The First Typographers and Bookbinders in Osijek, *Jubilarni almanah Kluba hrvatskih književnika i umjetnika* (Osijek, 1929), 60–88.

publish almost all the works of contemporary Slavonian authors – Kanižlić, Katančić, Lanosović, Velikanović, Josip Stjepan Reljković, and others. His successors, Martin Alojzije Divald (1806–35), Julije Divald (1835–50), and Dragutin Divald (1850–62), kept the press in the family until it was almost a century old, but shortly before his death, Dragutin Divald sold it to the printer Dragutin Leman (or Carl Lehman), who made his appearance in 1857. Leman operated it with a partner until 1869, after which it went into bankruptcy and was sold at auction in 1870.

In 1869 Ignjat Mederšicki (Ignatz Mederschitzky) founded a press, but after four years he moved to Vinkovci. Also in that year, Jakov Frank and Gustav Eagner opened a press so that Osijek had two presses from 1869 to 1873.

KARLOVAC

By the end of the eighteenth century, the city of Karlovac, one of the strongest provincial cultural centers, had a press owned by Gaspar Weitz. It is not known exactly when this printing house was founded, but we do know that a book was published there in 1791 – *Regulament zaderžavanja, muštranja i manovre pušaka* (Rules for the Maintenance, Handling and Tactical Use of Guns), perhaps the first military manual to be printed in the Croatian language. It was written by Daniel Rastić, a student at the Military Academy in Karlovac and later a general in Gospić.

During the time of the French occupation, the regime founded a state press in 1809 under the name "Civil i militarsko knjig pritiskanje" (Civil and Military Book Printing), which existed until 1813. It was here that *Pisma velikome Francie Maressalu od Marmond* was printed in 1810. This "Poem to the Great Marshal Marmont of France" was composed by a captain of the Karlovac city guard, Mirko Lopašić, during Marmont's sojourn in Karlovac, September 2, 1810. The book *Katekizmus u svih francuskoga cesarstva cirkvah upeljan* (The Catechism as Introduced into All Churches of the French Empire) was published in 1812 at the same press.

In 1822 Gaspar Weitz sold his press to Ivan Nepomuk Prettner, a brisk and ambitious man. After Prettner's death, the press was known as the "Tiskara nasljednika Ivana Pretnera" (The Press of the Successors of Ivan Prettner) until the year 1889.

Many important works of prominent patriots and writers were printed in Prettner's printing house. In 1832 a brochure by Count Janko Drašković, a patron of the Croatian National Movement, *Dissertacija iliti Razgovor, darovan gospodi poklisarom zakonskim* (A Dissertation or a Discussion Presented to the Honorable Delegates), was published. In the same year *Reč jezika narodnoga* (The Speech of the National Language) by Josip Kundek appeared. In 1835 the Bosnian Franciscan Martin Nedić published his *Razgovor koga vile Ilirkinje imadoše u Pramaletje godine 1835* (The Discussion which it is Said Took Place among the Illyrian Fairies in the Spring of 1835) there, and in 1840 he produced *Prigovor izmedj vila* (Chatter amongst the Nymphs). The great Croatian poet Ivan Mažuranić, who lived in Karlovac from 1840 to 1848, published his political study *Hrvati Magjarom: odgovor na proglase njihove od ožujka mjeseca i travnja, 1848* (The Croatians to the Hungarians: A Reply to Their Proclamations of the Months of March and April 1848) there. Prettner's press produced also a series of school manuals, collections of poems, prayer books, calendars, and periodicals. Prettner published German books too, and it is especially interesting that he printed the calendar *Karlstadskij Mesecoslov* (The Karlovac Calendar) both in Latin and in Cyrillic script.

Abel Lukšić founded a press in Karlovac in 1861 and began to issue the periodical *Glasonoša* (The Courier), to which many Croatian authors (J. E. Tomić, I. Trnski, Radoslav Lopašić, among others) contributed. Lukšić also issued a series of occasional publications, three books in the "Narodna knjižnica" (National Library) series, and a collection of poems, among other things.

SARAJEVO AND MOSTAR

The first printing shop in Bosnia-Hercegovina was founded in the sixteenth century, in the Orthodox monastery of Goražde in eastern Bosnia. It was small and short-lived. As was true of the other shops of that epoch, it printed only religious books. The Franciscans, who were the only Catholic priests and the principal educators in Bosnia-Hercegovina at that time, also tried to establish printing shops in their monasteries to print books in the vernacular, but the Turkish authorities did not encourage such endeavors. At the outset of the seventeenth century, the Franciscan Matija Divković (1563–1631), the founder of Bosnian Catholic religious literature, cherished the idea of a small printing shop in one of the Franciscan monasteries to supply edifying reading for the faithful.

Having failed to realize his plans at home, he went to Venice in 1611 to have his works published there.

More than two hundred years later, in the forties of the nineteenth century, the Franciscans moved again in the same direction. A writer, Ivan Franjo Jukić, sent his cousin, Ante Kajić, to Zagreb in 1844 to learn the printing trade in Ljudevit Gaj's printing shop. Three years later he sent Franjo Glavadanović as well, for the same purpose. Jukić, enthusiastic about Gaj's ideas on the Croatian national awakening, tried to establish the literary association Bosansko Kolo in Bosnia. Having laid down the by-laws for the new society in 1848, Jukić also sent a proclamation to his friends in Bosnia. Kajić returned from Zagreb only after thirteen years and decided to establish a Franciscan printing shop, but did not succeed in spite of the fact that the Franciscans supported his plea to the regional authorities in Sarajevo and the sultan in Istanbul, with whom they were on good terms.

The first printing shop in modern times in Bosnia-Hercegovina was opened in 1866. After administrative, scholastic, and judicial reforms, the vizier Topal Osman Pasha invited a young printer from Zemun, Ignjat (Ignac) Sopron, to come to Sarajevo to establish his printing shop there. Sopron complied with the vizier's request and opened his shop at the beginning of April 1866 in a house on Dugi sokak (Long Street) under the name of "Sopronova pečatnja" (Sopron's Printing Shop). In that very month he issued the first political newspaper in Bosnia-Hercegovina, *Bosanski vjestnik* (Bosnian Messenger). As early as May 16, 1866, *Bosna* was issued as the first official paper of the regional government, written in Turkish and Croatian or Serbian, and printed in Arabic and Cyrillic letters.

By the end of 1866, Topal Osman Pasha purchased Sopron's printing shop and named it "Vilajetska štamparija" (Government Printing Shop). As the word for government changed with successive political developments, the original name was changed first to "Zemaljska tiskara" and then to "Državna štamparija." After the conclusion of the sale, Sopron stopped publishing his weekly *Bosanski vjestnik*, and left Sarajevo.

While Bosnia was still under Turkish rule, the Government Printing Shop in Sarajevo issued several textbooks in Latin and Cyrillic letters as well as the above-mentioned papers. In 1869 it issued two textbooks for Catholic schools, a geography for the new schools, and a primer, *Bukvar s napomenkom članakah nauka vjere za katoličku mladež u Bosni* (A Primer with a Supplement Containing the Articles of Faith for the Catholic Youth in Bosnia). In 1871 the elementary geography of

Father Grga Martić was published. Aside from these textbooks, several calendars, a few collections of folk songs, and a Turkish-Croatian grammar were published.

In 1868 a young Muslim writer, Mehmed Šaćir Kurtćehajić, who at that time was managing the "Vilajetska štamparija," founded *Gjulšeni Saraj* (Sarajevo's Florilegium), a magazine of general interest. Kurtćehajić was the first Bosnian journalist born in Bosnia. Like *Bosna*, this new periodical was also published in two languages and two scripts: Croatian or Serbian and Turkish, Cyrillic, and Arabic. It was discontinued in 1872 on the death of its editor, at the age of 28.

In 1884, *Vatan*, the first Muslim political weekly, was published in Sarajevo in Turkish; later it changed its name to *Rehber*. In 1895 the first Serbian political weekly, *Prosvjeta* (Education), was issued, but it disappeared after about three years.

When the Hercegovinian administration was established in Mostar in 1876, a government printing shop was founded there with one part of the type sent by the Government Printing Shop in Sarajevo, and the Croatian typesetter Marko Šešelj as organizer. On February 19, 1876, *Neretva*, the official bulletin of the administration, was issued there under the editorship of Mehmed Hulusi. At the beginning of 1877, however, the Hercegovinian administration was suppressed, *Neretva* discontinued (its last issue being dated December 16, 1876), and the printing shop itself dismantled and taken back to Sarajevo.

In the 1860s the Hercegovinian Franciscans were determined to have their own printing shop, and after petitioning the regional government several times, Father Frane Miličević was finally given permission. The new shop was opened in Mostar at the end of 1872 under the name "Tiskara katoličkog poslaništva" (Printing Shop of the Catholic Mission). Father Miličević had learned the printing trade in Zadar, and in this undertaking he was both the typesetter and the main writer. He published primarily religious and ecclesiastical books, but later he published a newspaper as well. Before 1878, i.e., the year in which Bosnia and Hercegovina were occupied by Austria-Hungary, he issued the calendar *Mladi Hercegovac* (Young Hercegovinian), *Pravopis za niže učione katoličke u Hercegovini* (A Primer for Catholic Primary Schools in Hercegovina), and the popular *Bukvar za samouke* (Primer for the Self-Taught).

In 1878, with the arrival of the new Austro-Hungarian occupational authorities, instead of the official bulletin *Bosna*, a new one was immediately issued under the title *Bosansko-hercegovačke novine* (A Paper for Bosnia-Hercegovina). At first the paper was published twice a week and only in Latin script, but in 1879 a Cyrillic edition was added. That same year J. Lukeš and Heinrich Renner started to publish the weekly *Bosnische Korrespondenz.* As a correspondent of German and American newspapers, Renner traveled extensively in Bosnia and Hercegovina and recorded his impressions in his book *Durch Bosnien und die Herzegovina Kreuz und quer* (Berlin, 1896).

On January 1, 1884, Dr. Julije Makanec began to issue a German daily called *Bosnische Post*, printed in a shop of the same name. This periodical passed from him to the editor, E. Tepfer, then to Milena Mrazović, and finally to I. B. Schmard. *Bosnische Post* was issued weekly, then twice a week, and after 1896, daily, with a German and a Croatian edition.

In 1883, after five years of Austro-Hungarian occupation, Father Miličević was allowed to publish *Hercegovački bosiljak* (Hercegovinian Basil), a periodical of general interest. Rigid censorship led to suppression of the paper in 1885, since Father Miličević was not amenable to interference. Shortly thereafter, he started another paper, *Mladi Hercegovac* (Young Hercegovinian), but his collaborator, Nedjeljko Radičić, had to take over both paper and shop while Father Miličević lay ill. After his death, a nephew, the writer Ivan A. Miličević, continued the work of his uncle and in 1898 opened in Mostar the Croatian Printing Shop, Inc. and started to issue the weekly *Osvit* (Dawn), the first periodical in Bosnia-Hercegovina edited according to modern standards.

From the beginning of the Austro-Hungarian occupation until the end of the nineteenth century, about twenty periodicals were born in Bosnia-Hercegovina. Some are still in existence today, like *Glasnik Zemaljskog Muzeja u Bosni i Hercegovini* (Bulletin of the National Museum of Bosnia and Hercegovina). *Vrhbosna*, the paper of the archdiocese of Vrhbosna, and *Istočnik* (Source, Origin), the Orthodox religious review, were published until 1945.

By the end of 1910, thirty-three periodicals were being published in Bosnia-Hercegovina: eleven were political, seven religious, five vocational, four professional, two literary, two social, one scientific, and one official. Thirty were published in Sarajevo and three in Mostar. Twenty-six were published in Croatian or Serbian, i.e., nine in Latin, eight in Cyrillic script, and nine in both; two in German and Croatian or Serbian (Latin and Cyrillic); and one in Turkish. There were four dailies, eight weeklies or semiweeklies, eighteen monthlies or semimonthlies, and three periodicals published at irregular intervals. Nationally or religiously there were four Croatian, five Serbian, thirteen neutral, five Muslim, four Catholic, and two Orthodox. Their names and the years of their first appearance are given below.[27]

Sarajevski list 1878
Bosnische Post 1884
Školski vjesnik 1884
Bosanska vila 1886
Vrhbosna 1887
Istočnik 1887
Glasnik Zemaljskog muzeja 1889
Bošnjak 1891
Kršćanska obitelj 1900
Bosansko-hercegovački težak 1902
Srpska riječ 1905
Učiteljska zora 1905
Glasnik sv. Ante 1906
Hrvatski dnevnik 1906
Musavat 1906
Prosvjeta 1907
Srpska sloga 1907
Gajret 1907
Činovnički list 1908
Behar 1909
Hrvatska Bosna 1909
Rad 1909
Der Tourist 1909
Vjestnik 1909
Hrvatska zajednica 1909
Bosansko-hercegovački signal 1909
Bosansko-hercegovački željezničar 1910
Pregled 1910
Radnički list 1910
Sarajevski večernji list 1910
Samouprava 1910
Muslimanska sloga 1910

SOME SMALLER CITIES

In the middle of the nineteenth century, Ignjat (Ignac) Sopron (1824–94) began operating a press in Zemun. Among the works published in his shop were Josip Ettinger's *Srijemsko-slavonsko-hrvatske zvijeri i ptice* (Birds and Animals in Srijem, Slavonia, and Croatia), 1857, and *Zmaj sedmoglavi i sedam bojnih kopljah protiv njega* (The Seven-Headed Dragon and Seven Martial Lances to be used against it) by Mijat Stojanović. Also, at the invitation of Topal Osman Pasha, the military governor of Bosnia, Sopron printed a monograph on the city of Zemun. As noted above, Sopron also founded a press in Sarajevo.

In 1862, Požega's first publishing house was founded by Miroslav Kraljević (1823–77) and managed by the talented typographer Josip Senečić. By 1890, the "Trgovačka Tiskara" (The Commercial Press), directed by Gustav Kraljeta, was founded in Sušak; later it published *Novi List*, which was the continuation of Supilo's *Riječki Novi List*. The

27/Rudimir Rotter-Progonski, "Razvitak novinarstva u Herceg-Bosni s osvrtom na historijat štamparstva"/The Development of Journalism in Bosnia and Hercegovina in Relation to the History of Book Printing, *Grafička revija* (Zagreb), x, no. 4 (1936), 148–51.

"Primorski Štamparski zavod" (The Printing Establishment of the Littoral) was founded in 1929 in Sušak by Mario I. Banić, who owned not only a press but also bookbinding machinery and a paper warehouse. His establishment maintained four rapid-print machines, two smaller presses, two linotype-setting machines, and other machines in the bookbinding department. Banić was involved in the printing of newspapers, periodicals, books, and all kinds of stationery.

Between the two world wars, an especially prominent provincial press was that of Vinko Vošicki in Koprivnica; it published the series of books called "Svjetska Biblioteka" (The World Library) and also issued a series of works by August Cesarec and Miroslav Krleža.

In Croatia the following printing presses operated between the two world wars: in Zagreb, forty-seven printing presses; in Split, seven presses; in Osijek, fifteen; five in Šibenik and Karlovac; four each in Brod, Križevci, and Djakovo; three in Sisak, Varaždin, Vukovar, Virovitica, Čakovec, Dubrovnik, Daruvar, and Koprivnica; two in Slavonska Požega, Sušak, Samobor, Senj, Vinkovci, Bjelovar, Gospić, Glina, Kostajnica, Nova Gradiška, Ogulin, and Petrinja; and one in Podravska Slatina, Virje, Crikvenica, Donji Miholjac, Delnice, Kutina, Krapina, Jaska, Našice, and Pakrac. Croatian books were published during that period also in Bačka (in Subotica, for example, where at one time twelve presses were operating) and in Bosnia and Hercegovina, as described above.

LITHOGRAPHY

In 1841, forty-three years after Alois Senefelder invented lithography, S. Platzer, the Varaždin printer, set up the first lithographic press in Croatia. Karl Albrecht, an exceptionally gifted lithographic draftsman and engraver, worked a full six years in this establishment; then in 1851 he moved to Zagreb, where he managed a lithographic press under Platzer's name until 1868. Albrecht's engravings are veritable masterpieces.[28]

In 1854, Julije Hühn became the first lithographer in Croatia to utilize photography for his engravings, the process of photoengraving directly on stone being as yet unknown. At the end of the nineteenth century,

28/Eduard Molinari and D. Metzner, "Početci i razvitak litografije u Jugoslaviji"/ The Beginnings and Development of Lithography in Yugoslavia, *Grafička revija*, no. 3 (Zagreb, 1936), 68–79.

Trol, a Zagreb lithographer, became a specialist in the engraving of English letters. In 1904, Rudolph Mosinger began a lithographic and color-type press in Zagreb; he managed his shop until 1912.

In 1892, Vladimir Rožankovski started to use a small hand-operated lithographic press, 50 by 70 cm. Because of the quality of his work, he was recognized not only in Croatia, but also in Hungary, Poland, Bulgaria, and other countries.

When the more rapid offset presses began to supplant stone-lithography, Rožankovski purchased in Vienna an offset press from the factory of Waite and Saville Ltd. in Otley, Yorkshire, England. It was the first in Croatia, and he himself worked on this press for many years, until 1921. Rožankovski's establishment contained three single-color offset presses, six lithographic presses, and ten hand presses; in addition he managed a cardboard shop, a bookbindery, and a printing press. When he transferred to the "Tipografija" in 1921 as the director of the newly established lithographic section, he frequently traveled to western European countries to study the new lithographic process of photomechanical transferring. Rožankovski is noted as the most famous representative of the development of lithography in Croatia.

Between the world wars, the manager of the Narodne Novine Press in Zagreb, the engraver and artist Vladimir Kirin, perfected a lithographic department there. Like Rožankovski, Kirin equipped his establishment with excellent technical and photomechanical apparatus.

In 1928, M. Reputin set up a lithographic press which was later taken over by the Jugoslavenska Štampa (Yugoslav Press) in Zagreb. Between the two wars, in addition to those in Zagreb, there were three offset and three lithographic presses in Osijek, where lithography had made its appearance in 1882.

BOOKBINDING

The first mention of bookbinding in Croatia appears in the twelfth century when an artisan bound books on the Zagreb Kaptol, which suggests that he may have been a priest. The first definite evidence of the existence of bookbinding appears in 1515, when mention is made of a bookbinder named Paul. At that time, the titles of bound books were stamped on the back in gold with ready-made printer's letters. Bookbinders were considered true artists, and the municipalities and the Kaptol of Zagreb granted them building lots to encourage their trade. In 1664, Jesuit bookbinders were finishing book covers in the old Irish manner, that is, by placing the cover in leather and then enclosing it within metal plates. Old records mention a bookbinder in Samobor in the sixteenth century, one of whose works is so exquisitely gilded on the front, so precisely elaborated, that the cover is considered an antique masterpiece and is preserved in the University of Zagreb Library.

Later bookbinders include Franjo Zerauscheg (1763), who worked as a bookbinder in Zagreb. The first bookbinding establishment with the right of trade was opened there by the bookseller Franjo Župan in 1800. This was followed by another in 1806, operated by Franc Rudolf, who was interested mainly in the leather binding of church missals. Bookbinding developed rather slowly until 1873, when the discovery of mechanical techniques accelerated the process.

The greatest contribution to the development of bookbinding is usually ascribed to Ivan Schneider, who was working in Zagreb in 1856. His shop made many innovations and received recognition at the Paris Exhibition of 1864. Schneider also bound books for Matica Hrvatska. After his death, his son Ivan continued in his footsteps and made the firm into one of the largest bookbinders in Zagreb. Bookbinders Mučnjak and Senftleben also flourished in the trade and were chiefly occupied with the binding of books for the University of Zagreb Library.

The bookbinding shop of Josip Blecha, who trained a number of qualified and capable workers, was opened in 1872. Petar Ossek, who specialized in leatherbound books, opened his bookbinding shop in 1875. The first establishment to engage in illustrating was opened in 1880 by Stjepan Rusovan. In 1885, S. Schmidt founded his shop, complete with the most up-to-date bookbinding equipment in Zagreb. Schmidt's shop was taken over by Milan Ramuščak, who for the first three decades of this century concentrated on producing bookkeeping supplies for the entire country.

One of the most distinguished bookbinders was S. Jazbec (1863–1949), who learned his trade in Italy, Germany, and France. He provided modern machinery for his shop, and the quality of his binding is unusually fine. Of the more important twentieth-century bookbinders in Zagreb, it is worth mentioning Šoban, Strobach, Tkalec, Fezerinec, Čermak, Gril, Hönigsberg, Bartol Dimec, Žager, Kramer, and Franjo Štromar.[29]

Between the two world wars, bookbinding in Zagreb was done on

29/F. Štromar composed the first Croatian manual on the art of bookbinding. See Bibliography.

specially constructed machines, which could, in one hour, fold 3000 paper sheets, glue 500 pastedowns, sew up 60 books, and cover 200 of them, widen 150 book-backings, and cut the alphabet for 17 books of 200 sheets; these machines could also clip (finish) on all three sides simultaneously. All decoration, including gilding, was accomplished by mechanical means. Machinery was also of inestimable value in the binding of weighty technical-commercial books, as well as in preparing the backings and numbering the pages.[30]

DELUXE EDITIONS

A deluxe book is one that excels in external appearance: it is printed with perfectly formed letter-keys on first-quality paper; its typographical layout is good, and it is sometimes decorated with original engravings; finally it is enclosed in a lovely and sturdy binding. Quite a few Croatian books have always been and still are produced with an eye to esthetic as well as intellectual values. The Croatian engraver in his shop, and the artist in his studio, have endeavored to place as lovely a book as possible in the hands of the reader. Mirko Breyer has written on several occasions of the publishing of deluxe editions of old Croatian books. Here we shall mention but a few works of this century which can definitely be classified as such.

The Yugoslav Academy published, on the occasion of the fifteenth anniversary of the installation of its patron and founder, Bishop Josip Juraj Strossmayer, a deluxe edition entitled *Stolna Crkva u Djakovu* (The Cathedral in Djakovo). The book was printed in Prague, but it had been prepared by the director of the Academy's Gallery, the painter Nikola Mašić. *Zbornik Kralja Tomislava* (Symposium of King Tomislav), issued in commemoration of the millennium of the Croatian Kingdom (925–1925), was also beautifully decorated. The first volume of the catalogue listing the Academy Gallery's paintings was reproduced by Professor Artur Schneider (1897–1946) in a deluxe edition. The studies of the Academy's Art Department written by Professor Schneider, Dr. Ljubo Karaman, Dr. Cvito Fisković, Dr. Dragutin Kniewald, and others were sumptuously illustrated, as befitted a publication dealing with the monuments of the Croatian cultural past.

30/T. Katušić, "Knjigoveški obrt"/The Art of Bookbinding, *Grafička revija* (Zagreb, Nov.–Dec. 1925), III, 191ff.; Djuro Stojadinović, *Knjigoveźnja*/Bookbinding (Zagreb: Tehnička knjiga, 1950).

The Matica Hrvatska, founded in 1842, was careful of the appearance of even its very first editions, and especially the bindings (done by the Šoban Bookbindery). Among its deluxe editions are *Matica Hrvatska od godine 1842 do godine 1892* (Matica Hrvatska from 1842 to 1892) by Tade Smičiklas and Franjo Marković, *Starohrvatska umjetnost* (Ancient Art of Croatia) by Professor Joseph Strzygowski, *Zbornik o tisućugodišnjici hrvatskog kraljevstva* (Collection of Monographs on the Occasion of the Millennium of the Croatian Kingdom) in 1925, and *Dioklecijanova palača* (Diocletian's Palace) by Frane Bulić and Ljubo Karaman, in Croatian and German.

Croatian periodicals have also contributed to Croatian deluxe publishing, with issues such as the *Hrvatski salon* in 1898–9 and *Život* (Life) in 1900–1. In more recent times, a few deluxe volumes of *Savremenik* (The Contemporary Monthly) were artistically prepared by Professor Schneider. *Hrvatska Revija*, a literary monthly of Matica Hrvatska, has also appeared in fine editions, under the art editorship of Vladimir Kirin.

The Croatian Educational and Literary Association was founded in Zagreb in 1871 through the efforts of the leaders of Croatian teachers: Ivan Filipović, Stjepan Basariček, Skender Fabković, Mijat Stojanović, Ljudevit Modec, Tomislav Ivkanec, and others. This organization assumed the responsibility of further educating Croatian teachers, of stressing more professionalism among them, and of promoting the interests of school and national culture. The Association issued, in a lovely and valuable binding, the works of the great Czech pedagogue Jan Komensky, *didaktika* and *Velika Didaktika*; François Rabelais' *Misli o uzgoju* (Thoughts on Education); J. J. Rousseau's *Emil ili o uzgoju* (Emile or On Education); Herbert Spencer's *Nauk o uzgoju* (Studies on Education); Gabriel Compayre's *Intelektualni i moralni razvitak djeteta* (The Intellectual and Moral Development of the Child); and other essays. Later, the Association published, in four volumes, the work *Pedagogija* (Education) by Stjepan Basariček, followed by other school publications, and in 1895 it began the beautifully finished edition of the *Pedagogijska enciklopedija* (Encyclopedia of Education).[31]

The "Zabavna biblioteka" (Popular Library) of Dr. Nikola Andrić (founded in 1913) published several deluxe editions, among which we

31/The Association in its *Knjižnica za mladež* issued over 200,000 copies of the most outstanding Croatian children's and young people's books. Beginning in 1873, it issued one of the best children's magazines, *Smilje* (Cud-Weed), and a periodical, *Napredak* (Progress). The work of the Association is exhaustively presented in *Pedesetogodišnjica hrvatskoga pedagoško-književnog zbora*/The Fiftieth Anniversary of the Croatian Pedagogical-Literary Club (Zagreb, 1923).

may mention the five-hundredth book of that series, *Lijepa Naša* ... (Our Beautiful Country) by Josip Horvat. This book consists of eighteen commentaries on Croatia's loveliest landscapes, with thirty-eight original photographs. A number of copies of it appeared in a sumptuous binding bearing a golden design of the statue of Grgur Ninski by Ivan Meštrović.

The editors of the Minerva Publishing House and Bookshop produced a number of deluxe editions for the Croatian book market: *Kranjčevićeva djela, Novakova djela, Klasici ruske književnosti, Biblioteka općeg znanja, Minerva Leksikon, Svjetski atlas, Leksikon zdravlja, Pedagogijski Leksikon, Šta je šta,* and *Sto godina hrvatske književnosti* (The Works of Kranjčević, The Works of Novak, Classics of Russian Literature, Library of General Knowledge, The Minerva Lexicon, World Atlas, Encyclopedia of Health, Encyclopedia of Education, What's What [the Croatian version of the German *Duden*], and One Hundred Years of Croatian Literature [in six vols.]).

The intent of the Croatian Encyclopedia, later the Croatian Publishing Bibliographical Institute, was to publish books of an encyclopedic, lexicographic, or bibliographical nature. It took pride in a series of handsome editions: *Hrvatska enciklopedija, Znanje i radost, Svjetski klasici, Harambašićeva djela, Galovićeva djela, Jorgovanovićeva djela,* and *Hrvatska misao i riječ kroz stoljeća* (The Croatian Encyclopedia, Knowledge and Joy, World Classics, the Works of Harambašić, of Galović, and of Jorgovanović, and Croatian Thought and Word through the Centuries).

The Society of Engineers and Architects (founded in Zagreb in 1878) issued a magnificent edition of *Hrvatski gradjevni oblici* (Croatian Architectural Forms) in 1906.

The Vasić and Horvat Bookshop, later Radoslav Horvat (founded in 1918), distinguished itself with its deluxe editions, especially with some thirty books of the "Ilustrirana Omladinska biblioteka" (Illustrated Library for Young People) consisting of representative classical works from world literature, compiled for young people. These books are outstanding, not only for the graphic and technical art with which they were produced, but also for the purity of their Croatian diction, which is notably free from foreign words and idioms. This publisher also issued a selection of poems by Vidrić, Krklec, Pavić, and Sida Košutić and, later, an artistically executed work by Professor Gjuro Szabo, *Stari Zagreb* (Old Zagreb), and also *Hrvatsko Zagorje* (Croatian Zagorje), a book of scenic sights of northern Croatia. Vasić and Horvat prepared a large international exhibition of children's books in 1938, and displayed 5000 books, representative of all European nations. The firm was more than once internationally recognized, beginning in 1925 when it received a diploma in Florence at the "Seconda fiera internazionale del libro."

During the thirties, the publishing firm of A. Velzek (founded in 1930) successfully competed in the area of artistic book production. Particularly noteworthy was its preparation of the works of Josip Horvat: *Politička povijest Hrvatske* (The Political History of Croatia) in two volumes, *Kultura Hrvata kroz 1000 godina* (Croation Culture through 1000 Years) in two volumes, and later *Metropola Hrvata* (The Metropolis of Croatia) with reproductions by the photographer Tošo Dabac.

The Kugli Bookshop, founded in 1852, issued 163 volumes of the "Hrvatska biblioteka" (Croatian Library), which contained all the more important Croatian authors, and the six-volume *Povijest Hrvata* (History of the Croatians) with many original illustrations by Professor Vjekoslav Klaić.

Nova Evropa (New Europe), edited and published by the distinguished Serbian literary and cultural historian Dr. Milan Ćurćin (and printed by the Tipografija press in Zagreb), prepared a series of artistic publications dedicated to the work of Ivan Meštrović. Later, a series of *Nova Evropa* was dedicated to outstanding domestic and foreign celebrities and to various cities and provinces.

On the seventy-fifth anniversary of *Obzor* (Horizon) in 1935, a memorial volume of 326 folio pages appeared. This artistic work, finished by a domestic firm employing only domestic labor, and using paper from Croatian factories, was produced with letterpresses, copperplate and offset type. It is a small but pithy encyclopedia of Croatian national development during the period when *Obzor* was issued.

In 1925, Tipografija published an artistic album, *Zagreb*, by the painter and graphic artist Vladimir Kirin. The album contains a sixteen-page preface and notes on the paintings by Professor Schneider followed by twenty-four pages of reproductions of Kirin's drawings, and was prepared by the graphic technician Jan Novak and a group of fellow artisans, all experienced graphic artists. It is bound in vermilion-red cloth, and on its cover is an inscription in gold, "Vladimir Kirin, *Zagreb*. Published by the Municipality of Zagreb," and the decorative Zagreb coat of arms. The letters and coat of arms were drawn by Vladimir Kirin also. The title page and the preface are set in Walbaum's antique, an ancient classical font artistically recreated, cut and cast in the famous casting-house of H. Berthold in Vienna. The text of the preface was arranged *per extensum*, as one complete unit without indentation. The type-style is cut as a whole and is imprinted in gold on the paper. The fifteenth page carries the list of pictures, arranged both in "verse" and free style. The following twenty-four pages of fine reproductions illustrate different areas of old Zagreb, some better-known historical and architectural monuments, and the interiors of Rauch's palace and a number of churches. These impressions reveal delicate and dramatic artistic feeling on the part of both painter and graphic technicians.

Some issues of the graphic department of the Tipografija press in Zagreb were printed as deluxe editions. Dragutin Domjanić's collection of verses, *Kipci i popevke* (Pictures and Songs), prepared by Anka Krizmanić, and Vladimir Vidrić's poems were both printed by the Tipografija. In 1908, on the twenty-fifth anniversary of the poetic activity of S. S. Kranjčević (who died that same year), the Society of Croatian Authors issued his *Pjesme* (Poems) in a genuine deluxe edition of 500 copies with illustrations by Lina Virant, Branimir Petrović, Ljubo Babić, and Mihovil Kušlin.

Finally, it is worth noting the names of at least a few of the artists who, in their works, promoted deluxe editions: Ljubo Babić, Tomislav Krizman, Jerolim Miše, Vladimir Kirin, Ernest Tomašević, Oto Postružnik, Kamilo Ružička, Josip Restek, Mladen Veža, Petar Orlić, Vladimir Udatny, Julije Meissner, Dr. Vlado Miroslavljević, Dr. Pavao Gavranić, Zdenka Turkalj, Olga Höcker, Paul Goldoni, and Slavko Kopač. Considerable recognition has also been accorded the young and talented painter Fedor Vaić, who even after the Second World War, under difficult circumstances, continued conscientiously to practice the illustrator's art.

BOOKPLATING

The art of bookplating (*ex libris*) has also flourished in Croatia. In the history of Croatian graphic art, a few world-famous names may be noted, such as the copper-engravers Martin Kolunić-Rota and Andrija Medulić-Schiavone. In the sixteenth century Kolunić made bookplates for the nobility with coats of arms in the style of the Italian Renaissance. Bookplating, a favorite technique of modern European graphics, has also inspired Croatian artists, especially those who were occupied with xylography. Professor Miljenko Djurić, a particularly prolific artist in this field, and also a leader in the association of graphic artists, issued several albums of bookplates. Recent proponents of the art include Vjera Bojničić and Zvonimir A. Lukinović from Zagreb and Ivan Roch from Osijek.[32]

32/The reader may find more information on the subject treated in this section in the book *Ex libris* (Zagreb: Zaklada Narodnih Novina u Zagrebu, 1927).

At least a partial survey of the history of Croatian printing can be found in the Croatian Museum of Arts and Crafts in Zagreb. This museum has collected a large number of varied examples representative of the work of graphic artists, typographers, and photographers. Books illustrating the development of this craft are also deposited there. Included in the collection are works of well-known artists: Vlaho Bukovac, Bela Csikos-Sessia, Tomislav Krizman, Ljubo Babić, Jerolim Miše, Marijan Trepše, Olga Höcker, Zdenka Sertić, Ladislav Kralj-Medjimurac, and others. Some years ago graphic artists in Croatia prepared a series of representative exhibits of the history of publication, printing, and typesetting, and urged establishment of a permanent museum exhibition of graphic, printing, and bookbinding techniques.[33]

Bibliography

Alacevich, Angelico. "Stamperie e giornali di Zara nel secolo passato," *Il Dalmatino lunario* (Zadar), 1935.

Babić, Ljuba (Ksaver Šandor Gjalski). "Istina, pravica i ljepota"/Truth, Justice, and Beauty, *Omladina* (Zagreb), no. 7 (March 1931).

Bach, Ivan. "Grafika, tiskarstvo, knjigovežnja i fotografija u Hrvatskom narodnom muzeju za umjetnost i obrt u Zagrebu"/Graphics, Printing, Bookbinding, and Photography as Displayed in the National Museum of Arts and Crafts in Zagreb, *Grafička revija* (Zagreb), Jubilee Issue (1870–1940), no. 3 (1940).

Badalić, Josip. *Grafička produkcija Jugoslavije*/The Production of Graphics in Yugoslavia. Praha, 1928.

——— "Knjiga je glavni instrumenat civilizacije"/Books Are the Principal Instruments of Civilization, *Jutarnji List* (Zagreb), June 21, 1936. An interview.

——— "Američko javno knjižničarstvo"/American Public Libraries, *Alma Mater croatica* (Zagreb), no. 4–5 (1938–9). Summary in English.

——— *Za naše narodno knjižničarstvo*/For Our National Librarianship. Zagreb, 1943.

——— *Inkunabule u Narodnoj Republici Hrvatskoj*/Incunabula in the People's Republic of Croatia. ("Djela Jugoslavenske Akademije," 45.) Zagreb: Yugoslav Academy, 1952.

——— "Le Prime stamperie in terra jugoslava e Venezia," *Ricerche slavistiche* (Roma), 1954, 4.

33/Dr. Ivan Bach, "Grafika, tiskarstvo, knjigovežnja i fotografija u Hrvatskom narodnom muzeju za umjetnost i obrt u Zagrebu"/Graphics, Printing, Bookbinding, and Photography as Displayed in the National Museum of Arts and Crafts in Zagreb, *Grafička revija*, no. 3, 1940 (Jubilee issue, 1870–1940); and Dr. Eugen Sladović, "Knjigotiskarsko umijeće prema umjetnosti, orbtu, industriji i trgovini kao kulturnim pojavama"/The Art of Bookbinding as Compared to the Cultural Phenomena of Arts, Crafts, Industry, and Trade, *Grafički godišnjak*, I, ed. Jakov Keimal (n.d.).

—— *Jugoslavica – usque ad annum MDC. Bibliographie der südslawischen Frühdrucke.* Baden-Baden: Librairie Heitz, 1957. 2nd ed., *ibid.*, 1966.

Barge, Herrmann. *Geschichte der Buchdruckerkunst von ihren Anfängen bis zur Gegenwart.* Leipzig: Ph. Reclam, 1940. 521.

Benac, Alojz. "Uz jubilej Zemaljskog muzeja: Poslije sedamdeset i pet godina"/ For the 75th Anniversary of the Zemaljski muzej, *Oslobodjenje* (Sarajevo), xx (Sept. 29, 1963), 6.

Berkopec, Oto. "Die Anfänge des Buchdruckes bei den Südslaven," *Slavische Rundschau* 1940. *Der Buchdruck bei den slavischen Völkern* (Praha, 1940), no. 1–2, 42–63.

Bersa, Josip. *Dubrovačke slike i prilike (1800–1880)*/Life in Dubrovnik between 1800 and 1880. Zagreb: Matica Hrvatska, 1941.

Bjelica, Mihailo. "Da li je u Kosinju postojala štamparija prije Obodske?"/Did Kosinj Have a Press before Obod? *Naša Štampa* (Beograd), XII (Aug.–Sept. 1963), no. 118. *See also* Kulundžić.

Blažeković, Tatjana. *Fluminensia croatica.* ("Hrvatska bibliografija," ser. C, no. 4.) Zagreb: Yugoslav Academy, 1953. 172. This is a bibliography of books, periodicals, and newspapers published in the Croatian language in Rijeka.

—— "Hrvatske novine i štamparije u Istri (1870–1945)"/Croatian Newspapers and Presses in Istria from 1870 to 1945, *Riječka revija* (Rijeka), I, no. 1 (May 1952), 38–41.

Bogišić, Baltazar. *Zbirka slavenskih inkunabula*/A Collection of Slavic Incunabula. Dubrovnik, 1898.

Bösendorfer, Josip. "Povijest tipografije u Osijeku"/History of Typography in Osijek, *Gradja za povijest književnosti hrvatske* (Zagreb: Yugoslav Academy), XIV (1939), 113–46.

—— "Divaldiana u Osijeku"/The Divalds in Osijek, *Osječki zbornik* (Osijek: Croatian State Museum in Osijek, no. 1), 1942, 70–89.

Bošnjak, Mladen. "Može li se ustanoviti broj listova prve hrvatske tiskane knjige?"/Can One Establish the Number of Sheets of the First Croatian Printed Book? *Republika* (Zagreb), XI (1955), no. 1, 62–8.

—— "Sačuvani primjerci prve hrvatske tiskane knjige (Vajsov zbornik)" Preserved Copies of the First Croatian Printed Book (Miscellanea pro Vajs), *Slovo* (Zagreb), no. 6–8, 1957, 297–310.

—— "Drvorezi u primjercima prve hrvatske tiskane knjige (1483)"/Woodcuts in the First Croatian Printed Book (1483), *Bulletin Zavoda za likovne umjetnosti* (Zagreb: Yugoslav Academy), X (1962), no. 1–2, 54–62. A French summary on 142.

—— "O nalazima iz najstarijih tiskara"/Findings about the Oldest Presses, *Bulletin Zavoda za likovne umjetnosti* (Zagreb: Yugoslav Academy), XI (1963), no. 1–2, 108–22. A French summary on 163. *See also* Kulundžić.

Brčić, Ivan. *Chrestomatia linguae vetero-slovenicae charactere glagolitico.* Prague, 1859.

—— *Čitanka staroslavenskog jezika*/A Church Slavonic Reader. Prag, 1864.

—— "Njekoliko staroslavenskih i hrvatskih knjiga što pisanih što tiskanih glagolicom, kojim se u skorašnje doba u trag ušlo"/About a Few Church Slavonic and Croatian Books Recently Discovered, Some Written and Some

Printed in Glagolitic Script, *Rad* (Zagreb: Yugoslav Academy), LIX (1881), 166.

Breyer, Mirko. *Prilozi k starijoj književnoj i kulturnoj povijesti hrvatskoj*/Contributions to Older Croatian Literary and Cultural History. Zagreb, 1904.

—— "Der kroatisch Buchhandel," a reprint from *Börsenblatt für den deutschen Buchhandel*. Leipzig, 1910.

—— "Prilozi pvijesti dubrovačkog štamparstva"/Contributions to the History of Printing in Dubrovnik, *Rešetarov zbornik* (Dubrovnik), 1931.

—— "O štamparu i knjižaru dru. Ljudevitu Gaju"/Dr. Ljudevit Gaj, a Printer and Bookseller, *Grafička revija* (Zagreb), x, no. 4 (Dec. 1936), 152–4.

—— *Südslavische Rara und Rarissima, eine empfindsame bibliophile Exkursion*. Wien-Leipzig-Zürich: Herbert Reichner, 1937.

—— "Senj – kolijevka hrvatskoga tiskarstva"/Senj – The Cradle of Croatian Printing, in the work *Senj, Hrvatski Kulturni Spomenici*, I. Zagreb: Yugoslav Academy, 1940.

—— "Štamparstvo u Dubrovniku"/Printing in Dubrovnik, *Narodna knjiga* (Zagreb), no. 1 (Jan. 1950).

—— *O starim i rijetkim jugoslavenskim knjigama. Bibliografsko-bibliofilski prikaz*/Old and Rare Yugoslavian Books. A Study in Bibliography and Bibliophilism. Ed. Blanka and Tomislav Jakić. Zagreb: Yugoslav Academy, 1952.

Bučar, Franjo. *Povijest hrvatske protestantske književnosti za reformacije*/A History of Croatian Protestant Literature during the Reformation. Zagreb: Matica Hrvatska, 1910.

—— "O hrvatskoj protestantskoj tiskari u Njemačkoj u XVI stoljeću"/The Croatian Protestant Press in Germany in the 16th Century, *Grafička revija* (Zagreb), XVI (1942), 37–44.

Bučar, Franjo, and Fancev, Franjo. "Bibliografija hrvatske protestantske književnosti za reformacije"/A Bibliography of Croatian Protestant Literature in the Time of the Reformation, *Starine*, XXXIX (Zagreb: Yugoslav Academy, 1938).

Cecić, Vinko. *Historija organizacije i političkih borba grafičkih radnika Hrvatske 1870–1955*/History of the Organization and Political Struggle of the Graphic Workers of Croatia from 1870 to 1955. Zagreb, 1955. 369. Summaries in French, English, and Esperanto.

Dahl, Svead. *Geschichte des Buches*. Leipzig: Hiersemann, 1928.

Deanović, Mirko. "Dalmatinac u širokom svijetu"/Dalmatians throughout the World, *Savremenik* (Zagreb), XXII (1937).

Derossi, Josip. "Je li Kosinj prvi? U Lici prva tiskara na Slavenskom Jugu"/Is Kosinj First? The First Press among Southern Slavs was in Lika, *Ličke novine* (Gospić), XI (March 15, 1963), no. 6 (238), 4. *See also* Kulundžić.

Deželić, Velimir. *Inkunabule Zagrebačke Sveučilišne Biblioteke*/Incunabula of the University of Zagreb Library. Zagreb, 1902.

—— "Biskupska, a zatim Novoselova tiskaru u Zagrebu"/First Bishop's, then Novosel's Press in Zagreb, *Narodna Starina* (Zagreb), 1926.

Dizdarević, Branka, and Mišić-Jambrišak, Jelka. *Bibliografija knjiga ženskih pisaca štampanih u Hrvatskoj, Slavoniji, Dalmaciji, Bosni i Hercegovini do svršetka godine 1935*/A Bibliography of Books Written by Women Authors and Printed in Croatia, Slavonia, Dalmatia, Bosnia, and Hercegovina up to the End of 1935. Zagreb, 1936.

Dornik, Srećko. "Značajni kulturno-historijski jubileji u Senju. Prva štamparija Južnih Slavena u Kosinju kraj Senja?"/Important Historical and Cultural Anniversaries in Senj. Was the First Press among Southern Slavs in Kosinj near Senj? *Novi List* (Rijeka), XVII (April 7, 1963), no. 81, 6. *See also* Kulundžić.

Esih, Ivan. "Bibliopsihologija"/Bibliopsychology, *Obzor* (Zagreb), June 2, 1939.

—— "Knjiga kao pacijent u klinici knjiga"/Books as Patients in a Book Clinic, *Jutarnji List* (Zagreb), 1940, 21.

Ex libris. Zagreb: Zaklada Narodnih Novina u Zagrebu, 1927.

Firinger, Kamilo. "Pretplatnici jedne naše knjige g. 1823. štampane u Pešti"/ Subscribers of a Croatian Book Published in Budapest in 1823, *Osječki zbornik* (Osijek: Croatian State Museum in Osijek, no. 2–3), 1948, 275–7.

—— "Jedan pokušaj izdavanja novina u Osijeku 1813"/An Attempt to Publish a Newspaper in Osijek in 1813, *Historijski zbornik* (Zagreb), V (1952), no. 1–2, 190–2.

—— "Madžarska grana Divalda"/Hungarian Branch of the Divalds, *Osječki zbornik* (Osijek: Croatian State Museum in Osijek, no. 4), 1954.

Gabrščček, Andrej. *Goriški Slovenci 1830–1900*/Slovenes in the Gorica Region from 1830 to 1900. 2 vols. Ljubljana: Tiskarna Merkur, 1932.

Gjivanović, Niko. "Štampari u starom Dubrovniku"/Printers in Old Dubrovnik, *Dubrovački zabavnik* (Dubrovnik), 1928.

Goldschmidt, Hermann. "Incunabeln-Reisen in Oesterreich, I: Dalmatien," *Zentralblatt für Bibliothekwesen* (Leipzig), 1916.

Grafička revija, a Periodical of the Society of Graphic Workers of Yugoslavia, Zagreb, from 1922 to 1940.

Grafički almanah, 1938, issued by the Educational Center of the Society of Graphic Workers of Yugoslavia, Zagreb, 1938.

Gregov, Ljudevit. *Kalendar prvog tiskanog glagoljskog misala*. Izvadak iz doktorske disertacije "Prvi tiskani glagoljski misal"/Calendar of the First Printed Glagolitic Missal. Excerpt from the Doctoral Dissertation "First Printed Glagolitic Missal." Zagreb, 1952.

Hamm, Josip. "Glagoljica"/Glagolism, *Enciklopedija Jugoslavije* (Zagreb), III (1958), 462–8.

—— "Još uvijek Senj"/Senj Is Still First, *Vjesnik* (Zagreb), March 8, 1959. *See also* Kulundžić.

Hergešić, Ivo. *Hrvatske novine i časopisi do 1848*/Croatian Newpapers and Reviews up to 1848. Zagreb: Matica Hrvatska, 1936.

Hrvatski bibliofil, a Monthly for Bibliotechnical and Bibliographical Studies, edited by V. Deželić, Zagreb, 1905, nos. 1–3.

Ivšić, Stjepan. "Sredovječna hrvatska glagoljska književnost"/Croatian Glagolitic Literature in the Middle Ages, *Sveslavenski zbornik, spomenica o tisućugodišnjici hrvatskog kraljevstva*/All Slavic Collection, a Memorial Book of the Millennium of the Croatian Kingdom (Zagreb, 1930), 132–42.

—— "Izložba srpske knjige i štampe u Hrvatskoj od svojih početaka do godine 1918"/An Exhibition of Serbian Books and Printing in Croatia from the Beginning to the Year 1918, *Prosvjeta* (Zagreb), 1950. (The exhibition took place from April 30 to May 31, 1950.)

Jagić, Vatroslav. *Entstehungsgeschichte der kirchenslavischen Sprache.* Berlin: Weidmann, 1913.

—— "Hrvatska glagolska književnost"/Croatian Glagolitic Literature, in *Povijest hrvatske književnosti* by Branko Vodnik, I. Zagreb: Matica Hrvatska, 1913.

Jakić, Tomislav. "O našim najstarijim i najrjedjim knjigama od 1483–1625"/ Concerning our Oldest and Rarest Books from 1483 to 1625, *Narodna knjiga* (Zagreb), no. 4 (1949).

—— "Iz izdavačke prošlosti: Primorje i Dalmacija u XVIII I XIX stoljeću"/ From the History of Publishing: The Croatian Littoral and Dalmatia in the 18th and 19th Centuries. *Knjiga i svet* (Beograd), IV (June 1960), no. 31.

—— "Iz izdavačke prošlosti: Štamparstvo i knjižarstvo u Zagrebu za vrijeme ilirskog preporoda"/From the History of Publishing: Printing and Bookselling in Zagreb during the Illyrian Awakening, *Knjiga i svet* (Beograd), V (June 1961), no. 43, 6–7.

Janson, Stjepan. "Koje je godine Dr. Ljudevit Gaj otvorio svoju knjigotiskaru u Zagrebu"/What Year Did Dr. Ljudevit Gaj Start His Press in Zagreb?, Commemorative Issue (1870–1940) of *Grafička revija* (Zagreb), XIV (1940), no. 3, 135–6.

Jelić, Luka. *Fontes historici liturgiae glagolitico-romanae a* XIII *ad* XIX *saeculum.* Vol. I. Veglae, 1906.

Jokić, Gojko. "Izložba o štampi u Bosni i Hercegovini: Vijek svjedočanstava"/ Exhibit of Printing in Bosnia and Hercegovina: A Century of Evidence, *Oslobodjenje* (Sarajevo), XX (Sept. 29, 1963), 6.

Kabát, Karel. *Knihtisk a jeho vývoj v Československu*/Book Printing and Its Development in Czechoslovakia. Praha, 1937. 352.

Karlić, Petar. *Kraljski Dalmatin (1806–1810)*/Royal Dalmatian from 1806 to 1810. Zadar: Matica Dalmatinska, 1912.

Kasandrić, Petar. *Il giornalismo dalmato dal 1848 al 1860.* Zadar, 1946.

Katušić, T. "Knjigoveški obrt"/The Art of Bookbinding, *Grafička revija* (Zagreb), III, Nov.–Dec. 1925, 191ff.

Klaić, Vjekoslav. *Knjižarstvo u Hrvata. Studija o izdavanju i širenju hrvatske knjige*/The Book Industry among Croatians. A Study on the Publishing and Dissemination of Croatian Books. Zagreb: St. Kugli, 1922.

—— "Zagrebačke štamparije do osnutka Gajeve tiskare 1835"/Printing Presses in Zagreb to the Time of the Founding of Gaj's Press in 1835, *Grafička revija* (Zagreb), Nov.–Dec. 1925.

—— *Život i djela Pavla Rittera Vitezovića*/The Life and Works of Pavao Ritter Vitezović. Zagreb: Matica Hrvatska, 1941.

Kniewald, Dragutin. "Najstariji Zagrebački red i čin Mise"/The Oldest Zagrebian Ritual of the Mass, *Croatia Sacra* (Zagreb), 1938.

—— "Zagrebački liturgijski kodeksi XI.–XV. stoljeća/Codices Liturgici Zagrebienses a saeculo XI. usque ad finem S. XV.," *Croatia Sacra* (Zagreb), no. 19 (1940).

Kolendić, Petar. "Karačolov 'Quaresimale' u srpskohrvatskom prijevodu"/ Caracciolo's "Quaresimale" in a Serbo-Croatian Translation, *Godišnjak Skopskoga filozofskog fakulteta*, I (1930), 169–75.

—— "Mletački kaligraf Kamilo Zaneti kao štampar jednog dubrovačkog katekizma"/The Venetian Calligraphist Kamilo Zaneti as the Printer of a Dubrovnik Catechism, *Rešetarov zbornik* (Dubrovnik), 1931.

—— "Zadranin Šimun Kožičić i njegova štamparija na Rijeci"/Šimun Kožičić of Zadar and His Printing Shop in Rijeka, *Magazin Sjeverne Dalmacije* (Split), 1935, 95–107.

—— "Ars bene moriendi u glagolskom izdanju"/Ars bene moriendi in a Glagolitic Edition, *Južni Pregled* (Skopje), Sept. 1, 1936.

Kos, Milko. "Studija o Istarskom razvodu"/Study of Istrian Land Boundaries, *Rad* (Yugoslav Academy), CCXL (1931), 105–203.

Kostrenčić, Ivan. *Beiträge zur Geschichte der protestantischen Literatur der Südslawen in den Jahren 1559–1565.* Wien, 1874.

Kovijanić, Risto. "Trnavski univerzitet i Hrvati"/The University of Trnava and Croatians, *Novosti* (Zagreb), XXIX (Sept. 17, 1935), 11.

Krader, Barbara. "The Glagolitic Missal of 1483," *The Library of Congress* (Washington), XX, no. 2 (March 1963), 93–8.

Kreševljaković, Hamdija. "Štamparije u Bosni za turskoga vremena, 1529–1878"/Printing Presses in Bosnia during the Time of the Turks, 1529–1878, *Gradja za povijest književnosti hrvatske* (Zagreb: Yugoslav Academy), IX (1920), 1–41.

Krmpotić, Josip. "Razvoj tiskarskog obrta u Julijskoj Krajini"/The Development of the Printing Craft in the Julian Region, *Edinost* (Trieste), Jubilee Issue, 1926.

Kukuljević, Ivan. *Tiskari jugoslavenski* XV. *i* XVI. *vijeka*/Yugoslav Printers in the 15th and 16th Centuries. ("Arkiv za povjestnicu jogoslavensku," I.) Zagreb: Yugoslav Academy, 1851.

—— "Der Buchdruck in Kroatien im XVI. and XVII. Jahrhundert," *Kroatischen Revue* (Zagreb), 1882.

—— "Kroatische Bibliographie aus dem XVI and XVII Jahrhundert," *Kroatische Revue* (Zagreb), 1882. (*Agramer Zeitung* 1881, no. 265.)

Kukuljević-Sakcinski, Ivan. *Bibliografija hrvatska*/A Croatian Bibliography. Vol. I. Zagreb, 1860.

Kulundžić, Zvonimir. *Knjiga o knjizi*/A Book about Books, I: *Historija pisama*/A History of Scripts. Zagreb, 1957.

—— *Put do knjige*/The Way to the Book. Zagreb, 1959.

—— "Problem najstarije štamparije na Slavenskom Jugu/The Problem of the Oldest Press among Southern Slavs, *Narodna knjižnica* (Zagreb), III (1959), 21–8.

—— *Kosinj, kolijevka štamparstva Slavenskog Juga*/Kosinj, the First Press among Southern Slavs. Zagreb, 1960. 100. *See also* Bjelica, Bošnjak, Derossi, Dornik, Hamm, Petešić.

—— "Egzotične knjige u našim muzejima i kolekcijama"/Rare Books in Our Museums and Collections, *Narodna knjižnica* (Zagreb), 1961, 89–103.

—— "Prve naše štamparije"/Our First Presses, *Radio i televizija u školi* (Zagreb), 1963 (first semester of the school year 1962–3).

Lanović, Mihajlo. "Stjepan pl. Verböczy, veliki učitelj staroga našega prava"/S. Verböczy, the Famous Teacher of Our Old Civil Code, *Rad* (Yugoslav Academy), CCLXXVII (1943), 65–102.

Livadić, Branimir. "Knjige i život"/Books and Life (a lecture given in Sušak on the Day of the Croatian Book, April 29, 1937), *Jutarnji List* (Zagreb), May 30, 1937, 17.

Lozovina, Vinko. "Knjiga u prosvjeti i kulturi svjetskoj i narodnoj"/Books in National and International Education and Culture, *Jadranski dnevnik* (Split), in six continuations in the month of January 1938.

Malbaša, Marija. "Stodvadesetpet godina štamparske djelatnosti u Osijeku (1748–1873)"/One Hundred and Twenty-Five Years of Printing Activity in Osijek, *Osječki zbornik*, 4 (1954), 105–40; 5 (1956), 209–32; 6 (1958) (3 dio: "Izdavalačka djelatnost u Osijeku od sredine 18. do početka 20. stoljeća"), 257–301.

Maštrović, Vjekoslav. *Jadertina croatica.* Zagreb: Yugoslav Academy. I, 1949; II, 1954.

——— "Sto godina gospodarske štampe u Zadru"/One Hundred Years of Printing about Economic Life in Zadar, *Vjesnik* (Zagreb), no. 4, Jan. 4, 1953.

Medved, Ivan. "Prvi osječki tipografi i knjigoveže"/The First Typographers and Bookbinders in Osijek, *Jubilarni almanah Kluba hrvatskih književnika i umjetnika u Osijeku*/Jubilee Almanac of the Croatian Authors' and Artists' Club of Osijek (Osijek), 1929, 60–88.

Miholić, Stanko. "Bolesne knjige"/Books in the Deteriorated State, *Priroda* (Zagreb), XXVI (1936), no. 9, 303–10.

Mihovilović, Ivo. *Trst*/Trieste. Zagreb, 1945.

Milčetić, Ivan. "Prilozi za literaturu hrvatskih glagolskih spomenika"/Contributions to the Literature of Croatian Glagolitic Monuments, *Starine* (Zagreb: Yugoslav Academy), XXIII (1890), XXV (1892).

——— "Prethodni izvještaj o izučavanju hrvatske glagoljske književnosti"/A Preliminary Report on Research into Croatian Glagolitic Literature, *Ljetopis* (Zagreb: Yugoslav Academy), XXIII (1909), 182–3.

——— "Hrvatska glagoljska bibliografija Dio I, opisi rukopisa"/Croatian Glagolitic Bibliography, Part I, Descriptions of Manuscripts, *Starine* (Zagreb: Yugoslav Academy), XXXIII (1911).

——— "Berčićeva glagoljska zbirka u Petrogradu"/Berčić's Glagolitic Collection in Saint Petersburg, *Ljetopis* (Zagreb: Yugoslav Academy), XXVI (1911), 269.

Molinari, Eduard, and Metzner, D. "Početci i razvitak litografije u Jugoslaviji"/The Beginnings and Development of Lithography in Yugoslavia, *Grafička revija* (Zagreb), no. 3 (1936), 68–79.

Narodne Novine, January 5, 1935. An issue dedicated to the first hundred year anniversary of the *Narodne Novine*, 1835–1935. Zagreb, 1935.

Novak, Viktor, and Zwitter, Fran (eds.). *Oko Trsta*/About Trieste. Beograd: Državni izdavački Zavod Jugoslavije, 1945.

Olesnicki, Aleksej. "Naše orijentalno blago"/Our Oriental Treasures, *Hrvatska revija* (Zagreb), 1932.

Orel, Vladimir. "Glagolica u Istri"/Glagolism in Istria, *Primorski Dnevnik* (Trieste), Jubilee Issue, May 1950.

Pedesetgodišnjica hrvatskoga pedagoško-književnog zbora/The Fiftieth Anniversary of the Croatian Pedagogical-Literary Club. Zagreb, 1923.

Pejanović, Djordje. *Štampa Bosne i Hercegovine (1850–1941)*/Publications in Bosnia and Hercegovina from 1850 to 1941. Sarajevo, 1949.

——— *Štamparije u Bosni i Hercegovini (1529–1951)*/Printing Presses in

Bosnia and Hercegovina from 1529 to 1951. Sarajevo, 1952. 78.

Peruško, Tone. "Razvoj hrvatske štampe u Istri"/The Development of the Croatian Press in Istria, *Glas Istre* (Rijeka), Feb. 5, 1946.

—— "Istarski Hrvati su izdali prvu hrvatsku štampanu knjigu, editio princeps, glagoljski misal od 1483"/Istrian Croatians Issued the First Croatian Printed Book, Editio Princeps, the Glagolitic Missal of 1483, *Riječka revija* (Rijeka), I (1952), no. 1.

Petešić, Ćiril. "Najstarija štamparija Južnih Slavena"/The Oldest Printing Press among Southern Slavs, *Telegram* (Zagreb), March 23, 1963. 2. *See also* Kulundžić.

"Polonia typographica Saeculi Sedecimi," *Zbiór podobizn zasobu drukarsjiego tloczni polskich XVI. stulecia*, I, ed. Kazimierz Piekarski (Warsaw, 1936), tables 1–28; II, ed. Trzaska (Warsaw: Evert and Michalski, 1937), tables 29–60.

Putanec, Valentin. "Zapis žakna Jurja u Novakovu misalu"/Deacon George's Notice in Novak's Missal, *Riječka revija* (Rijeka), II (1953), no. 3–4, 127–30.

—— *Prva tiskara u Hrvatskoj i Jugoslaviji – Modruš 1482–1484*/The First Printing Shop in Croatia and Yugoslavia: Modruš 1482–4. Zagreb, 1959.

—— "Problem predsenjskih tiskara u Hrvatskoj (1482–1493)"/Printing Presses in Croatia before the Senj Printing Press (1482–93), *Jadranski zbornik* (Rijeka-Pula), IV (1959–60), 51–107.

Rački, Franjo. "Povjesnik Ivan Lučić Trogiranin. Na uspomenu 200. godišnjice njegove smrti"/The Historian Ivan Lučić of Trogir, on the Bicentennial of His Death, *Rad* (Yugoslav Academy), XLIX (Zagreb, 1879), 65–102.

Radojičić, S. Djordje. "Razvoj ćiriličkog štamparstva kod nas"/The Development of Our Cyrillic Printing, *Republika* (Beograd), no. 278 (Feb. 27, 1951).

Ravlić, Jakša, and Somborac, Marin. *Matica hrvatska 1842–1962*. Zagreb: Matica Hrvatska, 1963.

Reichnach, Pavao. "Uvod u izum štamparstva i razvoj u Osijeku"/Introduction to the Invention of Printing and Its Development in Osijek, Commemorative Issue (1870–1940) of *Grafička revija* (Zagreb), XIV (1940), no. 3, Osijek Supplement, v–xiv.

Rešetar, Milan. "Iz kulturnog života staroga Dubrovnika"/From the Cultural Life of Old Dubrovnik, *Jugoslavenska njiva* (Zagreb), VII (1923), nos. 9 and 10.

Rojnić, Matko. "Kulturne i književne veze Istre i Hrvatske u prošlosti, od prvih početaka do budjenja narodne svijesti"/Cultural and Literary Ties between Istria and Upper Croatia in the Past, from the Earliest Beginnings to the Awakening of National Consciousness. Zagreb, 1931. (Reprinted from the Zagreb daily *Obzor*, 1931, nos. 204–13.)

Rotter-Progonski, Rudimir. "Razvitak novinarstva u Herceg-Bosni s osvrtom na historijat štamparstva"/The Development of Journalism in Bosnia and Hercegovina in Relation to the History of Book Printing, *Grafička revija* (Zagreb), X, no. 4 (1936), 148–51.

Šafařik, Pavel Josef. *Geschichte der Südslawischen Literatur*. I. *Slowenisches und Glagolitisches Schrifthum*. Ed. Josef Jireček. Prag, 1864–5.

Schneider, A., and Rumann, A. *Prva hrvatska ilustrirana knjiga*/The First Illustrated Croatian Book. Zagreb (no date mentioned).

Sladović, Eugen. "Knjigotiskarsko umijeće prema umjetnosti, obrtu, industriji i trgovini kao kulturnim pojavama"/The Art of Bookprinting as Compared to the Cultural Phenomena of Arts, Crafts, Industry, and Trade, *Grafički godišnjak* (Zagreb, no date).

Spinčić, Vjekoslav. "Razvitak Narodnog preporoda u Istri"/The Development of the National Awakening in Istria, *Povijest Istre* (Zagreb: Braća Hrvatskog Zmaja), 1924.

—— *Crtice iz književne kulture Istre*/Sketches of the Literary Culture of Istria. Zagreb, 1926.

Spomen-knjiga o djelovanju tipografske odnosno grafičke organizacije u Zagrebu, 1870–1940/A Memorial Book on the Activity of the Typographical or Graphical Organization in Zagreb, 1870–1940. Zagreb: Savezna organizacija Saveza grafičkih radnika-ca, 1940.

Štefanić, Vjekoslav. "Jedan primjerak prve slovenske štampane knjige"/A Copy of the First Croatian Printed Book, *Glasnik Jugoslovenskog profesorskog društva* (Beograd), XIV (1933), no. 4, 361–5.

—— "Jedna hrvatskoglagoljska inkunabula iz godine 1491. Prilog izučavanju glagoljaškog kalendara"/A Croatian Glagolitic Incunabulum from the Year 1491: A Contribution to the Study of the Glagolitic Calendar, *Rad* (Yugoslav Academy), CCLXXXV (1951), 53–93.

—— "Josip Vajs: Najstariji hrvatski glagoljski misal"/Josip Vajs: The Oldest Croatian Glagolitic Missal, *Slovo* (Zagreb), I (1952), no. 1.

—— "Hrvatskoglagoljske inkunabule"/Croatian Glagolitic Incunabula, *Enciklopedija Jugoslavije* (Zagreb), IV (1960), 365–6.

Stojadinović, Djuro. *Knjigoveznja*/Bookbinding. Zagreb: Tehnička Knjiga, 1950.

Strohal, Rudolf. *Hrvatska glagolska knjiga*/Croatian Glagolitic Books. Zagreb, 1915.

—— "Pregled tiskara, u kojima su se štampale hrvatske knjige od najstarijih vremena do osnutka Jugoslavenske Akademije"/A Survey of Printing Presses which Published Croatian Books from the Oldest Times to the Founding of the Yugoslav Academy, *Nastavni vjesnik* (Zagreb), XXX (1921), 19–26.

Štromar, Franjo. *Knjigoveštvo*/Bookbinding. Zagreb: Zavod za promicanje obrta Obrtne komore u Zagrebu, 1939.

Šulek, Bogoslav. *Tiskarstvo i Pečatnja*/Printing and Typography. ("Novovjeki izumi," II.) Zagreb, 1883. For the history of printing among Southern Slavs, see pp. 102–238.

Tentor, Mate. *Pismo i postanak alfabeta*/Writing and the Origin of the Alphabet. Zagreb, 1931. (See the Zagreb paper *Obzor*, July 28, 1931, for a review of this book by Dr. B. Klaić.)

—— *Latinsko i slavensko pismo*/Latin and Slavic Scripts. Zagreb, 1932. (See the Zagreb paper *Obzor*, Sept. 24, 1932, for a review by Nikola Žic.)

Urlić, Šime. *Prva štamparija u Dalmaciji*/The First Printing Press in Dalmatia. ("Prilozi za književnost, jezik i folklor," III.) Beograd, 1923.

Vajs, Josef. *Rukovět hlaholské palegrafie. Uvedení do knizniho pisma hlahol-*

ského/Handbook of Glagolitic Paleography. Introduction to Glagolitic Literary Writing. Praha: Nakladem Slovanskeho ustavu, 1932.

—— *Najstariji hrvatskoglagoljski misal*/The Oldest Croatian Glagolitic Missal. ("Djela Jugoslavenske Akademije," 38.) Zagreb: Yugoslav Academy, 1948. With a bibliographical description of all Croatian Glagolitic missals.

Vidas, Kazimir. "450 godina našega štamparstva i naše štampe u Hrvatskom Primorju i Istri"/Four Hundred and Fifty Years of Our Printing and Publishing in the Croatian Littoral and Istria, *Riječki List* (Rijeka), IV, no. 1000 (May 27, 1950).

Vojnović, Kosta. "Bibliografski pabirci iz dubrovačkih arhiva"/Bibliographical Gleanings from Dubrovnik Archives, *Starine* (Zagreb: Yugoslav Academy), XXVII (1895) and XXVIII (1896).

Zellinger, Alojz. *Pantheon tyrnaviense, bibliographicam continens recensionem operum typis tyranaviensibus ab anno 1578–1930 editorum.* Tyrnaviae: typis Soc. S. Adalberti, 1931.

Žic, Nikola. "Bibliografijske bilješke o hrvatskim knjigama iz Istre"/Bibliographical Notes on Croatian Books from Istria, *Hrvatska Prosvjeta* (Zagreb), nos. 6, 7, 8 (1937).

—— "Prve štamparije u Trstu"/The First Printing Presses in Trieste, *Grafička revija* (Zagreb), no. 2 (1938).

6

Cultural Achievements of Bosnian and Hercegovinian Muslims

SMAIL BALIĆ

TRANSLITERATION OF ARABIC, PERSIAN, AND OTTOMAN TURKISH LETTERS

TRANSLITERATION OF ARABIC LETTERS

The transliteration system of Arabic characters used here corresponds generally to that of the *Encyclopedia of Islam*, new edition, vol. I, A–B, edited by H. A. R. Gibb, G. H. Kramers, *et al.* (London: Luzac and Company, 1960), transliteration table on page XIII. A few exceptions have been introduced in this article: the digraph *dj* has been rendered as *j*, and the lines set under the digraphs *th*, *kh*, *dh*, *sh*, and *gh* have been omitted for technical reasons. In the table below, the pronunciation of the transliterated letters is given. Both the transliterations and pronunciations are those used in most English-language scholarly publications.

TRANSLITERATION	PRONUNCIATION
Consonants	
ʾ (except when initial)	Glottal stop; as between the two words in "he?! aging?"
b	English *b*
t	like English *t*
th	English *th* in "tenth"
j (instead of dj)	English *j*
ḥ	velar *h* ("guttural")
kh	German *ch*, Spanish *j* (nearer *h* than *k*)
d	like English *d*
dh	English *th* in "that"

TRANSLITERATION	PRONUNCIATION
Consonants	
r	rolled *r*
z	English *z*
s	hissed *s* (in "this")
sh	English *sh*
ṣ	velar (emphatic) *s*
ḍ	velar (emphatic) *d*
ṭ	velar (emphatic) *t*
ẓ	velar (emphatic) *z*
ʿ	glottal scrape; to Anglophones barely audible
gh	voiced equivalent of *kh* above
f	English *f*
ḳ	velar (guttural) *k*
k	English *k*
l	English *l* (in "love")
m	English *m*
n	English *n*
h	English *h*
w	English *w*
y	English *y* (as consonant)
Short vowels	
a	short *a* as in "dart" (according to position)
i	short *i* as in "hit"
u	short *u* as in "pull"
Long vowels	
ā	long *a* as in "charter" (but held longer)
ī	long *i* as in "keen" (but held longer)
ū	long *u* as in "smooth" (but held longer)
Diphthongs	
aw	English *ow* in "now"
ay	English *y* in "style"
Final forms	
ī or īya (instead of iyy)	
uww	
Construct state	
a, at	
Definite article	
al- and ʾl-	

TRANSLITERATION OF PERSIAN AND OTTOMAN TURKISH

For the purposes of this article we do not offer here the complete transliteration of the Persian and Ottoman Turkish alphabets. Instead, both

Persian and Turkish words are treated as if they were Arabic, with the following additional consonants:

CONSONANTS	PRONUNCIATION
p	English "pot"
č	English "church"
ž	English "pleasure"
g	English "good"

The last consonant is pronounced sometimes in Ottoman Turkish as *n* (originally *ng*) and it is transliterated *ñ*. All Persian consonants are pronounced nearly as in English, except that *kh* and *gh* are as in Arabic.

Persian Vowels

The short vowels *a*, *i*, and *u* and the long vowels *ī* and *ū* are pronounced roughly as in Arabic. Long *ā* is close to that of "father" and short *e* like that of "bed" in English; short *o* is often pronounced like the *u* in "pull," and the diphthong *aw* like the *o* in "obey."

Ottoman Turkish Vowels

Vowels are transliterated as they are for Persian with the following two additions: *ö* as in German *öffnen* ("open") and *ü* as in German *über* ("over, above"). Diacritical signs proper to Arabic are, in principle, not used in words of Turkish origin.

MODERN TURKISH SPELLING

The official orthography adopted by the Turkish Republic in 1928 uses a modern Turkish Latin alphabet. Most *consonants* are pronounced approximately as they are in English with the following exceptions: *c* = *dj* (or *j*) as the English *j*; *ç* = *č* as the English *ch*; *ğ* = *gh* as in Arabic; *h* = *h*, *ḥ*, and *kh* as the Arabic *h*; *j* = *ž* as the French *j*; *ş* = *sh* as in English.

The *vowels* are *a*, *e*, *i*, *o*, *u*, pronounced as they are in Italian, with the variants *ö*, *ü* pronounced as in German; *ı* without a dot (sometimes marked with a circle or half-circle) is a slightly stifled vowel.

PREFATORY REMARKS

FOREIGN WORDS

Certain words of oriental origin (Turkish, Arabic, or Persian) which are used more frequently in the Croatian language as it is spoken in Bosnia than elsewhere occur in the text of this article. These foreign words have been briefly explained when they first appear. A glossary of foreign words has not been appended because it was felt to be unnecessary.

PERSONAL DATA ON THE BOSNIAN WRITERS

Bosnian writers in Arabic, Persian, and Turkish are referred to by their literary, oriental names here. They did have Croatian names as well, which were used in their private lives, but for many of these writers the native names have been lost, as have the dates and places of birth of most of them.

MUSLIM AND CHRISTIAN (GREGORIAN) CALENDARS

The Muslim calendar is a lunar calendar reckoned from the Hegira in A.D. 622 and organized in cycles of thirty years. To facilitate the reading of this article, Muslim dates have been converted to their Gregorian calendar equivalents.

INTRODUCTION

The Muslim community of Bosnia-Hercegovina embodies a viable culture, the roots of which go back to the middle of the fifteenth century and the arrival of the Ottoman Turks.

The culture of Islam is evident throughout Bosnia-Hercegovina, and especially in its principal intellectual and spiritual centers of Mostar and Sarajevo. The latter is an important center of Islamic education, for the Ghāzī Khusrew Beg Medresse and the great library of Ghāzī Khusrew Beg are located there. In addition, such monuments of Islamic civilization as mosques, clock-towers, mausoleums, and public baths have given a singularly Islamic stamp to the older Bosnian settlements.

Bosnia's connection with Islam probably dates from the tenth century. The new religion was brought in by the Hungarian Ismaelitak, or Ismaelites, who came into Bosnia between the tenth and fourteenth centuries as soldiers, financial advisors, and merchants, in the service of the Hungarian and Croatian kings.

During the twelfth century, groups of the Turkish Islamic tribe of Kalisians established settlements in Bosnia, Syrmium, and Mačva. Among the place-names which give us evidence, even today, of the life of these Kalisians in eastern Bosnia are Kalesije and Sarači (from Saracens) near Zvornik; Saračica, near Mali Zvornik; and Agarovići (deriving from Agarenians, that is, "descendants of Hagar"), near Rogatica. The most ancient mosque in Bosnia, in Ustikolina, was in use at least fifty years before the conquest of Bosnia by the Turks in 1463.

However, one cannot speak of any developing cultural influence of Islam before the arrival of the Ottomans; any monuments or other immediate cultural remains of these small medieval settlements were lost in the events that led to the formation of the first Slavic states in southeast Europe. It is in the late fifteenth century that the history of Islamic Bosnia really begins, for the Turkish advent was followed by the gradual spread of Islam. A large number of the Bosnian nobles and landowners did not share the prevailing Croatian allegiance to the Roman Catholic Church, but had long been members of a Manichean sect, called Bogomils, against whom thirteenth-century popes had launched crusades. Moreover, the Ottoman Turks offered what was virtually "first-class citizenship" in the Ottoman Empire and freedom from interference in local affairs. The Bosnian nobility therefore embraced Islam, and they have remained faithful to their commitment ever since. The resolve of the nobility being decisive in that era, Islam became the dominant culture of Bosnia. Finally, the Ottoman Turks, true to their word, granted Bosnia almost complete independence in local matters, and Bosnian Muslims came to play major roles in the cultural and political life of the Ottoman Empire.

On the other hand, for the non-Muslim Bosnian population, centuries of Turkish domination can certainly be viewed in an unfavorable light. Because the non-Muslim population was isolated from the mainstream of cultural and political life during the Ottoman period, a feeling of alienation developed which has made an objective view of the era difficult to achieve. The opinion persists among the South Slavs that this period was one of complete economic, social, and cultural darkness for the Balkan Peninsula, and this attitude is supported and intensified by the negative treatment of the period to be found in distinguished works of Croatian and Serbian literature, such as those of Nobel Prize winner Ivo Andrić (*Na Drini ćuprija*/The Bridge on the Drina River) and poets Ivan Mažuranić (*Smrt Smail-age Čengića*/The Death of Smail-Aga Čengić) and Petar Petrović Njegoš (*Gorski vijenac*/Mountain Wreath). But no serious objective assessment of the past can overlook the role of Croatian Muslims, especially those of Bosnia-Hercegovina, in the lively cultural life of the Ottoman Empire.

A number of historians and oriental scholars have attempted to achieve an objective approach in assessing the Ottoman period, among them Friedrich S. Krauss, Konstantin Jireček, Carl Patsch, Franz Babinger, Vladislav Škarić, Galab Galabow, Francesco Gabrielli, Josef Matl, Herbert Duda, and Hamdija Kreševljaković, but their influence has been limited.

Thus, although this essay will treat the culture of the Muslims of Bosnia-Hercegovina, it might be well to consider first some important aspects of the Ottoman period in order to correct the inevitable distortions already noted, and to bring into clear focus the context in which Bosnian Muslim culture flourished, a context containing characteristic resources as well as characteristic limitations.

The era of Croatian history with which we are concerned falls on the borderline between medieval and modern history. However, at its outset the prevailing world view throughout the Western world was medieval and gave preference to faith over reason. Moreover, since Islam does not divide human activities into religious and secular, the achievements of the Bosnian Muslims bore the hallmark of the time. Thus, on the whole, ordinary people, Muslim as well as Christian, remained medieval in mentality.

Cultural life in Bosnia under the Ottoman Turks was traditionalist. While neighboring Dalmatia was refreshed by the ideas of humanism in the fifteenth and sixteenth centuries, and Croatian humanists nurtured the new ideas of the West in their country, brilliant men of letters in Bosnia were almost exclusively occupied with religious, moralistic, and mystic themes. There was no cultural exchange between the Ottoman Empire and the West until the seventeenth century, and subsequent relations were very superficial and limited to diplomats and wealthy businessmen. Although western scholars concerned themselves with Turkish chronicles and Arabic literature and science, scholars in the Ottoman Empire showed little interest in these subjects except for the medical works of Arab scholars, which they copied and studied for obvious practical reasons. All cultural achievement was viewed in the light of religious tradition and remained subservient to it. Understood in a religious light, the Ottoman period left a deep impact on the spirit, mind, and external cultural profile of the Bosnian Muslims, an impact expressed in literature, art, and historical development.

The Bosnian population, if only in the upper middle classes, reached a considerable educational level and held firm ethical beliefs. Islam was the decisive factor in the transformation: it advocated discipline and cleanliness of body and soul, starting with the ablutions that preceded the five daily prayers. Also the regulating force of religion was brought to bear on the fulfillment of social duties, such as the surrender by the faithful of two and one-half percent of net income over and above subsistence as alms (*zakāt*), used to establish institutions for the common good (mosques, poor-relief kitchens, baths, bridges, clock-towers, etc.). This religious and moral influence of Islam was the deep impulse which led to the architectural achievements of Muslim Bosnia.

In addition, the Bosnians gave outstanding service to the empire. In spite of their distance from Constantinople and the difference in language and temperament, they succeeded immediately in entering into positions of central power, and in the most brilliant century of the Empire, the sixteenth, they were the leaders. In the years 1544 to 1612, nine grand viziers came from Bosnia, and Bosnia gave to the Empire most of the twenty-four grand viziers of Croatian ancestry in addition to many pashas, sandžak-begs, begler-begs, and other dignitaries. During that century Croatian was the second language in the Porte, and all principal military experts spoke both Turkish and Croatian. When, after disasters in the seventeenth century, Turkey was weak in its defense of Bosnia, Bosnian Muslims defended their own borders and even resumed their ancient incursions into Croatian Catholic territory. When the sultan ceded Bosnia to Austria, at the Congress of Berlin in 1878, Bosnian Muslims stood up to defend themselves and offered exceptionally strong resistance to Austria.

As pointed out earlier, the total cultural achievement of Bosnian-Hercegovinian Muslims is often overlooked. In modern times this neglect results not only from the prejudice and concomitant lack of sufficient scholarly effort noted above, but also from the cleavage of the political bond with the Orient; because of it, and because oriental languages are no longer as well known as in earlier times, native Bosnian-Hercegovinian scholars cannot adequately assess the considerable contribution of their Muslim compatriots to oriental Muslim culture.

The literary and scientific contributions written in the Croatian language, from the inception of Austro-Hungarian rule in 1878 until the present, will not be presented here. They can be found in other surveys of Croatian national culture in this collection. In this essay an attempt will be made to survey briefly the culture of Bosnian-Hercegovinian Muslims as it has been shaped by four centuries of Ottoman rule.

FOLK CULTURE

POETRY

It was the Muslim folk poetry of Bosnia and Hercegovina which drew world interest to the folklore of the Southern Slavic lands. Certain Muslim songs are, indeed, not only the most beautiful folk songs of the South Slavic lands, but probably among the most beautiful in the world.[1] Unfortunately, the Muslim origin of these poems was obscured because they were erroneously called "Morlak" or "Serbian" songs. Also, their intrinsic value was neither recognized nor acknowledged because of the frequent corruption of the texts.[2] Only with the aid of recent research, free from religious and nationalist bias, have the merit and true national origin of these poems been clearly recognized.

EPIC FOLK POETRY

The South Slavic folk epic was carefully cultivated by the Bosnian Muslims. Many nobles, the begs and aghas, kept personal singers who glorified their prowess in battle and that of their forefathers, and spurred the people on to new acts of heroism.

Of the patrons of this art, the following are worth mentioning: Aḥmad Pasha Hersek-Oghlu (died 1517); Beg of Lipa (presumed to be seventeenth century); Murād Beg Beširović and Captain Murād of Gradačac (both eighteenth century); Beg Novoselac (time unknown); Captain Mustaj Beg Kulenović from Bosanski Petrovac (in office as captain from 1821 until 1835); Ḥājj Rustam Beg Biščević from Bihać, and Smail Aga Čengić and his son Ded'Aga (all nineteenth century). Some famous singers were: Ćerim Ćaić, singer of Murād Beg Beširović;[3] Ahmad Bauk, singer of Smail Aga Čengić; and Avdo Karabegović, singer of Ḥājj Rustam Beg Biščević. Some singers made their art available to folklorists: Mehmed Kolak Kolaković, Hamid Kunić, Salko Vojniković-Pezić, Meho Beba (nineteenth century);[4] Omer Šestanović,[5] Meho Morić,[6] Ibro

1/Matthias Murko, "Auf den Spuren der Volksepik durch Jugoslavien," *Slavische Rundschau,* III (1931), no. 3.

2/Friedrich S. Krauss, *Slavische Volkforschungen* (Leipzig, 1908), 341; Smail Balić, "Die muslimische Volkspoesie in Bosnien," *Oesterreichische Osthefte* (Wien, July 1965), 386–7; Antun Šimčik, "Hasanaga Kuna," *Novi Behar* (Sarajevo), XIII (1939), 141.

3/Hamdija Kreševljaković, *Kapetanije u Bosni i Hercegovini*/District Captaincies in Bosnia and Hercegovina (Sarajevo, 1954), 61.

4/Hamid Dizdar, *Sevdalinke. Izbor iz bosansko-hercegovačke narodne lirike*/ Sevdalinkas: Selected Bosnian and Hercegovinian Lyric Folk Poems (Sarajevo, 1944), 17.

5/Biographical data on this folk-singer may be found in Friedrich S. Krauss's article "Vidirlijić [*sic!*] Ahmo's Brautfahrt. Ein moslimisches Guslarenlied," in *Festschrift für Adolf Bastian zu seinem Geburtstage 26. Juni 1896* (Berlin, 1896).

6/Hamid Dizdar, *Sevdalinke*, 17–18.

Topić, Avdo Medjedović, Ćor-Huso Husović,[7] and Ahmed Bucman-Jamaković (twentieth century).

Deliberate cultivation under patronage contributed to the high quality of the Bosnian-Muslim epic songs. Authoritative scholars unanimously affirm the value of Bosnian-Hercegovinian Muslim folk poetry. Friedrich Krauss writes: "My comprehensive collection of Muslim-Slav epics testifies to the fact that the South-Slav national characteristics found their supreme and artistic expression in these creations. None but the ancient Greek epics of Homer are equal to the Muslim-Slav epics; no other people among the so-called Indo-Germanic peoples have brought forth from their innermost heart such meaningful folk epics."[8]

In evaluating Kosta Hörmann's collection of Muslim epics Vatroslav Jagić, an expert on Slavic culture, said of the song "Filip Madžarin i gojeni Halil" (Philip the Hungarian and Fat Halil) that it was very beautiful and deserved its reputation as one of the best examples of Slavic folk poetry.[9] Isidor Kopernicki, an anthropologist from Cracow and also a Slavic expert, also commented on the Hörmann collection. Referring to a battle description in the song "Buljubaša Džanan i pô muhura carskog" (Captain Janan and Half of the Emperor's Seal), he declared it a "masterpiece." "Nowhere have I found an equal description of battle scenes."[10]

Writers and men of learning, such as Luka Marjanović, Petar Grgec, Alija Nametak, Olinko Delorko, Alois Schmaus, Gerhard Gesemann, Kosta Hörmann, Matthias Murko, Maximilian Hoelzel, Milman Parry, and Albert Bates Lord, all affirm the high quality of these Muslim epic poems. Indeed, with Krauss, Georg Stadtmüller compares some Muslim heroic songs to the Greek epics of Homer and also to the *Nibelungenlied*.[11]

The songs from northwestern Bosnia, the Military Frontier country, the Krajina are the most distinguished of this folk poetry. Because of the

7/Albert Bates Lord, Parry Homer, and I. Huso, in *Transactions of the American Philological Association*, LXVII (1936), 107ff., and A. B. Lord, Parry Homer, and I. Huso, in *American Journal of Archeology*, LII (1948), 31–44.

8/Krauss, *Slavische Volkforschungen*, 7.

9/Cited in Kosta Hörmann, *Narodne pjesme Muhamedovaca u Bosni i Hercegovini*/Folk Songs of the Muslims of Bosnia and Hercegovina (Sarajevo, 1889), II, 9. The song itself is no. XXXII in vol. I of this collection.

10/Krauss, *Slavische Volkforschungen*, 221.

11/Georg Stadtmüller, "Bosanski islam – most Evrope islamskom svijetu"/ Bosnian Islam – Europe's Bridge to the Muslim World, *Glasnik Vrhovnog Starješinstva Islamske Vjerske Zajednice*/Messenger of the Supreme Headquarters of the Islamic Religious Community (hereafter cited as *GVSIVZ*) (Sarajevo, July 1943).

common occurrence of border battles, the minstrels of the region added continually to the content of the folk songs. As a result, these epics closely approximate historic truth and thus differ greatly from most other South Slavic heroic songs. The folk poetry of the Krajina has its own unique style and construction and constitutes a separate branch of the South Slavic epic.[12] The Krajina songs are sung in all regions where Croatian Muslims live: in Bosnia and Hercegovina, including the Sandžak of Novi Pazar, Kosovo, and Metohija. Their influence extends to northern Albania, where they are sung by the Muslim Gegas, and where they are known as *krahinë*.

Muslim heroic poetry is distinguished by its characterization of people and by its decorative style and expression. The poetry is fundamentally dramatic, but betrays strong moralistic tendencies.

Among the rich selection of characters in the gallery of folk songs, sharply profiled heroic figures emerge, such as the dignified and calm Mustaj Beg of Lika; the aged grandfather Ćejvan Aga ("the empty case of his chin rattles/his last tooth has flown to the devil"); the brothers of "potbelly" Mujo, "The Falcon" Halil, and the little Omer Hrnjica, as well as their loyal and courageous sister, Ajkuna; the jester Tale Ličanin, Kovačina Ramo; the youthful sword-wielder Nukica; and little Radojica. Behind this band of heroes who defend the foremost borders of the empire – at the Serhat – other battle companions, no less important, are active: the pious dervish Gjergjelez Alija, with his mythological features; Ago Šarić, Buljubaša Džanan, Ghāzī Khusrew Beg, Ḥifẓī Beg Djumišić, Smail Aga Čengić, and others, of the most distinguished of whom, the Beg Ljubović, the folk song says:

> Lend ear, forsooth, my Beg, you Ljubović,
> From the wolf only wolf, from the brigand a brigand springs.
> Always was a falcon only of a falcon born,
> And always falcons have been given birth
> At the hearth of Beg Ljubović's home![13]

The following translation is an example of the epic poetry of the Bosnian Muslims. The song concerns the marriage of Ajkuna, the sister of Beg Ljubović (no relation to the Hrnjica brothers).

12/Alois Schmaus, "Studije o krajinskoj epici"/Studies on the Military Frontier Epic, *Rad*, 297 (Zagreb: Yugoslav Academy, 1953); Vito Morpurgo, "I fratelli Ibro e Paso Moric nell'intuizione popolare della balata Bosniaca," from *Annali del Corso di lingue e literature straniere presso l'Università di Bari* (Bari, 1962), 44.

13/Croatian text: Haj aferim, beže Ljubovićul/Vuk od vuka, hajduk od hajduka,/ A vazda je soko od sokola./Vazda su se sokolovi legli/Na odžaku bega Ljubovića.

Never, since the world had its beginning,
Never did a lovelier flow'ret blossom
Than the flow'ret we ourselves saw blooming
In the white court of the Bey Ljubović.
High above the level Nevesinje
Tower'd the fascinating maid Ajkuna;
She, the Bey Ljubović's lovely sister.

She was lovely – nothing e'er was lovelier;
She was tall and slender as the pine tree;
White her cheeks, but tinged with rosy blushes,
As if morning's beam had shone upon them,
Till that beam had reach'd its high meridian;
And her eyes, they were two precious jewels;
And her eyebrows, leeches from the ocean;
And her eyelids, they were wings of swallows;
Silken tufts the maiden's flaxen ringlets;
And her sweet mouth was a sugar casket;
And her teeth were pearls array'd in order;
White her bosom, like two snowy dovelets;
And her voice was like the dovelet's cooing;
And her smiles were like the glowing sunshine;
And the fame, the story of her beauty
Spread through Bosnia and through Hercegovina.

Many a suitor on the maiden waited:
Two were unremitting in their service;
One, the old grey-headed Mustaf'-Aga –
He of Krajina, from the Novi fortress,[14]
And the other, Suko of Udbina,[15]
Both together met the self-same evening,
When they came to court the lovely maiden.
Thousand golden coins the old man proffer'd,
And, besides, a golden drinking vessel;
Round the vessel twined a mighty serpent,
From whose forehead shone so bright a diamond,
That at midnight, just as well at noonday,
By its light you might indulge your feastings.
Suko offered but a dozen ducats;
All the youth possessed, except his sabre,
His good sabre, and his steed so trusty.
Suko dwelt upon the country's border,
As the falcon dwells among the breezes.
Then her brother thus address'd Ajkuna:
"Lo! Ajkuna, my beloved sister!

14/In Bosnia, on the river Una.
15/A town on the frontiers of Lika and Bosnia. Today Titova Korenica.

When my mother bore thee, she betrothed thee –
She betrothed thee to another lover.
Many a lover, maiden! now would woo thee;
But the best of all those wooing lovers
Are those twain to-day that seek thy presence.
One the venerable Mustaf'-Aga;
He that comes from Vraine [Vranje] out of Novi.
Countless are the old Mustafa's treasures:
He will clothe thee all in silk and satin,
Will with honey and with sugar feed thee.
Suko of Udbina is the other:
But this Suko nothing more possesses
Than his trusty steed and his good sabre.
Now, then choose, Ajkuna; choose, my sister;
Say to which of these I shall betroth thee."

Thus his sister answer gave her brother:
"Thine shall be the choice, my brother! only;
Him alone I'll wed whom thou wilt give me;
But I'd rather choose a youthful lover,
Howsoever small that youth's possessions,
Than be wedded to old age, though wealthy.
Wealth – it is not gold it is no silver;
Wealth – is to possess what most we cherish."
Little did he listen to his sister,
For he gave the maid to Mustaf'-Aga;
To that old white-bearded man he gave her.
He with speed to his own court departed,
Brought the bridal guests, to lead the maiden
To his dwelling; and among them Suko
Lifted o'er the rest the bridal banner;
And they hasten'd to the maiden's dwelling.

At the dwelling of the lovely maiden,
Three white days the bridal crowd had linger'd, –
When the fourth day dawn'd, at early morning,
Forth they led the maiden from her dwelling;
And ere they far off had proceeded,
Ere they reach'd the flat and open country,
Turn'd the lovely maiden to the leader,
And into his ear these words she whisper'd:
"Tell me now, my golden ring, my brother!
Who is chosen for the maiden's bridegroom?"
Softly did the marriage leader answer:
"Sweetest sister! fairest maid, Ajkuna!
Look to right, and look to left about thee;
Dost thou see that old man in the distance,
Who like an effendi sits so proudly
In the farthest palaquin of scarlet,

Whose white beard o'ercomes all his bosom?
Lo! it is the aged Mustaf'-Aga;

He it is who is chosen for thy bridegroom."
And the maiden look'd around the circle
And within her sad heart sighing deeply,
Once again she asked the marriage leader:
"Who is he upon that white horse seated,
He who bears so high aloft the banner,
On whose chin that sable beard is growing?"
And the leader answers thus the maiden:
"He's the hero Suko of Udbina;
He who for thee with thy brother struggled, –
Struggled well indeed, but could not win thee."
When the lovely maiden heard the leader,
On the black black earth, anon she fainted:
All to raise her, hastening, gather round her,
And the last of all came Mustaf'-Aga;
None could lift her from the ground, till Suko
Sticks into the earth his waving banner,
Stretches out his right hand to the maiden.
See her, see her! from the ground upspringing,
Swift she vaults upon his steed behind him;
Rapidly he guides the courser onwards,
Swift they speed across the open desert,
Swift as ever star across the heavens.

When the old man saw it Mustaf'-Aga;
Loud he screamed with voice of troubled anger;
"Look to this, ye bidden for the wedding!
He, the robber! bears away my maiden;
See her, see her borne away for ever,"
But one answer met the old man's wailings:
"Let the hawk bear off the quail in safety, –
Bear in safety – she was born to wed him;
Thou, retire thee to thy own dwelling!
Blossoms not for thee so fair a maiden!"[16]

Muslim heroic songs are often unusually long because of the Muslim way of life. In the long nights of Ramaḍān, the month of fasting, during which pious Muslims are at their most sociable after having abstained from food and drink all day, long songs that could fill the evening were needed, and thus emerged.

With the increasing decline of the older social institutions, the heroic song was condemned to fade from social life. It seems unlikely that it

16/The translation was made by John Bowring. See his book *Servian Popular Poetry* (London, 1827).

will again flourish as it did in the seventeenth century when, throughout the Ottoman Empire, Muslims were beginning their struggle to maintain a European existence, and when a national consciousness began to emerge among Bosnian Muslims.

LYRIC FOLK POETRY

In the Balkan lands, where poetry and the epic were virtually synonymous, lyric poetry was hardly understood or appreciated. Yet despite the fact that the Bosnian and Hercegovinian Muslims poured their greatest love and gifts into the cultivation of epic poetry, ballads and romances also developed. Their contrast with the epic is twofold: whereas the epic songs are sung to the accompaniment of the tamburitza or the gusle, these ballads and romances are recited simply and naturally, without melody or instrumental accompaniment. Then, too, they focus on feminine concerns.[17]

Their content accounts for their virtual absence from all but the Muslim Croatian culture. These songs of the lives of women are found only in the "western domain of the Serbo-Croatian language"[18] because of the comparatively higher social status enjoyed by the women in these territories. In the Bosnian-Muslim milieu, the chivalrous treatment of women, who are veritably coddled as young wives and highly honored as aged mothers, is in sharp contrast with the attitudes of the Orthodox hinterlands of the East.[19] The medieval, oriental non-Islamic conception of woman as something intrinsically evil, as the vessel of sin, was always entirely foreign to Muslim culture in contrast to Byzantine culture where the concept of woman's defectiveness reigned for a long time.[20] The Muslim woman had her hereditary rights from time immemorial according to the Sharīʿa (the canon law), and was not dependent upon the goodwill of father or brothers.

In the early days, most of the Muslim folk songs, as well as most other literary works, were composed in the melodic Ikavian speech common

17/Franz Miklosich, "Ueber Goethe's Klaggesang von der edlen Frauen des Asan Aga," *Sitzungsberichte der Wiener Akademie der Wissenschaften* (Wien, 1883); Camilla Lucerna, *Zur Hasanaginica* (Zagreb, 1909); Gerhard Gesemann, "Die Asanaginica im Kreise ihrer Varianten," *Archiv für slavische Philologie*, VII (1923).

18/Matthias Murko, *Das Original von Goethe's Klaggesang von der edlen Frauen des Assan Agas (Asanaginica) in der Literatur und im Volksmunde durch 150 Jahre* (Brünn-Prag-Leipzig-Wien, 1937), 4.

19/Josef Matl, "Okzidentale und eurasische Auffassung der slavischen Geschichte," *Saeculum*, IV (Munchen, 1953), 307.

20/*Ibid.*

to both Muslims and Catholics. The Muslim ballads and romances deal with the inner conflicts between mother-love, pride, love for one's husband, and the longing for security. These conflicts arise mainly from the specific morality of the Muslim Bosnians[21] and, above all, from the inculcated modesty of their women, particularly those belonging to the aristocracy. These Bosnian ballads also testify to a refined lyric sense, are dramatic, and offer deep psychological insight. Their plots are highly original, and their wealth of expression and euphony among the richest in South Slavic folk poetry.

The first Bosnian ballad to become known in a foreign country was *Hasan-Aginica,* which was introduced into world literature by Herder and Goethe as *Klagegesang von der edlen Frauen des Asan Aga* (The Lamentation of the Noble Wife of Hasan-Aga). It had already been published in Venice in 1744 by Alberto Fortis in his travel reminiscences, *Viaggio in Dalmazia.* This ballad, the "pearl of South Slavic folk poetry," aroused the interest of the cultural world in South Slavic folk poetry. Many famous poets admired its beauty and translated it into their languages. Its most famous German translation or paraphrase, namely Goethe's "Lament of the Noble Wife of Hassan Aga," can be found among Herder's *Volkslieder.* Some other translators were: Prosper Mérimée, Walter Scott, John Boyd, George G. N. Byron,[22] Alexander S. Pushkin, Michail J. Lermontov, Ernst Ludwig Gerber, Jakob Grimm, Friedrich August Clemens Werthes (1748–1817), Therese Albertine Louise Robinson (pseud. Talvj), Wilhelm Gerhard (1780–1858), Charles Nodier, Anne Elisabeth Voïard, Auguste Dozon, Sir John Bowring, Ferencz Kazinczy, František-Ladislav Čelakovsky, Karel Hynek Mácha, Georg Ferić (Ferrich), France Prešeren, Samuel Rožnay, Johann Ludwig Runeberg, and Camilla Lucerna. Thus, besides the original, there exist translations in German, English, French, Russian, Italian, Malayan, Slovenian, Hungarian, Czech, Latin, and Swedish. Poets and scholars of standing like Goethe, Scott, Byron, Michael Lermontov, Alphonse de Lamartine, Adam Mickiewicz, Jernej Kopitar, Matthias Murko, Gerhard Gesemann, and many others were filled with delight. Herder had the boldness to liken this "noble song" of the misjudged wife of the Slavic Muslim to the magnificent creations of women's tragedy by Shakespeare–to Desdemona and Ophelia. "The incomparable feeling for the germs of humanity and its first springs, the sense of touch and tone which showed him the inner form and the actions of all true songs des-

21/See the commentary by Vladimir Ćorović in *Srpski Književni Glasnik,* VII (1931), 549.

22/Dragutin Subotić, *Yugoslav Popular Ballads* (Cambridge, 1932), pp. 222–5.

pite the darkness in language, has won this elegy a place for its quality of judgment of the heart."[23]

An English translation of this ballad follows:[24]

THE WIFE OF HASAN AGA

What shows white in the wood? A flock of swans or a bank of snow?
Swans would have flown and a snow bank would have melted long ago.
It is not snow, nor a milk-white swan, but Hasan Aga's tent;
Sore wounded was he. His mother and sister to him went;
For very shame his wife came not. When his wounds were healed aright,
He charged his faithful wife withal: "Come not into my sight;
Await me never, woman, my fair white house within;
Nor yet do thou abide me in the houses of my kin."
When the faithful woman heard it, sad was her heart indeed.
Suddenly from the house she heard the trampling of the steed.
To the window she ran, to break her neck by leaping down from the tower;
But the daughters of Hasan Aga pursued her in that hour:
"Return to us, dear mother! Our father comes not," said they;
"It is thy brother, our uncle, Pintórovich the Bey."
The wife of Hasan Aga, to her brother's breast she came:
"Ah, brother, from my children five doth he send me! It is shame!"
Naught said the bey; in his silken pouch forthwith his hand he thrust
For a bill of divorce that granted her her dower held in trust,
And bade her go to her mother. When the purport thereof she wist,
Forthwith upon the forehead her two fair sons she kissed,
And on their rosy cheeks she kissed her little daughters twain.
But the little son in the cradle she could not leave for pain.
Her brother took the lady's hand; and hard it was to lead
That wretched woman from her babe, but he threw her on the steed;
He brought her unto the white house, and there he took her in.
A little while, but scarce a week, she stayed among her kin.
Good is the matron's parentage, men seek her in marriage withal;
But the great Cadi of Imotski desires her most of all.
"So should I not desire it," imploringly she said.
"Brother, I prithee, give me not to any to be wed,
That my heart break not with looking on my children motherless."
But the bey no whit he cared at all because of her distress;
To the great Cadi of Imotski he will give her to be wed.
Still the matron with her brother most miserably she pled,
That he a milk-white letter to the cadi should prepare,
And send it to the Cadi:
"The matron greets thee fair,
And implores thee: when that thou has brought the wooers from every side,
And when thou comest to her white house, do thou bring a veil for the bride,

23/Camilla Lucerna, *Die südslavische Ballade von Asan Agas Gattin und ihre Nachbildung durch Goethe* (Berlin, 1905), 2–3.

24/*Heroic Ballads of Serbia*, trans. George Rapall Noyes and Leonard Bacon (Boston: Sherman, French and Company, 1913), 271–5.

That she see not by the aga's house her children motherless."
When the letter came to the Cadi, with pomp and lordliness
He gathered many wooers; ah, nobly did they come!
And splendidly the wooers they brought the fair bride home!
But when they were by the aga's house, forth looked her daughters fair,
And her two sons came before her, and spoke to their mother there:
"Return with us, dear mother, to eat with us again!"
When the wife of Hasan Aga heard, she spake to the groomsman then:
"Brother in God, my groomsman, stop the steeds, of gentleness,
By my house, that I may give fair gifts to my children motherless."
They checked the steeds at the house for her.
She gave her children gifts;
To either son a gilded knife, to her daughters fair long shifts,
To her babe in the cradle a garment in a bit of linen tied.
When Hasan Aga saw it, to his two sons he cried:
"Hither, my children motherless! and from her stand apart!
Pity and mercy hath she none within her stony heart!"
She heard. Her face smote on the ground in the deep of her distress,
And her soul departed as she saw her children motherless.

The ballad *Lament of the Noble Woman of the Bajram Beg* portrays the fate of a nobleman's young widow, who, because her son is still an infant, can find no one to marry other than a common ruffian. He declares that he will care for the child and takes the young woman and her son to his home town. En route, the child begins to wail piteously, and all the mother's efforts to soothe him fail. Because she is too modest to disrobe before this young man to whom she is not yet married, the young woman has neglected to nurse the child. She tries to comfort him with her rings, but in vain. Angered by the continuous crying, the heartless man snatches the baby and throws it from the moving coach onto the branches of an almond tree.

The ballad *Hasan Aga* is the counterpart to the *Hasan Aginica,* and treats in a psychologically and ethically fascinating way the surprising settlement of a marital dispute. Behind the verses of this song, which sounds like the prologue to a play, "there is hidden, despite the gloomy atmosphere of the introduction, a certain comic element which makes for an even stronger and more original effect."[25]

The ballad *Omer i Merima,*[26] a Bosnian counterpart to the classic love story *Romeo and Juliet,* is very beautiful. This poem is the more interesting in that it follows neither the Eastern pattern (such as that of *Majnūn and Laylā, Farhād and Shīrīn,* or *Ṭāhir and Zuhrā*) nor the

25/Camilla Lucerna, "Balladen der Unbekannten," *Neue Ordnung* (Zagreb, June 4, 1944).

26/In the English translation under the title "The Death of Omer and Merima," in *The Slavonic Review,* VIII (1929), 198–202.

Western pattern (such as that of *Romeo and Juliet*). The Western pattern is characterized by murder and/or suicide barring the union of lovers; in the Eastern poems death is the tragic denouement, but it is not violent death. Death ensues as a result of the separation and the yearning this loss of love renders unbearable. In the former case, violent death is the cause of separation; in the latter, lingering death is a result. The Bosnian tragic love poem occupies a mid-point between these two.

The following two poems offer examples of the subtle ideas of the Bosnian Muslim lyric songs:

THE VIOLET

How captivating is to me,
Sweet flower! thine own young modesty!
Though did I pluck thee from thy stem,
There's none would wear thy purple gem.
I thought, perchance, that Ali Beg –
But he is proud and lofty – nay!
He would not price thee – would not wear
A flower so feeble though so fair:
His turban for its decorations
Had full blown roses and carnations.

VIRGIN AND WIDOW

Over Sarajevo flies a falcon,
Looking round for cooling shade to cool him.
Then he finds a pine in Sarajevo;
Under a well of sparkling water;
By the water, Hyacinth, the widow,
And the Rose, the young, unmarried virgin.
He look'd down – the falcon – and bethought him:
"Shall I kiss grave Hyacinth, the widow;
Or the Rose, the young, unmarried virgin?"
Thinking thus – at last the bird determined –
And he whisper'd to himself sedately,
"Gold, though long employ'd, is far, far better
Than the finest silver freshly melted."
So he kiss'd – kiss'd Hyacinth, the widow.
Very wroth wax'd then young Rose, the virgin:
Sarajevo! let a ban be on thee!
Cursed be thy strange and evil customs!
For thy youths they love the bygone widows,
And the aged men the untried virgins."[27]

27/Stevenson B. Stanoyevich (ed.), *An Anthology of Yugoslav Poetry – Serbian Lyrics* (Boston: Richard G. Badger, The Gordham Press, 1920). The two poems "The Violet" and "Virgin and Widow" are translated by Sir John Bowring; they are found on pages 24 and 35 of his work *Servian Popular Poetry* (London, 1927).

Another example of the many poems dealing with conjugal emotion and love is the so-called *sevdalinka.* Predominantly love songs, the sevdalinkas contain lyric poetry that is, as Krauss notes, flowery and rich in fantasy, intimate and sensitive, and full of ingenious accents.[28] However, Krauss's stress on their sensuality is unwarranted, as the sevdalinkas are only in small part sensual. On the whole they display a notable reserve, and, indeed, are inclined to moralize. The genuine sevdalinkas are refined and discreet, and wanting in the least frivolity. In addition to the amorous affections, these songs explore esthetic, religious, patriotic, social, and ethical sentiments. Despite certain elements of fantasy, they are basically realistic.

"In the sentiments expressed in the sevdalinkas," writes one South Slavic scholar, "we recognize our common tradition, our philosophy, our character, and all that forms our unique personality."[29] Indeed, according to authoritative literary critics, the sevdalinkas are the most beautiful and most artistically valuable parts of South Slavic folk poetry.[30]

FOLK MUSIC

According to Ludvik Kuba, the folk music of Bosnia and Hercegovina has three scales more than are common to European folk music with its "major" and "minor" scales.[31] Kuba was able to discover eleven scale-schemes in evaluating the tonality of the sevdalinkas, the Bosnian love songs. Despite the influence of the Arabian-Turkish musical tradition through the appearance of Turkish songs in the Balkans and through Islamic religious hymns, the main elements of Bosnian music remain autochthonous and unique, and the assumption that the melodies of Bosnian folk lyrics are of oriental origin is fallacious. Only the religious song is oriental in heritage, and then only partially so.[32] With few exceptions, the influences of oriental music upon the Bosnian folk song are reflected more in tonality and nuance than in musical structure.[33]

28/*Slavische Volkforschungen*, 12.

29/Čeda Mitrinović, *Naši muslimani*/Our Muslims (Sarajevo, 1926), 101.

30/Jovan Kršić, "Udeo muslimana u našoj književnosti"/*Gajret Kalendar za god. 1939* (Sarajevo, 1939), 197.

31/Ludvik Kuba, *Pjesme bosansko-hercegovačke*/Bosnian and Hercegovinian Poems (Praha, 1927). Cited by H. Dizdar, *Sevdalinke*, 28.

32/The melodies of the modern Mawlids, for example, are free of oriental influence. The Mewluds are poems written in honor of and sung in chorus on Muḥammad's birthday.

33/Just how much the Bosnian-Muslim folk songs differ melodically from those of Turkey the author was able to discover during a stay in Turkey (1955–6). At first I was surprised to hear, again and again, in streets and shops, the singing of "pious songs" like the Bosnian. Later, in learning the meaning of the songs I discovered that they were not religious songs, but very worldly national "hit" songs.

While the cradle of the Bosnian folk song and music was the feminine world with its fragile beauty, its characteristic hopes, longing, love, and sorrow, the poetic and musical creativity of the Bosnian Muslims was nurtured by the vagaries of their existence, the perpetual fluctuation between happiness and sorrow, security and insecurity, pulsating life and agonizing desolation, hope and despair. Wars, plague, and natural catastrophes ravaged this land, but the many fires in the cities where the majority of the inhabitants were Muslims claimed the greatest number of victims from the Muslim community. Bosnian music thus was conceived in joy, matured in faith and perseverance, and born in blessed sorrow.[34]

The rhythmic, melodic Bosnian music testifies to the existence of an old and carefully cultivated chamber music. Some of the instruments played by Bosnian-Hercegovinian musicians came principally from the Orient: the flute (*diple, nāj*); violin (*ćemāne*); guitars with oral resonance chamber (*tambura*); a long-necked instrument played by plucking (*tamburica*); oboe (*zurna*); tambourine (*def*); drum (*davul*); castanets; and the fiddle (*gusle*), a primitive string instrument.

The vocal solo with instrumental accompaniment, especially with the tamburitza, was carefully developed. Each of the sevdalinkas has its own melody through which the folk of Bosnia have given worthy expression to their creative musical urge, preserved in a wealth of ancient vocal techniques and a variety of tonality and song forms; thus, a proper interpretation of the sevdalinkas demands, in addition to a good voice, a special technical ability and a feeling for folk music.

Choral music was not particularly fostered during the Turkish period, and the only choral presentations in older times were certain types of religious song, improvised congregational chants for festive occasions, and the song of the dervishes (which, in the case of the Mawlawi dervishes, also had instrumental accompaniment).

The organization of orchestras and the performance of polyphonic instrumental music followed the introduction of reforms in military and governmental affairs (after 1832). The first such groups were military bands which presented concerts on religious and public holidays. The Turks, with the participation of the Bosnian Muslims, were the first to introduce military music into Europe. From this period of reform comes the stirring "Nizamski rastanak" (The Nizam's Farewell), which might be called the Croatian Muslim counterpart to the "Marseillaise" or the

34/A similar formulation was given by a Bosnian folk-singer: "Ja ne pjevam, što pjevati znadem,/Već ja pjevam, da teret rastjeram." ("I sing not because I can sing, but rather do I sing to banish my sorrow.")

"Wacht am Rhein." Vladimir Dvorniković notes that "The music of the sevdalinkas goes deeper into the heart and grips the soul more strongly than all the modern instrumentation that is used in Europe can."[35]

Bosnian folk music has become a source of inspiration and artistic strength for native Croatian composers and writers such as Jakob Gotovac, Krešimir Baranović, Milan Ogrizović, Ahmed Muradbegović, and Rasim Filipović. In recent times this music has aroused interest in wider European circles. For example, the folk song "Kad ja pojdoh na Bendbašu ... " (When I went to Bendbaša [district of Sarajevo] ...) became quite popular after it was heard in the successful German film *Die letzte Brücke* (The Last Bridge).

FOLK DRAMATIC ART AND FOLK TALES

The oriental shadow theater with Ḳara-Göz[36] as its main character was well known during the Turkish period. Unfortunately, this aspect of the Bosnian popular entertainment of the past has not as yet been studied critically and we lack precise information on the subject.

The beloved tales and humorous anecdotes of Bosnia have come down to us intact, and they preserve, as do their Turkish counterparts, the flavor of various dialects and provincial peculiarities. The Turkish meddah-burlesques have a long tradition in Bosnia, although, quite naturally, this heritage has been extensively transformed. Of oriental origin also are the humorous tales about Naṣr-ad-Dīn Khwāja (1208–83): "These little stories, well known in Yugoslav folklore, are a mixture of wit, finesse, shrewdness and, also, stupidity; however, the first quality noted is the prevailing one. And it is this which helps Naṣr-ad-Dīn Khwāja to be successful occasionally, or to get out of a mess in spite of his making quite a few foolish moves."[37]

Examples of Bosnian Muslim folk tales have been collected by Friedrich Krauss in his book *Tausend Sagen und Märchen der Südslaven* (A Thousand Sagas and Fairy Tales of the South Slavs).[38] Krauss has shown that in addition to the ancient Slavic folk tradition, the once famous Milesian fairy tales, as they exist in a collection of late Greek tales, and

35/Vladimir Dvorniković, *Karakterologija Jugoslovena*/Characterology of Yugoslavs (Beograd, 1939). Cited by H. Dizdar, *Sevdalinke*, 32.

36/Ḳara-Göz, "Dark-eyed," is the main figure of the Turkish shadow theater. See Helmuth Ritter, *Karagöz. Turkische Schattenspiele* (Series 1, Hanover, 1924; Series 2, Istanbul, 1941; Series 3, Wiesbaden, 1953).

37/Jovan Cvijić, *La Peninsule Balkanique* (Paris, 1918), 351. Cited by Balagija Abduselam, "Les Musulmans Yugoslaves," *Étude sociologique*, IX (1940), 54.

38/Collected and translated by Friedrich S. Krauss (8 vols.; Leipzig: Ethnologischer Verlag, 1914), I.

brought over by the Turks, have been preserved to the present time among Croatian Muslims.[39] In modern Yugoslav literature, the strong influence of Bosnian narrative art is noticeable. It is significant that one of the best contemporary storytellers of Yugoslavia, Nobel Prize winner Ivo Andrić, a Croatian from Bosnia, derives his material and style chiefly from the Bosnian Muslim folk milieu.[40]

DECORATIVE FOLK ART

Bosnian craftsmanship is a venerable tradition. During the Turkish period Muslim and Christian artisans produced various types of ornamental and useful weapons (rifles, sabres, lances, knives, axes), armor, and other military accessories, many of which were made in the Balkan lands.[41] Famous armorers were to be found in the cities of Fojnica, Busovača, Travnik, Visoko, and Mostar. According to Carl Peez: "In 1836 Malte-Brun praised the Damascus-blades which were forged there [Mostar]. The shining blades from Mostar and also those from Foča and Travnik were so popular with the Turks that they often paid enormous prices for them."[42]

Rug weaving as a home industry in eastern Hercegovina maintains its excellent reputation to our own day. Colorful, striped, thick carpets were specialties in both the commercial and home industry in Mostar.

In many Muslim homes cloth and fabric were produced for family use. The embroideries of the women and young girls, often in gold and silver, were frequently small masterpieces of color, composition, and original motif. These embroideries as well as the peasant costumes are rich in imaginative decoration and color harmony. A special type of Bosnian embroidery, the *banjaluka* (French: *benalouka*; Turkish: *banaluka*), became famous abroad.[43] The making of fine bez-fabrics (gauzy, cobweblike fabrics of wool or silk) and embroidery reached, at one time, a high degree of artistic excellence.[44]

Beautiful silver and gold inlay-work (damascene) on black steel was

39/*Ibid.*, 241. "Milesiaca," Milesian stories largely lascivious in content, were known through Aristeides (probably second century).

40/See his novels *Travnička Kronika*/The Chronicle of Travnik and *Na Drini ćuprija*/The Bridge on the Drina.

41/Vejsil Ćurčić, *Starinsko oružje*/Ancient Weapons, with fifty-six text illustrations (Sarajevo, 1926), 4.

42/Carl Peez, *Mostar und sein Kulturkreis: Ein Städtebild aus der Hercegovina* (Leipzig: Brockhaus, 1891), 86.

43/Celal Esad Arseven, "Banaluka," *San'at Ansiklopedisi* (Istanbul, 1943), fasc. I, 206.

44/Rif'at Pasha Gvozdović, "Bosnia's Artistic Handicraft, Heritage from the Turks," *Die Islamische Welt*, v (Berlin, 1917), 304.

also done in Bosnia, where excellent artisans were at work, especially in Sarajevo, Livno, and Foča. Three masters of this craft in the nineteenth century, when the art was already dying out, have been identified: Mustafa Letić of Foča and his two pupils whose names, unfortunately, have not come down to us.[45] However, although we don't know the artists, we know that the art flourished. As R. Gvozdović says: "Then, with many able exponents, inlaid work was produced in the land, the special merits of which were exquisite grace in design and ingenious ornamentation."[46]

In the vicinity of Visoko, the Muslim peasants produce wooden musical instruments (pipes and flutes) as well as beautiful tobacco pipes. The ceramics of Kiseljak near Fojnica and Visoko also have artistic merit. During the Turkish rule, luxuriously ornamented tents, powder and ammunition containers, Ḳur'ān portfolios (*enʿamlīḳ*) of leather, and water jugs fashioned of wood were produced throughout Bosnia and Hercegovina. Mostar is famous for its leather industry, its fine finished sheep leather, and morocco.

Traditional filigree work in gold, silver, and copper is still a flourishing industry today, and the ancient art of fine wood carving has also persisted. Wood carving and relief painting are specialties of the distinguished artist Ismail Mulić (born in 1895). His home and workshop in the small town of Konjic, Hercegovina, are a center of interest, and his gallery is well attended. Mulić's works are eagerly sought in other countries as well as in his homeland.

The craftsmanship of the Bosnians is especially evident in the execution of small, useful objects. They produce very lovely brooches, cigarette holders and cases, clocks, plates, mocha and punch sets, basins, pitchers, pots, and shoes with gold embroidery.

The skillful ornaments of artists of Mostar, Hercegovina, deserve special attention. They have created an extremely attractive and solid architecture, not only in their native town but also in the surrounding area, e.g., in Počitelj on the Neretva.[47]

DWELLINGS

Three types of Muslim dwellings distinguished for their individuality, solidity, and beauty are the *kula*, the *čardak*, and the *odžak*.

The kulas, built on a round or quadrangular foundation, are massive castles of two, three, or four stories which formerly served as family seats and fortresses for the Bosnian nobility. An interesting feature of these

45/*Ibid.*, 303.
46/*Ibid.*
47/Peez, *Mostar und sein Kulturkreis*, 16.

buildings is an extended, alcovelike upper story, sometimes enlarged into a pavilion. Some of these towerlike buildings have an additional story built of wood and a roof of pyramid shape; others are covered by a dome.[48] The lower levels have only a few small windows or loopholes, which served for defense against attackers. Except for this feature, the interior architecture corresponds largely to that of other Muslim dwellings.

With the decline of the Bosnian nobility in the nineteenth century, the kulas fell into ruin. Today only seven remain standing. Two of these, built of handsome, rough-hewn stone, are in Odžak near Bugojno and in Bila between Brčko and Gradačac. In 1943, the lovely castle of the Idrizbegović family in Vrili, near Kupres, became a casualty of the last war. The beautiful Kolaković-House in Buna near Mostar, which "owes its origin to the wish of a cultured person for peace in a beautiful house and for the pleasure to be derived from observing nature,"[49] looks much like a lordly castle.

The čardaks are two-storied homes, built partly of stone, partly of wood, belonging to wealthier Bosnians. In the upper story the windows are fashioned with semipointed arches in the oriental style, and the interiors contain beautifully furnished reception rooms or women's quarters. Frequently the upper story is built with adjoining alcoves. Larger čardaks, whose roofs have peculiar little chimneys about a foot and one-half high, are called odžaks. These are homes of the wealthiest and most elegant families. At the tip of the chimneys rises the family emblem, a so-called "apple" (*jabuka*), made of carved wood or silver or gold-plated metal. This "apple" served as a sign for travelers that a free night's lodging and board could be obtained in the house. Special quarters, called *akhars, musāfirkhānes, konačniks,* and *baškaluks,* were provided for the lodging of guests.

Whatever the type of dwelling, however, the religious influence led Muslims to place their doors so that the back of the entering visitor would not be turned to the southeast, i.e., towards Mecca. Such religious scruples are rare even in Arabia, the cradle of Islam.

The interior decoration of Muslim houses is more beautiful than the exterior. The carved wooden ceilings, with their meticulously executed central rosettes, are especially handsome. The carved wooden railings and the fronts of the wardrobes (*musanderas*) are frequently very beautiful too. Despite the fact that most of the decorative motifs and building materials used in the wainscotting came from the East, native craftsmen

48/Kreševljaković, *Kapetanije u Bosni i Hercegovini*, 23.

49/Vejsil Ćurčić, "Bauweise des muselmanischen Wohnhauses in Bosnien," *Neue Ordnung* (Zagreb, Nov. 22, 1942).

in time brought so much originality to their work that one may speak of a particular Bosnian art in this field.[50]

As a rule, the wood floors in the wealthier homes are covered with magnificently colored carpets. One often sees beautiful wall hangings and, here and there, decorative panels in calligraphy (*levha* = Arabic *lawḥa*) containing wise proverbs from the Ḳur'ān or from Arabian philosophy. Almost every sturdy house had a bath chamber or washroom with adjoining large tile stove, and every Muslim residence always had its own privy.[51]

In the finer Muslim homes, the pavement of the courtyard was often laid in geometrical figures. Behind the house, one usually found a vegetable garden or an orchard. Along the sides and in the middle of the courtyard were flower beds, with fragrant carnations, roses, tulips or lilacs, hyacinths, and (in Hercegovina) pomegranates. Frequently, a stream or a fountain splashed nearby, and century-old vines covered entire courtyards with their shade. "Noble types of roses," C. Peez writes, "flower in the gardens of the Muslims, tended with love and pious care, because a religious legend has it that the queen of flowers grew out of the sweat exuded by the Prophet during battle."[52]

In contrast to earlier history, the Turkish period meant progress in the development of housing throughout the Balkans. For example, in pre-Turkish Serbia in the first half of the fourteenth century, as the Italian writer-traveler Brokar relates, even the palaces and houses of kings and other magnates were built of wood. In Bosnia, however, there were many castles of Bans and kings in the Middle Ages and shortly after the arrival of the Turks in the fifteenth century, and there were about one thousand houses built of stone and many solidly built caravansaries with lead-covered roofs.[53]

ADVANCED CULTURE

LITERARY ACTIVITY OF THE BOSNIAKS IN ORIENTAL LANGUAGES

Soon after the Bosnian kingdom lost its independence in the year 1463, the Bosnians and Hercegovinians (to be referred to as Bosniaks) began to contribute to Turkish, Arabic, and Persian literature as new, but equal

50/Refik Bešlagić, "Srednjevjekovni nadgrobni spomenici"/Medieval Tombstones, *Kupres*, v (Sarajevo, 1954), 158.

51/Milenko S. Filipović, *Privreda, saobraćaj i naselja u Visočkoj Nahiji*/Economy, Communications, and Settlements in the District of Visoko (Beograd, 1929), 62.

52/Peez, *Mostar und sein Kulturkreis*, 66.

53/P. Matković, "Dva talijanska putopisa po Balkanskom poluotoku iz 16. vijeka"/Two Italian Travelogues on the Balkan Peninsula from the Sixteenth Century, *Starine*, x (Yugoslav Academy, 1878), 201–56.

members of the Ottoman Empire. From this time until the occupation of the country by troops of the Austro-Hungarian monarchy in 1878 the two provinces gave the Ottoman Empire roughly three hundred scientists and artists. About half of these were active as poets in one of the three official languages, Turkish, Arabic, or Persian. Some wrote in two, some even in all three languages.

Turkish was more or less the official language of the empire, Arabic was preferred in scientific circles, and Persian was limited mainly to literature. Under the circumstances, it is understandable that educated people preferred to use these languages, since their use smoothed the way to high government positions. Thus, the Bosniaks' richest literary production in these languages coincides with the period of their most powerful influence on affairs of state, from 1544 to 1612.

WRITERS IN ARABIC

The Bosnian-Hercegovinian Muslims were interested in the Arabic language chiefly for religious reasons. They aimed to teach every child at least to read and write vocalized Arabic texts,[54] so that they could read the Ḳur'ān on their own, although this reading, more often than not, was purely mechanical. However, knowledge of this alphabet proved most useful, because not only were Arabic, Turkish, and Persian written in Arabic characters, but their native Croatian was as well.

The primacy of the religious interest helped considerably to determine the type of literature produced in Arabic. The predominant subjects were religion, pedagogy, and mysticism, followed by the history of Islam and Arabic philology. The following Bosniaks wrote distinguished commentaries on orthodox religious manuals: Mawlā ʿAbd-al-Karīm (died 1471), Ḥasan ibn Turkhān al-Kāfī al-Aḳḥiṣārī (died 1616), Ḍiyāʾ-ad-Dīn Bayāḍī-Zāde (died 1686), Muṣṭafā ibn Yūsuf al-Mostārī Ayyūbī-Zāde (called Shaykh Yuyo) (died 1707), Aḥmad Khātam ibn Shahdī Aḳowalī-Zāde (died 1754), Muṣṭafā Ṣidḳī Ḳara-Beg (murdered 1878), Ḥasan Spaho (1841–1915), and Sayfallāh al-Bosnawī Proho (1859–1932). Original religious works were written by Al-Aḳḥiṣārī, Ḍiyāʾ-ad-Dīn al-Mostārī (died 1679), and Ayyūbī-Zāde.

Mystical works were more highly valued in the Orient than were scholastic treatises. Some of the former, such as the commentaries of ʿAbdallāh ʿAbdī ibn Muḥammad al-Bosnawī (died 1644), remain forever linked to the history of Islamic mysticism and are classics of this

54/Arabic is most often written without indicating the short vowels, which appear as diacritical marks above or below the consonants. It is obviously easier to read vocalized texts.

type of literature. The two volumes of Al-Bosnawī's commentaries on the famous work *Fuṣūṣ al-ḥikam* (Jewels of Wisdom) by Muḥyī-ʾd-Dīn ibn-ʿArabī (died 1240) were printed in Cairo in 1837 and in Istanbul in 1873. This work of Al-Bosnawī had been copied by hand and enjoyed great popularity, and the Bosnian scholar himself is generally known as "Shāriḥ al-Fuṣūṣ," i.e., the commentator on the famous work of Ibn-ʿArabī. Equally valuable are the mystical commentaries of Nūrallāh Munīrī al-Beligrādī al-Bosnawī (died 1617), of Ibrāhīm ibn Tīmūr al-Bosnawī (died after 1618), and of ʿAlī-Dede ibn al-Ḥājj Muṣṭafā ʿAlāʾ-ad-Dīn al-Bosnawī (died in battle in 1598), who is also known for a didactic work on Islamic history.

In politics and philosophy, remarkable essays were written by Burhān-ad-Dīn ibn Ibrāhīm ibn Bakhshī-Dede Khalīfa al-Bosnawī (died 1565) and Ḥasan ibn Turkhān al-Kāfī al-Aḳḥiṣārī.

Works on jurisprudence and ritual took account of the practical requirements of everyday life. Apart from the scholastics and representatives of the orthodox conception of Islam, the following were active in this area: ʿAlī ibn al-Ḥājj Muṣṭafā (died 1640), Muṣṭafā al-Aḳḥiṣārī (died 1755), Muḥammad Muḥtashim Shaʿbān-Zāde (died 1694), and Muḥammad (Meḥmed) Rafīḳ Efendī, the only Bosnian-born religious chief of all Muslims living in the Ottoman Empire (Shaykh al-Islām; died 1872). Ḍiyāʾ-ad-Dīn al-Mostārī, whose collection of sound juridical expert opinions (*Fatāwā-i Aḥmadīya*) became famous throughout the Balkans, was truly creative in his writings.

In the field of Arabic philology, valuable contributions were made by Muḥammad ibn Mūsā as-Sarāyī (died 1635), Maḥmūd ibn Khalīl al-Mostārī (died 1688), Ayyūbī-Zāde, Muḥammad ibn Čelebī (1711–69), Bayāḍī-Zāde, and ʿAlī Fahmī Džabić (died 1918). Maḥmūd ibn Khalīl and Fahmī Džabić, both from Mostar, were distinguished stylists, and their works are of permanent literary value. An important work on Arabic metrics was written by Meḥmed ʿArūḍī (died 1673).

The Bosniaks were not greatly interested in the natural sciences, and their contribution was limited to translating a number of scientific works from Arabic into Turkish. In this way, Aḳowalī-Zāde, for his translation of the work of *Al-Lumaʿ fī ʿilm al-ḥisāb*, and Darwīsh Ḥusām Boshnāḳ, for his translation of the *Lumʿat al-fawāʾid*, were reputed mathematicians. Muḥammad Boshnāḳ (dates unknown) translated the famous work on zoology *Ḥayāt al-ḥayawān* by Ad-Damīrī from Arabic into Turkish, and Muḥammad Rashīd (Hafizović) (died 1865) translated a treatise on hygiene. As-Suyūṭī (1445–1505), whose gifts shone in many disciplines, was made familiar to the Turks by two Bosniaks, Naṣūḥ al-Miṭraḳī (died 1547) and ʿAlī-Dede al-Bosnawī.

In history, Mīr Muḥammad (Meḥmed) ʿAfwī (died 1732) and Muṣṭafā al-Khurramī (also eighteenth century) were distinguished translators from Arabic into Turkish. Al-Aḳḥiṣārī wrote a political treatise, *Uṣūl al-ḥikam fī niẓām al-ʿālam*, in which he was one of the first to recognize and point out, at the zenith of its power, the causes of the ultimate decline of the Ottoman Empire. This treatise became world famous.

Muḥammad ibn Mūsā al-Bosnawī as-Sarāyī (died 1635) and Ayyūbī-Zāde were masters of logic, and also wrote literary works on Arabic rhetoric. In belles-lettres Bosniaks produced *Risālāt al-ḳalamīya*, an essay on the power of the written word, and *Risālāt as-sayfīya*, an essay on heroism, both written in rhymed prose by Aḥmad Shams-ad-Dīn (died 1575). After him, the best Arabic poet of Bosnian origin is Ḥasan ibn Muṣṭafā Boshnāḳ (al-Bosnawī), who lived in the latter half of the eighteenth century.

WRITERS IN PERSIAN

In regard to both Persian culture and the language itself the Bosniaks felt superior to their Turkish coreligionists. Perhaps they learned the language easily because of its Indo-European character. In any case, the best commentator on and interpreter of Persian classics in the Ottoman Empire was a Bosniak, Aḥmad Sūdī al-Bosnawī, who died in 1591 or 1592, and whose extensive and thorough works are still appreciated by scholars. The Turks seem to have been aware of this feeling of superiority of the Bosniaks; thus ʿUmar Muʿallim Nājī (1880–1916), in the course of observations in which he (wrongly) accuses Sūdī of having committed an error, says in his work *Şöyle, böyle* that the Bosniaks fancy that theirs is the priority in the mastery of the Persian language.[55]

Bosniaks used Persian almost entirely for literary works, while Arabic and Turkish were the languages of scholarship, religion, and politics. Sūdī himself, despite his pre-eminence as a Persian scholar, wrote non-literary works in Turkish. However, many Bosniak professors and scholars of religion were active as reciters and translators of classical Persian poetry such as the famous double-rhyme poem *Al-Mathnawī*[56] by Jalāl-ad-Dīn ar-Rūmī (1207–73). Reading poems by Persian poets remains today a favorite pastime of Bosnian Muslims educated in religion.

Many Bosnian Muslims who have been educated in literature and trained in writing have tried to write poetry in Persian. The most pro-

55/See Mehmed Handžić, *Književni rad bosansko-hercegovačkih Muslimana*/ The Literary Activity of Bosnian and Hercegovinian Muslims (Sarajevo, 1934), 63.

56/The *mathnawī* is a double-rhyme poem, mostly of philosophical or religious content.

ficient of these was Darwīsh Pasha Bāyazīd-Agha-Zāde (died 1603); he wrote a Persian *dīwān*[57] and a poetic counterpart to Ar-Rūmī's *Al-Mathnawī*, but this work was subsequently lost. Muḥammad Nergisī as-Sarāyī (died 1634) was also a skillful and very prolific poet. On the whole, however, except perhaps for the shorter lyric poems, his work has lost its appeal because of the affected and exaggerated style. In the middle of the eighteenth century Fawzī Blagaylǐ wrote an entertaining and instructive work, *Bulbulistān* (Nightingale Grove) in the manner of the famous *Gulistān* (Rose Garden) of Shaykh Saʿdī.

Other poets writing in Persian were Khiḍr (Hǐzǐr) Āsāfī (died 1621) and Muṣṭafā Mukhliṣī Boshnāḳ of the eighteenth century. Muṣṭafā Ladunnī, famous for his commentary on the Persian poet Shawkat, was a virtuoso in Persian rhyme. He is also believed to have written a commentary on Ar-Rūmī's *Al-Mathnawī*.

WRITERS IN TURKISH

These writers are by far the most numerous; they wrote mainly in Turkish and were more often than not Western-minded and, to some extent, the vehicle of Western or Bosnian cultural elements. Thus Naṣūḥ al-Miṭraḳī, the historian and miniature painter, seems more western than oriental in his approach; Ibrāhīm Pečewī (died *ca.* 1650 or a few years earlier) used Western sources for his historical works; ʿUthmān ibn ʿAbd-ar-Raḥmān al-Beligrādī of the latter half of the eighteenth century translated the six volumes of Dioskurides' *De materia medica* (On Medicinal Plants); ʿAlāʾ-ad-Dīn Thābit Užičewī (died 1712) and Wuṣlatī (died in battle 1688) brought elements of Croatian national poetry into Turkish poetry; and Muhammad (Meḥmed) Ṭāhir Boshnāḳ (died 1903), with his many translations from German, created an opening for the introduction of Western thought.

However, as in Arabic, religious and mystical-ethical themes dominated in works written in Turkish. Many works were translated from Arabic into Turkish and vice versa. The most prominent writers in this field were: ʿAbdallāh al-Bosnawī ("Shāriḥ al-Fuṣūṣ"), ʿAlī-Dede al-Bosnawī, Ḥasan al-Aḳḥiṣārī, Muṣṭafā Ayyūbī-Zāde, and Muṣṭafā Ṣidḳī Ḳara-Beg, of whom the first two, as we have noted, were distinguished mystics, while the others were orthodox *ʿulamā*.

The most valuable contributions in Turkish were those of the historians and chroniclers. Of value for the contemporary study of Ottoman

57/*Dīwān*, a collection of poems. It means also, in different contexts, an Imperial Turkish Council.

history are the treatises of Naṣūḥ al-Miṭraḳī, Ibrāhīm Pečewī, Muḥammad Nergisī (author of a biography of Murtaḍā Pasha, a just and brave vizier of Budim), ʿUmar Efendī, Ḳāḍī of Novi (died 1740), Ṣāliḥ Muwaḳḳit (died about 1883), author of a chronicle of his time, and Muḥammad Anwarī [Kadić] (died 1931), the greatest collector of historical documents on Bosnian Turkish history. The two latter works are absolutely essential for the study of Bosnian history.

Ibrāhīm ibn Ḥājj Ismāʿīl al-Mostārī, who died about the middle of the eighteenth century, left a beautifully written biography of the great scholar Ayyūbī-Zāde (Shaykh Yuyo). Nūrallāh Munīrī al-Beligrādī and ʿAbdallāh al-Khurramī al-Mostārī of the eighteenth century wrote on geography, and Naṣūḥ al-Miṭraḳī on mathematics and the art of fencing.

Of the many poets who wrote in Turkish the most prominent are: ʿAlī ibn ʿAbdallāh ʿĀlī al-Bosnawī (died 1646), a philosophical-mystic poet, whose beautiful language mirrors profound personal experience; Darwīsh Pasha Bāyazīd-Agha-Zāde, who wrote patriotic poems; Thābit Užičewī, one of the classical writers of the oldest Ottoman poetry; and ʿĀrif Ḥikmat Hersekli (died 1903), the last great representative of the so-called *dīwān*-literature, the most important pre-modern literary genre in Turkish. Poems by ʿĀlī and Thābit have been translated into German by Josef von Hammer-Purgstall, Jan Rypka, and Herbert Jansky.

Additional names of the more important writers are listed alphabetically in the appendix; however, the author does not claim completeness for the list of writers in either part of this essay. The alphabetical listing of the writers offers additional details, both biographical and bibliographical.

The Bosniaks did not stop writing in Oriental languages when Ottoman rule ended in their country in 1878. Bosnian Muslim writers who emigrated to those areas where the Ottoman Empire remained intact continued their tradition. At the present time there are educated Bosniaks in the country itself as well as in the Orient who, despite deep-felt allegiance to their homeland, still consider Arabic, Persian, and Turkish their literary languages.

POETRY IN CROATIAN

Although among the Ottoman diplomatic writings there are some (such as the Croatian) which are composed in the tongue of the conquered peoples, as we have noted, the Bosniaks used the three oriental languages for their cultural activities. Nevertheless, a small number of literary works were written in their native language, Croatian.

As Maximilian Braun has pointed out,[58] the lack of development of literature in the mother-tongue may also be attributed to the flourishing of folk-poetry, and the lively tales which indicate a well-developed narrative art and imply no real need for any other kind of literature.

Mainly religious-didactic works and, less frequently, love poems were written in Croatian. This literature, meant mostly for the simple folk, was begun by a certain Mehmed from Transylvania (*Mehmed od Erdelja*) with his poem "Khǐrwat türkisi" (The Croatian Song; 1588–9). With very few exceptions, all poems of this kind are written in a language interspersed with countless Arabic, Turkish, and Persian words, and according to the principles of Arabic metrics.

Of the approximately thirty poets of the Turkish period who composed their works in Croatian, barely three or four can stand the test of rigorous literary criticism. These are: Muḥammad Hawāʾī Üskūfī (1601–*ca.* 1651); Muṣṭafā or, as Otto Blau calls him, ʿAbd-al-Muṣṭafā, whose dates cannot be ascertained; and Fejzo Softa of the nineteenth century.

From Muḥammad Hawāʾī Üskūfī we get a rhymed dictionary of the "Bosnian Language" for the Turks, *Maḳbūl-i ʿārif* (approximately: Favorite Child of the Expert); several pious poems in quatrains; a mystic poem, "Tabshirat al-ʿārifīn" (Happy Message to Searchers for Knowledge); a poetic reflection on women; a love poem; and several comic epistles.

Blau has translated into German a beautiful amorous plaint by Muṣṭafā who wrote half in Turkish and half in Croatian.[59]

The simple poetry of Fejzo Softa, which forms the basis of a unique primer of the Arabic language, is beautiful in language and thought. Each letter is explained with a little verse of four or five lines.

All writings of the Bosnian Muslims prior to 1878 are in Arabic script. The national alphabet, the *bosančica*, which was based on the Greek alphabet, was used mainly for private and sometimes for diplomatic correspondence. Because of its completely independent development, the Muslim literature in Croatian remained devoid of influence and enrichment from the other national territories. This separate existence led to an ossification of form and thought, and the language remained poor and stunted. Despite these deficiencies, this literature has fulfilled three tasks: (a) it has proved that the national consciousness of the Bosnian Muslims remained alive even during the Turkish reign, (b)

58/*Die Anfänge der Europäisierung in der Literatur der muslimischen Slaven in Bosnien und der Herzegowina* (Leipzig, 1934), 27.

59/Otto Blau, *Bosnisch-türkische Sprachdenkmäler* (Leipzig, 1866), 118–20.

it has helped to explode the myth of the "cultureless Turkish past," and (c) it has enriched the common Croatian literature with a new tone.

MINIATURE PAINTING, CALLIGRAPHY, AND DECORATIVE BOOKBINDING

The Persian and Turkish arts of book-illustration were practiced in Bosnia, and survive mainly in litanies in praise of the prophet Muḥammad, in other books of prayer, especially the so-called *ḥamā'il* (*hamajlije*), as well as in anthologies of poems and in historical monographs. We find representations of sacred places in Mecca, Medina, and Istanbul; drawings of historical buildings; portraits of ʿAlī, the son-in-law of the Prophet; animal-drawings; various geometrical figures; hunting scenes and love scenes. Most of the historically significant motifs are borrowed from Persian miniature painting, and the style, characteristically Persian, is distinguished by its harmony of color.

It is difficult to determine how many Ottoman artists were Bosnians.[60] The greatest Turkish painter of Bosnian origin was Naṣūḥ as-Silāḥī al-Miṭraḳī al-Wisoḳawī (died 1547), a man of wide-ranging ability: he was a successful fencing master, a historian, mathematician, and calligrapher. His *Majmaʿ al-manāzil*, a description of the war expedition of Sultan Suleiman to Iraq (1533–5), contains 132 valuable miniatures. "He paints all localities in a most characteristic way. He omits every human aspect, especially everything vulgar. Because of this the artist succeeds in filling his miniatures with a colorful serenity which gives every place the shining appearance of a higher existence."[61]

Ornamental border designs, and title-page illustrations, preferably executed in gold, colored medallions, and rosettes adorned manuscripts.[62] The graceful ornamental Arabic calligraphy, which blossomed

60/According to Oktay Aslanapa there are in Topkapĭ-Saray in Istanbul approximately 10,000 miniatures, a veritable gallery of islamic art. Regrettably, only very few of these pieces have been made accessible to the public. See Ernst Diez-Oktay Aslanapa, *Türk Sanʿatĭ*/Turkish Art (Publication of the Department of Philosophy," no. 627; Istanbul, Turkey: University of Istanbul, 1955), 272.

61/*Turkische Miniaturen vom 13. bis zum 18. Jahrhundert.* Introductory Text by Richard Ettinghausen. "Piper: UNESCO Taschenbucher der Kunst" (München, 1965), 16; also see Hüseyin G. Yurdaydĭn, *Matrakçĭ Nasuh* ("Ankara Universitesi Ilahiyat Fakultesi Yayĭnlarĭ 43," Ankara, 1963); C. F. Sybold, "Ein anonymer alter turkischer Kommentar zum letzten Drittel des Korans in drei Handschriften zu Hamburg, Breslau und im Britischen Museum," 17 and 50; in *Festschrift Eduard Sachau zum siebzigsten Geburtstage gewidmet von Freunden und Schulern*, ed. by Gotthold Weil (Berlin, 1915), 329.

62/Alija Nametak, *Islamski kulturni spomenici turskog perioda u Bosni i Hercegovini*/Islamic Cultural Movements of the Turkish Period in Bosnia and Hercegovina (Sarajevo, 1939), 36.

all during the Ottoman reign, is still exercised today, albeit only modestly. The decorative panels (*levha*) painted in gold, embroidered on cloth, or carved in wood, on which are written in Arabic letters verses of the Ḳur'ān, or other sayings from the teachings of Islam or of Arabic philosophy, are of special interest.

The following Bosnians were distinguished calligraphers: Ḥusayn ibn Naṣūḥ al-Wisoḳawī, who finished copying a Turkish Ḳur'ān commentary on April 3, 1579 (this commentary is to be found in the city library of Breslau); Muḥammad Nergisī (died 1634); Sulaymān Mazāḳī (died 1677); Zakarīya Sukkarī (died 1687); Darwīsh Ḳahramān Muḥammad al-Gradičawī (seventeenth century); ʿAbd-al-Ḳādir; Muḥammad Cato; Aḥmad Bayāḍi-Zāde; Zakarīya ibn Ḥusayn ibn Masīḥ; Ibrāhīm ibn Ṣāliḥ; Ismāʿīl ibn Ibrāhīm; Muṣṭafā ibn Ismāʿīl; Aḥmad Khātam Aḳowalī-Zāde (died 1754); ʿUthmān Bosnawī; Muḥammad Muhtashim [Šabanović] (died 1694); Yaḥyā Bosnawī; Kimyāger (Chemist) ʿAlī Zakī; ʿĀṣim Yūsuf; ʿAbdallāh Māhir (died 1710); Ṣāliḥ Ṣalāḥī; Muṣṭafā ibn Ibrāhīm al-Mostārī; Muṣṭafā al-Ḥāfiẓ; Muṣṭafā Pasha Bosnawī; Sulaymān ʿĀrif; Ismāʿīl Bosnawī; Dawūd ibn Ismāʿīl; Darwīsh Ḥusām-ad-Dīn; Ḥusayn ibn ʿAbdallāh; Sulaymān Bosnawī; ʿAbd-ar-Raḥmān; Sayyid Muḥammad ibn Rajab; Ṭāhir Ibrāhīm; Ḥurram Bosnawī; Aḥmad Bosnawī; Aḥmad ibn ʿAlī al-Ghazghānī al-Bosnawī (first half of the eighteenth century); Muḥammad Islamović (nineteenth century); ʿAlī Faginović; Sālim Niyāzī; Derviš Korkut (died 1942); Ḥājj Ḥāfiẓ Muṣṭafā Čadordžija (died 1933); Aḥmad Jamal Dervišević (died in Cairo 1936); Sulaymān Čučak; Bahā'-ad-Dīn Sikirić; Wahbī Smailkadić; Fawzī Djulić; Muḥammad Mujagić (twentieth century); and Muḥammad Wahbī al-Bosnawī (died in Cairo 1948).[63]

Figured miniatures of trees, plants, animals, and arabesques appear on various utility items such as cradles, chests, coffee tables, and weaving looms, as well as on such parts of rooms and houses as doors, cupboards, pillars, railings, and ceilings. The Kolaković-House in Buna near Mostar and the Ottoman-Turkish School, "Rushdīya," in Sarajevo are especially rich in such ornamentations. In the many richly decorated Ḳur'ān reading-desks, book covers, and frames for hand-mirrors, the extensive use of mother-of-pearl is specially striking.

SCHOOLS, SEMINARIES, AND OTHER INSTITUTIONS

Universities, in the western sense of the term, did not exist during the period of Ottoman rule. Attendance at lectures in the theological semi-

63/"Bosna," *Türk Ansiklopedisi* (Ankara, 1954), VII, 410.

naries (*medresses*), which gave one a secondary education, was voluntary, and could be continued over an indefinite period of time. By means of question-answer periods following lectures, a kind of seminar approach was introduced; thus a veritable university system was employed in a number of these medresses. From the end of the nineteenth century to the year 1932, the Ghāzī Khusrew Beg Medresse in Sarajevo even had a college, the so-called ʿAlīya.

In the popular lecture halls, *Dār al-hadīth* and *Dār al-tafsīr*, Islamic tradition and exegesis of the Ḳurʾān were taught. At the same time, an interest in Arabic and its literature was fostered. Through the general courses and the courses in the famous religious poem of Jalāl-ad-Dīn ar-Rūmī (1207–73), *Al-Mathnawī*, an understanding of Persian and its poetry was awakened, and the horizons of the mind were enlarged. In the medresses, where books were of prime importance, Arabian calligraphy and ornamental decorative arts were fostered. In the religious schools for girls, the girls were taught embroidery, knitting, rug-making, lace-making, and weaving. And so were created in schools and private homes the variety of handwork that assured Bosnian women a widespread reputation.[64]

Popular tradition transmitted much in the line of factual knowledge, verse, and tales with numerous points. Only fragments of this monumental oral culture have been preserved to the present day.

For the calculation and regulation of exact times of prayer, and for the establishment of the time of the new moon, a small astronomical station (*muwaḳḳitkhāne*) was operated in Sarajevo. Astronomy and mathematics were developed there.

In the monasteries of the Mawlawi dervishes, oriental music was cultivated. The virtuosity of these dervishes in playing the flute was unsurpassed.

In the monastery of Ḥājj Sinān, in Sarajevo, there was for a time a hospital for the mentally ill. Whether or not music was used as a method of therapy there, as it was in a few other Ottoman sanatoriums, is unknown.

In addition to the regular practice of the *ḥakīm* (physician), the art of healing was practiced also by barbers, druggists, and barber-surgeons. Despite the decay which crept in during the eighteenth and nineteenth centuries, the old Arabian medicinal practices were preserved until quite recently. A famous popular healer, Sadik Sadiković,

64/*Hrvatski Dnevnik* (Zagreb, July 21, 1940).

still applied Arabian medical principles with success at the beginning of the twentieth century.

Medical books were used and copied when additional or new copies were needed. There is a Bosnian copy of the Canon of Medicine (*Ḳānūn aṭ-ṭibb*) by Ibn Sīna (died 1037), produced at the beginning of the nineteenth century, in Istanbul.[65] An additional copy of unknown date has recently been discovered in a remote village at the foot of Ivan Mountain.[66]

Modern European medicine found its way into Bosnia during the second half of the eighteenth century. In 1779, an Italian physician, Ludovico of Naples, who had been converted to Islam enjoyed great popularity. In about the year 1770, the Belgrade physician ʿUthmān ibn ʿAbd-ar-Raḥmān translated Andrea Mattioli's commentary on the six volumes of Dioskurides' *De Materia medica* on pharmacology and botany. The first general hospital was founded in the year 1866, with government aid and funds from pious Muslim institutions (*awḳāf*).

Bosnia produced one significant Ottoman inventor, the land surveyor ʿAbdallāh Muẓaffarī Čelebī, called "Master of many tricks," who died in 1750. His flexible bridges made the great military transports possible, and contributed much toward the victories of Hakīm Oghlu ʿAlī Pasha (1689–1758).

ARCHITECTURE

The spiritual influence of the Orient on the culture of Bosnia and Hercegovina manifests itself in song and story, literature and learning, religion and philosophy, language and social customs. Tangibly, this influence is embodied in Islamic religious and secular monuments.

As in the rest of the empire, the building activity of the Bosniaks stemmed from religion. Thus its origin lies in the piety, altruism, and individual initiative of those who strove to create something that would be pleasing to God and forever remembered by posterity.

The *āthār-i mufīda* (i.e., "useful works") that sprang from this spirit comprise sacred buildings, mosques, medresses or training colleges for students of theology, monasteries (*teke*), mausoleums (*turba*), and

65/Lujo Thaller, "Zdravstvo Hrvatsko-Slavonske Vojne Krajine"/Health Conditions of the Croatian-Slavonian Military Frontier, *Liečnički Viestnik* (Sarajevo, January 1944); Sadik Sadiković, *Narodno zdravlje/People's Health* (Sarajevo: Jugoslavenski List, 1928), 314.

66/Editorial: "Velike hvale vrijedan primjer g. Sulejmana Alića"/An example of Mr. Suleiman Alić Worthy of Special Praise, *GVSIVZ*, xxvi, no. 11–12 (Sarajevo, 1963), 561.

other tombs. The secular buildings include clock-towers, baths, libraries, hospices (*musāfirkhānes*), caravansaries, fountains, aqueducts, and paved roads. I shall discuss briefly each of these types of buildings.

Monuments of Sacred Character

Mosques

From the point of view of the history of art, the big, domed mosques of which about thirty are still standing[67] are most valuable. These mosques are massive buildings flanked by beautiful stone minarets. Their fronts consist of pillared stone halls, usually crowned by three cupolas, and their interior of numerous arches, capitals, bases, and abundant stalactite ornaments. Arabesques and vegetable and geometric patterns dominate the surface decoration. Through the use of well-calculated spatial proportions and tasteful architectural and surface ornamentation, the builders have achieved a pleasant and intimate atmosphere, even though the mosque appears larger than it really is. Here is a foreign visitor's impression of the interior of one of these mosques: "Despite the rich use of very brilliant colors in the cupolas, on the columns and their capitals, on the walls, and on the carpets which covered the floor without a gap, the room was full of the purest harmony. And when the sun shone through one of the windows, all the colors seemed to burst into flame, and so filled the room with their life, that I dared not step further, and remained confined to the portal."[68]

The exterior effect is enhanced by the surroundings, which often include a nearby river or stream. Where natural beauty was wanting, architectural science intervened to beautify. Thus the small mosque in the court of Tashlĭ Khan in Sarajevo, which has now been destroyed by fire, lay beyond a fountain. The mosque of Sultan Aḥmad, in Kulen Vakuf, was built on a daringly constructed stone arch, beneath which the animated commercial dealings of the little town took place. Most mosques are situated among a profusion of trees – cypresses, plane trees, chestnut trees, limes, oaks, acacias, and others. In the shaded courtyards splashes the water of the fountains, which serve for the ritual washings, and afford a pleasant tableau to the eye and melody to the ear of the visitor.

The most beautiful mosques are the following: Ghāzī Khusrew Beg

67/Alija Bejtić, "Spomenici osmanlijske arhitekture u Bosni i Hercegovini"/ Monuments of Ottoman Architecture in Bosnia and Hercegovina, *Prilozi za orijentalnu filologiju i istoriju jugoslovenskih naroda pod turskom vladavinom,* III–IV (Sarajevo, 1952–3), 246.

68/A. Vetter, "Bericht über eine Studienreise nach Bosnien und der Herzegovina (September–Oktober, 1910)" (Wien: Museum für Völkerkunde, Ms. 2324), 15.

Mosque of Mehmed Pasha Ṣoqollu (Soko-lović) at Istanbul, Turkey, facade

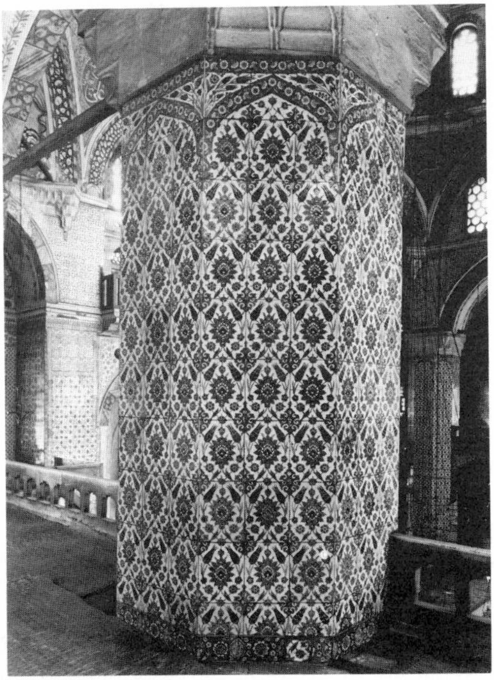

Pillar in the interior of the mosque of Rustam Pasha, the Croatian, at Istanbul, Turkey

The fortified city of Počitelj in Hercegovina, from the fifteenth century

Upper right
Mosque of Farhād-Pasha in Banjaluka

Model of the mosque of Ghāzī Khusrew Beg in Sarajevo (made by Husein Karišiković)

Courtyard of the Islamic Sheriat Theological School in Sarajevo

The Old Bridge on the Neretva River in Mostar, built in 1566

Mosque of Ḳara-Göz Beg at Mostar

The Old Bridge in Mostar at night

Ḥammām
(public bath)
at Mostar, from
the sixteenth century

(built in 1530), ʿAlī Pasha (1561), and Emperor's Mosque (1565) in Sarajevo; Farhād Pasha in Banjaluka (1579); Alaja in Foča (1560); Ḳarā-Göz Beg in Mostar (1570);[69] Sinān Beg in Čajniče (1582); Yūsuf Pasha in Maglaj (second half of the sixteenth century); and the Ḳi̇zlar Agha Mosque in Varcar-Vakuf (about 1591).

In the year 1938, the Khwāja-Kamāl-ad-Dīn Mosque (1540) in Sarajevo, famous for its interior facing, was destroyed.[70]

Medresses

Of the approximately seventy medresses (theological seminaries) only two still stand today: the Ghāzī Khusrew Beg or Kurshunlu Medresse in Sarajevo (1537) and the Shishman Ibrāhīm Pasha Medresse in Počitelj (1665). The Ghāzī Khusrew Beg Medresse consists of a large domed hall, which served as lecture room, and twelve identical rooms, each vaulted with a cupola. The whole building is planned around a small, intimate courtyard, in the center of which water bubbles from the many shells of a fountain. The area before the rooms is also domed, and surrounded by a stone colonnade. Special emphasis is given the building by the high, stalactite-adorned portal and several pointed chimneys reminiscent of small minarets. Despite its modest scale the Ghāzī Khusrew Beg Medresse gives the impression of monumental proportions. This famous theological seminary was enlarged early in 1930 into a really modern college and equipped with modern furniture. It was subsequently confiscated by the state at the end of the last world war and attached to the University of Sarajevo, to house the faculty of liberal arts. All efforts of Bosnian Muslims to regain ownership of this famous school have been in vain.

The medresse in Počitelj on the Neretva, despite the heavy destruction caused by an incompetently executed renovation and the devastating influences of weather, still retains many beautiful features of the old, horizontally developed architecture of the Ottomans.

Under Austro-Hungarian rule (1878–1918), two new medresses, in Travnik and Gračanica, and a school for Ḳāḍī candidates (later the College of Islamic Studies) in Sarajevo, were built in the Moorish style.

69/According to the research findings of Hazim Šabanović, Mehmed Karā-Göz Beg, a great founder of institutions in Mostar, was a brother of Khi̇rwāt Rustam Pasha.

70/From 1941 to 1945, 756 Muslim houses of prayer in Yugoslavia were bombed, burned, or destroyed; cf. *Jugoslawien* (Belgrade, 1954), 88. On December 15, 1958, there were 946 mosques and 232 smaller Islamic places of prayer (*masjid*); *Glasnik Vrhovnog Islamskog Starješinstva u SFRJ*/Official Paper of the Supreme Islamic Authority in SFRY (hereafter cited as *GVIS*), x, no. 1–3 (Sarajevo, 1959), 115.

Dervish Schools and Monasteries

Until 1931, Ṣarajevo had a dervish school (*khānḳāh*). This was set up by the founder of Sarajevo, Ghāzī Khusrew Beg (1480–1541), who founded more cultural institutions than did any other Bosnian. The architectural details were the same as those of the Ghāzī Khusrev Beg Medresse. This school was extensively rebuilt after 1931. Of the other dervish schools, the number of which is not known, not one survived into the nineteenth century. On the other hand, several dervish monasteries still exist, although they have lost their original function. The massive Ḥājj Sinān Monastery in Sarajevo (1640), which stands beautiful and serene on a hill, is of architectural value. There are plans under consideration to use this building as an Islamic museum.

Monuments of Memorial Architecture

The Muslim tombs in Bosnia are either completely closed octagonal mausoleums, open mausoleums supported by a colonnade, or simple blocklike tombstones. The mausoleums set up in honor of dead army commanders, aristocrats, sages, or saints, display beautifully constructed arches, pillar capitols, and ornaments of noteworthy originality.

The ornamental decoration of tombs originated partly in the Orient, partly in the Bosnia of the patarene period; the plant and animal representations especially are of Croatian origin. The verse or prose decoration is composed in Arabic calligraphy. It is only on the most ancient gravestones that one sees inscriptions in *bosančica* (the Bosnian script).

Since Islam frowns upon realistic likenesses of men, the Bosnian stonemason tried to capture the character and social significance of the deceased through delicately modulated representations of headgear, or through symbolic rendering of significant moments in his life. Thus, one finds on grave monuments figures of turban and fez, and, in addition, the crescent moon, sword, spear, bow, morning star, stylized flowers, plants and leaves, vases with water as a symbol of life to come, and complete hunting scenes. Man is symbolized by an outstretched hand. On one tomb below the Jahorina Mountains near Sarajevo, one sees the person as a large silhouette of a rider. Dj. Mazalić has found an ancient Muslim tomb near Prusac which bears the torso of a human body.[71]

The best-preserved mausoleums are those of Ghāzī Khusrew Beg and Murād Beg Tardić in Sarajevo (built in the sixteenth century); that of Ibrāhīm Beg in Foča (sixteenth century); and that of Perīshān Muṣṭafā Pasha (1798) in Banjaluka.

71/A. Bejtić, "Spomenici osmanlijske arhitekture," 287.

Monuments of a Secular Character

Bridges, Caravansaries, Bezistans, and Clock-Towers

Great architectural and technical courage is displayed in the Turkish stone bridges, constructed in a single bold arch, on the Neretva River in Mostar (built in 1566), on the Žepa River in Žepa (sixteenth century), on the Bregava River near Počitelj (1517), and on the Miljacka River near Sarajevo (before 1550). No less impressive are the massive bridges resting on several arches, such as the Drina bridge in Višegrad, which has been described in numerous narratives and novels, which is 175 meters long (built 1571); the bridge in Goražde (now destroyed); and the one on the Neretva River in Konjic (built 1682–3). The famous Mostar bridge has been a favorite subject not only of folk poetry, but also of literature and films ("The Last Bridge"). Jean Cassut, the French author, overcome by its beauty, calls the bridge "a petrified crescent across water." Other stone bridges linking the banks of the Neretva, Buna, Vrbas, Bosna, Čehotina, Radobolja, and Lim rivers are equally noteworthy.

The remains of former Bosnian caravansaries are now lying in ruin; two of these once magnificent caravansaries, first surveyed by the Viennese archeologist Moritz Hoernes, are located at the bridges of Višegrad and Goražde.

The only *bezistān* (market-hall) still preserved is the massive sexpartite domed building, covering an area of 27 by 18 meters, which stands in Sarajevo. It was built in 1551 by Khǐrwāt (the Croatian) Rustam Pasha.

Among the once numerous clock-towers, the most beautiful is that of Ghāzī Khusrew Beg in Sarajevo, which stands beside the mosque bearing his name.

Hydraulic Architecture

Architecturally, the most valuable fountains, watering-places, stations for drinking-water (*sabīl*), and public baths came into being in the fifteenth and sixteenth centuries. The first Turkish aqueducts were built at that time also.

Many of the fountains have beautiful ornamental and figure decoration (such as representations of flowers). On the wall surfaces of these objects, Arabic ornamental script is usually engraved, giving information about donors and the years in which they were built. Only in those fountains found in sacred buildings – *shadrewān* or *šadrvan* – and in public baths do we find round, square, octagonal, or hexagonal basins, in which the water level is raised to about one meter above the earth. Along the outside of the encircling walls which frame the building, several water-taps are arranged in a row. In the center there are usually stone cups on flowers from which the water bubbles forth and rushes down to the lower level. Most of the shadrewans are roofed and surrounded by ornamented stone columns.

The sabils, which have now entirely disappeared, were small drinking-water stations near the market-places, directed by an official, and they provided the populace with good drinking-water. The last sabil in Sarajevo, a square, domed building erected by Mehmed Pasha Kukavica in 1775, was destroyed in the year 1891.

In addition to numerous aqueducts and a swimming-pool in Sarajevo, the old Bosnians left behind some fifty-six public baths (*ḥammām*). The most beautiful of these were: the Ghāzī Khusrew Beg bath (built in 1557), the two largest baths of Mostar, and the baths of Stolac, Počitelj, and Blagaj in Hercegovina. The Ghāzī ʿĪsā Beg bath in Sarajevo, built by the founder of the mosque and medresse in Üsküb (Skopje),[72] is still standing. The interior paneling of these baths consisted of lovely woodcarvings. In the center of the reception rooms were gaily splashing fountains.

In the sixteenth century Sarajevo had seven public baths, and the institution was not lacking even in smaller towns, such as Kladanj, Prača, Rudo, Kostajnica, and Jasenovac. Medicinal springs in Kiseljak and Ilidža, near Sarajevo, and other places, were carefully maintained and used extensively. Public lavatories were also known, two existing in Sarajevo and two in Banjaluka (sixteenth century).

Bosnian Town-Planning

The development of Bosnian towns is closely connected with the building of Muslim religious establishments (*awḳāf*). Most towns were founded in the fifteenth and sixteenth centuries, when the building activity springing from religious motives was at its peak. The Croatian historian, Hamdija Kreševljaković was able to prove that a large number of these religious establishments were donated by the simple faithful, who literally earned their bread in the sweat of their brows.[73] Finally, we might note that in this era the empire had reached its zenith, and for almost fifty-two consecutive years Bosniaks had held the chair of grand vizier in Istanbul.

72/Herbert W. Duda, *Balkantürkische Studien* (Wien, 1949), 24, 25, 44–49, 58ff.

73/Alija Bejtić, "Spomenici osmanlijske arhitekture," 232.

Two essential characteristics of Bosnian city-planning are the choice of site and the ingenious placement of objects. In order to provide the building sites with a pleasant view, the houses were either built, terrace-like, above one another, or, in rigorous observation of social considerations, separated from one another by gardens and vacant areas. For reasons of both sanitation and esthetics, building near running water was preferred. Because of the strong ritual emphasis on cleanliness in Islam, Sarajevo, the capital of Bosnia, got its first water system as early as 1461; it was a pious donation by ʿĪsā B. Ishaković (died 1469). In the latter half of the sixteenth century a number of smaller Bosnian villages and towns such as Banjaluka, Foča, Livno, Mostar, and Travnik already had water systems and public fountains. During the seventeenth and eighteenth centuries the paved streets of the business quarters (*çarşĭ*) of several Bosnian towns, which were constructed with a slope, were washed almost daily by means of diverted waters of a river canal or brook, which were made to flow down them.[74]

The esthetic gain is impressive. In the ancient vizier-city of Travnik, for example, water flows through nearly every courtyard. Everywhere one hears the splashing, and senses the freshness of nature. A general tendency to extend the green of nature into the dwelling is evident and, thus, most of the older Bosnian cities are characteristically gardenlike.[75]

Architects

The outstanding architects of the Turkish period were: Khayr-ad-Dīn, builder of the old bridges in Mostar; Meḥmed, architect of the Ghāzī Khusrew Beg Mosque in Sarajevo; Ramaḍān Agha, architect of the Ala-ja Mosque in Foča; Najjār Ḥājj Ibrāhīm and Sinān al-Bosnawī, all of the sixteenth century. In the eighteenth century there were two architects of Greek-Orthodox faith, Staniša and Tanasije, who also designed buildings consecrated to Islam, and K. Jireček reports the occasional engaging of Italian architects to work in Bosnia.[76]

Juraj Neidhardt, the leading architect in Bosnia today, characterizes Bosnian culture in architecture as follows: "The basic principles of Bosnian architecture are in accord with modern prerequisites: its foremost principle is humanity. The other principles are derived therefrom: a way

74/"Neki detalji o pozitivnom djelovanju islama na našu kulturu"/A Few Details of the Positive Influence of Islam on Our Culture, *Takvim za godinu 1966* (Sarajevo, 1966), 115.

75/Enthusiastic tributes to the beauty of Bosnian cities are offered by Ewliya Čelebi, *Siyāḥatnāme* (Istanbul, 1936), v, 425–61 and 492–95; and R. Pelletier, *Sarajevo et sa région* (Paris, 1932), 257–8.

76/Alija Bejtić, "Spomenici osmanlijske arhitekture," 240; Robert Anhegger, "Die Römerbrücke von Mostar," *Oriens*, VII (1954), 87–107.

of building conforming to the scale of Man, a close relationship to Nature, a logical disposition in urban texture and a clear differentiation of its component parts according to their individual function."[77]

APPENDIX

Bosnian Authors Who Wrote in Oriental Languages

The following exposition will provide the reader with the most important biographical and bibliographical data on authors of Bosnian origin who wrote in Arabic, Turkish, and Persian. It should be noted that this survey also includes writers who lived and worked long after the Ottoman period, some of whom are our contemporaries. The names are in alphabetical order. No claim is made for the completeness of the list.

PROSE WRITERS

ʿAbd-al-Karīm, Mawlā (died 1471) wrote several works on Islamic law and was a glossographer of the Super-commentary of the Ḳurʾān by Sayyid Sharīf.[78]

ʿAbd-al-Karīm ibn Muḥammad al-Bosnawī as-Sāmiʿī (died 1685), a hagiographer.

ʿAbdallāh ʿAbdī ibn Muḥammad al-Bosnawī,[79] called "Commentator of Fuṣūṣ," head of a monastery of the Bayramī dervishes (died in Konya, 1644),[80] wrote a commentary to the work *Fuṣūṣ al-ḥikam* (Jewels of Wisdom) by the famous philosopher of the gnostic school Muḥyī-ʾd-Dīn ibn-ʿArabī (died 1240); a mystical treatise, *Maṭāliʿ an-nūr* (Rising Spots of Light); and several other books on Islamic theology and mysticism.

Aḥmad Ḥājj Nasīm-Zāde (Hadžinesimović), who died in the second half of the eighteenth century, is the author of a historical monograph on the Turko-Austrian and the Turko-Russian wars in the years 1736–9.

Aḥmad ibn Ḥasan Bayāḍī-Zāde (died 1686) interpreted in the work *Ishārāt al-marām min ʿibārāt al-imām* (Marks of the Ultimate Intention in the Texts of the Master) the dogmatic views of the founder of the Ḥanafite law-school, Abū Ḥanīfa (died 767).[81]

Aḥmad ibn ʿUthmān Shāhdī Aḳowalī-Zāde, son of the founder of a public library in Sarajevo (died 1754), left commentaries to the mathematical

77/B. Gabrijan and J. Neidhart, *Arhitektura Bosne i put u savremenost*/The Architecture of Bosnia and the Road to Contemporaneity (Sarajevo, 1958). Quoted according to Matko Meštrović in *Literatura* (Zagreb), 1958, 111.

78/Where there is no other source mentioned, see Safvetbeg Bašagić, *Bošnjaci i Hercegovci u islamskoj književnosti*/Bosnians and Hercegovinians in Islamic Literature (Sarajevo, 1912).

79/The epithet "Al-Bosnawi" (Bosniak, Bosnian) was applied to a great number of these writers.

80/The year of death is according to Carl Brockelmann, *Geschichte der arabischen Literatur* (hereafter cited as *GAL*), Suppl. I (Leyden, 1937), 193. According to the *Türk Ansiklopedisi*, VII (1954), Fasc. 55, p. 408, he died in 1640.

81/The title of this commentary is *Tajallīyāt ʿaraʾis an-nuṣūṣ fī minaṣṣāt ḥikam al-fuṣūṣ*.

manual *Al-Lumaʿ fī ʿilm al-ḥisāb* (Rays of Light on the Science of Arithmetic), to the manual of jurisprudence *Multaḳā al-abḥur* (Confluence of the Lakes) by Burhān-ad-Dīn al-Ḥalabī (died 949), and to the Persian vocabulary *Shāhidīya* and the *Risālāt alfāẓ al-kufr* (Treatise on Blasphemous Words). Aḳowalī-Zāde also tried his hand at poetry. Apart from his mother tongue, he also had command of Arabic, Turkish, and Persian.[82]

Aḥmad Shams-ad-Dīn as-Sarāyī (died 1575), in his works *Risālāt al-ḳalamīya* (Essay on the Pen) and *Risālāt as-sayfīya* (Essay on the Sword), contributed to belles lettres.[83]

Aḥmad Sūdī al-Bosnawī (died 1591 or 1592) is one of the best commentators on the Persian classical poets, Ḥāfiẓ (*ca.* 1325–90), Saʿdī (1184?–1291), and Ar-Rūmī (1207–73). His philological interpretations of their poetry are excellent.[84] Whereas the earlier Orient interpreted the first two poets, in particular Ḥāfiẓ, allegorically, this eminent Bosnian man of learning gave careful attention to the text in a more nearly Western approach.[85]

ʿAlī-Dede ibn Muṣṭafā ʿAlāʾ-ad-Dīn as-Sigetwārī al-Bosnawī, head of a dervish monastery, fell during the siege of Sziget in 1598. He wrote an entertaining historical work, *Muḥāḍarat al-awāʾil wa musāmarat al-awākhir* (Lesson on the First, and Discourse on the Last Events).[86] In it the author describes socio-historical and political events as they occurred, developed, and were resolved in the Islamic world. These reports are in each case supplemented by anecdotes from the lives and works of kings and learned men of the Orient. The author was strongly influenced by the Arabic sage As-Suyūṭī (1445–1505), but he intended his work for entertainment only. Another work by this author, *Ḥall ar-rumūz wa kashf al-kunūz* (Unravelling of the Symbols and Discovery of the Hidden Treasure), deals with Ḳurʾān philosophy from the mystical viewpoint. His work *Anwār al-mashāriḳ* (Eastern Lights) also delves into mysticism.

ʿAlī Fahmī al-Mostārī Džabić (died 1918), the mufti of Mostar and later university professor in Istanbul, conducted research into the Arabic art of style and the history of literature. His study *Ḥusn aṣ-ṣiḥāba fī sharḥ ashʿār aṣ-ṣaḥāba* (Beauty of the Discourse on the Interpretation of the Poems of Muḥammad's Companions) is highly valued. This interpretation, in three volumes, of the poetry of the Prophet's companions has been the subject of review and annotation by a great many Arabic scholars, among whom were Aḥmad Shākir al-ʿAlūsī and Muḥammad Makkī ibn ʿAzūz from Tunisia; the latter composed a poem in which he praised the author as one to whom literary men are in debt forever.[87] The mufti also wrote *Ṭilbat aṭ-ṭālib fī Lāmiyat Abī Ṭālib* (What Does the Student Require in Order to Understand the Poem "Lāmiya" by Abū Ṭālib"), and *Taʿlīḳāt ʿalā kitāb al-Kāmil* (Glossary to the Book "Al-Kāmil" of Muḥammad ibn Yazīd al-Mu-

82/Mehmed Handžić, *Književni rad bosansko-hercegovačkih Muslimana*/The Literary Activity of Bosnian and Hercegovinian Muslims (Sarajevo, 1934), 12–14, 114.

83/*Türk Ansiklopedisi*, VIII, 4, 403.

84/According to Jan Rypka *et al.*, *History of Iranian Literature* (Dordrecht, 1968), 266.

85/*Ibid.*, 103, 262.

86/*GAL*, II, 427; II, 197, 635.

87/Mehmed Handžić, *Al-jawhar al-asnā fī tarājim ʿulamāʾ wa shuʿarāʾ Bosna*/

barrad, on Arabic grammar). Džabić, one of the best of Arabic scholars, was head of the movement of Bosnian-Hercegovinian Muslims for religious and cultural self-administration (1899–1909).[88]

ʿAlī Zakī, called *Kimyāger* (Chemist), from an unknown time, dedicated himself to the studies of chemistry and the Persian language.

Burhān-ad-Dīn ibn Ibrāhīm ibn Bakhshī-Dede Khalīfa al-Bosnawī (died in Amasya, 1565) published a composition on the art of governing, *Risālāt as-siyāsa ash-sharʿīya*, which was translated into Turkish by Shaykh al-Islām Muḥammad ʿĀrif Efendi.[89]

Darwīsh Ḥusām Boshnāḳ, whose life-story is unknown to us except for the report that he lived in Izmir (Smyrna), translated from Arabic into Turkish under the title *Lumʿat al-fawāʾid* (Rays of Light of the Advantages) a mathematical treatise by ʿAbdallāh ibn Ḥajjāj al-Yāsamīnī (died 1204).

Ḍiyāʾ-ad-Dīn Aḥmad ibn Muṣṭafā al-Mostārī, teacher at a theological seminary (died 1679), is the author of two manuals on Islamic law and the art of preaching: *Fatāwā-i Aḥmadīya* (Ahmad's Expert Opinion on Questions Pertaining to Jurisprudence), and *Anīs al-wāʿiẓīn* (Preachers' Friend); he also wrote *Tanwīr al-ḳulūb* (Clearing of the Hearts), a commentary to Al-Ḳudurī's *Al-Mukhtaṣar* (Compendium).[90]

Ḥasan ibn Ṣāliḥ ibn Muḥammad al-Podgorijawī (=Podgoričanin) commented on several excerpts from the theological-mystical work *Al-Futūḥāt al-makkīya fī maʿrifat asrār al-malakīya* (Meccan Revelations Concerning the Knowledge of Angelic Secrets) by Muḥyī-ʾd-Dīn ibn-ʿArabī (died 1240).[91]

Ḥasan ibn Turkhān al-Kāfī al-Akḥiṣārī (=Pruščak), a socio-political critic and one of the most original authors of the Ottoman Empire, was teacher and judge in Prusac, western Bosnia (d. 1616).[92] He was one of the first to recognize the signs and causes of the coming decline of the Ottoman Empire, and at a time when it was at its zenith. His treatise *Uṣūl al-ḥikam fī niẓām al- ʿālam* (Bases of the Wisdom for the Order of Ruling the World), in which, from the religious viewpoint, he explains the principles of the art of ruling, won him the epithet of "Bosnian Macchiavelli." This work was translated into Turkish, French, Hungarian, German, and Croatian.[93] Other works of Al-Akḥiṣārī have a marked religious character. Worthy of mention are: *Rawḍāt al-jannāt fī uṣūl al-iʿtiḳādāt* (Gardens of Eden within Dogmatics), *Ḥadīḳat aṣ-ṣalat allatī hiya raʾs al-ʿibādāt* (Garden of the Fruit

The Sparkling Ring-Jewel in the Biographies of the Scholars and Poets of Bosnia (Cairo, 1931), 106–7.

88/H. I. Mehinagić, "U spomen velikom merhumu Ali Fehmi ef. Džabiću"/In Memory of the Late Great Sir Ali Fehmi Džabić, *GVIS*, VII, no. 1–3 (Sarajevo, 1956), 22–30.

89/*GAL*, II, 665.

90 'Mostar," in *Enciklopedija Jugoslavije* (Zagreb: Leksikografski Zavod, 1955).

91/*GAL*, II, 443, 659.

92/*GAL*, I, 792.

93/The first translation into Turkish is by the author himself. A second Turkish translation was published in the newspaper *ʿAṣr* (Aṣir) *Istanbul* before the First World War. The French is by Garcin de Tassy, and the Hungarian by Janos Karacsónyi. From this last version E. Thallóczy made a German translation. The authors of two separate Croatian translations are Safvet Beg Bašagić and Mehmed Handžič. The last-mentioned commented on and edited this work in Arabic in 1927, in Cairo.

of Prayer, the Pearl of Devoutness), and *Samt al-wuṣūl fī ʿilm al-uṣūl* (Direction of Entry into Islamic Jurisprudence).

Ḥasan Spaho, Professor at the Islamic School for Judges in Sarajevo (died 1915), is the author of several works on the principles of jurisprudence. His work *Muntakhab al-Uṣūl li intidāb al-wuṣūl* (Selections for the Principles of Islamic Jurisprudence) was printed in 1906 in Cairo. This work has no originality but purports to reproduce selections from the ancient writers. A treatise on the Arabic metaphor and a commentary on the treatise *Fann-i munāẓāra* (The Art of Disputing) by his compatriot, Muṣṭafā ibn Yūsuf Ayyūbī-Zāde (see under relevant heading), have remained to us in manuscript.[94]

Ḥusayn Efendi al-Bosnawī called *Ḳoja Müʾerrikh* ("Great Historian"), a famous chronicler and administrator of the court-chancery in Istanbul (died 1644 or 1645), wrote a chronicle *Badāʾiʿ al-waqāʾiʿ* (Wonderful Events).[94a]

Ḥusayn Lā-Makānī (died 1625), author of a treatise on the oneness of the divine being in the mystical sense.

Ibrāhīm al-Ḳazzāz (died 1617), a philosopher of mysticism.

Ibrāhīm Adham Beg Bash-Agha-Zāde (Bašagić) of Nevesinje, Hercegovina (died 1902), was the first Bosniak to study the literary work, in oriental languages, of his compatriots. To this specialized interest we owe the biographies on *Darwīsh Pasha al-Mostārī, Muḥammad Nergisī as-Sarāyī*, and *Ḥasan al-Kāfī al-Aḳḥiṣārī*, which he published in the annals of the Bosnian government, the *Bosna Salnāmeleri*, shortly before the Austro-Hungarian occupation of 1878. Ibrāhīm Bash-Agha-Zāde, father of Safvet Beg Bašagić, one of the greatest Bosnian poets of the period between the world wars, also left a number of Turkish poems.

Ibrāhīm ibn ʿAbdallāh Pečewī (Alajbegović), financial administrator of Bosnia (died *ca.* 1650), is the author of a well-written history of the period 1520–1640. This man of learning is one of the rare early Ottoman historians who used western European sources as well as Muslim ones for their work. Apart from Turkish and Bosnian, Pečewī also knew Hungarian, which helped lead him to Latin sources.[95] Excerpts of Pečewī's history have been translated into German and Hungarian.

Ibrāhīm ibn Ḥājj Ismāʿīl al-Mostārī [Opijač] (born 1678; died in the first half of the eighteenth century) is the author of a biography of his teacher, Muṣṭafā ibn Yūsuf Ayyūbī-Zāde (see under relevant heading), one of the most learned Croatian Muslims of his day. His book is studded with sociopolitical observations, making reading a real pleasure, and has been translated into Croatian.[96]

94/*Tridesetgodišnji izvještaj Šeriatske sudačke škole u Sarajevu*/Thirty Years' Report of the Shariʿa School for Judges in Sarajevo (Sarajevo, 1917), 49.

94a/Edited by Turtinova: *Husayn, Qoja Müʾerrikh, Bedāʾiʿ ul-vekāʾiʿ* (Udivitelʾnye sabytija), Izdan. tekstra, ovedenie i obšč. red. A. S. Tvertinovoj, Č. 1. 2 (Moscow, 1961).

95/Franz Babinger, *Die Geschichtsschreiber der Osmanen und ihre Werke* (Leipzig, 1927), 192–5; Bursalĭ Meḥmed Ṭāhir, *ʿOthmanlĭ müellifleri*/Ottoman Writers, III (Istanbul, 1914–15), 333ff.; F. v. Kraelitz, "Ibrāhīm Pečewī," *Der Islam*, VIII (1918), 282–60.

96/Muhamed Mujić, "Biografija Mustafe Ejubovića (Šejh Jujo)"/Biography of Mustafa Ejubović (Shaykh Yuyo), *GVIS*, VIII, no. 1–3 (Sarajevo, 1956), 13.

Ibrāhīm ibn Tīmūr Khān al-Bosnawī, an established mystic writer, was head of a monastery of the Bayramī dervishes (died after 1618). His well-known work is *Muḥriḳat al-ḳulūb fī-ʾsh-shawḳ li ʿallām al-ghuyūb* (Stimulus of Hearts to the Love of the Omniscient).

Maḥmūd ibn Khalīl al-Mostārī (died 1688) is the author of commentary on Arabic metrics, *Kitāb al-ʿarūḍ*, by Muḥammad Abū-ʾl-Jaysh al-Andalūsī al-Anṣārī (died 1229), and of a work on Arabic rhetoric and stylistics, *Al-Badīʿ*.[97]

Meḥmed ʿAfwī, Mīr (died 1732), son of the Doghanjĭ Ḥusayn Pasha, is the author of a brief Turkish history. He also collaborated in the translation of the work *ʿIqd al-jumān fī taʾrīkh ahl az-zamān* (Chain of Pearls), a work on contemporary history, by Badr-ad-Dīn Aḥmad ibn Mūsā ʿAynī (died 1451), from the Arabic into Turkish.[98]

Meḥmed ʿArūḍī (died 1673) concerned himself with metrics in particular and poetry in general. He also worked as translator, translating from Arabic to Turkish the book *Talkhīṣ al-Miftāḥ*, an excerpt of As-Sakkākī's (died 1229) work on Arabic grammar, syntax, and rhetoric.

Meḥmed Čajno (died 1791) wrote a commentary to the *Isagoge* on logic.

Meḥmed Kāmil (died 1897), a hagiographer.

Meḥmed Tawfīk Okić (Yayčalĭ Mehmed Tawfīḳ), a historian of Turkish literature in Bosnia, lived in the second half of the nineteenth century.

Muḥammad Anwarī [*Kadić*] (1855–1931) was the greatest collector of records pertaining to the Turkish period of Bosnian history. He left more than 10,000 pages of neatly and legibly entered chronicles and copies of whole documents. The work covers the period from 1346 to 1921. The original is kept in the Ghāzī Khusrew Beg Library in Sarajevo.

Muḥammad Hawāʾī Ǚskūfī (died about 1651) is the author of a rhymed Turkish-Bosnian dictionary, *Maḳbūl-i ʿārif* or *Potur Shāhidīya*.

Muḥammad ibn Muḥammad al-Bosnawī al-maʿrūf bi-ʾl-Khānjī (Mehmed Handžić),[99] professor of the Islamic College in Sarajevo, died in 1944. When still a student he published in Cairo a survey on the history of literature, *Al-jawhar al-asnā fī tarājīm ʿulamāʾ wa shuʿarāʾ Bosna* (The Sparkling Ring-Jewel in the Biographies of the Scholars and Poets of Bosnia). In the course of his later life, he wrote numerous articles and studies as well as several poems in Arabic. Handžić (al-Khānjī) was primarily a teacher and transmitter of knowledge on the Orient. Only secondarily was he a research scholar. Nevertheless, in his historical work and his contribution to the history of literature he pointed out the contribution of Bosnian Muslims to oriental culture, and he also called attention to the new discoveries of research regarding the islamization of Bosnia. However, the major part of his work focused on theology.

Muḥammad ibn Mūsā as-Sarāyī al-Bosnawī,[100] chief justice for the region of Aleppo, Syria (died 1635), became famous for his encyclopedic knowl-

97/*GAL*, I, 544.

98/Babinger, *Die Geschichtsschreiber der Osmanen und ihre Werke*, 266–7.

99/Mustafa Busuladžić, "Lo scrittore Hadži Mehmed Handžić di Sarajevo"/ Hadži Mehmed Handžić, the Writer of Sarajevo, *Oriente Moderno*, XXII (1942), 173–8.

100/*GAL*, I, 417, 466, 516, 534, 740.

edge. Thus he was called "ʿAllāmek" ("The Little Know-all" as distinct from "ʿAllām," which means "omniscient," i.e. God). Apart from an unfinished commentary to the Ḳurʾān-exegesis of Bayḍāwī (died 1286), *Anwār at-tanzīl wa asrār at-taʾwīl* (Lights of Revelation and the Secrets of Interpretation), he also wrote a glossary to the manual on logic, *Ar-Risālat ash-shamsīya fī-ʾl-ḳawāʿid al-manṭiḳīya* (Essay Full of Sunlight on the Rules of Logic) by Al-Ḳazwīnī al-Kātibī (died 1283); a commentary to *Miftāḥ al-ʿulūm* (Key of the Sciences), a famous work on Arabic grammar, syntax, and rhetoric by As-Sakkākī (died 1229); and a number of other commentaries and supplements.[101]

Muḥammad Muḥtashim Shaʿbān-Zāde [or Šabanović] (died 1694) wrote a treatise on legal proceedings under Islamic law entitled *Ādāb al-ḥukkām* (The Deportment of Judges); and a paper, "Risālāt as-sayfīya wa-ʾl-ḳalamīya" (Essay on the Sword and the Pen).[102]

Muḥammad (Meḥmed) Rafiḳ Efendī (Hadžiabdić), head of the Islamic community of the Ottoman Empire (Shaykh al-Islām) (died 1872), wrote *Nuḳūl al-fatāwa al-fāʾidīya* (Transmission of Valuable Expert Opinions on Jurisprudence).

Muṣṭafā ibn Yūsuf al-Mostārī Ayyūbī-Zāde (Ejubović), called *Shaykh Yuyo*, mufti of Mostar (died 1707), acquired a reputation as an expert on logic, rhetoric, philology, astronomy, geometry, and Islamic philosophy. The following are a few of his works, some original, some commentaries: commentary to the *Kitāb al-Isāgūjī* (Book Isagoge) by Athīr-ad-Dīn al-Abḥārī (died 1265); *Khulāṣat al-adab* (Extract of Literature), commentary to the work *Tahdhīb al-manṭiḳ wa-l-kalām* (The Teaching of Logic and Apologetic) by Saʿd-ad-Dīn at-Taftāzānī (died 1390); a commentary on the manual of Arabic grammar *Kitāb al-unmūdhaj* (Model-Book) by Az-Zamaksharī (died 1144); a glossary to *Ar-Risālat ash-shamsīya fī-ʾl-ḳawāʿid al-manṭiḳīya* (Essay Full of Sunlight on the Rules of Logic) of Al-Ḳazwīnī al-Kātibī; and a commentary on *Miftāḥ al-ḥuṣūl li Mirʾāt al-uṣūl fī* sharḥ Mirḳāt al-wuṣūl (Key to the "Mirror of Jurisprudence" in the Commentary "Mirḳāt al-wuṣūl").[103]

Muṣṭafā Ṣidḳī Ḳarā-Beg, mufti of Mostar, murdered on the eve of the occupation of Bosnia in 1878, left commentaries on various works on Islamic law, among which is a commentary on *Mirʾāt al-uṣūl* (Mirror of Jurisprudence) by Mullā Khusraw aṭ-Ṭarsūsī. Ḳarā-Beg wrote in Arabic.

Naṣūḥ ibn ʿAbdallāh (Ḳarā-Göz) as-Silāḥī al-Wisoḳawī al-Miṭrāḳī (Matrakčǐ Nasuh) (died *ca.* 1564) was famous as a mathematician, historian, calligrapher, painter, and fencing-master;[104] however, little is known of his personal life history. His works are a Turkish translation of the *Universal History* of Aṭ-Ṭabarī (died 923), *Majmaʿ at-tawārīkh* (Historical Collection), *Tuhfat al-mulūk* (Gift of the Kings), *Jamāl al-kitāb wa kamāl al-ḥisāb* (The Beauty of the Book and the Perfection of Mathematics), two

101/Mehmed Handžić, *Al-jawhar al-asnā*, 116–18; *GAL*, I, 516.

102/*Türk Ansiklopedisi*, VII, 403.

103/*Mirʾāt al-uṣūl* was written by Mullā Khusraw aṭ-Tarsūsī (died 1480).

104/Huseyin G. Yurdaydǐn, *Matrakçǐ Nasuh* (Ankara: University of Ankara, 1963), 30; *GAL*, II, 1024 (F *6*). "As-Salāmī," given in Brockelmann in place of "As-Silāḥī," is incorrect.

mathematical treatises, *Tuḥfat al-ghuzāt* (Gift for the Heroes), a manual of fencing, and many more.

Nūrallāh Munīrī al-Beligrādī al-Bosnawī (died 1617) wrote a geographical study in Turkish, *Sabʿīyāt* (The Seven Climatic Regions), and some other primarily mystical works.

Sayfallāh al-Bosnawī Proho, teacher at the Sharīʿa college of judges at Sarajevo (died 1932), wrote in Arabic quite a few studies on Islamic law, theology, and pedagogy. The following deserve mention: *Kitāb an-nikāḥ* (Book on Matrimony), *Zubdat al-farāʾid* (Cream of Science on the Law of Inheritance), *Hadiyat aṭ-ṭullāb fī uslūb muṭālaʿat al-Kitāb* (Gift to the Pupils for Mastering the Methodology of Reading the Ḳurʾān), and *Aḥsan al wasīla fī maʿrifat al-waṣāyā wa-ʾl-waṣīya* (About the Testament).[105]

Tayyib Okić, professor of theology in Ankara, worked in Islamic tradition and historical research. His major works in Turkish are: *Bazĭ hadis meseleleri üzerinde tetkikler* (Studies on Some Ḥadīth Questions), *Osmanlĭ devrinde Balkanlardaki ihtidalarla ilgili bazĭ vesikalar* (Some Deeds in Connection with Conversions to Islam in the Balkans during the Ottoman Era), *Bir tenkidin tenkidi* (Criticism of Critique),[106] *Uṣūl al-ḥadīth* (Terminology and Methodology of the Science of Tradition), and *Sarĭ Saltĭka ait bir fetwa* (A Legal Vote Pertaining to Sarĭ Saltiq̌).

ʿUmar Efendī (Elkazović-Čaušević), judge in Bosanski Novi (died 1740), is the author of a beautifully compiled history of the defensive wars of Bosnia under Ḥakīm-Oghlu ʿAlī Pasha (1735–40). This book, *Ghazawāt-i diyār-i Bosna* (Victorious Campaigns of the Country of Bosnia), has been translated into German, English, and Swedish.[107]

ʿUthmān ibn ʿAbd-ar-Raḥmān al-Beligrādī, a medical practitioner, translated into Turkish, sometime around 1770, Mattiolis' commentary to the six books by Dioskurides (*De materia medica*) on pharmacology and botany.

ʿUṯhmān ibn Ibrāhīm Boshnāḳ, a contemporary of ʿUmar Efendī (Elkazović-Čaušević), is the author of the work *Taḥḳīḳ an-nīyāt* (Examining the Intentions), in which he compiles what has been handed down on the moral value of religious deeds, taking as his basis for judgment the intent of the author in each individual case.[108]

The Turkish Encyclopedia (*Türk Ansiklopedisi*),[109] without giving adequate biographical and bibliographical data, mentions in addition the following learned Bosniaks of the Ottoman era:

ʿAbdallāh al-Khurramī al-Mostārī, writer of travel stories, drawer of geographical diagrams and sketches.

Ḥājj Yūsuf, a *muʾadhdhin* from Duvno in western Bosnia, wrote in 1618 an account of his travels to Mecca. It is the oldest of a dozen extant descrip-

105/*GAL*, II, 870.

106/The work contains data on the spread of Islam in southeastern Europe in pre-Ottoman days.

107/The German translation by J. H. Dubski, published in Vienna in 1789, is very good.

108/According to the *Türk Ansiklopedisi*, the title of this work is *Taḥḳīḳ aḳsām an-nīyāt* (see the article "Bosna").

109/*Türk Ansiklopedisi*, VII, 403, 408–9.

tions of travels to Mecca written in Turkish, Arabic, and Croatian during the Ottoman period. It is, as far as we know to date, also the best.[110]

Ḥusayn Ḥusnī al-Mostārī, writer of essays on logic and the art of preaching.

Meḥmed Emīn Serdarević (died about 1920), scholar of the art of preaching.

Meḥmed Khalīfa ibn Ḥusayn (died 1634 or 1635), a chronicler.

Muḥammad ibn Yūsuf Sūdī-Čelebī of Fojnica, mufti and author of treatises on rhetoric.

Muḥammad Rifāʿī-Zāde Khalīl Ṣidḳī al-Bosnawī, author of works on Arabic philology.

Muṣṭafā Aḥmad-Zāde al-Beligrādī, a chronicler.

Muṣṭafā al-Bosnawī, a commentator on the mystical poetic work *Al-Mathnawī* by Jalāl-ad-Dīn ar-Rūmī (died 1273).

Muṣṭafā al-Khurramī (eighteenth century), a biographer.

Ṣāliḥ Ṣidḳī al-Bosnawī, author of a methodology of historical research, *Uṣūl at-taʾrīkh.*

The following Bosnians have continued to work in the tradition of the Ottoman period, writing in various fields in Oriental languages since the late nineteenth century:

Haris Korkut and *Kāmil Y. Avdić*, in Egypt and Lebanon, have done research on the earliest Arab-Slav relations and on the history of Islam. The former wrote a study on the historical background of the present situation of the Bosnian-Hercegovinian Muslims (in Arabic), a study on mixed marriages in the light of the Sharīʿa, and a treatise on the forgiveness of sins and repentance, *Risāla fī-ʾl-kaffārāt* (in Croatian and partly in Arabic). The latter served on the editorial staff of several Arabic and Pakistani magazines.

Ali Šuliak wrote several works on the nature of cooperatives and interest-free banking systems, such as *Waqāʾiʿ al-iḳtiṣād at-taʿawunī* (also under the French title: Les Faits de l'économie coopérative) and *Makān at-taʿāwun fī- ʾl-ḥayāt ar-rīfiya* (La Place de la coopération dans la vie rurale).

Hasanefendić, a Hercegovinian scholar about whose career and work we have, unfortunately, no details, worked in the years between the two world wars, in Lahore, a center of Islamic culture in Asia.[111]

The following Bosniaks were journalists of the late Ottoman Empire and the late nineteenth and early twentieth centuries:

Muḥammad Shākir (Kurtćehajić) (died 1870), editor of the bilingual periodical *Bosna* (Sarajevo, in Turkish and Croatian).

Hersekli Aḥmad Sharīf, editor of the newpaper *Sharq we Kurdistān* (Istanbul, beginning in 1908), published twice a week.

Bosnalǐ Meḥmed Nūr-ad-Dīn, publisher and editor of the weekly *Bosna* (Istanbul, beginning 1908).

Ziya Shakir Soko, journalist and writer.

110/Hasan H. Ljubunčić, *Put na hadž*/Pilgrimage to Mecca (Sarajevo: Veselin Masleša, 1955), 96.

111/According to information from Mr. Mehmed Reszulović, a former officer of the Hungarian army, who visited India (today's Pakistan) in 1936 or 1937 as a member of a Hungarian delegation.

POETS

ʿAbd-al-Karīm ibn Muḥammad al-Bosnawī as-Sāmiʿī of Sarajevo (died 1685) wrote poems in Arabic and Turkish. Whereas the first are without exception beautiful and pleasing, the latter seem artificial and, therefore, of lesser value. Works: a dīwān; an appendix to the *Siyar-i Nabī* (Biography of the Emissary of God), by Uways ibn Muḥammad Waysī; and *Munshaʿāt,* a collection in which he vies with Muhammad Nergisī (see under proper heading) in composing epistles.

ʿAbdallāh al-Bosnawī al-Ghāʾibī of the seventeenth century was known as a mystic poet and saint. His poems are collected in a dīwān.

ʿAbdallāh Efendī Ṣarī was a poet from Užice who died in 1687; he composed a dīwān as well as a "Ghazānāme" (Victory Book) and several epitaphs.

ʿAbdallāh Efendī Fāʾiḍ (died 1688) was the youngest son of the poet ʿAbd-al-Karīm as-Sāmiʿī (see under that name), and also wrote dīwāns.

ʿAbdallāh ibn Bashīr ibn Muḥyī-ʾd-Dīn al-Bosnawī (died in 1710) was called by the nickname "Māhir," i.e. "The Skillful." He was a teacher, and then judge at Mecca and several other places, and was author of a dīwān.

Abū Bakr Agha Dhikrī, a feudal tenant of Užice (died 1688), wrote poems about his love of his native country.

Aḥmad Efendī Ṭālib, called Süleymaniyeli Aḥmad (died 1669), was a poet well versed in both Turkish and Persian, who held the position of army camp commandant under the grand vizier Ahmad Köprülü (Čuprilić).

Aḥmad ibn ʿUthmān Shāhdī Aḳowalī-Zāde (died 1754), son of the founder of a public library in Sarajevo, wrote a number of poems in Arabic, Turkish, and Persian. He left, apart from his scientific works, a complete dīwān and a poem on ethics.

Aḥmad Pasha Hersek Oghlu (died 1514), grand vizier under Mehmed II, Bayazid II, and Selim I, composed poems under the assumed name of "Shīrī."

Aḥmad Walī of Novi Pazar (died 1598) deserves mention as an author of love poems.

ʿAlāʾ-ad-Dīn ʿAlī ibn ʿAbdallāh al-Bosnawī Thābit of Užice (died 1712), judge, mufti, and mulla, left, apart from two complete dīwāns, four other rhymed works: *Edhem we Humā* (Edhem and Huma),[112] *Berbernāme* (The Book of the Berber), *Derenāme* (The Book of the Valley), and *Ẓafernāme* (The Book of Victory). Thābit was unusually versatile, and could express well-known proverbs and other familiar phrases and sayings in neat epigrams, often enlivened by a dash of humor, which at once gained for him great popularity, of which the shadow at least remains to the present day. "Thābit may fairly claim to be the first to introduce the spirit of humour into Ottoman poetry."[113] In Thābit's dīwāns we meet descriptions of spring, winter, the new moon, the hyacinth, as well as poems to celebrate festivals and special occasions, such as the promotion of military judges and professors; a beautiful peace poem on the occasion of the signing of the peace treaty of Karlowitz in 1699; a poem on the nocturnal ascent into

112/Josef Hammer-Purgstall, *Geschichte der osmanischen Dichtkunst* (4 vols.; Pesht, 1836–8), IV, 41.

113/E. J. W. Gibb, *A History of Ottoman Poetry,* ed. E. G. Browne (6 vols.; London: Luzac and Co., 1900–9), IV, 16.

heaven of Muḥammad; and several *ḳaṣīdas*.[114] From the poem on the nocturnal ascent of Muḥammad into heaven ("Miʿrājīya") the two following passages have been translated by E. J. W. Gibb.[115] The first of the two passages opens the poem and describes the night when the Ascension of the Prophet into heaven took place. The second relates what happened to the Prophet when in his heavenly journey he reached "the Lote-Tree beyond which none may pass," and had to leave behind his guide Gabriel and his steed Burāḳ.

MIʿRĀJĪYA

All hail to thee. O happy-starred, o favoured and most blessed night,
The title of whose fame's the head-line of the chapter *Isrā* hight.[116]
Before the sun-bride's radiant face the evening hung a rosy veil.
The stellar largesse[117] yielded matchless gems untold and infinite.
'Twas ne'er the lunar disc; the gloomy deep of night did surge and swell,
Whereon the raying waves cast up a fish with golden scales and bright.
The hour had o'er its gold-embroidered raimenture of orange-hue
A flowered cloak of ambergris with flashing jewelled buttons dight.[118]
Th' Efrāsiyāb-night laid beneath his hand the Khusrew-day's domain;[119]
And let illumine all the skies in honour of his conquering might.

* * *

What time they reached unto the Lote-Tree[120] still the Bird Celestial
  bode[121]
For unto him the Lote-Tree formed the term of his permitted flight.
The heaven-scouring steed Burāk[122] did likewise cease to prance and
  play,
For this that neither horse nor steed had part on yonder peerless site.
Thereon the Refref[123] came anear with lowly reverence to serve,

114/The *ḳaṣīda* is a longer lyrical poem or poem for a set purpose, with the two first lines rhyming with one another and with every subsequent second line. The *ḳaṣīda* is used mainly for panegyrics.

115/The verses that follow can be found in their original text in Gibb, *A History of Ottoman Poetry*, VI, 234–5; the English text appears in the same work (IV, 22–23), and the explanations of foreign words given below are taken from Gibb's notes on 22–23).

116/The seventeenth chapter of the Ḳurʾān is entitled "Isrā," because the word *isrā*, meaning "night journey," occurs in the opening verse.

117/[*Sachi*, like the Arabic *nithār*, denotes coins cast about on occasions of rejoicing. Ed.]

118/The starry night succeeding the sunset.

119/Efrāsiyāb was the legendary Turanian King whose wars with Rustam and other Persian heroes in the time of Kay-Kāʾūs and Kay Khusraw fill so large a portion of the Shāh-Nāme.

120/The Lote-Tree which marks the spot in Heaven beyond which even the angels may not pass, hence called *Sidrat al-muntahā*, "the Lote-Tree of the Limit."

121/I.e., Gabriel the Archangel.

122/Burāḳ, "the Flashing Steed," that bore the Prophet from earth to this point in Heaven.

123/The Refref, presumably a kind of throne, is the name of the last vehicle which bore the Prophet on this famous journey.

And sky-like gave its heart as station for yon Sun of beauty bright[124]
Therewith he passed through many an hundred thousand veils of light and dark,
Then stopped the Refref too, and Ahmed[125] went alone without affright.
He reached unto a region where the six directions were no more,
Where earth and sky were not, and where all roof and floor were lost to sight.
A wondrous world was yonder world, with no beginning and no end,
Where voice and ear and speech and mind and reason were forgot outright.

The following is one of Thābit's *ghazals*:[126]

Fain to hid his wine, the zealot passioned to his bosom's core
Hangs his prayer-rug as a curtain there before the tavern-door.
In his night-clothes sweat the lover as 'twere with the sweat of doom
While he stripped that wanton beauty even to the shift she wore.
Casting down her hook-like tresses, searcheth she her chin's sweet well
For the heart therein that's fallen of her lover all forlore.
That she looks not on her lover comes of her abounding grace;
From her eyen's shafts she guardeth him who doth herself adore.
Loosen not thy locks, let not them fall, by that fair head of thine!
Bind not Thābit's still free spirit in the chains of anguish sore.[127]

ʿAlī-Beg Shīrī, son of the grand vizier Aḥmad Pasha Hersek-Oghlu, educated at the court of Selim I (1467–1520), died a young man in 1528. He was an author of emotional ghazals and of a treatise on the conquest of Egypt by the Turks in 1517, *Taʾrīkh-i fatḥ-i Miṣr.*

ʿAlī-Beg Užičewī al-Wuṣlatī, son of a pasha, commandant of Smederevo, fell in battle against the Germans in 1688. He created one of the most beautiful epics of Turkish literature, *Ghazānāme-i Čehrin* (Book on the Victory at *Czygrihn*, 1678), and several chronograms as well as a poem in praise of the sultan on the occasion of the building of the summer palace.

ʿAlī ʿĀlī al-Bosnawī (Bosnewi-Baba),[128] whose life history is still unknown, was a judge and talented lyricist whose "mastery of poetry stood unques-

124/I.e. the Prophet.
125/I.e. Muḥammad.
126/The *ghazal* has the same rhyming sequence as the *ḳaṣīda* but is shorter and more varied in content. It consists of no fewer than five and no more than seven distiches, and the last one usually contains the name or pen-name of the poet.
127/E. J. W. Gibb, *A History of Ottoman Poetry*, IV, 26.
128/It is not known when ʿAlī ʿĀlī al-Bosnawī lived. Mehmed Handžić, *Književni rad bosansko-hercegovačkih muslimana*/The Literary Activity of Bosnian and Hercegovinian Muslims (Sarajevo, 1934), gives the year 1646 as the date of his death. The Turkish literary historian Sadeddin Nuzhet Ergun has discovered a poem by al-Bosnawī in which persons of the nineteenth century are mentioned, which would mean that he was one of the late poets. However, it seems to me that, because the possibility of interpolation in this poem cannot be ruled out, the question of the death date of al-Bosnawī must be left open. Ergun did not find any concrete data about him. See S. N. Ergun, *Bektaşi edebiyatï antolojisï*/Anthology of Bektaşi Literature (Istanbul, 1965), vol. 3, p. 139.

tioned by anyone" (*Ṣafā'ī*). Author of a complete dīwān, ʿAlī left among his philosophical-mystical poems several of winning beauty and depth.

ʿAlī ibn Ḥājj Muṣṭafā Boshnāḳ (died in Sarajevo, 1640) wrote simple and lucid verses. He is the author of a book written in prose and poetry on the merits of battle, *Faḍā'il al-jihād*.

ʿĀrif Ḥikmat Beg ibn Dhī-'l-Fiḳār Nāfidh Pasha Hersekli from Mostar (died 1903) was considered a great poet by his contemporaries. He is the last of the great dīwān poets and in a certain sense the last Ottoman classicist. His works include a large and a small dīwān, *Lawā'iḥ al-ḥikam* (The Tablets of Wisdom), *Lawāmiʿ al-afkār* (Highlights of Thoughts); *Fuṣūṣ al-islām* (The Great Pearls of Islam), a treatise in which he refutes several passages of the famous code of laws, *Majalla*. ʿĀrif Ḥikmat was a judge by profession.

ʿĀzim ibn Muḥammad, a member of the *Šabanović* (Shaʿbān-Zāde) family (died 1712), was a teacher at a medresse, completed the epic *Laylā and Majnūn* by Ḳāf-Zāde, and composed a dīwān.

Darwīsh Muḥammad Maylī of Sarajevo, Ḳadarite mystic (died 1781), was looked upon by the other members of his order as a distinguished poet.

Darwīsh Pasha Bāyazīd-Agha-Zāde (Bajezidagić) al-Mostārī (died 1603), governor of Bosnia, favorite of Sultan Murād III, to whom he dedicated a poem *Murādnāme*, translated the *Sakhānāme* (Book on Generosity) by Binā'ī from Persian into Turkish and wrote simple and beautiful love, religious, and patriotic poems. One of his two or three dīwāns is in Persian. Darwīsh Pasha also wrote an equivalent of the *Al-Mathnawī* of Jalāl-ad-Dīn ar-Rūmī and lovely poems in praise of his home town, Mostar.[129]

Darwīsh Serwī (died 1494) was one of the oldest Ottoman poets of Bosnia.

Fawzī, shaykh of a dervish monastery in Blagaj (died *ca.* 1747), ranked among the best poets of his day in European Turkey. Apart from a dīwān of his own, he left a Persian poem called *Bulbulistān* (Nightingale Grove) as a compliment to Saʿdī's *Gulistān* (Rose Garden).

Ḥabīb Ḥabībī-Dede (died 1643), a Mawlawī mystic, preached renunciation. Old Turkish records and chronicles tell of his witty though extravagant sallies.

Ḥabība, daughter of the vizier ʿAlī Pasha Rizvanbegović-Stočević of Hercegovina (died 1890), became well known as a composer of emotional ghazals.

Ḥasan Efendī Ḍiyā'ī of Mostar (died 1564/65), teacher at a medresse, is the author of a dīwān.

Ḥasan ibn Muṣṭafā al-Bosnawī, who died at the beginning of the nineteenth century at Medina, was one of the most well-known Bosnian poets writing in Arabic; he left a dīwān. His patriotic poem on the scenic beauty of Bosnia also deserves mention.

Ḥasan Naẓmī-Dede of Sarajevo (died 1713), member of the Mawlawī order, is the author of a dīwān dedicated to problems of more profound devoutness.

Ḥasan Ḳā'imī Baba (died 1691), senior of the Khalwatī dervish congregation and a fighter against the arbitrariness of the feudal lords in eastern Bosnia,

129/Poems can be found in Gibb, *A History of Ottoman Poetry*, v, 105.

died in exile. He left a dīwān, a prophetic mystic poem called "Wāridāt," and several didactic poems. Some of his literary works were written in his native Croatian.

Hižir (Khiḍr) Āsāfī (died 1621), a humorist, was a skillful composer of riddle-poems and an expert writer of Persian.[130]

Ḥusayn Agha Sipāhī (died 1605) wrote mediocre love poems.[131]

Ḥusayn Efendī Mīrī Alaybeg-Zāde (died 1691), teacher at Firūz Agha's Medresse in Sarajevo, was the author of a dīwān.

Ḥusayn Lā-Makānī (died 1625), a Bayramī shaykh, preached loving God to the point of self-abnegation.

Ibrāhīm Bezmī, son of Ramaḍān (died 1683), clerk and secretary, took part in the siege of Vienna as commandant of a military unit. Severely wounded, he died at the walls of the besieged city. He left a dīwān.

Ibrāhīm ibn Ḥājj Ismāʿīl al-Mostārī [Opijač] (died in the first half of the eighteenth century), jurist and biographer (see entry under prose writers), successfully tried his hand at poems in Turkish. His attempts at poetry in Arabic, however, were a failure.

Intiẓāmī al-Bosnawī, of the seventeenth century, suspected of heresy, wrote a poetic work, *Tuḥfat al-ikhwān* (Gift of the Brothers), treating Islamic moral teachings and the Turko-Austrian war.

Khalwatī-skaykh Muḥammad Fawzī of Sarajevo (died 1673), wrote poems expressing a reaction, characteristic of mystics, against the formalism of the scribes and their rational methods of teaching.

Meḥmed-Beg Yaḥyā-Pasha-Zāde, Ghāzī (died 1597 or 1591) was the author of a dīwān.

Meḥmed Efendī Rifdī (died 1721/22), son of ʿAbd-al-Karīm as-Sāmiʿī of Sarajevo, a teacher and mulla, left a dīwān.

Muḥammad Čāqī ʿArshī of Novi Pazar (died 1570), author of several ghazals and numerous chronograms, is more highly thought of as a scientist, though his poems are equally deserving of mention.

Muḥammad Nergisī as-Sarāyī (died 1634), historian, "deserves to be called the Turkish Narcissus for his works as composer of letters and prose writer."[132] Virtuoso in allegoric presentations and plays on words, Nergisī knew how to make his prose and poetry colorful and interesting. The collection of his prose writing, punctuated by poems, makes up a *Khamsa* (Quintet): (1) *Nihālistān* (Nucleus), (2) *Kīmiyā-i saʿāda* (Chemistry of Bliss), (3) *Ḳānūn ar-rushd* (Canon of the Right Way), (4) *Mashāḳḳ al-ʿushshāḳ* (The Torments of the Lovers), and (5) *Ghazawāt-i Maslama* (Maslama's Campaigns).[133]

Mulḥid Waḥdatī or *Bosnalı Vahdeti* is the pseudonym of a free-thinking gnostic who died in 1598, and whose thoughts remind one of a certain patarene slant. As his pseudonym, under which he is recorded in literary history, reveals, he was suspected of heresy. Works: a dīwān and *Waḥdetnāme* (Book on the Oneness of God).

Muṣṭafā is a poet of an unidentified period, who wrote in a language which is

130/Hammer-Purgstall, *Geschichte der osmanischen Dichtkunst*, IV, 74.
131/Gibb, IV, no. 2, 115.
132/Hammer-Purgstall, 15.
133/Gibb, III, 208; IV, 254; V, 16.

a mixture of Croatian and Turkish. Otto Blau translated into German a beautiful amorous complaint written by him.[134]

Muṣṭafā Ladunnī, secretary of the Imperial Dīwān (Council) and head of the office of the *vojvoda* of Walachia, was killed when the Germans took his master prisoner in 1715. He worked on a commentary of the Persian poet Shawkat, and became famous when he improvised a Persian poem before the shah during a visit to Isfahan.

Muṣṭafā Mukhliṣī Boshnāḳ of Gornji Vakuf lived in the eighteenth century and left a versified description of his pilgrimage to Mecca in 1748. Apart from this work in Turkish, Mukhliṣī, inspired by Persian works, wrote several beautiful Persian poems.

Muṣṭafā Sipāhī, or perhaps *Siyāhī* (died 1651), left two kasīdas as well as lamentations on the deaths of two statesmen of his time, Khusrew and Ḥāfiẓ Pasha, who were executed.

Niʿmatī of Novi Pazar (died 1603) is a "poet-Bohemian" who indulged in the pleasures of life.

Rajab-Dede ʿAdanī (died 1684), head of the Mawlawī monastery in Belgrade, wrote rhymed glossaries under the title *Nakhl-i tajallī* (Palm of Ecstacy) to the love poems from ar-Rūmī's *Al-Mathnawī.*

Ṣāliḥ Fākhir[135] (died 1715), imām of several begler-begs, Imperial Council secretary, and accountant of the state treasury, wrote mediocre verses.

Ṣāliḥ Shānī of Sarajevo (died 1601), teacher at a medresse, acquired some reputation for writing ghazals.[136]

*Sayf-ad-Dın Kemur*a, a dervish of Sarajevo (died 1917), did historical research and wrote, under the pseudonym Fahmī, occasional verses and inscriptions on tombstones.

Sayyid Muḥammad Fāḍil Pasha (died 1882/83), member of the Šerifović family, wrote a dīwān and a chronicle.

Shīr ʿAlī Ferīdūn of Sarajevo, a public scribe (died 1658), wrote some dīwān-lyrics.[137]

Sulaymān Mazāḳī of Hercegovina (died 1677), master at writing petitions and one of the gentlemen of the Imperial Dīwān (Council), may be regarded as the court poet of the grand vizier Aḥmad Pasha Köprülü (1635–76). Author of several ḳaṣīdas, ghazals, and chronograms, which sometimes reveal a real poetic gift, he forms with ʿĀlī, Thābit, Nergisī, al-Wuṣlatī, and ʿĀrif Ḥikmat Hersekli the group of the best Bosnian poets of the Ottoman period.[138]

Sulaymān Zulfatī al-Bosnawī was personal servant to Sultan Aḥmed II (1643–95) and brother of the vizier Mehmed Pasha. He left his post as teacher at the Serai and became a secretary. Zulfatī wrote mediocre verses in the manner of his times.

134/"ʿAbd-al-Muṣṭafā," Otto Blau, *Bosnisch-türkische Sprachdenkmäler*, 118–20.

135/Hammer-Purgstall, IV, 81, where he incorrectly gives the poet's name as Fakhri.

136/Aḥmad ibn Khalīl Taşköprü-Zāde, *Ash-Shaḳā'iḳ an-nuʿmānīya*, I, 457–8.

137/Muṣṭafā Ṣafā'ī, *Tadhkira-i Ṣafā'ī* (Manuscript in the Austrian National Library, HO 139), 181.

138/*Ibid.*, 225f.; Hammer-Purgstall, *Geschichte der osmanischen Dichtkunst*, III, 12–15.

ʿUthmān Ḥilmī Beg, ʿUmar Čelebi's son, member of the Bosnian aristocratic family Ljubović of Herceg Novi; died in the second half of the seventeenth century. He wrote nostalgic poems about his homeland and love.

Wajdī (died 1669), Mawlawī dervish, was head of the Yeni Shehir monastery; he left a dīwān.

Yūsuf Efendī ʿĀṣim, called Čelebī ʿĀṣim (died 1710), court scribe in Sarajevo, is the author of a dīwān. Among his most noteworthy works are an Ascension poem and several epitaphs.

Zakarīya ibn ʿAbdallāh as-Sukkarī (died 1687), secretary to the imperial chancellery, left a dīwān.

Bibliography

"Arabica," *Enciklopedija Jugoslavije,* I. Zagreb: Leksikografski Zavod, 1955.

Arseven, Celal Esad. "Banaluka," *San'at Ansiklopedisi*/Encyclopedia of Arts. Istanbul, 1943.

Ayverdi, Ekrem Hakkĭ. *Yugoslavya'da Türk abideleri ve vakĭflarĭ*/Turkish Monuments in Yugoslavia and Their Founders. (Vakĭflar Dergisi," III.) Ankara, 1956.

Babinger, Franz. *Die Geschichtsschreiber der Osmanen und ihre Werke.* Leipzig, 1927.

—— "Ein türkischer Stiftungsbrief des Nerkesī vom Jahre 1029 (1620)," *Mitteilungen zur osmanische Geschichte,* I (1921–32), 151–66.

—— "Fünf bosnisch-osmanische Geschichtsschreiber," *Glasnik zemaljskog muzeja,* XL (1930), 169–72.

—— *Aus Südslaviens Turkenzeit.* Zwei grossherrliche Schenkungsbriefe für Bosniaken Ibrahim Pascha und Mustafa Agha. Berlin, 1927.

Baghdādī, Ismāʿīl Pasha, Al-. *Hadīyat al-ʿārifīn: Asmā' al-mu'allifīn wa āthār al-muṣannifīn*/A Gift for the Experts: Names of the Authors and Works of the Writers. Vol. I. Istanbul, 1951.

Bajraktarević, Fehim. "Les Études islamiques en Yougoslavie," *Archiv orientalni,* III (1937), 492–509.

Balagija, Abduselam. *Les Musulmans Yugoslaves.* Étude sociologique. ("Publications de l'Institut d'études orientales," IX.) Alger: Faculté des lettres, 1940.

Balić, Smail. "Der orientalische Handschriftenschatz von Bosnien," in *Festschrift Ernst Trenkler.* Dargeboten von Freunden. Kollegen und Mitarbeitern. Wien: Hrsg. v. Josef Stummvoll. 1968. *Biblos,* XVII (1968). 19–25.

—— "Europas orientalische Kaligraphen und Miniaturmaler," *Biblos,* XVII (1968), 265–76.

Bartók, Béla, and Lord, Albert B. *Serbo-Croatian Folk Songs.* New York: Columbia University Press, 1951.

Bašagić, Safvetbeg. *Bošnjaci i Hercegovci u islamskoj književnosti*/Bosnians and Hercegovinians in Islamic Literature. Sarajevo, 1912.

—— *Znameniti Hrvati Bošnjaci i Hercegovci u turskoj carevini*/Famous Croats, Bosniaks, and Hercegovinians in the Ottoman Empire. Zagreb, 1931.

Begović, Mehmed. *De l'Évolution du droit musulman en Yougoslavie.* Alger, 1930.

Bejtić, Alija. "Spomenici osmanlijske arhitekture u Bosni i Hercegovini"/ Monuments of Ottoman Architecture in Bosnia and Hercegovina, *Prilozi za orijentalnu filologiju i istoriju jugoslovenskih naroda pod turkskom vladavinom.* III–IV (Sarajevo, 1952–3), 229–96.

Benac, A., Sergejevski, D., and Mazalić, Dj. *Kulturna istorija Bosne i Hercegovine*/Cultural History of Bosnia and Hercegovina. Sarajevo, 1955.

Bešlagić, Refik. *Srednjevjekovni nadgrobni spomenici*/Medieval Tombstones. ("Kupres." v.) Sarajevo, 1954.

Blašković, Jozef (ed.). *Handschriften, arabische, türkische und persische, der Universitätsbibliothek in Bratislava.* Bratislava, 1961.

Blau, Otto. *Bosnisch-türkische Sprachdenkmäler.* ("Abhandlungen für die Kunde des Morgenlandes," 52, 2.) Leipzig, 1866.

Bombaci, Alessio. "Das osmanische Reich," in *Historia Mundi: Ein Handbuch der Weltgeschichte*, VI. Bern, 1957.

"Bosna," *Türk Ansiklopedisi.* Ankara, 1954.

Bowring, John (tr.). *Narodne srpske pjesme – Servian Popular Poetry.* London, 1827.

Braun, Maximilian. *Die Anfänge der Europäisierung in der Literatur der muslimischen Slaven in Bosnien und der Herzegowina.* ("Slavisch-baltische Quellen und Forschungen," 7.) Leipzig, 1934.

—— *Die islamischen Slaven in Bosnien und der Herzegowina und der West Europäische Kultureinbruch.* ("Archiv für Kultur- und Universalgeschichte," 23, 2.) Berlin, 1932.

Brockelmann, Carl. *Geschichte der arabischen Literatur.* 2nd ed. adapted to the supplementary volume. Leyden, 1943. Supplementary vols. I, 1937; II, 1938; III, 1942.

Busuladžić, Mustafa. "Lo scrittore Hadži Mehmed Handžić di Sarajevo," *Oriente Moderno*, XXII (1942), 173–8.

Čelebī, Ewlijā. *Siyāḥatnāme*/Travelogue. Istanbul, 1936.

Ćorović, Vladimir. "Das Erwachen der jugoslavischen Moslims zum Modernen Leben," *Slavische Rundschau* (Praha), I (1929), 529–39.

Ćorović, Vladimir, and Kemura, Saifaddin. *Serbo-kroatische Dichtungen bosnischer Muslims aus dem* XVII, XVIII, *und* XIX *Jahrhundert.* ("Zur Kunde der Balkanhalbinsel. Quellen und Forschungen," 2.) Sarajevo, 1912.

Ćurčić, Vejsil. "Bauweise des muselmanischen Wohnhauses in Bosnien," *Neue Ordnung* (Zagreb), Nov. 22, 1942.

—— *Starinsko oružje u Bosni i Hercegovini*/Ancient Weapons in Bosnia and Hercegovina. Sarajevo, 1944.

Ćurić, Hajruddin. *Školske prilike muslimana u Bosni i Hercegovini 1800–1878* (with French summary): La Situation scolaire des Musulmans en Bosnie-Herzegovine. Beograd, 1965.

Cvijić, Jovan. *La Peninsule Balkanique.* Paris, 1918.

"The Death of Omer and Merima," *The Slavonic Review*, VIII (1929), 198–202.

Delorko, Olinko. *Narodne epske pjesme*/Epic Folk Songs. Zagreb, 1964.

Dizdar, Hamid. *Ljubavne narodne pjesme*/Folk Love Songs. Sarajevo, 1953.

—— *Sevdalinke. Izbor iz bosansko-hercegovačke narodne lirike*/Sevdalinkas: Selected Bosnian and Hercegovinian Lyric Folk Poems. Sarajevo, 1944.

—— *Narodne pripovijetke iz Bosne i Hercegovine*/Folk Tales from Bosnia and Hercegovina. Vol. I. Sarajevo, 1955.

Dobrača, Kasim. *Gazi Husrev-Begova Biblioteka. Katalog arapskih, turskih i perzijskih rukopisa*/Catalogue of Arabic, Turkish, and Persian Manuscripts. Vol. I. Sarajevo, 1963.

Ethé, Hermann. "Neupersische Literatur," *Grundriss der iranischen Philologie* (Strassburg, 1894–1904).

Ettinghausen, Richard (ed.). *Türkische Miniaturen vom 13. bis zum 18. Jahrhundert.* ("Piper: UNESCO Taschenbücher der Kunst.") München, 1965.

Filipović, Milenko S. *Privreda, saobraćaj i naselja u Visočkoj Nahiji*/Economy, Communications, and Settlements in the District of Visoko. Beograd, 1929.

Forrer, Ludwig. *Die osmanische Chronik des Rustem Pascha.* ("Türkische Bibliothek," 21.) Leipzig, 1923.

Gabrielli, Francesco. "Mohammed und der Islam als weltgeschichtliche Erscheinungen," in *Historia Mundi: Ein Handbuch der Weltgeschichte*, v. Bern: Frühes Mittelalter, 1956.

Gabrijan, B., and Neidhardt, J. *Arhitektura Bosne i put u savremenost*/The Architecture of Bosnia and the Road to Contemporaneity. Sarajevo, 1958.

Gerhard, Wilhelm. *W. Gerhard's Gesänge der Serben.* Hrsg. u. mit anm. versehen von K. Braun. 2nd ed. Leipzig, 1877.

Gesemann, Gerhard. "Die Asanaginica im Kreise ihrer Varianten," *Archiv für slavische Philologie*, XXXVIII (1923), 1–44.

—— "Der Klagegesang der edlen Frau'n des Asan Aga," *Slavische Rundschau*, IV (1932), 97–184.

Goethe, Johann Wolfgang. "Klaggesang von der edlen Frauen des Asan Aga," in *Herder's Volkslieder*. I. Teil. Leipzig, 1778. 309–14.

Gibb, E. J. W. *A History of Ottoman Poetry*. Ed. Edward G. Browne. 6 vols. London: Luzac and Co., 1900–9

Gövsa, Ibrahim Alaettin. *Türk Meşhurları Ansiklopedisi*/Encyclopedia of Famous Turks. Istanbul, [1947].

Grienberger, J. V. "Bosnische Holztüren," *Kunstgewerbeblatt N.C.* II (1891), 113.

Gvozdović, Rif'at Pasha. "Bosniens kunstgewerbliches Erbe der Türken," *Die islamische Welt*, v (Berlin, 1917), 302–4.

Hadžijahić, Muhamed. "Die Anfänge der nationalen Entwicklung in Bosnien und der Herzegowina, "*Südostforschungen*, XXI (1962), 168–93.

Hak, Abdul. *Ašiklije-Muslimanske sevdalinke*/Ašiklias-Muslim Love Songs. Sarajevo, 1906.

Hammer-Purgstall, Josef. *Geschichte der osmanischen Dichtkunst.* 4 vols. Pesth, 1836–8.

Handschriften, arabische, türkische und persische, der Universitätsbibliothek in Bratislava. Ed. Josef Blaškovičs. Bratislava, 1961.

Handžić, Mehmed. *Al-Jawhar al-asnā fī tarājīm 'ulamā' wa shu'arā' Bosna*/ The Sparkling Ring-Jewel in the Biographies of the Scholars and Poets of Bosnia. Cario, 1349 [1930].

—— *Ibrahim ef. Pečevija.* Narodna Uzdanica (Sarajevo), 1939.

—— *Književni rad bosansko-hercegovačkih Muslimana*/The Literary Activity of Bosnian and Hercegovinian Muslims. Sarajevo, 1934.

—— "Niẓām al-ʿulamāʾ ilā khātam al-anbiyāʾ"/The Sequence of Scholars Up to the Last Prophet of God, *Novi Behar*, VIII (Sarajevo, 1935).

Hangi, Antom. *Die Moslims in Bosnien und der Herzegowina.* Ihre Lebensweise, ihre Sitten und ihre Gebrausche. Ubers. v. H. Tausk. Sarajevo, 1907.

Herder, Gottfried J. *Volkslieder*. Leipzig, 1778–9.

Hille, Franz. *Kroatische und bosnische Novellen.* Wien, 1940.

Hoernes, Moriz. *Dinarische Wanderungen. Kultur- und Landschaftsbilder aus Bosnien und der Herzegowina.* 2nd rev. ed. Wien, 1894.

Horalek, Karel. "Türkische Volksbücher und balkanische Volksmärchen," *Les Études balkaniques tchécoslovaques* (Praha), II (1967), 69–86.

Hörmann, Kosta. *Narodne pjesme Muhamedovaca u Bosni i Hercegovini*/ Folk Songs of the Muslims of Bosnia and Hercegovina. 2 vols. Sarajevo, 1888–9.

—— *Narodne pjesme muslimana u Bosni i Hercegovini*/Folk Songs of the Muslims of Bosnia and Hercegovina (Iz rukopisne ostavštine. Red., uvod i koment. Djenana Buturović.) Sarajevo, 1966.

Hrvatske narodne balade i romance/Croatian Folk Ballads and Romances. 2 vols. Zagreb, 1951–6.

Hrvatske narodne pjesme/Croatian Folk Songs. 9 vols. Zagreb: Matica Hrvatska, 1896–1942.

Janc, Zagorka. "Islamski elementi u minijaturama Karanskog Jevandjelja"/ Islamic Elements in the Miniatures of the Karan-Gospel. *Godišnjak Balkanološkog Instituta* (Sarajevo), 2 (1961).

Janc, (Zagorka). *Islamski rukopisi iz jugoslavenskih kolekcija*/Islamic Manuscripts from Yugoslav Collections. Beograd, 1956.

Jenkins, H. D. *Ibrahim Pasha, Grand Vizier of Suleiman the Magnificent.* ("Columbia Univ. Studies.") New York, 1911.

Kemura, Sejfuddin. "Sarajevske džamije i druge javne zgrade turske dobe"/ The Mosques and Other Public Buildings of the Turkish Period in Sarajevo, *Glasnik zemaljskog muzeja* (Sarajevo), XXII (1909).

Kombol, Mihovil. *Poviest hrvatske književnosti do Preporoda*/History of Croatian Literature to the National Awakening. Zagreb, 1945. 2nd ed., 1961.

Kraelitz-Greifenhorst, F. V. "Ibrāhīm Pečewī," *Der Islam*, VIII (1918), 252–60.

Krauss, Friedrich Salomon. *Über den Einfluss des Orients auf die Südslaven.* Wien, 1886. Reprint from *Mitteilungen der Anthropologischen Gesellschaft.*

—— *Vom Derwisch-Recken Gazi Seidi. Ein Guslarenlied bosnischer Moslime.* ("Beiträge zur Kenntnis des Orients," 10.) Halle/S., 1912.

—— *Slavische Volkforschungen*, Leipzig, 1908.

—— *Tausend Sagen und Märchen der Südslaven.* 8 vols. Vol. I. Leipzig: Ethnologischer Verlag, 1914.

Kreševljaković, Hamdija. *Hanovi i karavansaraji u Bosni i Hercegovini* (with German Summary): Hane u. Karawansereien in B.-H. Sarajevo, 1957.

—— *Kapetanije u Bosni i Hercegovini*/District Captaincies in Bosnia and Hercegovina. Sarajevo, 1954.

——— *Vodovodi i gradnje na vodi u starom Sarajevu*/Aqueducts and Dike Constructions in Old Sarajevo. Sarajevo, 1939.

Kuba, Ludvik. *Pjesme bosansko-hercegovačke*/Bosnian and Hercegovinian Songs. Praha, 1927.

Kučukalić, Zija. *The Development of Musical Culture in Bosnia and Hercegovina*. Tr. Branka Bokonjić. Sarajevo, 1967.

Kurt, Džemaluddin Mehmed. *Hrvatske narodne ženske pjesme (muslimanske)*/Croatian Muslim Women's Folk Songs. Mostar, 1902.

Kus-Nikolajev, Mirko. "Der Islam und die jugoslavische Volkskunst," *Slavische Rundschau*, VII (1936), 242–6.

Ljubunčić, H. Hasan. *Put na hadž*/Pilgrimage to Mecca. Sarajevo: Veselin Masleša, 1955.

Lord, Albert V. *The Singer of Tales*. Cambridge: Harvard University Press, 1960.

Lucerna, Camilla. *Das Balladrama der Südslawen*. Leipzig, 1923.

———*Die südslavische Ballade von Asan Agas Gattin und ihre Nachbildung durch Goethe*. ("Forschungen zur neueren Literaturgeschichte," 28.) Berlin, 1905.

——— *Zur Hasanaginica*. Zagreb, 1909.

Marković, Stipo, and Popović, Cvetko. "Nekoliko podataka o livanjskom vezu srebrnom žicom u drvetu"/Some Information about the Art of Inlaying (Damiascene) in Livno. *Glasnik zemaljskog muzeja*, VI (1957).

Matković, P. "Dva talijanska putopisa po Balkanskom poluotoku iz 16. vijeka"/Two Italian Travelogues on the Balkan Peninsula from the Sixteenth Century, *Starine*, X (Zagreb: Yugoslav Academy, 1878).

Matl, Josef. "Okzidentale und eurasische Auffassung der slavischen Geschichte," *Saeculum*, IV (München, 1953).

——— *Die Kultur der Südslaven*. Frankfurt/M., 1966. (Handbuch der Kulturgeschichte. Liefer. 108–112, 1–5.)

Mazalić, Djoko. *Slikarska umjetnost u Bosni i Hercegovini u tursko doba. 1500–1878*/The Art of Painting in Bosnia and Hercegovina in the Turkish Period. Sarajevo, 1965.

Mehinagić, H. Ibrahim. "U spomen velikom merhumu Ali Fehmi ef. Džabiću"/ In Memory of the Great Ali Fehmi Dzabić, *Glasnik Vrhovnog Islamskog Starješinstva u SFRJ (GVIS)*/Official Paper of the Supreme Islamic Authority in SFRY, VII, nos. 1–3 (Sarajevo, 1956).

Milosich, Franz. "Ueber Goethe's Klaggesang von der edlen Frauen des Asan Aga," *Sitzungsberichte der Wiener Akademie der Wissenschaften* (Wien, 1883).

Morpurgo, Vito. "I fratelli Ibro e Paso Moric nell'intuizione popolare della balata Bosniaca," *Annali del Corso di lingue e literature straniere presso l'Università di Bari* (Bari, 1962).

"Mostar," *Enciklopedija Jugoslavije*, I. Zagreb: Leksikografski Zavod, 1965.

Muftić, Asim. *Moschee und Stiftung Ferhad Paša's in Banja Luka*. Gräfenhainishen, 1941. Leipzig, phil. Diss.

Mujić, Muhamed. "Biografija Mustafe Ejubovića (Šejh Jujo)"/Biography of Mustafa Ejubović (Shaykh Yuyo), *GVIS*, VII, nos. 1–3 (Sarajevo, 1956).

Muḥammad Nergisī. [Khamse-i Nergisī] Miṣr 1255, 138, 84, 69, 65, 56 S.

2nd ed. Istanbul, 1285, 164, 90, 37, 84, 67 S.
Murko, Matthias. "Auf den Spuren der Volksepik durch Jugoslavien," *Slavische Rundschau*, III, no. 3 (1931).
—— *Das Original von Goethe's "Klagegesang von der edlen Frauen des Assan Agas (Asanaginica)" in der Literature und im Volksmunde durch 150 Jahre*. Wien, 1937.
—— "Die Volksepik der bosnischen Mohammedaner," *Zeitschrift des Vereines für Volkskunde* (Berlin), XIX, I (1909), 13–30.
Nametak, Alija. *Narodne junačke muslimanske pjesme*/Muslim Heroic Folk Songs. Sarajevo, 1938.
—— *Islamski kulturni spomenici turskog perioda u Bosni i Hercegovini*/Islamic Cultural Monuments of the Turkish period in Bosnia and Hercegovina. Sarajevo, 1939.
"Naṣuḥ ibn ʿAbdallāh (Ḳara-Göz) as-Silāḥī al-Wisoḳawī al-Miṭrāḳī: Fetiḥnāme-i Ḳara-Boghdan," [Ruman] in *Cronici turçeşti privind tările române*. Extrase. I. Bucuresti, 1966. 219–32.
Okić, Tayyib M. *Hādim (ʿAtik) Ali Paşa kimder?*/Who is Khādim ʿAlī Pasha? Ankara, 1969.
—— *Gazi Husrev Beğ ve onun Saraybosnaʾdaki camiine bir minare daha ilâve edilmesine dair bir vesika* [with French summary]: Gazi Husrev Beg et un décret impérial au sujet de la construction d'un second minaret pour sa mosquee de Sarajevo. Ankara: Necati Lugat Armağani. 1969.
Orsini e Rosenberg, Giustiniana Contessa degli. *Die Morlaken*. Von. J. Wynne, Grafinn Von Ursini und Rosenberg. Aus dem Franz. von S. G. Bürde. Th. 1.2. Breslau, 1790–5.
ʿOmar Efendi Elkazović-Čaušević. *Aḥwāl-i ghazewāt der diyār-i Bosna*. Istanbul, 1741. New Prints: 1876, 1878, 1909.
Parry, Milman (collector), and Lord, Albert B. (ed. and tr.). *Serbocroatian Heroic Songs*. 2 vols. (I, English translations; II, Serbocroatian texts.) Cambridge, Mass., and Belgrade: Harvard University Press and the Serbian Academy of Sciences, 1954.
Past, The, of Bosnia and Hercegovina in the Light of the Collections in the National Museum in Sarajevo. [Sarajevo, 1950.]
Patsch, Carl. *Historische Wanderungen im Karst und an der Adria*. Mit. 82 Abb. T. *Die Herzegowina einst und jetzt*. ("Schriften zur Kunde J. Balkanhalbinsel," N.F. 1.). Wien, 1922.
Peez, Carl. *Mostar und sein Kulturkreis. Ein Städtebild aus der Hercegovina*. Leipzig: Brockhaus, 1891.
Pélletier, R. *Sarajevo et sa region*. Paris, 1932.
Pospišil, J[osef]. "Aus mohammedanischen Friedhofen," *Der Bautechniker* (Wien), Nov. 6, 1914, 741–2.
—— "Wie Man in Bosnien Djamien Baute," *Der Bautechniker* (Wien), Jan. 7, 1916, 1ff.
Prelog, Milan. *Povijest Bosne u doba osmanlijske vlade*/History of Bosnia during Ottoman Rule. 1.2. Sarajevo: Studnička, [about 1912].
Prohaska, Dragutin. *Das kroatisch-serbische Schrifttum in Bosnien und der Herzegowina von den Anfängen im* XI *bis zur nationalen Wiedergeburt im* XIX *Jahrhundert*. Zagreb, 1911.

Rycaut, Sir Paul. *The History of the Turkish Empire from 1623 to 1677 Containing the Reigns of the Last Three Emperors (Amurath* IV – *Mahomet* IV*)*. London, 1679.

—— *The Present State of the Ottoman Empire*. London, 1668.

Rypka, Jan. *Beiträge zur Biographie, Charakteristik und Interpretation des türkischen Dichters Sabit*, 1. Prag. 1924.

Rypka, Jan, *et. al. History of Iranian Literature*. Written in collaboration with Otakar Klima (and others). Ed. Karl Jahn. Dodrecht, (1968).

Šabanović, Hazim. "Upravna podjela Jugoslovenskih zemalja pod turskom vladavinom do Karlovačkog Mira 1699 godine"/Administrative Division of Yugoslav Lands under Turkish Rule up to the Peace of Karlowitz in 1699, *Istorisko Društvo Bosne i Hercegovine: Godišnjak* (1952), 171–204.

—— *Bosanski pašaluk. Pastanak i upravna podjela* (with German summary): Der bosnische Paschaluk. ("Naučno Društvo NR Bosne i Hercegovine," *Djela* 14.) Sarajevo, 1959.

Sadiković, Sadik. *Narodno Zdravlje*/People's Health. Sarajevo: Jugoslavenski List, 1928.

Safa'ī, Mustafā Efendī. "Tadhkira"/Biographies of the Ottoman Poets, 1640–1720. Austrian National Library, MS HO 139.

Šamić, Midhat. *Les Voyageurs français en Bosnie à la fin du 18ᵉ siècle et en début du 19ᵉ et le pays tel qu'ils ont vu*. Paris, (1960).

Schmaus, Alois. "Studije o krajinskoj epici"/Studies on the Military Frontier Epic, *Rad*, 297 (Zagreb: Yugoslav Academy, 1953).

Schmid, Ferdinand. *Bosnien und die Herzegowina unter der Verwaltung Österreich-Ungarns*. Leipzig, 1914.

Sertoğlu, Mithat. "Bosna ve Hersek müslümanlarĭnĭn Türk edibiyatĭ tarihindeki mevkii"/The Position of the Bosnian and Hercegovinian Muslims in the History of Turkish Literature. Library of the University of Istanbul, Istanbul, Turkey, MS Tez Nr. 47, 1938–9.

Seybold, C. F. "Ein Anonymer alter türkischer Kommentar zum letzten Drittel des Korans in drei Handschriften zu Hamburg, Breslau und im Britischen Museum," *Festschrift Eduard Sachau zum siebzigsten Geburtstage gewidmit von Freuden und Schülern*, ed. Gotthold Weil. Berlin, 1915.

Simčik, Antun. "Hasanaga Kuna," *Novi Behar*, XIII (Sarajevo, 1939).

Škaljić, Abdulah. *Turcizmi u srpskohrvatskom jeziku*/Turkisms in the Serbo-Croatian Language. Sarajevo: Svjetlost, 1965.

Škarić, Vladislav. *Uticaj turskog vladanja na društveni život*/The Influence of Turkish Rule on Social Life. Beograd, 1937.

Škrivanić, G. Review of *Bosanski pašaluk*/The Bosnian Pashalik, by Hazim Šabanović, in *Istoriski Glasnik* (Belgrade), April 4, 1960, 81.

Sladović, Eugen. *Islamsko pravo u Bosni i Hercegovini*/Islamic Jurisprudence in Bosnia and Hercegovina. Beograd, 1936.

Stadtmüller, Georg. "Bosanski islam, most Europe islamskom svijetu"/Bosnian Islam–Europe's Bridge to the Islamic World, *GVSIVZ*, July, 1943.

Stevenson, B. Stanoyevich (ed.). *An Anthology of Yugoslav Poetry: Serbian* Lyrics. Boston: Richard G. Badger, the Gorham Press, 1920.

Subotić, Dragutin. *Yugoslav Popular Ballads, Their Origin and Development*. Cambridge, Mass.: Harvard University Press, 1932.

Šunjić, Marijan. *Narodne junačke pjesme iz Bosne i Hercegovine*/Heroic Folk Songs from Bosnia and Hercegovina. 2nd ed. Sarajevo, 1925.

Tahir, Bursalī Mehmed. *Othmanlī mü'ellifleri*/Ottoman Writers. Istanbul, 1914–15.

Talat, Anīl. *Divan edebiyatinda Bosna we Hersekli şairler*/Bosnian and Hercegovinian Poets of Diwan Literature. Istanbul, 1941.

Taškӧprü-Zāde, Aḥmad ibn Muṣṭafā ibn Khalīl. *Ash-Shaḳā'ik an-nuʿmānīya fī manāḳib ʿulamā' wa mashāyikh ad-dawla al-ʿUthmānīya*/Red Anemones in the Biographies of Scholars and Grand Viziers of the Ottoman Empire. Būlāq, 1881.

Thallóczy, Ludwig von. Eine Staatsschrift des bosnischen Mohammedaners Molla Hassan Elkjafi "Über die Art und Weise des Regierens," *Archiv für slavische Philologie*, XXXII (1911), 139–58.

Tisma, O. "Islamic Relics in Yugoslavia," *Indo-Asian Culture*, VIII (1960), 292–300.

Tridesetgodišnji izvještaj Šeriatske Sudačke Škole u Sarajevu/Thirty Years' Report of the Shariʿa School for Judges in Sarajevo. Sarajevo, 1917.

Truhelka, Ćiro. "Ghazi Husrevbeg. Sein Leben und seine Zeit," *Südslaviche Revue*, 1, 2 (1912), 270–2.

Zambaur, Eduard von. "Prägungen der Osmanen in Bosnien," *Numismatische Zeitschrift*, N.F. 1 (1908).

7

The Ethnic and Religious History of Bosnia and Hercegovina

DOMINIK J. MANDIĆ

Along the eastern boundary of present-day Bosnia and Hercegovina runs the line which, for centuries, divided the eastern and western Roman empires, the eastern and western Christian churches, and eastern and western culture. In the fifteenth century the Turks created a fighting border between Islamic Turkey and the western Christian powers in western Bosnia. Because of its strategic and geographic location, radically divergent cultural influences have therefore been felt in Bosnia, creating a highly complicated internal state of affairs. Changes in the national religious and ethnic political makeup of Bosnia have occurred more frequently and penetrated more deeply than in other parts of Europe. In the past hundred years historians have attempted to extricate some of the salient features of this complex development and to explain the Bosnian enigma. Nevertheless, the problem of the religious and ethnic origin of the people of Bosnia and Hercegovina has remained unsolved.

During the past ten years, after much preparation and long research, I have published several historical works, carefully documented, in which I have tried to offer some new insights into the ethnic and religious history of Bosnia and Hercegovina.[1] The following pages present a brief survey of these studies. The reader who wishes to consider the problems in greater depth is invited to acquaint himself with the studies I have published in Croatian, where he will find copious documentation of appropriate sources in the original languages.

1/See the Bibliography.

CROATIANS IN BOSNIA AND HERCEGOVINA

THE SETTLEMENT OF SLAVS IN THE BALKANS

The Mongolian Hun invasion of Europe in A.D. 375 set in motion the migration of nations from eastern and northern Europe to the rich and spacious Roman Empire. The first to migrate to the Roman Empire were the Germans, followed by the Huns, then the Avars and Slavs. The most ferocious of these were the Huns and Avars, who destroyed both Roman settlements and their cultural institutions. The last migrants to the Balkans, the Slavs, came in two waves. In the first, which began in A.D. 375, over the course of about two hundred years, under the rule of the Huns and Avars or on their own, the Slavs populated the area from the Black Sea to the Tyrol and the Tagliamento River in Italy.[2]

The second Slavic migration began in A.D. 626, when Croatians crossed the Carpathian Mountains at the request of Heraclius I, Byzantine emperor (610–41), who needed allies in his war against the Avars, who were then besieging Constantinople. Within some ten years time, the Croatians defeated the Avars, driving them north of the Drava and Danube rivers. Then, according to their contract with Emperor Heraclius, they took over the entire Roman province of Dalmatia from the Raša River in Istria to the Drina River and to the city of Budva south of Boka Kotorska. One group also conquered South Pannonia and Illyricum.[3]

A short time after the arrival of the Croatians, the Serbs, who came from what are now northwestern Bohemia and Germany, entered the Balkans. Emperor Heraclius I granted them the northern section of the Roman province of Praevalis from the Drina to the Ibar River and Kosovo Field.[4] The Bulgars were the last to come as a conquering Turan-

2/V. N. Zlatarski, "Die Besiedlung der Balkanhalbinsel durch die Slaven," *Revue internationale des études balcaniques*, II (1936), 358–75; M. Vasmer, *Die Slaven in Griechenland*, Abh. der Preus. Akad., Phil.-Hist. Kl. 12 (Berlin, 1941), 1–350; D. Mandić, "Migrations of the Slavs into Danube Basin and the Balkans," *Croatian Review*, II (Chicago, 1959), 46–64.

3/L. Hauptmann, "Prihod Hrvatov"/The Arrival of Croatians, *Bulićev Zbornik/Strena Buliciana* (Zagreb-Split, 1924), 515–45; D. Mandić, *Rasprave i prilozi iz stare hrvatske povijesti*/Studies and Contributions to Ancient Croatian History (Rim, 1963), IV, "Dolazak Hrvata na Jadran"/The Arrival of Croatians on the Adriatic Sea, 51–76.

4/C. Porphyrogenitus, *De administrando imperio*, cap. 32, ed. Gy. Moravcsik and R. J. H. Jenkins (Budapest, 1949), 152–60; K. Jireček and J. Radonić, *Istorija Srba*/History of the Serbs, I (Beograd, 1922), 43–115; Mandić, *Rasprave i prilozi*, 226–54.

Altaian people, and occupied the northeastern section of the Balkans from the Black Sea up to Kosovo Field.[5]

These three nations gave their state organizations and national names to the Slavs of the first migration with whom they amalgamated ethnically and linguistically, each on its own national territory. Because of their small number, the Bulgars lost their Turco-Turanian language and the Serbs their western Slavic speech; both accepted the Ekavian language of the Slavs of the first settlement, who came from the Don River region in present-day Russia.

BOSNIA AND HERCEGOVINA WERE CROATIAN LANDS IN THE MIDDLE AGES

That the Croatians, when they arrived in the south, also took Bosnia and Hercegovina as their permanent homeland is attested to by the following documents:

1/The Emperor Constantine VII Porphyrogenitus (tenth century), on the basis of Croatian national tradition and historical materials in the Imperial Archives of Constantinople, writes that the Croatians, with the permission of the emperor Heraclius I, settled in the Roman province of Dalmatia; one group, he says, settled in Pannonia and Illyricum.[6] Present-day Bosnia and Hercegovina lay, for the most part, within the boundaries of Roman Dalmatia, a small part of it extending to the southernmost region of Pannonia.[7] If the Croatians had not taken possession of the whole of present-day Bosnia-Hercegovina, they would not have crossed into Illyricum and Pannonia.

2/An old Croatian chronicle of the eighth century relates this about the first Croatian ruler: "And his kingdom was Bosnia and Valdemin [Valde-vino or Vinodol, near the modern city of Rijeka] and extended

5/V. N. Zlatarski, *Istorija na b'lgarskata d'ržava*/History of the Bulgarian State, vol. I, part I (Sofija, 1918), 123–246.

6/"The Croats who now live in the region of Dalmatia are descended from the unbaptized Croats, also called 'white', who live beyond Turkey [Hungary] ... by command of the emperor Heraclius these same Croats defeated and expelled the Avars from those parts, and by mandate of Heraclius the emperor they settled down in that same country of the Avars, where they now dwell ..." Porphyrogenitus, *De administrando imperio*, cap. 31, 147–9.

"From the Croats who came to Dalmatia a part split off and possessed themselves of Illyricum and Pannonia ..." Porphyrogenitus, *op. cit.*, cap. 30, p. 145.

7/For the location and borders of Roman Dalmatia and Pannonia, see Th. Mommsen, *Römische Geschichte, Gesammelte Schriften*, V (Berlin, 1908), 561–88; B. Saria, "Dalmatia," in Pauly-Wissowa, *Real-Encycl., Suppl.* 8 (1956), 22–59; A. Mócsy, "Pannonia," in P.-W., *Real-Encycl., Suppl.* 9 (1962), 516–776, D. Mandić, "Dalmatia in the Exarchate of Ravenna," *Byzantion*, XXXIV (1964), 347–74.

to Polonia [Polina, the old Apollonia near Valona]: his kingdom was the coast-land and extended behind the mountains."[8]

3/The Croatian chronicle known as *Methodos*, written in A.D. 753, mentions that the provinces which composed the Croatian kingdom of that time were: White (western) Croatia, Red (southern) Croatia, and Bosnia.[9]

4/The authors of the chronicle *Kraljevstvo Hrvata* (The Kingdom of the Croatians), written between 1074 and 1080, and also of *Cronica Presbyteri Diocleatis* (Chronicle of the Priest of Dioclea), written between 1149 and 1153, allege the same thing.[10]

5/Since the earliest times, Bosnia, as an autonomous unit, had as its governor the Ban, and consequently was called Ban's Bosnia (Banovina Bosanska). The title "Ban" was specifically Croatian and unknown to the Serbs or, for that matter, to any other European nation before the twelfth century.[11] It would seem obvious, then, that Bosnia had been colonized and inhabited by Croatians from its very beginnings. Who else would have used the purely Croatian title of Ban for the governor, and called Bosnia "Ban's Country," but Croatians themselves?

6/The Byzantine writer John Cinnamus, describing the military expedition of 1155 of Emmanuel Comnenus, had this to say about Bosnia: "Bosnia is not subordinate to the ruler of Serbia. She is independent; a special nation who has its own way of living and who governs itself."[12] Thus, it is clear that in the twelfth century the nation of Bosnia was distinct from that of the Serbs. The people of Bosnia in this era had an autonomous government with its own customs and practices. It follows, then, that the people of Bosnia could have been none other than Croatian people; for in Bosnia and in Rascia or neighboring Serbia, from the

8/"I bi kraljevstvo njegovo Bosna i Valdemin deri do Polonije, tako primorsko kako i zagorsko kraljevstvo," "Kraljevstvo Hrvata"/The Kingdom of the Croatians, ch. 3 of F. Šišić (ed.), *Letopis Popa Dukljanina*/Chronicle of the Priest of Dioclea (Beograd-Zagreb, 1928), 388.

9/Šišić, *Letopis Popa Dukljanina*, ch. 9, pp. 305–8, 398–401.

10/*Op. et loc. cit.*; D. Mandić, *Crvena Hrvatska u svijetlu povjesnih izvora*/Red Croatia in the Light of Historical Sources (Chicago, 1957), 1–38.

11/V. Klaić, *Poviest Bosne do propasti kraljevstva*/A History of Bosnia to the End of the Kingdom (Zagreb, 1882), 42–54; V. Ćorović, *Historija Bosne*/History of Bosnia, I (Beograd, 1940), 126–64; D. Mandić, *Bosna i Hercegovina*, I (Chicago, 1960), 47–53; D. Mandić, *Etnička povijest Bosne i Hercegovine*/The Ethnic History of Bosnia and Hercegovina (Rim, 1967), 33–5; S. Ćirković, *Istorija srednjovekovne bosanske države*/A History of the Medieval Bosnian State (Beograd, 1964), 37–43.

12/"Ésti dè hē Bósthna oủ tō Serbíōn ȧrchizoupánō kaì aủtē̉ ḗikousa, ȧll' ĕthnos ȉdíā parà taútē kaì zōn kaì ȧrchómenon." Ioannes Cinnamus, *Historiarum epitome*, III, 7 (ed. A. Meineke; Bonn, 1836), 104.

eleventh century to our own day, there have been no other Slavic nations but the Serbs and Croatians.

THE CONVERSION TO CHRISTIANITY OF THE CROATIANS IN BOSNIA

When the Croatians arrived in the south, they were Iranian-Slavic pagans. At the request of Byzantium, Pope John IV (640–2) sent Catholic missionaries to the Croatian provinces. In 640 these missionaries converted Porga, the supreme ruler of Croatians, and also a great many of the clan under his immediate authority, to the Catholic faith.[13] This induced the Pope to re-establish the old archdiocese of Salona and transfer its See to the nearby city of Split (Spalatum). He also gave all the rights of the old archdiocese to the newly established archdiocese of Split, which included in its jurisdiction all the districts of the Croatian federated state with the region that is present-day Bosnia and Hercegovina, and covered all the territory extending from the Adriatic Sea to the Danube River in the north and to the Drina River in the east.[14]

THE BOGOMILS IN BOSNIA AND THEIR CONVERSION TO CATHOLICISM

During the reign of the Bulgarian emperor Peter (927–69), a Bulgarian Orthodox priest called Bogomil began to teach a new religious doctrine which thereafter bore his name, Bogomilism. Its main characteristic was its religious dualism, asserting that the world is governed by two principles, the principle of good and the principle of evil. This heresy rapidly spread throughout the neighboring countries, including Croatia. When Bosnia and Hercegovina came under the dominion of the Bulgarian emperors between 990 and 1018, they founded a separate diocese of Bogomilism in Bosnia for all the Croatian territories, and called it the Croatian Church, Ecclesia Sclavoniae. By the end of the thirteenth century and

13/"The emperor Heraclius sent and brought priests from Rome, and made of them an archbishop and a bishop and elders and deacons, and baptized the Croats; and at that time these Croats had Porgas for their prince." Porphyrogenitus, *De administrando imperio*, ch. 31, p. 149; Mandić, *Rasprave i prilozi*, VI, "Pokrštenje Hrvata"/The Christening of Croatians, 109–44.

14/"Interea summus pontifex misit quendam legatum Johannem nomine, patria Rauenatum, qui partes Dalmatie et Chroatie peragrando ... per dominum papam consecratione suscepta ... Ipsi concessum est a sede apostolica, ut totius dignitatis privilegium, quod Salona antiquitus habuit, obtineret ecclesia Spalatensium." Thomas Archidiaconus, *Historia Salonitana*, cap. XI (ed. F. Rački; Zagreb, 1894), 33; Mandić, *Rasprave i prilozi*, V, "Osnutak splitske nadbiskupije"/The Establishment of the Archdiocese in Split (Spalatum), 77–108.

the beginning of the fourteenth, the majority of the inhabitants of Bosnia and Hercegovina had become followers of the heresy.[15] After the failure of the Crusades of 1222–7 and 1235–9, the popes sent the Dominican Fathers and, a little later, the Franciscan Fathers to Bosnia to bring the Bogomils back to the Catholic Church. At the request of Pope Benedict XII (1334–42) Father Geraldus Eudes, general of the Franciscans, personally visited Bosnia in 1339 and established a special Franciscan unit, Vicaria Bosnae. From that time on, the Franciscans began sending their best missionaries from all over Europe to Bosnia, a practice they continued until Bosnia fell to the Turks in 1463.[16]

As a result of the dedicated zeal of the Franciscan missionaries, as Pope Boniface IX notes in a letter of March 7, 1402, about 500,000 followers of Bogomilism had been brought back to the Catholic Church.[17] Just prior to the Turkish conquest, the population of Bosnia and Hercegovina had the following religious and ethnic makeup: about 750,000 Croatian Catholics; 80,000–90,000 Croatians adhering to Bogomilism; 12,000–15,000 non-Slavic Vlachs; and 25,000–28,000 Serbs.[18] The Serbs lived in Podrinje, which had been taken away from old Serbia by the Bosnian ruler Tvrtko I and annexed to Bosnia between 1366 and 1373.

THE ORIGIN OF THE MUSLIMS IN BOSNIA AND HERCEGOVINA

First of all, it is a fact that Muslims from the Near East never settled in groups in Bosnia and Hercegovina. During their rule the Turks were unable to create anywhere in Bosnia and Hercegovina even a small settlement in which people would speak Turkish. Both Catholics and Muslims continued to speak exclusively in Croatian, in the Shtokavian

15/Ch. Schmidt, *Histoire et doctrine de la secte des Cathares ou Albigeois* (2 vols.; Paris and Genève, 1848–9); F. Rački, *Bogomili i Patareni*, 2nd ed. ("Posebna izdanja Srpske akademije nauka," 87; Beograd, 1931); D. Obolensky, *The Bogomils* (Cambridge, 1948); D. Angelov, "Der Bogomilismus auf dem Gebiete des byzantinischen Reiches," *Godišnjak Sofijskog univerziteta*, vol. 44, book 2 (Sofija, 1948); vol. 46, book 2 (Sofija, 1949–50); D. Mandić, *Bogomilska crkva bosanskih krstjana*/The Bogomil Church of the Bosnian Christians (Chicago, 1962).

16/Mandić, *op. cit.* 166–80.

17/"... per solicitas et continuas fratrum dicti ordinis in eadem vicaria existentium predicationes et inductiones quingenta milia personarum infidelium, vel circiter, cingulum veritatis amplectentes ad orthodoxe fidei sinceritatem unanimiter ... conversa fore noscuntur." Papal Bull of Boniface IX of March 7, 1402, *Arch. Secr. Vaticanum, Reg. Lat. vol. 104, f. 101r.* Mandić, *op. cit.*, 456.

18/Mandić, *Etnička povijest Bosne i Hercegovine*, 134–6.

dialect of Ikavian speech, the same language spoken and written during the Middle Ages, in the era of Bosnian Bans and kings. Only those Bosnians and Hercegovinians who were educated in Constantinople knew Turkish and wrote in it; in their families, in Bosnia, however, only Croatian was spoken.[19]

The present-day Muslims in Bosnia and Hercegovina are descendants of the Bosnian natives who are ethnically Croatians; their ancestors were followers either of the Catholic faith or of Bogomil's teaching.

It is fair to point out that, at the outset, the Turkish authorities in subjugated Bosnia did not use force to convert the local population to Islam. Mohammed II, the Conqueror, at the plea of Father Angjeo Zvizdović, superior of the Bosnian Franciscans, issued the famous imperial order known as *ʿAhd-nāme* on May 28, 1463. In it, he granted to the Franciscan Fathers and their faithful freedom to exercise their religious obligations, and protection for their lives and property. To this he added the stipulation: "as long as you remain faithful and obedient to my office and order."[20]

According to the official minute book of the Turkish government (Defter) of 1489, written twenty-five years after Bosnia had been conquered, 25,068 Christian families, 1332 Christian widows, 4026 unmarried Christian adults, 4485 Muslim families, and 2348 unmarried Muslim adults were living in the Sanjak area of Bosnia,[21] which was located between Novi Pazar and the Sana River, and Ivan Planina Mountain and the city of Maglaj. At that time, the average Bosnian family had at least eight members, which means that the Christian population in the Sanjak of Bosnia was then about 225,000 or 84 percent of all the inhabitants. The rest were Muslims, that is, about 40,000 or 16 percent. Almost all of these early Muslim converts were converts from Bogomilism.

During the early part of the sixteenth century, the relationship between the Bosnian Catholics and the Turkish government changed completely. At that time warfare between free Croatia and Islamic Bosnia or, more accurately, between the Turkish Empire and the Christian West, had become considerably intensified. Naturally, the Croatian Catholics of Bosnia along with the Franciscan Fathers felt sincere love and sympathy for their free brothers, and they manifested it by helping them in their struggle against the Turks. The Turks retaliated by drastic-

19/*Op. cit.*, 360–2.
20/*Op. cit.*, 150ff.
21/*Historija naroda Jugoslavije*/History of the Peoples of Yugoslavia, II (Zagreb, 1959), 121.

ally reversing their liberal attitude toward the Catholics of Bosnia and Hercegovina. In the first Statute-book for the Sanjak of Bosnia, written in 1516, the Turks issued the following decree: "Churches have been built in some places where they did not exist even during the reign of the infidels. Such newly built churches are to be demolished; those infidels and their pastors who attend those churches and who spy upon us and our movements and report them to the authorities of the infidel countries are to be severely punished, and physical tortures are to be applied to them."[22]

With this new law, the Bosnian Catholics and their spiritual leaders, the Franciscan Fathers, were officially proclaimed enemies of the Ottoman Empire, and bitter persecutions of the Catholic Church in Bosnia and Hercegovina were initiated. The Turkish authorities also resorted to economic sanctions against Catholics by imposing upon them heavy taxes from which Muslims were exempt.[23]

Suspicion was intensified in the Turkish authorities by the fact that the Bosnian Catholics and the Franciscan Fathers recognized the Roman Pontiff as their supreme spiritual leader. Since the popes had been the chief inspiration of military expeditions against the Turks, they were considered in Constantinople to be the principal enemy of the Ottoman Empire.[24]

To avoid persecution, great numbers of Croatian Catholics in Bosnia and Hercegovina began to emigrate to the free regions of Croatia, and many others moved to other free countries in Europe. However, the greater number of Catholics remained in Bosnia, especially peasants. To save themselves from economic destruction they usually embraced Islam, some of them wholeheartedly and others only outwardly, in their hearts remaining true to their Christian faith.

According to statistics gathered by Professor Omer L. Barkan from the official minute-books of the Ottoman Empire for the period between 1520 and 1530, there were 135,480 Muslims in the Sanjak of Bosnia and 221,328 in the entire region of Bosnia and Hercegovina.[25] This great increase of Muslims from 1489 to 1530 came partly from the members

22/*Kanuni i Kanun-name za Bosanski, Hercegovački, Zvornički, Kliški, Crnogorski i Skadarski sandžak*/Canons and Laws of the Bosnian, Hercegovinian, Zvornik, Klis, Montenegrin, and Scodra Sanjaks ("Monumenta Turcica," I; Sarajevo, 1957), 31.

23/Mandić, *Etnička povijest Bosne i Hercegovine*, 153–62.

24/*Op. cit.*, 367ff.

25/Omer Lufti Barkan, "Les déportations comme méthode de peuplement et de colonisation dans l'Empire Ottoman," *Revue de la Faculté des sciences économiques de l'Université d'Istambul*, XI (Istambul, 1949–50), 129; D. Mandić, "Bosnia y Herzegovina provincias croatas," *Studia Croatica*, VI (Buenos Aires, 1965), 176.

of Bogomil's church, but 120,000 to 150,000 Croatian Catholics had also become Muslims.

After 1530, because of the continuation of the persecutions begun in the previous two decades, the conversion of Catholics in Bosnia and Hercegovina to Islam was accelerated considerably. In 1624, the apostolic delegate, Peter Masarechi, submitted to the Congregation for the Propagation of the Faith in Rome the following report on the population of the Bosnian Pashalik: 900,000 Muslims, 300,000 Catholics, and 150,000 Greek Orthodox.[26]

The conversions of Catholics to Islam were not always total, however, as mentioned above, so that by the middle of the sixteenth century, there were a great number of "Poturs" in Bosnia, that is, half-Turks, who would have their children both circumcised and baptized. Outwardly, these people were Muslims, but at home they tried to live according to Christian teachings.[27] The practice continued into the seventeenth century. The Bosnian bishop Baličević, in his report of 1600 to the Holy See, confirms that: "There are many Muslim adults who firmly believe in Christ and receive baptism, but they are afraid of professing their faith publicly."[28] The apostolic delegate, Masarechi, in the year 1624, affirmed that the Bosnian Franciscan Fathers baptized the children of Muslims,[29] and in 1625 the Franciscans went so far as to ask the Holy See for permission to continue this practice, and it was granted them.[30] Again in 1628, Dominic Andriaš, OFM, bishop in central Hercegovina,

26/"La Prouintia di Bosna hauerà appresso trecento milla Catolici," K. Draganović, "Izvješće apostolskog vizitatora Petra Masarechija/Report of the Apostolic Delegate Peter Masarechi, *Starine* (Yugoslav Academy), XXXIX (Zagreb, 1938), 8. "... de Turchi saranno tre parti, et à pena de Catolici una, Schismatici saranno per la metà di Catolici, de quali saranno cento cinquanta milla anime in circa," *op. cit.*, 43.

27/Mandić, *Etnička povijest Bosne i Hercegovine*, 216–41.

28/"Cum multi fideles adulti baptisentur et credunt in Christum firmiter, tamen minime publice audent predicare amore [timore] poene," *Relatio ep. bos. F. Baličević an. 1600*. Arch. Vat., Fondo Borghese III 124 D, fol. 282r.

29/"In Bosna i frati batezzano, et non s'astengono n'anco fuori della Prouincia di batezzare li figliuoli de Turchi ...," K. Draganović, "Izvješće apostolskog vizitatora Petra Masarechija," 14.

30/Papal Bull of Urban VIII. *Cupientes*. Sept. 23, 1625, in Julijan Jelenić, "Izvori," *Glasnik Zemaljskog Muzeja*, IV (1912), 446f. J. B. Chaumette des Fossés, a chancellor of the French consulate in Travnik in 1807–8, studied the religious and social state of Bosnia at that day. He believed that the Bosnian and Hercegovinian native Muslims were Poturs of Catholic descent, who followed Catholic customs in many ways. He stated particularly that even then many seriously ill Muslims used to call Catholic priests to administer baptism and extreme unction to them. J. B. Chaumette des Fossés, *Voyage en Bosnie dans les années 1807 et 1808* (Paris, 1816), 53–56, 74, 88; M. Šamić, *Les voyageurs français en Bosnie* (Paris, 1960), 240–6.

asked the Holy See for instructions on how to deal with Muslims who were crypto-Catholics.[31]

There are a great many written documents from this period on the conversion to Islam, whether genuine or simulated, of the Croatian Catholics in Bosnia and Hercegovina. I will cite just a few.

The bishop of Zagreb, Simon Erdödi, states in a letter of November 24, 1536, that after the conquest of the city of Brod, on the Sava River, "over forty thousand Catholics have embraced Islam and others change sides every day."[32]

Jerolim Zlatarić, a Bosnian nobleman, wrote in 1599: "In that province there are a great number of Poturs who were at one time Christians [Catholics]. They embraced Islam for fear of their enemies, but they are neither good Muslims nor good Christians."[33]

In 1613, the Jesuit Bartul Kašić, after having visited Slavonia and southern Hungary, related to Pope Paul v that "many Christians [Catholics] in these regions and also in Bosnia have become Muslims."[34]

The papal delegate, Peter Masarechi, wrote to Rome in 1624: "In the district of the town of Sutjeska, in the past years, between six and seven thousands souls have fallen away from the [Catholic] religion."[35] The same year, the Franciscan Blasius of Gradac informed Rome that Catholics in the diocese of Trebinje "pass over to the Schism and Islam, and already nearly all have fallen into Schism and Islam."[36]

Atanazije Jurjević (Georgiceo), after his long journey through Bosnia in 1626, wrote: "The number of Muslims exceeds considerably the number of Catholics and Orthodox. It is necessary to note here that few of the Muslims working on farms are able to speak the Turkish language. If they were not afraid of the fire [rifle-shooting], almost all of

31/"Negotia ... Turcarum eandem fidem [catholicam] occulte profiteri volentium ab Episcopo Stephanensi signata, ad Sanctum Officium fuerunt remissa." Statement of the Sacred Congregation for the Propagation of the Faith, April 8, 1628, D. Mandić, *Acta Franciscana Hercegovinae*, I (Mostar, 1934), 17.

32/"... post expugnationem castri Brod, una cum his, qui misere praeda facti sunt, plusquam quadraginta millia animarum a fide christiana defecerunt, et desciscent in diem praeter numerum ..." E. Laszowski, *Monumenta Habsburgica*, II (Zagreb, 1916), 311.

33/"... et un numero grande de Pnoturi, li quali a un tempo sono stati christiani, et dalla grande tirannide de nemici fatti Turchi, et questi non sono ne Turchi buoni, ne christiani." *Glasnik Zemaljskog Muzeja*, XXI (1909), 60.

34/"Molti christiani di queste prouincie e della Bosna istessa si sono fatti Turchi." *Croatia Sacra*, IV (Zagreb, 1934), 250.

35/"Nel territorio di Sutieska nei anni andati mancarono dalla fede christiana appresso sei o sette milla anime." Draganović, "Izvješće apost. vizitatora," 45.

36/"... dette anime vanno traboccando nella scisma et turcismo ... et già tutti sono cascati nella scisma et turcismo." Relatio P. Blasii de Gradac, an 1624. B. Pandžić, *De dioecesi Tribuniensi et Mercanensi* (Roma, 1959), 115.

them would become Christians, knowing very well that their ancestors were Christians [Catholics]."[37]

The Croatian historian Ivan Tomko Mrnavić, who was originally from Bosnia, wrote in 1627: "Speaking in general, two-thirds of the population in Bosnia are Muslims, and almost all of them were converted from Christianity to Islam."[38]

In 1648, the Franciscan missionary Father Donatus Jelić informed the Sacred Congregation for the Propagatian of the Faith in Rome that "Christians in Bar [Antivari] passed to Islam, lest they lose their property and life, when they saw that the Turks decapitated seventy-four Christian leaders as rebels and traitors.[39]

In 1675, the Bosnian bishop Nikola Ogramić, OFM, reported to the Holy See on the district Bijela in northeastern Bosnia that there were only 995 Catholics in the entire district, and added: "The rest of the population are mostly Muslims and Orthodox who just a while ago belonged to the Catholic faith."[40]

It should be noted that some of the Muslims in Bosnia and Hercegovina today are descendants of Croatian slaves. Indeed, sad is the history of countless Catholic Croatians who were taken captive by the Turks in Bosnia and other Croatian lands and were sold as slaves at the markets of Sarajevo in Bosnia and Skopje in Macedonia, and dispatched to the Near East and North Africa. The Venetian historiographer Sanudo relates that by 1533 over 600,000 Catholics from Croatia had been captured by the Turks and sent into captivity in Turkey.[41] Of course, some of the captives remained in Bosnia and were forced to embrace Islam.[42]

A considerable number of Muslims living in Bosnia and Hercegovina

37/"Delli Turchi poi è molto maggior numero delli Cattolici e Scismatici; ma s'ha qui notare, che li Turchi che lavorano la terra, pouchi si trovano che parlano lingua turchesca: e però se non temessero il fuoco, quasi tutti quelli si farebbono Christiani sapendo bene che li loro maggiori sono stati Christiani." M. Batinić, "Relatione data all'imperatore dal Sign. Athanasio Georgiceo del viagio fatto l'anno 1626," *Starine* (Yugoslav Academy), XVIII (Zagreb, 1885), 128.

38/"Parlando però generalmente si tiene che siano al presente doi terzi d'habitanti Turchi, quasi tutti di raza christiana, et un terzo di christiani." *Glasnik Zemaljskog Muzeja*, XXI (1909), 357.

39/"Li christiani d'Antivari ... per non perder la vita e la robba, hanno professato la setta Mahomettana vedendo l'occisione de 74 christiani per ribelli et tradittori ..." B. Pandžić, "De Donato Jelić, O.F.M., Missionario Apostolico (1600–1676)," *Arch. Franc. Historicum*, LVI (1963), 8, ft. 5.

40/"Caeteri sunt omnes in gravi numero Turcae et schismatici, cum ante parvum tempus ferme omnes catholici fuerunt." J. Jelenić, "Spomenici," *Starine* (Yugoslav Academy), XXXVI (1918), 149.

41/L. Katić, *Pregled Povijesti Hrvata*/Survey of the History of Croatians (Zagreb, 1938), 160.

42/A. Solovjev, "Trgovina bosanskim robljem do god. 1661"/Trade in Bosnian

today are descendants of Croatians from Slavonia, Vojvodina, Lika, and Dalmatia, who had accepted Islam as their religion and had fled from these provinces when they were liberated from Turkish domination during the Viennese Wars of 1683–99 and thereafter, and came under Christian rule.[43]

Some present-day Muslims in eastern Bosnia, Hercegovina, and the Sanjak are descendants of the Croatian Muslims who lived in the medieval Croatian Dioclea, present-day Montenegro, and were expelled from their ancestral homeland during the eighteenth and nineteenth centuries. They were aware of their ancestral Croatian origin and gave Croatian names to several of their new settlements.[44]

The Serbs did not participate in spreading Islam in Bosnia. Under pressure from the Turks, the medieval Serbs did not retreat toward the west into Bosnia, but started to move toward the north across the Danube into present-day Vojvodina and southern Hungary.[45] Moreover, during the first centuries of their rule over Serbia, the Turks did not persecute the Greek Orthodox Church to which all the Serbs belonged.[46] The Patriarch of Constantinople and the Orthodox Vlachs cooperated closely with the Turkish government, so that this church was favored and privileged within the territory of the Ottoman Empire. According to Professor Omer L. Barkan's statistical research on the population of Serbia from 1520 to 1530, hence two complete generations after Serbia was subjugated by the Turks in 1459, there were only 4307 Muslim families as compared to 169,916 Greek Orthodox families in the Serbian Sanjaks.[47] Most of these Muslim families came from the outside, either as soldiers or craftsmen.

According to our research into the origin of the present-day Muslims in Bosnia and Hercegovina, the composition of the followers of Islam can be expressed as follows: 10–12 percent are descendants of Bosnian-Hercegovinian Croatians of the Bogomil sect, 70–75 percent come from Bosnian-Hercegovinian Croatian Catholics, 12–13 percent come from

Slaves up to 1661, *Glasnik Zemaljskog Muzeja*, N. S., I (Sarajevo, 1946), 139–146; V. Vinaver, "Trgovina bosanskim robljem tokom XIV veka u Dubrovniku"/Trade in Bosnian Slaves during the Fourteenth Century in Dubrovnik, *Anali Hist. Instituta* (Yugoslav Academy), II (Dubrovnik, 1953), 125–47; Mandić, *Etnička povijest Bosne i Hercegovine*, 242–51.

43/Mandić, *op. cit.*, 253–71.

44/Mandić, *op. cit.*, 271–4.

45/K. Jireček and J. Radonić, *Istorija Srba*, II, 73–214; IV, 95–104; *Historija naroda Jugoslavije*, I (Zagreb, 1953), 469–87; II (1959), 175–85, 818–28, 1118–21.

46/D. Mandić, "Herceg-Bosna i Hrvatska," *Hrvatska Revija*, XIII (Buenos Aires, 1963), 454–6.

47/O. L. Barkan, "Les déportations comme méthode de peuplement," 129.

Croatian Muslims of the neighboring Croatian provinces and Montenegro, 2–3 percent are of Turkish ethnic origin, and 1–2 percent are of Vlach ethnic origin.

WERE MUSLIM AND CATHOLIC INHABITANTS OF BOSNIA AND HERCEGOVINA DURING OTTOMAN RULE AWARE OF THEIR ORIGIN?

In the Middle Ages, Europe was a compound of many larger or smaller states, principalities, and free cities of varying degrees of independence. The boundaries of these political entities were constantly changing. It became customary to extend the names of the political units to the natives, though the natives might be of different origin or a part of a larger ethnic group. However, this political atomism did not prevent the spread and use of common languages and customs, and the preservation and development of spiritual unity within larger ethnic groups. Natives were always more or less aware that they belonged to a specific national entity.

The growth of political atomism among Croatians was promoted by specific geopolitical factors. At the outset of their political existence, the Croatians were organized into several autonomous principalities and political-geographic units populated by the same ethnic group. Thus, the ancient chronicles already mention certain Croatian principalities by name: White (western) Croatia, Red (southern) Croatia, Duklja (Dioclea), Zahumlje, Slavonia, etc.[48] The inhabitants of these principalities and provinces were interchangeably called by the name of the principality or by the common name Croatians.

In Bosnia, the extensive practice of designating the inhabitants by the name of the principality was reinforced by two factors. First, the people and leaders were concerned with preserving a maximum independence of the surrounding states; a specific name which would simultaneously identify the political unit and the populace was helpful. A second contributing factor was the appearance in Bosnia of the Croatian Bogomils who, to differentiate themselves from Croatian Catholics, began to call themselves Bosnians and their language the Bosnian language. This same practice was later adopted by the Muslims, whose origin lay in the conversion of almost all members of the Bogomil sect and a good many Croatian Catholics. Nevertheless, their common Croatian origin and name were not entirely forgotten. Both Muslims and Catholic Bosnians spoke the same Croatian language and were conscious of their common national origin and that they were only one branch

48/Mandić, *Crvena Hrvatska*. See Index for names mentioned.

of the Croatian nation which extended beyond the political borders of Bosnia.[49]

This awareness of their Croatian origin on the part of Bosnians is witnessed in the following facts:

I

1/In the year 1512, at the general convention of the Franciscan Order in the city of Naples, the official delegates of the Vicariate of Bosnia who were living on territory not yet under Turkish domination called themselves Croatians (Croatae) and requested that the convention change the ancient name of "Vicariate of Bosnia" to "Province of Croatia" (Provincia Croatiae).[50] At the subsequent convention of the order in Assisi in 1514, the Vicariate of Bosnia was divided into two separate units, and the larger unit, which was outside the territory under the control of the Ottoman Empire, was given the name Croatian Bosnia (Bosnia Croatiae).[51] This unit included the following monasteries from the territory of the present republic of Bosnia: Hlivno, Glamoč, Bihać, Jajce, Glaž on the Ukrina River, Modriča on the Bosna River, Tuzla and Bijeljina on the Drina River.

2/Those Catholics from Bosnia who left the Turkish-dominated territory after the first persecution of Catholics which began in 1516 called themselves "Croatians."[52]

3/The Franciscan Franjo Glavinich, born in 1585 in Glamoč, Bosnia, called the language *hrvatski* (Croatian) in his writings. In his work *Origine della provincia Bosna Croatia* (Origins of the [Franciscan] Province of Croatia-Bosnia) he wrote: "The Bosnians are the same people as the Croatians; and their language is also the same."[53]

4/The Franciscan Lovro Šitović (*ca.* 1680–1729), born to Muslim parents in Ljubuški, speaks in his writings about the "Croatian nation," the "Croatian language," and "Croatian rivers." In the introduction to his Latin-Illyrian Grammar (Venice, 1713), he calls himself and the youth of the Bosnian province to whom he directed his introduction "We Croatians."[54]

5/The Franciscan Nikola Lašvanin (died 1750), one of the best-

49/Mandić, *Etnička povijest Bosne i Hercegovine*, 285–446.

50/L. Waddingus, *Annales Minorum, ad. an. 1512, N. 6.*

51/*Op. cit. ad an. 1514 N.* 6; F. Glavinich, *Origine della Provincia Bosna Croatia* (Vdine, 1648), 11.

52/Mandić, *Etnička povijest Bosne i Hercegovine*, 293–305.

53/"I Bosnesi sono l'istessa natione con i Croati, e tale è anco il linguaggio loro." Glavinich, *Origine della provincia Bosna Croatia*, 1.

54/"... mnozi narodi ... lascgne nauce gramatiku, nego mi Hrvati ..." *Grammatica*

known chroniclers of Bosnia, wrote that Croatians came from beyond the Carpathian Mountains in 640 A.D. "into Dalmatia and into today's Croatian and Slavic countryside. The Dalmatia (Roman-Byzantine) which extended from the sea to the Danube assumed the name Croatia as it has been called up until today."[55] In another place he wrote of "the Highlands of Croatia which is now called Bosnia."[56]

6/Before the Viennese wars (1683–99), within the military structure of the Ottoman Empire there were in Bosnia hired units composed of native Catholic Croatians. The official name of these units was *Hrvatski junaci* ("Brave Croatians").[57] Thus, the natives, both Catholic and Muslim, were steadily reminded of their origin and nationality.

II/The Croatians of Bosnia were introduced to Islam through the Turks. Therefore the converts to Islam were called "Turks" by Croatian Catholics. This expression was accepted by the Ottoman authorities, and because there were no native Turks in Bosnia upon whom the central government could rely, they even approved of and tried to extend and encourage the use of this appelation. With time the practice became so common that, at the end of the sixteenth century, the population was classified as "Turks" (Muslims), "Kršćani" (Christian Catholics), and "Hrišćani" (Christian Orthodox). However, the Ottoman authorities did not succeed in denationalizing the Muslims of Bosnia and destroying consciousness of their Croatian origin. Until the Viennese wars, Muslims and Catholics lived together amicably and in close quarters. Members of the same clan might be either Catholic or Muslim; often, in the same families the parents were Catholics and sons Muslims, or a husband was Muslim and his wife Catholic.[58] The common origin of and close kinship between Catholics and Muslims is evident in the fact that the Muslims of Bosnia and Hercegovina to this day have retained the old exclusively Croatian Ikavian speech combined with strong elements

latino-illyrica ... juventuti illyrice studiose accomodata a Padre F. Laurentio de Gliubuschi (Venetiis, 1742), I.

55/"640. Doidoše iz priko Babini(h) Gora Hervati naiparvo u Dalmaciju, i ove sadašnje harvatske i slovinske strane. ... I od nji Dalmacija, koja je od mora do Dunava dosegla, harvatsko ime prima i zove se do današnjega dneva." J. Jelenić, *Ljetopis fra Nikole Lašvanina*/Chronicle of Nikola Lašvanin (Sarajevo, 1916), 22.

56/"1131. Stipan ugarski kralj ... Ovi zadobi Ramu u gornjoj Harvatskoj zemlji, koja se sada Bosna imenu(j)e, i zato svi njegovi namisnici zovu se kralji od Rame, t.j. Bosne." Jelenić, *op. cit.*, 31.

57/Evlija Čelebija, *Putopis*/Travelogue, Croatian trans. by H. Šabanović (Sarajevo, 1957), I, 207, 211; II, 177, 226. On the meaning and usage of *Hrvatski junaci* see Mandić, *Etnička povijest Bosne i Hercegovine*, 354–7.

58/Mandić, *op. cit.*, 332–4.

of the exclusively Croatian dialect called Chakavian.[59] Furthermore, Muslims used the old Croatian system of numbering the years, and the Croatian names of months;[60] they wrote with a special Croatian variant of the Cyrillic alphabet called *bosančica*,[61] and they also practiced many old folk customs and clung to the same superstitions as did the Catholics.

The Turks were a relatively small nation at the period of their most rapid expansion. As soon as they controlled a vast territory, they were faced with a need for huge numbers of soldiers and administrative personnel. To meet this problem they created special military units called Janissaries, which they recruited from the Christian children in the occupied territories. Thus, beginning in 1472, at five or ten year intervals, children were taken from their Catholic and Potur parents (these children were called in Turkish *adžemi oglan*) in Bosnia[62] and turned over to the Janissary school in Istanbul where they were educated and trained. Selected pupils from the Janissary school were sent to continue their education at the great court school and graduates of this school were designated as the future military and administrative leaders of the empire. Although they were completely integrated into the most intimate state life of Turkey, Janissaries and high administrative officers born in Bosnia and Hercegovina did not completely forget their homeland, nor were they ashamed of their Croatian origin. They continued to speak Croatian in Istanbul and at the sultan's court, and even succeeded in making their language the second official language of the empire during the sixteenth and seventeenth centuries, thus giving testimony that their kinfolk were Croatians and their homeland, Bosnia, was a Croatian land. Here are some prominent examples:

1/The young Mehmed Sokolović, the future grand vizier, was born in eastern Bosnia; at the age of eighteen, when he had finished high court school in Istanbul at the head of his class, he was asked by Sultan Suleiman, the Magnificent, where he came from; he answered: "From the Croats."[63]

59/Mandić, *op. cit.*, 360–5.

60/F. Spaho, "Narodni nazivi mjeseci"/Croatian Names of the Months, *Kalendar "Napredak" 1935* (Sarajevo), 42–5.

61/On the Croatian Cyrillic script called *bosančica*, see the following: Ć. Truhelka, "Bosančica. Prilog bosanskoj paleografiji"/Bosnian Script. A Contribution to Bosnian Paleography, *Glasnik Zemaljskog Muzeja*, I (Sarajevo, 1889), 65–83; M. Tentor, *Latinsko i slavensko pismo*/Latin and Slavic Script (Zagreb, 1932); Mandić, *Etnička povijest Bosne i Hercegovine*, 50–61.

62/For the taking of *adžemi oglan* in Bosnia and Hercegovina, see Mandić, *Etnička povijest Bosne i Hercegovine*, 346–8.

63/H. Lamb, *Suleiman the Magnificent* (Garden City, N.J., 1957), 53.

2/The grand vizier Rustam-Pasha, who was probably born in Mostar,[64] proudly called himself "Croatian." In 1553 he received the envoys of King Ferdinand I, and he asked the Hungarian Francis Zay "whether he and his companion bishop Anton Vrančić spoke Croatian." When they acknowledged that they did, he began to converse with them in that language.[65]

3/Francis Bornamissa de Alsow, on May 2, 1553, declared under oath concerning the person of Cardinal Juraj Utišenović: "He speaks Croatian and he is a friend of the pashas; he is a relative of Mehmed-Pasha, who is of Croatian origin, and who was, as a child, captured and taken away to Turkey ... Also Murad-Beg (Tardić) is Croatian and a relative of Father George."[66]

4/In 1589, Hodaverdi, an envoy of the Sofi-Pasha, governor of Bosnia, made an agreement with the Venetian governor (Provveditore) of Dalmatia F. Nani. About that mission Hodaverdi wrote "two charters in Turkish and two charters in Croatian."[67]

5/Mehmed-Aga, born in Zvornik, commander of the Janissaries at the sultan's court, on the occasion of a visit by a delegation from the republic of Dubrovnik in 1631, told the members of the delegation: "I am proud of our language and enjoy speaking it."[68]

6/Imperial envoy Marco A. Pigafetta, in 1567, during official visits to the Turkish Begler-beg in Budim, and during his diplomatic visits to Istanbul, used to speak in Croatian. In his accounts of those missions he wrote: "In Istanbul it is customary to speak Croatian, a language which is understood by almost all official Turks, especially military men."[69]

64/Contemporary sources do not agree on the place of birth of Rustam-Pasha; see Mandić, *Etnička povijest Bosne i Hercegovine*, 337ff.

65/"Conversus passa ad Zay: Tu, inquit, scisne croatice? Scio, respondit. Et is collega tuus? Respondit: Ipse quoque ... miratusque quod tam bene ea lingua loqueretur Zay ..." Actio Antonii Verancii etc. apud principem turcarum anno 1553, mense Augusto. *Mon. Hung. Hist. Scriptores,* IV, *Pars* II, *vol. 4* (Pest, 1858), 66.

66/"Ille et linguam Croaticam noverat, et erat familiaris cum Bassis, et etiam sanguine junctus Mehmed Bassae, qui natione Croatus erat et puer captivus in Turciam ductus; id quod fr. Georgius ipsi, testi, dixit, ac preterea Murad Begum esse quoque Croatum et consanguineum ipsius fr. Georgii." A. Theiner, *Vetera monumenta Slavorum Meridionalium historiam illustrantia,* II (Zagreb, 1875), 39, no. 57.

67/"Za to mi rečeni Hodaverdi čauš, hotismo ... dvoje knjige pisati turske, a dvoje horvatske ..." *Starine* (Yugoslav Academy), x (Zagreb, 1878), 14.

68/"Ja se ponosim našim jezikom i uživam razgovarati ovim jezikom." *Historija naroda Jugoslavije*, II, 240.

69/"... parlar in croato ... et ciò usassi parimente a Constantinopoli ... in croata lingua parlavano, la quale è familiare à tutti quasi i Turchi, et specialmente a gli huomini di guerra." A. Pigafetta, *Itinerario* (London, 1685); *Starine* (Yugoslav Academy), XXII 1890), 88.

7/The well-known Turkish historian Muṣṭafā ʿAlī, an official of the governor of Bosnia in the city of Banja Luka (1569–77), wrote in his book that "the Bosnians belong to the Croatian nation."[70]

8/In 1609, in Banja Luka in Bosnia, *mudāris* Muslī-ad-Dīn ibn ʿAlī wrote in his book *Munjetul-talibin ve gunjetur ragasin.* In the preface he said that he wrote the book "in the province of Croatia."[71]

9/The Turkish travelogue writer Evlija Čelebija, passing through Bosnia in 1660–4, mentions in several places in his book that the people of Bosnia speak "Croatian" and that Croatian is "the language of the Bosnian and Croatian people."[72]

During the Viennese wars (1683–99), when the Turkish might was definitely broken, the Bosnians protected Bosnia from the Western powers with their own military resources. They would defend and safeguard Bosnia throughout the eighteenth century. During those confrontations and hostilities, in which the Muslims of Bosnia were at war with the Croatians in the Kingdom of Croatia, Slavonia, and Dalmatia, the religious zeal and national separatism of the Bosnian Muslims became very strong, and led them to emphasize and to use even more the name Bosnia. But they rebelled as well against Istanbul when they thought that it went too far in attempting to control and regulate their specific Bosnian culture and interests, as did Husein Gradašćević in 1832 and the other Bosnian begs in 1850–51.[73]

THE AWAKENING OF CROATIAN NATIONAL CONSCIOUSNESS AMONG MUSLIMS IN BOSNIA AND HERCEGOVINA IN THE NINETEENTH CENTURY

The cultural and national renewal in Croatia proper – accelerated after Napoleon's intervention in the Balkans at the beginning of the nineteenth century – known as the Illyrian Movement and the Croatian National Awakening[74] soon spread into Bosnia, and it affected not only Catholics but also Muslims. Nevertheless, a genuine renewal of aware-

70/*Taʾrīkh-i ʿAlī*, IV, I, 12 s; S. Bašagić, "Bošnjaci i Hercegovci u islamskoj književnosti"/Bosnians and Hercegovinians in Islamic Literature, *Glasnik Zemaljskog Muzeja*, XXIV (1912), 6f.

71/H. Bošnjanin, *Hrvati i Herceg-Bosna*/Croatians and Bosnia Hercegovina (Sarajevo, 1940), 27.

72/Čelebija,*Putopis*, I, 49, 136, etc.

73/Mandić, *Etnička povijest Bosne i Hercegovine*, 408ff.

74/D. Šurmin, *Hrvatski preporod*/Croatian Renascence, I–II (Zagreb, 1903–4); F. Fancev, *Dokumenti za naše podrijetlo Hrvatskoga Preporoda (1790–1832)*/Documents for the Origin of Our Croatian Renascence (Zagreb, 1933); J. Horvat, *Politička povijest Hrvatske*/The Political History of Croatia (Zagreb, 1936), 88–197; F. Šišić, "O stogodišnjici Ilirskoga pokreta"/On the Centennial of the Illyrian Movement, *Ljetopis Jugosl. Akad.*, 49 (Zagreb, 1937), 99–130.

ness of belonging to the Croatian national community did not come until the last decades of the nineteenth century. The young Muslim students who went to the universities of Vienna, Prague, and Zagreb after Bosnia and Hercegovina were occupied in 1878 by the Hapsburg imperial forces were acquainted with modern political and national ideas which were not based on religious premise. As they studied the characteristics of their people's speech and the political and religious history of Bosnia, it became clear to these young Bosnians that Bosnian and Hercegovinian Muslims had descended from medieval Croatian Bogomils and Catholics, and that they (Muslims) belonged to the community of the Croatian nation. These new political concepts were carried by the students first to the progressive city dwellers and then to the broad strata of the Muslim people of Bosnia. This national awakening was supported by the leading Muslim magazines such as *Behar* and *Novi Behar* in the city of Sarajevo and *Biser* in the city of Mostar.

In the forefront of the Croatian National Awakening among the people of Bosnia and Hercegovina were the following prominent Muslims: poet and historian Safvet-Beg Bašagić (1870–1934) from Nevesinje; several members of the old aristocratic families of Kulenović and Džinić from Banja Luka; Edhem Mulabdić from Maglaj; the mayors of the city of Sarajevo, Esad Ef. Kulović and Edhem Bičakčić; poet Musa Ćazim Ćatić from Odžak in Bosnian Posavina; writer Hivzi A. Bjelavac; the Muslim religious leaders Reis-Ulema Hadži Mehmed Džemaludin Čaušević (1870–1938) and Reis-Ulema Fehim Spaho (1877–1942); business man and philanthropist Adem-aga Mešić (1866–1945); Džafer Beg Kulenović, a congressman for many years between the first and second world wars and political leader and president since 1938 of the Muslim political party (JOM) in the Belgrade Parliament.[75]

When the kingdom of Serbs, Croatians, and Slovenes was created after the first world war in 1918, and the outline of the new constitution was submitted to Parliament in Belgrade in 1920, the Muslim political party from Bosnia and Hercegovina sent twenty-four elected representatives to the Congress. It is an interesting fact that twenty-two members of this group were officially registered as Croatians. Only the president and the secretary of the official Parliament Club indicated their nationality as Yugoslav. This was interpreted by the close political associates of these two representatives as a move to facilitate the work of the club in the congress in which the Serbs were a majority.[76]

75/Mandić, *Etnička povijest Bosne i Hercegovine*, 412–26.

76/*Op. cit.*, 423; See also R. Bičanić, *Ekonomska Podloga hrvatskog pitanja*/The Economic Basis of the Croatian Problem (Zagreb: Dr. V. Maček, 1938), 3.

Of interest is a comment of Svetozar Pribićević, one of the chief founders of the Kingdom of Serbs, Croatians, and Slovenes and for many years a political power in the centralized political structure of Royal Yugoslavia. In his testamentary book *Diktatura kralja Aleksandra* (Dictatorship of King Alexander) he wrote in 1932 about the national awareness of Muslims from Bosnia and Hercegovina: "The huge majority of their intellectuals are Croatian-oriented. And in political action the masses follow the intellectuals blindly. There is no doubt ... that Muslims from Bosnia and Hercegovina in their aspirations and their outlook are in complete agreement with the Croatians. A Serbian statesman who does not recognize this fact, could not be considered a man of political stature.[77]

ORIGIN AND COLONIZATION OF THE PRESENT-DAY SERBS IN BOSNIA AND HERCEGOVINA

There were neither Serbs nor followers of the Greek-Orthodox Church in Hercegovina until the end of the twelfth century when the dynasty of the Nemanjići came into power in Serbia. There were none in Bosnia until the middle of the fifteenth century when Bosnia was subjugated by the Turks. The Nemanjić rulers were the first to spread the Orthodox faith by force among the Croatian Catholics in Hercegovina. During the Turkish rule in Bosnia and Hercegovina this practice was continued by the Serbian Orthodox patriarchs and clergy, and was successful especially in those regions in which Catholic clergy were scarce or had disappeared altogether.

FORCIBLE CONVERSION OF CROATIAN CATHOLICS TO THE ORTHODOX FAITH

The forcible conversion of native Croatian Catholics to the Orthodox faith was initiated by the Serbian prince Miroslav who was appointed by the Byzantine emperor Emmanuel Comnenus in 1173 to rule Zahumlje, the region which is today central Hercegovina. Pope Alexander III, in a letter of June 7, 1181, complains that Miroslav did not permit the consecration of the Catholic bishops. Moreover, he refused to receive the pope's delegate or to read his letter.[78] Serbian King Stefan Uroš II

77/Sv. Pribičević, *Diktatura kralja Aleksandra*/The Dictatorship of King Alexander (Beograd, 1952), 28ff.

78/"Alexander episcopus ... Miroslauo comiti ... nec legatum nostrum recipere nec nostris parere litteris voluisti ... Accepimus etiam, quod loca illa, in quibus

Milutin (1282–1321) adopted an even more aggressive policy, seizing a great many parishes, monasteries, and churches from the Catholic clergy and placing them in the hands of Orthodox priests.[79] By the middle of the sixteenth century, when the Turks intensified their persecution of the Catholic Church, a much larger number of Croatian Catholics in Hercegovina embraced the Orthodox religion. During these persecutions the Catholic clergy, along with some of their faithful, left Hercegovina; the majority of the Croatian Catholics, who remained in the country, were forced to accept Islam or the Orthodox faith.

From the sixteenth century until the end of the eighteenth a great many Croatian Catholics in Bosnia too were impelled to embrace the Orthodox religion. Most of these were forced conversions, initiated by the Patriarchs of Constantinople and Peć (Serbia) who considered themselves the only legitimate representatives of Christianity in the Ottoman Empire. These Patriarchs endeavoured, by every means in their power, to place the Croatian Catholics of Bosnia and Hercegovina, together with their spiritual leaders, the Franciscan Fathers, under their own jurisdiction.[80]

The Bosnian bishop Nikola Ogramić wrote to Rome in 1672: "The schismatics, led by their very bad bishop, keep persecuting our Catholics with the help of the Turks, forcing them to adopt their rite and pay them tithes. To this end they often bring severe letters patents from the Turkish emperor and use them to force us, in Turkish courts, to leave our holy Church and to become subject to them.[81]

Jesuit Father Daniel Farlati writes in his work *Illyricum Sacrum* about the pressure exerted by the Orthodox clergy upon the Catholics in Bos-

cathedrales sedes olim fuisse noscuntur, ordinari libere non permittas ..." Letter of Alexander III, the Pope, to Miroslav, the Prince of Zahumlje. T. Smičiklas, *Codex diplomaticus regni Croatiae, Dalmatiae et Slavoniae*, II (Zagreb, 1904), 176, n. 174.

79/"... monasteria, ecclesias, insulas ac villas ... nonnulli reges Rassie predecessores tui ... suis temporibus occuparunt et tu nunc ea occupas et detines occupata." Letter of the Pope Clement VI to the Serbian king Stefan Dušan, 1345. Smičiklas, *Cod. dipl.*, XI (1913), 179, n. 134; Theiner, *Vet. mon. Slav. Merid.*, I, 215, n. 280.

80/K. St. Draganović, "Massenübertritte von Katholiken zur Orthodoxie im Kroatischen Sprachgebiet zur Zeit der Türkenherrschaft," *Orientalia christiana Periodica*, III (Roma, 1937); L. Hadrovics, *Le Peuple Serbe et son église sous la domination turque* (Paris, 1947), 37–101; Mandić *Etnička povijest Bosne i Hercegovine*, 450–494.

81/"Schismatici ... cum nequissimo suo Vladica seu ritus eorum episcopo, non cessant catholicos nostros acerrime coram Turcis expugnari eosque ad ritum suum cogendo et ad tributum; in quem finem frequentissime adversus nos Turcarum imperatoris districtissima deferunt diplomata, quibus nos in tribunalibus Turcicis urgent sanctam N(ostram) E(cclesiam) deserere eisque subiici." *Relatio ep. bos. N. Ogramić an. 1675*. J. Jelenić, "Spomenici," *Starine* (Yugoslav Academy), XXXVI (1918), 138.

nia and Hercegovina. He says, on the basis of information furnished by the Bosnian historian Father Filip Laštrić, a Franciscan: "They are our enemies, worse than the Turks themselves, because they never stop their efforts to bring us under their power."[82]

About one-third of the Serbs in present-day Bosnia are descendants of the native Croatians. One group of these descended from members of the Bogomil sect, but they are predominantly descendants of Croatian Catholics. These Serbs in Bosnia and Hercegovina are rather reddish in complexion.[83]

THE ROMAN COLONIZATION OF MOORS IN THE BALKANS AND IN OTHER REGIONS OF EUROPE

Most of the Serbs living in Bosnia and Hercegovina today have a strikingly dark complexion, inherited from the Balkan Vlachs of the Middle Ages. All historians agree that the Vlachs were not ethnically Slavic. In the Middle Ages they spoke their own language, derived, in large part, from Latin. Historians disagree, however, on how they came into possession of their dark brownish complexions or, rather, on which black or semi-black race these Vlachs descended from.

In my study *Postanak Vlaha* (The Origin of the Vlachs), published in 1956, I have proved that the medieval Vlachs were the descendants of Moors who lived in Mauretania in northwest Africa. As war veterans, they were settled by the Romans along the Danube in the Balkans and in other regions of Europe.[84]

The Roman army was composed of mercenaries, who, for the most part, came from Dalmatia, Gaul, and Mauretania. Toward the end of the Roman Empire many of them were recruited from Germany also. Soldiers of a common ethnic and language group were organized in separate military contingents so that they might better understand one another and thus function more effectively in battle. Military service lasted for twenty-five years, and all veterans, after serving their military term, were given Roman citizenship and property in some place near the last camp at which they had served. The Roman authorities began

82/"Plerumque catholici promiscue domos habent cum Turcis et schismaticis Graeci ritus, et quidem hos infestiores hostes toleramus, quam turcas ipsos. Nunquam enim nobis non insidiantur, quo nos suae jurisdictioni subjiciant, sunt autem in hac patria numero et opibus majores catholicis duplo." D. Farlati, *Illyricum Sacrum*, IV (Venetis, 1769), 87.

83/Mandić, "Bosnia y Hercegovina provincias Croatas," 192–204.

84/D. Mandić, *Postanak Vlaha prema novim poviesnim iztraživanjima*/Origin of the Vlachs in the Light of New Historical Research (Buenos Aires, 1956). Second edition in Mandić, *Rasprave i prilosi*, 515–67.

to settle the Moors in the Balkans during the reign of Emperor Claudius (A.D. 41–54), and continued to do so until the fall of the Western Roman Empire in A.D. 476.[85]

An original brass military diploma which dates from the middle of the second century A.D. mentions Moorish soldiers in Moesia, which is modern Serbia.[86] Another military diploma of A.D. 158 speaks of Moorish soldiers from Africa in Dacia, or modern Rumania, and also of auxiliary troops of the Dacian Moors.[87] A Roman document, *Notitia Dignitatum*,[88] which dates from the beginning of the fifth century A.D., mentions several Moorish battalions in the Balkans and the Moorish military colony *Ad Mauros* which was located on the Inn River near Vienna;[89] and in what is modern Besarabia, there was a city called Maurocastrum.[90] According to the document *Notitia Dignitatum*, 2500 to 5000 Illyrian Moorish soldiers, in five separate military units, had served in the Near East.[91] From this document we must deduce that at the beginning of the fifth century at least 100,000 descendants of Moors lived in Illyricum, which was located in the present-day Balkans.

Writing about the settlement of the Bulgarians in A.D. 681, the old Croatian chronicles mention the Mauro-Vlachs under the name the "Black Latins."[92] Old Russian[93] and Hungarian chronicles[94] mention the Vlachs by the end of the ninth century, and place them in the Car-

85/*Digesta* XLIX, *16, 1–16; Cod. Justin.* XII, *35, 1–18*; Fl. Vegetius Renatus, *Epitome rei militaris*, ed. C. Lang (Lipsiae, 1885); M. J. Roman, *L'Organisation militaire de l'empire romain* (Paris, 1867); Mandić, *Rasprave i prilozi*, 519–28.

86/"... Mauris equit(ibus) et pedit(ibus), qui sunt in Moesia Super(iore) equitum Maurorum ..." *Diplomata militaria. Corpus Inscriptionum Latinarum*, XVI (Berolini, 1936), 103, n. 114.

87/"... et vexil(lariis) Afric(ae) et Mau(r)et(aniae) Caes(arinensis), qui sunt cum Mauris gentilib(us) in Dacia Super(iore) et sunt sub Statio Prisco leg(ato) ..." *Diplomata militaria. Corp. Inscript. Lat.*, XVI, 98, n. 108.

88/O. Seeck, *Notitia dignitatum accedunt Notitia urbis Constantinopolitanae et Laterculi prouinciarum* (Berolini, 1876).

89/"Sub dispositione uiri spectabilis ducis Pannoniae et Norici Ripensis: ... Equites promoti, Ad Mauros." O. Seeck, *Notitia dignitatum*, Occidentis 34, n. 31, p. 197.

90/Mandić, *Rasprave i prilozi*, 526.

91/"Sub dispositione uiri spectabilis ducis Foenicis: 18. Equites Mauri Illyriciani, Otthara ... 21. Equites Dalmatae Illyriciani, Lataui." O. Seeck, *Notitia dignitatum*, Orientis 32, 67ff. Likewise Orientis 33, 34, 35, 37, pp. 70, 73, 75, 81.

92/"... debellando ceperunt totam Macedoniam; post haec totam provinciam Latinorum, qui illo tempore Romani vocabantur, modo vero Maurovlachi, hoc est Nigri Latini vocantur." F. Šišić, *Letopis Popa Dukljanina*, 298; V. Mošin, *Ljetopis Popa Dukljanina* (Zagreb, 1950), 45. Likewise: *Kraljevstvo Hrvata*, Šišić, *op. cit.*, 389; Mošin, 45.

93/D. S. Lihačev, *Povest' vremennyh let*/Story of Olden Times II (Moskva-Leningrad, 1950), 11 and 21.

94/E. Szentpétery, *Scriptores rerum hungaricarum*, I (Budapest, 1937), 45, 48, 65ff., 156ff., 162ff.

pathian Mountains. Byzantine writers rarely speak of Vlachs before the end of the ninth century; they usually call them Mauro-Vlachs,[95] a name given to them because of their Mauretanian origin.

The principal settlements of the medieval Mauro-Vlachs, sometimes simply called Vlachs, are found in the Carpathian Mountains north of the Danube; in the Balkan Mountains, in present-day Bulgaria; around the Pind Mountains in Greece; around the Kopaonik Mountains in Serbia, and also in the Durmitor Mountains in Montenegro.

The Mauro-Vlachs spoke the Romance language which they learned from the Romans during their military service. They lived in segregated groups among Greeks, Bulgarians, Serbs, and other Slavic nations, in the Middle Ages. During this time the Serbs were forbidden by state law to marry Vlach girls.[96] The medieval Mauro-Vlachs led a nomadic life, their primary occupation being the raising of cattle, horses, and sheep. They had many horses, which resulted in their being engaged to transport merchant goods from the cities on the eastern shores of the Adriatic Sea to the interior. During the Middle Ages, many entered the army and fought on behalf of various rulers.[97]

The Mauro-Vlachs began to emigrate into Duklja, present-day Montenegro, during the Bulgarian rule from 990 to 1018. From the thirteenth to fifteenth centuries the great commercial center, Dubrovnik, attracted a great many of them from all over the central Balkans. They settled close by in eastern Hercegovina, where they formed many colonies.[98] Prior to the Turkish occupation, the Mauro-Vlachs in Hercegovina were Catholics.

The Vlachs from the middle Balkans started to move into Bosnia along with the Turks as the latter's auxiliary troops. These Vlachs were of the Orthodox faith, and the Turkish documents and chronographers often speak of this. In 1530 Benedict Kuripešić writes that the majority of the population in Bosnia was Catholic: "The ancient Bosnians of the Christian religion." He has this to say about the Vlachs: "The other inhabitants [of Bosnia] are Surrfen [Serbians] and are called Vlachs by the local

95/S. Dragomir, *Vlahii si Morlacii*/Vlachs or Mauro-Vlachs (Cluj, 1924); R. Lee Wolff, "The Second Bulgarian Empire." *Speculum* (1949), 167–206; Mandić, *Rasprave i prilozi*, 533–7.

96/"Sr'bin' da se ne ženi u Vlaseh'; ako li se oženi, da ju vede u merop'he." "Decanska povelja," *1330*, A. V. Solovjev, *Odabrani spomenici srpskog prava*/ Selected Monuments of Serbian Law (Beograd, 1926), 114. Likewise in "Banjska povelja," Solovjev, *op. cit.*, 93.

97/K. J. Jireček, "Die Wlachen und Maurowlachen in den Denkmälern von Ragusa," *Sitzungsber. boehm. Gess. der Wiss. in Prag. Jahrg. 1880*, 109–25; Dragomir, *Vlahii si Morlacii*; Mandić, *Rasprave i prilozi*, 537–64.

98/M. Vego, *Naselja bosanske srednjevjekovne države*/Settlements of the Bosnian Medieval State (Sarajevo, 1957), 127–132; Mandić, *Rasprave i prilozi*, 554–8.

population, and we call them Zitten or Martholosen. They came from Smederevo and Greek Belgrade."[99]

General Ivan Lenković informed King Ferdinand I in 1551 that the Turks had brought several thousands of Mauro-Vlachs into western Bosnia from the interior of the European section of the Turkish Empire.[100] In 1540 there were in the Bosnian Sanjak 9879 Vlach households, that is, about 80,000 souls, mostly of the Orthodox faith.[101]

Most of the present-day Serbs in Bosnia and Hercegovina descend from the medieval, non-Slavic Vlachs.

THE ROLE OF THE BULGARIANS, ALBANIANS, GREEKS, AND ARMENIANS IN CREATING THE SERBIAN ETHNIC GROUP IN BOSNIA AND HERCEGOVINA

A great many Bulgarians, Greeks, Albanians, Armenians, and other national groups of the Orthodox faith came into Bosnia and Hercegovina along with the Turks and settled in the cities and towns. Their principal occupations were either commerce and crafts or employment with the local Turkish government. By the end of the eighteenth century, and at the beginning of the nineteenth, in the religious communities of the Orthodox faith in Sarajevo, Banja Luka, Travnik, Zvornik, Foča, Mostar, and elsewhere a considerable proportion of the membership was composed of Bulgarians and other non-Slavic ethnic groups. These foreigners, living and associating with the native Croatians of the Muslim, Catholic, and Orthodox faiths, learned the native tongue. By the middle of the nineteenth century, all of them, owing particularly to the activity of the Serbian Orthodox Church, began to consider themselves Serbs.[102]

COLONIZATION OF BOSNIA AND HERCEGOVINA BY THE ETHNIC SERBS

The first ethnic Serb immigrants began to move into Hercegovina in very small numbers during the reign of the Serbian Nemanjić dynasty at the end of the twelfth century because Hercegovina was more densely populated and its cultural level higher than that of Serbia. At that

99/"Item wir haben in berürtem khünigreich Wossen dreyerley nation und glaubens völkher gefunden. Die ersten sein die alten Wossner; die sein des Römischen Christlichen Glaubens ... Die anderen sein Surrfen, die nennen sie Wallachen und wir nennens Zisttzen oder Marthalossen. Die khamen von dem *Ort Smedravo* und Khriechisch Weissenburg ... Die drit nation sein die rechten Türggen ..." B. Curipeschitz, *Itinerarium ... nach Konstantinopel 1530,* ed. Lamberg-Schwarzenberg (Innsbruck, 1910), 34.

100/"... aus der tyeffe des Turgkhey mit souil tausendt Morlagkhen oder Walachen pesezt worden." E. Laszowski, *Monumenta Habsburgica,* III (Zagreb, 1917), 414.

101/*Historija naroda Jugoslavije,* II, 141.

102/Mandić, *Etnička povijest Bosne i Hercegovine,* 513–18.

time the government officials in Hercegovina were as a rule native Croatians. Most of them were Catholic, and a few were of the group who had adopted the Orthodox religion.[103]

A certain number of Serbs had already settled in Bosnia and Hercegovina looking for a better livelihood when the Bosnian Ban Tvrtko I in 1366–73 occupied the region of Podrinje which had been formerly a part of the Serbian kingdom and inhabited by the Serbs.[104] An indication that the ethnic Serbs never immigrated to Bosnia and Hercegovina in great numbers during the Ottoman rule is given by the fact that no community speaking the Serbian Ekavian speech was ever formed on the territory of those provinces. The greatest number of ethnic Serbs settled in Bosnia and Hercegovina during the Austro-Hungarian occupation (1878–1918), and during the periods of the first (1918–41) and second (1945–) Yugoslavia, either as soldiers, government officials, or tradesmen. The colonization of Bosnia by the ethnic Serbs was considerably intensified after 1945 when Serbian workers were settled in many industrial centers.

SERBIZATION OF VLACHS, ORTHODOX CROATIANS, AND NON-SLAVS

Under the influence of the French revolutions of 1789, 1830, and 1848 strong national movements arose all over Europe. The Balkan countries were no exception. In the first half of the nineteenth century, at first on the territory of the Austro-Hungarian Empire and later in Bosnia and Hercegovina, a rigorous and carefully planned propaganda campaign was inaugurated among members of the Orthodox Church. Its sole aim was to convince them that they were Serbs. This campaign was executed primarily by teachers in the Serbian parochial schools and by the athletic organization "Sokol," but above all by the Orthodox clergy. In 1863, under the guidance and sponsorship of the Serbian minister of state, Ilija Garašanin, special committees were created in Sarajevo and in other cities all over Bosnia and Hercegovina with the sole purpose of systematically teaching the Vlachs and Croatians of Orthodox faith that they should call themselves Serbs since they belonged to the Serbian Orthodox Church.[105] Among the Vlachs, who had previously called themselves Rumanians, this process was finally accomplished not long ago.[106]

103/Mandić, *Bosna i Hercegovina*, I, 300–18; *idem*, *Etnička povijest Bosne i Hercegovine*, 508–10.

104/*Mandić, Etnička povijest Bosne i Hercegovine*, 125–7.

105/Vl. Škarić, *Sarajevo i njegova okolina*/Sarajevo and Its Environs (Sarajevo, 1937), 223ff; Mandić, *op. cit.*, 515–18.

106/See national population censuses of Bosnia and Hercegovina in 1910, 1921, 1948, and 1953.

According to our research, the ethnic origin of the present-day Serbs in Bosnia and Hercegovina can be given in percentages as follows: 2–3 percent from the ancient Croatians of Bogomil's sect; 30–32 percent from Croatian Catholics forcibly converted to the Orthodox church; 50–52 per cent from the non-Slavic Mauro-Vlachs; 6–7 percent from the Bulgarians, Greeks, Armenians, Albanians, and other, non-Slavic, ethnic groups; 8–10 per cent from Serbian immigrants from Serbia proper.

SUMMARY AND STATISTICAL DATA

During the migration of the European nations the Croatians settled in Bosnia and Hercegovina. They have dwelt permanently in those two provinces up to the present day. At the beginning they were pagans; then they became Catholics during the period from the middle of the seventh to the end of the ninth centuries. Bogomilism began to spread at the end of the tenth century, and the great majority of Bosnian and Hercegovinian Croatians had embraced this sect by the beginning of the fourteenth. Dominican missionaries began to work for the return of the Bogomils to the Catholic faith in about 1228[107] and Franciscan missionaries continued this work in 1291.[108] About a century later, Pope Boniface VIII stated in a letter dated March 7, 1402, that up to that date the Franciscans had converted about 500,000 Bogomils to the Catholic faith.[109] In the year 1463, when Bosnia fell to the Turks, the population of Bosnia and Hercegovina was composed as follows: about 750,000 Croatian Catholics (83%), 80,000–90,000 Croatian Bogomils (*ca.* 10%), about 15,000 Orthodox Croatians (2%); 10,000–12,000 Catholics and 4000–5000 Orthodox Mauro-Vlachs (constituting 2% altogether); and 25,000–28,000 Orthodox Serbs (*ca.* 3%), mostly in Podrinje, east of the Drina River.

With the Turkish occupation of Bosnia in 1463 the Bogomils began to embrace Islam. In the second decade of the sixteenth century, when the Catholic persecutions began, some Catholics emigrated to the free countries, but a great many of them, particularly the farming population,

107/N. Pfeiffer, *Die ungarische Dominikanerordenprovinz von ihrer Gründung 1221 bis zur Tatarenverwüstung 1241–1242* (Zürich, 1913), 50–74; J. Šidak, "Ecclesia Sclavoniae i misija dominikanaca u Bosni"/"Ecclesia Sclavoniae" and the Dominican Mission in Bosnia, *Zbornik Fil. fakult. u Zagrebu*, III (Zagreb, 1955), 11–40; D. Mandić, *Bogomilska crkva bosanskih krstjana*, 149–62.

108/J. Šidak, "Franjevačka 'Dubia' iz god. 1372/3," *Istor.časopis*, V (Beograd, 1954–5), 207–31; Mandić, *Bogomilska crkva*, 262–80.

109/See footnote 17.

accepted Islam, though, at least at the beginning, only externally. Some Catholics, particularly in the eastern parts of Bosnia and Hercegovina, accepted the Orthodox faith. The Mauro-Vlachs of the Orthodox faith began to immigrate into Bosnia and Hercegovina from diverse parts of the middle Balkans together with the Turks as part of the latter's troops. The population of Bosnia and Hercegovina in 1624, according to contemporary statistics, was composed as follows: 900,000 Muslims (66.7%), 300,000 Catholics (22.2%), 150,000 Orthodox (11.1%).[110] Ethnically, the Muslims and Catholics were descendants of the native Croatians of the Bogomil and Catholic faiths, both together making up about 89 percent, and the members of the Orthodox Church were partly Croatians and partly non-Slavic Mauro-Vlach immigrants. A great many Catholics emigrated into neighboring free Croatian and other lands during the Viennese wars (1683–99) and the following struggles.[111] Muslim begs, landowners, brought in a considerable number of the Slavicized Vlachs mostly from Nikšić and the regions around Durmitor Mountain. The Muslims strengthened their ranks by the immigration of huge numbers of Croatian Muslims from the neighboring Croatian provinces which were liberated from the Turks.[112] In spite of this, the Muslims were reduced to half of their former numbers in the seventeenth and at the beginning of the eighteenth centuries because of the losses through wars, starvation, and epidemics.[113] In Bosnia and Hercegovina there were 39,831 Catholics in the year 1743, and 60,061 in the year 1768, according to the list of families compiled by names by apostolic vicars.[114] The 3000 Catholics in the diocese of Trebinje should be added to the above numbers.[115] In addition, in 1768 there were about 400,000 Muslims (69%) and 125,000 Orthodox (20%).

The population of Bosnia and Hercegovina grew from the latter part of the eighteenth century, but the increase was proportionately smaller for the Muslims than for the other groups because of losses in wars with Serbia (1804–25), epidemic plagues in the years 1813–17, and emigration to Macedonia and Turkey in 1878–1910. During the Turkish rule in the eighteenth century, and later during the Austro-Hungarian occupation (1878–1918), a number of the descendants of the Bosnian and

110/See footnote 26.

111/Julijan Jelenić, *Kultura i bosanski Franjevci*/Culture and Bosnian Franciscans, I (Sarajevo, 1912), 202–4.

112/Mandić, *Etnička povijest Bosne i Hercegovine*, 253–74.

113/Mandić, *op. cit.*, 521.

114/D. Mandić, *Chroati catholici Bosnae et Hercegovinae in descriptionibus annis 1743 et 1768 exaratis* (Chicago-Roma, 1962).

115/B. Pandžić, *De Dioecesi Tribuniensi et Mercanensi* (Romae, 1959), 120, 131, 146.

Hercegovinian Catholics who lived as emigres in Dalmatia and other Croatian lands returned to Bosnia and Hercegovina. At the time of the Austro-Hungarian occupation, a few thousand foreign Catholics came to Bosnia, among them Ukrainians, Poles, Slovaks, Czechs, Italians, and Germans; most of these, however, left during the periods of the first and second Yugoslavia. A small part of those who remained have been Croatized. In addition, from the eighteenth century to date, there have been large internal migrations of peoples of all faiths from Hercegovina and the southwestern Bosnian regions to middle and northern Bosnia.[116]

The population of Bosnia and Hercegovina, according to official government censuses of the past century, has been distributed by religious affiliation as follows:

CENSUS	CATHOLICS	MUSLIMS	ORTHODOX	TOTAL POPULATION
1879	209,391 (18.1%)	448,613 (38.7%)	496,485 (42.9%)	1,158,440
1921	453,617 (24%)	588,173 (31.99%)	829,360 (43.9%)	1,890,440
1948	607,425 (23.67%)	885,689 (34.52%)	1,064,125 (41.48%)	2,565,277
1953	601,489 (21.1%)	917,720 (32.2%)	1,002,737 (35.2%)	2,847,790

(Other religious groups: 15,375 (0.6%). Without religion: 310,469 (10.9%))

The last official census taken in 1961 gives no data on the religious affiliation of the population.

Bibliography

SOURCES

Acta Bosnae potissimum ecclesiastica (925–1752). Ed. Eusebius Fermendžin. MSHSM, XXIII.) Zagreb,1892.

Čelebija, Evlija, *Putopis*/Travelogue. Tr. H. Šabanović. Vols. I, II. Sarajevo, 1957.

Draganović, Krunoslav. "Izvješće apostolskog vizitatora Petra Masarechija o prilikama katoličkog naroda u Bugarskoj, Srbiji, Srijemu, Slavoniji i Bosni g. 1623 i 1624"/Report of the Apostolic Delegate Peter Masarechi on the Conditions of Life of the Catholic People in Bulgaria, Serbia, Syrmium, Slavonia, and Bosnia in 1623 and 1624. *Starine* (Yugoslav Academy), XXXIX (1938), 1–48.

116/Mandić, *Etnička povijest Bosne i Hercegovine*, 404–7, 521.

Jelenić, Julijan. *Spomenici kulturnoga rada franjevaca Bosne Srebreničke/* Documents of the Cultural Work of Franciscans of the Province of Bosnia Argentina. Vol. I. Mostar, 1927.

——— *Ljetopis fra Nikole Lašvanina*/Chronicle of Father Nikola Lašvanin. Sarajevo, 1916.

Kanuni i Kanun-name za Bosanski, Hercegovački, Zvornički, Kliški, Crnogorski i Skadarski sandžak/Canons and Laws of the Bosnian, Hercegovinian, Zvornik, Klis, Montenegrin, and Scodra Sanjaks. Vol. I. ("Monumenta Turcica," I.) Sarajevo 1957.

Kraljevstvo Hrvata/The Kingdom of the Croatians. In Ferdo Šišić (ed.), *Letopis Popa Dukljanina* (Beograd-Zagreb, 1928), 383–416.

Laszowski, Emil. *Monumenta Habsburgica. Habsburški spomenici.* Vols. I–III. Zagreb, 1914–17.

Letopis Popa Dukljanina/Chronicle of the Priest of Dioclea. Ed. Ferdo Šišić. Beograd-Zagreb, 1928.

Ljubić, Šime. *Listine o odnošajih izmedju južnoga Slavenstva i mletačke republike*/Documents Concerning Relations between the South Slavs and the Venetian Republic. Vols. I–X. Zagreb, 1868–91.

Lopašić, Radoslav. *Spomenici Hrvatske Krajine*/Documents Concerning the Croatian Military Frontier. 3 vols. Zagreb, 1884–9.

Mandić, Dominik. *Acta Franciscana Hercegovinae.* Vol. I. Mostar, 1934.

———*Chroati Catholici Bosnae et Hercegovinae in descriptionibus annis 1743 et 1768 exaratis.* "Monumenta Chroatiae Vaticana," I. Chicago-Roma, 1962.

Miklosich, Franz. *Monumenta Serbica.* Wien, 1858.

Monumenta Spectantia Historiam Slavorum Meridionalium. Vols. 1–46. Zagreb, 1868–1951. (MSHSM.)

Mošin, Vladimir. *Ljetopis Popa Dukljanina. Latinski tekst s hrvatskim prijevodom i "Hrvatskom kronikom"* [= "Kraljevstvo Hrvata"]/Chronicle of the Priest of Dioclea. Latin Text with Croatian Translation and "Croatian Chronicle" [= The Kingdom of the Croatians]. Zagreb, 1950.

Porphyrogenitus, Constantine VII. *De administrando imperio.* Ed. Gy. Moravcsik and R. J. H. Jenkins. Budapest, 1949. (*De adm.imp.*)

Rački, Franjo. *Documenta historiae chroaticae periodum antiquam illustrantia.* (MSHSM, VII.) Zagreb, 1877. (*Doc.*)

Seech, Otto. *Notitia dignitatum.* Berlin, 1876.

Šišić, Ferdo (ed.). *Letopis Popa Dukljanina*/Chronicle of the Priest of Dioclea. Beograd-Zagreb, 1928.

Smičiklas, Tadija. *Codex diplomaticus regni Croatiae, Dalmatiae et Slavoniae.* Vols. II–XV. Zagreb, 1904–34. (*Cod.dipl.*)

Solovjev, Aleksander. *Odabrani spomenici srpskoga prava (od* XII *do* XV *veka)/* Selected Documents of Serbian Law (from the 12th to 15th Centuries). Beograd, 1926.

Theiner, Augustinus. *Vetera monumenta historica Hungariam sacram illustrantia.* Vols. I–II. Romae, 1859–62. (*Mon.Hung.*).

——— *Vetera monumenta Slavorum Meridionalium historiam illustrantia,* I, Romae, 1863; II, Zagreb, 1875.

Thomas Archidiaconus. *Historia Salonitana.* Ed. Franjo Rački. (MSHSM, XXVI.) Zagreb, 1894.

STUDIES

Barkan, Omer L. "Les déportations comme méthode de peuplement et de colonisation dans l'Empire Ottoman," *Revue de la Faculté des sciences économiques de l'Université d'Istambul*, XI (Istambul, 1949–50).

Bašagić, Safvet-beg. *Znameniti Hrvati Bošnjaci i Hercegovci u Turskoj carevini*/Famous Bosnian and Hercegovinian Croatians in the Turkish Empire. Zagreb, 1931.

Bošnjanin, Hrvoje [Kr. Draganović]. *Hrvati i Herceg-Bosna*/Croatians and Bosnia-Hercegovina. Sarajevo, 1940.

Byzantion. Vols. I–XXXIV. Paris-Liège-Bruxelles, 1924–64.

Ćirković, Sima. *Istorija srednjevekovne bosanske države*/A History of the Medieval Bosnian State. Beograd, 1964.

Ćorović, Vladimir. *Historija Bosne*/History of Bosnia. Vol. I. Beograd, 1940.

Croatia Sacra. Vols. I–XIV. Zagreb, 1931–44.

Draganović, Krunoslav St. *Massenübertritte von Katholiken zur 'Orthodoxie' im Kroatischen Sprachgebiet zur Zeit der Türkenherrschaft, Orientalia christiana periodica*, III (Roma, 1937).

Dvornik, Francis. *Les Slaves, Byzance et Rome au* IXe *siècle*. Paris, 1926.

Farlati, Daniel. *Illyricum Sacrum*. Vols. I–VIII. Venetiis, 1751–1819.

Glasnik Zemaljskoga muzeja. Vol. I–LV. Sarajevo, 1890–1944. New Series, Vols. I–XIX. Sarajevo, 1946–64.

Hadrovics, Ladislas. *Le Peuple Serbe et son église sous la domination turque*. Paris, 1947.

Jireček, Konstantin, and Radonić, Jovan. *Istorija Srba*/History of the Serbs. Vols. I–IV. Beograd, 1922–3.

Klaić, Vjekoslav. *Poviest Bosne do propasti kraljevstva*/A History of Bosnia to the End of the Kingdom. Zagreb, 1882.

Mandić, Dominik. *Postanak Vlaha prema novim poviesnim iztraživanjima*/ Origin of the Vlachs in the Light of New Historical Research. Buenos Aires, 1956.

—— *Crvena Hrvatska u svijetlu povjesnih izvora*/Red Croatia in the Light of Historical Sources. Chicago, 1957.

—— *Bosna i Hercegovina*, I. *Državna i vjerska pripadnost sredovječne Bosne i Hercegovine*/Bosnia and Hercegovina. I. The State and Religious Affiliation of Medieval Bosnia and Hercegovina. Chicago, 1960.

—— II. *Bogomilska crkva bosanskih krstjana*/The Bogomil Church of the Bosnian Christians. Chicago, 1962.

—— III. *Etnička povijest Bosne i Hercegovine*/The Ethnic History of Bosnia and Hercegovina. Rim, 1967.

—— *Rasprave i prilozi iz stare hrvatske povijesti*/Studies and Contributions to Ancient Croatian History. Rim, 1963.

—— *Franjevačka Bosna*/The Franciscan Bosnia. Rim, 1968.

Pandžić, Bazilije. *De dioecesi Tribuniensi et Mercanensi*. Romae, 1959.

Pfeiffer, Nikolaus. *Die ungarische Dominikanerordensprovinz von ihrer Gründung 1221 bis zur Tatarenverwüstung 1241/42*. Zürich, 1913.

Poviest hrvatskih zemalja Bosne i Hercegovine/A History of the Croatian Lands of Bosnia and Hercegovina. Vol. I. Sarajevo, 1942.

Šabanović, Hasim. *Bosanski pašaluk. Postanak i upravna podjela*/The Bosnian Pashalik. Origin and Administrative Division. Sarajevo, 1959.

Šišić, Ferdo. *Povijest Hrvata u vrijeme narodnih vladara*/History of the Croatians in the Times of the National Rulers. Zagreb, 1925.

Solovjev, Aleksandar. "Nestanak bogomilstva i islamizacija Bosne"/The Disappearance of the Bogomils and the Islamization of Bosnia, *Godišnjak*, I (Sarajevo, 1949), 42–79.

Starine. Jugoslavenska Akademija znanosti i umjetnosti/Antiquities. Yugoslav Academy of Sciences and Arts. Zagreb, 1869–.

Thallóczy, Ludwig. *Studien zur Geschichte Bosniens und Serbiens im Mittelalter*. München, 1914.

Wissenshaftiche Mitteilungen aus Bosnien und Herzegowina. Vols. I–XIII. Wien, 1893–1916.

8

The Croatian Immigrants in the United States of America

GEORGE J. PRPIĆ

HISTORY

CROATIAN IMMIGRATION BEFORE 1880

Historical evidence indicates that numerous Croatians had arrived in America prior to the "new immigration" after the 1880s. Although the theory that ships of the Croatian republic of Dubrovnik (Ragusa) preceded Columbus is not plausible, there are speculations that at least two Croatian sailors, one from Dubrovnik and another from Šibenik, were present on Columbus' ships when he discovered America in October 1492.[1]

Following the conclusion of a commercial treaty between Dubrovnik and Spain in 1492, ships from Dubrovnik, chartered by Spain, sailed regularly between Spain and her colonies in America. There is evidence in the Ragusan archives that the first Croatian emigrants embarked for America as early as 1510–20; these settlers were among the very first European immigrants in America and included the brothers Mato and Dominko Kokendović and Bazilije Basiljević. Ragusan vessels were at that time among the finest and largest in the world, and were quite capable of trans-Atlantic voyages.[2]

Some American and Croatian writers are of the opinion that the first

1/Josip Horvat, *Kultura Hrvata kroz 1000 godina*/One Thousand Years of Croatian Culture (Zagreb: Tipografija, 1939), 345–64; Tijas Mortidjija, "Die kroatische 'Hansestadt' Dubrovnik"/The Croatian "Hanseatic" City Dubrovnik, *Croatia*, VI (Zagreb: Hrvatski Bibliografski Zavod, 1943), 54.

2/Mortidjija, *ibid.*; W. F. Wingfield, *A Tour in Dalmatia, Albania, and Montenegro* (London: Richard Bentley, 1859), 290.

English colonists in the years 1584–7 found, among the friendly Indians off the shores of present-day North Carolina, descendants of some shipwrecked Croatian sailors. Francis L. Hawks, in his *History of North Carolina*, quotes from original English reports Indian stories of shipwrecked white men in 1558 whom they saved. Englishmen gave the name "Croatan" to those Indians, whose real name was Hatteras, and who inhabited one of the Carolina islands. It is not certain that "Croatoan" or "Croatan" is an Indian word. If instead the word is English, then it indicates that the English colonists had evidence of Croatian ancestry for applying this name to the island and the Indians.

Governor White, who was sent by the crown to lead the settlers, left a colony of over 120 men at Roanoke Island in 1587. Upon his return in 1590 he found the colony deserted and two inscriptions in the bark of a live oak: "Croatoan" and "Cro." According to their promise to White before he left for Europe, the colonists indicated through these signs that they had gone to live with the Indians on Croatan Island. Prevented by bad weather from searching for the colonists, White returned to England, and the group from Roanoke Island thus passed forever out of history. The "lost colony" was probably amalgamated with the Croatans whose descendants live today in Robeson County, North Carolina. Francis Hawks, and later Hamilton McMillan, stated that "what may have been the origin of the tribe, known to us through the English colonists as Croatan, can only be a matter of conjecture."[3]

Although it is not confirmed, it is supposed that the first Croatian settlement in America was in the sixteenth century, when the peasant uprising in Croatia in 1573 was crushed and many peasants left the country. While some of these went to Prussia, others allegedly traveled to America as sailors or immigrants, and some may have come by way of Prussia. Father Ivan Ratkaj (Juan Ratkay), S.J., who arrived at Mexico City in the fall of 1680, is the first known Croatian missionary in America.[4] An early immigrant to Lower California was the Reverend Ferdinand Konšćak (Fernando Consag), a Jesuit missionary who died

3/Francis L. Hawks, *History of North Carolina* (2 vols.; Fayetteville, N.C.: E. J. Hale and Son, 1857), I, 80–2, 99–100; Hamilton McMillan, *Sir Walter Raleigh's Lost Colony* (Wilson, N.C.: W. Taylor, 1888), 62; *Congressional Record*, Appendix, April 8, 1957, A2798. For an analysis and summary of the early contacts between Croatia and America, see George J. Prpić, "Early Croatian Contacts with America and the Mystery of the Croatans," *Journal of Croatian Studies*, I (New York, 1960), 6–24.

4/*Za Dom* (Zagreb), April 1, 1944, 1; L. Adamic, J. S. Roucek, and other writers mention in some of their works Croatians living during this early period in Ebenezer, Georgia. For Ratkaj, see J. Stoecklein (ed.), *Der neue Welt-Bott* (Augsburg and Graetz: [S.J.], 1726), I, 77–84; this was a regularly published Jesuit report on missionary activities. Also on Ratkaj, see H. E. Bolton, *Rim of Christendom* (New York, 1936), 51–5.

there in 1759. Another early Croatian immigrant was the Reverend Josip Kundek, who died in Jasper, Indiana, in 1857.[5]

The Dalmatian Croatians were among the first to immigrate in larger numbers to the United States. Many of them arrived in New Orleans in the early nineteenth century and remained there. Sailing around the Horn, Dalmatians came to California, which attracted them because the climate and country were similar to their own. Croatians also joined the Gold Rush of 1849, many of them settling in and around San Francisco and in the mining districts. Quite a few of these various immigrants prospered in several branches of business.

Joining those from Dalmatia, Istria, and the Croatian Littoral, inhabitants of inland Croatia started to emigrate when they heard, around the middle of the last century, about the newly opened copper mines in Michigan, to which their neighbors, the Slovenians from Carniola, had been going for some time already. Between 1850 and 1865 there was an influx of Croatians into Pennsylvania's rising coal mining industry. A Croatian bank had already been founded in Pennsylvania in 1867 by a German, Max Schamberg. In St. Louis, Missouri, Croatians first settled around 1850, many moving there from New Orleans. By 1886 a few Croatians had settled in Cleveland, Ohio.

About 16,000 people from Dalmatia alone had established themselves in the United States by 1850,[6] and in the 1870s the number of Croatian immigrants increased to at least 1000 a year.

CROATIAN IMMIGRATION 1880–1900

It is hard to determine on the whole how many Croatian emigrants came to the United States during this period, for they were listed by American

5/M. D. Krmpotić, *Life and Works of the Reverend Ferdinand Konšćak*, S.J., *1703–1759* (Boston, 1923), 14–23; this excellent biography also contains translated reports of Konšćak about his expeditions. See also: *Apostólicos afanes de la Compañia de Jesús* (Barcelona, 1754), 391–429; M. Venegas, *Noticia de la California* (3 vols.; Madrid, 1757), III, 140–94; and for a summary see George J. Prpić, "Fernando Konschak, S.J., Misionero y Explorador en Baja California," *Studia Croatica*, III (Buenos Aires, March 1962), 58–68, and George J. Prpić, "Rev. Ferdinand Konšćak, S.J., a Croatian Missionary in California," *Croatia Press*, XIII, nos. 199–200 (New York, July-Aug. 1959), 2–9. On Kundek see Dunstan McAndrews, *Father Joseph Kundek, 1810–1857* (St. Meinard, Ind.: A Grail Publication, 1954); also George J. Prpić, "Josip Kundek, hrvatski misionar u Americi," *Novi Život*, III, nos. 5–6 (Rome, Italy, Sept.-Dec. 1964), 241–58, and Vjekoslav Meler (ed.), *The Slavonic Pioneers of California* (San Francisco: the Slavonic Pioneers of California, 1932), 17.

6/Mladen Lorković, *Narod i zemlja Hrvata*/The Croatian Nation and Country (Zagreb: Matica Hrvatska, 1939), 145–6; Stepan Gaži, *Croatian Immigration to Allegheny County 1882-1914* (Pittsburgh: Croatian Fraternal Union, 1956), 24.

authorities as natives of Austria and Hungary. Between 1880 and 1889 approximately 74,000 Croatians left Istria, Dalmatia, Bosnia, Hercegovina, and Croatia proper. The Croatian Sabor (Diet) undertook measures to control emigration from Croatia as early as 1883. During this period, while many Croatians went to California, their countrymen on the Atlantic seaboard were prospering. Since many of the early immigrants were experienced sailors, they were highly regarded in the ports of Boston, New York, Philadelphia, and Norfolk. New York attracted thousands of Croatians, most of them from Dalmatia and Istria.

The immigrants after 1880 who settled in the eastern United States were mostly people of the soil; a great many of them came from the vine-growing regions of Croatia which had been afflicted by phylloxera. They did not become as readily accustomed to the new conditions as had the earlier settlers. They had to work under far more difficult conditions than their countrymen in California, and were generally not as successful as those there and in Louisiana. These later immigrants originally intended to stay only a few years, to save some money and return home, and at least one-third of them did return to their homeland, some with their savings, others with no extra funds or with their health impaired or crippled for life. Their destinations in the United States were mainly the mining and industrial centers of the East and Middle West. They found work in the coal and ore mines, in steel and iron works, in smelters, quarries, on railroad lines, as longshoremen in New York, and as lumbermen or as stave-cutters in the South. One of the oldest and largest Croatian mining settlements was at Calumet, Michigan. About 9000 Croatians had settled in Pittsburgh and its vicinity by 1893.[7]

The exact number of Croatians that came to the United States in the nineteenth century will never be known. Unfortunately, there is confusion in the nomenclature of American immigration records: while distinct nationalities like the Croatians and Slovenians were classified together in official statistics, groups of Dalmatians, Bosnians, and Hercegovinians, all of whom came from Croatian-inhabited provinces, were counted separately. Austrian official statistics are also unreliable, since

7/Lorković, Lakatoš, and various writers on immigration estimate that during the period from 1825 to 1850 about ten thousand Croatians – mostly from the Littoral, Dalmatia, and Istria – left for overseas; most of them immigrated to the United States. For other periods see M. Lorković, *Narod i zemlja Hrvata* 145–6; also Anon., "Problem iseljivanja iz Hrvatske"/The Problem of Croatian Emigration, *Danica* (Chicago), July 31, 1956. See additional reference in footnote 8. The life of the first Croatian family – the Lesacs – that came to Calumet, Michigan, from Severin on the river Kupa, Croatia, is described in a short story entitled "Manda Evanich from Croatia" by Louis Adamic, which is included in his book *From Many Lands* (New York and London: Harper and Bros., 1940), 55–67.

many Croatians left the country without papers or passports, and thus were not included in the total number. According to Josip Lakatoš, a reliable source, 13,845 persons left Dalmatia between 1880 and 1890, and in the following decade over 12,000 Croatians sailed for America. Between 1900 and 1910, 31,814 Dalmatians left their homeland, and from the district of Istria another 25,000 people emigrated to America. There was, in the 1890s, an exodus of people from Croatia proper, and by 1900 about 17,000 had left the county of Modruš-Rijeka; over 11,000 had emigrated from the county of Zagreb, and over 5000 from Lika-Krbava. In some parts of Croatia virtually none of the entire younger male population was left.[8]

THE HIGH POINT OF CROATIAN IMMIGRATION

Most of the immigrants during the high tide of Croatian immigration, which is considered to be from 1900 to 1914, settled in Pennsylvania, Illinois, Ohio, New York, Missouri, Wisconsin, Minnesota, or Michigan. Official figures from records in Croatian lands are inadequate, for the numbers of emigrants recorded comprise only persons who left Croatia with a passport, whereas the majority of emigrants, noted the government officials in Zagreb, were leaving the country without passports.[9]

From 1899 to 1910 a total of 31,696 inhabitants of Dalmatia, Bosnia, and Hercegovina, and 335,543 immigrants grouped together by U.S. Immigration as Croatians and Slovenians were admitted into the United States.[10] In 1905, when Ante Tresić Pavičić visited the Croatian settlements and groups in America, he noted that he met his countrymen in every part of the country, in the small as well as the large communities.[11]

By 1910, there were in the United States at least 39,000 Croatians from the county of Zagreb, 38,000 from the county of Modruš-Rijeka, and 31,000 from the county of Lika-Krbava, all of these in Croatia proper. According to one estimate, in the year 1907, when the peak of Croatian immigration was reached, 83,000 Croatians entered the United States.[12]

8/Josip Lakatoš, *Narodna statistika*/National Statistics (Osijek: R. Bačić, 1914), 64; L. V. Südland, *Južnoslavensko pitanje*/The South Slav Question (Zagreb: Matica Hrvatska, 1943), 259–60; Lorković, *Narod i zemlja Hrvata*, 129.

9/Südland, *Južnoslavensko pitanje*, 250.

10/U.S. Senate, Immigration Commission, *Emigration Conditions in Europe* (Washington: Government Printing Office, 1911), 274–6.

11/Ante Tresić-Pavičić, *Preko Atlantika do Pacifika*/Across the Atlantic to the Pacific (Zagreb: Dionička Tiskara, 1907).

12/Ivan Mladineo, *Narodni adresar*/National Directory (New York: By the author, 1937), ix. See also numerous statistical data in cited works of Lakatoš, Südland, and Lorković and in Emily G. Balch's *Our Slavic Fellow Citizens* (New York: Charities Publications Committee, 1910). Balch based her statistics mostly on official Austro-Hungarian sources.

Most Croatian authorities agree that before the First World War between 600,000 and 800,000 Croatians had permanently emigrated to the United States.

Croatian political leaders strongly opposed this mass emigration. In the hall of the Sabor the members of the Croatian parties bitterly denounced the administration which had caused the flight of the people from their native soil. Professor Smičiklas, an eminent Croatian historian, commented for the press of that day: "The best of our people have emigrated, mostly to America. Should we proceed this way, Croatia will perish."[13]

In November 1911, the Croatian Sabor promulgated some additional measures concerning emigration from Croatia. Restrictions were imposed on emigration as well as on the activities of steamship agencies.[14] An Emigrant's Fund (Iseljenička Zaklada) was established by the authorities to aid the needy returned emigrants, and it was to be supported by a fee paid by all those leaving the country.

Millions of dollars were sent back to Croatia by Croatian immigrants living in the United States. Also, many of the returning emigrants brought their savings home, purchased new land in Croatia, improved their houses, and thus substantially aided the Croatian economy. However, there were others who returned crippled, sick, depleted by hard labor. The influx of immigrant money made itself felt in Croatia. All the improvements and the general rise in the standard of living were to a great extent the result of American dollars sent by immigrants to relatives and of the financial resources of those who returned to stay.

As we have already noted, during the decades of mass exodus to America most of the Croatian immigrants were listed in immigration and census statistics as natives of Austria-Hungary. A new feature of the census of 1910 was the inclusion in its population questionnaire of an inquiry concerning the mother tongue of the person; this was in addition to the usual question concerning the country of birth. Croatian newspapers and organizations eagerly awaited and later publicized the results of this census, since they revealed, at least with greater accuracy than previous censuses, the approximate number of Croatians living in the United States.[15]

After the last war approximately 40,000 new Croatian immigrants came to the United States, many of them under the Displaced Persons Act of the Truman administration. Then on October 3, 1965, President

13/*Dom* (Zagreb), May 28, 1903.

14/*Stenografički zapisnici Sabora*/Stenographic Records of the Sabor (Zagreb: Kr. Zemaljska Tiskara, 1911), II, 1–5.

15/Cf. *Hrvatski Glasnik* (Pittsburgh), March 26 and April 2, 1910.

Johnson signed the new Immigration Act. This historic event took place in the shadow of the Statue of Liberty, a familiar sight and symbol to millions of incoming immigrants. Among the representatives of nationality groups witnessing the signing of the new law was V. I. Mandich, Supreme President of the Croatian Fraternal Union, the largest Croatian organization in this country. This new Act inaugurated a new era in the history of American immigration and, consequently, a new era in the history of Croatian immigration. The discriminatory national origins quota system of the old laws (in force for 41 years) was removed. In practice, this means that thousands of close relations of American citizens, many skilled artisans, scientists, and scholars, will be coming, especially from those areas which, for over forty years, had been discriminated against under the old quota system. More east Europeans, and therefore more Croatians and peoples from the Balkans, will now be coming to the United States.[16]

The immigration after 1945 has been different in character from the previous one. Two factors may be singled out: (1) it is partly economic as well as a politically motivated immigration in flight from the Communist rule of Croatia, and (2) a great number of intellectuals are included among the immigrants. Hundreds of priests, physicians, university and college professors, teachers, journalists, writers, and artists have entered as well as many businessmen, skilled workers, mechanics, and various other technically trained people. It is no exaggeration to state that the Croatian immigration after 1945 has brought many more intellectuals and educated persons than had the entire Croatian immigration before 1945. The best known among the artists and intellectuals was the sculptor Ivan Meštrović, who preferred exile to life under Communism in Croatia. Meštrović died in February 1962, at South Bend, Indiana.

THE NUMBER OF CROATIAN IMMIGRANTS IN THE UNITED STATES

Some sixty years ago Emily Greene Balch, in her excellent book *Our Slavic Fellow Citizens*, complained about the confused immigration statistics and the lack on the part of the authorities of information on ethnic groups in the United States. For example, Serbs were grouped

16/For detailed information see the twelve-page document no. 54-259-(361)0-65 entitled "Public Law 89–236 89th Congress, H. R. 2580, October 3, 1965 – An Act to amend the *Immigration and Nationality Act*, and for other purposes." *Zajedničar* of October 6, 1965, carried on page 1 a report of the event, "President Johnson Signs Liberal Immigration Bill: V. I. Mandich at Historic Meeting." The last remnants of the quota system expired on July 1, 1968.

with Bulgarians and Montenegrins, Croatians with Slovenians. For almost seven decades, one of the greatest puzzles in the history of Croatian immigration has been: *How many Croatian immigrants did come to the United States?*

It should also be pointed out that by "Croatian immigrants" one may designate either only those of Croatian nationality or all the immigrants of different nationalities who came from several Croatian provinces: Croatia proper (Banska Hrvatska), Dalmatia, Bosnia-Hercegovina, and Istria. It is true that until the late nineteenth century or even the beginning of this century, nationalism was very weak in some Croatian provinces. Many Croatian immigrants came as Dalmatians, or even Illyrians, Slavonians, "Slavish people," Bosnians, Hercegovinians, and Istrians. Because of centuries of foreign oppression and the denationalization policies of the Venetians, Austrians, Hungarians, and partly the Ottoman Turks, the Croatians were, in this respect, in the same position as were, for instance, the Ukrainians who came to this country as Ruthenians, Russins, Russians, Galicians, Lemkos, and Ukrainians.

Perhaps there would have been less confusion about the number of Croatian immigrants had the American immigration authorities known more about the nationality problems of Austria-Hungary. For the sake of historical accuracy we should therefore count as "Croatian immigrants" only those who consider themselves Croatians (this is especially true for the immigration after the First and Second World Wars or who before the First World War were designated by American authorities as "Dalmatians, Bosnians, and Hercegovinians."

Until 1924 the Croatians were grouped together with the Slovenians, and the Dalmatians, Bosnians, and Hercegovinians were counted as one group by immigration authorities. According to the data of the official analysis, a total of 481,242 immigrants who were marked as "Croatians and Slovenians" arrived in America before 1924. It is usually assumed that there are twice as many Croatians as there are Slovenians in this country. According to the report in the *Monthly Labor Review*, XVIII, Jan. 1924, 51,840 "Dalmatians, Bosnians, and Hercegovinians" came to this country between 1899 and 1923.

The number of immigrants from Croatia to this country up to the time when the new restrictive immigration law closed the gates for "less desirable" immigrants in 1924 is a matter of conjecture.

After 1918 and the establishment of the Kingdom of Serbs, Croatians, and Slovenes – officially proclaimed Yugoslavia in 1929 – the Croatian immigrants were listed as immigrants from Yugoslavia. Since it has been the policy of the Immigration and Naturalization Service to list immigrants according to the country of their birth, a policy inevitable under the terms of the new quota system, a German or Magyar born in Yugoslavia, or what later became Yugoslavia (originally it may have been Austria-Hungary), was listed under immigrants from Yugoslavia or "Yugoslav quota immigrants." In studying the number of immigrants from Yugoslavia, in order to reach an approximate figure for the Croatian immigrants, the best formula would seem to be to count about 60 percent of all immigrants as Croatians.

According to the *Annual Report of the Immigration and Naturalization Service* (1965),[17] the following was the immigration from Yugoslavia by decades:

1911–20	1,888	1961	1,188
1921–30	49,064	1962	1,086
1931–40	5,835	1963	972
1941–50	1,576	1964	1,098
1951–60	8,225	1965	1,051

Thus, it appears that under "Immigration by Country, for Decades: 1820–1965," *71,983 people have been listed as immigrants from Yugoslavia.*[18] It is evident from the above figures that prior to 1941 (and this is the first war year for all territories in Yugoslavia) 56,787 people were listed as immigrants from Yugoslavia. During the decade 1921–30 alone, 49,064 such immigrants arrived in the United States. This is by any count a considerable number, and it is safe to assume that a majority of these immigrants were Croatians. This means that *some 34,000 Croatian immigrants came to this country between the two world wars.*[19]

It would appear, from the above figures, that only 15,196 immigrants from Yugoslavia arrived here between 1941 and 1965 (between the

17/The most reliable and readily available official source on immigration statistics is the *Annual Report of the Immigration and Naturalization Service* in Washington, D.C. The INS is under the jurisdiction of the United States Department of Justice and is headed currently by Commissioner Mr. Raymond F. Farrell. This well-documented official report (well over 100 pages long) is published annually, shortly after the expiration of the fiscal year, and is addressed officially to the Attorney General, United States Department of Justice; it is also made available to scholars and the general public. It is the most comprehensive and authoritative report on the enormous flow of millions of immigrants since 1820. For this analysis of the number of Croatian immigrants, especially after the early 1920s, we are using the *Annual Report* for the year ended June 30, 1965. The author has checked also the most recent issues of the Report up to that printed in 1968.

18/*Annual Report*, 1965, 48–9. Yugoslavia is termed here officially as "the country of the last permanent residence." In 1966 an additional 1611 arrived.

19/To compare the number of immigrants from Yugoslavia with the entire immigration for all years see the table entitled "Immigration to the United States: 1820–1965," in *Annual Report*, 1965, 22. See also Karlo Mirth, "Problem of Croatian Refugees," *Croatia Press*, XVIII, no. 239 (Nov. 1964), 2–10.

beginning of the war in Yugoslavia and the end of the last fiscal year for which data have been published). However, this is at least partly deceiving since most of these were only quota immigrants, and the number of non-quota immigrants from some countries in recent years has been considerably larger than that of quota immigrants. The annual quota – which was abolished by the new Immigration Law of October 1965 – was 942 for Yugoslavia. The *Annual Report* of 1965 lists, for instance, only 4630 Yugoslav quota immigrants for the years 1961–5: in 1961 only 932 quota immigrants came to the United States; in 1962, 888; in 1963, 915; in 1964, 969; and in the year ending June 30, 1965, there were 926, according to the same source.[20]

In the same official report there are statistics (p. 30) indicating the numbers of "Refugees Admitted by Country or Region of Birth: Years Ended June 30, 1946–1965," covering the entire period after the Second World War. There are in this category *58,261 persons from Yugoslavia,* which means that over 58,000 refugees from Yugoslavia came to this country during the two decades after the last war. This again is a significant number. Of these, 17,238 were admitted as Displaced Persons. For a variety of reasons – involving the political status of the Croatian refugees after 1945 in several European countries of exile – it is very likely that only a minority (perhaps about 30 percent of the total number) of the Displaced Persons were of Croatian nationality. We do not know how many of the 15,936 persons (among the 58,261 refugees) who were admitted during the same period as "German Ethnics" (*Volksdeutsche*) were actually people belonging to the Croatian nationality group, but who for various reasons (some were, during the war, members of the German armed forces), in order to get through the complicated red tape and long processes of screening, declared themselves *Volksdeutsche.* The fact is that hundreds of Croatians from Bosnia came to this country after the last war as "German Ethnics" from Yugoslavia.

Under the Refugee Relief Act of 1953, 17,425 refugees were admitted from Yugoslavia.[21] By the early 1950s the political status of many thousands of Croatian refugees in Austria, Germany, and Italy was improved. Many Croatians were then eligible for the care of the International Refugee Organization (and other subsequent organizations that succeeded IRO and were conducting the massive transfer of refugees across the sea to America). It is safe to assume that about 50 percent of these more than 17,000 immigrants from Yugoslavia were Croatian refugees; the same proportion could be applied to the 3002 immigrants

20/*Annual Report,* 1965, 34.
21/*Ibid.,* 30.

who came under the Act of September 11, 1957, and the Act of July 14, 1960 (Refugee Escapees), which brought 3577 immigrants from Yugoslavia.[22] We may conclude from the evidence given by reports of the religious charitable organizations, private Croatian organizations, and many individuals that, on the whole, about 60 percent of all immigrants under most categories from Yugoslavia are of Croatian nationality.

There is a very interesting table on page 51 of the *Annual Report* (1965) of statistics on "Immigrants Admitted by Country or Region of Birth: Years Ended June 30, 1956–1965." It gives the numbers of immigrants who were born in parts of what is now Yugoslavia and who arrived here during those years:

1956	8723	1961	1989
1957	9842	1962	1857
1958	2260	1963	2560
1959	4349	1964	3098
1960	2742	1965	2818

This includes, of course, all nationalities and various categories of immigrants who were born in Yugoslavia and emigrated to the United States either from their homeland or from another country. It is evident from this source of information that *during the last ten years alone 40,238 immigrants who were born in Yugoslavia came to the United States.* Taking into account that about 60 percent of these were of Croatian nationality, one comes to the startling conclusion that *during the last decade approximately 24,000 Croatians arrived as, or received the status of, immigrants in this country.*

As the same report lists (on p. 34) for the years 1961–5 only 4630 quota immigrants from Yugoslavia, and the table on page 51 lists for the same period 12,322 immigrants, it follows that almost 8000 during these five years were non-quota immigrants. In fact, a majority of the immigrants from Yugoslavia between 1946 and 1965 were non-quota immigrants and, as already pointed out, 58,261 were marked by our immigration authorities as "Refugees." This is a very significant fact, for it sheds additional light on the character of the entire Croatian immigration following the Second World War.

In the year ending June 30, 1965, under "Immigrants Admitted by Classes under the Immigration Laws and Country or Region of Birth" – as already pointed out on page 51 of the report – 2818 came from Yugoslavia (quota and non-quota). The largest group of these (596) were in the age group 20–29 years, and 431 were between 30 and 39 years of

22/*Ibid.*

age; 1510 of them were males and 1308 females. These facts, too, speak for themselves.[23]

Another significant fact is revealed in the same *Annual Report*: between July 14, 1960, and June 30, 1965, there were 6290 persons from Yugoslavia who were paroled under the "Refugee Escapees Act of July 14, 1960." This is the largest group of paroled refugees and escapees who gained the status of immigrants; it outnumbers all other groups from Europe (Rumania with 4339 and Hungary with 1625).[24] It follows from these official sources that at least during these six years *the largest number of refugees from Communist-dominated countries who have been given asylum in this country came from Yugoslavia.* It is safe to assume that about 3500 of these 6290 parolees are Croatians. Since the figures for Rumanian parolees would include many non-Rumanian refugees, it is only logical to conclude that *the Croatians as a nationality group represent the largest European refugee-parolee group in the United States* and are at present outnumbered only by the Cuban refugees who are coming from this hemisphere.

After careful study of the immigration statistics, and having taken into consideration all factors involved, it is the opinion of this writer that: *Between 1920 and 1940 approximately 34,000 Croatians came to the United States. About 5000 Croatian Displaced Persons arrived prior to the 1953 Refugee Relief Act; approximately 8000 arrived under the Act. Between 1945 and 1956 about 5000 Croatian immigrants came to the United States from the homeland* (non-refugees); *about 24,000 Croatian immigrants of all categories came between 1956 and 1965. The total number of all Croatian immigrants after 1945 amounts to approximately 42,000.* Counting the immigration between 1920 and 1940, we may safely conclude that roughly 75,000 Croatians have arrived in this country since the founding of the South Slav state.

It is certain that the number of Croatian immigrants after the Second World War exceeds the estimates which have been up to the present time circulating among various Croatian organizations and in the Croatian press. The American Society for Croatian Migration in Cleveland, headed by Mr. Joseph V. Bosiljević, has brought to the Greater Cleveland area alone over 5000 Croatian immigrants during the past eight years.[25] Virtually thousands of Croatians are joining their relatives and friends in this country. This, too, explains the high proportion of Croatian immigration, which is well over that of the Slovenians and Serbs.

23/*Ibid.*, 27, 39–40.
24/*Ibid.*, 52.
25/Interview with J. V. Bosiljević, Cleveland, July 7, 1966.

The authorities in the Croatian Republic of Yugoslavia admit the exodus of Croatians and indirectly confirm the accuracy of our report. According to one article on emigration, *almost 25 percent of all Croatians live abroad.* A majority of them have been going to the United States. Only 10 percent of the other nationalities in Yugoslavia are immigrants in foreign countries.[26]

The authorities in Yugoslavia have not published accurate statistics on Croatian emigrants; the American authorities do not list them by nationality. As long as we do not have precise statistics – and it seems unlikely that we shall ever have them – we may accept the statistically based conclusions of this report, which are a result of intensive analysis and careful research through the maze of the last official immigration reports.

We may conclude from all these data that the Croatian immigration to this country has been going on at an average rate of about 2000 a year for the past two decades, and is very likely to continue at at least the same rate.

Thus, the best estimate would seem to be that today there are about a million Croatians and their descendants in this country. According to the Croatian writer Mladen Lorković, at least 800,000 Croatian immigrants have come to the United States before 1939.[27] Professor C. S. Mihanovich of Saint Louis University claims the number of Croatians in the United States to be about 900,000. J. S. Roucek, in a new edition of his book on the immigrants, writes that "the Croatians number about 900,000 or somewhat more."[28]

There are about two hundred major Croatian settlements and one thousand smaller ones in the United States. The largest group of American Croatians – approximately 180,000 – live in Pennsylvania. There are about 20,000 Croatians in the state of New York, 15,000 living in New York City alone. In all of the New England States combined, only about 1000 Croatians are settled. There are 3000 in Texas, 5000 in Louisiana and Mississippi, about 3000 in New Mexico, and 2000 more in other areas of the south. In Ohio there are 50,000, 15,000 living in Cleveland. Michigan has about 15,000, Indiana 13,000, and Illinois 90,000, a larger number than any state after Pennsylvania. In the state of Wisconsin

26/A. Šeparović, "Iseljenici i domovina"/Emigrants and the Homeland *Vjesnik u Srijedu* (Zagreb), Jan. 5, 1966. See also the work of Većeslav Holjevac, *Hrvati izvan Domovine*/Croatians Abroad (Zagreb: Matica Hrvatska, 1967), which states that about 25 percent of Croatians live outside their homeland.

27/Lorković, *Narod i Zemlja Hrvata*, 165.

28/J. S. Roucek, *One America* (New York: Prentice-Hall, 1957), 171–2.

there are about 18,000, 20,000 in Minnesota, another 20,000 in Missouri, and approximately the same number in Kansas. Montana has 10,000; there are over 3000 in Nebraska, about 2000 in Arizona, 10,000 in Colorado, 2000 in Idaho, 5000 in Iowa, 2000 in Nevada, 1000 in North Dakota, 3000 in Utah, and over 10,000 in the state of Washington. At least 50,000 Croatians live in California; San Pedro alone has over 8000, mostly engaged in the fishing industry. In Oregon, the Croatian group numbers about 10,000, and over 1000 are residents of Alaska.[29]

LIFE WITHIN CROATIAN SETTLEMENTS

A PERIOD OF DEVELOPMENT

The last decade of the nineteenth century witnessed the establishment, and the years between 1900 and 1920 saw the development of settlements, parishes, organizations, and newspapers among the American Croatians. As we have indicated earlier, there is no way of accurately determining the number of Croatian immigrants in the United States at the beginning of the twentieth century. An American expert on Slavic immigration, Miss E. G. Balch, estimates that by 1910 the number of Croatians had risen to about 400,000.[30] They had settled in every state and every corner of the country and were engaged in mining, in steel and other heavy industries, in fishing and fruit-growing, in the forest industry, and in various trades. A very small percentage entered

29/These estimates are taken from many sources, which it is not feasible to indicate here.

30/Balch, *Our Slavic Fellow Citizens*, 280.

TABLE 23/Estimates of the Total Slavic Population in the United States (1910), by Nationality

Nationality	Lower estimate	Upper estimate
Bohemians	500,000	500,000
Slovaks	400,000	750,000
Poles	2,000,000	4,000,000
Ruthenians	200,000	350,000
Slovenians	100,000	100,000
Croatians, including Dalmatians	250,000	400,000
Servians	150,000	200,000
Bulgarians	40,000	50,000
Russians	60,000 (?)	70,000 (?)
Total	3,700,000	6,420,000

the professions. The city of Pittsburg eventually possessed the largest Croatian settlement in the country, and from 1900 until the 1920s it was also the cultural center for Croatian Americans.

RELIGIOUS LIFE

The first Croatian Catholic priest came to Pittsburgh only after about 200,000 Croatian immigrants had already settled in the United States. The Reverend Dobroslav Božić was pastor of the first Croatian parish in this country, formed in the fall of 1894, St. Nicholas parish, Allegheny City, Pennsylvania (now "North Side," Pittsburgh). The first Croatian church, St. Nicholas in Allegheny City, was dedicated on January 27, 1895. Father Božić published the paper *Novi Svijet* and a humorous magazine called *Puco* in Allegheny City before he left for Steelton, Pennsylvania in August 1888, where he founded another Croatian parish, St. Mary's. He died in January 1900. St. John the Baptist parish was organized by the Croatians in Calumet, Michigan, the largest Croatian mining settlement, in 1901. In 1897 St. Rochus parish was formed in Johnstown, Pennsylvania. The Croatian immigrants in Cleveland, Ohio, organized two parishes: St. Paul's in November 1902, whose newly built church was consecrated in the summer of 1904; and St. Nicholas, a Greek Catholic parish (Byzantine rite), founded in 1902.[31]

Indeed, American Croatians, who are largely Roman Catholic (although there are also a considerable number of Muslims and a small number of Eastern Orthodox, Catholics of the Byzantine Rite, and Protestants), established many parishes throughout their new homeland during the first half of the twentieth century. A Croatian-Slovenian parish, The Nativity of Saint Mary, was founded in August 1903 in San Francisco; in Los Angeles, St. Anthony's parish was organized in December 1910.

In August 1902, when the Reverend Dr. Mato Matina, a Croatian patriot, came to Rankin, Pennsylvania, he founded a new Croatian parish, St. Mary's, later administered by the Reverend Bosiljko Bekavac, who, when he died in August 1959, was the oldest Croatian priest in America. Holy Trinity Parish was formed in 1929 in Ambridge, Pennsylvania; St. Anthony's in Monessen, Pennsylvania, is the most recently consecrated Croatian parish in America (August 18, 1957). The first Croatian school in this country was organized by Father Božić at one of

31/Boniface Sorić (ed.), *Centennial, 1847–1947* (Pittsburgh: The Croatian Historical Research Bureau, 1947); Tomislav Firis, *Spomen Knjiga*/Souvenir Book (Cleveland: St. Nicholas Parish, 1942).

the earliest Croatian parishes – St. Mary's parish in Steelton, Pennsylvania – to give the Croatian children elementary education.

Sts. Peter and Paul Parish in Youngstown, Ohio, was founded in July 1911. The Croatians of Lorain, Ohio, formed a parish dedicated to St. Vitus in November 1922; Christ the King parish in Akron was founed in February 1935.

The Croatians of New York City have had a parish of their own – Sts. Cyril and Methodius – since September 1913. The Croatian Sacred Heart parish in Lackawanna, New York, was formed in January 1917. There are two Croatian parishes in Michigan: St. John the Baptist, in Calumet, founded in 1901; and St. Jerome's in Detroit, founded in December 1923. Holy Trinity parish in Gary, Indiana, was organized in February 1912 and now is known as St. Joseph the Worker; on May 6, 1956, the largest Croatian church in America, beautiful St. Joseph the Worker church in Gary, was dedicated. Sts. Peter and Paul parish in Whiting, Indiana, was established in June 1910, and Holy Trinity in East Chicago was organized in October 1916.

The city of Chicago has five Croatian parishes, the largest concentration of Croatian parishes in a metropolitan area: Assumption of the Virgin Mary (founded in December 1900); Sts. Peter and Paul Greek Catholic parish (1905); St. Jerome's (December 1912); Sacred Heart parish (January 1913); and Holy Trinity (May 1914). In Joliet, Illinois. the parish of the Nativity of the Blessed Virgin was founded in June 1906.

Sts. Peter and Paul in Omaha, Nebraska, was formed in June 1917. Kansas City, Kansas, has had a Croatian parish, St. John the Baptist, since May 1900. Its pastor from 1902 until his death in 1931 was Monsignor M. D. Krmpotić, writer, well-known Croatian patriot, and leader of American Croatians. In July 1904, St. Joseph parish was founded among the Croatians of St. Louis, Missouri. Sacred Heart in Milwaukee, Wisconsin, was organized in April 1917; and, in nearby West Allis, St. Augustine's parish was formed in August 1928.[32]

The Croatian Sisters of the Precious Blood, now teaching at seven Croatian parochial schools, arrived in the United States in August 1906. The Sisters of Divine Charity, who came in September 1926, are now teaching at another five Croatian schools. In all, there are twenty-one Croatian elementary schools in the United States with approximately 5000 students. A group of Croatian Franciscans (O.F.M.) settled in

32/The data on Croatian parishes are taken from various Croatian almanacs and newspapers as well as souvenir books published by individual parishes. See especially the old *Naša Nada* almanacs of the 1920s, which contain valuable articles.

Chicago in 1926 and now have a large monastery there. Franciscan priests fill the office of pastor at twelve Croatian parishes in various cities. Croatian Franciscan Tertiaries (T.O.R.) have been active in the United States since 1926 and in 1940 established an ecclesiastical center in Pittsburgh, from which three Croatian parishes in Pennsylvania and a monastery and study house in Washington, D.C. are controlled. Since the end of the second world war over a hundred Croatian priests have come to this country as refugees.

The history of Croatian parishes is an important part of the life and work of Croatians in the United States. In 1934 the archbishop of Sarajevo, Ivan E. Šarić, visited several Croatian settlements here. Jesuit missionaries have also visited settlements from time to time, and on such occasions the missions they have given have deeply affected the religious life of the immigrants.

During late April and early May 1966, two Croatian Catholic dignitaries were guests of the American Catholic hierarchy and paid visits also to various Croatian parishes. The bishop of Skopje, Smiljan Čekada, and Franjo Cardinal Šeper, the archbishop of Zagreb (historically the metropolitan of Croatia), visited many Croatian colonies, which contributed thousands of dollars. It was the first time in history that a Croatian cardinal had visited the Catholic congregations of American Croatian immigrants.[33] Yet the lack of Croatian priests in this country during the high tide of Croatian immigration was acutely felt, and it was this shortage which prevented the establishing of still more Croatian parishes. Proportionately, compared to other minority groups, the Croatians could have been expected to found 150 parishes; yet the actual number of their parishes in the United States is only 34. Only about 15–20 percent of Croatians belong to Croatian parishes, the same percentage belong to American parishes,[34] a great number are not practicing Catholics, and the others are scattered among many national parishes.

SOCIO-ECONOMIC ACTIVITY

A greater number of immigrants prior to 1914 were men who had left their families behind in Croatia. Many of them lived in boarding-houses;

33/The American press in numerous issues reported on the visits of these two ecclesiastics, especially on that of Cardinal Šeper. See for instance Cleveland *Plain Dealer*, May 6, 8, and 9, 1966; *America*, April 30, 1966, 625; all issues of *Danica* and *Naša Nada* during May 1966; *Hrvatski Glas* for the same period as well as many American dailies (such as the *New York Times*) and Catholic weeklies.

34/Dragutin Kamber, "Hrvati u Americi"/Croatians in America *Osoba i Duh*, v (Madrid, 1953), no. 3–4, 109–10.

some lived in groups called *društvo*, which means in Croatian "a society." These men were noted as liberal lenders and most generous in their hospitality. Some of the single men sent as much as 80 percent of their earnings to their parents and relatives in the old country. The lodgings of these immigrants were often very meager; sometimes many boarders would share a single bedroom, which was often so crowded that different sleeping "shifts" had to be arranged. Interestingly, proportionately more Croatian wives were keeping boarders or lodgers than those of any other nationality. Some of the boarding-houses were unfortunately kept in very poor and unsanitary condition.[35] Yet, in spite of such unfavorable conditions, Croatians committed fewer crimes than many other nationalities according to a federal report (*Immigration and Crime*) published by the Immigration Commission in 1911.

The working conditions in steel mills and mines were most unsatisfactory. Many immigrants lost their lives or were crippled in the frequent accidents which occurred on these hazardous jobs. Although at the beginning of their life in the United States many Croatians were skeptical of joining the labor unions, later a great number of them entered the ranks of the labor movement, taking part, for example, in a big strike at McKees Rocks (Pennsylvania) in 1909, and also in the great copper-miners' strike in Calumet, Michigan, in 1913. During the latter an unintended tragedy occured when a deputy sheriff was accidentally killed by Croatian strikers.

In the social life of the Croatian immigrants the saloon played a prominent part. Besides his proper work, the saloonkeeper was often also the banker for his compatriots, took subscriptions for Croatian newspapers, collected union dues, was a steamship agent, and indeed often the political straw boss. He was also judicial adviser, intermediary with civic authorities, and adviser to factory hands as well. The federal authorities estimated the proportion of illiterate Croatians to be as high as 28.7 percent in 1911.[36]

Among the most unhappy of circumstances for the immigrants, who in great majority had been peasants in Croatia, was the fact that in the United States they usually could not obtain farms of their own. To own a farm was the desire of a majority of Croatians, but only a few thousand of them succeded in realizing this dream.

In 1907, when economic depression destroyed many immigrant banks,

35/Immigration Commission, *Immigrants in Industries* (2 vols.; Washington: Government Printing Office, 1911), I, 534–5.

36/*Congressional Record*, March 3, 1911, 4229–31. Louis Adamic, *From Many Lands* (New York: Harper and Bros., 1940), 55–61.

Frank Zotti, who was nicknamed "king of the Croatians," became bankrupt, and some 8000 Croatian depositors lost over $600,000 in his bank. A special investigation of immigrant banks and their mode of business was described in detail in a very interesting federal publication, *Immigrant Banks.*[37] According to this publication, in the short period between 1892 and 1902, Croatian immigrants sent the significant sum of $13,000,000 to Croatia.

Around 1910 about 24 percent of Croatian immigrants owned their homes. In some cities, such as St. Louis, Missouri, a majority of home owners were helped to purchase or build homes by their Croatian home loan associations. Their disappointment with the Yugoslav Kingdom created after the First World War led many Croatians to a final decision to remain in the United States, and as a result of this decision, many more Croatians started to buy homes. Those who had managed to save some money moved to farms. As early as 1915, a Croatian farming settlement, "Velebit," had been founded at Eagle River, Wisconsin; later it developed into a thriving and successful Croatian farming community, numbering over five hundred families.

But the great economic depression of the late 1920s and early 1930s struck the Croatians very severely. Many had to abandon their homes and move elsewhere. Some who could afford to do so returned to Croatia. However, the majority who remained realized the same improvement economically as did the American population as a whole.

As pointed out earlier, the immigration after the Second World War has consisted largely of highly skilled technicians, professionals, artists, and intellectuals who have rapidly become contributing members to American economic life as well as to that of their compatriots.

SOCIAL AND POLITICAL ACTIVITY

Americanization of the Croatians

Like other nationalities, the Croatians were confronted by the important problem of Americanization. The willingness of the Croatian immigrant to integrate himself into American life was hampered by the prejudices of his environment, which sometimes attempted to belittle or eliminate his genuine cultural riches. The Croatian writer Ante Tresić-Pavičić, after his visit to the United States in 1906, stated satirically in his book on the Croatians in America: "Denationalization [seems] unavoidable, inescapable ... There are Croatians in every part of the world who do not

37/Compiled by the Immigration Commission (Washington: Government Printing Office, 1910); this volume contains many data on Croatian banks.

know they are Croatian. We have added to the number and strength of every nation while depopulating our oppressed homeland. Every sea contains the bones of our sailors. In every mine there are the corpses of our workers ..."[38]

It is absurd to think that the Croatians could escape the process of Americanization. Like other nationalities, sooner or later they were bound to enter into the "melting pot." The renowned sociologist Clement S. Mihanovich, himself the son of Croatian immigrants, writes that the Croatians – by nature rural, clannish, conservative, patriarchal – tended to conflict with American urban life and culture. Their introduction into the American environment was a difficult process because their social and psychological characteristics were in direct opposition to accepted American cultural standards. The collectivistic Croatian family "does not fuse with the individualistic tendencies of the average American family; the deep religious attitude of the Croats conflicts with the moral laxity of American city life."[39] Until a few decades ago, for instance, divorce was very rare among American Croatians.

Mihanovich shows, in the case of the St. Louis Croatian colony, that the Croatian immigrants, on the whole, married within their own class and "culture," a trend which is still apparent in other Croatian settlements. The physical seclusion resulting in the formation of virtual Slavic ghettos (as well as the so-called "Hunky-towns") between 1890 and 1920 was often the result of physical violence and discrimination directed against Croatians by the native population in many American cities. Living on their national islands, many Croatians thus did not fully live in America. In one way they learned too little about their new homeland; yet in many other matters, they ceased, under American influence, to be Croatians. They were alienated from their homeland, but they were not properly adjusting to the new world.

The seafaring Croatians from Dalmatia and the coastal regions generally adapted more easily to the American way of life than did the inland Croatians, people who had traditionally been confined to a localized piece of soil. But in spite of their difficulties in adaptation, we can say that today most second- and third-generation American Croatians are in fact completely American. And yet they are proud, too, of their origin. While a few Croatians, during the painful process of assimilation, may have felt a certain shame because of their background, far more have

38/Tresić-Pavičić, *Preko Atlantika do Pacifika*, 26.

39/Clement S. Mihanovich, "The Americanization of the Croats in St. Louis, Missouri, during the Past Thirty Years" (unpublished Master's thesis, St. Louis University, St. Louis, Mo., 1936), 22–3.

had the feeling expressed by Professor Mihanovich of St. Louis University: "I have never had occasion to be ashamed of the fact that I was of Croat descent ... I am proud that I am a Croat. This is a natural feeling, a feeling that is part of all human beings."[40]

Americanization has produced an occasionally hybrid vocabulary among American Croatians, who have developed some English words with Croatian endings. Croatian names have often been Anglicized in the process also, either by changing them completely to an English form or simply by shortening the family name.

Social Organization

Croatians followed the pattern common to most immigrant groups in the United States, and quickly formed fraternal organizations. As we shall see, some of these later grew to be strongly political in nature (with the homeland as the focus of political concern); at the outset, however, they were essentially mutual aid and social and cultural groups.

In 1857, Dalmatian Croatians founded in San Francisco the first Croatian beneficial and fraternal organization, called the Slavonic Illyrian Mutual Benevolent Society. A similar society was organized in New Orleans in 1874.[41] In Hoboken, New Jersey, Croatians organized a benevolent society on March 30, 1890, and in Chicago they formed a benevolent society called "Strossmayer" in January 1892. By the end of the century hundreds of Croatian organizations, tamburitza orchestras, singing societies, and other fraternal associations were in existence.

New organizations were being founded or increasing in strength during the early years of this century. In March 1905, the Croatian League of Illinois was formed in Chicago, and soon acquired a large membership. In April 1910, at the instigation of the Croatian society "Zvonimir" in San Francisco, the Croatian Unity of the Pacific was organized.

"Sokol," a patriotic and athletic organization (of the same kind as the German *Turnvereine*) was founded on August 28, 1908, in Chicago. Soon it spread throughout the Croatian settlements in this country. The high point of Sokol activities was reached in 1914–15; after the First World War this society declined in vigor. A variety of other organizations was founded among Croatian immigrants from 1900 to 1920. Prominent among them were the first singing societies, "Zora" in Chicago and "Javor" in Pittsburgh. By 1912 about 1500 Croatian organizations of all

40/C. S. Mihanovich, "Credo of American-Born Croats," *Naša Nada – Our Hope,* Nov. 12, 1952.

41/Meler, *The Slavonic Pioneers of California*, 17.

kinds were prospering, most of them belonging to the two great fraternal organizations, the Croatian League of Illinois and the National Croatian Society.

The latter, destined to play a vital role in Croatian-American life, came into being when Peter Pavlinac, Zdravko Mužina, Ivan Ljubić, and a few other farsighted leaders founded a fraternal organization, "Hrvatska Zajednica" (Croatian Union), in Allegheny City, Pennsylvania, on September 2, 1894. This society was "to assist members during sickness and assist their families after death"; it also paid the funeral expenses for its deceased members.[42] At first the union had only 600 members and a few lodges; soon, however, thirty more lodges were formed in various Croatian settlements all over the country. In June 1897, the Croatian Union changed its name to "Narodna Hrvatska Zajednica" (National Croatian Society), and by 1904 it numbered 22,384 members in 281 lodges.[43]

On December 15, 1915, a junior branch of the NCS was established in Kansas City, Kansas, by which time the society was the largest Croatian organization in America.

Many aspects of Croatian life in the United States changed after the First World War. People with leftist tendencies assumed the leadership of the National Croatian Society, and years passed before they were overthrown. This was an era of radicalism on the American scene, partly influenced by the Russian Revolution. Many east Europeans – including the Croatians – responded to the impact of these trends. It was also the era of the "Red Scare" in America, of "Palmer's Raids," and the coming of age of the immigration restriction. In opposition to the NCS a new fraternal organization, the Croatian Catholic Union, was founded on

42/*By-Laws of the Croatian Union of the U.S.A.* (Allegheny, Pa.: Croatian Union, 1896); *Kratki pregled povijesti Hrvatske Bratske Zajednice, 1894–1949*/A Short Survey of the History of the Croatian Fraternal Union (Pittsburgh: CFU, 1949), 254, gives a great deal of documentary information on the history of the CFU.

43/The third president of the National Croatian Society was Frank Zotti. He was born in Boka Kotorska. As an immigrant he became a very successful businessman, banker, steamship agent, and newspaper publisher in New York. He used undue influence to be elected by the NCS convention in October 1904 at St. Louis, Mo. A very controversial figure, he came into conflict with the rest of the NCS leadership and many members, and was deposed by the convention of the organization held in New York City in September 1906. In all present-day publications of the Croatian Fraternal Union (which succeeded the NCS) Zotti is not even listed as its third president, but rather Pavao Hajdić is. (See, for instance, CFU, *65th Anniversary* [Pittsburgh, 1959], 8.) After his ouster Zotti became the most violent opponent of the NCS, and through the years denounced its leaders in his *Narodni List*, the most influential daily among the American Croatians in the early 1900s.

October 12, 1921, in Gary, Indiana. This was later to become the second largest Croatian organization in America. The organ of this union is *Naša Nada – Our Hope.*

By the mid-twenties the National Croatian Society counted some 500 lodges, having over 55,000 adult and 23,000 junior members; the Croatian League of Illinois had about 250 lodges and a membership of 12,000; the Croatian Unity of the Pacific had 27 lodges and 1500 members. The National Croatian "St. Joseph" Beneficial Society in St. Louis had 4 lodges and over 600 members; the Croatian Fraternity in Montana, 4 lodges with 600 members; and the Young National Croatian Union in Whiting, Indiana, 8 lodges with over 1500 members. In 1925 all of these groups merged into the greatest Croatian organization in America, called the Croatian Fraternal Union of America. The first convention of the newly formed organization was held in Cleveland from May 3 to May 22, 1926. Since that time many other individual fraternal organizations have joined this powerful union.[44]

A great number of other organizations flourished between the two wars. A Croatian cultural-educational union (with Socialist leanings), "Hrvatski Radiša" (an organization for young tradesmen), various singing societies, tamburitza orchestras, kolo groups, theatrical clubs, and tian League of Illinois had about 250 lodges and a membership of 12,000; the Croatian Unity of the Pacific had 27 lodges and 1500 members. The National Croatian "St. Joseph" Beneficial Society in St. Louis had 4 lodges and over 600 members; the Croatian Fraternity in Montana, 4 lodges with 600 members; and the Young National Croatian organizations were in existence – though some of them only for a short time. Those years saw a number of noteworthy exchanges of cultural and human interests between American Croatians and native Croatians. In the summer of 1937, a large group of Croatians led by the president of the Croatian Fraternal Union, Ivan Butković, visited Croatia. Zagreb and the whole country gave them a royal welcome.

Since the Second World War the Croatian Fraternal Union has grown in members and financial assets. By 1947 it had 613 lodges with over 70,000 members and 500 junior groups with 29,000 members. The CFU changed leadership at the convention in 1947 when Ivan Butković, prominent leader among the Croatians and president of the organization, lost the presidency to Vjekoslav I. Mandić, who held the office for twenty years. The present membership of CFU is about 115,000.[45]

44/*Zajedničar*, Nov. 16, 1955.

45/For the most recent report on the state of the CFU see *Zajedničar*, March 30, 1966, 5–12.

Political Organization

Developing from the fraternal organization, concomitant with it, and often within it was the political organization. In September 1912, during the National Croatian Society convention in Kansas City, a great political organization and the first of its kind, the Croatian League, was founded. This league had considerable influence, even upon political life in Croatia. Within a few months of its inception 110 lodges of the new organization had sprung up all over the United States.[46]

Scarcely a year later, one of the emigrants who had returned to Croatia, Stjepan Dojčić, a member of a Croatian secret organization in the United States, was caught in an attempt to assassinate the Hungarian commissary Skerlecz on August 18, 1913. *Hrvatski Svijet* in New York and other Croatian newspapers in this country, together with a majority of American Croatians and the general public in Croatia, hailed Dojčić, who was sentenced to prison, as a patriot and an enemy of Austria-Hungary. Stjepan Radić, the leader of the rising Croatian Peasant Party, disapproved, however, of the revolutionary activities of the American Croatians, and begged them in a pamphlet which he wrote on this occasion to give up further attempts to murder representatives of foreign rule in Croatia.[47]

The Croatian League held a large national convention in Chicago on March 10, 1915, and on this occasion condemned the Austro-Hungarian rule in Croatia, and in a special resolution advocated the formation of a union of Slovenians, Croatians, Serbians, Montenegrins, and Macedonians. The Chicago resolution was the basis for the establishment of the Yugoslav Committee, which was formed in Paris in May 1915. This committee acted in allied countries as a representative of the oppressed South Slavic nationalities under the Dual Monarchy.

A group of Croatian patriots, led by the Reverend M. D. Krmpotić, opposed the policy of the Croatian League, which was under the leadership of Don Nikola Gršković, a former priest. The Croatians around Father Krmpotić, together with some Slovenian priests, propagated the formation of an independent Croatian state under the scepter of the Hapsburgs. At the outbreak of the First World War, the political feelings of American Croatians concerning their homeland were hopelessly divided into three groups: one loyal to Austria, another advocating a trialist Austrian Empire (which would include as third partner a

46/*Zajedničar*, Sept. 21, 1912.

47/Stjepan Radić, *Javna poruka hrvatskoj braći u Americi*/A Public Message to Croatian Brethren in America (Zagreb: Slavenska Knjižara, 1913). Throughout his political career until his violent death in 1928 Radić was in constant correspondence with the leading Croatians in America.

Croatian state), and the third desiring the destruction of Austria and creation of a South Slavic federation.

A group of Slovenian and Croatian priests signed a resolution in 1916, later published in a pamphlet, protesting against the activities of the "Great-Serbian" propaganda in the United States and voicing the desire of the Croatians and Slovenians to be given the right to decide their own future. In spite of this furor about whether or not an enlarged Serbia should be formed, many Croatian settlements were extremely pro-Austrian and rejected all other political designs.[48]

A national convention in Pittsburgh on November 29, 1916, with 615 delegates representing about 400 Croatian organizations, appealed to President Wilson for the destruction of Austria and the formation of a South Slavic union.[49]

During this period an office of the South Slavic National Committee for America was opened in Washington, D.C. Dr. Hinko Hinković, a member of the central South Slavic Committee, came to this country from London late in 1917. In a series of lectures he informed the authorities and the American public of the aims of the South Slavs under Austrian rule. He later published his impressions of the United States in a commendable book, *Iz Velikog Doba* (From a Great Era; Zagreb: Ćirilo-Metodska Nakladna Knjižara, 1927).

Wilson's policy was still directed toward the preservation of Austria – as evident from point ten of his Fourteen Points – but later, through the influence of Secretary Lansing and steady pressure from the South Slav Committee, he changed to the idea of advocating establishment of a South Slav state. Wilsonian ideas were very popular in Croatia, where he was especially praised by Stjepan Radić, then president of the Croatian Peasant Party.

During the historic session of the Croatian Sabor in Zagreb, on October 29, 1918, when Croatia dissolved all ties with Austria and Hungary, Wilson was enthusiastically hailed as the liberator of the small nations. The fears of many Croatian patriots that Italy (which by a secret treaty in London in April 1915 was promised, as the price for its entry into the

48/*Narodni List*, May 24, 1916; M(irko) K(ajić), *Naša izjava i k našoj izjavi*/ Our Declaration and about Our Declaration (New York: Narodni List, 1916). For an analysis and detailed discussion of the political activities of Croatians in the United States see G. J. Prpić, "The South Slavs," in Joseph P. O'Grady (ed.), *The Immigrants' Influence on Wilson's Peace Policies* (University of Kentucky Press, 1967), 173–203.

49/*Hrvatski Glasnik* and *Hrvatska Zastava*, Nov. 20–30, 1916. In regard to the first world war, the best discussion with much data on Croatians is Victor S. Mamatey, *The United States and East Central Europe 1914–1918* (Princeton University Press, 1957).

war, Dalmatia and Istria) would take possession of the Croatian provinces of Dalmatia and Istria were realized after the end of the war. All appeals from Zagreb to President Wilson were in vain. At the Paris Peace Conference the Adriatic question almost broke up the peace negotiations. Wilson tried in vain to save at least Rijeka and some parts of Istria for the South Slavs, but after the conference, although it did lose Dalmatia (except for Zadar and a few islands), Italy was awarded Rijeka and Istria by the treaty of Rapallo.

Later, as a result of the Serbian occupation, which introduced terror and oppression in Croatia, the whole South Slavic movement in the United States collapsed. A new Croatian League, which had in its program the liberation of Croatia, was formed in Cleveland on April 1, 1919, under the leadership of Monsignor M. D. Krmpotić.

A significant political organization, the Croatian Peasant Party, was formed after the war, and by 1925 it had thirty-six branches.

The effect in America was great when, in the summer of 1928, the leader of the Croatian people, Stjepan Radić, "the irrepressible Stjepan Radić" as the American press called him, was shot in the Belgrade parliament. As a result of the tragic events in Croatia, the Croatian Circle, a patriotic Croatian organization sponsoring the establishment of an independent Croatian state, was formed in New York City in August of that year. The publication of the Circle was *Hrvatski List i Danica Hrvatska* under the able leadership of Ivan Krešić.

Speaking in the name of its 90,000 members, the Croatian Fraternal Union at its third convention in Gary, Indiana, held between June 13 and 29, 1932, adopted a resolution condemning most emphatically "all the tyrannies and persecutions that have been and still are perpetrated by the Belgrade regime against Croatia and the Croatian nation."[50]

50/*Danica Koledar* for 1933, 148. Josip Kraja, "Narodna borba prvih hrvatskih useljenika u U.S.A."/The National Struggle of the First Croatian Immigrants in the U.S.A., *Hrvatska Revija* (Buenos Aires), XIII, no. 3 (Sept. 1963), 293–326. Mr. Kraja gives here and in the article below a well-documented survey of the political scene and activities of the Croatian Circle and some other organizations. As eyewitness accounts, they offer important information on political activities during the past sixty years. Also by Joseph Kraja, "The Croatian Circle, 1928–1946: Chronology and Reminiscences," *Journal of Croatian Studies*, V–VI (1964–5), 145–204, reproduces the entire text of the *Memorandum* which in October 1933 was submitted to President Roosevelt, American newspapers (see *New York Times*, Oct. 12, 1933), and various political leaders here and abroad. On October 26, the *Memorandum* issued by the Croatian National Council, Youngstown, Ohio, with thousands of signatures, was presented to the League of Nations in Geneva by Msgr. Ivan Stipanović. Kraja, former head (*starješina*) of the Croatian Circle, is in possession of thousands of documents on the history of the political activities of Croatians. For those who wish to travel to Croatia to do research in the same field, we would recommend the Historical Department of Matica Iseljenika (Zavod za Migraciju) in

The Croatian National Council, with headquarters in Youngstown, Ohio, issued a memorandum in the fall of 1933 addressed to the League of Nations, to the press, and to American and other leading statesmen of the free world, protesting against the persecutions of the Croatian people in Yugoslavia. This was in fact, as the document stated, a protest of "250,000 American citizens of Croatian descent." Monsignor Stipanović went to Geneva to present the memorandum to the League. Another group of Croatians, an offshoot of the Croatian Circle, founded an extremist nationalist organization, the "Hrvatski Domobran" (Croatian Home Defenders) with headquarters in Pittsburgh, and with its own publication *Nezavisna Hrvatska Država – The Independent State of Croatia.*

Period of the Second World War

The period from 1939 to 1945 was a fateful one for Croatia and for the Croatians in the United States. A Croatian state, organized under German and Italian auspices, was in existence between April 1941 and May 1945. On February 20, 1943, a huge congress of American Croatians, sponsored by the Croatian Fraternal Union, with representatives from 716 Croatian organizations, was held in Chicago. The congress condemned the new state, as well as the German and Italian occupation of large sectors of it. The result of this congress was the formation of a new Croatian National Council and a Central Council of American Croatians.

Various leftist organizations appeared in the United States during the Second World War, aiding the Communist Partisan movement in the old country. Notable among them was the United Committee of South Slavic Americans, presided over by the leftist writer of Slovenian descent, Louis Adamic. *Narodni Glasnik*, a Communist paper, formally an organ of the Croatian Benefit Fraternity, advocated the formation of a Communist Yugoslavia. The American Slav Congress, a confedera-

Zagreb. For the war period, see also: *Kratki pregled povijesti Hrvatske Bratske Zajednice, 1894–1949* and numerous issues of *Zajedničar*, 1941–5; also various passages in Gerald G. Govorchin, *Americans from Yugoslavia* (University of Florida Press, 1961). On wartime leftist activities see also: U.S. Senate, *Communist Activities among the Aliens and National Groups*, 81st Congress, 1st Session, 1949; various issues of *The Slavic American* in 1947–8 with comments on such activities and U.S. House of Representatives, Committee on Un-American Activities, *Guide to Subversive Organizations and Publications* (Washington: Government Printing Office, 1961). *Uspjesi i zadaće Narodnog Vijeća Amerikanaca Hrvatskog Porijekla/* Successes and Tasks of the National Council of Americans of Croatian Descent (Pittsburgh: NVAHP, 1949), is a good collection of documents on the wartime activities of American Croatians.

tion of thirteen Slavic ethnic groups in America, in which the Croatians were a most active element, was listed in 1948 by the Attorney General as a subversive organization.

Hrvatski List i Danica Hrvatska, edited by Ivan Krešić and still published during the Second World War by the Croatian Circle, opposed Communism and any foreign occupation and dictatorship in Croatia, while *Hrvatski Svijet* came out openly for the Communist Partisans. Another Croatian paper, which, in this time of confusion, was strongly anti-Communist and sympathetic to the Croatian state, was the publication of the Croatian Catholic Union, *Naša Nada – Our Hope*, published in Gary, Indiana. *Zajedničar*, the organ of the Croatian Fraternal Union, sympathized with the Partisans, but at the same time supported the Croatian Peasant Party. *Nezavisna Hrvatska Država* and the organization which it represented, Hrvatski Domobran, ceased to exist in 1941.

After the war, on March 17, 1946, the representatives of several Croatian national, Catholic, and anti-Communist societies founded a new political organization in Cleveland, naming it the United Croatians of America and Canada. It condemned the Communist rule and the terror which it imposed in Croatia. This organization was composed of some ten different organizations. On September 2, 1946, a large Croatian congress was held in Chicago, presenting as principal speaker Dr. Vladko Maček, the exiled leader of the Croatian Peasant Party. A virile group for over two years, the United Croatians began to split up toward the end of 1948, after the Croatian Peasant Party left its ranks. Yet the group continued to be active. The Second Croatian Congress of the United Croatians took place on February 27, 1949, in Chicago. It is still a very active political organization with some twenty chapters all over the country, and it publishes in New York a well-edited *Bulletin* in English and Croatian.

Very active in the movement for the Croatian cause has been a group of Croatians of the Franciscan religious order. In 1945 they purchased Ivan Krešić's newspaper *Hrvatski List i Danica Hrvatska*, renamed it *Danica*, and have since published it in Chicago. The *Hrvatski Katolički Glasnik* (Croatian Catholic Messenger), a monthly, was introduced by the Franciscans during the last war and is still in publication.

The Press

For Croatians as for other immigrant groups, the written word has served to help preserve traditional interests, to unify people scattered over a vast continent, and to disseminate information regarding matters of vital concern to them. Thus the founding of newspapers was an early activity of the Croatian immigrants.

It is alleged that the first Croatian newspaper in America, *Slavenska Sloga*, was founded in 1884 in San Francisco. In November, 1891, A. Škrivanić published in Hoboken, New Jersey, the first Croatian paper in the East, *Napredak*. In 1896, after its transfer from Hoboken to Pittsburgh, *Napredak* became the official organ of the Croatian Union, later the National Croatian Society.

The first issue of the newspaper *Hrvatska Zora* was published in Chicago, in August 1892, by Janko Kovačević. *Chicago*, first published in October 1892 by Nikola Polić, was later united with another of his publications and published under the name *Chicago-Sloboda*. A short-lived paper, *Hrvatska Sloboda*, was edited by Nikola Gršković.[51] *Danica* was published by Zdravko Mužina in Pittsburgh in 1894, and in that same year he also edited the first Croatian almanac in the United States entitled *Hrvatsko-Amerikanska Danica za Godinu 1895*. Josip Marohnić was the publisher of the paper *Hrvatski Glasnik*, which together with *Hrvatska Zastava* in Chicago was the official paper of the Croatian League. In addition, Marohnić published in Pittsburgh numerous Croatian books and pamphlets, English grammars and dictionaries, and aids for the immigrants.

Many early papers in the United States became organs for steamship agencies and immigrant banks, e.g., *Narodni List – National Gazette*, which became the best known and most popular newspaper among the Croatians. It was published in New York by a Croatian banker and steamship agency owner, Franjo (Frank) Zotti. Founded as a weekly in 1898, it became a daily in 1902 – the first Croatian daily in America – and remained in existence until the early 1920s.

A great many Croatian newspapers, representing a variety of organizations, business groups, and ideologies, have been published in the United States, and many of them changed their names as frequently as they changed ownership and locale of publication. Among the best known American Croatian journalists, publishers, publicists, and writers of the early part of the century were Franjo Zotti, Don Niko Gršković, Ivan Krešić, Stjepko Brozović, A. G. Škrivanić, Hinko Sirovatka, I. F. Lupis Vukić, Ivan Mladineo, Frano Akačić, and Gabriel Rački. The

51/Anthony Zuback, "Croatian Publications in Chicagoland," *Croatian Almanac for 1950* (McKeesport, Pa.: Dobroslav Sorić, 1949), 101–25; and George J. Prpić, "The Croatian Newspapers in America before 1918," *Croatia Press*, xv, no. 6 (Dec. 1961), 7–15.

most outstanding was Ivan Krešić, who dedicated forty years of his life as a writer, editor, and publisher in New York. Krešić's paper, a tri-weekly, *Hrvatski List i Danica Hrvatska,* which he edited from 1922 to 1945, is considered one of the best Croatian papers ever published in this country.

Zajedničar, published in Pittsburgh, has been issued since 1904 as the organ of the National Croatian Society (later the Croatian Fraternal Union). Since 1929 it has appeared weekly; it has a circulation of over 65,000, greater than that of all other Croatian papers combined. It is regularly published in twelve pages, six of which are printed in English, the other six in Croatian. It is the most important newspaper of the American Croatians, and is sent to all families of CFU members and to individual members with the exception of members of the Junior Order in America. Many copies are also mailed to members who live in retirement in Yugoslavia.

THE CROATIAN CONTRIBUTION TO THE UNITED STATES

The Croatians have contributed to practically every aspect of American life. The early settlers, sailors, pioneers, missionaries, priests, miners, steelworkers, factory laborers, tradesmen, journalists, publishers, scientists, teachers, artists, physicians, fishermen, fruit growers, railroad workers, mechanics, soldiers, sportsmen – all contributed to the development, growth, and progress of the United States by their skills and sacrifices in blood and lives. A few Croatians names are listed in encyclopedias and other reference works, but there are many others who deserve some recognition.

MISSIONARIES

Father Ivan Ratkaj (Juan Ratkay), S.J., was born on May 22, 1647, in the castle of Veliki Tabor, Croatia. Ivan studied philosophy and jurisprudence in Vienna, where he joined the Society of Jesus. Subsequently, he taught for three years at the Jesuit colleges in Zagreb and Gorizia. While he was studying for the priesthood he determined to go as a missionary to America. He therefore went to Seville, Spain, where he was trained with other future missionaries for the church's work in America. He arrived in Vera Cruz, Mexico, on September 25, 1680, the first Croatian missionary in North America. For a while he worked among the primitive Tarahumara Indians near the border of New Mexico. Eventually he was sent to Carichic, Mexico, where he died a martyr on December 26, 1683, poisoned by the Indians whose drinking orgies and pagan dances he had forbidden.

That Ratkaj was a Croatian is indicated by the title of one of his letters from Mexico printed in *Der Neue Welt-Bott*: "The Travel Account of Father Ratkay, a Born Baron of the Ancient Family of the Former Croatian Barons and Present Counts Ratkay."[52]

The Reverend Ferdinand Konšćak (Fernando Consag, S.J., also known in Spanish sources as Consago, Conzag, Gonsago, Konsag, and Konschak) was born in Varaždin, Croatia, on December 3, 1703, and went to Vera Cruz, Mexico, as a missionary in 1730. In 1733 he was transferred to the mission of San Ignacio in Baja California. In 1746 he explored the mouth of the Colorado River and drew the first scientific map of the peninsula of Lower California. Diaries of his explorations in 1746 and again in 1751, which have been reprinted in many works are of great significance for the student of the early history of California. In 1748 Konšćak became visitator of all Jesuit missions in California and the same year founded the mining village of San Antonio Real. He explored the entire region of Lower California, discovered important water sources, and founded a new mission, Santa Gertrudis, in 1752. In his missionary activities during this period he baptized over a thousand Indians. He was also a linguist: besides his mother tongue, Croatian, he was proficient in Latin, spoke several Indian dialects, and spoke and wrote in German, Spanish, and French. He was an expert in mathematics, geography, and geology, and accomplished as an engineer in developing mines, roads, and dams. Without his maps the development of California would have been delayed. As he was about to found another new mission, San Francisco de Borja, he died in San Ignacio on September 10, 1759. H. H. Bancroft, H. Bolton, P. M. Dunne, and other American and Mexican historians consider Konšćak one of the greatest of California missionaries, explorers, and pioneers. Consag Rocks, in the northern part of the Gulf of California, are named after him.[53]

52/P. Elesban de Guilhermy, *Ménologe de la Compagnie de Jesus* (Paris: Leroy, 1898), 507–8; Emilij Laszowski (ed.), *Znameniti i zaslužni Hrvati*/Famous and Reputed Croatians (Zagreb: Odbor za Izdanje Knjige, 1925), 227; Joseph Stoecklein (ed.), *Der neue Welt-Bott* (Augsburg and Graetz, 1726), I, 77–84 (containing two letters of Ratkaj from Mexico amply used as a source by American historians since they contain excellent information about the missionaries, trans-Atlantic voyages, and Mexico); H. E. Bolton, *Rim of Christendom*, 51–5, 71–2; Gerard Decorme, *La Obra de los Jesuitas Mexicanos* (2 vols.; Mexico City: José Potrua, 1941), I, 410, which lists Ratkay as "Croata."

53/M. D. Krmpotić, *Life and Works of the Reverend Ferdinand Konšćak*, S.J. *1703–1759* (Boston: Stratford Co., 1923), contains excellent information (it was

The Reverend Joseph Kundek, a secular priest, a gifted poet, and an ardent Croatian patriot, was born on January 21, 1809, in Ivanić, Croatia. Learning through the *Berichte der Leopoldinen Stiftung*, a publication of the Leopoldine Mission Society in Vienna, of the plight of the German settlers in America, he desired to come to the United States as a missionary. In May 1838 he was sent by the Leopoldine Society to Jasper, Indiana, where he spent many years as missionary caring for the Catholic Germans.

Father Kundek built up the parish at Jasper, founded the towns of Ferdinand, Celestine, and Fulda, and also established four parishes and four missions. In 1853 he, along with a group of secular priests, brought from Europe the first Benedictine priests to settle in the United States, from Einsiedeln, Switzerland. As a colonizer, he settled about 7000 Germans in Dubois and Spencer counties in Indiana. He also built the courthouse in Jasper. From Croatia he brought the Reverend Edward Martinović of Križevci, who later worked at the German parish in Madison, Indiana.

Kundek died on December 4, 1857, but his labor has left a lasting impression upon southern Indiana: in December, 1957, Jasper and St. Meinrad solemnly celebrated the centennial of his death. The governor of Indiana proclaimed December 8, 1967, "Father Kundek Day," in order "to pay tribute to a great missionary, pioneer and citizen who left Croatia, the land he loved, to come and colonize the wilderness of this great state, for which we owe him a huge debt of gratitude."[54]

EARLY PIONEERS

Many Croatians settled in the southern part of the United States in the early nineteenth century. They introduced and developed the oyster fishing industry in Louisiana and Mississippi; a Croatian settlement

Krmpotić who found Konšćak's diary of 1746 in the British Museum); *Apostólicos afanes* (Barcelona: Pablo Nadal, 1754), 391–429; Miguel Venegas (ed.), *Noticia de la California* (3 vols.; Madrid: M. Fernandez, 1757), III, 140–94, with map; H. H. Bancroft, *Works: History of the North Mexican States* (San Francisco: A. L. Bancroft, 1884), I, 452–70; P. M. Dunne, *Black Robes in Lower California* (Berkeley and Los Angeles: Univ. of California Press, 1952), 321–32, and passim; P. M. Dunne, "Lower California an Island," *Mid America*, 35, no. 1 (Jan. 1953), 37–66.

54/From a photostatic copy of the proclamation in the author's possession. About Kundek's life and activities, see M. D. Krmpotić, *Josip Kundek* (Virje, Croatia: published by the author, 1925); *Berichte der Leopoldinen Stiftung* (Wien, 1839–49) with many of Kundek's letters; Dunstan McAndrews, *Father Joseph Kundek* (St. Meinrad, Ind.: A Grail Publication, 1954), originally a doctoral dissertation; and Albert Kleber, *St. Joseph Parish, Jasper, Indiana* (St. Meinrad, Ind.: St. Meinrad Abbey, 1937).

existed in New Orleans as early as 1835, and not too much later in Biloxi, Mississippi. Some of the people came in their own vessels, while others worked their way to the new world as crewmen on commercial vessels. A few became successful merchants and traders in New Orleans, and many served as sailors in the Louisiana area or were engaged in shrimp and oyster fishing. In the Delta they developed America's greatest oyster center. Luka Jurišić, a Croatian from Dalmatia, began successful fishing enterprises in Bayou Creek in 1860; other early Croatian pioneers in oyster fishing were Luke and Miho Zibilić and Mate Mužina. The Croatians produced a new type of lugger, low and wide beamed, with a deep hold for large hauls. With the success of these early immigrant fishermen many more Dalmatians were induced to come to the Gulf area.

At the present time, over fifty descendants of these pioneer Croatian fishermen control a major part of the oyster and shrimp industry in Louisiana and Mississippi.[55] Peter Kopanica, who came to Empire, Louisiana, in 1893, gained control of a large part of the oyster business. Two other noted Croatian pioneers in the area were Mike Bačić and Šime Tucić.[56] Today, many prominent professional people and restaurateurs in New Orleans are of Croatian descent.

Croatians had long been in California when the first Americans reached the Pacific coast. Among the men who were seeking their fortune in San Francisco during the gold rush was John Owen Dominis, whose father was Captain John Dominis, a native of the island of Rab of the Croatian Littoral. The latter had settled in Honolulu, Hawaii, and built a mansion there called Washington Place, which was later to become the palace of the governor. His son John Owen returned to Hawaii in 1850 after his adventuresome days in California. In September of 1862, Owen married Princess Lydia Kamekaha Kapaadea, who later became the last Hawaiian queen, Liliuokalani. Prince Consort John Owen died in August 1891.[57]

One of the leading Croatian pioneers in San Francisco was Nikola Barović, who arrived there in June 1850. With two other prominent first settlers, Florio Antonović and Nikola Buja, in 1857 he founded the first Croatian Benevolent Society, called the Slavonic Illyrian Mutual Benevolent Society. A number of these first Croatians were experienced sea captains – e.g., Captain John Silovich and Captain Vincent Politeo – and

55/*Hrvatski List i Danica Hrvatska Koledar 1932* (New York: Ivan Krešić, 1931), 188–9; Hartnett Thomas Kane, *Deep Delta Country* (New York: Duell, Sloan and Pearce, 1944), 92–99 gives a detailed description of "Dalmatia in Mississippi."

56/*Danica Koledar za 1928*, 155, 61–62.

57/A. Z., "His Royal Highness the Prince Consort John Owen Dominis ...," *The American Croatian Historical Review* (Youngstown, Ohio), I (Aug. 1946), 3–9.

among the very successful businessmen should be listed Jerome Suić, John Ivankovich, John Uzovich, and Stephen Divizich.

Dr. Vincent Gelcich, a native of Starigrad on the island of Hvar, Dalmatia, was a physician and surgeon in the Union Army during the Civil War and held the rank of colonel. After the war he became the coroner of the city of Los Angeles. Also active in the Civil War was Jakov Mikulić from Rijeka, who had enlisted as a young boy in the U.S. Navy in 1860. However, it is impossible to determine the number of Croatians who participated in the Civil War.

John Ivankovic, a native of Lopud, near Dubrovnik, became a well-known wholesale fruit merchant in California. One of his sons joined the Jesuit Order and later became a member of the faculty of Santa Clara College.[58]

In the 1870s Marko Rabaša began to plant apple orchards in the Pajaro Valley near Watsonville, California. With his Croatian countrymen M. N. Letunić, Gjuro Stražić, Marinović, and Luka Škurić, he created a new business for California, that of growing apples for export all over the country. Among other things these men built packing-houses and introduced new methods of fighting apple diseases. Letunić was the first to export California apples to England. Sresović introduced new methods of packing apples. These inventive men developed new ways of drying apples, and in the later development of this industry other Croatians, among them Miladins, Cikuts, Milovićs, Kalićs, Rešetars, and Katušićs, introduced modern methods and sorting machines, trucks, tractors, and spray machines.[59] The writer Jack London described "New Dalmatia" in his book *Valley of the Moon*: a veritable "apple paradise" produced by industrious Croatian men from Dalmatia. London mentioned Peter Mongol, who was exporting apples to England and South America; Luka Skuric (*sic*) who owned a particularly large fruit business; and Mateo Lettunich (*sic*), who began work in California as a dish washer and eventually became a rich man in the apple-growing industry.

58/For a full picture of prominent Croatians in early California, cf. Meler, *Slavonic Pioneers of California*, 32–43; Stephen N. Sestanovich, *Slavs in California* (Oakland: Slavonic Alliance, 1937), 2–24; *Croatian Almanac for 1947* (Pittsburgh: D. Sorić, 1946), 201; Adam S. Eterovich, "Croatian Pioneers on the Barbary Coast of San Francisco 1849–1870," *Croatia Press*, XVII, no. 233 (Nov. 1963), 2–5; and also by the same: *Croatian Cemetery Records of San Francisco, California 1849–1930* (San Francisco: Slavonic American Historical and Genealogical Society, 1964); *Irish-Slavonians in California: 1849–1880* (San Francisco: By the author, 1964); issues of the bulletin by Eterovich in 1965 and 1966: *Balkan and Eastern European American Genealogical and Historical Society*. All these are primary sources recently published and so far have not been used in writing American Croatian history.

59/Meler, *Slavonic Pioneers of California*, 52–3.

London also notes that more than 12,000 acres were owned at that time by these apple farmers.[60]

Other new industries were created by the Dalmatian Croatians. Some immigrants took over old Spanish land grants in the Santa Clara Valley where they planted many varieties of fruit trees, but chiefly plums and apricots, which were dried for market. Near Fresno, the Croatians worked in the raisin and grape-growing industries. In the Sonora and Sacramento Valleys pear-growing became a specialty. Since 1882 many Croatians in the San Joaquin Valley have been successful grape growers or diversified farmers: raising cattle, hogs, sheep, goats, poultry, and bees or producing plums and figs, or lettuce, onions, and other vegetables on a large scale.[61]

Stephen N. Mitrović came from Dalmatia to Fresno in 1881. Up to that time Californians had planted fig trees around their homes and along the roads only for shade and landscape decoration. In 1883 Mitrović imported from his native village in Dalmatia one thousand fig cuttings which he planted and cultivated; eventually he introduced his own system of harvesting, curing, drying, and packing figs, and shipped dried figs by the carload to eastern American markets, where he obtained a higher price than was paid for the imported product. At the World's Columbian Exposition at Chicago in 1893, he exhibited his "Adriatic" figs, and was awarded the gold medal for the best cured and packed figs at the exhibition. The fig industry in California, which Mitrović alone introduced and originally developed, has through the years added many millions of dollars to the income of the people of that state.[62]

Numerous Croatian Americans of course continued in their traditional occupation as fishermen, working the California waters and along Puget Sound and the coast of British Columbia and Alaska. For decades these hardy men have been supplying the American market with sardine, salmon, mackerel, and tuna. Some founded their own canneries and not rarely made great fortunes. A few of these seafaring men have been highly successful shipbuilders. Many of these various businessmen have employed great numbers of their own countrymen.[63]

Other Croatians became restaurateurs. John Zvierkovich came to California in 1878 at the age of fourteen and worked for years as a waiter

60/J. London, *Valley of the Moon* (New York: Macmillan, 1914), 363–6.

61/Meler, *Slavonic Pioneer of California*, 56.

62/Paul E. Vandor, *History of Fresno County* (Los Angeles: Historic Record Co., 1919), 1621–4; Mladineo, *Narodni adresar* xviii.

63/I. F. Lupis-Vukić, "Hrvati kao stvaralački narod u tudjem svijetu"/Croatians as Creative People Abroad, *Godišnjak Hrvatski Radiša 1939* (Zagreb: Hrvatski Radiša, 1938), 63.

to save enough money to buy a restaurant of his own. John V. Tadich arrived in 1871 and eventually became one of the leading restaurateurs in San Francisco. His restaurant was a landmark of old San Francisco and was frequented by many prominent Americans of that time.[64]

Meanwhile, the Croatians on the Atlantic coast gained reputations as good sailors and navigators. A sturdy race of mariners, they were active and influential in all the ports of the East. Nick Jelusic, whose home port was Philadelphia, became one of the best-known ship captains in the area. Before he died, he was in charge of the entire fleet at Reading, Pennsylvania, consisting of forty ships. Through this fleet Jelušić offered employment to hundreds of his countrymen. Other prominent ship captains in the Atlantic ports were: the three Gladulić brothers, Erić, Marković, Randić, Tony Rudar, Sablić, and Vidović.[65]

Quite a few Croatians were employed during these years in tugboat crews in the New York harbor, and until recently more than fifty Croatian tugboat masters were directing harbor traffic there.

In Michigan between the 1880s and the end of the First World War thousands of Croatians invested their energy and lives in the prospering copper mines. Judge Anthony Lucas, son of the Croatian pioneer Mato Lesac from Severin (na Kupi) who settled in Calumet, Michigan, successfully supported the first safety laws in mining; he was the first Croatian to enter the Michigan legislature.[66]

Janko Kovačević, a former officer in the Austrian army and one of the few intellectuals coming from Croatia in the last century, settled in South Dakota, where he enlisted as a member of the militia in the last Sioux war in 1890. In August 1892, he began publication of the paper *Hrvatska Zora* in Chicago.[67]

Besides their contribution in farming, fruit-growing, fishing, and seafaring, Croatians also were working in large numbers in the forest industry, in steel mills, in railroad and other construction work, in mining, meat-packing, leather-manufacturing, and oil-refining. The production of staves for French claret barrels in Louisiana and Mississippi was done almost entirely by Croatian workers. In 1909, 50,000 Croatian immigrants were working as lumbermen, woodworkers, and stave-cutters.[68]

64/Anon., *A Memorial Biographical History of Northern California* (Chicago: Lewis Publishing Co., 1891), 390; Meler, *Slavonic Pioneers of California*, 50–1.

65/Jure Kvarnerski, "Hrvatski pomorci u Americi"/Croatian Sailors in America, *Danica Koledar*, 1934, 77–8.

66/*Hrvatski Glasnik*, Nov. 12, 1910.

67/*Narodni List*, Jan. 16, 1902.

68/Jeremiah W. Jenks and W. Jett Lauck, *The Immigration Problem* (New York and London: Funk and Wagnalls Co., 1912), 137; *Hrvatski Svijet*, Dec. 3, 1909.

NIKOLA TESLA, A GREAT INVENTOR

Nikola Tesla, the son of an Orthodox priest, was born on July 10, 1856, in Smiljan, Lika. In 1875 he entered the Polytechnic Institute in Graz, Austria, and in 1881 graduated in electrical engineering at the University of Prague. An excellent mathematician and a genius in the field of electrical engineering, he worked for a time for the American Edison Company in Paris, where he became acquainted with Charles Bachellor, a close friend of Thomas Alva Edison. In 1883 Tesla built his first two-phase-system dynamo, the greatest and most profitable invention in this field at that time. With Bachellor's recommendation he went to the United States, in 1884, to work for Edison in New York. Edison distrusted Tesla's alternating system of light power, and the two scientists soon separated. For the next few years Tesla worked at various jobs, even doing ditch-digging in New York for one year. Then, in 1887, with the backing of several financiers, he formed the Tesla Electric Company. On October 12 of that year, he registered a whole series of his important inventions with the U.S. Patent Office. It was the beginning of a new era in the history of American technology, indeed of American civilization, for by means of Tesla's alternating current inventions, electricity could be delivered economically at vast distances from the powerhouses.

Through his famous lecture at the Institute of American Electrical Engineers in New York, on May 16, 1888, Tesla's discoveries gained acceptance by a majority of American experts in the field. Almost immediately he became world-famous. In 1888–9 he worked with George Westinghouse, president of Westinghouse Electric Corporation, and in 1893 Chicago's World Fair was illuminated with his polyphase system of electricity. Tesla lectured in the United States and Europe and his name appeared in all of the newspapers and scientific magazines.

Fifty-one patents in the field of the polyphase system alone and a great number of other inventions are credited to Nikola Tesla. In 1888 he patented a form of electrical transmission of power, an electromagnetic motor, a system of electrical distribution, a dynamo electric machine, and regulations for alternating current motors. In 1891 he registered a method of operating arc lamps.[69]

69/John J. O'Neill's *Prodigal Genius: The Life of Nikola Tesla* (New York: Ives Washburn, 1944), 55–8, 70–2ff., is the best biography of Tesla to date. See also *Zajedničar*, April 11 and 18, 1956; Slavko Bokšan, *Nikola Tesla i njegovo djelo*/ Nikola Tesla and His Work (Beograd: Naučna Knjiga, 1950), 120–1. Thomas C. Martin's *The Inventions, Researches and Writings of Nikola Tesla* (New York: The Electrical Engineer, 1894) is very good also. Tesla described his inventions in the

Statue of Father Joseph Kundek,
Jasper, Indiana
(Courtesy of Mr. Anthony G. Zubak, the Croatian publicist, standing beside the statue)

The new headquarters of the Croatian Fraternal Union at Kingston and Delaney Drives, Pittsburgh

Duquesne University Tamburitzans of Pittsburgh

A young Duquesne tamburitzan with his instrument
(Courtesy Mr. Walter W. Kolar)

Maksimilian Vanka, painter, *Four Riders of the Apocalypse*, oil, 1957

Maksimilian Vanka, *Angelus in Croatia* (or *Faith in Croatia*)

Maksimilian Vanka, *The Morning Shift*

Paul Kufrin, sculptor,
David Lloyd George

Paul Kufrin, *After the Dream*

Paul Kufrin, *American Historical Indian*, looking intensely at approaching enemy from the top of a rock

Joseph Turkalj, *The Memories* (marble), 1961

Joseph Turkalj, sculptor, detail of *Moses*, an 18-foot bronze statue standing in front of the Notre Dame University Library

Paul Draženović, "Alaskan pioneer gold miner"
(reached Alaska in 1911; now living in Fairbanks)

One of many appraisals of Tesla's work gives the following summary:

His inventions and discoveries include a system of arc lighting (1886); the Tesla motor and alternating current power transmission system (1888); a system of electrical conversion and distribution by oscillatory discharges (1889); high frequency current generators (1890); the Tesla Coil, or transformer (1891); a system of wireless transmission of information (1893); mechanical oscillators and generators of electrical oscillations (1894–1895). Between 1896 and 1898 he carried on researches and made discoveries in radiations, material stream and emanations; in 1897 he invented his high potential magnifying transmitter; and between 1897 and 1905 worked on a system for the wireless transmission of power. However, he was perhaps best known for his epoch-making alternating current motors, and for his famous Tesla coil, or transformer. One of the outstanding geniuses in his field, in his later years he indulged in many ideas bordering on the fantastic. For example, on his 78th birthday he announced the invention of a death beam capable of destroying 10,000 airplanes at a distance of 250 miles and of wiping out an army of 1,000,000 men instantly.[70]

Tesla's inventions ushered in the age of electricity and of American mass production. He made radio and television possible; and without his induction motor, nearly everything that today moves on wheels would stop. His inventions made possible cheap electrical light and energy, as well as travel on street cars, electric trains, and subways. He discovered the nature of cosmic rays, and pointed the way to the automatic pilot, to the robot bomb, and to the rocket airplane. He is the originator of our system of power transmission. Though he was a great inventor, humanitarian, and pacifist, both during and after his lifetime this amazing man was alternately exploited, lied about, and ignored.[71]

Tesla had a literary flair also. He wrote poems, spoke perfect English, and was in fact a good friend of Mark Twain and other American literary figures. Though of Serbian descent, he always stressed the fact that his homeland was Croatia. Tesla created fortunes for others, but this honest yet impractical man himself died penniless as a bachelor at the age of 87, on January 7, 1943, in New York City.[72]

work *Experiments with Alternate Current of High Potential and High Frequency* (New York: McGraw, 1904).

70/"Tesla, Nikola," *The Encyclopedia Americana* (New York: Americana Corp., 1956), XXVI, 452–3.

71/E. H. Armstrong, "Nikola Tesla," *Scientific Monthly* (April 1943), 379–80; Leland T. Anderson (ed.), *Bibliography: Dr. Nikola Tesla (1856–1943)* (2nd ed.; Minneapolis: The Tesla Society, 1956).

72/*Zajedničar*, April 11, 1956; *The New York Herald Tribune*, Jan. 8 and 24, 1943; *New York Times*, Jan. 8 and 9, 1943.

CAPTAIN ANTHONY LUCAS

Anthony Lucas was another Croatian who helped to revolutionize American industry. Born on September 9, 1855, in Split, as the son of a sea captain, Franjo Lučić, he was educated at the Gymnasium in Trieste and the Polytechnic Institute at Graz, Austria (the same school which Tesla attended). Having graduated from the latter school in 1875 he joined the Austro-Hungarian navy. In 1879 he left the navy as second lieutenant and joined his uncle in Saginaw, Michigan, where he changed his name to Lucas. On May 9, 1885, at Norfolk, Virginia, he became an American citizen.

As a mining engineer from Washington, D.C., Lucas went to Louisiana and Texas in 1893, where he labored for years, hoping to find petroleum. In spite of general doubt at that time that there was any oil in Texas, Lucas insisted on drilling in Beaumont, at a spot called Spindletop. He and his crew struck oil on January 10, 1901. The entire country was agape at this new and significant achievement in the history of industrialized America.

Lucas, however, did not develop Spindletop but instead sold all his interests to the Mellon group for $400,000. In 1905 he returned to Washington, where he opened an office as consulting engineer. He died in Washington on September 2, 1921. The inscription on his tombstone at the Rock Creek Cemetery states that he was born in Spalato, Dalmatia, and that he was of "Illyrian [Croatian] parentage."

On October 9, 1941, the Texas Mid-Continent Oil and Gas Association unveiled at Spindletop a 58-foot granite monument honoring Lucas. The inscription notes that enormous industry that Lucas practically gave birth to.[73]

In 1936 the American Institute of Mining and Metallurgical Engineering, in recognition of the distinguished achievement of the discovery and production of petroleum, established the "Anthony F. Lucas Medal" as an award to all outstanding persons whose work contributes to the development of the oil industry.[74]

73/B. Sorić, *Centennial, 1847–1947* (Pittsburgh: The Croatian Historical Research Bureau, 1947), 85–99; T. A. Richard, *Interviews with Mining Engineers* (San Francisco: Mining and Scientific Press, 1922), 293; Anthony Zuback, "The Birth of a Great Discoverer," *The American Croatian Historical Review* (Youngstown, Ohio, July 1946), I, 4–5.

74/*The American Petroleum Institute Quarterly*, 15, no. 1 (New York, Jan. 1945), 9; *Who Was Who in America, 1897–1942* (Chicago: Marquis Co., 1942), 751, mistakenly states that Lucas was born in Trieste and that he was an Italian.

OUTSTANDING CULTURAL CONTRIBUTIONS

Sculptors

Croatia's greatest contribution to American art has undoubtedly been the work of Ivan Meštrović. He was born of Croatian parents in Vrpolje, Slavonia, on August 15, 1883, and died at South Bend, Indiana, on January 16, 1962, after gaining recognition as the greatest sculptor in the United States and one of the greatest in the world.

In 1924, 1926, and 1927, his exhibitions in the United States were a great success.[75] During the first of these exhibitions he met his countryman Nikola Tesla, and they became good friends. In 1926–7 he created his two famous equestrian Indians – one with a bow, and the other with a spear – for Grant Park in Chicago.

As a Croatian, a humanist, an artist, and a strong believer in liberty, he was disappointed after the First World War by conditions in Yugoslavia; he lived during the Second World War in Switzerland and chose to remain abroad. Soon after the end of the war, in 1946, he settled in Syracuse, New York, where he taught sculpture at the University of Syracuse. Later, from September 1955 until his death, he was a professor in the Art Department of Notre Dame University. Today there are Meštrović sculptures in several major American cities, and in most of the important museums and art galleries in the United States. The University of Syracuse published two representative books on his life with about four hundred reproductions of his work done both in Europe and America and including sculptures in stone, bronze, plaster, and wood as well as reliefs, drawings, and architectural works.[76]

In the course of his rich lifetime Meštrović produced a tremendous variety of works: statues, torsos, portraits, reliefs, and monuments, and a limitless number of plaster, clay, wood, stone, marble, and bronze pieces. His *My Mother* and *Moses* (found in the Chicago Art Institute) are original in style and expression and yet have a common quality of power; they are strong, muscular figures, resembling the Croatian peasant types. Even his saints reflect the features of his native peasant men

75/Christian Brinton, *The Meštrović Exhibition, The Brooklyn Museum, 1924* (New York: The Meštrović Exhibition Committee, 1924).

76/Harry Hilberry, *The Sculpture of Ivan Meštrović* (Syracuse University Press, 1948), with over 150 pages of reproductions; an excellent bibliography on 22–3. Lawrence Schmeckbier (Dean of the University of Syracuse School of Art), *Ivan Meštrović, Sculptor and Patriot* (Syracuse University Press, 1959), with 200 reproductions of Meštrović's artistry, arranged in chronological order. See also Meštrović's autobiography, *Uspomene na političke ljude i dogadjaje*/Recollections on Political People and Events (Buenos Aires: Knjižnica Hrvatske Revije, 1961).

and women. As his friend, painter Jozo Kljaković, has said, through his art "erupted centuries of suppressed national dynamism ... through him spoke up the pride and national stubbornness of Croatia."[77]

Meštrović became the most famous Croatian immigrant to the United States. In 1954 he became an American citizen, and in the same year he produced a bronze work, *Man and Freedom*, for the Mayo Clinic in Rochester, Minnesota. A bronze statue of St. Anthony for the University of Oxford is also a work of recent years. On June 8, 1955, he received an honorary doctor's degree from Marquette University.

At Notre Dame, where his mission was to build "the strongest, most respected department of sculpture in any American university," he was hard at work. In a single year he had been known to do as many as nine major works and a score of minor ones. Both a wood carver and a modeler in other materials, he produced in this country every kind of sculpture, from portrait busts to huge architectural pieces. Besides sculpturing, he also painted in fresco and oil, and produced engravings and lithographs.

A statue of Pope Pius XII for Saint Louis University, a bust of Cardinal Stepinac, one of former President Hoover, a monument to Nikola Tesla (besides a bust which he made in the 1930s), and another to Rudjer Bošković for the Atomic Institute in Zagreb – these were some of his many recent works. In April 1958, his monument to Francisco Lopez de Mendoza Grajales and his work *Pieta*, honoring modern Catholic martyrs, were unveiled in St. Augustine, Florida. The carved marble portraits on this latter work depict six persecuted churchmen, including Aloysius Cardinal Stepinac of Croatia. Two of Meštrović's works are at the National Shrine of the Immaculate Conception, Washington, D.C.: one is a statue of the Virgin Mary with two angels, and the other is a relief, twenty-five feet in height, entitled *Mary, Queen of the Universe.* His statue in bronze of St. Jerome is in front of the Croatian Franciscan Monastery in Washington, D.C.[78]

In an article published in 1958, two Americans thus summarized the significance of this great artist:

> Art critics compare him to Michelangelo. His own master, the great French sculptor Rodin, called him "the greatest phenomenon among sculptors." He was the first artist ever to be invited to hold an exhibition at the Metropolitan

77/Jozo Kljaković, *U Suvremenom kaosu*/In Contemporary Chaos (Buenos Aires: by the author, 1952), 168.

78/Vinko Nikolić, "Ivan Meštrović govori"/Ivan Meštrović speaks, *Hrvatska Revija*, IV (Sept. 1953), 327–32; *Hrvatski Katolički Pučki Kalendar 1954*/Croatian Catholic Popular Almanac, 198; *Danica*, Nov. 23, 1955; *Croatia Press*, XII, no. 4 (April 1958), 14 and the same, no. 5 (May 1958), 15.

Museum in his own lifetime ... Meštrović is one of those rare artists who are born, not taught ... He is the last living master of the human form ... As a man and as an artist, Meštrović must be put down as an epic type. Rising from peasant sources ... he has become his people's symbol of freedom and their spokesman and defender ... His art has been more than a creative outlet; it has been a social and political and religious statement. Through it, Meštrović speaks for man. And long after the oppressors have been forgotten, the art of Ivan Meštrović will remain to speak for him.[79]

Two young and talented sculptors assisted Meštrović in his many projects. Josip Turkalj, born in Rakovica, Croatia, on August 10, 1924, studied at the Academy of Arts, Zagreb, from 1948 until 1952, when he escaped to Italy. He graduated from the Accademia delle Belle Arti, Rome, in 1954. Meštrović sponsored Turkalj's immigration to this country and made him his assistant in January 1957. Turkalj has exhibited his sculptures a number of times. In the past few years, he has created several large sculptures, one of which *Moses* – a powerful eighteen-foot-high statue – stands in front of Notre Dame University's Library at South Bend, Indiana. Among his most recent creations are *St. Joseph with Jesus*, for the Holy Cross Brothers in South Bend, and a large sculpture of St. Paul for the Croatian St. Paul church in Cleveland where Turkalj now lives with his family.

Theodore Golubic, a young sculptor of Croatian descent, was born in this country and for several years worked with Meštrović at Notre Dame. His sculptures were exhibited at "Art U.S.A. '58" and at the exhibition of the National Academy of Design in New York in February 1959.[80]

Paul de Kufrin, a native of Croatia, has been working for many years as a sculptor in Chicago and has enriched the culture of his adopted country through many fine works. An excellent portraitist, he has produced busts of prominent Americans, including Franklin Delano Roosevelt. Among the famous men he has sculpted, he most admires Clarence Darrow; his bust of Darrow won for him the World's Fair gold medal in 1934. His awards include those from the Bohemian Arts Club, the Pallet and Chisel Academy, and the Chicago Painters and Sculptors Society.

The artist as man of ideas is beautifully exemplified in Kufrin. An outspoken critic of modern art as a symptom of the confusion of our time, he believes that the future of the arts in Western civilization requires a reappearance of the patron who would protect creative talents and allow

79/Jacques Lowe and Dennis Howard, "Mestrovic: Man and Artist," *The Sign* (March 1958), 42–6.

80/*Danica*, Oct. 9, 1957; *Croatia Press*, XII, 1–2 (Jan.-Feb. 1958), 22 and the same XIII, 4 (April 1959), 18.

them to develop free from external pressures. In an interview a few years ago Kufrin stated: "If art is supposed to be great, it must have spiritual depth; it must seek the truth."[81]

Painters

Vlaho Bukovac, born on July 4, 1855, in Cavtat, near Dubrovnik, one of the greatest Croatian painters, lived in the United States on two occasions and began his artistic career here. In 1866 he arrived in Brooklyn, New York, to live with his uncle, but he left the country shortly after. After several eventful years he arrived in San Francisco around 1875, and there he eventually took to painting portraits. Having saved some money, he returned to Europe, going to the Art Academy at Paris in 1877 to finish his education as a painter. In 1897 he rendered the "Diploma" of the National Croatian Society.[82]

Oton Iveković, a reputed Croatian painter, arrived in the fall of 1909 in Kansas City, Kansas, to decorate the Croatian St. John the Baptist church. For six months he painted huge frescoes on its walls, creating works of potentially enduring value. One fresco 39 feet long depicted Croatian peasants and workers. Unfortunately almost all of these excellent paintings were later destroyed by fire.[83] In 1910 he returned to Croatia, where he published his American impressions in a series of articles in the Croatian literary review *Vienac* in 1911.

Two notable American painters of Croatian origin at the beginning of this century were Ivan Benković and Lawrence Mazzanovich, the latter born in California. Benković was born in Rečica, near Karlovac, in 1887, and died in New York at thirty-one years of age in 1918. A very gifted artist, he studied under Bela Csikos in Zagreb; after graduating from art academy in Zagreb, he spent some time in Vienna and Paris. He had two successful exhibitions in Zagreb before coming with his family to the United States in 1913. Among his first works in this country was a huge oil painting, *Liberation of Croatia*, executed for Hrvatski Savez (The Croatian League).[84] He settled in Chicago, where economic pressures compelled him at first to make his living by drawing diplomas. Not long after, through the recommendation of Nikola Tesla, he obtained a job

81/Vlado Luburić, "Pojam umjetnosti kipara Kufrina"/The Artistic Concept of Sculptor Kufrin, *Naša Nada Kalendar za 1949* (Gary, Ind.: Stanko Borić, 1948), 136–42.

82/*Hrvat*, April 1, 1903; A. J-k, "Bukovac Vlaho," *Hrvatska Enciklopedija* (Zagreb: Hrvatski Izdavalački Bibliografski Zavod, 1942), III, 494–6.

83/*Danica Koledar*, 1927, 128–9; *ibid.*, 1932, 199–200.

84/*Hrvatski Svijet*, July 1, 1913, 1, with reproduction of the picture.

as illustrator with a Chicago newspaper. He also drew and painted scenes of Chicago and landscapes of the Atlantic coast, signing his works sometimes with the pseudonym "Benkov." Most of the paintings and drawings of this young artist are lost, although some of them were recovered in Slovenia and Croatia by his wife. His *Self-portrait, View of the Harbor in Chicago, Scarlet Sagebrush* (Atlantic coastal scene), and *Swamp* (drawn in the vicinity of Chicago) – all oil paintings – are preserved in Zagreb.[85]

Makso (Maksimilijan) Vanka, born of noble parents in Zagreb in 1890, was until his death in February 1963 the most outstanding Croatian painter in the United States. He graduated from the Academy of Arts in Brussels in 1914. After the First World War he taught painting for sixteen years at the Art Academy of Zagreb, where Meštrović was president, exhibited in Zagreb and many European capitals, and gained fame as the best portraitist in Croatia. In 1932 he met the American writer of Slovenian descent, Louis Adamic, who was then visiting Slovenia and Croatia. They became close friends. In one of his short stories, "My Friend Maxo Vanka," as well as in many places in his *Native's Return*, Adamic describes the life and works of Vanka, and his book *Cradle of Life* is based on the early life of Vanka.[86]

Induced by his American wife and by Adamic, Vanka finally left Croatia in 1934 for the United States. Although he settled in New York, he found time to travel widely across this new country which fascinated him tremendously. His first exhibitions in New York and Pittsburgh were successes. Many critics praised his floral drawings as well as his scenes of Croatian villages and of American slums, and his frequent drawings of people from the lowest levels of society. Returning to Zagreb in the spring of 1936, he exhibited there for the last time before his final departure for America, in October 1936.[87]

In an obscure Croatian American church, St. Nicholas in Millvale, Pennsylvania, at the request of the pastor the Reverend Albert Žagar, T.O.R., Vanka created more than ten large murals in the course of only two months in 1937. In the pictures depicting the religious life of the

85/A. J-k, "Benković, Ivan," *Hrvatska Enciklopedija* (Zagreb: HIBZ, 1941), II, 394–5 with two reproductions.

86/L. Adamic, *My America* (New York and London: Harper and Bros., 1938), 156–83; *The Native's Return* (New York and London: Harper and Bros., 1934), 116, 279, 296; *Cradle of Life* (New York and London: Harper and Bros., 1936).

87/*The New York Times*, Dec. 2, 1934; *The World Telegram*, Dec. 11, 1934; *Time*, Dec. 3, 1934; *The Art Digest*, Dec. 15, 1934; *The New York Herald Tribune*, April 21, 1935; *The Pittsburgh Press*, May 15, 1935; *Jutarnji List* (Zagreb), Oct. 2, 1936.

Croatians in America, as well as in his famous *The Croatian Death in Pennsylvania*, which portrays a man killed in a mine accident, the painter paid tribute to his Croatian countrymen in America.

Vanka's murals have been acclaimed as brilliant, the finest in any American church, even as "the finest ... in the world," according to the newspapers in Pittsburgh, an opinion which was later repeated by other critics. As one magazine put it, the St. Nicholas church had "made a precious gift from its Croatian culture to this land."[88]

Later, in 1941, Vanka worked for six months painting a number of additional murals in St. Nicholas church, this time covering the whole of the interior, and on the 16th of November his murals were consecrated. Again the whole art world of the United States hailed him. Besides portraying saints, Vanka had also specifically manifested in some of these murals his love for peace and justice. The artist said in an interview at that time that "these murals are my contribution to America – not only mine, but my immigrant people's."[89] A Pittsburgh paper, reporting on these "heroic murals," stated that the modest Croatian immigrant church in Millvale has become "one of the great American art centers."[90]

Vanka is thus far the only Croatian painter in the United States who has achieved a truly national reputation. His work shows a deep love for his fellow men and a profound understanding of all who suffer. An admirer of Impressionism, he nonetheless mastered various painting styles and techniques. Though not a modernist, he broke completely with the traditional conception of religious painting on church walls, and gave something new to American art.

From 1941 until his death in 1963 in an accident in Mexico, Makso Vanka lived on his farm in Bucks County, Pennsylvania, where he continued to paint, draw, sculpt, and prepare exhibitions.

Ivan Galantić came to this country after the last war, upon finishing his art education in Rome. In 1952, shortly after his arrival, he decorated the Croatian church Saints Cyril and Methodius in New York. Since

88/*Survey Graphic*, April 1939; *The Pittsburgh Press*, March 24 and June 12, 1937; *Time*, July 19, 1937; *The Pittsburgh Post Gazette*, March 21, 1937; and June 13, 1937; *The Bulletin Index*, April 8 and June 24, 1937; *Novosti* (Zagreb), Aug. 4, 1937.

89/*Pittsburgh Sun-Telegraph*, Aug. 22 and Nov. 12, 1941.

90/*The Pittsburgh Post Gazette*, Nov. 13, 1941; see also Jure Prpić, "Maksimilijan Vanka, zaboravljeni hrvatski slikar i njegov doprinos Americi"/Maximillian Vanka, the Forgotten Croatian Painter, and His Contribution to America, *Hrvatska Revija*, VIII, no. 2 (June 1958), 129–60; Herbert Kubly, "Pittsburgh," *Holiday*, 23 (March 1959), 84–5; also unpublished notes in the possession of George J. Prpić, a result of extensive interviews with Vanka during 1957–61.

then he has taught painting at Marygrove College in Detroit and Emmanuel College in Boston and has exhibited his oil paintings at Assumption University in Windsor, Canada.[91]

Gustav Likan, a well-known painter and successful portraitist in his homeland, had many exhibitions in Croatia before he joined the postwar exodus and went to Argentina. During his residence of more than ten years there he was highly praised by the local critics. Recently Likan immigrated to the United States and is now living in Chicago, where he is well known in the art life of the city.

There are other American painters of Croatian descent, such as Raymond Prohaska, Ivan Kovačević, Jure Salamunović, Boris Plenkovich, and Anthony Eterovich. Eterovich, a modernist painter, lives in Parma, Ohio, where he teaches in a high school. He regularly exhibits at Cleveland's May art shows, where he has won several prizes. Plenkovich, a graduate from the National Academy of Fine Arts, has painted portraits of Woodrow Wilson, Abraham Lincoln, Franklin Roosevelt, and the late John F. Kennedy and Mrs. Kennedy. His large painting, *Christopher Columbus Discovers the New World*, was accepted by the Congress of the United States and hangs in the Capitol Building.

Although Kristian Kreković is not living in the United States, he has become well known also in this country. An exceptionally talented painter who was educated in Paris, he found refuge in Peru after the last war. There he produced colossal paintings inspired by the past of the Incas. In 1955 over 126,000 people came to view his pictures (which dealt with the fabulous past of Peru) at an exhibition in the Smithsonian Institute in Washington. One reputable critic stated of Kreković: "Native to mountainous Croatia, where folk art and peasant craft have survived the ebb and flow of military, political and religious tides for centuries, he has maintained a reverence for tradition and time-tested quality."[92] Kreković's exhibitions in Washington, Philadelphia, Syracuse, and New York were significant events in American art.

Contributions in Music, Folk Music, Dance, Opera, Singing, and Motion Pictures

American Croatians love music and dancing. Their popular instrument, the tamburitza, is at least thirteen centuries old. The kolo (meaning

91/*Danica*, Jan. 30, 1952; *Croatia Press*, XII, nos. 7–8 (July-Aug. 1958), 17.

92/Thomas M. Beggs (Director of the National Collection of Fine Arts, Smithsonian Institute), "The Golden Brush of Kristian Krekovic," *American Artist*, Dec. 1955, 38.

"the circle" or the "wheel") is their favorite national dance, which they had traditionally danced in the "old" country, from the islands of the Adriatic to the mountains of the Dinaric Alps, the green hills of "Banska" (Ban's) Croatia, and the plains of Slavonia and Srijem.

Among the first Croatian societies in this country were tamburitza orchestras. The tamburitza itself is a stringed instrument with a pear-shaped body which somewhat resembles a mandolin but with a richer sound than the latter instrument. There are altogether six kinds of tamburitza, different in size and style as well as in the number of strings. In the course of years, tamburitza orchestras have formed an integral part of the customary activities in Croatian homes and in fraternal lodges and other organizations. Wherever there are Croatians there are tamburitza orchestras and, in many cases, affiliated kolo groups. Frequently tamburitza groups have performed before distinguished audiences. It is recorded that a Croatian tamburitza orchestra played in Carnegie Hall in New York on April 1, 1900,[93] and a famous tamburitza orchestra called "Živila Hrvatska" (Hail Croatia), dressed in Croatian national costumes, gave a concert at the White House to President Theodore Roosevelt.[94]

Ilar Spiletak, born in Dubrovnik, organized the "Croatian Tamburitza Society" in San Francisco some sixty years ago, reputedly one of the first Croatian tamburitza associations in the United States. He subsequently founded eleven other tamburitza orchestras. Through his propagation of the instrument many other such orchestras were formed in Croatian settlements, many of which are still active, especially among the third and fourth generation of American Croatians. With the development of radio in the 1930s the popularity of the instrument spread enormously. College students and other young men of Croatian and non-Croatian descent began giving tamburitza concerts before enthusiastic audiences throughout the country.[95]

In the 1930s St. Edward's University in Austin, Texas, publisher of *Tamburitza News*, became the first American university to introduce a tamburitza orchestra. Today, the best known of collegiate tamburitza and Croatian folklore groups is the Duquesne University Tamburitzans, an outgrowth of the group from St. Edward's. Most of the members of this troupe are Americans of Croatian descent. Performing in the colorful national costumes of Croatia, the "Tammies" work their way through college by interpreting songs and dances of the Croatian people and

93/*Croatian Almanac* 1950 (McKeesport, Pa.: D. Sorić, 1949), 252–3.
94/*Narodni List*, April 7, 1900.
95/Anon., "Croatian Musical Instrument Gains Favor," *Interpreter's Releases*, XII, Dec. 19, 1935, 445–6.

other Slavs. They have performed in hundreds of communities all over the country, and have made tours throughout Europe.[96]

Many Croatian groups also have had – and some continue to have – brass bands, singing societies, and dramatic groups. On May 30, 1949, a League of the Croatian Singing Societies (Savez Hrvatskih Pjevačkih Društava) was formed, uniting all of the major singing societies. This is a cultural and educational organization, supported by the CFU, which propagates Croatian songs, music, and folklore, stimulating among young American Croatians a love and knowledge of their Croatian cultural heritage.

Since tamburitza music has been played over hundreds of radio stations – being a part of many Croatian "radio hours" and of the programs of other Slavic nationalities – and since even American collegiate groups have popularized it, it is not surprising that the governor of Michigan proclaimed a special Tamburitza Day (December 8, 1957) and that the mayor of San Francisco proclaimed a "Kolo Week" (during November 23–30, 1957).[97]

At the annual "Holiday Folk Fair" in Milwaukee, Croatians have taken part in dances, music, exhibits of handicrafts, and the display of their native food.[98]

Many Croatian national customs, festivals, Christmas customs, celebrations of various saints' days – such as St. Martin's day – and memorial days for the Croatian national heroes Zrinski and Frankapan have attracted the attention of American folklorists. Rich, attractive, and colorful Croatian national costumes, various artistic handicrafts, as well as country fairs and festivals, have been praised as immigrant gifts to America. Some folklorists have noted the fact that entire choruses of Croatian singing societies are sometimes dressed in very picturesque national costumes, many of them made in Croatian villages.[99]

Zlatko I. Kerhin, who died recently in his eighties, came to the United States in 1898. He lived in Gary, Indiana, for over fifty years, and was

96/*Naša Nada*, Jan. 29, 1958. In innumerable issues of *Zajedničar* the work and performances of this group are reviewed and described. Carl A. Apone, "The Tamburitsans of Duquesne," *The Catholic Digest*, Oct. 1962, 61–6, maintains that this is the best Slavic folklore group in America.

97/*Zajedničar*, Nov. 27, 1957.

98/The State Historical Society of Wisconsin has published, in a book on the folklore of different nationalities, extensive information about the folklore of the Croatians in Wisconsin: William J. Schereck, *The Peoples of Wisconsin* (Madison, Wis.: State Historical Society of Wisconsin, 1956), 83–96.

99/Dorothy Gladys Spicer, *Folk Festivals and the Foreign Community* (New York: The Womans Press, 1923), 21; Allen H. Eaton, *Immigrant Gifts to American Life* (New York: Russell Sage Foundation, 1932), 54, 100, 122.

the founder (1902) and the first president of the singing society "Zora" in Chicago, one of the foremost American Croatian singing societies. He also founded the singing society "Javor" (1905) in Pittsburgh, and was the president of the excellent "Preradović" singing society in Gary. He was the president of Američko-Hrvatski Pjevački Savez. He presented as a gift to the University of Minnesota Immigrant Archives his great collection of Croatian handicrafts and a most valuable collection of materials and documents covering the history of the Croatian singing societies in the United States.[100]

The eminent soprano Milka Ternina, one of the greatest singers of her time, was enthusiastically hailed by New York opera lovers and critics throughout the country at the turn of the century. Famous for her Wagnerian roles, she sang for nine seasons at the Metropolitan Opera.

Miss Ternina, however, was not the first Croatian singer at the Metropolitan Opera. During the seasons of 1873–9 the Croatian singer Ilma de Murska was acclaimed as a "great coloratura soprano."[101]

Croatians Mate Ćulić Dragun of the San Francisco Opera, Tino Patiera and M. Nikolić of the Chicago Opera, and Piero Pierotić, Paško Alujević, Marin Mirčeta, J. Marion Vlahović, Simon Babin, and Marjorie Radovan excelled as singers in the United States between 1920 and 1940. But the greatest of all in recent times has undoubtedly been Zinka Kunc Milanov, a prominent star of the Metropolitan Opera. From 1940, when she came to the United States, until the spring of 1966, when she retired only a few days before the old "Met" was closed, she maintained, as a member of the ranking American opera house, a great reputation as an operatic singer, following in the tradition of the great Ternina.

Louis Svećenski (born in 1862 in Osijek, Croatia) was a graduate from the conservatories in Zagreb and Vienna. In 1885 he received a contract from the Boston Symphony Orchestra as first violinist. For thirty-three years he played viola in the famous Kneisel Quartet. On many occasions he toured America and Europe. He met Milka Ternina in New York, traveled to Croatia several times, and always considered himself a Croatian. In American music circles he gained fame as a great artist as well as a promoter of music. To this goal he contributed for many years as a director in New York's Institute of Musical Art. He was also one of the founders of the Curtis Institute of Music. He died in 1926.

100/Notes in my possession based on an interview with Mr. Kerhin in September 1962 in Cleveland, Ohio.

101/*Narodni List*, Dec. 23, 1899; Feb. 6, and Nov. 20, 1901; it also published a full-page picture of Milka Ternina. About Murska see *Matičin iseljenički kalendar 1958*, 75–9.

Arthur Rodzinski was for years director of the Cleveland Symphony Orchestra. Zlatko Baloković, world-renowned violin virtuoso, enjoyed tremendous success during the 1920s and 1930s in the finest concert halls of the United States as well as in other parts of the world. He lived in America for twenty years before his death in 1965, in Venice where he had stopped during a trip to Yugoslavia. He is usually considered one of the greatest artists that Croatia has contributed to this country.[102]

Božidar Kunc, composer and pianist (brother of Zinka Kunc Milanov), was born in Zagreb in 1903, and spent many years in the United States as an active artist. He died on April 1, 1964, while accompanying his sister on the piano at a concert of the Detroit Symphony Orchestra organized and sponsored by the Croatian Board of Trade of Detroit, Michigan.[103]

Among postwar arrivals in the musical field are Fedor Kabalin, composer and musician, and baritone Dragutin Šoštarko, a former member of the Croatian Opera in Zagreb. Šoštarko's audiences and critics have been repeatedly impressed by the quality of his voice and by his performances in both classic and native Croatian repertoires. On March 23, 1958, a celebration and Jubilee Concert were held in Chicago on the occasion of the twentieth anniversary of the beginning of Šoštarko's singing career.

The Hollywood actor Peter Coe, whose real name is Knego, was born of Croatian parentage. His family name was Marinović, and his parents came from Konavlje, near Dubrovnik. Josip Zolović, a star of RKO Studios, is also of Croatian descent. Slavko Vorkapić, born in Srijemska Mitrovica in 1884, has for decades been active as an actor, movie director, painter, and sculptor; he has also been a prominent innovator in motion picture techniques. The original name of actress Gloria Gray was Dragomanović. Mia Ćorak-Slavenska, a movie actress and prominent ballerina, excited American audiences for over fifteen years. An artist of high quality, she was prima ballerina of the Metropolitan Opera in 1954–5.[104]

Guy Mitchell, popular American singer and movie actor, was born Al Crnić, of Croatian parents. Mitchell is a member of the CFU lodge in Los Angeles, speaks Croatian well, and often performs before groups

102/Baloković's life story and numerous great successes are described in a series of eight articles in *Zajedničar*, beginning on January 15, 1958. For Svećenski, see an undated clipping from the Croatian periodical *Kolo*.

103/*Zajedničar*, April 8, 1964.

104/Vlaho Vlahović, *Manual of Slavonic Personalities* (New York: Slavonic Press, 1940), 25, 79; Adamic, *The Natives' Return*, 159.

of Croatian Americans. In the autumn of 1957, he had his own television show on the ABC network; many of his records have been best sellers.[105] Walter Kray (Krajačić), a Hollywood actor, is also of Croatian descent and very active in the American Croatian Community.

Scholars

Henry Suzzallo, a distinguished American scholar, educator, and onetime president of the Carnegie Foundation, was born of Petar and Ana Suzzallo in San Jose, California, on March 9, 1873. He received his B.A. from Stanford in 1899, an M.A. from Columbia University in 1902, a PH.D. from the same institution in 1905, and an LL.D. from the University of California in 1918. After a career in scholarship and educational writing, he became president of the University of Washington, where he remained from 1915 until 1926. During the First World War, Dr. Suzzallo was an advisor to President Wilson and worked quietly as an unseen figure in many progressive educational movements. In 1918 he became a member of the War Labor Policy Board under Wilson. In 1927 he was made the chairman of the board of trustees of the Carnegie Foundation for the Advancement of Teaching, the first Slav to occupy this position.[106]

During the First World War Suzzallo was engaged in the movement of west coast Croatian Americans for the establishment of a South Slavic union. He was of great assistance to Dr. Hinko Hinković when the latter was lecturing in Seattle. On April 27, 1918, on the occasion of the commemoration of the Croatian patriots Zrinski and Frankapan, he said to his immigrant countrymen: "You are not Austrians, but sons of Zrinski and Frankopan."[107] He himself was neither Austrian nor Italian (as he was incorrectly designated in American books and encyclopedias) but Croatian.

A brilliant scholar, Suzzallo wrote many books on education; among them are *Rise of Local School Supervision in Massachusetts* (New York: Teachers College, 1906); *Our Faith in Education* (Philadelphia and London: J. B. Lippincott, 1924); *The Teaching of Primary Arithmetic* (Boston and New York: Houghton Mifflin Co., 1913); *The Teaching of Spelling* (Boston and New York: Houghton Mifflin Co., 1913); with George E. Freeland, *Fact and Story Readers* (9 vols.; New York and

105/*Zajedničar*, Dec. 19, 1956; Oct. 3 and Dec. 18, 1957.

106/*The National Cyclopedia of American Biography*, c, 21; *Who's Who in America*, 17, 2228; Sorić, *Centennial*, 105.

107/H. Hinković, *Iz velikog doba*/From a Great Era (Zagreb: Ćirilo-Metodska Nakladna Knjižara, 1927), 109; I. F. Lupis-Vukić, *Medju našim narodom u Americi*/Among Our People in America (Split: Leonova Tiskara, 1929), 20.

Cincinnati: American Book Co., 1930–1). In 1932 he became an editor-in-chief of *The National Encyclopedia* (10 vols.)

The child of humble immigrant parents, Suzzallo sincerely loved the American ideal, and he inspired his friends and students to love it too. Profoundly devoted to human welfare, he looked at democracy as a way of life, a means of development for the individual and for the group.[108]

When Suzzallo died, the newspapers referred to him as "one of the nation's most distinguished educators" who devoted his life to the advancement of good education.[109]

Dr. Victor G. Djurkovečki, who later shortened his name to Vecki, was born in 1857 in Zagreb and emigrated to the United States in 1890. He was a physician and one of the few intellectuals among the early Croatian immigrants. Settling in San Francisco, he became one of the most distinguished doctors in California. He wrote a series of distinguished works in English and German in the field of medicine as well as a book on alcohol and prohibition. In 1931 he published a successful novel describing the life of a Croatian-American physician in San Francisco.[110]

Dr. Ante Biankini, also a physician and a contemporary of Dr. Vecki, was very active politically for the Croatians during the First World War; he was publisher of *Hrvatska Zastava,* and editor and a writer. He went to Chicago in 1898, where for many years he was a practicing physician and surgeon. He had a reputation as a physician among many American and Croatian patients, as a surgeon at Mercy and Columbus Hospitals in Chicago. As professor at Northwestern University he also produced a number of scholarly books on medical problems which he wrote in English and Croatian.[111]

American-born Dr. Edward Miloslavić was a well-known professor of medicine at Marquette University and the universities of Vienna and Zagreb. During the Second World War, while a member of the Faculty of Medicine at the University of Zagreb, he was one of the leading European pathologists and criminologists, and a member of the international commission which investigated the Katyn massacres near Smo-

108/*Henry Suzzallo 1875–1933: A Memorial Gathering* (New York: Columbia University, 1934), 5–15.

109/*New York Times,* Sept. 26, 1933.

110/Meler, *Slavonic Pioneers,* 26; Victor G. Vecki, *Alcohol and Prohibition in Their Relation to Civilization and the Art of Living* (Philadelphia and London: J. B. Lippincott, 1923); the novel is *Threatening Shadows* (Boston: The Stratford Co., 1931).

111/*Hrvatska Enciklopedija,* II, 467–8.

lensk, Russia. After the war he returned to the United States, where he died on November 12, 1952, at St. Louis, Missouri.[112]

Dr. Stephen L. Polyak was born in Zagreb, Croatia, in 1899. He was known in scholarly circles as one of the greatest neuroanatomists of our era. As a young medical doctor he was sent by the Rockefeller Foundation to London (1924–5) for further specialization. In 1925 he worked in Madrid under Professor Dr. Santiago Ramon y Cajal, a famous neurohistologist and Nobel Prize winner. In 1926 he came to the University of Chicago Medical School and then he returned for a short while to Zagreb where he found his position at the Medical School taken by somebody else. Invited by the University of California, he joined its faculty as an assistant professor of neuroanatomy. In 1930 he became a member of the University of Chicago Medical School, where he taught until his death on March 9, 1955. He devoted many years of research to the anatomy of the eye. His book *The Retina* (published in 1941 by the University of California Press) is a classic in this field. His most important work is *The Vertebrate Visual System*, a great scholarly study of some 1600 pages which was published after his death, in 1957.[113]

Dr. Karlo Marchesi is a professor at the Institute of Parapsychology at Duke University, Durham, N.C. He is an opponent of Freud's psychoanalysis, and has published a great number of scholarly studies in this field during the past thirty years. A scholar of great European reputation, he was invited by Duke University in 1950 when he finally left his homeland after many bitter experiences.[114]

Professor Francis Preveden, born in Croatia, was a historian, anthropologist, and linguist. He taught in the graduate school at Duquesne University; later he was head of the language department at De Paul University, and subsequently became a professor at the University of Chicago. He spoke and wrote many languages, and was a fellow of the American Association for the Advancement of Science. His *History of the Croatian People* (2 vols.; New York: Philosophical Library, 1955, 1962) was the first scholarly history of Croatia written in English.[115] Preveden died in September 1959 in Washington, D.C.

Stanko Guldescu, although born in Trieste (1908, then Austria) in

112/*Hrvatski Narod*, Zagreb, May 16, 1943; *Facts on File*, XII, no. 628, Nov. 7–13, 1952, 367.

113/Ragnar Granit, "The Grand Theme of Stephen Polyak", *Science*, 122, no. 3157 (July 1, 1955), 64.

114/Mahmud Muftić, "Dr. Karlo Marchesi," *Hrvatska Revija*, XIV, no. 1 (March 1964), 51–3.

115/*Naša Nada*, Jan. 19, 1949; *Danica*, April 25, 1956; Jure Prpić, "Život i djelo Franje Prevedena"/The Life and Work of Francis Preveden, *Hrvatska Revija*, X, no. 1 (March 1960), 87–98.

a family which has been connected with America for the last hundred years, is an American historian of Croatian descent. His background is most interesting; his grandfather was born in Istria, and came to Virginia as a young man, after fighting for Maximilian in Mexico. Guldescu earned his doctorate from the University of Chicago. His *History of Medieval Croatia* (The Hague, Netherlands: Mouton & Co., 1964) is a very good scholarly revisionist history of the Croatian lands until 1527. He has written extensively on Croatian history and is a contributor to this and the preceding volume of *Croatia*. His second volume of Croatian history is in process of publication.[116]

Professor John A. Zvetina, an eminent authority on international law, was born of Croatian parents on April 20, 1898, in Chicago, where he was teaching since 1925 at Loyola University. A prominent scholar and lawyer, he is active in numerous religious, social, and patriotic organizations. For his outstanding activities as a Catholic layman, he was appointed a Knight of St. Gregory in December 1954 by Pope Pius XII.[117]

Dr. Clement S. Mihanovich, professor of sociology and for many years head of the Department of Sociology and Anthropology, Saint Louis University, was born in St. Louis of Croatian parents. In his master's thesis,[118] and in numerous articles in sociological journals, he has dealt with the problem of the Americanization of the Croatians. Besides his many articles, he has published a number of books in the field of sociology: *Current Social Problems* (Milwaukee: Bruce Publishing Co., 1950), *Principles of Juvenile Delinquency* (Milwaukee: Bruce, 1950), *Social Theories* (Milwaukee: Bruce, 1953), and others, some of which are in use as textbooks at many Catholic universities and colleges. One of the foremost American Catholic sociologists, Mihanovich is proud of his Croatian descent and takes an active part in the cultural and religious activities of the American Croatians.

Dr. Dinko Tomašić taught at the University of Zagreb until 1939, at which time he came to the United States, where he has taught at various universities. He has been associated with Indiana University since 1943, and is at present a professor of Sociology and Area Studies. Tomašić is an expert in matters bearing on eastern Europe and has published

116/Francis H. Eterovich (ed.), *Biographical Directory of Scholars, Artists, and Professionals of Croatian Descent in the United States and Canada* (2nd ed.; Chicago: By the author, 1965), 31; letters of Stanko Guldescu in the possession of this author.

117/Basil and Steven Pandžić, *A Review of Croatian History* (Chicago: "Croatia," 1954), 71.

118/Clement S. Mihanovich, "Americanization of the Croats in St. Louis, Missouri, during the Past Thirty Years" (unpublished Master's thesis, St. Louis University, 1936) is probably the first scholarly thesis written on the American Croatians.

numerous articles on the problems of Croatia and eastern Europe. Notable among the books which he wrote in Croatian is *Politički razvitak Hrvata* (Political Development of the Croatians; Zagreb: Hrvatska Književna Naklada, 1938). In this country he has published *Personality and Culture in Eastern European Politics* (New York: George W. Stewart, 1948), *Some Problem Areas in Communist Society* (Bloomington, Ind.: Indiana University, 1952), *The Impact of Russian Culture on Soviet Communism* (Free Press, 1953), and *National Communism and Soviet Strategy* (Washington: Public Affairs Press, 1957).

Dr. Milislav Demerec (born on January 11, 1895, in Kostajnica; died April 12, 1966, in Laurel Hollow, Long Island) was widely known for his great scholarly work in the field of genetics. After his studies in Croatia and France he came to the United States in 1919. He earned his PH.D. from Cornell University, and worked for many years for the Carnegie Institution of Washington, D.C. From 1941 to 1960 he was director of the biological laboratories of the Long Island Biological Association in Cold Spring Harbor and also taught as associate professor at Columbia University. In 1960 he was appointed senior geneticist at Brookhaven National Laboratory at Upton, Long Island. For his discoveries and contributions he received many awards and honorary doctorates.

Croatian contributors to American scholarship also include Professor M. Krunić of the University of California and Matthew Braidech, an engineering specialist in industrial water supplies.[119]

Writers and Poets

Croatian Americans who have written in the Croatian language (some of whom we have already mentioned) are Josip Marohnić, Matija Šojat, Ivan Sikočan, Milan Gnjatović, Šime Sinovčić, Josip Mihećin, Toni Lulić, Z. Kostelski, Andro Janković, Dragan J. Jagrović, Stjepko Brozović, Viktor Vojvodić, the Reverend Bosiljko Bekavac, Frano Akačić, Monsignor M. D. Krmpotić, Ivan Mladineo, Slavko Nemec, Vjekoslav Meler, J. D. Božić, Milan Marjanović, Božo Milošević, Stephen Sestanovich, Vlaho Vlahović, Ivan Krešić, Ante Zubak, Antun Tanasković, Josip Kraja, Grgo Turkalj, Niko Gršković, and the Reverend Ilija Severović, among many others.

Josip Marohnić, a printer by profession, was one of the founders not only of the National Croatian Society but also of popular Croatian literature in the United States. As an editor of newspapers, almanacs, and other publications, a publisher of dictionaries, grammars, and histories,

119/These names were compiled both from works of Adamic and from various American and Croatian periodicals and publications. On Demerec, see *Croatia Press*, XX, 1–3 (Jan.-June 1966), 12–13.

he helped the Croatian immigrant to learn about his new environment. Marohnić published the first book of Croatian poetry in the United States. He also published the first large English-Croatian and Croatian-English dictionary, compiled by Francis Bogadek, a Croatian lawyer and writer from Pittsburgh. This dictionary is the best of its kind in the United States, and has been through many editions.

The real literature of the American Croatians began with S. R. Danevski, who published his *Pripovijesti* (Short Stories), which deal mostly with the life of the Croatian immigrants, in Chicago in 1911. Viktor Vojvodić published the first book of poetry among the Croatian immigrants, *Sabrane Pjesme* (Collected Poems).[120] The first Croatian priest in the United States, the Reverend Dobroslav Božić, who was a good writer and a newspaper editor, published a book of his recollections.[121] The Reverend B. Bekavac and Monsignor M. D. Krmpotić were outstanding historians among the Croatian immigrant priests. Krmpotić was also a contributor to the old *Catholic Encyclopedia.*

Ivan Krešić, who lived for forty years in New York City, made his living as an editor and publisher of several newspapers (*Hrvatski List i Danica Hrvatska* being the best known) and had a good literary style. From 1924 until 1943 he published his *Koledar*, one of the finest of Croatian almanacs. Krešić wrote in both Croatian and English and did considerable translating from English into Croatian.

A few Croatians have written books in the English language. As already noted, Victor V. Vecki wrote *Threatening Shadows* in 1931. Gabro Karabin, a young American-born Croatian, wrote a highly commended short story about the life of the Croatian steel-mill workers. His "Honorable Escape" won a thousand-dollar award from *Scribner's Magazine* in 1937, and it reflected a very capable and gifted writer. The editors of *Scribner's* praised Karabin as a writer who "has the qualities of a great artist."[122]

Srdjan Tucić came to the United States in 1917; he had already been a successful writer in his homeland. For a while he was in charge of the propaganda bureau of the South Slavic Committee in Washington, D.C. Disappointed with political conditions in the new state of Yugoslavia, Tucić remained an exile in this country after 1918. He was the first and finest Croatian playwright to live here. His plays *The Precipice*, *The Liberators*, and *Golgotha* were very successful in both London and Zagreb. A painstaking naturalistic and realistic writer, he even studied

120/San Jose, Calif.: Hrvatski Sokol, n.d.

121/D. Božić, *Zulum*/The Oppression (Senj: Hreljanović, 1906).

122/Gabro Karabin, "Honorable Escape," *Scribner's Magazine*, CII, no. 6 (Dec. 1937), 40–2, 80; editor on Karabin, 6.

the dialect of the "hillbillies" in the South: this knowledge he put to use in *The Precipice*. He died in New York in September 1940.[123]

In Silence is the autobiography of Louis Sanjek, a Croatian immigrant and a Lutheran minister. Besides many warm descriptions of Croatia and expressions of high admiration for his countrymen in the United States, it shows a deep concern for this country, which he loves and esteems, for having given him both a means of livelihood and freedom.[124]

Joseph George Hitrec was introduced to the publisher Harper through Louis Adamic while Hitrec was still in exile in India after the last war. Harper subsequently published Hitrec's *Ruler's Morning*, a collection of short stories about life in India. Later, Hitrec immigrated to this country, and encouraged by the literary success of his first book, he wrote two more: *Son of the Moon* and *Angel of Gaiety*, both using material from life in India.[125] Since coming to this country, Hitrec has been very active as a writer, and is undoubtedly one of the finest and most successful Croatian writers in the English language.

Barton Michael Phillips is the pen name of Phillip Michael Bavcevich, the son of Croatian immigrants, who was born in the Chicago slums in 1901. In 1955 he published *And the Angels Won't Blame Him*, a realistic novel set in Chicago.[126]

Bogdan Radica, a versatile and extremely productive writer, was born in Dalmatia on August 26, 1904, but has lived in the United States for over twenty years. Before settling here, he had already published books in Croatia and Italy. Although he is primarily a political writer, his style in both Croatian and English reflects high literary standards. The list of his articles in English – which have been published in many leading American newspapers, reviews, and magazines – comprises hundreds of titles. He also writes for all of the better-known Croatian publications and publishes frequently in Spanish and other languages as well. Since 1948 he has been professor of history at Fairleigh Dickinson University. Between 1929 and 1945, he served in the Yugoslav Foreign Service.

There are a considerable number of writers and poets among the large number of Croatian intellectuals who came to the United States as refugees after the last war. Some of the new arrivals were already writers

123/*Danica Koledar*, 1941, 101.

124/L. Sanjek, *In Silence* (New York: Fortuny's Publishers, 1938).

125/J. G. Hitrec, *Ruler's Morning and Other Stories* (New York: Harper, 1946); L. Adamic, "A Book on India," *Today and Tomorrow* (Milford, N.J.), II (March-May 1946), 13; J. G. Hitrec, *Son of the Moon* (New York: Harper, 1948) and *Angel of Gaiety* (same publisher, 1951).

126/B. M. Phillips, *And the Angels Won't Blame Him* (Dallas, Texas: The Story Book Press, 1955).

of distinction in Croatian: novelists, short-story writers, poets, and essayists.

The main organ of Croatian writers in the United States and the free world, the quarterly *Hrvatska Revija* (The Croatian Review), which has been in existence for more than eighteen years, is now published in Munich, Germany, by one of the leading Croatian writers in exile, Vinko Nikolić, who visited the United States in 1965 as an Argentine citizen. Many Croatian authors, among them Ivan Meštrović and Bogdan Radica, have been regular contributors to this periodical.[127]

Some of the poets active in American Croatian publications are Mladen Kabalin, Stjepan Hrastovec, Nada Kesterčanek, Antun Nizeteo, and Ante Bonifačić.

Nada Kesterčanek, for many years head librarian at Wilkes College, Pennsylvania, published three works of poetry and prose in Croatia. In the United States she has written *Short Stories* (Wilkes-Barre, 1954; mimeographed) and *Tragovi* (Footprints; Buenos Aires, 1959). She regularly contributes to *Hrvatska Revija* and *Croatian Voice.*

An outstanding writer in the ranks of Croatian immigrants is Ante Bonifačić, who came to the United States by way of Brazil. He had published several books of prose and poetry in Croatia and Argentina. Since coming to this country, he has collaborated with Professor Clement Mihanovich in editing a symposium, *The Croatian Nation* (Chicago: "Croatia," 1953). Essayist, novelist, and poet, Bonifačić has a style that is hardly matched by any contemporary Croatian writer. Unfortunately, he does not write in English.

Antun Nizeteo was well known in Croatia for two books of poetry which he published before coming to this country in 1950. In 1957 he published an excellent selection of his short stories entitled *Bez povratka* (Without Return; Buenos Aires: Knjižnica Hrvatske Revije, 1957), whose principal theme is that an emigrant may return physically but not psychologically or culturally to his native country. At present Nizeteo is a librarian at Cornell University in Ithaca, New York.[128]

Ante Kadić, who teaches Slavic languages and literatures at Indiana

127/George J. Prpić, "Petnaest godina *Hrvatske Revije*"/Fifteen Years of *Hrvatska Revije*, *Zajedničar*, Oct. 6, 1965, 10.

128/Letter of Ante Nizeteo, New York, May 23, 1958, to this writer. Ante Kadić gives a good review of Croatian immigrant writers in "Croatian Emigre Writers," *Croatia Press*, XIII, no. 5 (May 1959), 2–9. Bogdan Radica has contributed several historical studies on Croatia in the past few years, notably: *Supilova pisma Ferrerovima* Supilo's Letters to Ferreros (2 vols.), reprints from *Hrvatska Revija*, VII, no. 4 (Dec. 1957), 349–405 and *ibid.*, XII, nos. 1–2 (March-June 1962), 17–54. Also *Risorgimento and the Croatian Question: Tommaseo and Kvaternik*, reprint from *Journal of Croatian Studies*, V-VI (1964–5), 3–144.

University, edited a *Croatian Reader* (published in 1960 by Mouton and Co., The Hague, the Netherlands) and wrote a book on contemporary Croatian literature. He is a contributor to several American and European journals and reviews on the subjects of Croatian literature and Croatians in exile.

The Reverend Charles Kamber, who died in Toronto, Canada (after a long sojourn in the United States), published recently travel accounts and political and other essays; he enjoyed a good reputation as a writer in Croatian, English, and German. Monsignor Ivan Stipanović, the Reverends Vladimir Vančik, Silvije Grubišić, Ljubo Čuvalo, Častimir Majić (who for many years was editor of the independent weekly *Danica – Morning Star*, Chicago), Kvirin Vasilj,[129] Vendelin Vasilj, Theodore Badurina, Ante Livajušić, and many other priests have written numerous books and articles and served as editors of various almanacs, newspapers, and magazines.

The Reverend Dominik Mandić, O.F.M., who lives in Chicago, is foremost among Croatian historians in the United States. Author of numerous scholarly essays in his field, he also published *Crvena Hrvatska* (Red Croatia, Chicago: The Croatian Historical Institute, 1957), and has recently issued three scholarly books on the history of Bosnia and Hercegovina.[130] Mandić's works have been recognized even by contemporary historians in Croatia.

Dr. Vatroslav Murvar published a book in Croatian, *Hrvatska i Hrvati* (Croatia and the Croatians; Chicago: "Croatia," 1953), and recently also published *Russian Social Monism and American Social Pluralism* (Spokane, Wash.: Gonzaga University Press, 1959).

Dr. Vladko Maček published his memoirs under the title *In the Struggle for Freedom* (New York: R. Speller, 1957). Dr. Branko Pešelj, the first Croatian after the Second World War to receive a PH.D. at an American university, is a contributor to *The Encyclopedia Americana* and to several scholarly journals; he teaches Socialist Law at George-

129/Author of a unique work in the field of philosophy, *Analiza i Sinteza Čovjeka*/Analysis and Synthesis of Man (Chicago: Franciscan Press, 1958).

130/*Bosnia i Hercegovina*/Bosnia and Hercegovina, I, *Državna i vjerska pripadnost sredovječne Bosne i Hercegovine*/The State and Religious Affiliation of Medieval Bosnia and Hercegovina (Chicago: Croatian Historical Institute, 1960); II, *Bogomilska crkva bosanskih krstjana*/The Bogomil Church of the Bosnian Christians (same publisher, 1962); III, *Etnička povijest Bosne i Hercegovine*/The Ethnic History of Bosnia and Hercegovina (Rome, 1967). Also by Mandić: *Rasprave i prilozi iz stare hrvatske povijesti*/Studies and Contributions to Ancient Croatian History (Rome: Croatian Historical Institute, 1963), 631 pp. To pay tribute to historian Mandić on the occasion of his 75th birthday the Croatian Historical Institute in Rome (recently founded by Croatian scholars in Europe) published a symposium: *Mandićev Zbornik* (Rome, 1965), 319 pp.

town University's Law School, Washington, D.C. Stanko Vujica, head of the Philosophy Department at Wilkes College, contributes to American and Croatian publications. Dr. Vilko Rieger, a university professor, is an author of numerous articles and book reviews. The Reverend Dobroslav Sorić is an active publisher and editor of almanacs and religious magazines. Dr. Jozo Tomasevich wrote *Peasants, Politics, and Economic Changes in Yugoslavia* (Stanford, Calif.: Stanford University Press, 1955). Dr. Mirko Usmiani, the first Croatian to receive a doctorate from Harvard University, wrote for his dissertation, "Marcus Marulus, Life and Works" (Harvard University, Department of Slavic Studies, 1955), and now publishes articles in the field of Slavic studies. Dr. Francis H. Eterovich and Dr. Christopher Spalatin are editors of the present volumes, *Croatia: Land, People, Culture*, the first work of its kind in America. Previously, Professor Eterovich was editor of the Croatian Catholic quarterly *Osoba i Duh* (Person and Spirit), published in Spain (1949–52) and the United States (1952–5). Vlaho Vlahović, who has lived for many years in this country, has written books in English: *Manual of Slavonic Personalities* (New York: Slavonic Press, 1940) and *Two Hundred Fifty Million and One Slavs* (New York: Slav Publications, 1945). Jere Jareb, a Columbia University PH.D., is a political writer and historian, author of one book, and contributor to *Hrvatska Revija* and *Croatia Press*. Karlo Mirth is editor and publisher of *Croatia Press*, a review and news bulletin (now in the seventeenth year of its existence) published bimonthly in New York in both English and Croatian. Dr. Ivo Omrčanin, a professor at State College, Indiana, Pennsylvania, is author of several books in several languages on Croatian history. Dr. Charles Zudenigo, writer, playwright, and poet, teaches French at Southern Oregon College, Ashland, Oregon.

This list of Croatian scholars, writers, poets, publicists, and journalists does not pretend to be complete. During the past few years virtually hundreds of Croatian immigrants and visiting scholars, scientists, various experts, professionals, teachers, librarians, and writers have joined many American institutions of higher learning.

Croatians in Sports

Many Croatian names appear in the annals of American sport. As early as 1912, an American-born Croatian, Nikola T. Niric, had become the national champion in swimming the half-mile. Any compilation of Croatians and Croatian Americans who have been prominent in American athletic circles would have to include the following names, but since the writer is drawing extensively on sports literature published more than ten years ago, undoubtedly the list is not exhaustive of Croatian Americans prominent in sports more recently.

In college football the following are nationally known: John Andretich, from Purdue University; Mike Balen, Tulane University; Emil Banjavicich, Arizona University; Steve Belichik, Western Reserve University; Hugh Bogovich, Delaware University; Tony Butkovich, Illinois University; Joe Damanovich, Alabama University; Tony Gallovich, Wake Forest College; James Jurkovich, California University; Peter Kmetovic, Stanford University; Joe Lokanc, Northwestern University; Alex Lucacick, Boston College; Frank Medanich, Texas Christian University; Johnny Mihalic, Temple University; Mike Mihalic, Mississippi State University; Mike Miketinac, Michigan State University; Leo Mogus, Youngstown University; Steve Narick, West Virginia University; Emil Narick, University of Pittsburgh; George Paskvan, Wisconsin University; Chris Pavich, Georgetown University; Art Rebrovich, Vanderbilt University; Lou Saban, Indiana University; Mike Saban, Indiana University; Tony Samarzia, Northwestern University; Tom Senffner, Detroit University; Rudy Sikich, Minnesota University; Frankie Sinkovic, University of Georgia; Bill Telesmanich, San Francisco University; Andy Tomasich, Temple University; Emil Uremovich, Indiana University; Larry Visnic, St. Benedict's College; Steve Vuchich, St. Vincent's College; Mike Zeleznak, Kansas State University; George Zellick, Oregon State University; George Zorich, Northwestern University. In professional football Joe Styduhar of the Chicago Bears and Joe Kuharich gained national recognition.

Prominent basketball players have included Johnny Abramovich of Salem College; Rudy Baric, West Virginia University; Joe Camic, Duquesne University; Bill Hapac, University of Illionis; Eleanor Laich, Olson's All American Red Heads; Leo Mogus, Youngstown University;[131] and George Mikan of De Paul University, later to be called "Mr. Basketball."

Professional baseball players include John Babich, Philadelphia Athletics; Joseph Beggs, Cincinnati Reds; Walter Judnich, St. Louis Browns; Mike Kreovich, Chicago White Sox and the St. Louis Browns; Steve Mesner, Cincinnati Reds; George Metkovich, Boston Red Sox; and Johnny Pesky, Boston Red Sox.

Outstanding in bowling were Billy Arbanas, Eli Marichich, and Joe Sinkovich, all of Chicago, Illinois.

131/*Hrvatski Svijet*, June 27, 1912.

Well known as hockey players were Mike Karakas of the Chicago Black Hawks and Johnny Polich of the New York Rangers.

Nick Vukamic of Pennsylvania State was outstanding in performance with the javelin.

Among Croatians who have been coaches in various sports are Lou Zarza of the University of Arizona; Tony Blazina, the University of Illinois; Joseph L. Kuharich, formerly coach of the Washington Redskins and recently head football coach at Notre Dame University. George Mikan, who was three times an All-American in college, was at one time the coach of the Minneapolis Lakers professional basketball team. Eddie Erdelats is the present coach of the Navy football team at Annapolis.

William Mihal(ovich) was at one time world walking champ, and Helen Grlenkovich was once a world diving champion. Fritzie Zivich (Živčić), born of Croatian parents in Millvale, Pennsylvania, was world welterweight boxing champion in 1941.

Tom Rosandich, an athlete of distinction, was sent to the Far East by the U.S. Department of State in 1957 to help organize the Asiatic Games.[132]

OTHER CONTRIBUTIONS

Nick Bez (Bezmalinović), who arrived in Alaska some fifty years ago with five dollars in his pocket, owned a number of mines, an airline, the greatest fishing fleet on the west coast, and was often called the "King of Alaska." He died recently. John Radoš and Joe Martinac are prominent shipbuilders on the Pacific coast. Paul Draženović has been awarded several prizes in Fairbanks, Alaska, where he lives as one of the pioneers of gold mining.

Paul Martinis, who came from Dalmatia as a young boy before the First World War, lives in Everett, Washington, and is president of fishing enterprises. In 1957 he was named "king of salmon" and was personally congratulated by President Eisenhower. Steve M. Sekul, of Biloxi, Mississippi, was honored in 1958 as Mississippi's "shrimp king." John Drazick, a self-made man, a native of Bribir, is an eminent industrialist in Detroit; he is president of the Northeastern Tool and Die Co. Robert J. Breskovich is a very successful and prosperous industrialist in Seattle, and owner of large tuna canneries.

When gold was discovered in 1898 in Alaska, Miho Stjepović arrived from Dalmatia to join the gold rush. He enjoyed luck in gold mining, and

132/*Zajedničar*, Feb. 6, 1963.

later became a successful realtor. His son, Mike Stepovich, born in 1919, was the first native Alaskan and the first Catholic to become Governor of the Territory of Alaska. He is the proud father of thirteen children.

In the fishing industry, in fish-processing, and in the production of fishing equipment the Croatians have introduced many new methods and tools which have considerably modernized tuna, salmon, and sardine fishing. In the Seattle-Tacoma area alone there are over 120 Croatian fishing boats. When Mladineo compiled his *Adresar* in 1937, he listed one hundred Croatians who owned fishing boats in the largest Croatian fishing settlement in America, at San Pedro, California. It was there that Peter Dragnich produced many revolutionary innovations in fishing and Martin Bogdanović founded the large Star-Kist Tuna Company, which employs many hundreds of Croatians. Croatian businessmen own the Fisherman's Bank, the largest in San Pedro.[133] Several other large canneries in the coastal area are owned by Croatians, and Croatian fishing boats are operating in all waters between Alaska and Peru.

Croatians have performed similar services in the production and processing of fruits and vegetables in the west. John Slavich, who died in 1959 in Fresno, California, was one of the principal fruit processors in the United States. He was born in San Francisco of Croatian parents who immigrated in 1897. With his brother-in-law he entered the grape growing and transporting business and founded the nationally known Delmonte Fruit Company.[134] Marcus Nalley (Narančić) is also known as a food processor and grower and Pero Divizić, the Dulčić brothers, and the Lukas, Lučić, Lukšić, and Zaninović families are important vineyard owners in the vicinity of Delano, California, and own companies which are currently shipping grapes throughout the United States. Divizić owns 6000 acres where he cultivates grapes, other fruits, vegetables, and cotton. In Divizić's vicinity there are more than fifty Croatian families, each one owning up to 1000 acres of grapes.[135] Watsonville, California, and vicinity have for several decades been inhabited by a great number of prosperous Croatian American farmers and fruit growers. A large hotel, beautiful restaurants, and merchandising establishments of all kinds are owned by Croatian immigrants in the area. Numerous fruit processing plants, vegetable collecting and crating centers, and related industries are owned by Croatian firms.[136]

133/Billyana Niland, "Yugoslavs in San Pedro," *Sociology and Social Research,* XXVI (Sept.-Oct. 1941), 36–44.

134/*Zajedničar,* Aug. 19, 1959.

135/Bogdan Radica, "A West Coast Visit to Our Countrymen," *Croatia Press,* X (Oct. 1956), 1–6.

136/*Zajedničar,* Dec. 4, 1957.

Thousands of Croatians and their descendants are engaged in all types of industry and in many professions throughout California. Over eighty Croatian contractors are in business in Los Angeles. Especially prominent is Joe Jurich, former head of the national CIO Fisherman's Union. Many other Croatians have also participated in the leadership of various labor unions.

The Croatian contribution to the U.S. steel industry has been considerable; thousands of Croatians have worked for decades in many of the steel mills. There have been a number of recognized Croatian innovators in the steel industry, men who have invented techniques for saving time and for increasing production. Many useful tools and machine parts also have been invented by Croatians, some of them unknown workers, whose patents were never registered. Hugo Tomich is a well-known Chicago metal manufacturer and Nikola Šulentić, who came as a young man from Croatia, was an inventor and eventually became a prosperous industrialist in Waterloo, Iowa, before his premature death more than twelve years ago. Again, some Croatians have been engaged in the printing business, as is Joseph Kraja, who was born in Dubrovnik in the 1890s and came to this country in 1906. He succeeded in becoming a prominent printer in Youngstown, Ohio, where he owns the United Printing Co. One of the leaders of the Croatian Circle (Hrvatsko Kolo) in the 1930s and early 1940s, he has published many articles in various newspapers and almanacs and at present contributes articles to the Croatian journals about the history of the Croatians in America.

Thousands of Croatian miners throughout the United States have given their energy and their lives for the development of the American mining industry. The same may be said also for the meat packing and lumber industries. The Croatians of Eagle River, Wisconsin, the greatest Croatian farming settlement in this country, and of Beloit, Sanborn, Willard, and Park Falls in Wisconsin, are dairymen.

Many other Croatians have been prominent in industry and the professions. Michael Nosic, a worker from South Chicago, was chosen several years ago as the typical "Labor Day American Worker." Paul Gusdanovic, who died in 1959 in Shaker Heights, Ohio, at the age of eighty, came to this country some sixty-five years ago. He was a pioneer in the motion picture industry in Cleveland, where he owned fourteen movie theatres.[137] Police lieutenant Daniel T. Dragel, a lawyer and chemist, is director of the Police Crime Detection Laboratory in Chicago and is widely known as an expert in his field.[138] Vincent L. Knaus is a

137/*The Cleveland Press*, Sept. 5, 1959.
138/*Zajedničar*, Sept. 2, 1959.

prominent Chicago lawyer and a distinguished Catholic layman, whose name is frequently mentioned in the columns of the Chicago newspapers.

There are, besides these few whose names are mentioned, Croatian American professional men, businessmen, priests, industrialists, in fact, men in all walks of life, who are enriching American civilization and whose contributions are too numerous to be noted in this article. Hundreds of these names could some day well appear in a Croatian *Who's Who* in America.[139] The difficulty of compiling such a volume is, however, enhanced by the fact that many Croatians have Americanized their names.

Traditionally, the majority of Croatians have been members of the Democratic Party, although comparatively few are prominent in American politics. A few have served in state legislatures but none, to our knowledge, has been elected a senator or representative. However, a considerable number have been elected as mayors of larger cities, as city councilmen, and as sheriffs.

In American fraternalism the Croatians rank very prominently. The Croatian Fraternal Union celebrated in 1969 the seventy-fifth anniversary of its existence. It has been headed by John Badovinac, its first American-born president, since September 1967. It numbers over 115,000 members, prints the largest Croatian paper in this country, owns well over $37,000,000 in assets, has more than $136,000,000 active in insurance, and is one of the largest fraternal organizations in the country. It owns a Children's Home and hundreds of homes and halls throughout the nation. Many American-born priests, intellectuals, businessmen, and other prominent men of Croatian descent have risen to prominence from the ranks of this greatest Croatian organization in the country. The Croatian Fraternal Union represents in many ways the greatest achievement of the Croatian nationality group here. It is primarily a result of many years of labor and sacrifice contributed by the Croatian workingman for the benefit of all who needed the type of assistance which could be rendered by a fraternal organization. But the CFU also has stood in the forefront of many Croatian national, social, cultural, and on many occasions religious activities. The "Zajednica," as the CFU is popularly known among the Croatians of the United States, Canada, and Croatia, did sponsor some controversial issues, but on the whole the record of this organization is definitely a part of the overall Croatian success and achievement in this country and a significant contribution to American fraternalism during the past seventy-five years.

139/The first attempt at compiling such a volume was made and the results published by Francis H. Eterovich. See the bibliography for complete information.

One particular achievement which should be especially noted is the Scholarship Foundation of the CFU. The current president of this unique Croatian foundation is the well-known Croatian banker in Pittsburgh, A. D. Thomas (Tomašić). From June 27, 1958, through June 29, 1966, this foundation aided 624 college students, members of the CFU, to the extent of $124,675. This work is being continued. Most of the funds have been contributed by Croatian workers, businessmen, and professionals.[140] Each year the foundation pays tribute to an outstanding man from the ranks of the CFU by naming him Man of the Year and honoring him with a special banquet. Among those thus honored is Lt. General F. J. Chesarek of the U.S. Army a man with a distinguished military career and a member of CFU Lodge 4 in Etna, Pennsylvania.

The largest Catholic organization among the Croatian immigrants is the Croatian Catholic Union. Its headquarters are in Gary, Indiana, its supreme president is Joseph Šaban, and the membership is approximately 15,000. The organ of the organization is *Naša Nada – Our Hope*, published every first and third Wednesday of the month. Its editor has been for many years Stanley Borić. About 7000 copies of each issue are published in both English and Croatian.[141] This is the second largest Croatian organization in this country, and has a proud record of many achievements. At present the CCU is at work building a Croatian chapel devoted to Our Lady of Bistrica in the National Shrine, Washington, D.C.

In 1957 a group of Croatian Muslim immigrants from Bosnia and Hercegovina opened a mosque and a cultural-religious center for Croatian and other Muslims living in the Chicago area. This enterprise was aided by some other Muslim Chicagoans and by a few Catholic friends.

The Croatians have also built over one thousand national homes, halls, clubs, and cultural centers. Over three thousand organizations of all kinds have been in existence since the early nineteenth century. Many citizens' clubs and boards of trade, kolo groups, theatrical and educational societies, tamburitza orchestras, and singing societies are still very active throughout the United States.

Many Croatian intellectuals, including about a hundred priests, have come to this country between 1945 and 1969. Many of these have been writers, high-school teachers, librarians, university professors, artists, journalists, engineers, and members of various other professions. About one hundred Croatian laymen and priests, experts in many fields, are

140/*Zajedničar*, July 13, 1966, 1.

141/*Naša Nada*, June 29, 1966 lists all the lodges of the CCU in the United States and Canada.

teaching at American colleges and universities. Only some of the Croatian professionals are listed in the *Directory* published by Francis H. Eterovich (see Bibliography).

In Chicago, which is at present the cultural center of American Croatians, a group of Franciscans have established a successful printing shop where several Croatian publications are regularly printed and from which numerous Croatian and English books, almanacs, and journals have been published. A Croatian Academy of America, whose center is in New York, has existed for fifteen years and comprises over a hundred Croatian intellectuals. It publishes the *Journal of Croatian Studies*, the first Croatian scholarly review in the English language. In November 1955, Croatian intellectuals founded the Croatian Historical Institute in Chicago, which has published six historical books. The American Croatian Academic Club, founded in 1958 in Cleveland, Ohio, has organized many seminars discussing the problems of Croatia and has made an impact on the American cultural scene.

There has been considerable recognition in the United States of Croatia's Cardinal Aloysius Stepinac, "a man who stood up to the Communist oppressor," as the governor of Michigan stated when proclaiming October 13, 1957, as Cardinal Stepinac Day. On September 12, 1948, Archbishop Stepinac High School was dedicated in White Plains, New York by Cardinal Spellman. April 5, 1959, was proclaimed Cardinal Stepinac Day in Illinois, and a similar day was proclaimed in Ohio for May 3, 1959. Stepinac's contribution to the struggles of the free world against oppression was also honored by innumerable articles in hundreds of American newspapers and magazines, and he was hailed by many American ecclesiastical and political leaders. An excellent book paying tribute to him and to Croatia was written a few years earlier by Richard Pattee, *The Case of Aloysius Cardinal Stepinac* (Milwaukee: The Bruce Publishing Company, 1953).

SACRIFICE IN LIVES

Thousands of American Croatians have given their lives during the past several generations to build a better country. Thousands of known and unknown workers have died in mines, steel mills, factories, on railroads, in construction work, on the high seas, and in various other occupations. A search through many old Croatian American newspapers reveals the tragic story of numerous accidents, in some of which several members of the same family lost their lives. Thousands of others were crippled for life or died as a result of injuries sustained and sicknesses contracted on hazardous jobs. Thousands of these disabled workers returned from the United States to Croatia, only to die there. This contribution in lives and blood, though it was made by persons hardly known outside of their own families, has been just as important as that of the prominent inventors and pioneers.

Thousands of Croatians and Croatian Americans served in the First World War, and hundreds were killed in combat. Jake Alex (Andjelko Mandušić), Louis Cukela, Mate Koćak, and James Meštrović were decorated with the Congressional Medal of Honor, the latter two posthumously. Captain Cukela, USMC, was given this medal twice, the only living man to hold two such decorations for extreme bravery in a single war.

Many thousands of American Croatians served in the Second World War. One Croatian parish, in South Chicago, was cited on the floor of the U.S. Congress for sending 707 of its parishioners into the armed forces. More than 13,000 members of the CFU went to the battlefields, and, of these, 308 were killed in action. From the Croatian parish of St. Paul in Cleveland, Ohio, came twenty-three young men who were to lose their lives on the battlefield, and about one thousand members of other Croatian parishes were killed in action.

Officer Pavlić, an Annapolis graduate, lost his life in the battle of Guadalcanal on the U.S.S. *South Dakota*. Subsequently, a destroyer was named after him. Peter Tomich, chief water tender of the U.S.S. *Utah*, who died at Pearl Harbor, was awarded posthumously the Congressional Medal of Honor in 1944. In 1945, First Lieutenant John F. Tominac of Johnstown, Pennsylvania, was awarded the same decoration for exceptional heroism in France. Lieutenant J. Luksich of Joliet, Illinois, piloting a P-51 Mustang, shot down or destroyed on the ground twenty enemy planes.[142]

During the Second World War some Croatian families had four to seven boys and girls in the service; e.g., Matt Babic, a Croatian immigrant in Detroit, had six children in the armed forces and four working at essential war jobs. The majority of the Croatians worked in basic war industries, often up to eighteen hours a day for seven days a week. Since the Croatians excel especially in the making of steel and machine tools and in automotive-vehicle manufacturing, they made a great contribution to American war production. A number have also worked at the delicate and dangerous task of blast furnace relining. In 1943 a Croatian foreman, John Starcevich, and his crew (mostly Croatians) relined a

142/L. Adamic, *A Nation of Nations* (New York: Harper and Bros., 1944), 247–8; for Tomich, see *Naša Nada*, June 8, 1963.

furnace in a steel plant in Indiana Harbor, Indiana, in twenty-eight days, an astonishing feat considering that the previous record was approximately sixty days.[143] In the present Vietnam conflict many Croatians serve in the armed forces.

CONCLUSION

Contrary to the prevailing view that the Croatians are entirely "new" immigrants, their immigration to this continent and the United States began considerably earlier than the period of the "new" immigration. As thousands were leaving the Croatian lands at a time when Croatian nationalism was non-existent or very weak, a considerable number were listed in this country as Austrians, Magyars, and even Italians. Adam S. Eterovich of San Francisco, with his recent discoveries (in the state, county, city, and parish archives and in various other sources), is now shedding new light on the existence of thousands of Croatian pioneers in all walks of life in the West and Southwest. His findings prove even more conclusively that all the immigrants from Istria, Croatia-Slavonia, especially Dalmatia, and to a lesser degree Bosnia-Hercegovina should be treated as part of both the old and new immigration.

Because of the confusing classification system of the immigration authorities, which grouped Croatians and Slovenians together and separately classified "Dalmatians, Bosnians and Hercegovinians," we shall never know how many Croatians came to this country. It should also be noted that aside from those immigrants who were conscious of their Croatian nationality, there were many immigrants from Croatia of Serbian, German, Hungarian, Jewish, and other origins. For this reason we may speak in terms of "the immigrants from Croatia" rather than using only the term "the Croatian immigrants." Thousands of people from Croatia-Slavonia whose descendants are now listed as Serbian immigrants considered themselves Croatians of the Orthodox faith about sixty or seventy years ago.

Furthermore, not all people of Croatian nationality came from the Croatian provinces. A few thousand Croatians from Burgenland (before the First World War West Hungary and now a part of Austria), a few hundred from southern Italy, about two hundred families from Janjevo at Kossovo, and several thousands from southern parts of Hun-

143/*Ibid.*; also Jure Prprić, "Tisuće hrvatskih grobova: Hrvatski doprinos Americi u krvi i životima"/Thousands of Croatian Graves: The Croatian Contribution to America in Blood and Lives, *Hrvatska Revija*, x, no. 4 (Dec. 1960), 741–59.

gary (the region north of the Drava River, Medjumurje, Baranja, Bačka, and Banat) have all been almost completely forgotten by both Croatian and American historians of immigration. This writer believes that the members of the Croatian diaspora in Europe should be considered a part of the Croatian national emigration to the United States.

Because of social pressures to which the minorities have been subjected in the past and present in this country, many Croatians changed their names; hence it is most difficult to trace the origin of many who are present-day Americans. Many of the descendants of these immigrants now bearing Anglo-Saxon names are aware of their Croatian or at least Slavic origin. Many, however, are not conscious of their origin, but know only that their forefathers came from the Hapsburg Empire. Again, it will never be possible to discover the extent of the Croatian contribution because many conscious Croatians had German, Hungarian, Italian, and other names. Who can suspect that a Croatian is hidden behind such names as Suzzallo, Zotti, Marchesi, Guldescu, Lucas, and Knaus?

On the whole, the immigration from Croatia remains a fruitful area for investigation. Most of the writing done in the past decades, unfortunately, only repeats most of the old facts, refers to some legends and myths, and advances vague and romantic theories. It is most encouraging, therefore, to see in this field the new discoveries of Adam S. Eterovich. His findings definitely expand our knowledge of the life and contributions of the old Croatian immigrants. It is to be hoped, too, that more serious work will be undertaken by scholars living in Croatia, as thousands of documents and a great amount of historical evidence is being gathered by the organization "Matica Iseljenika Hrvatske" in Zagreb.[144] The establishment of the Immigrant Archives at the University of Minnesota – the largest repository of immigration documents in this country – will make it possible for scholars to do additional original research on the Croatian immigrants.

Judging from historical evidence, the number of Croatian immigrants is greater than is generally recognized by our historians of immigration. The Croatian contribution is also more significant and more extensive than is generally accepted by the historians. A new phenomenon – insufficiently stressed thus far – is the appearance of the new type of Croatian immigrant following the Second World War. The flow of thousands of new, mostly young, highly qualified and highly skilled immi-

144/The Historical Department under the direction of Professor I. Čizmić is doing a great deal to promote interest and actual work in the field of the history of Croatian immigrants. A good step in the right direction was taken by the former president of the Matica Iseljenika Hrvatske, Većeslav Holjevac, through the publication of his recent book *Hrvati izvan domovine* (1967 and 1968 editions).

grants still continues and will go on for a long time after the inauguration of the new Immigration Act of October 1965. Considering the fact that there were very few educated Croatian immigrants prior to 1914, the Croatian contribution to American culture, civilization, and industrial progress is an important part of the American past. With thousands of intellectuals and educated and skilled Croatians reaching our shores after 1945, the Croatian share in the making of America is considerably increasing.

Historiography on Croatia and Croatians in the English language is also increasing. This volume of *Croatia* is a part of it as well as an endeavor to do away with some misconceptions about the Croatians. And this study should be considered only a modest attempt to introduce to Americans and other English-speaking peoples the history of the life and contributions of the Croatian immigrants[145] in this country of freedom which has played so tremendous a role in the life of the Croatian nation in the homeland as well. The largest number of Croatians – their largest national group – outside Croatia is now located in this country. It is therefore with good reason that the Croatian historians at home refer to the American Croatians as a "Iseljena Hrvatska," which in a free English translation means "the Emigrated (or uprooted) Croatia."

Selected Bibliography

PRIMARY SOURCES

DOCUMENTS, RECORDS, AUTOBIOGRAPHIES, AND MONOGRAPHS

Anonymous. *Apostólicos afanes de la Compañia de Jesús* por un padre de la misma Sagrada Religion de su Provincia de México. Barcelona: Pablo Nadal, 1754. Indispensable in the study of Konšćak.

Bukovac, Vlaho. *Moj život*/My Life. Beograd: Srpska Književna Zadruga, 1925.

Consag, Fernando. "Derrotero del viage ..." In Venegas, Miguel (ed.), *Noti-*

145/In the spring of 1965 Vinko Nikolić, the editor of *Hrvatska Revija*, spent a few weeks visiting Croatian colonies in the United States and Canada. As a result of his visit and observations he published a book entitled *Pred vratima domovine*/At the Gates of the Homeland (Buenos Aires: Knjižnica Hrvatske Revije, 1966). Extensive parts of this good and interesting book deal with Croatian immigrants in the United States, with their activities, ideas, and accomplishments. After the book of Tresić-Pavičić some sixty years ago, Nikolić's is the best analysis and discussion of American Croatians written by a keen observer. See also Bogdan Radica, "Hrvatska emigracija u USA i Kanadi poslije dvadeset godina"/Croatian Immigrants in the United States and Canada after Twenty Years, *Hrvatski Glas* (Winnipeg), June 18 and 25, 1966, which reviews Nikolić's book and the last two decades of the Croatian immigrants in the United States and Canada.

cias de la California. Madrid: M. Fernandez, 1757. III, 140–94. This is Consag's log on his exploration of Baja California in 1746.

Decorme, Gerard. *La Obra de los Jesuitas mexicanos durante la Época Colonial: 1572–1767.* 2 vols. Mexico City: José Porrua, 1941. The first volume gives proof that Ratkaj was a Croatian.

Eterovich, Adam S. *Croatian Cemetery Records of San Francisco, Cal.: 1849–1930.* ("Slavonic: American Historical and Genealogical Society," I, no. 2.) San Francisco, 1964. "Slavonic ..." is the title of the publisher and the series.

—— *Yugoslav Survey of the West and South: 1850–1880.* ("Slavonic," I, no. 1.) San Francisco, 1964.

—— *Irish Slavonian Marriages in California: 1849–1880.* ("Slavonic," I, no. 3.) San Francisco, 1964.

—— *San Francisco Yugoslavs – Census – Voting – Business 1870.* ("Slavonic," I, no. 4.) San Francisco, 1964.

—— *Yugoslavs in Los Angeles: 1733–1900.* ("Balkan and Eastern European American Genealogical and Historical Society," II, no. 2.) San Francisco, 1965.

—— *Yugoslavs in Austin County, Texas; Census: 1870.* (*Ibid.*, II, no. 3.) San Francisco, 1965.

Hinković, Hinko. *Iz velikog doba*/From a Great Era. Zagreb: Ćirilo-Metodska Nakladna Knjižara, 1927.

Maček, Vladko. *In the Struggle for Freedom.* New York: R. Speller, 1957. Autobiography of the late president of the Croatian Peasant Party who died in exile in Washington, D.C.

Meštrović, Ivan. *Uspomene na političke ljude i dogadjaje*/Recollections on Political People and Events. Buenos Aires: Knjižnica Hrvatske Revije, 1961. Autobiographical work written by the late great sculptor and patriot who died in South Bend, Ind.

Nikolić, Vinko. *Pred vratima domovine*/At the Gates of the Homeland. Buenos Aires: Knjižnica Hrvatske Revije, 1966. An excellent survey and analysis of Croatian immigrants in the United States by the editor of *Hrvatska Revija.*

Sanjek, Louis. *In Silence.* New York: Fortuny's Publishers, 1938. A candid autobiography of a Croatian Lutheran minister in the United States.

Schereck, William J. *The Peoples of Wisconsin.* Madison, Wis.: State Historical Society of Wisconsin, 1956. Contains a good survey of the Croatians in that state; it was recorded on the scene.

Stoecklein, Joseph (ed.). *Der neue Welt-Bott.* 8 vols. Augsburg and Graetz: Societas Jesu, 1726. The first volume of these reports from Jesuit missions contains letters of Father Ratkaj.

Tresić-Pavičić, Ante. *Preko Atlantika do Pacifika: Život Hrvata u Sjevernoj Americi*/Across the Atlantic to the Pacific: Life of the Croatians in North America. Zagreb: Dionička Tiskara, 1907. A valuable first-hand report on the life of Croatian immigrants written during the author's sojourn in America. He was one of the leading Croatian writers and the first ambassador of the Kingdom of the Serbs, Croats, and Slovenes in Washington after 1918.

Venegas, Miguel (ed.). *Noticias de la California.* 3 vols. Madrid: M. Fernandez, 1757. A new edition was published in Mexico City by Editorial Layag in 1943.

Zrno, Rev. David (ed.). *Centennial: 1848–1948; the Life and Work of the Croatian People in Chicagoland.* Chicago: Croatian Franciscan Fathers, 1949.

Zuback, Anthony G. *50th Anniversary of the Life and Work of the Croatian People in the Mahoning Valley.* Youngstown, Ohio: Croatian Historical Research Bureau, 1946.

The above two monographs are well-done documentary surveys. The Croatian Historical Research Bureau was founded and conducted by A. G. Zuback and attorney Vincent L. Knaus and was responsible for the publication of many original documents and primary sources on Croatian immigrants.

OFFICIAL DOCUMENTS

Croatian Catholic Clergy of the U.S. *Memorandum to Various Governments, Leading Statesmen and Religious Leaders, Publicists and New Agencies.* Chicago: Croatian Franciscan Press, 1954.

Croatian National Council of North America. *Memorandum.* Youngstown, Ohio: Croatian National Council, 1933.

Croatian National Representation. *Memorandum ... to All Governments, Leading Statesmen and Publicists of the World Regarding the Struggle of Croatia For Independence.* Pittsburgh: CNR, 1939.

The above three are only a few of several such documents issued during the decades of political activity of the Croatian immigrants.

Croatia-Slavonia-Dalmatia, Sabor. *Saborski spisi* .../Minutes of the Diet. 14 vols. Zagreb: Kr. Zemaljska Tiskara, 1865–1918.

——— *Stenografički zapisnici*/Stenographic Minutes. Zagreb: Kr. Zemaljska Tiskara, 1889–1917.

The above two official documents refer on many occasions to the legislation on emigration and various problems related to emigrants.

The Secretary of Labor. "A Century of Immigration," *Monthly Labor Review*, XVIII, no. 1 (Jan. 1922), 1–19. This is an excellent authoritative and statistical analysis, a document in itself, based on official sources.

U.S. Congress. *Public Law 89–236 89th Congress, H.R. 2580, October 3, 1965 – An Act to Amend the Immigration and Nationality Act, and for Other Purposes.* Washington, D.C.: Government Printing Office, 1965. This twelve-page document is the official text of the new Immigration Act of October 1965.

U.S. Department of Justice. *Annual Report of the Immigration and Naturalization Service, 1965.* Washington: INS, 1965.

U.S. Department of State. *Papers Relating to Foreign Relations of the United States; the World War, 1918.* Suppl. I, vol. I. Washington: Government Printing Office, 1947.

U.S. House of Representatives; Committee on Un-American Activities. *Report on the American Slav Congress and Associated Organizations.* June 28, 1949. House Report No. 1951. Washington: Government Printing Office, 1950. This official document describes Communist activities among the Croatian immigrants during the Second World War.

U.S. Office of Strategic Services. *Foreign Nationality Groups in the United States.* Washington: OSS, 1945. Classified data on organizations, publications, and personalities among the immigrants during the Second World War.

U.S. Senate. Reports of the Immigration Commission. *Emigration Conditions in Europe.* Washington: Government Printing Office, 1911. A valuable eyewitness account compiled on the scene by members of the Immigration Commission. This and 41 other volumes of the *Reports* helped to inaugurate the anti-immigration legislation of the 1920s.

—— *Immigration and Crime.* Washington: Government Printing Office, 1911. Data on Croatians were favorable to them.

—— *Dictionary of Races or Peoples.* Same publisher as above, 1911.

—— *Immigrants in Cities.* 2 vols. Same publisher, 1912.

The last two volumes contain a great deal of primary information on Croatians.

SECONDARY SOURCES

BOOKS, PAMPHLETS, AND SOUVENIR BOOKS

Adamic, Louis. *The Native's Return.* New York: Harper and Bros., 1934.

—— *Cradle of Life.* New York and London: Harper and Bros., 1936.

—— *My America, 1928–1938.* New York: Harper and Bros., 1938.

—— *From Many Lands.* New York: Harper and Bros., 1940.

—— *Two-Way Passage.* New York: Harper and Bros., 1941.

—— *What's Your Name?* New York: Harper and Bros., 1942.

—— *My Native Land.* New York: Harper and Bros., 1943.

—— *A Nation of Nations.* New York: Harper and Bros., 1944.

All of Adamic's works treat immigrants, especially South Slav immigrants, and the background of their emigration. He wrote more about Croatian immigrants than did anybody else at that time. However, he was a better writer than historian. When he became one of the leading leftists in this country, he wrote with considerable bias.

Anderson, Leland (ed.). *Bibliography: Dr. Nikola Tesla (1856–1943).* 2nd ed. Minneapolis: The Tesla Society, 1956. A biblography on Tesla and a listing of his patents.

Anonymous. *Kažiput*/The Road Pointer. Hartford, Conn.: "Hrvatska Trobojnica," 1914.

Ardas, Vjenceslav. *Souvenir Book – Spomen Knjiga: Dedication of St. Joseph the Worker (Croatian) Church.* Gary, Ind.: V. Ardas, 1956.

Balch, Emily Greene. *Our Slavic Fellow Citizens.* New York: Charities Publications Committee, 1910. Parts of the book are primary sources, and many pages deal with Croatian immigrants. The best and most valuable source for the period before 1910.

Benković, Theodore. *The Tragedy of a Nation: An American's Eye-witness Report.* Chicago: Franciscan Press, n.d. (1947?).

Bolton, Herbert E. *Rim of Christendom: A Biography of Eusebio Francisco Kino, Pacific Coast Pioneer.* New York: Macmillan, 1936. Gives information on Ratkaj and Konšćak.

Bone, James. *Ivan Meštrović: Victoria and Albert Museum.* London: Victoria and Albert Museum, 1915.

Bone, James, and others. *Ivan Meštrović, a Monograph.* London: Williams and Norgate, 1919.

Bonifačić, Antun F., and Mihanovich, Clement S. (eds.). *The Croatian Nation in Its Struggle for Freedom and Independence.* Chicago: "Croatia" Publishing Co., 1955. A symposium with articles by numerous Croatian scholars; the first of its kind in the United States.

Botkin, Benjamin A. (ed.). *A Treasury of American Folklore.* New York: Crown Publishing Co., 1944. Contains the saga of Joe Magarac.

Brinton, Christian. *The Meštrović Exhibition, The Brooklyn Museum, 1924.* New York: The Meštrović Exhibition Committee, 1924.

Brown, Francis J., and Roucek, Joseph S. (eds.). *One America: The History, Contributions, and Present Problems of Our Racial and National Minorities.* New York: Prentice-Hall, 1945.

Bučar, Franjo. *Hrvatske kolonije u tudjini*/Croatian Colonies Abroad. Zagreb: Prosvjeta, 1907.

By-Laws of the Croatian Union of the U.S.A. Allegheny, Pa.: Croatian Union of the U.S.A., 1896.

Clinch, Bryan J. *California and Its Missions.* 2 vols. San Francisco: Whitaker and Ray, 1904. Vol. I discusses Konšćak's activities.

Commons, R. John. *Races and Immigrants in America.* New edition. New York: Macmillan, 1920. Gives valuable comments on Croatians as a race.

Constitution and By-Laws of the Croatian Catholic Union in the United States of America. Gary, Ind.: CCU, 1954.

Constitution and By-Laws of the Croatian Fraternal and Beneficial Association "Sloga." Pittsburgh: "Sloga," 1907.

Corsi, Edward. *In the Shadow of Liberty: the Chronicle of Ellis Island.* New York: Macmillan, 1935.

Croatian Fraternal Union. *65th Anniversary.* Pittsburgh: CFU, 1959.

Danevski, S. R. *Pripovijesti*/Short Stories. Chicago: By the author, 1911. The first Croatian literary work published here; it deals with the Croatian immigrants.

Dunne, Peter Masten. *Early Jesuit Missions in Tarahumara.* Berkeley and Los Angeles: University of California Press, 1948.

—— *Black Robes in Lower California.* Berkeley and Los Angeles: University of California Press, 1962. Points out the importance of Ratkaj and Konšćak.

Duquesne University Tamburitzans. *Duquesne University Tamburitzans. Programs for the 20th, 21st, 22nd, 23rd, and 24th Seasons.* Pittsburgh: Duquesne University Tamburitzans, 1957–61.

Easton, Allen H. *Immigrant Gifts to American Life.* New York: Russell Sage Foundation, 1932. All such books on immigration include Croatian immigrants; the quantity and quality of information vary from one book to another.

Eterovich, Francis H. (ed.). *Hrvati profesori na američkim i kanadskim visokim školama*/Croatian Professors at American and Canadian Schools of Higher Learning. Chicago: By the author, 1963.

—— *Biographical Directory of Scholars, Artists, and Professionals of Croatian Descent in the United States and Canada.* 2nd ed., 1964–5. Chicago: By the author, 1965. 3rd ed.; Chicago: By the author, 1970.

Firis, Tomislav. *55th Anniversary: St. Nicholas Croatian Greek Catholic Church*. Cleveland, Ohio: St. Nicholas Parish, 1957. All such souvenir books, of which a great number have been published in the United States, yield interesting and valuable and sometimes primary information.

Gaži, Stjepan. *Croatian Immigration to Allegheny County 1882–1914*. Pittsburgh: CFU, 1956.

Generalni Iseljenički Komesarijat. *Iseljenički propisi*/Rules for Emigrants. Zagreb: Generalni Iseljenički Komesarijat, 1922.

Govorchin, Gerald Gilbert. *Americans from Yugoslavia*. Gainesville, Fla.: University of Florida Press, 1961. First scholarly survey of all immigrants from Yugoslavia.

Guldescu, Stanko. *History of Medieval Croatia*. The Hague: Mouton and Co., 1964. A very good historical study.

Hilberry, Harry. *The Sculpture of Ivan Meštrović*. Syracuse, N.Y.: Syracuse University Press, 1948.

Holjevac, Većeslav. *Hrvati izvan domovine*/Croatians Abroad. Zagreb: Matica Hrvatska, 1967.

Horvat, Josip. *Kultura Hrvata kroz 1000 godina*/One Thousand Years of Croatian Culture. Zagreb: Tipografija, 1939.

Juricek, J. *Silver Jubilee of Saints Peter and Paul Church 1917–1942*. Omaha, Neb.: Sts. Peter and Paul Croatian Parish, 1942.

Kadić, Ante (ed.). *Croatian Reader with Vocabulary*. The Hague: Mouton and Co., 1960.

K(ajić), M(irko). *Naša izjava i k našoj izjavi*/Our Declaration and About Our Declaration. New York: Narodni List, 1916.

Kane, Harnett T. "Dalmatia on the Mississippi," in *Deep Delta Country* (series "American Folkways," ed. Erskine Caldwell). New York: Duell, Sloan and Pearce, 1944. 92–104.

Kljaković, Jozo. *U Suvremenom kaosu*/In Contemporary Chaos. Buenos Aires: Privately printed by friends of the author, 1952.

Kosier, Ljubomir St. *Srbi, Hrvati i Slovenci u Americi: Ekonomsko Socijalni Problemi Emigracije*/Serbs, Croats, and Slovenes in America: Economic and Social Problems of Emigration. Beograd: Biblioteka "Bankarstva," 1926. A detailed study with much valuable data.

Kostelski, Z. *The Croats*. Floreffe, Pa.: "Kolo" Publishing Co., 1950.

Krmpotić, Martin Davorin. *Life and Works of the Reverend Ferdinand Konšćak, S.J. 1703–1759, an Early Missionary in California*. Boston: The Stratford Co., 1923. The only monograph on Konšćak; it is a good study.

—— *Josip Kundek, Misionar u Jasperu, Dubois County, Ind. i generalni vikar vincenneskog biskupa (1809–1857)*/Joseph Kundek, Missionary in Jasper, Dubois County, Ind., and General Vicar of the Bishop of Vincennes (1809–1857). Zagreb: Tiskara S. Bartol u Virju, 1925.

Lakatoš, Josip. *Narodna statistika*/National Statistics. 2nd ed. Osijek: Naklada R. Bačić, 1914. Large parts are primary sources; it contains valuable data on emigration from Croatia.

Laszowski, Emilij (ed.). *Znameniti i zaslužni Hrvati*/Famous and Reputed Croatians. Zagreb: Odbor za Izdanje Knjige, Hrv. Štamparski Zavod, 1925.

London, Jack. *The Valley of the Moon*. New York: Macmillan, 1914. Describes "New Dalmatia" apple paradise in California.

Lorković, Mladen. *Narod i zemlja Hrvata*/The Croatian Nation and Country. Zagreb: Matica Hrvatska, 1939. A good scholarly work with many data on Croatians in the United States and containing statistics on emigration.

Lupis-Vukić, Ivo F. *Medju našim narodom u Americi*/Among Our People in America. Split: Leonova Tiskara, 1929. An interesting account on many Croatian settlements by a returned emigrant and writer.

Mamatey, Victor S. *The United States and East Central Europe, 1914–1918*. Princeton, N.J.: Princeton University Press, 1957. An excellent scholarly study containing an extensive discussion of the Croatian political movement during the first world war.

Marohnić, Josip. *Englesko-Hrvatski listar*/English-Croatian Letter Writer. Pittsburgh: Hrvatska Knjižara J. Marohnića, 1908.

—— *Popis Hrvata u Americi i kratki opis Sjedinjenih Država*/Census of Croatians in America and a Brief Description of the United States. Allegheny, Pa.: J. Marohnić, 1902. A valuable source containing a great deal of primary data.

Martin, Thomas Commorford. *The Inventions, Researches and Writings of Nikola Tesla*. New York: The Electrical Engineer, 1894. One of the basic works on Tesla.

Matina, Mato. *Official Souvenir*. Rankin, Pa.: St. Mary's Parish, 1904.

McAndrews, Dunstan. *Father Joseph Kundek: 1810–1857, a Missionary Priest of the Diocese of Vincennes*. St. Meinrad, Ind.: A Grail Publication, 1954. The first complete American biography of Kundek.

Meler, Vjekoslav. *Hrvati u Americi: Hrvatske kolonije u Chicagu i St. Louisu*/ Croatians in America: The Croatian Colonies in Chicago and St. Louis. Chicago: Adria Printing Co., 1927.

—— *Los Angeles and San Pedro*. Los Angeles: By the author, 1933.

—— *The Croatians of the Copper Country*. Calumet, Mich.: By the author, 1929.

—— (ed.). *The Slavonic Pioneers of California*. San Francisco: Slavonic Pioneers of California, 1932.

Milošević, Božo (ed.). *Americans of Slav Ancestry*. New York: "Slavia," 1936.

Misich, Joseph. *St. Paul's Church Fiftieth Anniversary: 1903–1953*. Cleveland, Ohio: Croatian St. Paul Parish, 1953.

Mladineo, Ivan. *Narodni adresar – National Directory*. New York: By the author, 1937. An extensive survey of Croatian organizations and personalities in the United States.

Narodno Vijeće Amerikanaca Hrvatskog Porijekla. *Uspjesi i zadaće Narodnog Vijeća Amerikanaca Hrvatskog Porijekla*/Successes and Tasks of the National Council of Americans of Croatian Descent. Pittsburgh: NVAHP, 1949.

Nemec, Slavko. *Povijest hrvatske naseobine u St. Louisu, Mo., 1862–1931*/ A History of the Croatian Settlement in St. Louis, Mo., 1862–1931. St. Louis: By the author, 1931.

Nizeteo, Ante. *Bez povratka*/Without Return. Buenos Aires: Knjižnica Hrvatske Revije, 1957. Short stories about Croatian immigrants written by a Croatian writer in the United States.

O'Neill, John J. *Prodigal Genius: The Life of Nikola Tesla*. New York: Ives Washburn, 1944. The standard biography of Tesla presenting him as the greatest inventor that ever lived in the United States.

Orr, Dorothea. *Portrait of a People: Croatia Today.* New York: Funk and Wagnalls, 1936. A sympathetic account of modern Croatia, commenting also on the fate of the returned immigrants.

Park, Robert. *The Immigrant Press and Its Control.* New York: Harper and Bros., 1922.

Pattee, Richard. *The Case of Aloysius Cardinal Stepinac.* Milwaukee, Wis.: The Bruce Publishing Co., 1953.

Paulova, Milada. *Jugoslavenski Odbor*/The South Slav Committee. Zagreb: Prosvjetna Nakladna Zadruga, 1925. This contains documents about the political activities of American Croatians during the first world war.

Poljak, J. (ed.). *Almanak i statistika južnih Slavena u Sjedinjenim Državama Sjeverne Amerike*/Almanac and Statistics of the South Slavs in the United States of North America. Chicago: By the author, 1925.

Potočnjak, Franko. *Iz emigracije: u Americi*/From the Emigration: In America. Vol. III. Zagreb: Tipografija, 1927,

Preveden, Francis. *A History of the Croatian People.* 2 vols. New York: Philosophical Library, 1955, 1962. First scholarly history of Croatia published in the United States.

Radić, Stjepan. *Moderna kolonizacija i Slaveni*/Modern Colonization and the Slavs. Zagreb: Matica Hrvatska, 1904.

——*Javna poruka hrvatskoj braći u Americi*/A Public Message to Croatian Brethren in America. Zagreb: Slavenska Knjižara, 1913.

Schmeckbier, Lawrence. *Ivan Meštrović, Sculptor and Patriot.* Syracuse, N.Y.: Syracuse University Press, 1959. A comprehensive and thorough biography of the artist.

Sestanovich, S. N. (ed.). *Slavs in California.* Oakland, Calif.: Slavonic Alliance, 1937.

Sliskovich, Anselm, and Zuback, Anthony G. *50th Anniversary of the Life and Work of the Croatian People in the Shenango Valley.* Farrell, Pa.: The Croatian Historical Research Bureau, 1944.

Sorić, Boniface (ed.). *Centennial: 1847–1947: The Life and Work of the Croatian People in Allegheny County, Pennsylvania.* Pittsburgh: The Croatian Historical Research Bureau, 1947. A well-documented survey.

—— *Sacred Heart Parish 50th Golden Jubilee.* McKeesport, Pa.: Croatian Sacred Heart Parish, 1956.

Steiner, Edward. *The Immigrant Tide.* New York: Fleming H. Revell, 1909.

Strossmayer Singing Society. *40th Anniversary: Strossmayer Singing Society, 1911–1951.* Youngstown, Ohio: Strossmayer, 1951.

Südland, L. V. *Južnoslavensko pitanje*/The South Slav Question. Zagreb: Matica Hrvatska, 1943. This book was also reprinted in its original German version by the same publisher under the title *Die südslawische Frage und der Weltkrieg* (zweite Auflage, 1944). This unique study by the Croatian scholar Pilar comments extensively on the problem of Croatian emigration.

Suzzallo, Henry 1875–1933: A Memorial Gathering Held in the Milbank Memorial Chapel, Teachers College, Columbia University, December 18, 1933. New York: Columbia University, 1934.

Tesla, Nikola. *Experiments with Alternate Currents of High Potential and High Frequency.* New York: McGraw Publishing Co., 1904.

—— *Lectures, Patents, Articles.* Beograd: Nikola Tesla Museum, 1956.

Vecki, Victor G. *Threatening Shadows*. Boston. The Stratford Co., 1931. A novel written by an American Croatian physician.

Vlahović, Vlaho. *Manual of Slavonic Personalities*. New York: Slavonic Press, 1940.

—— *Two Hundred Fifty Million and One Slavs*. New York: Slav Publications, 1945.

Vojvodić, Viktor. *Sabrane pjesme*/Collected Poems. San Jose, Calif.: "Sokol", n.d.

Vukelić, Philip (ed.). *Kratki pregled povijesti Hrvatske Bratske Zajednice, 1894–1949*/A Short Survey of the History of the Croatian Fraternal Union, 1894–1949. Pittsburgh: CFU, 1949.

Žagar, Albert. *Spomen Knjiga*/Souvenir Book. Millvale, Pa.: St. Nicholas Croatian Parish, 1950.

ARTICLES IN NEWSPAPERS AND PERIODICALS,
AND UNPUBLISHED THESES AND DISSERTATIONS

Adamic, Louis. "Woman from Croatia," *Saturday Evening Post*, CCXIII (Oct. 21, 1939), 23ff.

—— "The Millvale Apparition," *Harper's Magazine*, 176 (April 1938), 476–86.

Anonymous. "The Immigration Authorities and the Croatians," *Narodni List – National Gazette* (New York), Feb. 17, 1900.

Anonymous. "Croatian Musical Instrument Gains Favor," *Interpreter Releases*, XII (Dec. 19, 1933), 445–6.

Anonymous. "Millvale Murals," *Time*, July 19,1937, 22.

Anonymous. "Croatians in Sports Today," *The Croatian Almanac 1944* (Chicago: Croatian Franciscans, 1943), 247–50.

Anonymous. "Tesla, Nikola." *The Encyclopedia Americana* (New York: Americana Corp., 1956), XXVI, 452–3.

Bresson, Mary Alfred (Sister). "Contemporary Iowa Opinions Regarding the Influence of Croatians in Waterloo and Vicinity, 1907–1949." Unpublished Master's Thesis, Catholic University of America, Washington, D.C., 1951. This sociological thesis deals with a group of Croatians in Iowa.

Brkich, Stephen F. "President Johnson Signs Liberal Immigration Bill; V. I. Mandich at Historic Meeting," *Zajedničar*, Oct. 6, 1965, 1.

Dunne, Peter Masten. "Lower California an Island," *Mid America*, 35, no. 1 (Jan. 1953), 37–66. An excellent study by an expert stressing the importance of Konšćak's explorations in California.

Eterovich, Adam S. "Croatian Pioneers on the Barbary Coast of San Francisco 1849–1870," *Croatia Press*, XVII (Nov. 1963), 2–5.

—— "Jugoslav Immigrant Bibliography," *Balkan and Eastern European American Genealogical Society*, III, no. 1 (San Francisco, Jan. 1966), 1–18.

Grado, Arthur Benko. "Tričetvrt vijeka našeg prekooceanskog seljenja"/Three-quarters of a Century of Our Trans-oceanic Migration, *Obzor Spomen Knjiga: 1860–1935* (Zagreb: Tipografija, 1936), 6–7.

Granit, Ragnar. "The Grand Theme of Stephen Polyak," *Science*, 122, no. 3157 (July 1, 1955) 64.

J. D. "Hrvatski slavuj: burni život naše slavne pjevačice Ilme Murske"/The

Croatian Nightingale: The Stormy Life of Our Famous Singer Ilma Murska, *Matičin Iseljenički Kalendar 1958* (Zagreb: Matica Iseljenika Hrvatske, 1957), 75–79.

Kadić, Ante. "Jack London and Croatian Settlers in Watsonville," *Croatia Press*, IX, no. 146 (Feb. 1955), 6–7.

Kamber, Dragutin. "Hrvati u Americi"/Croatians in America, *Osoba i Duh*, V (Madrid, 1953), no. 3–4, 91–116.

Karabin, Gabro. "Honorable Escape," *Scribner's Magazine*, CII (Dec. 1957), 40–2, 80.

Kesterčanek, Vujica Nada. "Croatian Newspapers and Calendars in the United States." Unpublished Master's Thesis, Marywood College, Scranton, Pa., 1952. The first attempt to outline the history and plight of Croatian journalism in the United States.

Kraja, Josip. "Narodna borba prvih hrvatskih useljenika u U.S.A."/The National Struggle of the First Croatian Immigrants in the U.S.A., *Hrvatska Revija*, XIII, no. 3 (Sept. 1963), 293–326.

—— "The Croatian Circle, 1928–1946; Chronology and Reminiscences," *Journal of Croatian Studies*, V–VI (New York, 1964–5), 145–204. An excellent eyewitness account.

Krešić, Ivan (ed.). *Hrvatski List i Danica Hrvatska Koledar*/The Almanac of Hrvatski List and Danica Hrvatska, New York: Hrvatski (*sic*) Publishing Co., 1922–44. This was the best almanac published by American Croatians during the period covered. As Krešić was a very good journalist and writer, his almanacs are rich in primary and secondary sources.

Krmpotić, M. D. "Croatia," *The Catholic Encyclopedia* (New York: The Encyclopedia Press, 1907)), II, 510–13.

—— "Dalmatia," *The Catholic Encyclopedia*, III, 606–8.

Kvarnerski, Jure. "Hrvatski pomorci u Americi"/Croatian Sailors in America, *Hrvatski List i Danica Hrvatska Koledar 1934*, ed. Ivan Krešić, 77–8.

Meštrović, Ivan. "Iz Michelangelovih imaginiranih razgovora"/Imaginary Dialogues of Michelangelo, *Hrvatska Revija*, III (March 1953), 43–9.

Mihanovich, Clement S. "Americanization of the Croats in Saint Louis, Missouri, during the Past Thirty Years." Unpublished Master's Thesis, Saint Louis University, St. Louis, Mo., 1936. Based on primary sources, this contains a great deal of original information.

Mirth, Karlo. "Problem of Croatian Refugees," *Croatia Press*, XVIII, no. 239 (Nov. 1964), 2–10.

Mortidjija, Tijas. "Die kroatische 'Hansestadt' Dubrovnik"/The Croatian "Hanseatic" City Dubrovnik, *Croatia*, VI (Zagreb: Hrvatski Bibliografski Zavod, 1943), 50–60.

Muftić, Mahmud. "Dr. Karlo Marchesi," *Hrvatska Revija*, XIV, no. 1 (March 1964), 51–3.

Owen, Francis. "The Saga of Joe Magarac: Steelman," *Scribner's Magazine*, XC (Nov. 1931), 505–13.

Palmieri, Aurelio P. "Growth of Croatian Nationalism," *The Catholic World*, CIX (June 1919), 344–59.

Pavelić, Ante S. "Croatia," *Encyclopaedia Britannica* (Chicago: Encyclopaedia Britannica, Inc., 1965), VI, 783–6.

Pešelj, Branko M. "Croatia," *The Encyclopedia Americana* (New York: Americana Corporation, 1955), VIII, 214–17.

Prpić, George J. "The Croats in America." Unpublished Doctoral Dissertation, Department of History, Georgetown University, Washington, D.C., 1959.

—— "Rev. Ferdinand Konscak, S.J., a Croatian Missionary in California," *Croatia Press*, XIII, nos. 198–200 (July-Aug. 1959), 2–9.

—— "Fernando Konschak, S.J., Misionero y Explorador en Baja California," *Studia Croatica*, III (Buenos Aires, March 1962), 58–68.

—— "The Croatian Newspapers in America before 1918," *Croatia Press*, XV (Dec. 1961), 7–15.

—— "Josip Kundek, hrvatski misionar u Americi"/Joseph Kundek, Croatian Missionary in America, *Novi Život*, III, nos. 5–6 (Rome, Italy, Sept.-Dec. 1964), 241–58.

—— "Petnaest godina *Hrvatske Revije*"/Fifteen Years of *Hrvatska Revija*, *Zajedničar*, Oct. 6, 1965, 10.

—— "The South Slavs," in Joseph P. O'Grady (ed.), *The Immigrants' Influence on Wilson's Peace Policies* (University of Kentucky Press, 1967), 173–203.

—— "Razgovors hrvatskim kiparom Josipom Turkaljem u Washingtonu"/ Interview with the Croatian Sculptor Josip Turkalj in Washington, *Danica*, Oct. 9, 1957, 1, 6.

—— "Croatians in the U.S.," *The New Catholic Encyclopedia*, IV, 467–8.

—— "Maksimilijan Vanka, zaboravljeni hrvatski slikar i njegov doprinos Americi"/Maximilian Vanka, the Forgotten Croatian Painter, and His Contribution to America, *Hrvatska Revija*, VIII, no. 2 (June 1958), 129–60. Also published as a reprint under the title *Maksimilijan Vanka: Njegov Doprinos Umjetnosti Amerike*.

—— "Znanstveni rad Dra. Dinka Tomašića u S.A.D. i pitanje 'Nacionalnog Konunizma'"/Scholarly Work of Dr. Dinko Tomašić in the U.S.A. and the Question of "National Communism," *Hrvatska Revija*, IX, no. 4 (Dec. 1959) 448–52.

—— "Život i djelo Franje Prevedena"/The Life and Work of Francis Preveden, *Hrvatska Revija*, X, no. 1 (March 1960), 87–98.

—— "Tisuće hrvatskih grobova: hrvatski doprinos Americi u krvi i životima"/ Thousands of Croatian Graves: The Croatian Contribution to America in Blood and Lives, *Hrvatska Revija*, X, no. 4 (Dec. 1960), 741–59.

Radica, Bogdan. "A West Coast Visit to Our Countrymen," *Croatia Press*, X (Oct. 1956), 1–6. Professor Radica's articles, scattered throughout many Croatian publications in exile, yield a great deal of information on the life and activities of Croatian immigrants in the United States and other countries.

Raditsa, Bogdan. "Clash of Two Immigrant Generations," *Commentary*, 21, no. 1 (Jan. 1958), 8–15.

Šeparović, A. "Iseljenici i domovina"/Emigrants and the Homeland, *Vjesnik u Srijedu* (Zagreb), Jan. 5, 1966.

"Suzzallo, Henry," *The National Cyclopedia of American Biography* (New York: J. T. White and Co., 1930), C, 21.

Tomašić, Dinko. "Croatia in European Politics," *Journal of Central European Affairs*, II, no. 1 (April 1942); 63–85.

Vanino, Miroslav. "Martin Davorin Krmpotić (1867–1931)," *Hrvatski List i Danica Hrvatska Koledar 1932*, ed. Ivan Krešić, 193–201.
Zotti, Frank. "Croatians: Who They Are and How to Reach Them," *Advertising and Selling*, XXIX, no. 5 (July 5, 1919), 19.
Zuback, Anthony G. "Croatian Publications in Allegheny County, Pa., "*Croatian Almanac 1948* (McKeesport, Pa.: "Ave Maria," 1947), 101–25.
—— "Croatian Publications in Chicagoland," *Croatian Almanac 1950* (McKeesport, Pa.: "Ave Maria," 1949), 101–73.

APPENDIX

Croatian Papers and Periodicals in the United States 1884–1960[146]

American Citizen – Amerikanski Gradjanin, Pittsburgh, 1913–16.
American Croat – Američki Hrvat, San Jose, Calif., 1966–.
American Croatian Historical Review, Chicago and Youngstown, Ohio, 1946.
American-Croatian Pioneer, Cleveland, 1957–.
American Jugoslav, San Francisco.
American-Yugoslav Reflector.
Američki Hrvat, Chicago, 1905–22.
Američki Hrvat – The American Croatian, Pittsburgh, 1922–30.
Američki Hrvat – The American Croat, Gary, Ind., and Cleveland, 1945–6.
Američki Hrvatski Glasnik, Chicago, 1945–56.
Amerikansko-Hrvatski Glasnik, 1909.
Austrijska Zastava, California, 1915.
Ave Maria, Pittsburgh and McKeesport, Pa., 1944–.
Balkan, New York City.
Balkan and Eastern European American Geneological and Historical Society, San Francisco, 1964–.
Borbeni Zajedničar – Militant Fraternalist, Chicago, 1935.
Branik – The Defender, Chicago, 1898–1908.
Branitelj, Milwaukee, 1935.
Brico – The Barber, Allegheny, Pa., 1809–?
Budućnost, Detroit, 1922.
The Bulletin of the American Croatian Academic Club, Cleveland, 1965–.
California, San Pedro, Calif., 1920–3.
Chicago, Chicago, 1892–6.
Chicago – Sloboda, Chicago, 1896–1903.
Croatiapress, San Francisco, 1934–9.
Croatia Press, Cleveland and New York, 1946–.
Croatian Courier, Detroit, 1954–60.
Croatian Review – Hrvatska Smotra, Philadelphia, 1931.

146/Sources: The archives of the former Croatian Historical Research Bureau, New York, as well as numerous old issues of Croatian newspapers, almanacs, and pamphlets. The data presented are such as could be ascertained from available sources.

Croatian Review, Chicago, 1958.
Dalmacija, California, 1915.
Dalmatinska Zora, San Francisco, 1893.
Danica, Allegheny, Pa., 1894–96.
Danica – The Morning Star, Chicago, 1945–.
Danica Hrvatska, New York City, 1921–3.
Dom i Sviet – Home and World, New York City.
Domovina – The Homeland, New York City, 1915–17.
Društveni Vijesnik – Society Reporter, Chicago, 1926–8.
The Fraternalist, Cleveland, 1958–.
Glas, Youngstown, Ohio, 1917.
Glas – The Voice, Chicago, 1925–6.
Glas Istine – The Voice of Truth, Bennett, Pa., 1901–?
Glas Naroda – The Voice of the People, New York City, 1908–?
Glas Radnika, Chicago, 1920–4.
Glasnik Družbe Sv. Ćirila i Metoda, Kansas City, 1903–?
Glasnik Istine – The Herald of Truth, Chicago, 1915.
Glasnik Muslimanskog Vjerskog i Kulturnog Doma, Chicago, 1958.
Glasnik Župe Sv. Petra i Pavla, Youngstown, Ohio, 1942.
Hrvat – The Croat, Allegheny, Pa., 1903–6.
Hrvat u Americi, Rankin, Pa., 1902–3.
Hrvat u Americi, Chicago, 1927–8.
Hrvatska – Croatia, Official Organ of the Slovenian-Croatian Union, Calumet, Mich., 1905–29.
Hrvatska – Croatia (a daily), Allegheny, Pa., 1903–?
Hrvatska Republika – The Croatian Republic, Pittsburgh, 1922–?
Hrvatska Riječ – The Croatian Word, Youngstown, Ohio, 1935–7.
Hrvatska Sloboda – Croatian Liberty, Chicago, 1902–4.
Hrvatska Sloboda, Calumet, Mich.
Hrvatska Sloga, Calumet, 1915.
Hrvatska Štampa – Croatian Press, Youngstown, Ohio, 1915–17.
Hrvatska Zastava – Croatian Flag, Chicago, 1901–17.
Hrvatska Zora, Chicago, 1892–3.
Hrvatske Seljačke Novine – Croatian Peasant Newspaper, Pittsburgh, 1915.
Hrvatski Američki Sokol, Gary, Ind.
Hrvatski Borac, Chicago, 1924–?
Hrvatski Glasnik – Croatian Herald, Pittsburgh and Chicago, 1908–28.
Hrvatski Katolički Glasnik, Chicago, 1942–.
Hrvatski Katolički List, Youngstown, Ohio, 1915–?
Hrvatski List – Croatian News, New York City, 1922–3.
Hrvatski List i Danica Hrvatska, New York City, 1923–45.
Hrvatski Narod, St. Louis, Mo., 1914.
Hrvatski Narod – The Croatian Nation, Chicago, 1959–.
Hrvatski Pokret, 1932.
Hrvatski Radnički Pokret – Croatian Worker's Movement, Chicago, 1911–?
Hrvatski Radnik – Croatian Worker, Calumet, Mich., 1909.
Hrvatski Republikanac, Los Angeles, 1923.
Hrvatski Rodoljub – Croatian Patriot, Pittsburgh, 1915–19.
Hrvatski Svijet – Croatian World, New York City, 1908–56.
Hrvatski Vijesnik – Croatian Messenger, Chicago, 1924.
Hrvatsko-Amerikanske Novine, New York City.
Hrvatsko-Amerikanski Glasnik – Croatian-American Messenger, New York.
Hrvatsko Narodno Pravo – Croatian National Right, San Francisco, 1930–5.
Ilustrovani List – Illustrated News,

New York City, 1915.
Immaculate Conception, McKeesport, Pa., 1953–.
Industrialist, Detroit, 1925–?
Industrialni Radnik – Industrial Worker, Chicago, 1925.
Informativni Bulletin H.S.S., Cleveland, 1958–.
Iseljenik – The Emigrant, Pittsburgh, 1914–15.
Istrian World, Union City, N.J.
Jadran – The Adriatic, San Francisco, 1908–16.
Jedinstvo, Los Angeles, 1922.
Journal of Croatian Studies, New York, 1960–.
Jugoslaven, Detroit, 1933–40.
Jugoslaven, Los Angeles.
Jugoslavenska Zastava – South Slav Flag, Chicago, 1917.
Jugoslavenski Glasnik – The South Slav Herald, Chicago, 1905–45.
Jugoslavenski Jadran, San Francisco.
Jugoslavenski Soko, New York.
Jugoslavenski Svijet – South Slav World, New York, 1917–20.
Jugoslavija, Chicago.
Jugo-Slav Review, Chicago, 1917–20.
Junior Magazine, of the Junior Order Department of the Croatian Fraternal Union, Pittsburgh, Pa., 1916–.
The Kansas City Croatian – Kansaski Hrvat, Kansas City, 1948–?
Katolički Glasnik.
Kolo, New York, 1924–?
Kopriva, Great Falls, Mont.
Križ – The Cross, Gary, Ind., 1941–60.
Mjera.
Mladost, New York.
Napredak, Hoboken, N.J., and Allegheny, Pa., 1891–1906.
Narod, Oakland, Calif., 1925–48.
Narod – The Nation, Farrell, Pa., 1914.
Narodna Obrana – People's Defence, Duluth, Minn.
Narodni Glasnik, Chicago, 1907–.
Narodni Glasnik, Los Angeles, 1927–?
Narodni Glasnik, San Francisco, 1937.
Narodni List – National Gazette, New York City, 1898–1922.
Narodni Magazin, Milwaukee, Wis., 1925.
Naša Nada – Our Hope, Gary, Ind., 1922–.
Naša Sloga, San Francisco, ?–1906.
Naše Novine, Youngstown, Ohio.
The New Life – Novi Život, Fresno, Calif.
Nezavisna Hrvatska Država – The Independent State of Croatia, Pittsburgh, 1933–41.
Nova Domovina, Cleveland, 1908.
Nova Misao, Chicago, 1917.
Novi Hrvat, New York, 1914–15.
Novi Iseljenik.
Novi List — The New Gazette, New York, 1948–54.
Novi Rod — New Generation, Chicago, 1922–9.
Novi Svijet, Chicago, 1923–?
Novi Svijet – The New World, Allegheny, Pa., 1897–8.
Novo Vrijeme, Los Angeles, 1909–?
Organizator, Chicago, 1937.
Osa, New York, 1898–1922.
Oslobodjenje, 1918.
Osoba i Duh, Albuquerque, 1952–5.
Panslavian Review, New York, 1929–?
Pomladak Narodne Hrvatske Zajednice, Pittsburgh, 1916.
Pošta – The Post, South Chicago, 1933.
Pravda, Cleveland, 1931.
Pravda – Justice, Chicago, 1935–6.
Prognanik – The Exile, Calumet, Mich.
Pučki List — People's Gazette, Chicago.
Puco, Allegheny, Pa., 1898.

Radnička Borba, Cleveland, 1908–21.
Radnička Obrana, Duluth, Minn., 1916.
Radnička Straža, Chicago, 1907–17.
Radničke Novine, Johnstown, Pa., 1909.
Radničke Novine, Butte, Mont., 1918–20.
Radnički Glas.
Radnički Glasnik, Chicago, 1936–?
Radnik, 1898–1905.
Radnik – The Worker, Chicago, 1909–36.
Republika, Los Angeles, 1918.
Republika, Pittsburgh, 1921–5.
Rodoljub, Chicago, 1915.
Rodoljub – The Patriot, Calumet, Mich., 1902–?
Savjetnik, Chicago, 1908–15.
Slavenska Sloga, San Francisco, 1884–?
Slavenski Svijet – Slavic World, Washington, D.C., 1917.
Slavensko Jedinstvo, Butte, Mont.
Slavia, New York, 1934–9.
Slavjanska Sloboda, California.
Slavonic Bulletin, New York.
The Slavonic Monthly, New York.
Sloboda, Oakland, Calif.
Sloboda – Liberty, Chicago, 1893–?
Sloboda, Cleveland, 1905.
Sloboda, New York.
Slobodna Misao, Detroit, 1925.
Slobodna Tribuna, Seattle, 1914–25.
Sloga Hrvata.
Slovenski List, San Francisco.
Službeni Glasnik Hrvatske Zajednice Illinois, Chicago, 1915–33.
Sokol, San Jose, Calif.
Sokol, Saint Louis, 1931–5.
Sokol – American Sokol Messenger, Chicago, 1916–28.
Sokol-Republika, Los Angeles, 1922.
Sokolski Vijesnik, Chicago, 1922–4.
Sveti Rafael, New York.
Sveza – The Unity, San Francisco, 1910–?
Svijet – The World, New York, 1911–38.
Svijetlo, Chicago, 1911–14.
Svijetlo, Cleveland, 1914–18.
Svojan, 1904.
Tamburitza News, Austin, Texas, 1937–?
Trojedna Kraljevina, San Francisco, 1899–?
The Truth – Istina, Cleveland, 1957–.
United Lodges News, South Chicago, 1957–.
Vatra i Plamen, Chicago, 1901.
Velika Hrvatska – Great Croatia, McKeesport, Pa., 1903.
Vienac, Steelton, Pa.
Vijesnik Hrvatske Katoličke Zajednice, Gary, Ind., 1921–2.
Vinculum Caritatis, Organ of the League of Croatian Catholic Priests in America, New York and Cleveland, 1945–.
Vitez, Herald, Circle of Croatian Knights, Cleveland-Akron, Ohio; 1953–6.
Vjesnik Ujedinjenih Američkih Hrvata, Cleveland, 1958–65; New York, 1965–.
Volja, New York, 1911–?
Vukodlak – The Werewolf, Chicago, 1915.
Za Boga i Hrvatsku, Erie, Pa., 1952–3.
Zajedničar, Pittsburgh, 1904–.
Zdrav Razum – Common Sense, Youngstown, Ohio.
Znanje, Chicago, 1917–40.
Zora, Chicago.
Zora, Buffalo.
Zora, St. Louis.
Zora and Istrian World, Sacramento.
Život, New York.
Život – Life, Los Angeles, 1922–3.
Žumberačke Novine, 1934.

9

Croatians in Canada

NEDO PAVEŠKOVIĆ

IMMIGRATION

PRIOR TO THE FIRST WORLD WAR

It has been stated recently that two Croatian sailors were members of the crew of the expedition of Jacques Cartier and Le Sieur de Roberval in 1543. Their names are Giovanni Malogrudici (Ivan Malogrudić) from Senj, and Marino Masalarda from Dubrovnik. Allegedly, they had reached France by way of Venice and joined the expedition to the New World. The list of the crew, in which the two names appear, was published in the book *Le Sieur de Roberval* by Gagnon Gilles (Montreal, 1937).[1] A sailor called Kozulić came aboard a ship of Bodega y Quadra and visited the Canadian Pacific coast in 1779. In a sense, Kozulić may be considered among the first explorers of British Columbia. Other Croatians used to come to this part of Canada around 1800 for fishing, and fifty years later more came to British Columbia during the "Gold Rush." However, none of these remained in Canada but returned to their permanent settlements in the United States.

1/Michelle Brouillette, "Hrvati medju prvim osvajačima Kanade"/Croatians among the First Conquerors of Canada, *Zvono – La Cloche* (Montreal, October 15, 1969). Following is a list of books and articles dealing with the history of Croatian immigration to Canada: "Croats," in *The Canadian Family Tree* (prepared by the Canadian Citizenship Branch, Department of the Secretary of State, and published in cooperation with the Centennial Commission, Ottawa, 1967), 63; P. Stanković, "Croatian Origin, People of," in *Encyclopedia Canadiana*, III (1966), 159–60; Nedo Pavešković, "The Croats in Canada" (unpublished Master's Dissertation, Institute of Slavic Studies, University of Montreal, 1961), 123–4; Dr. Mladen Giunio-Zorkin, "Croatian Celebration of B.C. Centennial," in *Hrvatski Glas – Croatian Voice* (hereafter: *Croatian Voice*) (Winnipeg), July 2, 1966; Većeslav Holjevac, *Hrvati izvan domovine*/Croatians Abroad (Zagreb: Matica Hrvatska, 1967), 163.

In 1872, a Croatian sailing ship from Kostrena entered Vancouver harbor in order to load timber. One member of its crew, a sixteen-year-old seaman called George, whose family name remains unknown to us, left the ship and stayed behind on the Canadian shore in British Columbia. This young man may be considered the first Croatian immigrant to Canada.

Some Croatians came to British Columbia between 1880 and 1890, and in the latter year another sailing ship brought a group of families from Croatia to Vancouver. Kozulichs, Martinolichs, Radoslavichs, Vidulichs, and others made up the group. Soon after their arrival, these families moved from Vancouver to Ladner, where they settled. Thus, in the year 1890, real Croatian immigration into Canada began, with Ladner, British Columbia, as the first settlement.

During the 1890s the number of immigrants to British Columbia from Croatia's Adriatic shores steadily increased. In 1898, a small group of miners came from Chicago to Oyster Harbor (at present Ladysmith) on Vancouver Island looking for better wages. These men were soon followed by another group from Chicago, some of whom settled at Ladysmith and others at Cumberland, Nanaimo, and Wellington. All of these settlers had originally come from the Žumberak region of Croatia.[2]

A considerable, but unascertained, number of Croatians also immigrated to British Columbia from the United States between 1911 and 1914. Indeed, of the twenty-nine Croatian settlements established in Canada before the first world war, fourteen were in British Columbia.[3] Other Croatian immigrants from the United States moved eastward to the Northwest Territories into regions of today's provinces of Saskatchewan and Alberta. A group reached Saskatchewan in 1894, and settled at Bladworth, Hanley, and Kenaston. Two groups came to Lisgar near Prince Albert and to Regina in 1904. Also in 1904 another group came and settled at Calgary. This group named its settlement Lovinac, after the Croatian village from which they had come. A settlement at Edmonton was established in 1910. All these Saskatchewan and Alberta settlers had come from the province of Lika in Croatia, except for a small group at Lisgar, who were from Severin in the adjacent Pokuplje region.[4]

2/Joso Nikšić, "Hrvati i 100-god. British Columbia-e"/The Croatians and British Columbia's Centennial, *Croatian Voice Almanac* (Winnipeg, 1959), 96.

3/Arthur Benko Grado, *Migraciona Enciklopedija*, I: *Kanada* (Zagreb: Zaklada tiskare Narodnih Novina, 1930), 198–202.

4/*Ibid.*, 191–2, 194, 199, 208, 218.

Some Croatian farm hands came to Winnipeg a short time before 1909, and settled there and in neighboring areas, mainly in Transcona, Manitoba; however, the exact date of these settlements remains unknown.[5]

In Ontario, the first settlement was founded in Welland in 1907, the second in Schumacher in 1908, and the third in Hamilton in 1910. At about the same time the settlements in Sault Sainte Marie and Port Arthur were established.[6] During the same period, the settlements at Noranda and Rouyn, Quebec, came into existence, although the exact dates of their establishment are not known.[7]

Almost all the immigrants to inland Canada came through the United States and most were originally from villages in Croatia's interior.[8]

We may assume, on the basis of the data available, that there were 2147 Croatians in Canada in 1901 and 3891 in 1911. However, it is impossible to determine the exact number of Croatians who immigrated during this period and how many of them were in Canada at the beginning and end of the First World War.[9] At the beginning of the war, a

5/Ralph Connor, *The Foreigner* (Toronto: The Westminster Co. Ltd., 1909), 12–14, 83.

6/Stjepan Gaži, "Dvadeset godina hrvatskih seljačkih organizacija u Kanadi"/Twenty Years of the Croatian Peasant Society Organizations in Canada, and Ivan Krznarić, "Hrvati iseljenici u Kanadi i hrvatska narodna borba"/Croatian Immigrants in Canada and the Croatian National Struggle, in Glavni Odbor hrvatskih seljačkih organizacija u Kanadi (ed.), *Spomenica na dvadeset godina hrvatskih seljačkih organizacija u Kanadi*/Souvenir-Book on the Occasion of the Twentieth Anniversary of the Croatian Peasant Society in Canada (Winnipeg, 1952), 43–6, 88; Grado, *Migraciona Enciklopedija*, I, 198.

7/Pavešković, "The Croats in Canada," 202.

8/Nikšić, "Hrvati i 100-god. British Columbia-e," 98.

9/The figures for the number of Croatians in Canada are formed mainly on the basis of figures for Yugoslavs (Serbo-Croats, Croato-Serbs, Yugoslavic Group) available in Canadian statistics; cf. Canada Bureau fédéral de statistique (ed.), *Origines, pays de naissance, nationalités et langues de la population canadienne* (Ottawa, 1930), 44–5, 52, 60; Canada Dominion Bureau of Statistics, *Sixth Census of Canada: 1921. Population*, I, 356; *Seventh Census of Canada: 1931. Population*, I, 246, III; *Eighth Census of Canada: 1941. Population*, I, 222; *Ninth Census of Canada: 1951. Population*, I, table 31; *Tenth Census of Canada: 1961*, I, part II, 34/i, 35/2.

Croatians were not given a separate entry in the statistics published by the Canadian Census Division until 1921, but were lumped together with the Austrians and Hungarians or were even designated as "Americans" if they had come into Canada from the United States; cf. Grado, *Migraciona Enciklopedija*, I, 21, and Gabriel Vršić, "The Yugoslav Contribution to the Civilization of North America," unpublished Doctoral Thesis, Institute of Slavic Studies, University of Montreal, 1958, XXVIII. See also *Fourth Census of Canada: 1901. Population*, I; *Fifth Census of Canada: 1911. Population*, I; and *Sixth Census of Canada: 1921*, I, 356. In the census publication for 1921, Croatians appeared as part of the Racial Origin Group

large number of immigrants fearing difficulties as subjects or former subjects of the Austro-Hungarian Monarchy, which was then at war with Canada, left for the United States. Some of these returned after the United States went to war with Austria-Hungary, but the majority remained.[10] Moreover, at the end of the war a considerable number of immigrants, in British Columbia in particular, contracted Spanish flu and died.[11] Because of these two factors, and the fact that there was no immigration from Europe to Canada during the war, there were undoubtedly fewer Croatian settlers in Canada in 1918 than there had been in 1914.

BETWEEN THE TWO WORLD WARS

Croatian immigration in the immediate postwar years was slight; only 60 Croatians immigrated from 1919 to 1921, and the total number of Croatians in Canada in 1921 was about 5400.[12]

The subsequent heavy influx of Croatian immigrants began in 1923 and lasted until 1929. Between March 1923 and March 1929 10,060 Croatians entered Canada. The influx was slowed down by the great

"Serbo-Croats," which was subdivided as follows: "Albanian," "Croatian," "Hercegovinian," "Yugoslavic," "Montenegrin," "Serbian," and "Slovenian." In the censuses of 1931–61, these groups were combined in one larger group called "Yugoslavic." A similar situation prevails in the statistics published by the Canada Department of Citizenship and Immigration, which, from 1920 to 1925, used the term "Yugoslav" for the racial or ethnic origin of immigrants from Yugoslavia; from 1925 to 1946, the terms "Croatian," "Dalmatian," and "Yugoslavian"; and from 1950 onward "Yugoslavian." See "Immigration to Canada for the Period April, 1920 to March 31, 1925," *Annual Report Fiscal Year Ended March 31, 1950* (Ottawa, 1950), 31; "Immigration to Canada by Ethnic Origin, 1925–1958," *Annual Report Fiscal Year Ended March 31, 1959* (Ottawa, 1959), 31; and "Ethnic Origin, Age and Sex," *Quarterly Immigration Bulletin* (Ottawa, Dec. 1962), 20–1.

A careful estimate is that 60 percent of the Yugoslavs residing in Canada are Croatians. This proportion was used by the Yugoslav consulate in Montreal between the two wars, according to information given to the author in a personal interview by the late Mr. George Sigmund, notary public in Montreal, an official of the former consulate. The same figure was confirmed as probably correct in a letter to the author by the Canadian Citizenship Branch, Ottawa, September 30, 1960. A fraction quite close to 60 percent (59.51%) also was noted as the percentage of Croatians in relation to Yugoslavs in the United States in 1921; see Grado, *Migraciona Enciklopedija*, I, 24. Further substantiation for the use of this percentage can be found in Yugoslav reports on emigration.

From figures available in the entries "Iseljeništvo" and "Hrvati izvan domovine" in *Enciklopedija Leksikografskog Zavoda*, III (Zagreb, 1958), 576, 456, and Stjepan Gaži, *Croatian Immigration to Allegheny County 1882–1914* (Pittsburgh: Croatian Fraternal Union of America Printing Department, 1956), 20, it can be assumed, for example, that in 1938 58.33 percent of all Yugoslavs abroad were of Croatian derivation, and in 1958, just 60 percent.

10/Grado, 189, 191. 11/Nikšić, 98. 12/Grado, 20.

world depression, however, so that from March 1929 to March 1931 only 2080 Croatian immigrants entered Canada, compared with some 4000 between March 1927 and March 1929.[13] These immigrants came from all parts of Croatia, but a somewhat higher percentage came from the western interior.

Some settlers who became unemployed with the onset of the depression of the thirties left Canada, a certain number of these entering the United States illegally and others returning to Croatia.[14] Thus there were not more than about 12,600 Croatians in Canada in 1931.[15]

During the 1920s quite numerous settlements were established; indeed, at one time there were as many as 171. Most of these obviously comprised a small number of settlers, and were of short duration, for many of them disappeared during the depression. Better-known settlements established in this period were: Ford City near Windsor in 1923; Creighton Mine and Levack, Ontario, in 1924; Arvida and Montreal, Quebec, and Toronto, Ontario, in 1925; New Waterford, Reserve Mines and Stellarton and Sydney, Nova Scotia; Carson Mine, Kapuskasing, and Kirkland Lake, Ontario, in 1926; Taber and Wayne, Alberta in 1927. Three settlements at Allin, China City, and Dawson in the Yukon emerged during the 1920s also, but the exact date of their establishment remains unknown.[16]

The prolonged depression stopped immigration almost completely. A relatively small number of Croatians, amounting to some 2140, did immigrate into Canada between March 1931 and March 1941, but most of these were women, wives of earlier settlers. This decade was indeed the only period in which the number of male Croatian immigrants was surpassed by the number of female immigrants.[17] However, the increase in the total number of immigrants over the previous decade was negligible; the total number of Croatians in Canada in 1941 was only 12,728.[18]

13/Canada Department of Citizenship and Immigration, "Immigration to Canada from Overseas, and from U.S.A., for the Period April 1, 1925 to March 31, 1950," *Annual Report Fiscal Year Ended March 31, 1950,* 32–7; Gaži, "Dvadeset godina," *Spomenica*, 88.

14/Grado, 19–25, 206.

15/Canada Bureau of Statistics, *Seventh Census of Canada: 1931. Population*, I, 246/III; Vršić, 1; Grado, 22–5, 189.

16/Grado, 198, 202, 220; Križan Majić, "Organizacija HSS, Sydney, N.S."/The CPS Association at Sydney, N.S., *Spomenica*, 163; Anon., "Organizacija HSS, Stellarton, N.S."/The CPS Association at Stellarton, N.S., *Spomenica*, 165.

17/Canada Department of Citizenship and Immigration, *Annual Report Fiscal Year Ended March 31, 1950*, 32–7.

18/Canada Bureau of Statistics, *Eighth Census of Canada: 1941. Population*, I, 222.

AFTER THE SECOND WORLD WAR

Croatian immigration to Canada virtually ceased during the Second World War, and after the war it did not show any considerable revival until 1948; thus from March 1941 to March 1948 only some 312 Croatians entered Canada.[19] Before the new influx began, some prewar immigrants returned to Croatia.[20] Most of these soon tried to return to Canada, however, and some succeeded although no figures are available on the actual number of persons who did so. The experience gained by these "returnees" discouraged other immigrants from returning to their native land.[21]

Meanwhile, the number of new Croatian immigrants was slowly increasing, and from March 1948 to March 1951, inclusive, 5500 entered Canada, 2505 in 1951 alone.[22] Despite this increase in the number of immigrants, a comparison of population census data for 1951 with those for 1941 shows a slight increase of 114 persons, for the total number of Croatians in Canada in 1951 was 12,842, compared to 12,728 in 1941.[23]

There was a substantial influx of Croatian immigrants into Canada between 1951 and 1961. In 1957, for example, 3435 entered Canada,[24] the largest immigration for any one year up until 1968. During the decade 1951–61 natural increase must have also been high, for the

19/Canada Department of Citizenship and Immigration, *Annual Report ... 1950*, 32–7.

20/Andrija Josipović, "Kuća u Welland-u"/A Home in Welland, in *Matica iseljenički kalendar*/Matica Emigrants' Almanac (Zagreb, 1961), Ill. Josipović contends that two thousand of them returned, but the real figure was obviously higher. A number of Croatians emigrated to the United States, which explains the slight difference in the total number of Croatians in Canada in 1941 and 1951.

21/Nikšić, 105.

22/Canada Department of Citizenship and Immigration, *Annual Report ... 1959*, 31.

23/Canada Bureau of Statistics, *Ninth Census of Canada: 1951. Population*, I, table 31. See footnote 21.

24/Canada Department of Citizenship and Immigration, *Annual Report ... 1950*, 31; Letter and an Appendix to letter from Citizenship Branch, Ottawa, Sept. 30, 1960; "Origin of Post War Immigration and the Total from the United States" and "Immigration to Canada by Origin, Cal. Year – 1962," *Quarterly Immigration Bulletin* (Ottawa, Dec. 1962), 3, 24. In 1962, 1266 Croatians entered Canada; in 1963, 1320; in 1964, 1869; in 1965, 1932; in 1966, 2593; in 1967, 1493; and in 1968, 2796. See Bureau of Statistics, *Canada Year Book, 1965*, "Immigration and Citizenship," 210–11; *Canada Year Book, 1968*, "Immigration and Citizenship," 235; Department of Manpower and Immigration, *Annual Reports for the Fiscal Year 1966–1967*, Appendix 12; *idem for 1967–1968*, Appendix D; Department of Manpower and Immigration, Canada Immigration Branch, *1968 Immigration Statistics* (Ottawa, 1968), 14.

Canadian population census of 1961 showed 41,152 Croatians residing in Canada.[25] In all, 50,659 had entered Canada from 1918 to 1968 inclusive.[26]

LIFE WITHIN CROATIAN SETTLEMENTS

PRIOR TO THE FIRST WORLD WAR

Most of the first Croatian immigrants to Canada had been sailors and fishermen in their native country, and upon their arrival, quite naturally they tried to continue doing the same kind of work, generally with success. For these reasons they came to settle on the Pacific coast.[27]

The next group, which settled in the Canadian interior, consisted mainly of peasants, people of the land, who also tried to continue in their former type of work. Not many of these succeeded in turning to farming, but those who did settled in southeastern British Columbia, southwestern Alberta and the Peace River region in the north of that province, Saskatchewan, and southeastern Ontario from Cooksville to Niagara Falls and from Toronto to Windsor. Most of that group of immigrants found jobs in the mines of British Columbia, Alberta, northern Manitoba, and northern Ontario and Quebec. A sizable group secured employment in the industrial centers of southern Ontario, and still another group in forestry or in public works such as railroads and public buildings.[28]

Most of these early immigrants were males, bachelors between the ages of 21 and 40 who had emigrated for economic reasons. Only a few of them had a higher education. Feeling lonely in a new country, most of them did not easily adapt to their new surroundings. They found it difficult to learn English or French, the official Canadian languages;

25/Canada Bureau of Statistics, *Tenth Census of Canada: 1961*, I, part II, 34–1, and *Canada Year Book, 1968*, "Immigration and Citizenship," 235. At the end of 1968 there would seem to be about 55,000 Croatians in Canada, assuming the rate of natural increase to be the same as for all Canada between the last two censuses.

26/Grado, 20; Canada Department of Citizenship and Immigration, *Annual Report ... 1950*, 31, 32–7; *Quarterly Immigration Bulletin* (Dec. 1962) distributed by Canadian provinces and territories, 3, 24; *Canada Year Book, 1965*, 210–11. (In 1961 there were 26,138 Croatians in Ontario, 5136 in British Columbia, 3344 in Quebec, 3197 in Alberta, 1468 in Manitoba, 1442 in Saskatchewan, 228 in Nova Scotia, 69 in the Yukon, 68 in New Brunswick, 34 in the Northwest Territories, 6 in Newfoundland, and 2 in Prince Edward Island. It should be understood that these figures are approximate. [See *Tenth Census of Canada: 1961*, quoted above.])

27/Nikšić, 100–2, 104; Pavešković, "The Croats in Canada," 145–6.

28/Grado, 191, 192, 198–219; Nikšić, 99, 100.

consequently they did not easily succeed in approaching and communicating with native Canadians.[29] Considering the language barrier, and the fact that literate Croatians concentrated on reading their own publications (published in the United States), one can easily understand why the integration of these settlers was slow and why the number of naturalized Croatians in Canada at this time was not as large as it might have been under different circumstances.

The only Croatian social, cultural, and religious life in evidence before the end of the First World War was centered in the few lodges of the Croatian Fraternal Union (henceforth CFU), the first of which, no. 268, named "Saint Nicholas," was founded on October 21, 1903, at Ladysmith, British Columbia. The members of CFU subscribed to *Zajedničar* (Fraternalist), the CFU organ, and some of them subscribed, as well, to *Danica* (Morning Star), *Narodni List* (Peoples' Newspaper), and *Hrvatski Svijet* (Croatian People), all published in the United States.[30]

The first to adapt to the new living conditions and circumstances were the fishermen in British Columbia. Some of these became prosperous in a relatively short time, as did, for example, Franjo Cvitanović in Vancouver. A number of business-minded settlers in the interior of British Columbia were also highly successful financially.[31]

A good many of these early settlers had very unpleasant experiences during the war as subjects of a hostile nation, Austria-Hungary. Treated as enemies, they were arrested and imprisoned. Fortunately, 2000 of them were released when CFU president Joseph Marohnić intervened on their behalf with Canadian General Otter. The remaining prisoners for whom Marohnić was unable to vouch were also released eventually, but more gradually.[32]

BETWEEN THE TWO WORLD WARS

The immigrants between the wars differed from prewar immigrants in several respects. Of course, as we have seen, this immigration was larger. Furthermore, peasants from the Croatian interior outnumbered sailors

29/Pavešković, 173.

30/Nikšić, 97; Krznarić, "Hrvati iseljenici u Kanadi," 43, 46. Also on the CFU see the chapter on "The Croatian Immigrants in the United States of America" by George J. Prpić in this volume.

31/Nikšić, 97–8; Grado, 192, 198–219; Pavešković, 143, 145, 146, 171.

32/Josip Marohnić, President of CFU, Report to 12th Convention of CFU (1914?) as cited in *A Brief Historical Review of the Croatian Fraternal Union of America 1894–1949*, ed. CFU of America (Pittsburgh, 1949), 137–8.

and fishermen coming to Canada from the Adriatic coast. The percentage of semi-illiterates among the newcomers was smaller than it had been before the war. Nevertheless, among these immigrants there were only two persons with a higher education, the journalist Petar Stanković and Špiro Sinovčić, an official of Cunard Lines, and the only person with a college education was the Reverend Zvonimir Mandurić. Unfortunately, Sinovčić and Fr. Mandurić did not remain in Canada, Sinovčić returning to Croatia and Mandurić to his permanent home in the United States. The language difficulty, especially during the 1920s, continued to be the main barrier to integration and naturalization, but integration and naturalization did accelerate during the 1930s.[33]

Between the wars Croatian immigrants showed a tendency to seek employment in mines or in factories rather than on farms. Although initially they were to go to Winnipeg, the center for the farming labor force, and then to disperse to farms all over the Prairie Provinces, during the depression years, many did not even reach Winnipeg. The news of unemployment in the West received en route led them to decide to remain in Ontario and, in a smaller number, in Quebec and to try to get employment in industries in the southern or in mines in the northern regions of these provinces. During this period the existing older Croatian settlements in these two provinces therefore increased in size and new ones sprang up, in southern Ontario in particular.[34]

Naturally, social and cultural activities in this region were remarkably lively. A number of CFU lodges were growing during the 1920s. There were twenty-six lodges in all Canada by the end of 1929, most of them in southern Ontario. At the same time, a few fraternal associations were founded: two in Ontario in Sault Ste. Marie and Toronto, which assumed educational functions as well; and one in Manitoba, in Winnipeg. In addition, three choirs were founded in Ontario, in Toronto, Hamilton, and Levack. Quite a few tamburitza groups also were formed: in Niagara Falls, Ford City, Kirkland Lake, Schumacher, Timmins, Sudbury, and Sault Ste. Marie, Ontario; then in Winnipeg, with the Croatian Unity association, and finally in Regina, Saskatchewan, and Calgary and Taber, Alberta.

At the end of this decade, the Yugoslav government financed the founding of a few libraries. The Reverend Z. Mandurić in Schumacher

33/Pavešković, 149, 153, 180; Grado, 203–10, 228.

34/Gaži, "Dvadeset godina," *Spomenica*, 88–90; J. M. Gibbon, *Canadian Mosaic – The Making of a Northern Nation* (Toronto, 1938), 342; Stjepan Bradica, "Otkriće Kanade"/Discovery of Canada, *Spomenica*, 34–42.

and Franjo Cvitanović and Ivan Raić in Vancouver were in charge of the libraries, and Špiro Sinovčić was in charge of teaching English to Croatian settlers in Winnipeg and its vicinity.[35]

The year 1929 was marked by two important cultural events. In March, *Kanadski Glas – The Canadian Voice*, a weekly, and at the end of the same year an almanac of the same name, both in Croatian, appered in Winnipeg. Petar Stanković was the founder and has been editor up to the present time. The name of both publications was later changed to *Hrvatski Glas – Croatian Voice.*

The first Croatian National Home, or Hall, a center for social, political, and cultural activities, was also founded in 1929, in Hamilton, Ontario, and a year later another hall was established in the same city. In the course of the thirties, despite the harsh economic conditions of the depression, Croatians established halls in the following Ontario communities: Welland, Schumacher, Sudbury, Kirkland Lake, Windsor, Port Arthur, and Sault Ste. Marie. Halls also were established in Noranda, Quebec, in Taber, Alberta, and in Vancouver. Eight of these halls were owned by the Croatian Peasant Society of Canada.

In the same decade, nineteen chapters of the Croatian Peasant Society were founded:

1930 Toronto
1931 Cooksville, Hamilton, Welland, Windsor, Schumacher, Kirkland Lake, Sudbury, all in Ontario, and Noranda in Quebec
1932 Winnipeg, Manitoba; Montreal, Quebec; Sault Ste. Marie and Port Arthur in Ontario; Nanaimo and Vancouver in British Columbia
1933 Stellarton, Nova Scotia
1934 Iron Springs, Alberta
1937 Bourlamaque, Quebec
1938 Sydney, Nova Scotia

and six women's chapters (all in Ontario):

1934 Welland and Port Arthur
1935 Windsor and Hamilton
1936 Schumacher
1938 Sudbury

Some of the chapters kept small libraries, and within these chapters five choirs, four amateur acting groups, and twenty tamburitza groups were

35/Grado, 203–16, 222–4. See also Bradica, "Otkriće Kanade" and Petar Perković, "Za pravicu"/In the Struggle for Justice, *Spomenica*, 34–43, 71–75 on the difficulties encountered by Croatian laborers during the 1930s due to calumnies and intrigues of Yugoslav official representatives in Canada.

founded. The best-known tamburitza groups were the two in Hamilton, which were heard over a Hamilton radio station each Sunday in 1938–9. In 1938, together with the foundation of the chapter in Sudbury, a young people's athletic team, "Hrvatski Sokol" (The Croatian Falcon), was founded.[36]

Some young Croatians also became members of the Canadian Scouts. In this connection, J. M. Gibbon, in his book *Canadian Mosaic – The Making of a Northern Nation* (Toronto, 1938), mentions that Croatian was among the languages spoken by the Canadian Scouts. Gibbon also pointed out the Croatians' great appreciation of their mother tongue.[37] It is understandable then that the Croatians have resented the irregularities in the name applied to their native language and the designation for the Croatian ethnic origin in Canadian official statistics publications. Croatians of Hamilton, for example, in 1931, on the occasion of the Canadian population census, vigorously protested against the use of the term "Yugoslavian" to designate their ethnic origin and "Serbo-Croatian" their native language.[38]

AFTER THE SECOND WORLD WAR

Immigration since the Second World War has differed from that of both of the earlier periods in many ways. In the first place, the influx has, of course, been much greater. In addition, the new immigrants have come from all professions and trades, most of them being craftsmen and skilled workers and a sizable number of them well educated. Illiteracy has been almost unknown among them. These postwar immigrants naturally have not faced as many problems in the new country as did the prewar immigrants; they have learned the Canadian languages more rapidly and adjusted more readily to new living conditions. Though they still prefer to marry among themselves, the percentage of mixed marriages has been much higher than it was previously. For these reasons integration and naturalization have come sooner. Though more Croatian men than women have continued to enter Canada, the percentage of men in relation to women has not been as high as it was generally before the war.

The first postwar immigrant groups were of both sexes and of various ages. Most were part of the emigration that left Croatia in 1945. In more

36/Gaži, "Dvadeset godina"; Peter Stanković, "Naše Glasilo"/Our Organ; Pavešković, 183–7.
37/Gibbon, *Canadian Mosaic*, 418, 419.
38/Pavešković, 187–8.

recent years, immigrants have tended to be considerably younger.[39] Both groups are preponderantly political refugees.[40]

In regard to occupation and employment, one may say that the majority of the Croatian immigrants are still manual workers. This is especially true of those who immigrated between the wars, although many of them have improved their economic conditions and working responsibilities. A certain number of them are, for example, engaged in the hotel business, and many others work as foremen in their occupations; a good number are well-to-do, particularly the fishermen in British Columbia.

The most economically successful of the postwar immigrants are craftsmen who have continued to work at their own trade. College-educated immigrants in certain high-level professions, such as physicians and engineers, have in general eventually succeeded in doing the work for which they were educated, and a great many immigrants with other high qualifications have gone through Canadian universities and secured adequate positions.

It is not possible to give a systematic and complete review of the professions of Croatians in Canada, but some general statements can be made. A large proportion in British Columbia are fishermen, particulary in Vancouver, but some are farmers, planters, and fruit growers in the southeastern part of the province, and those who live in the interior are mainly miners and lumberjacks. In Alberta and Saskatchewan they tend to work in towns in the local industries, although a number are farmers in the southwestern sections of those provinces and in the Peace River region of Alberta. They are miners in the Northwest Territories. In Manitoba Croatians are employed in the mines and in a variety of industries and occupations in the towns. In northern Ontario they are, in most cases, miners residing in Schumacher, Timmins, Kirkland Lake, Larder Lake, and Sudbury; in the south and west, notably in Toronto, Hamilton, Welland, Windsor, Sault Ste. Marie, and Port Arthur, factory

39/The approximate sexual composition of Croatian immigrants in 1961 was 56 male to 44 female; in 1931 it was 70.2:19.8 and in 1921 83:17. Some figures on the age of these immigrants may be interesting also: 8 percent of the 1961 immigrants were in the range of 15–19 years, 10 percent 30–34 years, 18 percent 25–29 years, and 25 percent 20–24 years. These percentages remain almost constant for the various periods of Croatian immigration to Canada, with the exception of the 1940s. See *Quarterly Immigration Bulletin* (Dec. 1962) of the Department of Citizenship and Immigration, 20–21, table 8; *Population Census: 1931*, 296, table 31; and *Population Census: 1961*, I, part II, 35–2; and *Origines, pays de naissance, nationalités et langues de la population canadienne* (Ottawa, 1930), 68, 70 of the Canada Bureau of Statistics.

40/Nikšić, 100–5.

workers and craftsmen predominate; and in the Hamilton area quite a few are still engaged in farming. As in Ontario, Croatians in northern Quebec are miners in mining centers such as Bourlamaque, Malartic, Noranda, Rouyn, and Val d'Or. In the south of the province, that is, in Montreal, they are mainly factory workers or craftsmen. In Nova Scotia they are generally miners and factory workers in Sydney and New Waterford.

There are, of course, in many Canadian towns and cities, such as Toronto, Vancouver, and Montreal, a certain number of Croatians engaged in various private enterprises, and some with college education in various professions, especially engineering.

Except for a few settlements in Nova Scotia, Croatian settlements in Canada are found only in the six largest provinces, the greatest number being in Ontario and British Columbia. The total number of settlements in Canada is uncertain, but there are eighty-one that are fairly well known. The locations of the better known ones are listed below.

In British Columbia, there are twenty-two settlements. The largest is in Vancouver, and the others are at Chemainus, Cumberland, Duncan, Kamloops, Ladner, Ladysmith, Nanaimo, Nelson, New Westminster, Oliver, Penticton, Port Alberni, Prince George, Prince Rupert, Princeton, Richmond, Smithers, South Wellington, Summerland, Trail, and Victoria.

Alberta has eleven settlements, at Calgary, Coaldale, Edmonton, Lethbridge, Widewater, Iron Springs, Leader, Mercoal, Picture Bute, Roycroft, and Taber; Saskatchewan has six, at Bladworth, Hanley, Kenaston, Saskatoon, Lisgar, and Regina; and Manitoba has five, in Flin Flon, Transcona, Selkirk, Winnipeg, and St. Boniface.

Ontario has twenty-eight settlements, of which eight may be termed large: in Hamilton, Port Arthur, Sault Ste. Marie, Schumacher and Timmins, Sudbury, Toronto, Welland, and Windsor. Somewhat smaller, but still significant, settlements are found at Kirkland Lake, Kitchener, Larder Lake, London, and Ottawa. The other known settlements are at Bothwell, Cooksville, Creighton, Elliot Lake, Fort William, Garson, Geraldton, Grimsby, Huntsville, Levack, Port Colborne, Sarnia, South Porcupine, St. Catharines, and Wawa.

Quebec has ten settlements, at Arvida, Bourlamaque, Chicoutimi, Malartic, Montreal, Noranda, River Bond, Rouyn, Schefferville, and Val d'Or; and Nova Scotia has four, at New Waterford, Reserve Mines, Stellarton, and Sydney.

The largest settlements are in Toronto, comprising some 12,000 settlers in 1961; Vancouver, including New Westminster and Ladner, with some 4000; the Welland area, with around 3000; Hamilton and its surrounding area, with somewhat more than 3000; Windsor, with 1600; Schumacher and Timmins, with 1500; Montreal, with around 1300; Sudbury and its neighboring region, with 1000; and Sault Ste. Marie, with 900.[41] Religious, social, cultural, and athletic activities and entertainment naturally are most developed in these larger settlements.

Religious activities are, of course, centered in the churches within parishes. Some Croatian Catholic churches have been erected, or buildings purchased to be used as churches, the first in Windsor in 1950. In Toronto, the old church purchased in 1958 was destroyed by fire in 1962, but an impressive new structure was erected in its place in 1965. A church was erected in Hamilton in 1958, and a provisional church building acquired in Sault Ste. Marie in 1963. A church building was bought in Montreal in 1964, and a church was built in Vancouver in 1968. As of December 1968, there were six Croatian Catholic parishes and three missions, the latter in Calgary, Winnipeg, and London. There are ten Croatian Catholic priests in Canada and thirteen Croatian Dominican sisters, who are now directing three humanitarian institutions in Sherbrooke, Quebec: a Retarded Children's Centre, Centre Notre-Dame de l'enfant, that is, a home for emotionally disturbed children, and an Aged Ladies' Centre.[42]

The centers of social, cultural, and recreational activity are Croatian Homes, or halls, of which there are seventeen in all. Two are in Hamilton; two each in Toronto, Welland, and Windsor; one each in Montreal, Kirkland Lake, Port Arthur, Sault Ste. Marie, Schumacher, Sudbury, Sydney, Welland, and Vancouver. Four of these halls belong to the local Croatian Catholic parishes, one each in Hamilton, Montreal,

41/Pavešković, 197–239.

42/Pavešković, 213–31; Anon., "Nova hrvatska katolička župa bl. Nikole Tavelića, Montreal, Kanada"/The New Croatian Catholic Parish of the Blessed Nicholas Tavelić, Montreal, Canada, *Hrvatski Kalendar* (Chicago, 1964), 157–8; "Nova hrvatska katolička župa Majke Božje zaštitnice putnika Sault Ste. Marie, Ont., Kanada"/The New Croatian Catholic Parish of the Mother of God the Protector of Travelers in Sault Ste. Marie, Ont., Canada, *ibid.*, 188–90; Editorial, "Prva velika hrvatska katolička crkva u Kanadi"/The First Croatian Catholic Church in Canada, *Croatian Voice* (Winnipeg), Oct. 23, 1965; Francis H. Eterovich (ed.), *Biographical Directory of Scholars, Artists, and Professionals of Croatian Descent in the United States and Canada* (2nd ed., 1964–5; Chicago, 1965), 4, 42, 131, 137; Archevêché de Montréal (ed.), *Le Canada Ecclésiastique 1964* (Montréal: Librairie Beauchemin Limitée, 1964), 186, 363, 378, 420, 543, 1307, 1417, 1489; "Hrvatske župa i misije u Kanadi"/Croatian Parishes and Missions in Canada, *Hrvatski Kalendar* (Chicago: "Danica," 1969), 23.

Toronto, and Windsor. The Croatian Peasant Society (CPS) is chartered owner of seven of these homes, owner of two more, and joint owner of two of the remaining.[43]

CPS comprises twenty-six active and five less active chapters, mainly for men, and in addition there are nine women's clubs affiliated with some of the chapters. The CPS organ is the weekly *Hrvatski Glas – Croatian Voice*, published in Winnipeg.

In addition to CPS and its chapters, there are other Croatian associations in Canada. The Croatian Fraternal Union (CFU), with headquarters in Pittsburgh, has around 10,000 members and sixty-six lodges in Canada, most of which have Youth Nests and sports sections, with emphasis on bowling. *Zajedničar*, a weekly published in Pittsburgh, is the organ of the Union.

The Croatian Catholic Union (CCU), with headquarters in Gary, Indiana, has thirty-four lodges and 1548 members in Canada. Its organ is *Naša Nada* (Our Hope).

United Croatians in Canada (UCC) counts up to seventeen chapters and periodically publishes its own organ, *Nezavisna država Hrvatska* (Independent State of Croatia), in Toronto. A small monthly newspaper, *Naš Put* (Our Way), is also published there.

Savez Hrvatskih Društava u Kanadi (The Federation of Croatian Societies in Canada) consists of seven chapters. The Montreal chapter publishes a periodical *Jadran* (The Adriatic). The group of Croatians in Montreal publishes a fortnightly *Zvono – La Cloche* (The Bell).

The Catholic parish in Windsor sponsors three small associations of religious character, and publishes a small mimeographed weekly, *The Bulletin*. The parish in Toronto also publishes a small weekly called *The Bulletin*.

Besides these groups there are other, local, Croatian associations. The better known are the "Katarina-Zrinska" women's association and the "Erich Lisak" association in Toronto. Toronto has also the "Croatian Credit Union," which publishes a small mimeographed bulletin, *Vjesnik* (The Messenger) once every two weeks. In London, Ontario, there is

43/*Spomenica*, 113–65; Nikšić, 105; Stjepan Margetić, "Svečana proslava otvorenja H. N. Doma"/The Croatian Hall Opening Ceremony, *Croatian Voice*, Oct. 10 and 30, 1960; Juraj Krnjević, "Domovi hrvatskih seljačkih organizacija u Kanadi ponos su svega hrv. naroda"/CPS Halls in Canada Should Make Us All Proud, *Croatian Voice*, Oct. 24, 1960; Matt Janjac, "Svečano otvorenje H. N. Doma u Wellandu"/Opening Ceremonies of the Croatian Hall in Welland, *Croatian Voice*, Nov. 5, 1966; Anon., "Nova hrvatska katolička župa ..."/A New Croatian Catholic Parish ..., *Hrvatski Kalendar* (1964), 157–8; Paveškovič, 198, 241.

a club called "Zagreb," and in Calgary one called "King Zvonimir," in which Croatian Muslims are especially active.[44]

Within these associations, mainly within the CPS chapters, numerous choirs, dancers' groups, and kolo and tamburitza (a native stringed instrument) groups are organized. There are eleven better-known choirs, seven kolo groups, and twenty-four tamburitza groups. Through these musical organizations Croatian culture expresses itself in Canada and makes its contribution to Canadian culture.

CONTRIBUTION TO CANADA

FOLKLORE AND FOLK MUSIC

Many performances of folk music, folk songs, folk dances, and plays are presented in the national halls. There are also displays of tools and national dishes, and portrayals of national customs.

Special pageants and celebrations are held in the halls on the occasion of particular Croatian anniversaries. Prominent Canadians have often attended these, including representatives of Parliament, members of the federal, provincial, and municipal governments, members of the Catholic Church hierarchy, and representatives of other ethnic groups in Canada. Such dignitaries are drawn particularly to the pageants held at the conventions of the Croatian Peasant Society once every three years in southern Ontario, usually in the Croatian National Home in Toronto. This performance also attracts the attention of the Toronto press, radio, and television.

Groups of chapters of CPS in northern Ontario and Quebec, in southern and western Ontario, and in the vicinity of Vancouver also organize an outdoor pageant known as "Hrvatski dan" (Croatian Day). On these occasions one may hear tamburitza players and folk singers, see dancers in colorful national costumes, and enjoy special meals prepared according to Croatian traditions. Many Canadian dignitaries and other Canadians attend these celebrations.

Aside from performing within the community, Croatian groups appear and perform in public with other Canadian ethnic groups. For

44/This information was gathered between 1960 and the end of 1965 from the following Croatian newspapers and almanacs published in Canada and the United States: *Hrvatski Glas – Croatian Voice*, weekly and almanac (Winnipeg); *Nezavisna država Hrvatska* and *Naš Put* (Toronto); *Danica*, a weekly, and *Hrvatski Kalendar* (Chicago); *Naša Nada* (Gary, Ind.); *Zajedničar* (Pittsburgh). Because most of the information was obtained from many short notices and advertisements, it is virtually impossible to cite the sources in detail in an essay as brief as the present one.

example, singers, dancers, and tamburitza players perform in the yearly Festival of Neo-Canadians in Montreal, where, too, Croatian youth appear in national costumes; performers participate in the Toronto Exhibition, the Toronto International Festival, and the International Freedom Festival at Windsor, Ontario; they appear also at the Easter Parade and the Pacific National Exhibition and Folk Festival in Vancouver.[45]

MUSIC

A few Croatians have made significant individual contributions to the musical culture of Canada. Hilda Irek, a gifted child pianist, was born in Croatia in 1956. She and her parents settled in Toronto for a time and then moved to California in the fall of 1965. She began to play the piano when she was four years old, and to compose when she was six. She has appeared frequently on television in Toronto, Hamilton, and Buffalo, and has given performances in Sudbury, Hollywood, and at the World's Fair in New York. She has won several prizes, among them the First Prize at the Kiwanis Music Festival in Toronto, and is acknowledged to be an extraordinarily gifted child and a musical prodigy.[46] Another exceptionally gifted pianist is Andriana Kalanj of Van-

45/Gaži, "Dvadeset godina," 110–12; Nikšić, 105–8; Paveškovič, 224–5, 240–2; *Croatian Voice Almanac* (Winnipeg), 1964, 89 and 1965, 133-5, 137, 158, 206 (these two editions of *Croatian Voice Almanac* comprise photographs and information on Croatian folklore in Canada); letter from Dan Campbell, Minister of Municipal Affairs, B.C., to the CPS chapter in Vancouver, Nanaimo, and Victoria, June 1965; undated extract from a letter to the CPS chapter in Vancouver from E. B. (Ted) Sexsmith, regional liaison officer, Canadian Citizenship Branch, Vancouver; undated "Greetings" from Wm. G. Rathie, mayor of Vancouver, to CPS chapter, Vancouver; letters and greetings cited in *Souvenir Programme Eighth Croatian Day ... Sponsored by Croatian Peasant Societies (chapters) "Ivan Gundulić" and "Ban Jelačić" Sunday, June 13, 1965, in Vancouver, B.C., Canada* (Vancouver, 1965), 7, 9, 10. Souvenir programs such as this have been published by CPS chapters in Vancouver and Nanaimo each year since 1958 on the occasion of the Croatian Day celebrations in Vancouver in June.

A Croatian folklore group appeared with the other ethnic groups at Dominion Square and Parliament Hill in Ottawa to participate in the celebration of Dominion Day, July 1, 1965.

46/Leon Kossar, "29 Ethnic Groups Honor Prime Minister. She Composed Her Own Tribute," *The Telegram* (Toronto), Nov. 18, 1961, 32; Bill Brown, "Pint Sized Pianist," *Weekend Magazine*, XII, no. 24 (Toronto, 1962), 6, 8–9; John Kraglund, "Hilda, 6, Is Offered Hollywood Contract," *The Globe and Mail* (Toronto), June 27, 1962; Jane Becker, "Profile: The Life and Times of a Child Prodigy," *Maclean's* (Toronto), Feb. 10, 1962, 52; Anon., "4-Year-Prodigy Girl Plays Piano, Composes," *Toronto Daily Star*, July 26, 1962, 29; [Bob Blackburn] "Bob Blackburn's Column," *The Telegram* (Toronto), Sept. 6, 1963, 40; "Toronto Child Pianist to Play Own Work," *Toronto Daily Star*, May 22, 1965, 70; Fra Častimir Majić, "Hrvati na svjetskoj veleizložbi u New Yorku,"/Croatians at the World Fair in New York, *Hrvatski Kalendar* (1965), 106, 108, 109.

couver who, as a young child, won first prize in a piano contest in Vancouver in 1958.[47]

EDUCATION

Canadian Croatians have made contributions as teachers in many fields. Some are distinguished teachers of music and allied arts as well as performers. Vlado Miloslavić teaches music in the Canadian Navy, Emilia Zaharia teaches at the Royal Conservatory in Toronto,[48] and Nenad Lhotka was ballet-master of the Royal Ballet of Winnipeg, and now has his own school of ballet in the same city.[49]

Seven Croatians are teaching at Canadian universities: Mladen Vranić, associate professor of physiology at the University of Toronto, who has published many research articles in scholarly journals; Augustine Filipović, sculpture lecturer at the University of Toronto; Stjepan Krešić, associate professor of Classic Languages and Literature at the University of Ottawa; Milivoj Mostovac, associate professor of Constitutional Law and Constitutional History at the University of Ottawa; Emil Primorac, lecturer in economics at the University of Western Ontario; Fr. Joseph Zaufar, chemistry professor at the Royal Military College, St. Jean, Quebec; and Krešimir Krnjević, outstanding medical expert in the physiology of the lymphatic system, who is professor of research in anaesthesia at McGill University in Montreal.[50]

In teaching and related areas we might also mention Veljko Duboković, a high school teacher in Trail, British Columbia, who is engaged in research on the history of seamanship.[51] Neda Leipen-Madirazza, Associate Curator of the Greek and Roman Department, Division of Art and Archaeology, Royal Ontario Museum in Toronto, does research from time to time in the United States and in Europe and is a contributor to the *Quarterly* of the Royal Ontario Museum.[52]

ARTS, LITERATURE, AND JOURNALISM

In the arts and literature in Canada there are also some prominent Croa-

47/Nikšić, 107.

48/Margetić, "Svečana proslava"; Pavešković, 212.

49/Stanković, "Naše Glasilo"; Eterovich, *Biographical Directory*, 135.

50/Interview with A. Filipović, Toronto, Sept. 4, 1962; Eterovich, *Biographical Directory*, 49, 50, 69, 80, 115, 135.

51/Eterovich, *op. cit.*, 18; see *New Croatia* (London), Mar.-Apr. 1960, and *Croatian Voice*, June 20, 1960: Duboković's treatise, "The History of Seamanship," appeared in *The Rudder*, no. 10 (New York, 1960), and, as a result, Duboković was appointed director of an international expedition engaged in salmon migration research.

52/Eterovich, *Biographical Directory*, 54; Pavešković, 212.

tian names. Sculptors Ivan Meštrović and Augustine Filipović are major figures. The former, although he never lived in Canada, helped to enrich her culture with the marble relief, *Canadian Phalanx*, created for the War Memorial in Ottawa, and with his figure of a Croatian peasant woman which belongs to the Art Gallery of Ontario in Toronto.[53]

Augustine Filipović, sculptor and painter, member of the Ontario Association of Art and the Sculpture Association of Canada, was born in 1931 and is now living in Toronto. He studied at the Academy of Plastic Arts in Zagreb and at the Accademia di Belle Arti di Roma, where he also taught. His main field is sculpture, but he has exhibited both sculpture and paintings on nine occasions in Rome and once in Stockholm. In 1958, in Rome, he won an international award, the "Roma Patria." In 1959, his reputation established, he came to Canada, and since his arrival he has had successful showings several times in Toronto and Hamilton. His works are exhibited among those of Butler and Moore in Toronto's Art Gallery, and some of his sculptures are in the National Gallery in Ottawa. In November 1960, with financial aid from the Canada Council, Filipović founded a post-graduate art school in Toronto; there he makes his home, lecturing at the University of Toronto as well.

Filipović's creative activity has met with an attentive and, on the whole, highly appreciative critical response. Art critics Robert Fulford and Paul Duval consider his works interesting and a valuable contribution to the arts in Toronto and to the development of Canadian sculpture. He has been commended by Henry Moore and is accepted as one of Canada's leading young sculptors.[54]

Two Croatians have made noteworthy contributions to Canadian literature. The first, Alan Horić, is a Muslim born in the province of Bosnia in 1923. He holds a master of arts degree in Slavic literatures, and is a poet and member of the Canadian Writers' Association. He has lived in Montreal since 1951. Horić's poems are written in French and have been appearing in the literature sections of French-Canadian newspapers and in literary reviews. His principal creative work comprises

53/Vršić, "The Yugoslav Contribution," LXVI.

54/Marie Flanagan, "300 Invitation Cards for an Exhibition with Correct Birth Place," quoted by "K" in *Hrvatska Revija*, II–III (Buenos Aires, 1960), 241; "You Can See Chips Flying When This Group Gets Together," *Toronto Daily Star*, Mar. 21, 1960 and Apr. 10, 1961; Robert Fulford in *Toronto Daily Star*, Mar. 26, 1960, and Earl Duval in *The Telegram* (Toronto), Apr. 9, 1960, both quoted "K" in *Hrvatska Revija*, II–III (1960), 241 (Mr. "K," however, does not mention either pages or titles of respective papers and articles); Mario Rivosecchi, "Augustin Filipović," *Hrvatska Revija*, II (1959), 233–4; Enzzo Maizza, "Augustin Filipović," *Hrvatska Revija*, IV (1956), 378–81; Pearl McCarthy, in *The Globe and Mail* (Toronto), Mar. 26, 1960, quoted by "K," *Hrvatska Revija*, I–II (1960), 241; W. Dorroch, "Hart House Was Gay with Spanish Music," *Toronto Daily Star* (Social Whirl Section), Feb. 13, 1961; interview with A. Filipović, Toronto, Sept. 4, 1962.

three published collections of poems: *L'Aube assassinée* (Montreal, 1957), with twenty-one poems; *Nemir duše* (Madrid, 1959), with eighteen poems; and *Blessure au flanc du soleil* (Montreal, 1962), with twenty-seven poems. The publication of the last collection was sponsored by the Canada Council. Horić's poems also appear occasionally in *Amérique française*, a literary revue published in Montreal; and two poems were printed in *Livre d'or de la poésie française contemporaine* (Paris, 1962), and six in the anthology *Littérature du Québec*, edited by G. Robert (Montreal, 1964).[55] His fifteen poems appeared under the title "Atomises" in the anthology *Ecrits du Canada français* (Montreal, 1965).

On the whole, Canadian literary critics have received Horić's work favorably.[56] In 1957, J. G. Pilon pointed out that Horić was the only Canadian immigrant poet who had written successfully in one of Canada's official languages. Even more noteworthy is Pilon's assessment of that success; because Horić has encountered a number of cultures and civilizations in his lifetime, he has brought, according to Pilon, a certain freshness to Canadian poetry.[57]

Nada Stipković is also a poet. She has written a motion picture scenario for the National Film Board, and published her first collection of poetry, *Lignes*,[58] in 1961.

Journalism has also attracted Croatians. The Croatian contribution of Petar Stanković to the mosaic of the Canadian ethnic press is noteworthy. He is the founder and, since 1929, editor-in-chief of *Hrvatski Glas – Croatian Voice*, a weekly and almanac published in Winnipeg, and is a member of long standing of the Winnipeg Press Club and Ethnic Press Federation of Canada.[59]

55/Eterovich, *Biographical Directory*, 33; interview with A. Horić, Montreal, Apr. 14, 1963; George J. Prpić, *The Croatian Publications Abroad after 1939, a Bibliography* (Cleveland: The Soviet and East European Institute, John Carroll University, 1969).

56/Andrée Maillet, "Alan Horic un vrai poète," *Le Petit Journal* (Montréal), Oct. 20, 1957, 93; Clement Marchand, "L'Aube assassinée," *Le Bien Public* (Trois-Rivières), Oct. 18, 1957, 23; F. St. Martin, "Aspects d'une poésie sociale," *La Presse* (Montréal), Oct. 26, 1957, 78; Roger Duhamel, "C'est sûrement la poésie qui emporte parmi nos jeunes écrivains ...," *La Patrie* (Montréal), Nov. 10, 1957, 26; Gilles Marcotte, "Poésie d'aujourd'hui ...," *La Presse*, Feb. 16, 1963, 8; André Renaud, "Blessure au flanc du ciel," *Le Droit* (Ottawa), Dec. 22, 1962. It is also interesting to note the comment of a Croatian critic: Ante Kadić, "Hrvatsko emigrantsko pjesništvo,"/Croatian Poets Abroad, *Hrvatska Revija*, IV (1960), 454–5.

57/Jean-Guy Pilon, "Début de saison," *Journal Musical Canadian* (Montréal), Dec. 1957, 3.

58/Nada Stipković, *Lignes* (Montréal: Beauchemin, 1961); Jean Menard, "Nada Stipković," *Le Droit*, Oct. 28, 1961.

59/Anon., "Dvogodišnja konvencija stranojezične štampe"/Biannual Foreign Press Convention, *Croatian Voice*, June 22, 1959.

POLITICS

The participation of Croatians in Canadian politics is slight. Joseph Mavrinac, Jr., of Schumacher, ran as a candidate for the Progressive-Conservative party in the 1963 federal elections, Andrew Mihalich was an official delegate representing the Hamilton New Party Ethnic Club at the founding convention of the Canadian New Democratic Party in Ottawa on August 1, 1961, and Dr. M. G. Zorkin ran as a candidate for the Liberal party in the 1968 federal elections.[60]

SPORTS

The Croatian contribution to Canadian sports is considerable. There are seven soccer teams: in Calgary, Hamilton, London, Sudbury, Toronto, Windsor, and Vancouver. With the exception of the one in Sudbury, "Adria," all bear the name "Croatia."[61] Also Ante Kosta, the soccer ace of Split's Hayduk, Yugoslavia's First Division, played for Montreal's "Cantalia."[62]

There are a number of other Croatian sports figures in Canada. Frank Mahovlich, who has an outstanding record as a member of the Toronto Maple Leafs hockey team, at his best was rated with the hockey "Stars" of North America.[63] Ken Magličić, formerly with the Notre Dame football team, was an outstanding member of the Winnipeg Blue Bombers.[64] Željko Pokupec of Hamilton is a well-known member of a Canadian cycling team.[65] Jack Stulac from Toronto was, for a time, a well-known Canadian hammer thrower.[66] George Chuvalo of Toronto was the Canadian heavy-weight boxing champion.[67] Mladen Peroš of Schefferville,

60/Anon., short notice on Mavrinac in *Croatian Voice*, Dec. 25, 1957, 19; interview with the late George Sigmund, Montreal, Apr. 10, 1963; "Ethnic Delegate Seeks Party Role for Immigrants," *The Montreal Star*, Aug. 1, 1961, 25. The author has personal knowledge of Dr. Zorkin's candidacy in 1967.

61/Zvonimir Peroš, *Sport i Hrvati*/Sports and Croats (Buenos Aires: Frederico Grote, 1954), 21; *Croatian Voice Almanac* (Winnipeg), 1964, 185, and 1965, 206; Petar Listes, "Zadnja pobjeda Hamiltonske Croatiae"/Recent Victory of "Croatia" from Hamilton, *Croatian Voice*, Nov. 20, 1965.

62/"Cantalia Star," *The Ottawa Citizen*, June 2, 1961 (photograph and short caption).

63/T. Alderman, "Big Frank Mahovlic: Maple Leafs' Reluctant Dragon," *Liberty* (Toronto, Jan. 1961), 33; Anon., "Voici les equipes d'étoiles de la LHN – La Première," *La Presse*, June 15, 1963, 25.

64/A short notice on Magličić and his photograph in *Croatian Voice*, Nov. 13, 1965.

65/Anon., "Nešto o našim sportašima u emigraciji"/Croatian Sportsmen Abroad, *Croatian Voice*, Oct. 2, 1961.

66/Anon., photograph of Štulac with short caption in *Naš Kalendar* (Toronto, 1958), 142.

67/Anon., "Chuvalo Stops Forte in 2nd," *The Ottawa Journal*, May 16, 1966,

Quebec, was one of six Canadians who received from the hands of Queen Elizabeth II a decoration which he earned as a distinguished boy scout.[68] Finally, Anton Furlany, of Toronto, was active in the Canadian Volleyball Association as the editor of *Canadian Volleyball Annual and Rule Book*, and a referee in chief.[69]

INDIVIDUAL CONTRIBUTIONS IN VARIOUS FIELDS

Individual Croatians have contributed to Canadian life in a variety of activities. Stjepan Bradica of Hamilton, former president of CPS, and his successor, Ivan Krznarić Sr. of Schumacher, should be mentioned in view of their work in the organization and preservation of CPS chapters, which, as we have noted, own a considerable number of Croatian National Halls and which have been contributing for years to Croatian culture through the activities of choirs, dance groups, and Canadian tamburitza groups. In acknowledgment of the efforts of Croatians in Canada in peace and war, Bradica was decorated by King George VI.[70]

Of some interest is the modest but unique contribution of Nicholas Žunić Sr., from Winnipeg, who, having lost his sight in a mine explosion in northern Manitoba in 1931, turned to handicrafts: in knitting small items like purses he has earned recognition as one of the best Canadian craftsmen in this domain.[71] His son, Nicholas Žunić Jr., an architectural engineer, was chairman of Manitoba's Chamber of Commerce and vice-chairman of the Manitoba Architects' Association. In April 1964, he was appointed member of the Board of Directors of the Central Mortgage and Housing Corporation.[72] A very successful travel agent, Joseph M. Torbar, the secretary-general of the Universal Organization of Travel Agents Associations in Montreal for the year 1967, deserves special mention also.

Finally we should take note of the numerous activities of Mladen Giunio Zorkin, LL.D., president of M. G. Zorkin & Co. Ltd., Nanaimo, B.C., commercial and industrial brokerage, development and investment brokers, property management, real estate, mortgages, insurance,

21; Moca, "Terrell i Čuvalo: 1 Studenoga u Toronto"/Terrell and Chuvalo on November 1 in Toronto, *Danica*, Sept. 29, 1965.

68/Anon., short notice (information) in *Croatian Voice*, Aug. 4, 1960.

69/Anton H. Furlani (ed.), *Canadian Volleyball Annual Rule Book 1963* (Toronto: The Canadian Volleyball Association, 1962), 1, 3, 51.

70/Pavešković, 237.

71/Anon., short notices on Žunić in *Croatian Voice*, May 4, 1959, and Nov. 7, 1960. Žunić was for a time cribbage champion of Canada and the United States.

72/Short notice with photograph in *Croatian Voice Almanac* (1946), 127; Anon., short notice in *Croatian Voice*, May 18, 1959 and April 27, 1964.

and appraisals. Zorkin, a first president of the Nanaimo Real Estate Board, was a president of the Real Estate Boards of British Columbia and a vice-president of Canada's Association of Real Estate Boards. He was the Canadian representative to three congresses of the International Real Estate Federation which has its headquarters in Paris. Credit goes to Zorkin for his contribution to establishing a Real Estate Chair at the University of British Columbia in Vancouver in 1960, the first such in the Commonwealth.[73]

ECONOMY

The major Croatian contribution to the Canadian economy is found in west coast fishing, a comparatively smaller one in mining, industry, forestry, and farming, and a very slight one in canal digging.

As noted earlier, the first Croatian immigrants were fishermen who settled in British Columbia and followed anew their traditional calling. Thus, the history of the Croatian contribution in fishing began with the arrival and settlement of the early immigrants. However, there were no significant achievements in this area before 1925, when a considerable number of Croatians started work in Canadian fisheries with Japanese fishermen. They gained many new ideas from the Japanese and thus improved their fishing abilities and skills brought from their homeland. These fishermen were quite industrious, working more than twenty hours a day at times during the fishing season, and in the course of a short time, by their diligence and frugality, they amassed enough funds to buy fishing craft, often by co-operative means with up to ten fishermen owning one craft. As J. Nikšić states, thanks to the efforts of Norwegian, Indian, and Croatian fishermen, the United Fishermen and Allied Workers Union was established in Vancouver.

During the Second World War, when the Japanese were moved to the interior of Canada, the Norwegians and Croatians bought their fishing craft and tools. Croatian fishermen were thus given a chance to play a greater role in the Canadian fishing industry.[74] Nikšić says that these Croatian fishermen owned ninety large and forty small fishing vessels

73/Anon., "TC-Man of the Month, Mladen Zorkin – Success in a Decade," *Trade and Commerce, a Monthly Report on Western Industry* (Winnipeg, June 1960), 14; Jack Haskett, "Artisan Metro Mart a Canadian First," *Trade and Commerce* (a reprint from March 1962 issue); Anon., short notices on Zorkin in *Croatian Voice*, May 4, 1959 and Nov. 7, 1960; Anon., *Croatian Voice*, Oct. 23, 1965 and May 7, 1966. Zorkin is also president of the CPS Pacific league comprising CPS chapters on the Canadian and American Pacific coast, and in 1965 he was elected vice-president of CPS in Canada.

74/Nikšić, 100, 102, 104.

in 1958.[75] According to an article of Ivan Pribanić, "Naši u izgradnji zapadne Kanade" (Our People in the Building of Western Canada) in *Jedinstvo* (Toronto, 1955), it is thought that one out of three Canadian fishermen on the Pacific coast is of Croatian origin, and that these fishermen, along with the Norwegians, are an important factor in the Canadian west coast fishing industry.[76] However, success did not come without sacrifice and loss, sometimes tragic loss, since many fishermen have lost their lives in the Pacific.[77]

Second only to fishing is the field of mining. In proportion to their number, Croatians have made their greatest contribution to mining in the following areas:

Aluminum: Arvida, Que.; Kitimat, B.C.
Coal: New Waterford, N.S.; Brule Mines, Cadomin, Fernie, Mercoal, Moutain, and Wayne, Alta.; Blackburn, Copper Mountain, Cranbrook, Ladysmith, Nanaimo, Premier Mine, Rossland, and Wedgewood, B.C.
Copper: Bourlamaque and Val d'Or, Que.; Nelson, Princeton, and Stewart, B.C.
Gold: Bourlamaque, Malartic, Rouyn, and Val d'Or, Que.; Schumacher, Ont.; Britannia Mine, Copper Mountain, and Stewart, B.C.; Allin, China City, and Dawson, Yukon Territory
Nickel: Creighton Mine, Garson and Levack near Sudbury, Ont.; Thomson, Man.
Silver: Britannia Mine, B.C.
Quarries: Allenby and Granite Falls, B.C.[78]

Of course, there were several accidental deaths among the first Croatian miners; the first vicitims were Juraj Berdik, Bill Keserić, Janko Bulić, and Loje Jurkas, who died in a mine explosion in 1915.[79]

Contributions have also been made in the following industries:

Automobiles: Ford City and Windsor, Ont.
Cotton: Welland, Ont.
Foundries: New Waterford and Sydney, N.S.; Hamilton, Ont.; Trail, B.C.
Iron and Pipes: Sault Ste. Marie and Welland, Ont.
Nickel: Levack, Garson, and Sudbury, Ont.
Oil Refinery: Calgary, Alta.

75/*Ibid.*
76/See p. 54.
77/Nikšić, 101–4. According to the *Croatian Voice* of March 31, 1961, the most recent victims were two sons of Joseph Katnić from Vancouver, who together with their fishing craft, "Northview," went to the bottom of the Pacific on February 23, 1961.
78/Grado, 190–220; Gaži, "Dvadeset godina," 86–100; Gibbon, *Canadian Mosaic*, 323, 324; Vršić, "The Yugoslav Contribution," XLVIII; Nikšić, 97–104; Pavešković, 235–6.
79/Nikšić, 97.

Paper: Arvida and River Bend, Que.; Sault Ste. Marie, Ont.; Ocean Falls and Powell River, B.C.

In forestry, contributions have been made in lumber loading, sawmills, and factories at Rouyn, Que.; Port Arthur, Ont.; Campbell River, Ocean Falls, and Swift Creek, B.C. Croatians have been lumberjacks or diggers in forests in Edmonton, Legal, and Wayne, Alta.; and in Canal Flats, Cranbrook, Crows' Nest, Nelson, Prince George, and Revelstoke, B.C.

Farming has benefitted from Croatian participation in the Hamilton region in Ontario; at Avonlea, Colier, Hanley, Kenaston, Leask, Lisgar, Regina, and Truax in Saskatchewan; at Lovinac (near Calgary), Drumheller, Edmonton region, Edson, Rob, Roycroft, and Taber, Alberta; at Cassaday, Chemainus, Fraser River Valley, Okanagan Valley, Oliver, Penticton, Prince George, Smithers, Summerland, Trail, and Wellington in British Columbia.

Croatians have also contributed to canal digging in Hamilton and Welland.[80]

CONTRIBUTION IN WARS

We have little information on the Croatian contribution during the First World War. However, one very valuable source, *The Book of Remembrance* in the Parliament Buildings in Ottawa, lists, among others, the following names: Borich, Michael; Somek, Stepan; Zigich, Milan; and Zindich, Nich., who fell on the battlefields in 1917; and Milatovich, Marko, who fell in 1918.[81]

The Croatian contribution during the Second World War is somewhat more fully documented. Like other Canadians, Croatians purchased Victory Loan Bonds. The Croatians of Hamilton presented an ambulance car to the Canadian Red Cross.[82] The essential contribution, however,

80/Grado, 190–220; Gaži, "Dvadeset godina," 86–100; Nikšić, 97–100. In Montreal and Toronto, Croatians have for many years been working in various factories and industries, but no distinctive work could be mentioned. For Schumacher, see also *Encyclopedia Canadiana*, 9 (Ottawa, 1963), 243; Pavešković, 235–7.

81/*The Book of Remembrance: Names of the Canadians ... Who Served in the Canadian and Other Forces of the British Empire and Gave Their Lives in the Great War 1914–1918. In the Parliament Buildings, Ottawa, Great War 1914–1918* (Ottawa: Edmond Cloutier, Printer to the King's Most Excellent Majesty, 1934), 204, 330, 355, 470.

82/"Bond Sale Upped $2,500 by Maltese and Croat," *Toronto Globe and Mail*, Oct. 21, 1942. The article mentions Croatian Stanley Misitich (Mišetić), factory worker, who contributed to the Victory Loan, having bought $1000 worth of bonds. His photograph is included. See also "Slavs Pledge Aid to Loan," *Windsor Star*, Oct. 8, 1942 (among twenty-four organizations mentioned there the "Croats" are

was made on the battlefields with the Canadian armed forces. Among other Croatians, the better-known active participants were: Stanley Majich, a parachutist; Antony Milosh, naval engineer; Dragutin (Charles) Neralić; Captain Marijan Zadrijevac, commander of a warship; and Nicholas Žunić, Jr., an air force officer.[83]

We do not have exhaustive data on all those who fell in battle. A few Croatians who died for Canada and whose names are recorded are: J. Duralia and J. Zajc, in the army; M. Ostović, armored cars, Camp Borden Ontario Unit; V. Brozović, navy; and M. Popović (theology student, Ottawa), air force.[84]

These few lines on the Croatian contribution to Canada during the two world wars serve as a fitting ending to this survey on Croatians in Canada.

Bibliography

PUBLIC DOCUMENTS

DOMINION BUREAU OF STATISTICS, OTTAWA

Fifth Census of Canada: 1911. Population. Vol. I. Ottawa, 1913.
Sixth Census of Canada: 1921. Population. Vol. I. Ottawa, 1925.
Origines, pays de naissance, nationalités et langues de la population canadienne. (Une étude basée sur les données du recensement de 1921 et autres renseignements supplementaires.) Ottawa, 1930.
Seventh Census of Canada: 1931. Population. Vol. I. Ottawa, 1936.
Eighth Census of Canada: 1941. Population. Vol. I. Ottawa, 1950.
Ninth Census of Canada: 1951. Population. Vol. I. Ottawa, 1953.
Tenth Census of Canada: 1961. Population. Vol. I. Ottawa, 1963.

included), and Bradica, "Postanak," 31–2; Povrženić, "Proslava 30. god. H. N. Doma-Hamilton."

83/Photographs of Milosh, Neralic, Zadrijevac, and Zunic, with captions, in *Croatian Voice Almanac* (1945), 161; "Umro je Stanley Majich"/Stanley Majich Is Dead, *Croatian Voice*, Aug. 21, 1965, a short notice on the occasion of Majich's death.

84/From I. Krznarić, personal letter, Schumacher, Nov. 15, 1965. This letter does not give the full names of the victims. Popovich, Flying Officer Nicholas, is probably identical with "M. Popovic, teol. Ottawa, zrakoplovstvo" (M – Mike – Popovic, theology student, Ottawa, Air Force). This Nicholas Popovich, from Ladysmith, B.C., fell at the age of 24, after the end of the great European war on July 13, 1945. See *The War Dead of the British Commonwealth and Empire: The Register of the Names of Airmen Who Fell in the 1939–1945 War and Have No Known Grave*, The Ottawa Memorial (London: Compiled and Published by Order of the Imperial War Graves Commission, 1959), 27. A letter of December 9, 1965, from Canadian Forces Headquarters Information Services, Ottawa, to the author makes it clear that the records of Canadians who fell during the Second World War have not yet been published.

DEPARTMENT OF TRADE AND COMMERCE, OTTAWA

Cañada Year Book, "Population" and "Immigration" sections, published in Ottawa each year. For our subject, editions since 1916 are relevant.

DEPARTMENT OF CITIZENSHIP AND IMMIGRATION AND
DEPARTMENT OF MANPOWER AND IMMIGRATION, OTTAWA

Annual Report, Fiscal Year ended March 31 each year, published in Ottawa. The editions since 1950 offer sufficient information on our subject.

Canadian Family Tree. Prepared by the Canadian Citizenship Branch, Department of Manpower and Immigration and published in cooperation with the Centennial Commission, Ottawa, 1967.

Naturalization Records since 1890 stored with the Public Archives Records Centre, Ottawa.

BOOKS AND THESES

Connor, Ralph. *The Foreigner*. Toronto: The Westminster Co. Ltd., 1909.

Gibbon, John Murray. *Canadian Mosaic – The Making of a Northern Nation*. Toronto: McClelland & Stewart, 1938.

Glavni Odbor hrvatskih seljačkih organizacija u Kanadi (ed.). *Spomenica na dvadeset godina hrvatskih seljačkih organizacija u Kanadi*/Souvenir-Book on the Occasion of the Twentieth Anniversary of the Croatian Peasant Society in Canada. Winnipeg, 1952.

Grado, Arthur Benko. *Migraciona Enciklopedija*. I. *Kanada*/Canada – A Migration Encyclopedia. Zagreb: Tiskara Narodnih Novina, 1930.

Holjevac, Većeslav. *Hrvati izvan domovine*/Croatians Abroad. Zagreb: Matica Hrvatska, 1967.

Kratki pregled Povijesti Hrvatske Bratske Zajednice 1894–1949/A Brief Historical Review of the Croatian Fraternal Union of America. Pittsburgh: CFU, 1949.

Pavešković, Nedo. "The Croats in Canada." Unpublished Master's Dissertation, Institute of Slavic Studies, University of Montreal, 1961.

Prpić, George J. *The Croatian Publications Abroad after 1939, a Bibliography*. Cleveland: The Soviet and East European Institute, John Carroll University, 1969.

Vršić, Gabriel. "The Yugoslav Contribution to the Civilization of North America." Unpublished Doctoral Thesis, Institute of Slavic Studies, University of Montreal, 1958. (In Slovenian; summary in English.)

ENCYCLOPEDIAS

Grolier of Canada Ltd. (ed.). *Encyclopedia Canadiana*. Vol. III. Ottawa, 1966. 159–60.

Leksikografski Zavod FNRJ (ed.). *Enciklopedija Leksikografskog Zavoda*/ Encyclopedia of the Lexicographic Institute. Vol. III. Zagreb, 1958.

ALMANACS

Stanković, Petar (ed.). *Kalendar Hrvatski Glas – Croatian Voice Almanac*. Winnipeg, since 1929.

Uprava Hrvatskog Katoličkog Glasnika i Danice (eds.). *Hrvatski Kalendar/* Croatian Almanac. Chicago, since 1943.

Savez jugoslavenskih Kanadjana i *Jedinstvo* (ed.). *Naš Kalendar*/Our Almanac. Toronto, since 1948.

Matica iseljenika Hrvatske (ed.). *Matica iseljenički kalendar*/Matica Emigrants' Almanac. Zagreb, since 1955.

WEEKLY, FORTNIGHTLY, AND MONTHLY NEWSPAPERS

Hrvatski Glas – Croatian Voice, Winnipeg.
Jadran/The Adriatic, Montreal.
Jedinstvo/Unity, Toronto.
Naš Put/Our Way, Toronto.
Nezavisna Država Hrvatska/Independent State of Croatia, Toronto.
Zvono – La Cloche/The Bell, Montreal.

APPENDIXES

APPENDIX A

Biographies of the Authors

FRANCIS H. ETEROVICH

Francis H. Eterovich was born in Pučišća, on the island of Brač. He is a member of the Dominican Order and studied philosophy and theology at the Dominican Institute in Louvain, Belgium, from 1937 until 1939. He received his M.A. in classical languages from the Croatian University in Zagreb in 1944, and his PH.D. in theology at the Dominican University in Etiolles, near Paris, France, in 1948. He studied Anglo-American analytic philosophy at the University of Chicago and was awarded an M.A. in philosophy in 1965.

Professor Eterovich has taught at several universities since 1945. He came to the United States in 1952, and since that time has taught philosophy at various colleges in the American Mid-west. Since 1962 he has taught at DePaul University in Chicago, where he is associate professor of moral, social and political philosophy.

Dr. Eterovich was founder and editor of the quarterly journal for contemporary moral and social problems *Osoba i Duh* (Person and Spirit), first published in Madrid in 1949. He continued to publish the journal in the United States at Albuquerque, New Mexico, until the end of 1955. At that time he began work on the multi-volume project *Croatia: Land, People, Culture*, of which volume I was published in 1964, and to which he contributed a study entitled "Geographic and Demographic Statistics of Croatia and Bosnia-Hercegovina" (3–19) and another entitled "Ethical Heritage" (191–225).

In addition to the numerous editorials, studies on ethical problems, and book reviews he has written for *Osoba i Duh*, Professor Eterovich has contributed to many magazines and journals, especially to those published by Croatian emigres in various countries after the Second World War. Among these journals are *Hrvatska Revija* (Croatian Review), published in Munich, and *Journal of Croatian Studies*, published in New York. Of particular interest is his article, "Subjective Demands of Human Action," published in Spanish in *Revista de Filosofia* (XI, no. 41, 1952), a journal of the Philosophical Institute of the University of Madrid. He is co-author of the textbook anthology, *Approaches to Morality*, published by Harcourt, Brace, and World in 1966. He has compiled, edited, and published *Biographical Directory of Scholars, Artists, and Professionals of Croatian Descent in the United States and Canada* (Chicago: 1st ed., 1963; 2nd ed., 1965; 3rd ed., 1970).

Professor Eterovich has received entries in *Who's Who in American Education, 1967–68* (Hattiesburg, Miss., 1968); *Who's Who in the Midwest* (10th ed.; Chicago, 1967); *Illinois Lives: The Prairie State Biographical Record*, ed. Clyde C. Walton (Chicago, 1969); *Directory of American Scholars*, vol. IV: *Philosophy, Religion and Law* (5th ed.; New York, 1969); *Dictionary of International Biography* (6th ed., 1969–70, general editor Ernest Kay; London, 1969).

STANKO GULDESCU

Stanko Guldescu was born in Trieste (then part of Austro-Hungary) in 1908. He studied the history of central and eastern Europe at the universities of Zagreb, Madrid, and Chicago. At the University of Chicago, he obtained both his M.A. and his PH.D. degrees in history. He has taught at St. John's University, Shanghai (1945–6), New Mexico State Teachers College (1947–8), Indiana University, Extension Division (1954), Washington and Lee University (1956), South Dakota State Teachers College (1957), Central Methodist College, Fayette, Missouri (1958–65), and is at present on the faculty of Fayetteville State College, Fayetteville, North Carolina.

Among Professor Guldescu's numerous studies are: "The Kossuth Tradition and Hungary's Delusion of Grandeur," "The Background of the Croatian Nationalist Movement," and "Austria's Economic Future," all in the *South Atlantic Quarterly*; "Spain and Totalitarianism," *Thought* (Fordham University); "The Habsburg Hysteria," *Social Science Quarterly*; "The Slovenes," *Social Studies*; "Austrian Attitudes towards the Anschluss from October 1918 to September 1919," *Journal of Modern History*; "The Rumanians of Istria," *New Pioneer*; "Submarine Warfare in the Adriatic: The Otranto Barrage, 1915–1918," *U.S. Naval Institute Proceedings*; and "Titos Kärntner Aspirationen," *Austria*. Other important articles and reviews by Dr. Guldescu have appeared in the *Hungarian Quarterly*, the *Danubian Review*, and the *China Press* (Shanghai).

In recent years, Professor Guldescu has devoted his time almost exclusively to the study of Croatian history. His book *History of Medieval Croatia* (The Hague: Mouton and Company) was published in 1964, and its continuation is due in the fall of 1970. His article "Political History to 1526" appeared in volume I of this series, pp. 76–130.

WILLY A. BACHICH

Willy A. Bachich was born in Pula in 1896. He was graduated from the Naval Academy in Rijeka in 1914, and then studied at the Ecole de Guerre Navale (French Academy of Naval Warfare) from which he graduated as *officier d'état major* (Naval Staff Officer) in 1927. In 1929 he was awarded the degree of Doctor Juris by the Croatian University in Zagreb. He pursued his studies in that field subsequently, and received equivalency for his degree of Doctor of Law in 1952 from the Catholic Pontifical University in Lima, Peru.

Bachich's naval career includes service in both the Austro-Hungarian (1914–18) and the Royal Yugoslav (1919–41) navies, in the latter of which he has served as commanding officer of a number of ships, chief of operations in the Admiralty, vice-director of the Naval Academy in Dubrovnik and its acting director for two years, and finally, consultant to the navy on International Maritime Law. During the Second World War (1941–5) he was in the civil service of the Croatian Ministry of Foreign Affairs.

Mr. Bachich is a specialist in international and maritime law and naval history. His published works include the following books: *Uvod u medjunarodno pomorsko javno i ratno pravo*/Introduction to International Maritime, Public and War Law (Belgrade: M. J. Stefanović, 1933); *Dubrovački bro-*

dovi u doba procvata dubrovačkog pomorstva u XVI vijeku/Ships of Dubrovnik in the Golden Era of Ragusan Seamanship in the Sixteenth Century (Zagreb: Vasić i Horvat, 1941); *Povijest prvog svjetskog rata na Jadranu*/History of the First World War on the Adriatic Sea (Zagreb: Hrvatski Izdavalački Bibliografski Zavod, 1944); Liburnicus, *Der Kampf um die Ostküste der Adria; eine geschichtliche Darstellung* (Zagreb: HIBZ, 1944); *La Soberana Militar Orden de Malta: Historia de los caballeros de San Juan, Rodes y Malta en su pasado, sus obras y luchas relacionadas con la historia de Tierra Santa y del Mediterraneo* (Lima: Editorial Continental, 1968).

Many of his articles have appeared in Yugoslavia in the magazine *Mornarički Glasnik*, Zemun (1933–9), all of them concerning either naval history or maritime law. He has also published articles on maritime law in Peru, these have appeared in the yearbook *Derecho* (Universidad Catolica de Lima, 1951–8). The article "La condicion juridica del buque" appeared in *Revista de Marina del Peru*, no. 2 (1954).

CHRISTOPHER SPALATIN

Christopher Spalatin was born in Ston, Croatia, on October 15, 1909. He attended the Gymnasium in Šibenik, graduating in 1927. He studied French and Latin languages and literatures, as well as Croatian and Serbian literatures, at the University of Zagreb, obtaining his M.A. degree in 1931. He obtained his doctorate at the University of Zagreb in 1934. His doctoral thesis, on Saint-Evremond, was written in French and published in Zagreb in 1934. He continued his graduate studies at the University of Paris. Dr. Spalatin has taught French language at the University of Zagreb, Croatian language at the University of Rome, Croatian and Serbian literatures at the Naples Oriental Institute, and French, German, and Latin at Wesleyan College in Mount Pleasant, Iowa. At present he teaches French at Marquette University, Milwaukee, Wisconsin.

Among his published works are the Croatian translations of two books from the French, *Komunizam i Kršćani*/Communism and Christians (1937) and *Seksualni Problemi*/Sexual Problems (1939), both published in Zagreb. Dr. Spalatin's articles have been published in French, Italian, English, and Croatian, and he has contributed a number of studies to *Hrvatska Revija*. Especially noteworthy is his work in the field of informing the Croatian people about trends, ideas, theories, and systems in other European countries. Professor Spalatin is currently writing a book on the subject of rendering Croatian foreign terms into English, French, Italian, and German, and frequently contributes articles in English about the Croatian language to various journals and periodicals.

As early as 1955 he joined Francis H. Eterovich as an associate editor of *Croatia: Land, People, Culture*.

FRANJO TROGRANČIĆ

Franjo Trogrančić was born on September 2, 1913, in Vareš, Bosnia, Croatia. He studied at the Franciscan Gymnasium in Visoko (Bosnia) until 1934. From 1937 to 1942 he studied at the University of Zagreb, and in 1942 went to Rome, where he received first his doctorate in philosophy in 1943 and then his doctorate in romance languages in 1945 from the University of Rome.

Professor Trogrančić is a philologist, specializing in Croatian and Serbian languages and literatures, which he taught at the University of Florence from 1945 to 1947, and at the University of Pisa from 1947 to 1949. He is at present professor of Croatian and Serbian at the University of Rome, where he has taught since 1949.

Among his publications are the following: *Letteratura medioevale degli Slavi meridionali* (Rome, 1950); *Storia della letteratura croata* (Rome: Ed. Studium, 1953); various critical introductions to Italian translations of both Croatian and Serbian literary works (such as those of Ivana Brlić-Mažuranić, Fran Mažuranić, Ivo Ćipiko, Ljubomir Nenadović, Vladimir Vidrić, and Ivan Mažuranić); anthologies of Croatian poetry, both in the original and in Italian translation, such as: *Antologija hrvatske lirike*/Anthology of Croatian Poetry (Rome, 1953), *Poeti croati moderni* (Milan, 1965), *Novellieri croati moderni* (Rome, 1967), and *Narratori croati* (Rome, 1969).

IVAN ESIH

Ivan Esih was born in Ljubuški, Hercegovina, on August 7, 1898. After studying at the Gymnasium in Sarajevo, he began his Slavic studies in Prague at Karl University and completed his work in Zagreb, where he received his doctorate in 1923, submitting a dissertation entitled "Psychology of a Dream." Subsequently he specialized in Polish studies at the Yagellon University in Krakow.

Dr. Esih was an editor of *Omladina* (Youth), a magazine for secondary school students. He served as secretary of the "Društvo hrvatskih književnika" (Association of Croatian Writers), and spent many years as a librarian, archivist, and scholarly contributor to the Yugoslav Academy of Sciences and Arts. He retired in 1957.

During fifty years of his active life Dr. Esih wrote numerous studies and articles in foreign and Croatian journals. The topics of his studies are remarkably variegated. He was a polyhistor and, at the same time, a polyglot. He knew, besides the principal west European languages, all the Slavic languages and translated several important literary works from Russian and Polish into Croatian.

Dr. Esih died while working at his desk on January 23, 1966, in Zagreb. His article was largely completed at that time, and we have decided to honor his memory by publishing his contribution.

SMAIL BALIĆ

An orientalist born in Mostar on August 26, 1920, Professor Balić began his academic career after completing his studies in 1940 at the Ghazi Khusrev Beg Secondary School in Sarajevo, where he spent the following year studying at the Higher School for Islamic Law and Oriental Studies. He continued his Islamic, Turkish, Arabic, and Slavic studies at the universities of Vienna, Leipzig, and Breslau, and was awarded the PH.D. degree by the University of Vienna in 1945.

From 1945 to 1962 Dr. Balić lived in Vienna, lecturing on the Turkish language at the Superior School of Commerce; during this period he made a number of extensive trips to Turkey, and was employed by the Turkish Embassy in Vienna, by the High Commission of the United Nations for Displaced Persons, and by the Muslim Humanitarian and Educational Foundation at Jami ʿat al-Islam, Inc. On October 1, 1962, he accepted a position as teacher of German in a private college in Salmiya, Kuwait. He returned to Vienna in 1963, and at the present time he is a state librarian there in the Orientalist Section of the National Library.

Dr. Balić founded, edited, published, and has written for *Muslimanska Biblioteka* (Muslim Library), in Vienna, a publication aimed at the education of Croatian Muslims. He is a regular contributor to a variety of journals, such as *Islamic Literature* (Lahore), *Wissenschaftlicher Dienst Sudosteuropa* (Munich), and *Bustan* and *Furche* (Vienna). Among his publications are the following: *Die geistigen Triebkräfte im bosnisch-herzegowinischen Islam: Ideengeschichtiche und soziologische Ansätze* (Doctoral dissertation; Vienna, 1945); *Etičko naličje bosansko-hercegovačkih muslimana*/Ethical Outlook of the Bosnian-Hercegovinian Muslims (Vienna, 1952); *Islam – Njegova nauka i njegovo značenje*/Islam, Its Doctrine and Its Significance (Vienna, 1954); "Osmanische Bauten in Bosnien," *Wiener Zeitschrift für die Kunde des Morgenlandes* (1960), Jubilee issue dedicated to Professor Herbert Duda, pp. 1–8; "Podunavski muslimani srednjeg vijeka"/Danubian Muslims in the Middle Ages, *Bosanski Pogledi*, no. 14 (1962), pp. 3–5; and *Ruf vom Minarett. Ein Lehrbuch des Islam für Jugend und Erwachsene* (Vienna, 1962).

DOMINIK MANDIĆ

Dominik Mandić was born in Lise, Hercegovina, in 1889. He entered the Franciscan Order in 1906, and from 1910 to 1914 studied theology and history in Fribourg, Switzerland, where he was ordained to the priesthood in 1912. In 1921 he earned his doctorate in theology with highest honors.

In 1918 Fr. Mandić started to publish *Savremena Pitanja* (Contemporary Problems), a collection of essays on topics of religious and scientific interest. By 1939 twenty-three studies, written by various authors, had been printed in thirty-nine volumes of that collection. In 1924 he published his work *De legislatione antiqua Ordinis Fratrum Minorum*. In 1927 he began to collect source materials for the history of the Franciscan Order in the South Slavic lands, and these were published in two volumes, the first in 1927 and the second in 1934. In 1927 he also published his *Conspectus chronologicus vitae S. Francisci Assisiensis* (Chronological Survey of the Life of Saint Francis).

In 1928 Fr. Mandić was elected Provincial of the Hercegovinian Franciscan Province, and at the general meeting of the Franciscan Order at Assisi in 1939 he was elected Representative of the Slavic Provinces in the High Council of that order, and became general treasurer of the Franciscans. While serving as treasurer, he conducted construction of the general headquarters and its adjoining church in Rome. The art work in the interior of the church is rich in Croatian folk motifs.

In 1952 he moved to Chicago, and became a superior of the Croatian Franciscan Commissariat in the United States. In Chicago, in 1953, he founded the Cultural Publishing Center "Croatia," which has published six books thus far, and in 1955 he founded the Croatian Historical Institute which transferred its headquarters to Rome in 1963.

Among Fr. Mandić's extensive publications, the more recent are the following: *Crvena Hrvatska u svijetlu povijesnih izvora*/Red Croatia in the Light of Historical Sources (Chicago, 1957); *Bosna i Hercegovina,* I. *Državna i vjerska pripadnost sredovječne Bosne i Hercegovine*/Bosnia and Hercegovina, I. The State and Religious Affiliation of Medieval Bosnia and Hercegovina (Chicago, 1960); II. *Bogomilska crkva bosanskih krstjana*/The Bogomil Church of the Bosnian Christians (Chicago, 1962); III. *Etnička povijest Bosne i Hercegovine*/The Ethnic History of Bosnia and Hercegovina (Rim, 1967); *Rasprave i prilozi iz stare hrvatske povijesti*/Studies and Contributions to Ancient Croatian History (Rim, 1963).

GEORGE JURE PRPIĆ

George J. Prpić was born on November 16, 1920, in Djala, Banat, Yugoslavia. He took his B.A. degree from the Real Gymnasium in Požega, and then studied jurisprudence at the University of Zagreb where he received his M.A. degree in February 1944. Just prior to receiving the doctorate he left Croatia in early 1945 when it was occupied by the Communists. He studied history at the universities of Vienna and Graz in Austria, and arrived in the United States in May 1950. He earned his M.A. in history at John Carroll University in Cleveland in 1956 and a doctorate in American history at Georgetown University in Washington, D.C., in 1959, submitting a dissertation entitled "The Croatians in America." At the present time Dr. Prpić is professor of East European history at John Carroll University in Cleveland, Ohio.

Among his publications are the following: "Early Croatian Contacts with America and the Mystery of the Croatans," *Journal of Croatian Studies,* 1 (New York, 1960), 6–21; "The Croatian Newspapers in America Before 1918," *Croatia Press,* XV, no. 6 (Dec. 1961), 7–15; "Fernando Konschak, S. J. Misionero y Explorador en Baja California," *Studia Croatica* (Buenos Aires), III, no. 1 (March 1962), 58–68; *East Central Europe and Its Sovietization, a Bibliography* (University Heights, Ohio: John Carroll University, Institute for Soviet and East European Studies, 1962); "Josip Kundek, hrvatski misionar u Americi"/Josip Kundek, Croatian Missionary to America, *Novi Život,* III, nos. 5–6 (Sept.-Dec. 1964), 241–58; "Kroatische Auswanderung nach Amerika vor 1914," *Der Donauraum* (Vienna), IX (Sept. 1964), 167–74; "The Croatian Immigrants and the Americans from Yugoslavia: Marginalia on the Book: Gerald Gilbert Govorchin, *Americans from Yugoslavia: A Survey of Yugoslav Immigrants in the United States* (Gainesville, Fla.: Univ. of Florida Press, 1961), XII, 352," in *Journal of Croatian Studies,* III–IV (March 1964), 166–72; "French Rule in Croatia: 1806–1813," *Balkan Studies* (Thessaloniki), V (Dec. 1965), 221–76; *World Communism: Selective Chronology, 1917–1964* (Cleveland, Ohio: John Carroll University, Institute for Soviet and East European Studies, 1965); *Eastern Europe and World Communism: A Selective Annotated Bibliography in English* (Cleveland, Ohio: John Carroll University, Institute for Soviet and East European Studies, 1966); *Fifty Years of World Communism* (Cleveland, Ohio: same publisher, 1967); *The Croatian Publications Abroad after 1939, a Bibliography* (Cleveland, Ohio: same publisher, 1969).

NEDO PAVEŠKOVIĆ

Born in 1921 in Tugare, Croatia, Nedo Pavešković graduated from the Classical Gymnasium in Zagreb in 1942, and received his law degree (LL.M.A.) from the University of Croatia there in 1948. He studied at the University of Montreal in 1960–3, where he received his M.A. (1961) and PH.D. (1969) degrees. He also studied at Sir George Williams University, Montreal, and at Carleton University, Ottawa.

The title of his M.A. thesis was "The Croats in Canada," and his PH.D. dissertation was entitled "L'Activité littéraire et politique d'Ante Starčević" (The Literary and Political Activity of Ante Starčević).

His major field of study has been the history, culture, and civilization of eastern and central European countries.

Mr. Pavešković practiced law from 1953 to 1956 in Croatia. He has been a college teacher in Croatia and Canada, and since 1965 an archivist with the Public Archives in Ottawa.

APPENDIX B

Geographical Names

Since a number of cultures have left traces on the lands today inhabited by the Croatians, it is helpful to know the most frequently used variant forms of Croatian place-names. The Croatian names are followed in the list by any Croatian variants (*Cr.*), and by the appropriate ancient (*anc.*), English (*Eng.*), French (*Fr.*), German (*Ger.*), Greek (*Gr.*), Hungarian (*Hung.*), Italian (*It.*), Latin (*Lat.*), or other equivalents. The Croatian forms of some non-Croatian place-names are also given. The abbreviation *obs.* is used to indicate a variant form that is now obsolete.

ADIDŽA, *see* Adige
ADIGE (river), *Cr.* Adidža, *Ger.* Etsch
ADRIATIC SEA, *Cr.* Jadransko More or Jadran
AEGEAN SEA, *Cr.* Egejsko More, *Serbian* Jegejsko More
AKVILEJA, *see* Aquileia
ALSACE (region of France), *anc.* Alsatia, *Cr.* Elzas, *Ger.* Elsass
ANCONA (Italy), *Cr.* Jakin (*obs.*)
AQUILEIA (Italy), *anc.* Aquileia, *medieval* Aglar, *Cr.* Oglaj (*obs.*) or Akvileja
ARDEAL, *see* Transylvania
ATENA, *see* Athenai
ATHENAI (Greece), *Cr.* Atena, *Serbian* Atina, *Eng.* Athens

BAKAR, *Lat.* Volcera, *It.* Buccari
BANOVIĆ, *see* Banovići
BANOVIĆI OF BANOVIĆ
BAR (Montenegro), *Gr.* Antibaris, *Lat.* Antibarum, *Albanian* Tìvari or Tivari, *It.* Antivari
BAŠKA (on the island of Krk) or BAŠKANOVA, *It.* Besca (nuova)
BEČ, *see* Wien
BEČKO NOVO MJESTO, *see* Wiener Neustadt
BENKOVAC, *It.* Bencovazzo, *Ger.* Benkovatz
BEOGRAD (Serbia), *Lat.* Singidunum, *Fr.* and *Eng.* Belgrade, *It.* Belgrado
BERAM (near Pazin), *It.* Vermo
BIHAĆI, *see* Bijaći
BIJAĆI (near Trogir), a popular form of Bihaći
BIOGRAD OF BIOGRAD NA MORU (White City on the Sea), *It.* Zaravecchia
BIOKOVO (mountain), *It.* Monte Biloco or Monti Albii
BIŠEVO (island), *It.* Busi
BITOLA (Macedonia), *Cr.* Bitolj
BITOLJ, *see* Bitola
BJELOVAR, *Hung.* Belovár
BLATO (on the island of Korčula), *It.* Blatta (di Curzola)
BOHEMIA (part of Czechoslovakia), *Cr.* Češka, *Czech* Čechy, *Ger.* Böhmen
BOKA KOTORSKA, *It.* Bocche di Cattaro, *Eng.* Gulf of Kotor
BOSANSKA GRADIŠKA, *Lat.* Servitium
BRAČ (island), *Lat.* Brattia, *It.* Brazza
BRATISLAVA (Czechoslovakia), *Cr.* Požun, *Ger.* Pressburg, *Hung.* Pozsony
BRIJUNI OF BRIONI (islands), *Lat.* Insulae Pullariae, *It.* Isole Brioni
BRIONI, *see* Brijuni
BROD, BROD NA SAVI, OF SLAVONSKI BROD, *Lat.* Marsonia
BROD NA SAVI, *see* Brod
BUCARESTI (Rumania), *Cr.* Bukurešt, *Eng.* Bucharest
BUDAPEST (Hungary), *Cr.* Budimpešta, Budim or Buda, or Pešta
BUDIM, *see* Budapest
BUDIMPEŠTA, *see* Budapest
BUDVA, *It.* Budua
BUKAREŠT, see Bucaresti
BURGENLAND (Austria), *Cr.* Gradišće

ČAKOVEC, *Ger.* Csakathurn, *Hung.* Csáktornya
CARIGRAD, *see* Istanbul
CARINTHIA (region in central Europe), *Cr.* Koruška, *Ger.* Kärnten

CARNIOLA (region in Yugoslavia), *Cr.* Kranjska, *Ger.* Krain
CAUCASUS, *Cr.* Kavkaz
CAVTAT, *anc.* Epidaurus, *Lat.* Civitas Vetus, *It.* Ragusavecchia
ČEDAD, *see* Cividale del Friuli
CELJE (Slovenia), *anc.* Claudia Celeia, *Ger.* and *It.* Cilli
CELOVAC, *see* Klagenfurt
ČEŠKA, *see* Bohemia
CETINA (river), *anc.* Tilurius
CHINA, *Cr.* Kina or Kitaj (*obs.*)
ĆIĆARIJA (region), *It.* Cicceria
ČIOVO (island), *Lat.* and *It.* Bua
CIPAR, *see* Cyprus
ČITLUK (near Sinj), *Lat.* Aequum
CIVIDALE DEL FRIULI (Italy), *anc.* Forum Julii, *Slovenian* Čedad
CRES (island), *Lat.* Crepsa; Cres and Lošinj had a common name in antiquity, Apsyrtides; *It.* Cherso
CRETE, *anc.* Creta or Candia, *Cr.* Kreta or Kandija (*obs.*), *Serbian* Krit
CRNA GORA, *Eng.* and *It.* Montenegro
CYPRUS, *Cr.* Cipar, *Serbian* Kipar

DALJ (near Osijek), *Lat.* Teutoburgium
DANSKA, *see* Denmark
DANUBE (river), *Cr.* Dunav; Danube River Basin, *Cr.* Podunavlje
DARUVAR, *Lat.* Aquae Balissae
DENMARK, *Cr.* Danska
DEVIN, *see* Duino
DINARA (mountains), *It.* Alpi Dinariche
DJAKOVO, *Hung.* Diakovár
DJURDJEVAC OR GJURGJEVAC, *Ger.* Sankt Georgen
DRAČ, *see* Durrës
DRAGONJA (river), *It.* Dragogna
DRAVA (river), *Ger.* Drau, *Hung.* Dráva; Drava River Basin, *Cr.* Podravina
DRAŽDJANI, *see* Dresden
DRENOPOLJE, *see* Edirne
DRESDEN (Germany), *Cr.* DRAŽDJANI (*obs.*)
DRVENIK (island, *It.* Zirona
DUBROVNIK, *Gr.* Rausion, *Lat.* Rhagusium or Racusa, *It.* Ragusa
DUGI OTOK (island), *It.* Isola Lunga or Isola Grossa
DUINO (Italy), *Slovenian* Devin, *Ger.* Tibein
DUNAV, *see* Danube
DURRËS (Albania), *Lat.* Dyrrachium, *Cr.* Drač, *It.* and *Eng.* Durazzo, *Turkish* Dradj, Draj, or Draç
DUVNO OR TOMISLAV-GRAD, *Lat.* Delminium

EDIRNE (Turkey), *anc.* Adrianopolis or Hadrianopolis, formerly Adrianople, *Cr.* Jedrene or Drenopolje
EGEJSKO MORE, *see* Aegean Sea
EGIPAT, *see* Egypt
EGYPT, *Cr.* Egipat or Misir (biblical)
EISENSTADT (town in Burgenland, Austria), *Cr.* Železno (*obs.*), *Hung.* Kismarton
ELBE (river), *Cr.* Laba
ELZAS, *see* Alsace
ERDELJ, *see* Transylvania

FALAČKA, *see* Palatinate
FILIPJAKOV, *It.* Santi Filippo e Giacomo
FIRENCA, *see* Firenze
FIRENZE (Italy), *Cr.* Firenca, *Eng.* and *Fr.* Florence
FRIULI (region in Italy), *Friulian* Furlanei, *Cr.* Furlanija, *Ger.* Friaul
FURLANIJA, *see* Friuli

GALIPOLJE, *see* Gallipoli
GALLIPOLI (Turkey), *Cr.* Galipolje
GENÈVE (Switzerland), *Cr.* Ženeva, *Eng.* Geneva; Lake of Geneva, *Cr.* Ženevsko Jezero
GERMANY, *Cr.* Njemačka
GJURGJEVAC, *see* Djurdjevac
GOMILICA, *It.* Castel Abbadessa
GORICA, *see* Gorizia
GORIZIA (Italy), *Slovenian* and *Cr.* Gorica, *Ger.* Görz
GORJANCI, *see* Žumberačka Gora
GORNJI GRAD, *see* Grič
GRADAC, *see* Graz
GRADEŽ, *see* Grado
GRADIŠĆE, *see* Burgenland
GRADO (on the Adriatic, near Aquileia, Italy), *Cr.* Gradež (*obs.*)
GRAZ (Austria), *Cr.* (Štajerski) Gradac (*obs.*)
GRIČ OR GORNJI GRAD, part of the city of Zagreb
GRUŽ, *It.* Gravosa

HAVAJI, *see* Hawaii
HAWAII, *Cr.* Havaji

HERCEG-NOVI, *It.* Castelnuovo (di Cattaro)
HUNGARY, *Cr.* Madjarska, Madžarska, or Ugarska
HVAR (island), *Gr.* Pharos, *Lat.* Pharia or Pharus, *It.* Lesina

IMOTSKI, *It.* Imoschi
IST (island), *It.* Isto
ISTANBUL (Turkey), *anc.* Byzantium, *Cr.* Carigrad, Stambol (obs.), or Stambul (obs.), *Fr.* and *Eng.* Constantinople
IŽ (island), *Lat.* Esum, *It.* Eso

JABUKA (island), *It.* Pomo
JADRAN, *see* Adriatic Sea
JADRANSKO MORE, *see* Adriatic Sea
JAKIN, *see* Ancona
JEDRENE, *see* Edirne

KALAMOTA, *see* Koločep
KAMBELOVAC, *It.* Castelcambio
KANDIJA, *see* Crete
KANFANAR, *It.* Canfanaro
KARLOBAG, *It.* Carlopago
KARLOVAC, *Ger.* Karlstadt, *Hung.* *Károlyváros*
KARLOVCI (Serbia), *Ger.* Karlowitz, *Hung.* Karlócza
KASTAV, *It.* Castua
KAŠTEL-SUĆURAC, *see* Sućurac
KAŠTELA KOD SPLITA, *It.* Castelli di Spalato
KAVKAZ, *see* Caucasus
KERKYRA (Greece), *anc.* Corcyra, *Cr.* Krf, *Eng.* Corfu
KINA, *see* China
KITAJ, *see* China
KLAGENFURT (Austria), *Cr.* Celovac, *Slovenian* Celovec
KLIS, *It.* Clissa
KNIN, *It.* Tenin
KOBARID (Slovenia), *It.* Caporetto, *Ger.* Karfreit
KOLOČEP (island) or KALAMOTA, *It.* Calamotta
KOPAR, *see* Koper
KOPER (Slovenia), *anc.* Capris, *Cr.* Kopar, *It.* Capodistria
KOPRIVNICA, *Ger.* Kopreinitz, *Hung.* Kapronca
KORČULA, *Lat.* Corcyra Nigra, *It.* Curzola
KORNAT (island), *It.* (Isola) Incoronata
KORUŠKA, *see* Carinthia
KOTOR, *Gr.* Dekatera, *Lat.* Catharum, *It.* Cattaro
KRALJEVICA, *It.* Porto Re
KRANJSKA, *see* Carniola
KREMLIN, *Cr.* Kremlj
KREMLJ, *see* Kremlin
KRETA, *see* Crete
KRF, *see* Kerkyra
KRIŽEVCI, *Ger.* Kreuz, *Hung.* Körös
KRK (island), *Lat.* Curicum or Curicta, *It.* Veglia
KRKA (river), *Lat.* Titius, *It.* Cherca
KVARNER, *It.* Quarnaro or Carnaro

LABA, *see* Elbe
LABIN, *anc.* and *It.* Albona
LANGOBARDIJA, *see* Lombardy
LASTOVO (island), *Lat.* Ladesta, *It.* Lágosta
LAVOV, *see* Lwiw
LEIPZIG (Germany), *Cr.* Lipsko (*obs.*)
LIPSKO, *see* Leipzig
LISABON, *see* Lisboa
LISBOA (Portugal), *anc.* Olisipo, *Cr.* Lisabon, *Eng.* Lisbon
LOMBARDY, *Cr.* Langobardija, *It.* Lombardia
LOPUD (island), *It.* Isola di Mezzo
LORRAINE, *Cr.* Lotaringija, *Ger.* Lothringen
LOŠINJ MALI (*see* Cres), *It.* Lussinpiccolo
LOŠINJ VELI, *It.* Lussingrande
LOTARINGIJA, *see* Lorraine
LOURDES (France), *Cr.* Lurd
LOVĆEN (mountain), *It.* Monte Leone
LOVRAN, *It.* Laurana
LUKŠIĆ, *It.* Castel Vitturi
LURD, *see* Lourdes
LUSATIA (region in Germany and Poland), *Cr.* Lužica, *Polish* Luźyca, *Ger.* Lausitz
LUŽICA, *see* Lusatia
LWIW (Ukraine), *Cr.* Lavov, *Eng.* Lvov, *Polish* Lwów

MADŽARSKA, *see* Hungary
MAIN (river), *Cr.* Majna
MAJNA, *see* Main
MAKARSKA, *It.* Macarsca
MARIA-THERESIOPEL, *see* Subotica
MARIBOR (Slovenia), *Ger.* Marburg
MARMARA, SEA OF, *Cr.* Mramorno More
MARTINŠĆICA, *It.* San Martino in Valle
MAUN (island), *It.* Maon or Maoni

MEDITERRANEAN SEA, *Cr.* Sredozemlje or Sredozemno More
MEDJIMURJE or MEDJUMURJE (region), *Ger.* Mittelmurgebiet or Murinsel, *Hung.* Muraköz
MEDJUMURJE, *see* Medjimurje
METKOVIĆ, *It.* Metcovich
MISIR, *see* Egypt
MITROVICA, *see* Srijemska Mitrovica
MLECI, *see* Venezia
MLETAKA, *see* Venezia
MLJEĆANI, *see* Mljet
MLJET (island), *It.* Meleda; Mlječani are the inhabitants of the island
MOHAČ, *see* Mohács
MOHÁCS (Hungary), *Cr.* Mohač
MOLAT (island), *anc.* Mel(i)ta, *It.* Melada
MONAKOV, *see* München
MOŠĆENICE, *It.* Moschiena
MOTOVUN, *It.* Montona
MRAMORNO MORE, *see* Marmara
MUĆ (near Split), *It.* Mucci
MÜNCHEN (Germany), *Cr.* Monakov (*obs.*), *Fr.* and *Eng.* Munich, *It.* Monaco di Baviera
MURA (river), *Ger.* Mur
MURTER (island), *It.* Morter

NAPOLI (Italy), *anc.* Neapolis, *Cr.* Napulj, *Eng.* and *Fr.* Naples
NAPULJ, *see* Napoli
NERETVA (river), *Lat.* Naro, *It.* Narenta
NEREŽIŠĆE (on the island of Brač), *It.* Neresi
NETHERLANDS, *Cr.* Nizozemska
NIN, *It.* Nona
NIZOZEMSKA, *see* Netherlands
NJEMAČKA, *see* Germany
NOVI, NOVI VINDOLSKI, or VINODOL
NOVI VINDOLSKI, *see* Novi
NOVIGRAD (Dalmatia), *It.* Novegradi
NOVIGRAD (Istria), *anc.* Neapolis, *It.* Cittanova

ODER (river), *Cr.* Odra
ODRA, *see* Oder
OGLAJ, *see* Aquileia
OLIB (island), *It.* Ulbo
OLOVO (a mine), *Lat.* Plumbum
OMBLA, *see* Rijeka Dubrovačka
OMIŠ, *anc.* Oneum, *It.* Almissa
OPATIJA, *It.* Abazzia
OPRTALJ (Istria), *It.* Portole
ORAŠAC (near Dubrovnik), *It.* Valdinoce
ORMOŽ (Slovenia), *Ger.* Friedau
OSIJEK, *Lat.* Mursa, *Ger.* Esseg, *Hung.* Eszek
OŠLJE (near Ston), *It.* Oseglie

PAD, *see* Po
PAG (island), *It.* Pago
PALAGRUŽA (island), *It.* Pelagosa Grande
PALATINATE (region in Germany), *Cr.* Falačka, *Ger.* Pfalz
PARIS (France), *Lat.* Lutetia Parisiorum, *Cr.* Pariz, *Eng.* and *Ger.* Paris
PARIZ, *see* Paris
PAŠMAN (island), *Lat.* Postumiana, *It.* Pasman
PASSAROWITZ, *see* Požarevac
PAZIN, *It.* Pisino, *Ger.* Mitterburg
PEČ, *see* Pécs
PÉCS (Hungary), *Cr.* Pečuh (*obs.*) or Peč, *Serbian* Pečuj (*obs.*)
PEČUH, *see* Pécs
PELJEŠAC (peninsula) or STONSKI RAT, *It.* Sabbioncello
PERAST, *It.* Perasto
PEŠTA, *see* Budapest
PETROVARADIN, *Ger.* Peterwardein, *Hung.* Pétervárad
PIRINEJI, *see* Pyrenees
PLANINSKI KANAL, *see* Velebit Channel
PLITVICE, *see* Plitvička Jezera
PLITVIČKA JEZERA or PLITVICE, *Eng.* Plitvice Lakes
PLOMIN, *It.* Fianona
PO (river, Italy), *Cr.* Pad
PODGORSKI KANAL, *see* Velebit Channel
PODRAVINA, *see* Drava
PODUNAVLJE, *see* Danube
PORAJNJE, *see* Rhine
POREČ, *Lat.* Parentium, *It.* Parenzo
POSAVINA, *see* Sava
POSTOJNA (Slovenia), *It.* Postumia, *Ger.* Adelsberg
POŽAREVAC (Serbia), *Ger.* Passarowitz
POŽEGA (Slavonska), *anc.* Incerum, *Hung.* Pozsega
POŽUN, *see* Bratislava
PRAG, *see* Praha
PRAHA (Czechoslovakia), *Ger.* and *Cr.* Prag, *Fr.* and *Eng.* Prague
PRESSBURG, *see* Bratislava
PROVANSA, *see* Provence
PROVENCE (region in France), *Cr.* Provansa
PRVIĆ (island), *It.* Pervicchio

PTUJ (Slovenia), *anc.* Petovia, *Ger.* Pettau
PULA, *Lat.* Pietas Iulia, *Slovenian* Pulj, *It.* Pola
PYRENEES (mountains), *Cr.* Pirineji, *Spanish* Pirineos, *Serbian* Pireneji

RAB (island), *Lat.* Arva, *It.* Arbe
RAJNA, *see* Rhine
RAŠA (river), *It.* Arsa
RHINE (river), *Cr.* Rajna; Rhine River Basin, *Cr.* Porajnje
RIJEKA, *It.* Fiume
RIJEKA DUBROVAČKA or OMBLA, *It.* Ombla
RIM, *see* Roma
ROMA (Italy), *Cr.* Rim, *Eng.* and *Fr.* Rome
ROVINJ, *It.* Rovigno (d'Istria)

SAD, *see* USA
SASKA, *see* Saxony
SAVA (river), *Lat.* Savus, *Ger.* Sau, *Hung.* Száva; Sava River Basin, *Cr.* Posavina
SAVINJA (river), *Ger.* Sann
SAXONY, *Cr.* Saska, *Ger.* Sachsen
ŠĆEDRO (island), *anc.* Tauris (?), *It.* Torcola
SEDMOGRADSKA, *see* Transylvania
SELCA (on the island of Brač), *It.* Selza
SENJ, *Lat.* Senia, *It.* Segna, *Ger.* Zengg
SENTA, *Hung.* Zenta
SESTRUNJ (island), *It.* Sestrugno or Sestro
SHKODËR or SHKODRA (Albania), *anc.* Scodra, *Cr.* Skadar, *Turkish* Iskenderiye, *It.* and *Eng.* Scutari
ŠIBENIK, *It.* Sebenico
SIGET, *see* Szigetvár
SILBA (island), *It.* Selve
SINJ, *It.* Signo
ŠIPAN (island), *It.* Giuppana
SISAK, *Lat.* Siscia or Segestica
SKADAR, *see* Shkodër
SKOPJE (Macedonia), *anc.* Scupi, *Cr.* Skoplje, *Turkish* Üsküb
SKOPLJE, *see* Skopje
SKRADIN, *It.* Scardona
SLOVONSKI BROD, *see* Brod
SMRDELJE (near Skradin), *It.* Lentischeto
SNJEŽNIK (mountain), *Slovenian* Snežnik, *It.* Monte Nevoso, *Ger.* Schneeberg
SOČA (river), *anc.* Sontius, *It.* Isonzo
SOLIN, *Lat.* Salona, *It.* Salona
ŠOLTA, *see* Sulet
SOLUN, *see* Thessalonike
SPIČ, *It.* Santa Maria degli Ospizi
SPLIT, *Gr.* Aspalathos, *Lat.* Spalatum, *It.* Spalato
SPREE (river), *Cr.* Spreva (*obs.*)
SPREVA, *see* Spree
SREBRENICA or SREBRNICA, *Lat.* Domavia
SREBRNICA, *see* Srebrenica
SREDOZEMLJE, *see* Mediterranean Sea
SREDOZEMNO MORE, *see* Mediterranean Sea
SRIJEM (region), *Serbian* Srem, *Ger.* Syrmien, *Hung.* Szerém
SRIJEMSKA MITROVICA or MITROVICA, *Serbian* Sremska Mitrovica, *Lat.* Sirmium
SRIJEMSKI KARLOVCI or KARLOVCI, *Serbian* Sremski Karlovci, *Ger.* Karlowitz
ŠTAJERSKA, *see* Styria
STAMBOL, *see* Istanbul
STAMBUL, *see* Istanbul
STARIGRAD (on the island of Hvar), *It.* Cittavecchia
STON, *Lat.* Stagnum, *It.* Stagno
STONSKI RAT, *see* Pelješac
STYRIA (region in Austria), *Cr.* Štajerska, *Ger.* Steiermark
SUBOTICA, *Hung.* Szabadka, *Ger.* Maria-Theresiopel
SUĆURAC or KAŠTEL-SUĆURAC, *It.* Castel San Giorgio
SUĆURAJ (on the island of Hvar), *It.* San Giorgio (di Lesina)
SUKOŠAN, *It.* San Cassiano
SULET or ŠOLTA, *Lat.* Solentia, *It.* Solta
SUPETAR (on the island of Brač), *It.* San Pietro (di Brazza)
SUPETARSKA DRAGA (on the island of Rab), *It.* San Pietro in Valle or Valle di San Pietro
SUSAK (island), *It.* Sansego
SUŠAK, *It.* sometimes Porto Baross
SUTOMORE, *Lat.* Sancta Maria, *It.* Santa Maria
ŠVAJCARSKA, *see* Switzerland
SVETAC (island), *It.* Sant'Andrea
SVETI VID, *see* Vidova Gora
ŠVICARSKA, *see* Switzerland
SWITZERLAND, *Cr.* Švicarska or Švajcarska

SZABADKA, *see* Subotica
SZIGETVÁR, formerly Sziget (Hungary), *Cr.* Siget

TARANTO (Italy), *anc.* Tarentum, *Cr.* Tarent
TARENT, *see* Taranto
TEMZA, *see* Thames
THAMES (river), *Cr.* Temza
THESSALONIKE (Greece), *Cr.* Solun, *Eng.* Salonica, Salonika, or Saloniki
TKON (on the island of Pašman), *It.* Tuconio
TOMISLAV-GRAD, *see* Duvno
TRANSILVANIJA, *see* Transylvania
TRANSYLVANIA or ARDEAL (Rumania), *Cr.* Transilvanija, Erdelj (*obs.*), or Sedmogradska (*obs.*), *Hung.* Erdely, *Ger.* Siebenbürgen
TRENTO (Italy), *anc.* Tridentum, *Cr.* Trident, *Eng.* Trent
TRIDENT, *see* Trento
TRIESTE (Italy), *anc.* Tregeste, *Slovenian* and *Cr.* Trst, *Ger.* Triest
TRILJ (near Sinj), *It.* Treglia
TROGIR, *Gr.* Tragurion, *Lat.* Tragurium, *It.* Traù
TRSAT, *Lat.* Tarsatica, *It.* Tersatto
TRST, *see* Trieste
TRSTENO, *It.* Cannosa
TRVIŽ, *It.* Terviso

UČKA (mountain), *It.* Monte Maggiore
UDINE (Italy), *Slovenian* Videm
UGARSKA, *see* Hungary
U(G)LJAN (island), *It.* Ugliano
ULCINJ, *Lat.* Ulcinium, *It.* Dulcigno
UNIJE (island), *It.* Unie
USA, *Cr.* SAD (Sjedinjene Američke Države) or USA
USKOČKE PLANINE, *see* Žumberačka Gora

VANDEJA, *see* Vendée
VARAŽDIN, *Lat.* Aqua Viva, *Ger.* Warasdin, *Hung.* Varasd
VARŠAVA, *see* Warszawa
VELEBIT (mountain), *It.* Alpi Bebie
VELEBIT CHANNEL, *Cr.* Velebitski Kanal, Podgorski Kanal, or Planinski Kanal, *It.* Canal della Morlacca
VELEBITSKI KANAL, *see* Velebit Channel
VENDÉE (region in France), *Cr.* Vandeja
VENEZIA (Italy), *Lat.* Venetia, *Cr.* Mleci (genitive: Mletaka), *Eng.* Venice; Venetians, *Cr.* Mlečani, Mlečići, or Venecijanci
VIDEM, *see* Udine
VIDOVA GORA (mountain on the island of Brač), VIDOVICA, or SVETI VID, *It.* San Vito
VIDOVICA, *see* Vidova Gora
VINODOL, *see* Novi
VIR (island), *It.* Puntadura
VIROVITICA, *Hung.* Veröcze
VIS (island), *Lat.* Issa, *It.* Lissa
VISLA, *see* Vistula
VISTULA (river), *Cr.* Visla
VODNJAN, *It.* Dignano d'Istria
VOGEZI, *see* Vosges
VOLOSKO (suburb of Opatija), *It.* Volosca
VOSGES (mountain), *Cr.* Vogezi
VRSAR, *anc.* Ursaria, *It.* Orsera
VUKOVAR, *Lat.* Valdasus, *Hung.* Vukovár

WARSZAWA (Poland), *Cr.* Varšava, *Eng.* Warsaw
WIEN (Austria), *Lat.* Vindobona, *Cr.* Beč, *Eng.* and *It.* Vienna
WIENER NEUSTADT (Austria), *Cr.* Bečko Novo Mjesto
WROCLAW (Poland), *Cr.* Breslava (*obs.*), *Ger.* Breslau

ZADAR, *Gr.* Diadora, *Lat.* Jadera, *It.* Zara
ZAGORA (Dalmatian hinterland), *It.* Il Montano
ZAGREB, *anc.* Zagrabia, *Ger.* Agram, *Hung.* Zágráb, *It.* Zagabria
ZATON (near Dubrovnik), *It.* Malfi
ŽELEZNO, *see* Eisenstadt
ZEMUN, *Ger.* Semlin, *Hung.* Zimony
ŽENEVA, *see* Genève
ZENICA, *Lat.* Bistue Nova
ZENTA, *see* Senta
ZIDANI MOST (Slovenia), *Ger.* Steinbrück
ŽIRJE (island), *It.* Zuri
ZLARIN (island), *It.* Slarino
ZRMANJA (river), *Lat.* Tedanium, *It.* Zermagna
ŽUMBERAČKA GORA, GORJANCI, or USKOČKE PLANINE, *Eng.* Uskok Mountains
ŽUMBERAK, *Ger.* Sichelburg, *Hung.* Sarlovar
ŽUT (Island), *It.* Zut

APPENDIX C

Pronunciation of Croatian Letters

In the Croatian language, a Latin alphabet consisting of thirty letters is used. Five of these letters correspond to vowel sounds, and the rest to consonants. With four exceptions, which are indicated below, each letter represents one definite speech sound, and each sound corresponds to one definite letter.

CROATIAN	ENGLISH	ENGLISH PRONUNCIATION
Consonants		
c	ts	ca*ts* – always, even before *a*, *o*, and *u*
č	ch	*ch*ur*ch*
ć	t (+y)	as in hi*t you*
š	sh	*sh*oe
ž	z (+y)	vi*s*ion, plea*su*re
dj, gj	d (+y)	as in di*d you*
dž	j	*j*udge
g	g	go, even before *e* and *i*
j	y	*y*outh, *y*ell
lj	ll (+y)	mi*lli*on
nj	n (+y)	ca*ny*on, o*ni*on
r	r	*r*oom

The remaining consonant sounds (b, d, f, h, k, l, m, n, p, s, t, v, z) correspond closely to the English pronunciation of the same letters.

Vowels		
a	a	f*a*ther
e	e	b*e*st
i	ee	k*ee*n
o	au	c*au*ght
u	oo	sm*oo*th

Index

ʿAbd-al-Ḳādir, 331
ʿAbd-al-Karīm, Mawlā, 324, 340
ʿAbd-al-Muṣṭafā, 329
ʿAbd-ar-Raḥmān, 331
ʿAbdallāh ʿAbdī ibn Muḥammad al-Bosnawī, 324, 325, 327, 340
ʿAbdallāh al-Khurramī al-Mostārī, 328, 346
ʿAbdallāh Māhir, 331
ʿAbdallāh Muẓaffarī Čelebī, 333
Abram, 256
Abramovich, Johnny, 454
Actium, 121, 122
Adamic, Louis, 420, 437, 450
Ad-Damīrī, 325
Adresar, 456
"Adria" (soccer club), 498
Adrianopole, 11
Adriatic, 11, 12, 15, 45, 50, 121, 134, 137, 138, 147, 516; and Austria, 137–45, 181; Byzantium in, 125; coast, shore, 120, 123, 126, 134, 176, 214; eastern-, 119–54, 122, 141, 146, 385, 440, 480, 486; "figs," 428; fleet, 129, 131; islands, 37, 120; Legion, 79; northern-, 141, 146, 147; question of, 419; ports, 127; Saracens in, 124; sea, 129, 171, 366, 385; southern-, 146, 148
Adriatic Printing Press, 272
Aegean, 119, 516
Aesop, 216, 231
Africa, 133, 372, 383, 384
Agar, 256, *see also* Hagar
Agarenians, 303
Agarovići, 302
Agron, 120, 121
Aḥmad, Sultan, 334
Aḥmad Bayāḍī-Zāde, 331
Aḥmad Bosnawī, 331
Aḥmad ibn ʿAlī al-Ghazghānī al-Bosnawī, 331
Aḥmad Jamal Dervišević, 331
Aḥmad Shams-ad-Dīn as-Sarāyī, 326, 341
Aḥmad Sūdī al-Bosnawī, 326, 341
Akačić, Frano, 422, 448
akhar, 322
Aḳowalī-Zāde, Aḥmad Khātam ibn ʿUthmān Shāhdi, 324, 325, 331, 340, 348
Akron, Ohio, 409
Al-Aḳḥiṣārī, *see* Ḥasan ibn Turkhān
Al-Bosnawī, *see* ʿAbdallāh ʿAbdī
Alabama University, 454
ʿAlāʾ-ad-Dīn ʿAlī ibn ʿAbdallāh al-Bosnawī Thābit Užičewī, 327, 328, 348–50
Alaja Mosque, 335, 339
Alaska, 407, 428, 455, 456
Albania, 38, 74, 86, 92, 137, 146, 147, 148, 219, 256, 308; coast of, 126, 147
Albanian settlers, 9, 386, 388
Albert, Archduke, 50
Alberta, 480, 483, 485, 487, 488, 490, 491, 501, 502
Albioni or De Albis, *see* Zoranić
Albrecht, Karl (Dragutin), 269, 281
Aldo's press (Venetian), 261
Aletić, P., 219
Alex, Jake (Andjelko Mandušić), 461
Alexander I of Russia, 38
Alexander III, Pope, 177, 381
Alexander, king of Yugoslavia, 381
Algiers, 133
ʿAlī, 330
Ali Beg, 316
ʿAlī-Dede ibn al-Ḥājj Muṣṭafā ʿAlāʾ-ad-Dīn as-Sigetwārī al-Bosnawī, 325, 327, 341

ʿAlī Faginović, 331
ʿAlī Fahmī al-Mostārī (Džabić), 325, 341
ʿAlī ibn ʿAbdallāh ʿAlī al-Bosnawī, 328
ʿAlī ibn al-Ḥājj Muṣṭafā al-Bosnawī, 325, 351
ʿAlī Pasha Mosque, 334
ʿAlī Zakī, Kimyāger, 331, 342
ʿAlīya (college), 332
Allegheny City, Pennsylvania, 408, 415
Allenby, British Columbia, 502
Allin, Yukon Territory, 483, 502
Almissa (Omiš), 128
Alujević, Paško, 442
Aluta River, 28
Ambridge, Pennsylvania, 408
America(s), 73, 77, 79; and Croatians, 394–464 *passim*; and Croatian seamen, 154; German settlers in, 425; and Ivan Meštrović, 433; Slavic ethnic groups in, 421; *see also individual countries*
American(s): art, 438, 439; audiences, 443; authorities, 397, 401, 406; Catholic hierarchy, 410; Croatian organizations, 416, 418, 420; Croatians, 406–9 *passim*, 413–17 *passim*, 420, 422, 428, 429, 430, 435, 439, 440, 441, 443, 444, 447, 456, 460, 464, *see also* Croatian Americans; in First World War, 84; folklorists, 441; forces, 91; fraternalism, 458; historians, 424, 446, 463; ideal, 445; impressions, 436; journals, press, newspapers, 279, 419, 450, 452; life, 412, 413, 423; for Serbo-Croatian unity, 82; slums, 437; tradition, 22
American Association for the Advancement of Science, 446
American Croatian Academic Club, 460
American Croatians, Central Council of, 420
American Edison Company, 430
American Institute of Mining and Metallurgical Engineering, 432
American Slav Congress, 420
American Society for Croatian Migration, 405
American Union, 62
Americanization of Croatians, 412–14, 447, 458
Americans, United Committee of South Slavic, 420
Ammann, 266
Amsterdam, 263
Ančić or Anitius, Ivan, 208
Ancona, 120, 261, 516
Andrassy, Count, 51
Andjelinović, 82
Andreolo, printer, 271
Andretich, John, 454
Andriaš, Dominic, 370
Andrić, Ivo, 303, 320
Andrić, Nikola, 285
Anglicized, 414
Anglophones, 300
Anglo-Saxon, 87, 463
Anitius (Ančić), Ivan, 208
Annapolis, 455, 461
Anschluss, 87
Antonius, 121
Antonović, Florio, 426
Appendini, F. M., 206, 222, 238, 271
Apsorus (Osor), 122, 176
Apulia, 120, 125
Arabia(n), 317, 322, 332, 333
Arabic: calligraphy, 330–1, 336; letters, script, and use in printing, 277, 278, 299, 329, 331, 337; literature, 304, 323, 324–6, 332; metrics, 325, 329; philology, 325; translations from, 325–6; use of, 207, 324, 328, 332; use of words in Croatian, 301–2, 329
Arandjelovac, 71
Arba, *see* Rab
Arbanas, Billy, 454
Arcadia, Academy of, 222, 239
Archbishopric Press, 270
Ardiaei, 120–1
Aretino, Pietro, 189
Argentina, 439, 451
"argosy," 133
ʿĀrif Ḥikmat Beg ibn Dhī-ʾl-Fiḳār Nāfidh Pasha Hersekli, 328, 351
Ariosto, 184, 199, 216
Arizona, 407; University, 454, 455
Armanini, A., 273
Armenians, 386, 388
Arpad (dynasty), 126
Ar-Rūmī, Jalāl ad-Dīn, 326, 327, 332
Arsenale (in Venice), 127
"Art U.S.A. '58," 435
Artaleo, Spiro, 273
Arumanians, 158
Arvida, Quebec, 483, 491, 502, 503
Asia, 158
Asiatic Games, 455
ʿĀṣim Yūsuf, 331
Aspern, 36
Assumption of the Virgin Mary (parish), 409
Assumption University (Windsor), 439

As-Suyūṭī, 325
āthār-i mufīda (useful works), 333
Atlantic: coast, 397, 429, 437; Ocean, 134, 153, 394
Attila, 203, 256
Auersperg, General Count, 11
Auffenberg, Moritz von, 62
Augustus Caesar, 121
Austin, Texas, 440
Austria, 11, 21, 27, 35, 43, 52, 86, 91, 96, 145, 236, 403, 417, 418, 430, 432, 446, 462; absolutism in, 16; Bavarians against, 24; and Boka Kotorska, 37, 38; and Bosnia, 305; Cisleithanian, 44, 56; and Croatia, 17, 23, 35, 42, 53, 196; and Ferdinand I, 5, 135; and France, 34, 36, 37; Germanic, 87, 95; and Germany, 90; "Great Austria," 60, 61, 62; House of, 10; and Hungary, 53, 55, 63, 72, 73, 92, 143, 397, 418; Inner, 48; Lower, 10, 13; and Matthias Corvinus, 3; and Narodna Odbrana, 67; and "Nationalists," 39, 44; and nationality question, 61, 68; nobility in, 43; and Polish succession, 27, 227; and Spanish succession, 24; and *Srbobran*, 54; and Steed, 87; Transleithanian, 44; Upper, 10, 13; wars waged by, 17, 20; and Zrinski-Frankapan conspiracy, 23; *see also following entries*
Austria-Hungary, 51, 65–70 *passim*, 79, 84, 87, 88, 140, 274, 399, 401, 402, 417, 482, 486; and Bosnia-Hercegovina, 278; dissolution of, 91, 92, 96; South Army of, 71; troops of, 86
"Austriaki," 78, 79, 82
Austrian, 38, 56, 63, 75, 86, 401; anti-, 40, 57, 58, 67; army, military forces, soldiers, 5, 13, 16, 29, 40, 86, 146, 147, 193, 429; authorities, 76; capital, 38, 46; Catholics, 18; Command, 94; constitution, 63; delegation, 48; emperor, ruling house, 18, 45; Empire, Monarchy, state, 42, 51, 72, 138, 211, 226, 417; flag, 138, 140; fleet in Otranto Strait, 147; government, 41, 46, 138, 139; Hapsburg countries, 10; harbors (Dalmatian coast), 35, 137, 146; Hussars, 43; lands, provinces, 10, 17, 21, 23, 25, 85; -Magyar Compromise, 46; military men, 29, 62, 63; navy, 143–7 *passim*; Pan-Germans, 89; Part of Monarchy, 72, 75, 88; "party," 23; pressure on Italy, 80; prisons, 227; pro-, 53, 76, 96, 418; Protestants, 18; Reichsrat, 72, 77, 82, 88; rule, 42, 67, 138, 143, 144, 175, 271; sea power, 48; Slovenian-Croatian nucleus, 91; Social Democrats, 89, 90; statistics, 397; Suzzallo, 444; -Turkish wars, 228
Austrian Lloyd, 141, 149
Austrians, 158, 462; in Belgrade, 28; and Budapest, 78; after Campo Formio, 34–5; and Croatian question, 64; in Dalmatia, 35; and the Frontier, 8; German-speaking, 83; in Montenegro, 83; and Pribićević, 93; and the seacoast, 48; and seaplanes, 148; and the Turks, 10, 28; in 1918, 91
Austro-Croatian: *Anschluss*, 24; forces, 130
Austro-Hungarian, 141, 143, 146, 148–51 *passim*, 175, 278; Agreement, 138, 140; army, troops, 61, 71, 80, 81, 84, 87, 93, 94; *Ausgleich*, 47; coast, 142, 143; Command, 87; Dual Monarchy, Empire, state, 53, 61, 62, 63, 66, 67, 70, 71, 72, 74, 78, 80–7 *passim*, 90, 91, 140, 143, 144, 146–9 *passim*, 267, 268, 335, 387, 389, 482; dualism, 51, 62; Embassy, 79; general headquarters, 94; navy, 432; occupation of Bosnia-Hercegovina, 278, 279, 305, 324, 387; offensive, 71; public, 75; rule in Croatia, 417; Slavs, 68; union, 46, 53, 70, 83, 90
Avars, 122, 363
Avonlea, Saskatchewan, 503
awḳāf, 333, 338
Ayyūbī-Zāde, *see* Muṣṭafā ibn Yūsuf al-Mostārī

Baba, Pietro, 272
Babić, Ljubo, 288, 289
Babich, John, 454
Babich, Matt, 461
Babin, Simon, 442
Babinger, Franz, 303
Bach (Alexander) era, 41–3
"Bach Hussars," 43
Bachellor, Charles, 430
Bachich, Willy A., 510–11
Bačić, Mike, 426
Bačka, 281, 463
Badovinac, John, 458
Badurina, Theodore, 452
Baglioni Press, 271
Bahāʾ-ad-Dīn Sikirić, 331
Bajram Beg, 315

Bakar, 135, 140, 516
Balch, Emily Green, 400, 407
Balen, Mike, 454
Balić, Smail, 512–13
Baličević, 370
Balkan (daily paper), 259
Balkan(s), 27, 66, 84, 86, 90, 92, 95, 157, 158, 317, 323, 325, 363, 364, 379, 384, 385, 389, 400; countries, 387; front, 70; lands, 312, 320; peoples, 175
Balkan Mountains, 158, 385
Balkan Peninsula, 176, 190, 303, 383, 384
Balkan War, 145
Baloković, Zlatko, 443
Baltic, Balts, 157
Ban, 12, 24, 26, 41, 49, 93, 95, 323; administration, office of, 10, 51, 62; appointment or nomination of, 47, 48; authority or control of, 12, 13, 17, 18, 29, 30, 33; and Crna Ruka, 68; and the Hungarian Council of Lieutenancy, 30; Ivan Skerlecz, 64; jurisdiction of, 14, 17, 19, 23, 26, 40; list of Bosnian bans, 117; list of Croatian bans, 114–17; Magyar, 51; Pejačević, 55; Petar Erdödi, 193; and sovereignty, 211; Zrinski, 191, 210, 262; *see also* Banal
Ban's Bosnia, 365, 387
Banal (Ban's): authorities, 13, 19, 24; Bench, 26; Border (Banija or Banska Krajina), 14; *četas*, 9; (Civil) Croatia, 12, 13, 14, 21, 23, 25, 30, 35, 36, 38, 401, 440; *see also* Ban
Banat, 67, 71, 462
Bancroft, H. H., 424
Banić, Mario I., 281
Banija (Banal Border), 14
Banjaluka, 335, 336, 338, 339, 379, 380, 386
banjaluka (embroidery), 320
Banjavicich, Emil, 454
Banovina: elections in, 59; regiments from, 40
Banska Krajina (Banal Border), 14
Bar (Antivari), 372, 516
Baraković, Juraj, 203, 220
Baranja, 30, 463
Baranović, Krešimir, 319
Barčić, Erazmo, 257
Bari, 124
Baričević, Adam Alojzij, 238
Barich, Rudy, 454
Barilović, 14
Barkan, Omer L., 369, 373
Barleti, Marino, 266
Baromić, Blaž, 254, 255
Baronius or Baronio, Caesar, 177, 225
Barović, Nikola, 426
Bartulović, 82
Bašagić, Safvet-Beg, 380
Basariček, Stjepan, 285
Basiljević, Bazilije, 394
Baška Tabletts, 159, 516
baškaluk, 322
Battara, Anton Luigi, 273
Battara brothers, 272
Bauk, Aḥmad, 306
Bavaria(ns), 24, 28, 29, 31, 36, 193
Bavcevich, Phillip Michael (Barton Michael Phillips), 450
Bayādī-Zāde, *see* Ḍiyā-ad Dīn
Bayou Creek, Louisiana, 426
Beaumont, Texas, 432
Beba, Meho, 306
Bedeković, Josip, 234
Bedeković, Kazimir, 234
Bedričić, Silvestar, 254, 255
Beggs, Joseph, 454
Begler-beg, 378
Begna-Kožičić, Šimun, 255
Behar, 280, 380
Bekavac, Bosiljko, 408, 448, 449
Belgrade, 28, 68, 71, 159, 333, 516; and the Coalition, 57; and the Dual Monarchy, 66; Greek-, 386; Parliament, 380, 419; regime, 419; Serbian Academy of, 262; and Supilo, 58; and Yugoslav Committee, 79
Belichik, Steve, 454
Beloit, Wisconsin, 457
Belostenec, Ivan, 206, 266
Bembo, 184
Bendbaša (district of Sarajevo), 319
Bendulović, Ivan, 208
Benedict XII, Pope, 367
Benedictine, 184, 202, 203, 206, 215, 261, 425
Beneš, 95
Benger, Nikola, 234
Benignus, Georgius (Juraj Dragišić), 179
Benković (Benkov), Ivan, 436
Berdik, Juraj, 502
Berlin, 73, 78, 85, 86; Congress of, 51, 305
Bernardin of Split, Brother, 253
Berthold, H., 287

Bertolini, 149
Besarabia, 384
Beširović, Murād Beg, 306
Besse (Wesse), Andrija, 267
Bethlen, Prince Gabriel of Transylvania, 18
Betina, 143, 150
Betondić, Josip, 217
Bettera, Baro, 202
Bez (Bezmalinović), Nick, 455
bezistān (market-hall), 337
Biankini, Ante, 77, 273, 445
Bible or Sacred Scripture, 180, 182, 183, 193
Bičakčić, Edhem, 380
Bihać, 5, 8, 10, 14, 306, 375
Bijela, 372
Bijeljina, 375
Bilan, Petar, 273
Bilo Mountain, 8, 15
Biloxi, Mississippi, 426, 455
Bindoni and Pasini, 253
Biograd, 126, 516
Biščević, Ḥājj Rustam Beg, 306
Biser, 380
Biskupska Tiskara, 268
Bistrica, Our Lady of, 459
Bjelavac, Hivzi, A., 380
Bjelovar, 28, 268, 281, 516
Black Sea, 153, 363, 364
Blackburn, British Columbia, 502
Bladworth, Saskatchewan, 480, 491
Blaeu, Johannes, 263
Blagaj, 338
Blagojević, Adam Tadija, 232
Blasius of Gradac, 371
Blašković, Andrija, 268
Blau, Otto, 329
Blazina, Tony, 455
Blecha Josip, 283
Blinja, 14
Bobaljević, Vuk, 178
Bobovac, 14
Bočać (Donji Kosinj), 15
Bocskay rebellion, 13–15
Bodega y Quadra, ship of, 479
Bogadek, Francis, 449
Bogdanovich, Martin, 456
Bogomil(s), Bogomilism, 367, 388; in Bosnia, 303, 366–7, 368, 370, 373, 389; Croatian, 367, 374, 380, 383, 388
Bogović, Mirko, 257
Bogovich, Hugh, 454
Bohemia, 3, 10, 61, 65, 83, 363, 516
Bohemian, 12, 435
Bojničić, Vjera, 288
Boka Kotorska (Gulf or Bay of Kotor), 34, 37, 38, 129, 131, 138, 139, 148, 363, 516, *see also* Kotor; navy base, 144, 145, 146, 148, 151, 152
Bokau, Karl, 269
Bokeška mornarica, 131
Bol, 203
Bologna, 178
Bolton, H., 424
Bona, Jacobus de (Jakov Bunić), 180
Boniface VIII, Pope, 388
Boniface IX, Pope, 267
Bonifačić, Ante, 451
Boninis, Boninus de (Dobruško Dobrić), 251, 270
Boranić Press, Stjepan, 270
Border, 9, 10, *see also* Military Frontier
Borić, Michael, 503
Borić, Stanley, 459
Bornamissa de Alsow, Francis, 378
Borojević, General, 87
bosančica, see Cyrillic
Bosanka vila, 280
Bosanski Petrovac, 306
Bosanski vjestnik, 277
Bosansko-hercegovačke novine, 278
Bosansko-hercegovački seljak, 280
Bosansko-hercegovački signal, 280
Bosansko-hercegovački željezničar, 280
Bosansko Kolo, 277
Bosiljević, Joseph V., 405
Bošković, Petar, 218
Bošković, Rudjer Josip, 221, 434
Bosna, 277, 278
Bosna River, 337, 375
Bosnia, 14, 20, 27, 36, 52, 68, 71, 178, 219, 237, 276, 278, 279, 302, 304, 308, 318, 320, 330, 333, 339, 364, 365, 374, 375, 376, 497; and Archduke Albert, 51; (Bosnia) argentina, 228; and Austria, 305; and Bogomilism, 366, 374; (Bosnia) Croatiae, 375; Croatian Catholicism in, 382; Croatians of, 376, 385; dialect of, 205, 376, 377; Dominicans in, 367, 388; eastern, 303; Eugene of Savoy in, 27; in First World War, 72, 92; Franciscans in, 207, 208, 209, 223, 226, 227, 228, 367; governor of, 280, 378, 379; historic right to, 27; invasion of, 71; and Islam (Islamic), 302, 303, 305, 336, 371; Italian architects in, 339; Kingdom of, 3;

Muslims of, 207; Ottoman possession of, Turks in, 3, 128, 175, 228, 256, 303, 362, 368, 372, 381, 388; "Poturs" in, 370; Serbs in, 158, 373, 386, 387; tales of, 319; in Turkish history, 328; Vicaria Bosniae, Vicariate of Bosnia, 367, 375; viziers from, 305; and Vlachs, 385; western, 386; *see also* Bosnia-Hercegovina, Bosnian, Bosnians

Bosnia-Hercegovina, 50, 67, 71, 93, 138, 139, 195, 277, 279, 309, 321, 364, 366, 367, 377, 380, 388, 389, 390, 397, 398, 401, 452; annexation of, 50, 51, 61, 65; and Bogomilism, 366; Catholics in, 370, 371, 382; and Croatians, 27, 68, 234, 363–7, 388; Croatians of, in First World War, 70, 75, 76, 83, 85, 92; between East and West, 362; folk music of, 317–19; and Franciscans, 276; and a "Great Serbia," 50; and heresy, 367; immigrants from, 462; and Kašič, 205; Muslims in, 302, 304, 305, 367–81, 459; occupation of, 51, 175, 278; and Orient, 333; and Palmotić, 199; partition of, 89; printing in, 276–80, 281; and Serbian nationalists, 67, 72; Serbs in, 387, 388; and Trialism, 63; and Triune Kingdom, 61, 89, 213; and Turks, 255, 367, 381, 386; and Vlachs, 389

Bosniaks, 323–6 *passim*, 328, 333, 338, *see also* Bosnian-Hercegovinian

Bosnian, 37, 66, 67, 69, 278, 319, 320, 325, 327, 383; art, 323; ballads, 307; Ban(s), 368, 387; begs, 14; bishop, 370, 372, 382; caravansaries, 337; Catholic literature, 276; Catholics, 364, 369, 374; craftsmanship, 320, 321; Croatian union, 51; culture, 339, 379; Cyrillic script, 207; dialect, language, 208, 239, 374; embroidery, 320; enigma, 362; folk songs, 317, 318; Franciscans, 368, 370; kings, kingdom, 323, 368; love songs, 317; music, 317, 318; Muslim epic songs, 307; Muslim folk tales, 319; Muslim lyric songs, 316; Muslims, 303–6 *passim*, 312, 313, 318, 320, 326, 329, 335, 379; nobles, nobility, 3, 303, 321, 371; Pashalik, 370; population, natives, 304, 368; Posavina, 380; province, 375; Sandjak Beg, 7; script, 336; Serbs, 67, 68, 76; settlements, 302; towns, 338, 339; tragic love, 316; villages, 339; women, 332; writers, 302; *see also* Bosnia, Bosnians

Bosnian-Hercegovinian, 368, 397; (Bosniaks), 323; Catholics, 374, 390; Croatians, 373, 388; immigrants, 401, 462; musicians, 318; Muslim poetry, 307; Muslims, 299–361, 305, 309, 312, 324, 380; regiments, 70; scholars, 305

Bosnians, 330, 331, 374, 375, 378, 379, 385, 397

Bosnische Korrespondenz, 279

Bosnische Post, 279, 280

Bošnjak, 280

Bošnjak, Blaž, 230

Bošnjak, Petar, 263–4

Boston, 397, 439, 442; Red Sox (baseball team), 454; College, 454

Bothwell, Ontario, 491

Boué de Lapeyrère, Auguste, 146

Bourlamaque, Quebec, 488, 491, 502

Bowring, Sir John, 313

Boyd, John, 313

Božić, Dobroslav, 408, 448, 449

Brač, 123, 127, 130, 204, 516

Bracher, Melchior, 274

Bradica, Stjepan, 500

Braidech, Matthew, 448

Bratislava, 264, 516

Braun, Maximilian, 329

Brazil, 451

brazzere (ships), 139

Bregava River, 337

Brescia, 223

Breskovich, Robert J., 455

Breslau, 331, 521

Breyer, Mirko, 252, 270, 284

Brezovački, Tito, 235, 238

Bribir, 128, 455

Brindisi, 147, 148

Brist, 224

Britannia Mine, British Columbia, 502

British, 36, 41, 52, 87, 93, 132; firms, 150; flag, 137; forces, 140, 146, 147, 148, 152; frigates and ships, 137

British Columbia, 428, 479, 480, 482, 485, 486, 488, 490, 500, 501, 502; University of, 501

Brlić, Andrija Torkvat, 257

Brod, 259, 281, 371, 516

Brokar (Italian writer-traveler), 323

Bronze Age, 119

Brookhaven National Laboratory at Upton, Long Island, 448

Brooklyn, New York, 436
Brozić, Mikula, 253
Brozović, Stjepko, 422, 448
Brozović, V., 504
Bruère Desrivaux, Marc, *see* Bruerović
Bruerović or Bruère Desrivaux, Marko, 218–19
Brule Mines, Alberta, 502
Brussels, 437
Brussilov, 80, 81
Bubalini, Antonio, 273
Bučić, Mihajlo, 262
Bucks County, Pennsylvania, 438
Bucman-Jamaković, Ahmed, 307
Buda, 7, 13, 36, 48
Budapest, 44,46, 49, 56, 57, 59, 75, 76, 78, 88, 143, 149, 516; journals, 51; Kačić in, 224; library of the National Museum, 255, 262; non-Croatian businessmen in, 142; and the Sabor, 59; University Library, 262
Budim, 328, 378
Budinić, Šime, 205, 212
Budva, 144, 363
Buenos Aires, 80
Buffalo, New York, 495
bugarštice (poems), 217, 220
Bugojno, 322
Buja, Nikola, 426
Bukovac, Vlaho, 289, 436
Bukovina, Bukovinian, 74, 75
Bulgaria, 52, 90, 158; and lithography, 282; and Turks, 256; and Vlachs, 385
Bulgar(s), Bulgarian(s), 52, 66, 71, 86, 157, 158, 163, 363, 385, 401; emperor, 366; forces, 81; language, 157, 158; Orthodox, 366; settlers, 9, 384, 386, 388
Bulić, Frane, 285
Bulić, Janko, 502
Bulletin (Toronto and Windsor), 493
Bulletin (United Croatians), 421
Buna (near Mostar), 322, 331, 337
Bunić, Ivan, 203
Bunić, Jakov (Jacobus de Bona), 180
Bunić, Luka,127
Bunić, Nikola, 202
Bunić Vučićević, Dživo, 195, 200–1, 216
Burgenland, 274, 462, 516
Burhān-ad-Dīn ibn Ibrāhīm ibn Bakhshī-Dede Khalīfa al-Bosnawī, 325, 342
Busovača, 320
Butković, Ivan, 416
Butkovich, Tony, 454
Butler, 496
Buzet, 260
Byron, George G. N., 313
Byzantine, Byzantium, 126, 366; (towns in the) Adriatic, 125; culture, 312; emperor, 363, 381; governor, 122; rite, 408; vessels, 122; writers, 365, 385

Cadi of Imotski, 314
Cadomin, Alberta, 502
Ćaić, Ćerim, 306
Cairo, 325, 331
Čajniče, 335
Čakavian or Chakavian, 39, 159, 160, 204, 205, 206, 210, 212, 377
Čakovec, 262, 281, 516
Calgary, Alberta, 480, 487, 491, 492, 494, 499, 502
California, 396, 397, 407, 426, 427, 436, 456, 495; figs from, 428; Gulf of, 424; Lower, 395, 424; University of, 444, 446, 448, 454
Calumet, Michigan, 397, 408, 409, 411, 429
Camic, Joe, 454
Campbell River, British Columbia, 503
Campo Formio, 34
Canada: Association of Real Estate Boards of, 501; Council, 497, 498; Croatians in, 458, 479–503; Ethnic Press Club of, 498; Federation of Croatian Societies in, 493; *see also* Canadian
Canadian(s): cycling team, 499; economy, 500; Festival of Neo-, 495; fisheries, 501; interior, 485, 501; languages, 489, 497; literature, 496; navy, 495; newspapers, French-, 497; Pacific coast, 479; Parliament, 493; poetry, 497; politics, 498; Red Cross, 503; scouts, 489; sculpture, 496; sports, 498; universities, 490, 495; Volley-ball Association, 500; Writers' Association, 497; *see also* Canada
Canadian Phalanx, 497
Canal Flats, British Columbia, 503
Candia (Crete), 119, 129
Candiano, Pietro, 124, 125
Canisius, Peter, 212
"Cantalia" (soccer club), 498
Caorle, 124

Caporetto, 84–6, 87, 518
Capuchin press, 258
Caracciolo, Roberto, 255
čardak, 321, 322
Carichic, Mexico, 424
Carinthia, 8, 10, 12, 18, 25, 26, 37, 91, 265, 516
Carnegie Foundation, 444, 448
Carnegie Hall, New York, 440
Carniola, 8, 10, 12, 18, 25, 26, 37, 85, 89, 91, 193, 264, 396, 517
"Carolina" highway, 27
Carpathian, 74, 157, 363, 376, 385
çarşĭ (business district), 339
Carson Mine, Ontario, 483
Carthage, 121
Cartier, Jacques, 479
Cassaday, British Columbia, 503
Cassius (Kašić), Bartol, 204, 371
Cassut, Jean, 337
Castaldo, John, 8
Catholic(s), Catholicism, 18, 54, 69, 193, 200, 280, 382, 455, 493; bishop(s), 255, 381; in Bosnia-Hercegovina, 3, 13, 367, 369, 371, 379, 382, 385, 388, 389; Church, 208, 213, 266, 303, 367, 369, 382, 494; clergy, priests, 77, 276, 381, 382; countries, 236; Croatian(s), 9, 14, 61, 67, 70, 305, 367, 368, 370, 372, 376, 377, 381, 382, 388, 491; crypto-, 371; faith, 366, 368, 372, 386, 388; layman, 447, 457; martyrs, 434; missionaries, 366; organization, 459; quarterly, 453; schools, 277; universities, 447
Ćatić, Musa Ćazim, 380
Čaušević, Hadži Mehmed Džemaludin, 380
Cavtat, 122, 128, 132, 436, 517
Čazma, 14
Čehotina River, 337
Ćejvan Aga, 308
Čekada, Smiljan, 410
Čelakovsky, František-Ladislav, 313
Čelebija, Evlija, 379
Celestine, Indiana, 425
ćemāne, 318
Čengić, Smail Aga, 306, 308; his son Ded'Aga, 306
Central Powers, 81
Cerauscheg(g), *see* Zerauscheg
Čermak, 283
Cerovšek, *see* Zerauscheg
Cerva, Aelius Lampridius (Ilija Crijević), 179, 180
Cesarec, August, 281
Česmički, Ivan (Janus Pannonius), 178
Cetin, 3, 5
Cetina River, 34, 123
Charles I, king of Spain, 4, 5
Charles V, 9, 133, 135
Charles VI, 135
Chemainus, British Columbia, 491, 503
Chemin des Dames, 84
Chernovtsy (Ukraine), 198
Chesarek, F. J., 459
Chicago, 409, 410, 414, 417, 420, 421, 422, 429, 435, 436, 439, 442, 443, 447, 449, 452, 459, 460, 480; Art Institute, 433; Bears (football team), 454; Black Hawks (hockey team), 455; Columbian Exposition at, 428, 430; Columbus Hospital, 445; Grant Park, 433; Mercy Hospital, 445; newspapers, 437, 457; Painters and Sculptors Society, 435; Police Crime Detection Laboratory in, 457; slums, 450; University of, 446, 447; White Sox (baseball team), 454
Chicago Sloboda, 422
Chicoutimi, Quebec, 491
China City, Yukon, 483, 502
Chlopy, 56
Christ, 213, 370
Christ the King (parish), 409
Christian(ity), 178, 184, 197, 198, 202, 204, 210, 227, 304, 382; artisans, 320; ascetics, 181; Catholics, 376; children, 377; churches, 362; doctrine, 232; edification, 204; faith (religion), 226, 369, 385; leaders, 372; Orthodox, 376; population, 175, 368; and Poturs, 371, 372; powers, 362; rule, 373; teaching, 370; thought, 182; values, 196; West, 368
Christian Social Party (Austria), 89
Christianization, 177, 235, 390
Christina of Sweden, 200
Christmas customs, 441
Chuvalo, George, 499
Čikulin, Baron Ivan, 264
Cikuts, 427
Ciminelli, S., 180
Cincinnati Reds (baseball team), 454
Cinnamus, John, 365
Činovnički list, 280
Civil Croatia, *see* Banal
Civil War (American), 427

Clam-Martinitz, Count, 83
Claudiano, 197
Claudius, Emperor, 384
Cleveland, 77, 396, 405, 406, 408, 416, 419, 421, 435, 439, 443, 457, 460, 461
Coaldale, Alberta, 491
Coalitionists, 61, 62, 64, 75, *see also* Serbo-Croatian Coalition
cocas (vessels), 132
Coe, Peter (Knego), 443
Colier, Saskatchewan, 503
Cologne, 251
Colorado, 407
Columbia University, 444, 448, 453
Columbus (Christopher), 394, 439
Commonwealth, 501
Communism, 421
Communist, 171, 400, 405, 460; anti-, 421; paper, 420; Partisans, 420, 421; rule, 421; Yugoslavia, 420
Comnenus, Emmanuel, 365, 381
Compayre, Gabriel, 285
conduras (vessels), 125
Congregation for the Propagation of the Faith, 206, 209, 370, 372
Congress (in Belgrade), 380
Consag(o) or Conzag, Fernando, 395, 424, *see also* Konšćak
Consag Rocks, 424
Consilium or Dicasterium (Croatian Council of Lieutenancy), 30
Constantine VII Porphyrogenitus, 176, 364
Constantinople, 7, 13, 20, 21, 132, 157, 213, 305, 363, 368, 369; Imperial Archives of, 364; Patriarchs of, 373, 382
Cooksville, Ontario, 485, 488, 491
Copper Mountain, British Columbia, 502
Ćorak-Slavenska, Mia, 443
Corcyra, 121
"Cordon" (Kordun), 9
Corfu, 79, 82, 121, 147, 518
Corinth, 130
Corneille, 218
Cornell University, 448, 451
Coron in Morea, 133
Ćorović, historian, 9
Cortona, St. Margaret of, 232
Corvinus, Matthias, 3, 178
Cosulich, 149
Counter-Reformation, 180, 205, 206, 207; in northern Croatia, 208–9
Cracow, 307
Cranbrook, British Columbia, 502, 503
Creel Committee (CPI), 88
Creighton Mine, Ontario, 483, 491, 502
Cres, 122, 130, 139, 142, 144, 517
Crescenzio, Bartolomeo, 134
Crete (Candia), Cretan, 119, 129
Crew House, 88
Crewe, Lord, 78
Crexa or Crepsa, *see* Cres
Crijević, Ilija (Aelius Lampridius Cerva), 179, 180
Crijević Tuberon, Ludovik, 271
Crikvenica, 281
Crimea(n), 28, 140
Crna Ruka (Black Hand) or "Union of Death" Society, 68
Crnić, Al (Guy Mitchell), 443
Crnko, Ferenc, 195
Croat(s), 33, 65, 79, 377, 413, 414, *see also* Croatians
"Croatan," 395
Croatia, 27, 41, 42, 55, 63, 141, 178, 210, 214, 215, 223, 238, 264; as a battleground (armed camp), 7, 11; and (I.) Benković, 437; and Bogomilism, 366; eastern, 171; in First World War, 76; and the Frontier, 8; governor of, 366; a "Great Croatia," 50, 53, 55, 61, 76, 96, 212; Hungarian legislature in, 17; and Hungary, 23, 44, 47, 48, 126, 127, 417; Independent State of, 153; and Inner Austria, 18; and Istria, 253, 254; and Istro-Rumanians, 158; and Maria Theresa, 29; medieval, 126; and (I.) Meštrović, 433; minister for, 49; mountainous, 439; northern, 194, 195, 199, 208, 210, 211, 213, 215, 233–6 *passim*, 238, 239; proper, 7, 397, 398, 401; Provincia Croatiae, 375; Radić in, 60; and (B.) Radica, 450; and Reformation, 192, 193, 194; Red-, 365, 374; after (the Peace of) Schönbrunn, 36; southern, 36, 54, 194, 211, 263; and (N.) Tesla, 431; and Trialism, 63, *see also* Trialism; Turks in, 3, 8; Upper, 193, 195, 196, 210–14, 259, 286; and Uskoks, 126; and Venice, 124, 125, 126; weakness of, 19, 24; western, 18, 27; White-, 314, 365; *see also* Croatian, Croatians
Croatia (soccer club), 498
Croatia, Liberation of, 436
Croatia Press, 453

Croatia-Slavonia, 5, 7, 10, 13, 24, 26, 32, 37, 38–40, 41, 42, 51, 52, 55, 56, 62, 64; and Archduke Albert, 50; under Bach, 42; Ban of, 12; civil, 52; and Croatian language, 59; and Croatian-Serbian identity, 57; and Dalmatia, 32, 34, 44, 46; in eighteenth-century, 24–33; in the First World War, 72, 75, 81, 85, 91; and Francis-Joseph, 63; and Hungary or Magyars, 32, 38, 45, 47, 48, 59, 65, 83, 175; immigrants to the United States from, 462; and Mayerling, 56; and Paul Rauch, 59, 60; and Pejačević, 55; and Radić, 60; and Rijeka Resolutions, 57; separate nation, 49; and Serbia, 58, 72; Serbians of, 50, 54; and serfdom, 39; *see also* Triune Kingdom

Croatian: agricultural development, 54, 62; Americans, 64, 77, 78, 79, 126, *see also* American Croatians; ancestry, descent, origin, parents, 305, 336, 373, 375, 376, 377, 436, 439, 440, 443, 444, 446, 447, 456, 458, 463, 488, 501; culture, 50, 254, 438, 493, 499; economic recovery, economy, 26, 399; immigrants to USA, 399, 402, 405–14 *passim*, 422, 429, 434, 438, 445, 448, 449, 453, 459, 461–4; immigrants to Canada, 479–86 *passim*, 489, 500; nation(ality), people, 39, 50, 53, 55, 57, 60, 62, 73, 78, 85, 119, 175, 238, 254, 256, 365, 375, 378, 380, 419, 420, 440, 458, 462, 464; paper factories, 287; pioneers, 426, 429, 462; sailors, 143, 144, 395; Serbs, 50–60, 64, 70, 73, 75, 77, 88, 89, 92, 95; settlements in USA, 406, 408, 410, 413, 414–33, 458; settlements in Canada, 480, 487, 490, 491; settlers, 14; shipping industry, 131; *slavonski, slovinski, ilirički* for, 213, 233; *see also following entries*

Croatian (arts, crafts, leisure): acting (in USA), 443–4; book-plating, 288; book-printing, 251, 254, 256, 259; composers, 319; graphic art, artists, 288, 289; heraldic work, 212; lithographic press, 281; music (in USA), 439–43, (in Canada), 493–5; national costumes, 440, 441, 494; painters (in USA), 436–9, (in Canada), 496; press, printing, 254, 255, 257, 259, 278, 405, (of church melodies or songs), 265, 267; sculptors (in USA), 433–6, (in Canada), 496; sportsmen (in USA), 453–5, (in Canada), 498–9

Croatian (language, literature, scholarship): almanacs, 265, 422, 449, 460; alphabet, 205, 212; authors, writers, 178, 191, 193, 208, 229, 236, 237, 258, 263, 264, 394, 412, 450, (in USA), 448–53, (in Canada), 496; books, 225, 252, 265, 266, 268, 274, 284, 460; chronicle, 364, 365, 384; dialects, 160; dictionaries (-English), 449, (-Latin-Italian), 271, (-Turkish), 207; Encyclopedia, 286; folk poetry, 178, 180, 184, 221, 327; folk tales, 236; grammar, 165–71, 205, 206, 213; historians, 338, 372, 399, 463, 464; humanists, 176, 179, 219, 304; journals, periodicals, 285, 457, 460; language, 39, 41, 58, 64, 77, 157–74, 177, 178, 183, 186, 191, 192, 199, 206, 207, 210, 212, 213, 215, 219, 229, 252, 253, 254, 260, 262, 275–9 *passim*, 285, 301, 305, 328, 362, 367, 368, 375, 378, 421, 445, 447; latinists, 221, 222; lawyers, 42, 499; literary renaissance, 39, 212; literature, 159, 176, 181, 182, 184, 185, 186, 188, 191, 193, 196, 197, 198, 204, 206, 207, 210, 214, 226, 228, 230, 231, 303, 330, 448, 452; metrics, 232; names, 302, 373, 377, 423, 453, 463, 496; newspapers, 85, 259, 280, 399, 411, 417, 422; plays, 235, 449; poetry, poets, 178, 180, 200, 226, 233, 449, (in USA), 448–53, (in Canada), 497–8; professors, teachers, 263, 285, (in Canada), 495–6; Protestant literature, 192–4, 261, 262; scholars, (in USA), 444–8, 453; schools in the United States, 408, 409; translation, 185, 193, 262

Croatian (political, geographical, historical): administration, 72, 76; aspirations, 50, 51, 52, 64, 68, 69; authorities, 71, 399; autonomy, 25, 31, 64; -Bosnian union, 51; boundaries, 27; -Bulgarian community, 52; character of Medjumurje, 45; coast, 120, 134, 137, 139, 144, 153, 154, 239, 253; conflicts with the Hapsburgs, 12; constitution, 22, 38, 39, 51; Council of Lieutenancy, 30; county regimes, 29, 30, 32, 49;

defeat in 1493, 256; delegates, deputies, representatives, 13, 17, 32, 44, 47, 48, 82; Dioclea, 373; domestic affairs, 33, 49, 55; education, 62; estates, 8, 11, 12, 13, 17, 19, 21, 29, 30, 31, 32, 38, 39; flag, 51, 82; fleet, navy, ships, 123, 124, 125, 137, 139, 140, 141, 142, 143, 153, 176, 192; forces, regiments, troops, units, 18, 29, 33, 34–7 *passim*, 40, 51, 70, 73, 74, 80, 81, 84, 85, 89, 91, 94, 125, 191, 223; freedoms, 17; generals, 92, 93; history, 195, 206, 210, 225, 234, 256, 266, 304, 446, 447, 453, 456; -Hungarian garrison, 10; interior, 481, 486; judicial independence, 26; king, kingdom, crown, 3, 7, 12, 14, 19, 24, 26, 27, 30, 34, 35, 40, 45, 48, 52, 54, 64–70, 75, 95, 126, 127, 128, 134, 225, 284, 365, 379; lands, regions, 6, 9, 15, 23, 24, 27, 29, 32, 35, 36, 38, 39, 52, 53, 55, 62, 63, 64, 71, 75, 76, 78, 86, 88, 89, 90, 95, 207, 228, 232, 256, 369, 372, 398, 401, 403, 404, 447, 462; leaders, 399, 419; Littoral, 15, 27, 29, 128, 134, 135, 138, 139, 141, 142, 143, 180, 203, 208, 253–60, 396, 426; loyalty, 73; masses, population, 11, 37, 228; National Awakening, *see* Illyrian; (national) cause, 260, 421; national tradition, 364, 494; nobles, nobility, 3, 6, 9, 12, 16, 20, 23, 24, 29, 32, 35, 228; parties, 45, 53, 59, 399; patriotism, patriots, 196, 417; peasants, 417; problem, question, 64, 75, 83; provinces, 196, 199, 223, 228, 234, 236, 237, 366, 374, 389, 397, 401, 419, 462; refugees, 129, 229, 252, 253, 254, 260, 275, 276; Republic, 406; rights, 25, 26, 32, 40, 41, 43; - Serbian identity (unity), 56, 57, 58, 70, 72, 95, 96; serfs, 27; slaves, 372; -Slavonian Dicasterium, 43; soil, 14, 15, 192, 255; sovereignty, 95, 211; state, 53, 86, 152, 366, 417, 419, 420, 421; students, 50; supreme executive, 26; taxes, 32, 33; territory, 58, 65, 67, 75, 83, 85, 206, 232, 237, 366; towns, 69; Trialism, 62; unification, 63, 85, 89; villages, 441; wars against Turks, 27; *župa*, 256; *see also* Croatia, Croatians

Croatian (religious): allegiance to Catholic Church, 303; bishops, 6; Bogomils, 367, 374, 380, 388; Capuchins, 268; Catholic(s), 367, 371, 374, 376, 380–3 *passim*, 388, 408, 410, 491, 492; Church (Ecclesia Slavoniae), 366; Muslims, 304, 308, 318, 320, 373, 374, 381, 389, 459, 493; parishes (in USA) 408–10, 461, (in Canada) 492; priests, 408, 418, 492; Uniate Church, 52

Croatian (societies and organizations): Academy of America, 460; Authors, Society of, 288; Beneficial and Fraternal Organizations, 414; Benefit Fraternity, 424; Benevolent Society, 426; Catholic Union, 415, 421, 459, 493; Circle, 419, 420, 421, 457; Credit Union, 493; Cultural-Educational Union, 416; Educational and Literary Association, Zagreb, 285; Fraternal Union of America (CFU) or "Zajednica," 400, 416, 419, 420, 421, 423, 486, 487, 493; Fraternity of Montana, 416; Historical Institute, 460; League, 414–7 *passim*, 419, 422, 436; Museum of Arts and Crafts, Zagreb, 289; National Council, 420; National Homes, 416; National Home or Hall (Canada), 488, 492, 494, 500; Pacific Unity, 414, 416; Peasant Party, 60–2, 64, 68, 69, 76, 417, 418, 419, 421; Peasant Society (CPS) of Canada, 488, 493, 494, 499; "St. Joseph" Beneficial Society, 416; secret organization in the United States, 417; Singing Societies, League of, 441, 442; Society, National, 415, 416, 417, 422, 423, 448, 456; Society of Illinois, 415, 416; Sokols, 72; Tamburitza Society, 440; Union, 415, 422; Union, Young National, 416; Unity, 414, 416, 487

Croatian Athens, 196

Croatian Day, 494

Croatian Press, 270

Croatian Printer's Establishment, 269

Croatian Printing Shop, Inc., 279

Croatian Voice (*Kanadski Glas*), 451, 488, 493, 498

Croatians, 62, 65, 67, 68, 73, 78, 122, 123, 137, 157, 158, 176, 224, 363, 364, 374, 376, 380, 386, 388, 397, 399, 462; after 1849, 40, 41; Americanization of, 412–14; in the Americas, 77, 79; and Archduke Ernst, 13; and Austrian federalism, 61; of the Banovina,

55, 56; and the Black Sea, 140; and Bocskay, 14; of Bosnia, 376, 403; and Bosnia-Hercegovina, 27, 206, 389; Burgenland, 274; civilian, 50; in Canada, 479, 482, 488, 493–503; and Czernin, 83; and Dalmatia, 34, 35, 140; and their Dicasterium in Vienna, 30; divided, 6; of Dubrovnik, 37; (borne away to the) East, 8; exodus of, 406; in First World War, 70, 72, 73, 74, 85, 86, 89, 91, 92, 93; and fishing, 456, 501; and France, 21, 37; and Francis Ferdinand, 56, 69; and Francis Joseph, 44–7 *passim*; and Garibaldi, 62; and German language, 31; and "Great Croatia," 50, 55; and Hapsburg absolutism, 19; and Hapsburg allegiance, 18, 25, 26, 34, 40, 42; Humanism and Renaissance among, 175–95; in Hungarian counties, 31; and Hungarians (Magyars), 25, 28, 31, 32, 33, 44, 49, 56, 58, 64, 75, 82, 86, 89, 93, 206; illiterate, 411; Istrian, 258, 260; and Kačić-Miošić, 226; *Kaisertreue*, 45, 62; at Karlowitz, 23; and Khuen, 54; and Kossuth, 40, 53; of Kotor, 38; and Magyar language, 32, 38; and Matthias Corvinus, 3; and Matthias II, 17; and Maximilian I, 4; and Nagodba, 51; naïveté of, 45; and Napoleon, 33, 37; as a nation, 239; and navigation on the Adriatic, 142, 144, 149, 151; and Old Illyrians, 39; of Orthodox faith, 386, 387, 388; protest, 13, 38; and a separate statehood, 50; of Slavonia, 206; in Srijem, 7; and Sylvester Patent, 42; and tamburitza, 440; and taxes, 43; and Thirty Years War, 18; and Tisza, 76; in Trieste, 259; and Turkish attacks, 5, 28; and Turkish pressure, 4; in the United States, 394, 396, 397, 398, 401, 408–10, 412, 420, 423–62; and Venetian fleet, 129, 130; and Venetians, 15, 124, 125; and Vienna, 13, 18, 19, 36, 46; and Yugoslav Committee, 77, 80, 84; and Zrinski-Frankapan conspiracy, 22, 23, 56; *see also* Croatia, Croatian

Croatians, United, of America and Canada, 420

Croatoserbian language, 159, 171, *see also* Serbo-Croatian

Crows' Nest, British Columbia, 503

Crusades, 367

Csikos-Sessia, Bela, 289, 436

Cuban, 405

Čubranović, Andrija, 185, 261

Cukela, Louis, 461

Ćulić Dragun, Mate, 442

Cumberland, British Columbia, 480, 491

Cunard Lines, 487

Ćurćin, Milan, 287

Curicum, *see* Krk

Curtis Institute of Music, 442

Cuvaj, Slavko, 64, 68

Čuvalo, Ljubo, 452

Cvečić, Juraj, 194

Cvitanović, Franjo, 486, 488

Cyrillic: alphabet, 163, 193, 213, 276–9 *passim*; Bosnian script (*bosančica*), 207, 227, 256, 261, 329, 336, 376; manuscript, 254

Czarist: army, 84; government, 68; Russia, 80

Czech, 59, 71, 83, 92, 94, 96, 163, 267, 285, 390; aspirations, 90; capital, 49; Committee, 88; hussars, 43; kingdom, 61; language, 157, 171; leaders, 95; legionnaires, 87, 91; "Mafia," 84; politicians, 83; pressure, 95; Protestants, 18; translation of *Hasan-Aginica*, 313

Czech-American Austrophobe Society, 79

Czernin, Ottokar, 83

Dabac, Tošo, 287

Dacia, 384

Daco-Rumanian, 158

Dalmacija Company, 150

Dalmata, Antonius (Antun Dalmatin), 193

Dalmata, Georgius (Juraj Dalmatin), 251

Dalmata, Gregorius (Grgur Dalmatin), 251

Dalmatia, 20, 32, 34, 37, 38, 45, 52, 62, 139, 176, 188, 195–213, 229, 304, 390, 396, 397, 398, 401, 427, 455, *see also* Triune Kingdom; Austrians in, 35, 36; central, 185; cities, towns of, 126, 127, 128, 176, 177; counts of Bribir in, 128; and Croatia, 35, 42, 45, 51; and Croatian-Serbian identity, 57; Croatians from, 413, 428; and Dubrovnik, 203; during the First World War, 70, 72, 83, 85, 91, 92; and folk literature, 220; and Francis Joseph, 63; Franciscans in, 226; and General Rukavina, 34; and Glagolitic books,

252; governor of, 378; highways, 143; history of, 196, 234; immigrants from, 462; -Istria, 56; Kačić in, 224, 228, 273; after fall of Klis, 15; and London Pact, 78, 419; northern, 186, 191, 253; poets of, 180, 186, 227; Protestant books in, 193; and Renaissance, 175; reunion with Croatia-Slavonia, 44, 46, 48, 50, 56; and Rijeka Resolutions, 57; in Roman times, 121, 122, 123, 171, 363, 364, 376, 383; and Serbs, Serbia, 54, 58, 67, 72; and shipping, 142; and Trialism, 63; and Turks, 128, 175; and Venice, 125, 128, 129, 136, 196, 206, 214, 223; *see also* Dalmatian, Triune Kingdom
Dalmatian(s), 34, 37, 55, 56, 77, 176, 198: coast, 35, 121–9 *passim*, 138, 147, 154, 171, 175, 414; Croatians, 35, 57, 70, 82, 171, 396; "our Dalmatian sea," 126; deputies, 72; and the Hapsburgs, 36; islands, 123, 136; literature, 177; newspapers, 85; nobility, 35; ports, 122; sabor, 42; Serbians, 57; thema (province), 122; and Turkish rule, 129; in the USA, 396, 397, 398, 401, 426, 428, 462; and the Uskoks, 196; and Venice, 129, 130; writers, 203, 210; *see also* Dalmatia
Dalmatin, Antun (Antonius Dalmata), 194
Dalmatin, Grgur (Gregorius Dalmata), 251
Dalmatin, Juraj (Georgius Dalmata), 251
Damanovich, Joe, 454
Damascus, 320
Danevski, E. R., 449
Danica (Pittsburgh), 422, *see also Danica Hrvatska*
Danica Hrvatska (later *Danica*), 419, 421, 423, 449, 452, 486
Danica ilirska, 268
Dante, 186, 270
Danube, Danubian, 28, 34, 50, 61, 86, 89, 91, 95, 157, 158, 363, 366, 373, 376, 385, 517
dār al-hadīth and *dār al-tafsīr* (lecture halls), 332
Darrow, Clarence, 435
Darsa, Marin, *see* Držić
Daruvar, 281, 517
Darwīsh Ḥusām-ad-Dīn, 331
Darwīsh Ḥusām Boshnāḳ, 325, 342
Darwīsh Ḳahramān Muḥammad al-Gradičawī, 331
Darwīsh Pasha Bāyazīd-Agha-Zāde al-Mostārī, 327, 328, 351
davul, 318
Dawson, Yukon, 483, 502
Dawūd ibn Ismāʿīl, 331
Déak, Francis, 38, 46, 47, 49
Debrecen, 262
def, 318
Defoe, 235
Delano, California, 456
Delaware University, 454
Delić, Colonel, 80
Della Bella, Ardelio, 205
Del Monte Fruit Company, 456
Delnice, 281
Delorko, Olinko, 307
Demarchi-Rougier Press, 273
Demerec, Milislav, 448
Demetrius of Pharos, Admiral, 121
Democratic Party (American), 458
Denmark, 18
De Paul University, 446, 454
Der Neue Welt-Bott, 424
Der Tourist, 280
Derviš Korkut, 331
Dervish: *see* Darwīsh and Derviš; schools and monasteries, 336
Descartes, 222
Desdemona, 313
Detroit, 409, 439, 455, 461; Croatian Board of, 443; Symphony Orchestra, 443; University, 454
Deželić, Velimir, 268
Diadora or Jadera (Zadar), 122
Dicasterium or Consilium (Croatian Council of Lieutenancy), 30
Dimec, Bartol, 283
Dinaric Alps, 440
Dioclea, *see* Duklja and Pop Dukljanin
Diogeneš, 235
"Dionička Tiskara," 257
Dioskurides, 333
diple, nāj, 318
Divald or Divalt, Dragutin, 275
Divald or Divalt, Ivan Martin, 274
Divald or Divalt, Julije, 275
Divald or Divalt, Martin Alojzije, 275
Divizić, Pero, 456
Divizich, Stephen, 427
Divković, Matija, 208, 227, 228, 239, 276
Divulje (Split), 152

dīwān (collection of poems), 327, 328
Ḍiyāʾ-ad-Dīn Aḥmad ibn Muṣṭafā al-Mostārī, 324, 325, 342
Ḍiyāʾ-ad-Dīn Bayāḍi-Zāde, Aḥmad ibn Ḥasan, 324, 325, 340
Djakovo, 44, 281, 517
Djordjić (Djurdjević) or Giorgi, Ignjat, 215–17, 227, 228, 229, 236, 239
Djordjić (Djurdjević) or Giorgi, Stjepo, 203, 216
Djumišić, Ḥifẓī Beg, 308
Djurdjevac, 9, 517
Djurdjević, *see* Djordjić
Djurić, Miljenko, 288
Djurkovečki (Vecki), Victor G., 445
Dniester River, 157
Dobrić (Dobričević), Dobruško (Boninus de Boninis), 251, 270
Dobrila, Juraj, 259
Dobrota, Boka Kotorska, 131
Doglioni, 225
Dojčić, Stjepan, 417
Dolci (Slade), Sebastijan, 217
Dolenc, Viktor, 259
Dom, 61
Domagoj, 124
Dominican(s), 206, 208, 261; in Bosnia, 367, 388; sisters, 492
Dominis, Captain John, 426
Dominis, John Owen, 426
Dominis, Marcus de (Gospodnetić), 193
Domjanić, Dragutin, 288
domobran (*ska vojska*) (home defense force): in Banal Croatia, 35; in the First World War, 70, 80
Don River, 364
Donji Kosinj (Old Bočać), 15
Donji Miholjac, 281
Donji Vakuf, 208
Doria, Andrea, 133
Došen, Vid, 232
Dozon, August, 313
Dragel, Daniel T., 457
Dragišić, Juraj (Georgius Benignus), 179
Dragnich, Peter, 456
Dragoljub (calendar), 269
Dragomanović (Gray), Gloria, 443
Drašković, Ivan 24
Drašković, Janko, 276
Drašković, Juraj (bishop), 193
Draškovićs, 18
Drava River, 8, 14, 15, 16, 228, 256, 363, 463, 517
Draženović, Paul, 455
Drazick, John, 455
Drina River, 27, 45, 71, 337, 363, 366, 375, *see also* Podrinje
dromons (vessels), 122
Drosaicus (Družak), 123
Drumheller, Alberta, 503
Družak (Drosaicus), 123
Držić (Darsa), Džore (Georgio), 180, 181, 184
Držić (Darsa), Marin, 188–9, 191, 192, 203, 218, 261
Dual Monarchy, *see under* Austro-Hungarian
Dubica, 14
Dubois County, Indiana, 425
Duboković, Veljko, 496
Dubourdieu, Commodore, 137
Dubrovačka plovidba, 142, 150
Dubrovčani, 37
Dubrovnik (Ragusa), 132, 135, 138, 139, 141, 161, 171, 178, 196, 201, 206, 217, 256, 261, 378, 427, 436, 440, 443, 457, 479, 517; and America, 384; and Austrian rule, 219; and book-printing, 270–2, 281; and Bruerović, 219; Croatians of, 37; culture of, 196; diplomatic service of, 271; and Djurdjević, 228, 239; and M. Držić, 189; fleet, ships, 134; and folk literature, 220; Franciscan Library in, 220, 260; Great Council of, 188; and Gundulić, 197, 198; and Hanibal Lucić, 184; history of, 131, 196; Humanism in, 179, 192; Jesuit Library in, 253; and Kačić, 226; literature, poets of, 181, 184, 185, 186, 188, 195–201, 202, 205, 208, 210, 214, 215, 217, 218, 219, 223, 225, 227, 229, 237, 238, 239, 272; and Louis the Great, 127; and Molière, 218; merchant shipping in, 132; and Nalješković, 187; nobility of, 180, 222; (Ragusium), 122; Republic of, 128, 131–4, 137, 190; Romanized, 176; Senate, 218, 271; Slavic, 177; theater in, 186–92, 199, 218, 229; and Venice, 128, 175, 251; and Vetranović, 184; and Vlachs, 385; and Zrinski, 201; and Zvonimir, 126
Dubrovnik (destroyer), 152
Duda, Herbert, 304
Duke University, 446
Duklja (Dioclea), 374, 385
Dulčić brothers, 456
Dunne, P. M., 424

Duncan, British Columbia, 491
Duquesne University, 446, 454; Tamburitzans, 440
Duralia, J., 504
Durham, North Carolina, 446
Durmitor Mountains, 385, 389
Duval, Paul, 497
Duvno, 208, 517
Dvorniković, Vladimir, 319
Džamanjić, Brno, 222
Džanan, Buljubaša, 308
Džemaludin (Čaušević), Hadži Mehmed, 380
Džinić family, 380

Eagle River, Wisconsin, 412, 457
Eagner, Gustav, 275
East(ern), 322: (American), 397, 422, 429; Christianity, 213; Orthodox, 312; pattern, 315, 316
East Chicago, 409
Edinost (Slovenian daily), 259
Edison, Thomas Alva, 430, *see also* American Edison Co.
Edmonton, Alberta, 480, 491, 503
Edson, Alberta, 503
Einsiedeln, Switzerland, 425
Eisenhower, President, 455
Eisenstadt, 31, 517
Ekavian, 158, 160, 364, 387
Elizabeth II, Queen, 500
Elliot Lake, Ontario, 491
Emmanuel College (Boston), 439
Emmanuel Comnenus, 365, 381
Emperor's Mosque, 335
Empire, Louisiana, 426
Engineers and Architects, Society of, 286
England, 73, 84, 87, 133, 152, 282, 395, 427
English, 62, 77, 78, 87, 133; colonists, 395; -Croatian dictionary, 449; dictionaries and grammars, 422; language, 160, 161, 163–71 *passim*, 299, 300, 301, 421, 431, 445, 446, 452, 459, 460, 463, 485, 487; letters, 282; literature, 222; translation of *Hasan-Aginica*, 313, 314; use of words in Croatian, 414; *see also* British
Entente (Powers), 78, 84–8 *passim*, 90–4 *passim*
Eötvös, Joseph, 38
Epidaurum, *see* Cavtat
Epirus, 121
Epistles, 252
Erdelats, Eddie, 455
Erdödi, Nikola, 23, 24
Erdödi, Petar, 193
Erdödi, Simon (bishop), 6, 371
Erdödis, 18, 24
Erić, 429
Erich Lisak (association), 493
Ernst, Archduke, 13
Esih, Ivan, 512
Esztergom, 31
Eterovich, Adam S., 462, 463
Eterovich, Anthony, 439
Eterovich, Francis H., 453, 460, 509
Etna, Pennsylvania, 459
Ettinger, Josip, 280
Ettoreo, *see* Hektorović
Eudes, Father Geraldus, 367
Eugene of Savoy, Prince, 27, 28
Europe(an), 38, 91, 95, 132, 178, 198, 217, 286, 302, 303, 312, 318, 319, 362, 363, 365, 369, 374, 383, 386, 387, 388, 395, 400, 415, 425, 441, 442, 445, 446, 463, 482, 496; and book-printing, 251; and Bošković, 221, 222; and V. Bukovac, 436; capitals, 437; Central, 87, 88, 90, 138; countries, 403; Eastern, 171, 447; folk music, 317; graphics, 288; medicine, 333; and I. Meštrović, 433; missionaries, 367; powers, 27; south-central, 236; struggle, 130; territory, 158; Tesla in, 430; and Uskoks, 136; Western, 59, 171, 236, 282
Everett, Washington, 455

Fabković, Skender, 285
Fahmi Džabić, *see* ʿAli Fahmī al-Mostārī
Fairbanks, Alaska, 455
Fairleigh Dickinson University, 450
Far East, 141, 145, 455
Farhād and Shīrīn, 315
Farlati, Daniel, 382
Farhād Pasha Mosque, 335
Fawzī Blagaylī, 327, 351
Fawzī Djulić, 331
February Patent, 44
Fehim Spaho, 380
Fejzo, Softa, 329
Ferdinand, archduke of Austria, 5, 136
Ferdinand (son of Maximilian I), 4–10 *passim*
Ferdinand of Styria, Archduke, 18
Ferdinand I, 135, 378, 386
Ferdinand II, 18

Ferdinand v, 45
Ferdinand, Indiana, 425
Ferhat Pasha, 11
Ferić Gvozdenica, Djuro, 220, 221, 313
Fernie, Alberta, 502
Ferrara, 178
Ferrari, Josip, 273
Fezerinec, 283
Figaro, 235
Filipović, Augustine, 496, 497
Filipović, Ivan, 285
Filipović, Rasim, 319
First World War, 144, 145–9, 150, 399, 401, 412, 414, 415, 417, 429, 433, 437, 444, 445, 455, 481, 485, 503
Fisherman's: Bank, 456; Union, 457
Fisković, Cvito, 284
Flatius Illyricus (Matija Vlacić-Franković), 193
Flin Flon, Manitoba, 491
Florence, 261, 287
Florentine: songs, 185; models, 187
Flori Giuseppe, 272
Florida, 434
Foča, 320, 321, 335, 336, 339, 386
Fojnica, 320, 321
Ford City (near Windsor, Ontario), 483, 487, 502
Fort William, Ontario, 491
Fortis, Alberto, 220, 225, 312
Fracasso, Dominik, 273
France, 11, 18, 21, 33, 152, 218, 283, 448, 461; and Austria, 21, 34, 36, 37, 38; Croatian horse in, 33; diplomacy of, 5, 7; in the First World War, 70, 73, 84, 87; and London Pact, 78; and Uskoks, 136; *see also* French
Francis II, 33, 34, 35, 268
Francis Ferdinand, 56, 61, 65, 69
Francis Joseph, 41, 43–7 *passim*, 56, 62, 63, 70
Franciscan(s) or Minor Friars, 205, 207, 224, 229, 255, 274, 276, 277, 375, 421; in Bosnia, 207, 208, 209, 223, 226, 227, 228, 276, 367, 368, 369, 375, 376, 382, 383; in Dalmatia, 226; in Hercegovina, 226, 276, 382; and Katančić, 232; Library, 220; missionaries, 367, 372, 388; monastery, 257, 265, 276; and Pavao Modruški, 253; of Požega, 230; and Reljković, 232; in Slavonia, 226, 228, 230, 232; Tertiaries, 410; in USA, 409, 410, 434, 460
Frangipani, *see* Frankapan
Frank, Jakov, 275
Frank, Dr. Josip, and Frankists, 54, 55, 59, 60, 62, 63, 64, 68, 69, 72, 75, 76, 82, 83, 86, 89, 93, 95
Frankapan, Bernardin, 5, 6
Frankapan, Fran(o) Krsto, 21, 210, 211, 216, 220, 227
Frankapan, Katarina, 210
Frankapan, Krsto, 5, 6
Frankapan, Nikola, 18
Frankapans or Frankopans, 11
Frankfurt on the Oder, 230, 266
Franklin, Benjamin, 89
Franks, 124
Fraščić, Father, 253
Fraser River valley, British Columbia, 503
Freeland, George E., 444
French, 5, 7, 9, 37, 38, 77, 78, 84, 91, 120, 137, 337, 434, 497; anti-revolts, 35; claret barrels, 429; culture, 230; in Dalmatia, 35, 36; in Dubrovnik, 271; firms, 150; forces, 140; in Istria, 36; in Karlovac, 275; language, 160, 162–71 *passim*, 219, 221, 232, 424, 453, 485; literature, 215, 218, 222; navy, 137, 146, 147; Maison Blanche, 88; at Malta, 147; Ministry of the Navy, 87; prisoners, 37; regime, 19, 37, 38; Republic(ans), 33, 219; revolution(s), 215, 268, 387; translation, 220, 230, 313; war, 24, 28, 29, 33–8; and Zrinski, 21; *see also* France
Fresno, California, 428, 456
Freud, 446
Freundsberg or Frundsberg, Ivan Sanf Sangilla von, 274
Friuli, 139, 144
Fuček, Stjepan, 266
Fulda, Indiana, 425
Fulford, Robert, 497
Furjan, 27
Furlany, Anton, 500

Gabrielli, Francesco, 304
Gabršček, Andrej, 258, 259, 260
Gacka River, 15
Gaj, Ljudevit, 44, 213, 235, 238, 239, 268, 269, 270, 277
Gaj, Velimir, 269
Gajret, 280
Galabow, Galab, 304
Galantić, Ivan, 438
Galicia(n), 61, 74, 75, 90, (Ukrainians), 401

Gallic, 37
Gallovich, Tony, 454
Galović, 286
Ganz-Danubius Company, 143
Garašanin, Ilija, 387
Garibaldi, 62
Garmogliosi, Ivan, 270
Garson, Ontario, 491, 502
Gary, Indiana, 409, 416, 419, 421, 441, 442, 459, 493
Gasparotti, Hilarion, 234
Gaul, 383
Gavranić, Pavao, 288
Gazarović or Gazzari, Marin, 204
Gāzī Husrev-beg, *see* Ghāzī Khusrew Beg
Gazzari, *see* Gazarović
Geel, Brothers, 260
Gegas, 308
Gelčić, Josip, 272
Gelcich, Vincent, 427
Genesis, book of, 194
Geneva, 420
Genoa, 127
George (seaman), 480
George VI, King, 500
Georgetown University, 452, 454
Georgia, University of, 454
Geraldton, Ontario, 491
Gerber, Ernst Ludwig, 313
Gerhard, Wilhelm, 313
German(s), 38, 71, 78, 83, 158, 179, 221, 269, 279, 299, 301, 319, 363, 396, 402, 404, 420, 462, 463; army, 70, 72, 81, 84, 90, 92; of Austria, 83; in Bosnia, 390; Catholic, 425; and Croatians, 85; culture, 192, 231; Dominican, 208; emperor, 123; folk tales, 236; in Indiana, 425; language, 31, 162–71 *passim*, 194, 195, 232, 233, 267, 279, 285, 327, 424, 445, 451; libraries, 261; navy, 145, 147, 153; offensive, 261; officers, 16; papers, 268, 279; Protestants, 9, 18, 21, 261; Reich, 70, 83; settlers, 425; Slavic grammar, 231; texts, works, 266, 268, 276; translation, 220, 230, 232, 235, 313, 328, 329; *Turnvereine*, 414; *see also following entries*
Germanic, 43, 60, 83, 171; elements, 72; generals, 12; non-Germanic, 31, 83
Germanies, 5, 383
Germanism, 65
Germanization, 31, 214
Germany, 11, 82, 87, 90, 91, 95, 96, 135, 145, 151, 152, 214, 236, 283, 363, 403, 451, 517; and rationalism, 228; and Reformation, 192; *see also preceding entries*
Gesemann, Gerhard, 307
Ghāzī ʿĪsā Beg, 338
Ghāzī Khusrew Beg, 302, 308, 339; clock-tower, 337; or Kurshunlu Medresse, 332, 335, 336; Mosque, 339; public bath, 338
Gibbon, J. M. 489
Giorgi, *see* Djordjić
Giulli Printing Press, 272
Giustiniani, L., 180
Gjergjelez Alija, 308
Gjulšeni Saraj, 278
Gjurković, 38
Gladstone, 52
Gladulić brothers, 429
Glagolitic, 181, 193, 194, 195, 208; area, 253; books, 209, 252, 253, 254; breviary, 254; literature, 253; missal, 255; priests, 254; script, 256, 257, 258, 261, 262
Glamoč, 208, 375
Glasnik sv. Ante, 280
Glasnik Zemaljskog Muzeja (u Bosni i Hercegovini), 279, 280
Glasonoša, 276
Glavadanović, Franjo, 277
Glavinić, Fran(jo), 209, 257, 375
Glaž, 375
Gledj, Timotej, 218
Gledjević, Antun, 201
Glina, 14, 27, 281
Glinica, 27
Gnjatović, Milan, 448
Goethe, 221, 312
Goldoni, Carlo, 218, 235
Goldoni, Paul, 288
Golubić, Theodore, 435
Goražde, 276, 337
Gorica (Gorizia), 10, 259, 423
Gorizia, province of, 136
Gorgonzola Mediolanensis, Damianus de, 252
Gorlice-Tarnow, 74
Gösl, Milan, 272
Gospel, 194, 195, 197, 209, 252
Gospić, 275, 281
Gospodnetić (Dominis), Marcus de, 193
Gothic script, letters, 252, 253, 255
Goths, 256
Gotovac, Jakob, 319

Gozze (or Gučetić), A., 219
Grabovac, 223–4, 225, 227
Grabrovnica, 9
Gračanica, 335
Gradac, 371
Gradačac, Captain Murād of, 306
Gradaščević, Husein, 379
Gradić, St., 202
Gradisca War, 136
"Grand Army," 37
Graničari (Frontiersmen), 9, 16, 20, 21, 27
Granite Falls, British Columbia, 502
Granitz Press, Ignatz, 269, 270
Gray, Gloria (Dragomanović), 443
Graz: and Borders, 17, 18, 263; and Katarina Zrinski, 210; Polytechnic Institute in, 430, 432; prison, 227; and school texts, 258; Styrian capital, 12; and Uskoks, 136; and Venice, 135; War Council, 12, 23
Great Britain, 78
Greece, 130, 256, 385
Greek(s), 66, 79, 232, 385; alphabet, 329; Belgrade, 386; –Catholic, 213, 408, 409; classics, 214, 222; colony, 121; epics, 307; fleet, 121; literature, 190; merchants, 120; Modern language, 167; –Orthodox, 339, 370, 373, 381; settlers, 9, 386, 388; ships, 121; tales, 319; territory, 158
Gregorian calendar, 302
Gregory VII, Pope, 126
Grgec, Petar, 307
Grgur Ninski (Bishop Gregory of Nin), 286
Gril, 283
Grimm, Jakob, 313
Grimsby, Ontario, 491
Grlenkovich, Helen, 455
Gršković, Niko(la), 77, 417, 422, 448
Grubišić, Sivije, 452
Gruž, 141, 517
Guadalcanal, 461
Guarini, 187, 191
Gubec, Matija, 11
Gučetić or Gozze, A., 219
Gučetić, Ivan or Gjivo, 201
Guiscard, Robert, 126
Guldescu, Stanko, 446–7, 463, 510
Gundulić or Gondola, Dživo or Ivan, 186, 191, 195, 196–8, 200–4 *passim*, 216, 217, 218, 229, 237, 239, 261, 271
Gundulić, Dživo Šiško, 201, 217
Gusdanovic, Paul, 457
gusle, 221, 318
Gutenberg, 252, 270
Gvozdanović (Quosdanovich), 33
Gvozdović, Rif'at Pasha, 321

Habdelić, Juraj, 206, 209
Hagar, 303, *see also* Agar
Ḥājj Ḥāfiẓ Muṣṭafā Čadordžija, 331
Ḥājj Sinān (monastery), 332, 336
ḥakīm (physician), 332
Ḥakīm Oghlu ʿAlī Pasha, 333
Hale, Nathan, 22
ḥamāʾil (*hamajlije*), 330
Hamilton, Ontario, 481, 487–92 *passim*, 496, 498, 499, 502, 503
hammām (public baths), 338
Hammer-Purgstall, Josef von, 328
Hanley, Saskatchewan, 480, 491, 503
Hapac, Bill, 454
Hapsburg: anti-, 63, 72, 73, 79; army, 70, 74, 87, 88, 90, 380; authority (-ies), 67, 68, 73, 93; castle, 95; Croatians, 79; dynasty, throne, 41, 61; Empire, Monarchy, 60, 65, 78, 83, 135, 194, 463; flag, 135; High Command, 84; House (Law), 4, 25, 28; Imperialists, 61; Istria, 192; nationalities, 77, 83, 85; peoples, 41, 42, 62; princess, 25; pro-, 48, 76; provinces, 10, 23, 36, 42, 89; regime, 68; ruler, 9, 27, 85; Serb(s), Serbian(s), 57, 73, 75, 83; service, 5; Slavonia, 11; sovereignty, 13, 41, 86, 214; state, 14, 27, 33, 43, 44, 63, 68, 82, 135, 136; territories, 83; treasury, 11; -Zápolya struggle, 7
Hapsburgs: in Boka Kotorska, 38; claims of, 4; and Croatian allegiance, 18, 25, 28, 34, 37; Croatian conflicts with, 12; in Dalmatia, 36; in the First World War, 73, 75, 85, 417; lands of, 67; and the Military Frontier, 8, 9, 16; and Pragmatic Sanction, 27; and Transylvania, 14; and Uskoks, 136; and Venice, 135; and Zrinski, 20, 210
Harambašić, 286
haramije, 12, 13, 16
Harl, Kajetan Franjo, 267
Harper, 450
Hartman and Company (Press), 269
Harvard University, 453
Hasan Aga, 314–15
Hasan Aginica, 313
Ḥasan ibn Muṣṭafā Boshnāḳ (al-Bosnawī), 326, 351

Ḥasan ibn Turkhān al-Kāfī al-Akḥiṣārī, 324–7 *passim*, 342
Ḥasan Spaho, 324, 343
Hasse's Press (Prague), 268
Hatteras, 395
Haus, Admiral, 146
Hawaii, 426, 517
Hawks, Francis L., 395
"Hayduk" (soccer club), 498
Hegira, 302
Heivel or Heyvl, Jakob Vjenceslav, 265
Hektorović, Petar (Ettoreo), 185–6, 219, 260
Heraclius I, 363, 364
Hercegnovi, 129, 518
Hercegovački bosiljak, 279
Hercegovina, 52, 175, 189, 321, 323; Croatians in, 387; eastern-, 320, 385; feudal lords of, 3; Franciscans in, 226, 370; Greek-Orthodox Church in, 381, 382, 387; public baths, 338; Serbs in, 386, 388; western-, 32
Hercegovinian(s), 66, 278
Herder, 221, 313
Herolt, Johannes, 208
Hersek-Oghlu, Aḥmad Pasha, 306
Hesiod, 222
Hinković, Hinko, 418, 444
Hitler, 87
Hitrec, Joseph George, 450
Hlivno, *see* Livno
Hoboken, New Jersey, 414, 422
Höcker, Olga, 288, 289
Hodaverdi, 378
Hoelzel, Maximilian, 307
Hoernes, Moritz, 337
Hofer, Andreas, 36
Hoffhalter, Raphael, 262
Hoffhalter, Rudolf, 262
Holland, 18
Hollywood, 443–4, 495
Holofernes, 183
Holy Cross Brothers, 435
Holy League, 133, 135
Holy Roman or German Emperor, 5, 10, 11, 124, 135
Holy See, 370, 371, 372
Holy Trinity (parish): in Ambridge, Pennsylvania, 408; in Gary, Indiana, 409; in East Chicago, 409
Homer, 307
Hönigsberg, 283
Honolulu, Hawaii, 426
Hoover, President, 434
Horace, 201, 217, 219
Hörer, Ivan, 269
Horić, Alan, 497–8
Hörmann, Kosta, 307
Horn, Cape, 396
Hörner, Franjo, 268
Horvat, Josip, 286, 287
Horvat, Radoslav (Vasić and Horvat Bookshop), 286
Hoste, Sir William, 137
Hötzendorff, Conrad von, 62, 70, 71, 80, 86, 87
Hraste, Mate, 158
Hrastovec, Stjepan, 451
Hrastovica, 11, 14
Hrnjica, Ajkuna, 308–11
Hrnjica brothers, 308
Hrnjica, Halil, 308
Hrnjica, Mujo, 308
Hrnjica, Omer, 308
Hrvatska Bosna, 280
Hrvatska misao, 60
Hrvatska Revija (abroad), 451
Hrvatska Revija (Zagreb), 285
Hrvatska Sloboda, 422
Hrvatska vila (magazine), 257
Hrvatska zajednica, 280
Hrvatska Zastava, 422, 445
Hrvatska Zora, 422, 429
Hrvatski dnevnik, 280
Hrvatski Domobran, 420, 421
Hrvatski Glasnik, 422
Hrvatski Katolički Glasnik, 421
Hrvatski List (New York), 419, 421, 423, 449
Hrvatski Radiša, 416
Hrvatski salon, 285
Hrvatski Svijet (New York), 417, 421, 486
Hrvatsko-Amerikanska Danica za Godinu 1895, 422
Hueber, Josip Antun Fortunat, 274
Hühn, Julije, 281
Hulusi, Mehmed, 278
Hun, 363
"Hunky-towns," 413
Hungarian, 14, 59, 76, 191, 232, 262, 378, 462, 463; Adria Company, 149; armies, 40; authorities, 57, 76; -Bosnian division, 91; cabinet, 49; chronicles, 384; commissary, 417; control of Croatia, 24, 30, 32, 46; "constitution," 39; Council of Lieutenancy, 26, 30, 32; count palatine, 19, 41, 264; counties, 30, 31; Court Chancellery, 43; crown, kingdom, king, 12, 32, 40, 43, 45, 53, 56, 88, 126; destinies, 53; domination, 175,

208; elections, 56; estates, 5, 21; flag, 60, 140; half of the Monarchy, 48, 63, 75, 88; Independence Party, 52, 54, 56, 57, 58; internal affairs, 56; Ismaelitak, 302; historiography, 3; lands, 9, 45; law invalid in Croatia, 19, 25; Nationality Law, 49; noble families, 20; Parliament, Diet, 4, 17, 19, 24, 25, 26, 32, 33, 38, 45, 46, 48, 59, 65; Port Authority, 138; Protestants, 14, 18, 21; regiments, 94; royal symbols, 5; seacoast, "Littoral," 38, 48; Serbs, 53, 60, 89, 92, 94; sources, 58; state, 7, 51, 65; taxes, 32; territory, 53, 83; throne and the Jagellons, 4; translation, 313; usurpation, 33; writers, 209; *see also* Hungarians, Hungary, Magyar

Hungarian-Croatian, 9, 24, 25, 32–5 *passim*, 38, 39, 51, 58, 64; affairs, 47; diet, 47; king(s), 127, 128, 252, 302; railways, 59; steamship company, 142

Hungarians, 17, 38, 49, 59, 158, 206, 401; and Croatian aristocrats, 32; and Croatian kingdom, 45; and France, 21; and Hapsburg House Law, 28; and Medjumurje, 18, 45; and Protestants, 39; and Supilo, 58; and Venetians, 15; and Vienna, 19; after Zsitva-Török, 19; *see also* Hungarian, Hungary, Magyar

Hungary, 41, 52, 56, 59, 75, 94, 178, 234, 264, 405, 518; and "annexed parts," 19, 24; and *Ausgleich*, 47; and Austria, 53, 55, 65, 88, 89, 138, 175, 211; and Croatia, 17, 25, 26, 33, 38, 42, 47, 48, 49, 52, 54, 59, 68, 83, 86, 128, 175; and Dalmatian coast, 35, 127; eastern- (Transylvania), 5; and Ferdinand I, 7, 135; and Francis Joseph, 56; and Gradiška Border, 16; history of, 274; and Karl IV, 88; king of, 88; and Kossuth(ists), 39, 40, 57; levies in, 10; and lithography, 282; and Medjumurje, 41; nobility in, 43; and Ottomans, 7, 8; "Royal"-, 10, 13, 14, 17, 19, 20, 21; and Ruthenians, 88; southern, 7, 58, 67, 371, 373, 462; and Supilo, 57; "Turkish," 20; uprising in, 24; west, 462; *see also* Hungarian

Huntsville, Ontario, 491

Ḫurram Bosnawī, 331

Ḥusayn ibnʿAbdallāh, 331

Ḥusayn ibn Naṣūḥ al-Wisoḳawī, 331

Ḣusović, Ćor-Huso, 307

Hvar (Pharos), 119, 120, 121, 123, 127, 130, 131, 183, 186, 204, 206, 427, 518; and Hektorović, 185; and Lucić, 260; Romanized, 176

Hyacinth, 316

Iapyges, 120

Ibar River, 363

Ibn-ʿArabī, Muḥyī-ʾd-Dīn, 325

Ibn Sīna, 333

Ibrāhīm Beg, 336

Ibrāhīm ibn Abdallāh Pečewī, 327, 328, 343

Ibrāhīm ibn Ḥājj Ismāʿīl al-Mostārī, 328, 343, 352

Ibrāhīm ibn Ṣāliḥ, 331

Ibrāhīm ibn Tīmūr Khān al-Bosnawī, 325, 344

Ibrāhīm Pečewī, *see* Ibrāhīm ibn Abdallāh Pečewī

Idaho, 407

Idrizbegović family, 322

Ijekavian, 158, 160, 198, 204

Ikavian, 160, 204, 205, 208, 210, 211, 229, 312, 368, 376

Ilidža, 338

Illinois, 398, 406, 414, 415, 460, 461; University of, 454, 455

Illyria(n): ideal, 41; immigrants, 401, 432; kingdom, 37, 38; language, 253, 373; Moorish, 384; National Awakening (Movement), 39, 159, 212, 226, 233, 236–9 *passim*, 254, 268, 276, 277, 379, 380; naval power, 120; Provinces, 137; Romanized, 176; shores, 120; tribes, 120; wars, 121

Illyricum, 121, 363, 364, 384

Illyrism, 44

Ilova River, 8, 15

Immigration Act, 464

Imotski, 314, 518

Impressionism in painting, 438

Incas, 439

Independent National Party, 46, 48, 52, 53

India, 450

Indian (western), 395, 406, 424, 501; dialects, 424; equestrian (sculpture), 433

Indian Ocean, 141

Indiana, 409, 416, 419, 421, 435, 441, 453, 459, 462, 492; University, 447, 451, 454

Indiana Harbor, Indiana, 462
Indo-European or Indo-Germanic, 119, 307, 326
Inn River, 383
Inner Austria (Carinthia, Carniola, Styria), 8, 10, 11, 16, 18
Innsbruck, 64
Invincible Armada, 134
Ionian Sea, 121
Iowa, 407
Iranian(s), 157, 366
Iraq, 330
Irek, Hilda, 495
Irish, 283
Iron Springs, Alberta, 488, 491
Islam, Encyclopedia of, 299
Islam(ic), 322, 333, 339, 368, 369, 370; Bosnia, 303; culture, 302, 303, 304; history, 325; museum, 336; religion, 305, 312, 317, 333, 371, 372, 373, 376, 382, 388, 389; studies, 335; tradition, 332; *see also* Muslim
Ismael, 256
Ismaelites or Hungarian Ismaelitak, 302
Ismāʿīl Bosnawī, 331
Ismāʿīl ibn Ibrāhīm, 331
Isolani(s), 18
Isonzo (Soča) River, 74
Issa (Vis), 120, 121
Istanbul, 325, 330, 338, 377, 378, 379, 516
Istočnik, 279, 280
Istria, 10, 36, 37, 50, 56, 126, 128, 137, 138, 144, 363, 396, 397, 398, 446; and book-printing, 253–60; and Croatia, 253, 254; and Domagoj, 124; economy of, 143; in First World War, 70, 75, 85, 90; and Francis Joseph, 63; and Glagolitic books, 252; immigrants from, 462; and Istro-Rumanians, 158; and London Pact, 78, 419; and Narrantani, 124; and the Paris Peace Conference, 419; people of, 259; and Protestant books, 193; and Reformation, 192; and Rijeka Resolutions, 57; and shipping, 142; and Slavic liturgy, 258; Slovenian-, 258, 260; and Trialism, 63; and Triune Kingdom, 89, 213; and Venice, 196
Istrian(s): books, 258; coast, 122, 136; concern, 260; Croatians, 56, 258; Glagolitic priests, 253; immigrants, 401; municipalities, 253; Slovenes, 258; towns, cities, 124, 260
Isvolsky, Alexander, Russian Ambassador, 58
Italian(s), 62, 78, 80, 87, 88, 91, 93, 94, 153, 201, 222, 258, 323, 420, 462, 463; academy, 239; actors, 218; agents, 86; architects, 339; army, 84, 147; in Bosnia, 390; catechism, 208; coast, ports, 146, 148, 153; culture, 236; Dalmatians, 44; debacle, 84; domination, 259; euphuism, 204; farce, 189; fashion, 199; fleet, 74, 137, 144, 145, 148, 152; language, 162, 167–71 *passim,* 183, 190, 192, 203, 204, 229, 232; literature, 180, 182, 185, 187, 190, 192, 196, 207, 212, 214, 218, 219, 221, 222, 225, 232; models, 190; Napoleon Kingdom, 137; newspapers, 257; pastoral drama, 191; poets, poetry, 180, 181, 199; prison camps, 95; Renaissance, 288; Risorgimento, 62; schools, 176; Supreme Command, 94; translation, version, 221, 230, 261, 263, 313; in Valona, 147; writers, 191, 323; *see also* Italy
Italianization, 44, 259
Italy, 11, 27, 35, 36, 74, 77, 80, 86, 90, 91, 92, 95, 145, 149, 176, 178, 179, 188, 202, 214, 283, 363, 403, 435, 450; in First World War, 145, 146, 149, 419; Gradisca, 136; and Hapsburgs, 135; Humanism in, 178; and London Pact, 78, 236, 418; and Rab, 131; and Rijeka, 258, 419; in Second World War, 153; southern, 462; *see also* Italians
Ithaca, New York, 451
Iura Municipalia, 26
Ivan Planina (Mountain), 33, 268
Ivanić, 11, 425
Ivanišević, Ivan, 204
Ivankovich, John, 427
Ivanošić, Antun, 230
Iveković, Oton, 436
Ivelja, Petar, 134
Ivkanec, Tomislav, 285

Jablanac, 15
jabuka (family emblem), 322
Jacob de Cesamis, 127
Jacobin, 33
Jadera (Zadar), 122
Jadran, 493
Jadranska Plovidba, 150

Jagellon, Anna, 4
Jagellon, Louis, 4, 5
Jagellons and Croatians, 3–5
Jäger battalions, 70
Jagić, Vatroslav, 307
Jagrović, Dragan J., 448
Jahorina (Mountains), 336
Jajce, 3, 5, 32, 375
Jakić, Antun, 269
Jalāl-ad-Dīn ar-Rūmī, 326, 327, 332
Jambrešić, Andrija, 239, 266
Jandera, Anton, 267; his widow nee Maglić, 267
Jandrić, Matija, 235
Janissaries, 377, 378
Janjevo (Kosovo), 462
Janković, Andro, 448
Jansky, Herbert, 328
Japanese, 84, 501
Jareb, Jere, 453
Jasenovac, 338
Jaska, 281
Jasper, Indiana, 396, 425
"Javor" (singing society), 414, 442
Jazbec, S., 283
Jelačić (baron), 33
Jelačić, Joseph (Ban), 41, 42, 89
Jelaške (Vareš), 208
Jelić, Donatus, 372
Jelušić, Nick, 429
Jesuit(s), 196, 198, 205, 209, 211, 215, 221, 228, 229, 232, 234, 235, 371, 382, 423, 427; bookbinders, 282; College, 264; missionaries in America, 395, 410, 424; Press, 266; of Slavonia, 237; in Zagreb, 264
Jesus, 204
Jeszer, General, 80
Jewish, 39, 51, 462
Jews, 36
Jireček, Konstantin, 303, 339
John, Archduke, 35
John IV, Pope, 266
John VIII, Pope, 124
Johnson, President, 400
Johnstown, Pennsylvania, 408, 461
Joliet, Illinois, 409, 461
Jorgovanović, 286
Journal of Croatian Studies, 460
Jozefić, Frano (bishop), 6
Joseph II, 40; against clergy and nobility, 31, his era, 30–1, 228, 232
Judith, 182
Judnich, Walter, 454
Jugonovinsko Inc. (Press), 270
Jugoslavenska Brodogradilišta, 150
Jugoslavenska Štampa, 270, 282
Jugoslavenski Lloyd, 150
Jukić, Ivan Franjo, 277
Jurich, Joe, 457
Juričić, Juraj, 194
Jurišić, Luka, 426
Jurjević, Atanazije, 371
Jurjević, Gabrijel, 209
Jurkas, Loje, 502
Jurkovich, James, 454
Jutarnji List, 270

Kabalin, Fedor, 443
Kabalin, Mladen, 451
Kačić (clan), 128
Kačić Miošić, Andrija, 220, 223–6, 227, 228, 230, 231, 239
Ḳāḍī, 335, *see also* Cadi
Ḳadić, Ante, 451
Kadlec, Karlo, 262
Kajić, Ante, 277
Kajkavian, 39, 158, 160, 162, 194, 206, 209–12 *passim*, 233, 236, 239, 262; literature, 194–5, 239; novel, 236; poetry, poets, 209, 234; writers, 235
Kalanj, Andriana, 495
Kalesije, 302
Kalićs, 427
Kalisians, 302
Kamber, Charles, 452
Kamengrad, 3
Kamloops, British Columbia, 491
Kanadski Glas, see Croatian Voice
Kanavel(ov)ić, Petar, 202, 272
Kanfanar, 257
Kanisza, 14, 20
Kanižlić, Antun, 229, 230, 237, 239, 275
Kansas, 407; State University, 454
Kansas City, Kansas, 409, 415, 417, 436
Kapaaḍea, Princess Lydia Kamekaha, 426
Kapela Mountains, 15
Kaptol Press, 267
Kapuskasing, Ontario, 483
Karabegović, Avdo, 306
Karabin, Gabro, 449
Karadžić, Vuk Stefanović, 159, 213, 220
Ḳara-Göz, 319
Ḳara-Göz Beg Mosque, 335
Karakas, Mike, 455
Karaman, Ljubo, 284, 285
Karaman, Matija, 210

Karl, Archduke, 10, 12; and Napoleon, 34
Karl III (VI of Austria), 26–9 *passim*
Karl IV (VII of Austria), 81, 82, 88, 91, 93, 94, 95
Karlecki, Lovrenc, 257
Karlobag, 15, 138, 258, 518
Karlovac, 18, 193, 436, 518; Border, 15, 23; (Karlstädter) Generality, 15, 16, 17; Military Academy, 275; presses, 269, 275–6, 281; prison, 227
Karlowitz, 23, 34, 208, 228, 518
Karoyli (government), 94
Kašić or Cassius, Bartol, 204, 371
Kastav, 260
Katančić, Matija Petar, 232, 236, 237, 239, 268, 275
Katarina-Zrinska (association), 493
Katolička Hrvatska Tiskarna, 273
Katušićs, 427
Katyn (massacres), 445
Kavanjin, Jerolim, 204
Kazinczy, Ferencz, 313
Kemal Atatürk, Mustafa, 89, 93
Kenaston, Saskatchewan, 480, 491, 503
Kennedy, Jacqueline, 439
Kennedy, John F., 439
"Kerensky Offensive," 81
Kerhin, Zlatko I., 441
Keserić, Bill, 502
Kesterčanek, Nada, 451
khānḳāh (dervish school), 336
Khayr-ad-Dīn, 339
Khiḍr (Hīzīr) Āsāfī, 327, 352
Khīrwāt (Croatian) Rustam Pasha, 337
Khotin, 198
Khuen-Hederváry, Karl, 49, 51, 52, 54, 55
Khwāja-Kamāl-ad-Dīn Mosque, 335
Kimyāger (Chemist) ʿAlī Zakī, 331, 342
Kirin, Vladimir, 282, 285, 287, 288
Kirkland Lake, Ontario, 483, 487, 488, 490, 491, 492
Kiseljak (near Fojnica), 321, 338
Kitchener, Ontario, 491
Kitimat, British Columbia, 502
Kiwanis Music Festival, 495
Ḳīzlar Agha Mosque, 335
Kladanj, 338
Klaić, Vjekoslav, 265, 287
Klis, 5, 15, 518
Kljaković, Jozo, 434
Ključ, 3
Kmetovich, Peter, 454
Knaus, Vincent L., 457, 463
Knego (Peter Coe), 443
Kneisel Quartet, 442
Knezović, General, 36
Kniewald, Dragutin, 284
Koćak, Mate, 461
Kokendović, Dominko and Mato, 394
Kolaković, Mehmed Kolak, 306
Kolaković-House, 322, 331
Koledar, 449
kolo, 221, 439
Kolo Week (San Francisco), 441
Koločep, 132, 518
Koloman, 126
Kolunić-Rota, Martin, 288
Komárno, 31
Komensky, Jan, 285
konačnik, 322
Konavle Polje, 128
Konjic, 321, 337
Konšćak, Konsag, or Konschak, *see* Consag
Konzul Istranin, Stjepan, 194
Kopač, Slavko, 288
Kopanica, Peter, 426
Kopaonik Mountains, 385
Kopar, 193, 258, 518
Kopernicki, Isidor, 307
Kopitar, Jernej, 313
Koprivnica, 9, 11, 193, 281, 518
Korana, 14, 15, 30
Korčula, 127, 138, 203, 272, 518; and boat-builders, 143, 150; and ship-building, 131; and Venice, 128
Kordun ("Cordon"), 9
Korošec, Msgr., 83, 86
Kosovo (Field), 308, 363, 364
Kossuth, Louis, 38, 40, 41, 47, 53; his son, 52
Kossuthist(s), 39, 54, 57, 58
Kosta, Ante, 499
Kostajnica, 8, 14, 23, 281, 338, 448
Kostelski, Z., 448
Kostrena, 480
Košutić, Sida, 286
Kotor, 45, 131, 138, 518; and M. Držić, 189, 203; printer, 271; and Venice, 128, 130, 202
Kotsche, Joseph Karl, 267, 268
Kovačević, Ivan, 439
Kovačević, Janko, 422, 429
Kovačina Ramo, 308
Kožičić, *see* Begna Kožičić
Kozulić or Kozulich (Cosulich), 480
Kragujevac, 71
Kraja, Josip, 448, 457

Krajačević Sartorius, Nikola, 209
Krajačić (Kray), Walter, 444
Krajina, *see* Military Frontier
Kraljeta, Gustav, 257–8, 280
Kraljević, Miroslav, 280
Kraljevica, 135, 140, 518; printing in, 257; shipyards, 143, 150
Kralj-Medjimurac, Ladislav, 289
Kramer, 283
Kranjčević, Silvije Strahimir, 286, 288
Krapina, 281
Krauss, Friedrich Salomon, 303, 307, 317, 319
Kray (Krajačić), Walter, 444
Krbava Polje, 4
Krčelić, Adam Baltazar, 234, 238, 266, 267
Kreković, Kristian, 439
Kremsier diet, 42
Kreovich, Mike, 454
Kreševljaković, Hamdija, 304, 338
Krešić, Ivan, 419, 421, 422, 423, 448, 449
Krešić, Stjepan, 496
Krešimir I, 124
Krešimir IV, 126
Krimeja, 140
Kristijanović, Ignjat, 236
Kristolovec, Ivan, 234
Križanić, Juraj, 213–14
Križevci, 11, 26, 425, 518; "circle," 30; county, 263; printing presses in, 281
Krizman, Tomislav, 288, 289
Krizmanić, Anka, 288
Krizmanić, Ivan, 235
Krk (Curicum), 122, 142, 144, 253, 518; Romanized, 176; and Venice, 128, 130, 139, 255, 259
Krka River, 34, 518
Krkavce, 258
Krklec, 286
Krleža, Miroslav, 281
Krmpotić, 239
Krmpotić, Josip, 259
Krmpotić, M.D., 409, 417, 419, 448, 449
Krnarutić, Brne, 191, 212, 260
Krnjević, Krešimir, 496
Kršćanska obitelj, 280
Krunić, M., 448
Krupa, 5
Krznarić Sr., Ivan, 500
Kuba, Ludvik, 317
Kufrin, Paul de, 435–6
Kugli (bookshop), 287
Kugli Press, Stjepan, 270
Kuhačević, Mateša Antun, 227
Kuharich, Joseph (Joe) L., 454, 455
Kukuljević-Sakcinski, Ivan, 42
kula, 321, 322, 331
Kulen Vakuf, 334
Kulenović (family), 380
Kulenović, Džafer Beg, 380
Kulenović, Mustaj Beg, 306
Kulmer, baron, 41
Kulović, Esad Ef., 380
Kunc Milanov, Božidar, 443
Kunc Milanov, Zinka, 442
Kundek, Joseph, 276, 396, 425
Kunić, Hamid, 306
Kunić, Rajmund, 222
Kupa River, 8, 11, 13, 14, 15, 18, 30, 194, 228, 429, *see also* Pokuplje
Kupres, 322
Kuprili (Köprülü) viziers, 21, 28
Ḳur'ān, 324, 331, 332
Ḳur'ān portfolios (*en'amlïḳ*), 321
Kuripešić, Benedict, 385
Kurshunlu Medresse, *see* Ghāzī Khusrew Beg Medresse
Kurtćehajić, Mehmed Šaćir, 278
Kurykta (press), 259
Kurzbeck, 258
Kušlin, Mihovil, 288
Kutina, 281
Kutlina (stream), 15
Kutzo-Vlachs or Macedo-Rumanians, 9, 158
Kvarner, Gulf of, 138, 518
Kvarner Islands, 144, 252, 253, 254

Lackawanna, New York, 409
Ladislas: of Naples, 34, 128; Polish prince, 198
Ladner, British Columbia, 480, 491, 492
Ladysmith, British Columbia, 486, 491, 502, *see also* Oyster Harbor
Laginja, Matko, 260
Laich, Eleanor, 454
Lakatoš, Josip, 398
Lakić, Juraj Žigmond, 263
Lamartine, Alphonse de, 313
Landsturm, 10
Lanosović, 239, 275
Lansing, Robert, 91, 92, 418
Larder Lake, Ontario, 490, 491
Lastovo, 129, 251, 518
Laštrić, Filip, 228, 383
Lašvanin, Nikola, 375
Latin, 38, 73, 162, 167, 169, 170, 177,

178, 180, 183, 192, 194, 195, 199, 200, 203, 218, 221, 222, 224, 227, 229, 232, 234, 264, 383; alphabet, script, 163, 181, 227, 252, 257, 261, 276, 277, 279; books, works, 207, 225, 230, 260, 262, 263, 265, 266, 268, 274; calendar, 266; catechism, 208; chronicles, 265; Church-, 252; church melodies, 267; -Illyrian grammar, 375; in Istria, 258; literature, 190, 214; newspaper, 267; official language, 208, 233; original, 255; poems, 179, 181, 212, 219, 222, 233; poets, 182, 219, 220; translation, 313; verses, 179, 211
Latin America, 79
Latinists, 221–2
Latins, Black, 384
Laurel Hollow, Long Island, 448
Lauterbourg, 33
Lazarić, Captain, 37
Leader, Alberta, 491
League of Nations, 420
Leask, Saskatchewan, 503
Legal, Alberta, 503
Leibnitz, 222
Leipen-Madirazza, Neda, 496
Leipzig, 251, 518
Leitha River, 44
Leman or Lehman, Dragutin or Carl, 275
Lemberg (Lvov), 71
lembi (vessels), 120
Lemkos (Ukrainians), 401
Lenković, Ivan, 10, 386
Leoben, 33, 34
Leopold I, 21, 23, 29; and Zrinski, 22, 201; and Varaždin Military Generality, 24
Leopoldine Mission Society, 425
Lepanto (battle), 130
Lermontov, Michael J., 313
Lesac, Mato, 429
Lethbridge, Alberta, 491
Leto, Pomponio, 179
Letunić, M. N. (Mateo Lettunich), 427
leuti (ships), 139
Levack, Ontario, 483, 487, 491, 502
Levaković, Rafael, 209
levha (Arabic *lawḥa*), 323, 331
Leykam and Widmanstad, 258
Lhotka, Nenad, 496
Library of Congress, Washington, 252
Liburnia, *liburnae*, 120, 121, 122
Lignes (Montréal), 498
Lika (and Krbava), 7, 20, 23, 24, 227, 373, 398, 430, 480
Lika, Mustaj Beg of, 308
Likan, Gustav, 439
Liliuokalani, Hawaiian queen, 426
Lim River, 337
Lincoln, Abraham, 439
Lindar (Pazin), 253
Linotype Co. (Press), 270
Linz, 64
Lipa, Beg of, 306
Lisgar, Saskatchewan, 480, 491, 503
Lissa (Vis), 48, 120, *see also*Vis
Lithuania, 3
"Little Wallachia," 28
Livajušić, Ante, 452
Livanjsko Polje, 3
Livno or Hlivno, 3, 321, 339, 375
Ljubić, Ivan, 415
Ljubljana, 90, 262, 263, 264, 274
Ljubović, Beg or Bey, 308, 309
Ljubuški, 375
Lobkowitz, Wenzel, 22
Löffler's Hungarian Honved Brigade, 80
Lokanc, Joe, 454
London, 77, 84, 221, 418, 446, 449; Pact, 418
London, Ontario, 491, 492, 493, 498
London, Jack, 427–8
London Times, 87
Long War of 1593–1606, 13–14
Longobards, 123
Lopašić, Mirko, 275
Lopašić, Radoslav, 276
Lopud, 132, 427, 518
Lorain, Ohio, 409
Lord, Albert Bates, 307
Lorković, Ivan, 75
Lorković, Mladen, 406
Los Angeles, 408, 427, 443, 457
Lošinj, 139, 141, 143, 149, 518
Lothair, king of Germany, 124
Louis II, emperor of the Franks, 124
Louis II Jagellon, 5
Louis the Great (of Croatia-Hungary), 127, 128, 252
Louis XVI, 33
Louisiana, 397, 406, 425, 429, 432
Lovinac, Alberta, 480, 503
Lovrenčić, Jakob, 235, 274
Lower Austria, 10, 13
Loyola University, 447
Lucacick, Alex, 454
Lucas, 463
Lucas, Anthony (engineer), 432

Lucas, Anthony (judge), 429
Lucerna, Camilla, 313
Lučić, 456
Lučić (Lucas), Franjo, 432
Lučić or Lucius, Ivan, 206, 263
Lucić or Lucio, Hanibal, 183, 184, 260
Luck, 81
Lucretius, 222
Lukarević, Jakov, 271
Lukas family, 456
Lukeš, J., 279
Lukinović, Zvonimir, 288
Lukšić, 456
Lukšić, Abel, 276
Luksich, J., 461
Lulić, Toni, 448
Lusatian, 157
Lutheran (minister), 450
Lybia, 219
Lyons, 218

Macedonia, 66, 158, 372, 389
Macedonian(s), 157, 158, 163, 417; language, 157, 158, 159, 171
Macedo-Rumanians, *see* Kutzo-Vlachs
Maček, Vladko, 96, 421, 452
McGill University, 496
Mácha, Karel Hynek, 313
McKees Rocks, 411
McMillan, Hamilton, 395
Mačva, 302
Madison, Indiana, 425
Madrid, 136, 446
Maffei, 218
Magdalenić, Matijaš, 209
Maglaj, 335, 368, 380
Maglić, Konstantin, 73, *see also* Jandera, Anton
Magličić, Ken, 499
Magyar(s), 7, 24, 25, 35, 38, 40, 44, 45, 50, 56, 72, 88, 94, 405, 462; anti-, 44, 76; bureaucrats, 73; capital, 49; claims, 19, 32; constitution, 32; in Croatia, 28; and Croatian affairs, 63; and Croatian-Bosnian union, 51; -Croatian-Serbian opposition, 57; Déak and, 47; delegates, 44; and Francis Joseph, 46, 47, 56; against Germanization, 31; Hungary, 60; language, 32, 38, 49, 59, 64; legislative body, 4; after Nagodba, 48; officers, 59; oligarchy, 75, 76, 78; pro-, 39, 44; and Radić, 60; and Serbs, 50; in Slavonia, 6; after 1849, 40; *see also* Hungarian, Hungary
Magyarization, 38, 49
Magyarone, 32, 47, 60
Maḥmud ibn Khalīl al-Mostārī, 325, 344
Mahovlich, Frank, 499
Mainz, 251
Majić, Častimir, 452
Majich, Stanley, 504
Majnūn and Laylā, 315
Makanec, Julije, 279
Makarska, 124, 224, 518
Malartic, Quebec, 491, 502
Malaspalli, Belisari, 261
Malayan, 313
Mali Zvornik, 302
Malogrudici, Giovanni, 479
Malta, Maltese, 119, 130, 147
Malte-Brun, 320
Mandelc (Mannel or Manlius) Hans, 262, 273–4
Mandić, 239
Mandić, Dominik, 452, 513–14
Mandić, Vjekoslav I., 400, 416
Mandurić, Zvonimir, 487
Mandušić, Andjelko (Jake Alex), 461
Mani and Mlinar, 273
Manichean (sect), 303
Manitoba, 480, 485, 488, 490, 491, 499, 500, 501
Mannel, Hans, *see* Mandelc
Mannerheim, 98
Mantua, 178
Marano in Friuli, 135
Marchesi, Karlo, 446, 463
Marči, Nikola, 217
Marcus Aurelius, 453
Marenigh, Ivan, 258
Maretić, Toma, 162, 253
Maria (daughter of Maximilian I), 4
Maria Theresa, 27, 28, 85, 214, 228, 266, 267, 274; and the Croatians, 29–30; and Trieste, 135
Mariani, *see* Narrantani
Marichich, Eli, 454
Marini or Marino, G. B., 201, 217
Marinović, 427, 443
Marjanović, Luka, 307
Marjanović, Milan, 448
Markovac-Margitić, Stjepan, 228
Marković, 429
Marković, Franjo, 285
"Marlak," 306
Marmont, Marshal, 272, 275
Marne River, 71
Marohnić, Josip (Joseph), 422, 448–9, 486
Marquette University, 434, 445, 511
"Marseillaise," 318

Marseilles, 218
Martecchini, Antun, 271–2: Fran Petar, his son, 271–2
Martholosen (Zitten), 386
Martić, Grga, 278
Martinac (priest), 256
Martinac, Joe, 455
Martinis, Paul, 455
Martinolić or Martinolich, 260, 480
Martinović, Edward, 425
Martinšćica, 140
Marulić, Marko (Marcus Marulus), 180–3, 184, 260
Mary, Virgin (statue), 434
Marygrove College (Detroit), 439
Marxist, 67, 88
Masalarda, Marino, 479
Masarechi, Peter, 370, 371
Masaryk, Thomas, 50, 60, 95, 96
Mašić Nikola, 284
Maštrović, Vjekoslav, 272–3
Matica Hrvatska, 283, 285
Matica Iseljenika Hrvatske, 463
Matijašević, Djuro, 220
Matijević, Stjepan, 208
Matina, Mato, 408
Matl, Josef, 304
Matthias II, 17, 18, 136
Mattioli, Andrea, 333
Mauretania(n), 383, 385
Maurocastrum, 384
Mauro-Vlachs, *see* Vlachs
Mavrinac Jr., Joseph, 499
Mawlawi (dervishes), 318, 332
Maximilian (in Mexico), 447
Maximilian I, 4, 25
Maximilian II, 10, 11
Mayerling, 56
Mayo Clinic, 434
Mazilić, Dj., 336
Mažuranić, Ivan, 46, 52, 53, 63, 64, 276, 303
Mazzanovich, Lawrence, 436
Mecca, 322, 330
Medanich, Frank, 454
meddah-burlesques, 319
Mederšicki or Mederschitzky, Ignjat or Ignatz, 275
Medina, 330
Mediterranean, 119, 122, 133, 134, 137, 145, 147, 153, 519; countries, 126; eastern-, 141; ports, 127; struggle, 121, 146; submarines in, 148, 152; trade, 150
Medjedović, Avdo, 307
Medjumurje, 14, 18, 41, 262, 463, 519
medresse, 332
Medulić-Schiavone, Andrija, 288
Medved, Ivan, 274
Meḥmed (architect), 339
Mehmed-Aga, 378
Meḥmed Arūḍī, 325, 344
Mehmed from Transylvania, 329
Mehmed-Pasha, 378
Mehmed Pasha Kukavica, 338
Meissner, Julije, 288
Meler, Vjekoslav, 448
Mellon, 432
Menčetić or Menze, Šiško, 180, 184, 202, 219
Menčetić or Menze, Vladislav, 201, 203
Mendoza Grajales, Francisco Lopez de, 434
Menze, *see* Menčetić
Mercoal, Alberta, 491, 502
Mérimée, Prosper, 313
Merkantile Press, 270
Mešić, Adem-Aga, 380
Mesner, Steve, 454
Meštrović, Ivan, 76, 286, 287, 400, 433–5, 437, 451, 497
Meštrović, James, 461
Metastasio, 218, 232
Metković, 139, 519
Metkovich, George, 454
Metohija, 308
Metropolitan Museum, New York, 434
Metropolitan Opera, New York, 442, 443
Metternich, 44, 72
Mexican, 424
Mexico, 423, 424, 426, 438, 447
Mexico City, 395
Micaglia, Jakov, 205
Michelangelo, 434
Michigan, 396, 397, 398, 408, 409, 411, 429, 432, 441, 443, 460
Mickiewicz, Adam, 313
Middle Ages, 175, 183, 225, 236, 263, 323, 368, 374, 382, 385
Middle West (American), 397
Mihal(ovich), William, 455
Mihalic, Johnny, 454
Mihalic, Mike, 454
Mihalich, Andrew, 499
Mihanović, Antun, 239
Mihanovich, Clement S., 406, 413, 414, 447, 451
Mihećin, Josip, 448
Mikan, George, 454, 455
Mikloušić, Tomo, 236, 238, 274
Mikoci, Josip, 234, 236

Mikula, Father, 253
Mikulić, Aleksandar Ignjat, 264
Mikulić, Jakov, 427
Miladins, 427
Milanov, *see* Kunc Milanov
Milatovich, Marko, 503
Milesian, 319
Miličević, Frane, 278, 279
Miličević, Ivan A., 279
Military (Croatian) Frontier(s), Confines or border (Vojna Krajina), 8–26 *passim*, 35, 45, 52, 144, 308, 309; and France, 36; and "Great Croatia," 51; and Kuhačević, 227; liquidated, 52; and Maria Theresa, 30; officers of, 50; Posavina part of, 29; restored, 38
Miljacka River, 337
Millvale, Pennsylvania, 437, 438, 455
Milošević, Božo, 448
Milosh, Anthony, 504
Miloslavić, Edward, 445
Miloslavić, Vlado, 496
Milovićs, 427
Milton, 235
Milwaukee, Wisconsin, 409, 411
Minerva Publishing House, 286
Minneapolis Lakers, 455
Minnesota, 398, 407, 442; University of, 454, 463
Mīr Muḥammad (Meḥmed) ʿAfwī, 326, 344
Mirčeta, Marin, 442
Miroslav, Croatian king, 125
Miroslav, Serbian prince, 381
Miroslavljević, Vlado, 288
Mirth, Karlo, 453
Miše, Jerolim, 288, 289
Mislav, 123
Mississippi, 406, 425, 429, 455; State University, 454
Missouri, 398, 407, 445
Mitchell, Guy (Al Crnić), 443
Mitrović, Stephen N., 428
Mladi Hercegovac, 279
Mladineo, Ivan, 422,448, 456
Mljet, 129, 202, 261, 519
"Mobilization" (*Ustanak*), 10, 24
Modec, Ljudevit, 285
Modriča, 375
Modruš, 255, 398
Modruški, Pavao (Paul of Modruš), 253
Moesia, 384
Mogus, Leo, 454
Mohács, 5, 58, 228, 519
Mohammed II, the Conqueror, 368
Mohović, E., 257
Moldavia, 28
Molière, 215, 218
moneres (vessels), 122
Monessen, Pennsylvania, 408
Mongol, Peter, 427
Mongolian Hun invasion, 363
Montana, 406
Monte Rocherii (Rotherii), Guido de, 255
Montecucculi, Count Raymond, 20, 22
Montenegrin(s), 37, 71, 74, 401, 417
Montenegro, 34, 37, 50, 70, 79, 83, 86, 145, 146, 373, 374, 385, 517
Montreal, Quebec, 483, 488, 491, 492, 494, 495, 497, 498, 500
Moore, Henry, 497
Moors, Moorish, 335, 383, 384
Moravia, 10, 61, 83, 227
Morić, Meho, 306
Moscow, 27
Moses (sculpture), 433, 435
Moslavina, 14, 256
Moson, 31
Mostar, 278, 279, 302, 320, 321, 322, 325, 335, 336, 338, 339, 378, 380, 386
Mostovac, Milivoj, 496
Moutain, Alberta, 502
Moysett, Henri, 87
Mrazović, Milena, 279
Mrnavić, Tomko, 203, 372
Mučnjak, 283
Mueller, Johannes, 221
Muḥammad (the Prophet), 323, 330
Muḥammad Anwarī (Kadić), 328, 344
Muḥammad Boshnāḳ, 325
Muḥammad Cato, 331
Muḥammad ibn Čelebī, 325
Muḥammad ibn Mūsā as-Sarāyī al-Bosnawī, 325, 326, 344
Muḥammad Hawāʾī Üskūfī, 329, 344
Muḥammad, Islamović, 331
Muḥammad Muḥtashim Shaʿbān-Zāde (Šabanović), 325, 331, 345
Muḥammad Mujagić, 331
Muḥammad Nergisī as-Sarāyī, 327, 328, 331, 352
Muḥammad (Meḥmed) Rafīḳ Efendī (Hadžiabdić), 325, 345
Muḥammad Rashīd (Hafizović), 325
Muḥammad (Meḥmed) Ṭāhir Boshnāḳ, 327
Muḥammad Wahbī al-Bosnawī, 331
Muḥyi-ʾd-Dīn ibn-ʿArabī, 325
Mulabdić, Edhem, 380

Mulić, Ismail, 321
Mulih, Juraj, 234, 266
Munich, 252, 451, 519
Murād Beg Tardić, 336, 378
Muradbegović, Ahmed, 319
Muratori, Lodovico Antonio, 263
Murko, Matthias, 307
Murska, Ilma de, 442
Murtaḍā Pasha, 328
Murter, 143, 150, 519
Murvar, Vatroslav, 452
musāfirkhāne (hospice), 322, 334
musandera, 322
Musavat, 280
Muscovites, 28
Muslī-ad-Dīn ibn ᶜAlī, 379
Muslim(s), 8, 9, 11, 14, 37, 280, 312, 497; begs, leaders, 380, 389; in Bosnia-Hercegovina, 304, 305, 312, 326, 367–81; calendar, 302; Croatian(s), 67, 70, 207, 308, 313, 333, 338, 379, 386, 389, 408, 459, 493; culture, way of life, 311, 312; dwellings, 321–3; folk poetry, 306, 307, 312; folk tales, 319; Gegas, 308; homes, 320; literature, 321; party, 380; peasants, 321; students, 380; tombs, 336; writers, 328; *see also* Islam(ic)
Muslimanska sloga, 280
Mustaf-Aga, 309, 310, 311
Muṣṭafā al-Aḳhiṣārī, 325
Muṣṭafā al-Ḥāfiẓ, 331
Muṣṭafā al-Khurramī, 326, 347
Muṣṭafā ᶜAlī, 379
Muṣṭafā Ayyūbī-Zāde, *see* Muṣṭafā ibn Yūsuf al-Mostāri
Muṣṭafā ibn Ibrāhīm al-Mostārī, 331
Muṣṭafā ibn Ismāᶜīl, 331
Muṣṭafā ibn Yūsuf al-Mostārī Ayyūbī-Zāde, 324–8 *passim*, 345
Muṣṭafā Ladunnī, 327, 353
Muṣṭafā Mukhliṣī Boshnāḳ, 327, 353
Muṣṭafā Pasha Bosnawī, 331
Muṣṭafā Ṣidḳi Ḳara-Beg, 324, 327, 345
Mustaj Beg of Lika, 308
Mustang (plane), 461
Mužina, Mate, 426
Mužina, Zdravko, 415, 422
Myriam press, 258

Nadažd (Nadasdy), Ban, 267
Nagodba (Compromise), 47–50, 58–9
nāj (*diple*), 318
Najjār Ḥājj Ibrāhīm, 339
Nalješković, Nikola, 184, 188, 191
Nalley (Narančić), Marcus, 456
Nametak, Alija, 307
Nanaimo, British Columbia, 480, 488, 491, 500, 502
Nani, F., 378
Naples, 133, 375, 519
Naples, Ludovico of, 333
Napoleon (Bonaparte), 33, 34, 36, 37, 38, 134, 137, 379
Napoleonic: Illyrian Provinces, 137; Wars, 137, 139
Napredak, 422
Narančić (Marcus Nalley), 456
Narick, Emil, 454
Narick, Steve, 454
Narodna Odbrana, 66, 67, 68
Narodna Tiskara, 257
Narodne (ilirske) novine, 75, 268, 269, 282
Narodni Glasnik, 420
Narodni List (Zadar), 273
Narodni List - National Gazette (New York), 79, 422, 486
Narona (Vid), 122
Narrantani or Mariani, 123–5, 127, 128
Naš Put, 493
Naša Nada, 416, 421, 459, 493
Naša Sloga, 259
Našice, 281
Naṣr-ad-Dīn Khwāja, 319
Naṣūḥ ibn ᶜAbdallāh (Ḳarā-Göz) as-Silāḥī al-Wisoḳawī al-Miṭrāḳī, 325, 327, 328, 330, 345
National Academy of Design, New York, 435
National Academy of Fine Arts, 439
National Council (Zagreb, 1918), 92, 93, 95
National Party (Nationalists), 39, 44, 45, 47, 52
National (Printing) Press, 264–7
National Shrine of the Immaculate Conception (Washington), 434, 459
Nativity: of the Blessed Virgin (parish), 409; of Saint Mary (parish), 408
Nazi(s), 87
Near East, 367, 372, 384
Nebraska, 407
Nedelišće, 195, 262, 273
Nedić, Martin, 276
Neidhardt, Juraj, 339
Nelson, British Columbia, 491, 502, 503
Nemanjići or Nemanjić dynasty, 381 386
Nemec, Slavko, 448

Nemirov, 27
Neolithic, 119
Neralić, Charles (Dragutin), 504
Neretva, 278
Neretva River, 15, 120, 123, 129, 138, 139, 321, 335, 337, 519
Netherlands, 5, 33, 519
Nevada, 407
Nevesinje, 309, 380
New Democratic Party (Canada), 499
New England States, 406
New Jersey, 414, 422
New Mexico, 406, 423
New Orleans, 396, 414, 426
New Testament, 194
New Waterford, Nova Scotia, 483, 491, 502
New Westminster, 491, 492
New York (City), 77, 79, 397, 406, 409, 417, 419, 422, 423, 430, 431, 436–9 *passim*, 449, 450, 460; harbor, 429; Institute of Musical Art, 442; Rangers (hockey team), 455; World's Fair, 495
New York (State), 406, 451, 460
Newton, 222
Nezavisna država Hrvatska (Toronto), 493
Nezavisna Hrvatska Država, 420, 421
Niagara Falls, Ontario, 485, 487
Nibelungenlied, 307
Nicolini de Sabio, 253, 261
Nikolić, M., 442
Nikolić, Vinko, 451
Nikšić, 389
Nikšić, J., 501
Nirić, Nikola T., 453
Niš, 158
"Nizamski rastanak," 318
Nizeteo, Antun, 451
Njegoš, Petar Petrović, 303
Njegovan, Maximilian, 144
Nobel Prize, 303, 320, 446
Nodier, Charles, 313
Noranda, Quebec, 481, 488, 491
Norfolk, Virginia, 397, 432
Norman ruler of Sicily, 126
North America, 62, 499
North Carolina, 395, 446
North Dakota, 407
Northcliff, Lord, 87
Northeastern Tool and Die Co., 455
Northwest Territories (Canada), 480, 490
Northwestern University, 445, 454
Norwegian, 502
Nosic, Michael, 457
Notre Dame, Indiana, 433, 435, 455, 499
Nova Evropa, 287
Nova Gradiška, 281
Nova Scotia, Canada, 483, 488, 491, 501, 502
Nova Ves (Nova Villa), part of Zagreb, 267
Novak family, 252
Novak, Jan, 270, 287
Novak, Vjenceslav, 286
Novi, Bosnia (on Una River), 23, 27, 309, 310
Novi Behar, 380
Novi List, 56, 280, *see also Riječki Novi List*
Novi Pazar, 368
Novi Svijet, 408
Novi Vinodolski (Croatian Littoral), 256
Novigrad, 258
Novosel, Antun, 268; his widow, Francisca, 268
Novoselac, Beg, 306
Nukica, 308
Nūrallāh Munīrī al-Beligrādī al-Bosnawī, 325, 328, 346
Nuremberg, 251, 262

Obrovac, 15
Obzor (former *Pozor*, *Zatočnik*, and *Branik*), 269, 270, 287
Obzoraši, 53, 54
Occhi, Carlo Antonio, 271, 272
Ocean Falls, British Columbia, 503
Oceania Corporation, 150
October Diploma, 43–4
Oder River, 157
odžak, 321
Odžak (near Bugojno), 322, 380
Ogramić, Nikola, 372, 382
Ogrizović, Milan, 319
Ogulin, 11, 281
Ohio, 398, 406, 439, 457, 460, 461
Okanagan Valley, British Columbia, 503
Oliver, British Columbia, 491, 503
Olovo, 208
Olson's All American Red Heads, 454
Omaha, Nebraska, 409
"Omer i Merima," 315
Omiš (Almissa), 128, 519
Omišalj, 253
Omrčanin, Ivo, 453

Ontario, 481, 483, 485, 487, 488, 490, 491, 494, 501, 502, 503; Art Gallery of, 497; Association of Art, 497; Museum, Royal, 496; Western-, University of, 496
Opatija, 259, 519
Ophelia, 313
Orbini, Mavro, 206, 212, 217, 225, 261
Oregon, 407, 454
Orient(al), 202, 305, 318, 324, 328, 333, 336
Orlić, Petar, 288
Orseolo, *see* Pietro Orseolo
Oršić, Adam, 36
Oršićs, 18
Orthodox, 34, 52, 54, 280, 312; in Bosnia, 371, 372, 386, 389; Bulgarian, 366; Church, Serbian, 386, 387; clergy, priest(s), 77, 340, 382, 387; Croatians, 388, 408; faith, 381, 386, 388, 389, 462; Greek-, 339, 370, 373; immigrants, 17, 66, 67; monastery, 276; religious review, 279; Rumanian, 229; Serb(ian)(s), 9, 213, 229, 388; settlers, 9; Vlachs, 373, 385
Osijek, 37, 288, 442, 519; and book-printing, 274, 281, 282; and Franciscan Press, 274
Osman, Sultan, 198, 204
Osoba i Duh, 453
Osor, 122, 176
Ossek, Petar, 283
Ostović, M., 504
Osvit, 279
Otley, Yorkshire, 282
Otočac, 15
Otranto, Strait of, 147, 148
Ottawa, Ontario, 491, 497, 499, 502, 504; University of, 496
Otter, General, 486
Ottoman: architecture, 335; artists, 300; conquest, 8, 9, 15; control, rule, 15, 16, 23, 305, 328, 331, 387; Empire, 20, 133, 197, 198, 202, 303, 304, 305, 312, 324, 325, 326, 328, 368, 369, 373, 375, 376, 382, 386; history, study of, 327–8; menace, 3, 20; period, 303, 304; poetry, 328; policy, 9; provocations, 20; raids, 8; sanatoriums, 332; Turkish, 299, 300, 301, 331; Turks, 302, 303, 304, 401; *see also* Turkish
Ottomans, 10, 13, 27, 28, 303, 333; defeated by Zrinskis, 20; and Ferdinand I, 9; on Krbava Polje, 4; and Kupa River, 11; losing soil, 14, 24; at Sisak, 13; in Transylvania, 8, 14; and "Turkish Croatia," 23; and Una River, 14; and Zápolya, 7; and Zsitva-Török Treaty, 19; *see also* Turks
Ovid, 183, 185, 199, 216, 217, 261
Oxford, University of, 434
Oyster Harbor (Ladysmith), on Vancouver Island, 480

Pacific coast, 426, 455, 479, 485, 501
Pacific National Exhibition, 494
Pacta Conventa, 47
Padua, 178, 191
Pag, 138, 205, 519
Pajaro Valley, 427
Pakrac, 281
Pallas, Ivan Bartolomej, 265
Pallet and Chisel Academy, 435
"Palmer's Raids," 415
Palmotić (Palmotta) Dionorić, Jaketa, 202
Palmotić (Palmotta), Junije or Džono, 195, 196, 199–200, 201, 203, 204, 211, 217, 218
Palmotta, *see* Palmotić
Paltašic of Kotor, Andrija (Andreas Paltasichis Cattarensis), 251
Paltasichis Cattarensis, Andreas, *see* Paltašić of Kotor, Andrija
Panama, 154
Pan-German(ic), 73
Pannonia (South), 363, 364
Pannonius, Janus (Ivan Česmički), 178
Pan-Slavism, Pan-Slavist, 39, 68, 213, 214, 225, 261
Pantero, Pantera, 134
Papić, Pavao, 208
Papušlić, Antun, 274
Paris, 60, 84, 179, 221, 417, 430, 519; Art Academy in, 436; Bibliothèque nationale in, 256; and book-printing, 251; Exhibition of 1864, 283; and Ivan Benković, 436; and Kristian Kreković, 439; Peace Conference, 419; Real Estate Federation in, 501
Parisians, 153
Park Falls, Wisconsin, 457
Parma, Ohio, 439
Parry, Milman, 307
Participatius, Ursus, 124
Party of Croatian Rights (Pravaši), 48, 53
Party of Pure Right, 54–5
Pašić, Nicholas, 82

Pasini, *see* Bindoni and Pasini
Paskvan, George, 454
Passarowitz, 27, 34
Patiera, Tino, 442
Patsch, Carl, 303
Pattee, Richard, 460
Paul v, Pope, 371
Paul (bookbinder), 282
Paulist(s), 233–4, 235; cloister, 256; college, 218
Pavešković, Nedo, 515
Pavić, Emerik, 230
Pavić, Nikola, 286
Pavich, Chris, 454
Pavišević, Josip, 230
Pavlić, 461
Pavlinac, Peter, 415
Pazin, 253, 260, 519
Peace River, Alberta, 485, 490
Pearl Harbor, 461
Peć (Serbia), 382
Pećine, 140
Pécs, 58, 178, 519
Peez, Carl, 320, 323
Pejačević, Count, 55
Pelješac (Sabioncello), 128, 137, 138, 519
Pelješac, Maritime Association of, 141
Pellico, Silvio, 227
Peloponnesus, 157
Pennsylvania, 396, 398, 406, 410, 411, 415, 437, 438, 451, 459, 461; State College, 455
Pennsylvania, Croatian Death in, 438
Penticton, British Columbia, 491, 503
Perast, 131, 203, 519
Pergošić, Ivan, 195, 262, 274
Perīshān Muṣṭafā Pasha, 336
Peroš, Mladen, 499
Persian, 299–302 *passim*; arts, 330; language, 324, 326, 328, 332; literature, 323, 332; painting, 330; use of words in Croatian, 301–2, 329
Peru, 439, 456
Pesaro, 261
Peselj, Branko, 452
Pesky, Johnny, 454
Pest "circle," 31
Peter, Bulgarian emperor, 366
Petrarch(ans), 180, 181, 184, 185, 186, 190, 191, 203, 215
Petretić, Petar, 209
Petrinja, 13, 14, 18, 281
Petrović, Branimir, 288
Petrović Njegoš, Petar, 303
Philadelphia, 397, 429, 439, 454
Philip II of Spain, 133
Phillips, Barton Michael (Phillip Michael Bavcevich), 450
Pharos, *see* Hvar
Piave River, 84, 87, 88, 91
Picenum (Piceno), 120
Picture Bute, Alberta, 491
Pierotić, Piero, 442
Pietro Candiano, 124, 125
Pietro Orseolo, Venetian doge, 125
Pietro Tradonico, Venetian doge, 123
Pigafetta, Marco A., 378
Pilon, J. G., 498
Pind Mountains, 385
Pindar, 222
Pintórovich Bey, 314
Piombi (Venetian prison), 223, 227
Pirot, 71
Pittsburgh, 78, 79, 397, 408, 410, 418, 420, 422, 423, 437, 438, 442, 449, 454, 459, 493
Pius v, Pope, 130
Pius XII, Pope, 434, 447
Platonist, 178
Platzer, Josip, 269, 274, 281
Plautus, 190
Plemić, Juraj, 24
Plenkovich, Boris, 439
Plitvice, 15, 519
Počitelj, 321, 335, 337, 338
Podravina, 193, 519
Podravska Slatina, 281
Podrinje (Lower Drina River Basin), 367, 387, 388
Pokupec, Željko, 499
Pokuplje (Kupa River Basin), 480
Pola, *see* Pula
Poland, 6, 21, 213, 227; and lithography, 282; *see also* Polish
Poland-Lithuania, 3
Polić, Martin, 257
Polich, Johnny, 455
Polish (Poles), 80, 83, 163, 390; Committee, 88; kingdom, 61; language, 157, 171; prince, 198; victory, 197; and Vienna, 90; *see also* Poland
Politeo, Captain Vincent, 426
Poliziano, A., 180
Polonia (anc. Apollonia), or Polina, 365
Polyak, Stephen L., 446
Pop Dukljanin (Priest of Dioclea), 182, 199, 365
Popović, M., 504
Popovici, Aurel, 61, 62
Poreč, 258, 518
Porga, 366

Porphyrogenitus, Constantine VII, 176, 364
Port Alberni, British Columbia, 491
Port Arthur, Ontario, 481, 488, 490, 491, 492, 503
Port Colborne, Ontario, 491
Porte, *see* (Sublime) Porte
Posavina (Sava River Basin), 29, 380
Posilović, Pavao, 208
Postružnik, Oto, 288
Potiorek, Oskar, 71
Potočnjak, Franko, 77
"Poturs" (half-Turks), 370–1, 377
Powell River, British Columbia, 503
Požega, *see* Slavonska Požega
Pracatović, Miho, 132
Praevalis, 363
Pragmatic Sanction, 24–9
Prague, 50, 60, 95, 260, 268, 284, 519; University of, 49, 269, 380, 430
Prairie Provinces, 487
Pravaši, 48, 53
Prčanj, Boka Kotorska, 131
Predavec, 9
Pregled, 280
Prekomurje, 193
Premier Mine, British Columbia, 502
Preradović (singing society), 442
Prešeren, France, 313
Pressburg or Pozsony (Bratislava): Hungarian capital, 13; Hungarian (-Croatian) diet at, 32, 38; Peace of, 35
Prettner, Dragutin, 272
Prettner, Ivan Nepomuk, 275, 276
Preveden, Francis, 446
Pribanić, Ivan, 502
Pribićević, Svetozar, 54, 55, 64, 69, 72, 73, 75, 92, 381
Priboevus, *see* Pribojević
Pribojević or Priboevus, Vinko, 206, 261
Primorac (magazine), 257
Primorac, Emil, 496
Primorje, 23, *see also* Croatian Littoral
Primorska Tiskara, 257
Primorski Štamparski zavod, 281
Primović, Paskoje, 201, 203
Prince Albert, Saskatchewan, 480
Prince George, British Columbia, 491, 503
Prince Rupert, British Columbia, 491
Princeton, British Columbia, 491, 502
Prodan, Ivo, 273
Progressive Party (Croatia), 55
Progressive-Conservative Party (Canada), 499
Prohaska, Raymond, 439
Propagation of the Faith, *see* Congregation for the Propagation of the Faith
Prophet (Mohammed), 323, 330
Prophets, book of the, 194
Prosvjeta, 278, 280
Protestant(ism), 16, 18, 39; books, 193, 274; Croatian, 408; literature, 192–4, 256, 261; movement, 192, 193
Prpić, George Jure, 514–15
Prusac, 336
Prussia, Prussian(s), 28, 29, 31, 230, 395
Prvi Dubrovački (ship), 141
Psalms, book of, 216
Pucić Soltanović, Vice, 201
Pučki Prijatelj, 259
Puco (magazine), 408
Puget Sound (Pacific Ocean), 428
Pula, 122, 144, 148, 520; bishop of, 193; navy base, 145, 146; printing press in, 259, 260
Pulci, L., 180
Punic Wars, 121
Pupin, Michael, 52
Purdue University, 454
Pushkin, Alexander S., 313

Quebec, 481, 483, 487, 488, 491, 494, 499, 501, 502
Queipo de Llano, 93
Quosdanovich (Gvozdanović), 33

Raab, 31
Rab, 122, 130, 131, 138, 176, 520; and Baraković, 203; and Captain John Dominis, 426
Rabaša, Marko, 427
Rabatta, General, 136
Rabelais, François, 285
Račić Company, 150
Rački, Franjo, 44, 263
Rački, Gabriel, 422
Rad, 280
Radić, Ante, 60
Radić, Stjepan, 60, 61, 62, 70, 95, 418, 419; and the American Croatians, 417; and the Czechs, 95–6
Radica, Bogdan, 450, 451
Radičić, Nedjeljko, 279
Radivojević, Field Marshal, 37
Radnički list, 280
Radobolja River, 337
Radojica, 308
Radonja, 11

Radoš, John, 455
Radoslavichs, 480
Radovan, Marjorie, 442
Radovinović, Luka, 270
Ragnina, *see* Ranjina
Ragusa, Ragusium: archives, 394; vessels of, 394; *see also* Dubrovnik
Raić, Ivan, 488
Rakóczi, 24
Rakos: Field, 4; resolution, 4
Rakovica, 435
Ramaḍān, 311
Ramaḍān Agha, 339
Ramon y Cajal, Santiago, 446
Rampazetti, G. A., 253
Ramuščak, Milan, 283
Randić, 429
Ranjina (Ragnina), Dinko, 190, 261
Ranjina (Ragnina), Nikša, 180, 185
Ranjina (Ragnina) Songbook, 189
Rankin, Pennsylvania, 408
Rapallo, Treaty of, 419
Rapić, Djuro, 231–2
Raša River, 363
Rascia, 365
Rastić, Daniel, 275
Rastić or Resti, Džono or Junije, 22
Ratkaj, Juraj, 211
Ratkaj or Ratkay, Ivan or Juan, 395, 423–4
Ratković, Franjo, 256
Rauch, Levin, 48
Rauch, Palace (in Zagreb), 288
Rauch, Paul, 59, 62, 63
Reading, Pennsylvania, 429
Rebrovich, Art, 454
Rechberg, Count, 44
Rečica, near Karlovac, 436
Reformation, 192–3, 208, 209
Regina, Saskatchewan, 480, 487, 491, 503
Rehber, 278
Reichsrat (Austrian), 72, 77, 82, 88
Reiner, Antun, 266–7
Reis-Ulema, 380
Reljković, Josip Stjepan, 275
Reljković, Matija Antun, 230–2, 233, 234, 236
Renaissance: in Dalmatia, 175; Italian, 288; and Marin Držić, 188; and Marulić, 182
Renner, Heinrich, 279
Reputin, M., 282
Reserve Mines, Nova Scotia, 483, 491
Rešetar, Milan, 167
Rešetars, 427
Restek, Josip, 288
Resti, *see* Rastić
Reuchlin, J., 179
Revelstoke, British Columbia, 503
Rhine River, 33, 519
Richmond, British Columbia, 491
Rieger, Vilko, 453
Riječki Novi List (Rijeka New Paper), 257, 280, *see also Novi List*
Rijeka, 37, 38, 41, 44, 55, 56, 58, 61, 128, 134, 135, 136, 140, 142, 144, 254, 398, 427, 520; and Italy, 149, 419; Naval Academy in, 144; printing (house) in, 255, 257, 258; Resolutions, 57; shipyards, 143; United Press of, 257, 258
Rinuccini, 196
Risman, Josip, 274
River Bend, Quebec, 491, 503
Rivoli (French ship), 137
Roanoke Island, 395
Rob, Alberta, 503
Robert, G., 498
Roberval, Le Sieur de, 479
Robeson County, North Carolina, 395
Robinson, Therese Albertine Louise, 313
Roch, Ivan, 288
Rochester, Minnesota, 434
Rockefeller Foundation, 446
Rodin, Auguste, 434
Rodzinski, Arthur, 443
Rogatica, 303
Rojnić, Matko, 254
Roman(s), 39, 121; army, 383; in the Balkans, 158, 383, 385; Catholic, 175, 303, 408; cities in Dalmatia, 176; citizenship, 383; colonists, 176; domination, 122; Empire, 363, 383, 384; province, 363, 364; wars, 121; *see also* Rome
Romani, 176
Romanized cities, 176, 177, 186
Romance language(s), 160, 167, 171, 176, 177, 385
Rome, 52, 78, 84, 93, 94, 134, 179, 205, 206, 520; Accademia della Belle Arti, 435, 438, 497; (ancient), 121, 126; and Bošković, 221; and book-printing, 251, 257; and M. Držić, 189; and Glagolitic missal, 252; and Gundulić, 261; and Križanić, 213, 214; and Kunić, 222; and the Orthodox, 229; Papal, 136, 370, 371, 372, 382; and Vrančić, 260; *see also* Roman
Romeo and Juliet, 315, 316

Roosevelt, Franklin Delano, 435, 439, 440
Rosandich, Tom, 455
Rose, 316
Rossi, Josip, 268
Rossland, British Columbia, 502
Rotherii, *see* Monte Rocherii
Roucek, J. S., 406
Rousseau, 222, 285
Rouyn, Quebec, 481, 491, 502, 503
Rovišće, 14
Royal Ballet, Winnipeg, 495
Royal Conservatory of Music, Toronto, 496
Royal Council in Croatia, 267
Royal Hungarian Port Authority, Rijeka, 138, 139
Royal Ontario Museum, Toronto, 496
Roycroft, Alberta, 491, 503
Rožankovski, Vladimir, 282
Rožić, Antun, 274
Rožmanić Press, Kuzma, 270
Rožnay, Samuel, 313
Rudar, Tony, 429
Rudo, 338
Rudolph II, 12, 13, 17
Rudolf, Crown Prince, 56
Rudolf, Franc, 283
Rukavina, Petar, 34
Rumania, 383
Rumanian(s), 60, 61, 81, 86, 158; Istro-, 158; language, 158, 163; Megleno-, 158; Orthodox, 229; refugees (from), 405; of Transylvania, 53
Runeberg, Johann Ludwig, 313
Rushdīya (school), 331
Rusovan, Stjepan, 283
Russia, 28, 38, 60, 66, 68, 70, 71, 74, 77, 81, 84, 86, 88, 90, 181, 364; and Križanić, 213, 214; and London Pact, 78
Russian(s), 38, 39, 40, 67, 77, 80, 81, 140, 163; advance into Moldavia, 28; agents, 72; chronicles, 384; collapse, 90; Front, 71, 74; language, 157, 171, 213; and Montenegro, 37; naval officers, 131; public, 68; and Radić, 61; religious thinkers, 213; Revolution, 84, 415; -Slavonic language, 159, 209; support, 27; translation, 206, 313; (Ukrainians), 401; White-, 157, 163
Russins (Ukrainians), 401
Rustam-Pasha, 378
Ruthenes (Ruthenians) or Carpatho-Russians, 53, 60, 80, 88, 94, 401
Ružička, Kamilo, 288
Rycaut, Sir Paul, 132
Rypka, Jan, 328

Šaban or Saban, Joseph, 459
Šaban or Saban, Lou, 454
sabīl, 337
Sabioncello, *see* Pelješac
Sablić, 429
Sabor (Croatian Diet), 12, 13, 24, 26, 42; and Archduke Karl, 12; and Austro-Hungarian union, 46; Ban responsible to, 48; and Ban Tomašić, 63; and the Central Parliament in Vienna, 46; and clergy and nobility, 31; control, 29; and Croatian constitution, 38; and Croatian Council of Lieutenancy, 30; and Croatian Sovereignty, 95; and emigration, 397, 399; and Ferdinand, 5; and Francis II, 33; and Francis Ferdinand, 69; in Glina, 27; and "Great-Croatian" kingdom, 51; and the Hungarian Council of Lieutenancy, 26, 32; and Hungarian diet (parliament), 32, 38, 39; and Inner Austria, 18; and *iura municipalia*, 26; jurisdiction, 14, 17, 24, 26, 33; and Maria Theresa, 30; and Mobilization, 18; and Paul Rauch, 59; and the Pragmatic Sanction, 28; and President Wilson, 418; and Radić, 60; and Rudolph II, 13; and Serbians, 69; for Slavonia, 39; and the Trialist idea, 53; and the union of Croatian lands, 75; and Unionist Party, 44; in Varaždin, 19, 264; after Zsitva-Török, 19; of 1712, 25; of 1740, 28; of 1797, 34; of 1908, 62
Sacramento Valley, 428
Sacred Heart (parish): in Chicago, 409; in Lackawanna, New York, 409; in Milwaukee, Wisconsin, 409
Sacred Scripture, *see* Bible
Sadiković, Sadik, 332
šadrvan (shadrewān), 337
sagenas (vessels), 125
Saginaw, Michigan, 432
Sagredo, 225
St. Anthony (statue), 434
St. Anthony's (parish): in Los Angeles, 408; in Monessen, Pennsylvania, 408
St. Augustine, Florida, 434
St. Augustine's (parish), 409
St. Benedict College, 454
St. Blaise, 133, 197
St. Boniface, Manitoba, 491

St. Catherines, Ontario, 491
St. Edward's University, 440
St. Francis Xavier, 182
St. Gotthard, 20
St. Gregory, Knight of, 447
St. Jean, Quebec, 496
St. Jerome's (parish): in Chicago, 409; in Detroit, 409; (statue) in Washington, D.C., 434
St. John the Baptist (parish): in Calumet, Michigan, 408, 409; in Kansas City, Kansas, 409, 436
St. Joseph's (parish): in Gary, Indiana, 409; in St. Louis, Missouri, 409
St. Louis, Missouri, 396, 409, 412, 416, 446; Croatian colony in, 413; University, 406, 434, 447
St. Louis Browns, 454
St. Mark, 34, 195
St. Martin in Poljica, 123
St. Martin's Day, 441
St. Mary's (parish): in Steelton, Pennsylvania, 408; in Rankin, Pennsylvania, 408
St. Meinrad, Indiana, 425
St. Nicholas (parish): in Allegheny City, 408; in Cleveland, 408
St. Paul's (parish), 408, 435, 461
St. Petersburg, 61
St. Rochus (parish), 408
St. Stephen's Crown, 5, 26, 38, 56
St. Susan, 232
St. Theresa, 232
St. Vincent's College, 454
St. Vitus (parish), 409
Sts. Cyril and Methodius (parish), 409, 438
Sts. Peter and Paul (parish): in Chicago, 409; in Omaha, Nebraska, 409; in Whiting, Indiana, 409; in Youngstown, Ohio, 409
Salem College, 454
Ṣāliḥ Muwakkit, 328
Ṣāliḥ Ṣalāḥī, 331
Sālim Niyāzī, 331
Salm, Nicholas, 5
Salona, *see* Solin
Salonika or Salonica, 86, 158, 521
Salumonović, Jure, 439
Samarzia, Tony, 454
Samobor, 281, 283
Samouprava, 280
San Antonio Real (village), 424
San Francisco, 396, 408, 414, 422, 426, 428, 436, 440, 456, 462; "Kolo Week," 441; Opera, 442; University, 454
San Francisco de Borja (mission), 424
San Ignacio, Baja California, 424
San Joaquin Valley, 428
San Jose, California, 444
San Pedro, California, 407, 456
Sana River, 3, 368
Sanborn, Wisconsin, 457
Sandžak, *see* Sanjak
Sangilla von Freundsberg (Frundsberg), Ivan Sanf, 274
Sanjak or Sandžak (area of Bosnia), 7, 308, 368, 369, 373, 386
Sanjek, Louis, 450
Sannazzaro, 186, 187
Santa Clara College, 427
Santa Clara Valley, 248
Santa Gertrudis (mission), 424
Sanudo, 372
Sappho, 222
Saracens (Arabs), 124, 302
Sarači, 302
Saračica, 302
Sarajevo, 63, 69, 71, 76, 83, 208, 278, 280, 302, 316, 319, 321, 335, 386, 387; archbishop of, 410; astronomical station in, 332; *bezistān* in, 337; *Dugi sokak* in, 277; founder of, 372; markets of, 372; mausoleum in, 336; mayors of, 380; mosques in, 334, 335; murders of, 63–70; periodicals in, 279, 380; public baths in, 338; public lavatories in, 338; *sabīl* in, 338; school in, 331, 332; University of, 335; water system in, 339
Sarajevski list, 280
Sarajevski večernji list, 280
Šarić, Ago, 308
Šarić, Ivan E., 410
Sarkotić, General, 93
Sarnia, Ontario, 491
Saskatchewan, 480, 485, 487, 490, 491
Sault Ste. Marie, Ontario, 481, 487, 488, 490, 491, 492, 502, 503
Sava River, 8, 12, 14, 28, 36, 37, 38, 71, 157, 228, 256, 371, 519, *see also* Posavina
Savez Hrvatskih Društava u Kanadi (Federation of Croatian Societies in Canada), 493
Savonarola, 179
Savremenik, 285
Saxons, 31
Sayfallāh al-Bosnawī Proho, 324, 346
Sayyid Muḥammad ibn Rajab, 331
Schamberg, Max, 396
Schefferville, Quebec, 491, 499

Schmard, I. B., 279
Schmaus, Alois, 307
Schmerling, Anton, 43
Schmidt, S., 283
Schneider, Artur, 284, 285, 287
Schneider, Ivan, 283
Scholz Press, Antun, 270
Schönbrunn, Peace of, 36, 37
Schönfeld Press, Enrik, 273
Schotter, Josip Ivan, 267
Schreyer, Jacobus, 274
Schulhof, Dragutin Stjepan, 270
Schumacher, Ontario, 481, 487, 488, 490, 491, 492, 499, 500, 502
Schwarzenberg, Felix, 40, 41–3, 60
Sclavi, *see* Slavs
Sclavonia, 366
Scocchi, *see* Uskoks
Scott, Walter, 313
Scotland, 152
Scribner's Magazine, 449
Scutari, 219, 266, 520
Seattle, 444, 455, 456
Second World War, 152–4, 171, 401, 403, 405, 410, 412, 416, 420, 421, 433, 452, 461, 463, 484, 489, 501, 503
Sekul, Steve M., 455
Selkirk, Manitoba, 491
Senečić, Josip, 280
Senefelder, Alois, 281
Senffner, Tom, 454
Senftleben, 283
Senj, 10, 128, 134, 227, 479, 520; bishop of, 6; and book-printing, 254, 257, 281; Captaincy, 15; Grgur of, 255; missal, 255; and Ungaro-Croata, 142; Uskoks of, 135, 136; and Vitezović, 211, 264
Šeper, Franjo Cardinal, 410
Serb-Croatian-Slovene government, kingdom, state, 82, 86, 149, 380, 381, 401
Serbia, 27, 52, 54, 58, 67, 68, 70, 71, 77, 79, 86, 95, 181, 382, 384, 385, 386, 388; and Bosnia, 365; and Bosnia-Hercegovina, 65, 66, 389; part of "Great Croatia," 50; or Great Serbia, 55, 67, 73, 79; and Narodna Odbrana, 66; pre-Turkish, 323; and the Turks, 373
Serb(ian)(s), 37, 38, 52, 55, 62, 65, 69, 70, 71, 76, 77, 79, 82, 157, 158, 163, 303, 363, 364, 380, 381, 385, 387, 400, 405, 417, 419, 462; Academy, 262; agents, 66; anti-, 54; army, 66, 74, 77, 79; and Ban, 365; of Bosnia, 383, 385, 386, 388; of Bosnia-Hercegovina, 65, 89, 367, 387; campaign of 1914, 28; claims, 66, 67; and the Coalition, 59; of Croatia-Slavonia, 50, 54, 228; Croatian-, 55; deputies in Reichsrat, 82; and Dual Monarchy, 67, 83, 90; extremists, 68; in the First World War, 71, 74; flag, 60; government, 77; "Great Serbian," 50, 418; Hapsburg-, 57, 62; immigrants, 17, 386, 388; Independent Party, 54; and Islam, 373; and Khuen, 52; king(dom), 68, 387; language, 77, 157–71 *passim*, 277, 278, 279; literature, 303; minority, 51, 52, 70, 72; nationalists in Americas, 77, 431; officers, 67; and old Illyrians, 39; Orthodox, 9, 213, 229, 381, 386, 387; peasant, speech of, 159; policy, 68; political power, 54, 55; press, 68; refugees, 14; of Serbia, 57, 58; settlers, 9, 36; -Slavonic language, 159; and Slovenes, 89; soldiers, 71, 79; southern Hungary, 50; state, 86, 366; and Strossmayer, 52; and Supilo, 56, 58; weekly, 278, 280; writers, 159; in Zagreb, 60
Serbo-Croatian: and Ban Tomašić, 63; Coalition, 57, 58, 59, 62, 64, 68, 69, 72, 75, 76, 86; "fallacy," 79; identity, 75; language, 158, 159, 171, 312, 489; -Slovenian, 93, 96; unity, 59, 67, 76, 82
Serenissima, 34
Serhat, 308
Sertić, Zdenka, 289
Seton-Watson, R. W., 78, 87
Šešelj, Marko, 278
Šestanović, Omer, 306
Sestanovich, Stephen, 448
sevdalinka, 317
Seven Years War, 33, 228, 230
Sever, Josip, 274
Severin (na Kupi), 29, 30, 429, 480
Severović, Ilija, 448
Seville, 423
shadrewān or *šadrvan*, 337
Shaker Heights, Ohio, 457
Shakespeare, 313
Sharīʿa (canon law), 312
"Shāriḥ al-Fuṣūṣ," 325
Shawkat (Persian poet), 327
Shaykh Saʿdī, 327
Shaykh Yuyo, *see* Muṣṭafā ibn Yūsuf al-Mostārī
Sherbrooke, Quebec, 492

Shishman Ibrāhīm Pasha Medresse, 335
Shtokavian, *see* Štokavian
Šibenik, 126, 179, 205, 520; and America, 394; navy base, 144, 145, 151, 152; canon of, 203; printing presses in, 281; and Šižgorić, 219; and Venice, 128, 130; and Vrančić, 260
Siberia, 213
Sicily, 126
Siena, 188
Sigismund, 128
Sigismund III, Polish king, 198
Sikich, Rudy, 454
Sikoćan, Ivan, 448
Silesia, 10, 61, 83
Silovich, Captain John, 426
Šimunić, Mihajlo, 264
Sinān al-Bosnawī, 339
Sinān Beg Mosque, 335
Sinj, 5, 520
Sinkovich, Frankie, 454
Sinkovich, Joe, 454
Sinovčić, Šime, 448
Sinovčić, Špiro, 487, 488
Sioux, 429
Šipan, 132, 520
Sirovatka, Hinko, 422
Sisak, 8, 14, 60, 281, 520
Sisgoreus, Georgius (Juraj Šižgorić), 178
Sisters of Divine Charity, 409
Sisters of the Precious Blood, 409
Sitović Ljubuški, Lovro, 228, 375
Šižgorić, Juraj (Georgius Sisgoreus), 178
Škarić, Vladislav, 304
Skenderbeg, 266
Skerlecz (Škrlec), Ivan, 64, 417
Skerlecz (Škrlec), Nikola, 32
Školski vjesnik, 280
Skopje, 158, 338, 372, 520
Skradin, 129, 520
Škrinjarić, 274
Škrivanić, A., 422
Škrlec, *see* Skerlecz
Škurić, Luka, 427
Slade or Dolci, Sebastijan, 217
Slano, 132, 133
Slav(s), 41, 122, 123, 124, 363, 364, 441, 444; in the Balkans 363–6; in Dalmatia, 176; Eastern, 158; and Gundulić, 197; Western, Southern, 157, 158
Slavenska, Mia, *see* Ćorak-Slavenska
Slavenska Sloga, 422
Slavic, 34, 52, 65, 73, 78, 157, 158, 165, 166, 170, 171, 177, 181, 199, 206, 213, 214, 219, 225, 230, 313, 363, 376, 383, 385, 453, 463; ethnic groups in America, 421; folk tradition, 319; -German grammar, 231; ghettos, 413; (im)migration, 363, 407; language(s), 177, 217, 451; literatures, 497; Middle Ages, 225; non-, 367, 386, 388, 389; patriotism, 196; population in USA (table), 407; states, 303; western-, 364; *see also* South-Slav
Slavich, John, 456
Slavism, 65
Slav(ic)ization, 171, 177, 389
Slavonia, 5, 6, 20, 24, 25, 41, 50, 51, 54, 195, 213, 374, 440; as a battleground, 7; Border of, 9, 11, 12; counties of, 28, 49; Franciscans in, 226, 228, 230; history of, 234; Jesuits of, 237, 371; literary activity in, 228–33; northern-, 18; Protestantism in, 193; and Reljković, 231; Sabor, 5; after the Treaty of Karlowitz, 23; and Trialism, 63; Turkish-held, 15, 26, 196, 228, 373; and Turks, 7, 8; *see also* Croatia-Slavonia, Triune Kingdom, *and following entry*
Slavonian: authors, 275; Croatians, 7; dialect, 239; immigrants to the USA from, 401; *see also preceding entry*
Slavonic, 39; Church-, 181, 209, 213, 252; Common-, 157; Illyrian Mutual Benevolent Society, 414, 426; lands, 256; -Serbian language, 159
Slavonska Požega or Požega, 519; and book-printing, 280, 281; "circle," 30; county, 28; Franciscan, 230; and the Jesuits, 228, 229; pashalik of, 8; *župa*, 15
Sloboda (daily paper), 257
Slovak(s), 38, 53, 60, 88, 94, 163, 390; Catholicism, 263; language, 157, 171
Slovakia, 263
Slovene(s), Slovenian(s), 37, 55, 79, 83, 157, 163, 264, 396, 397, 398, 401, 405, 408, 417, 418, 462; and Austria-Hungary, 86, 92; and Austrians, 89; clergy, 89; descent, 420, 437; Hussars, 43; Istria, 258, 260; language, 77, 157, 158, 159, 171, 193; leader, 259; National Committee, 90; newspapers, 259; and old Illyrians, 39; press, 258; Protestant literature, 193; and the

Reichsrat, 82; and Reljković, 231; state, 86; translation, 194, 313; in 1918, 91
Slovenia, Slovene lands, 50, 83, 85, 89, 256; and Ivan Benković, 437; and Reformation, 192, 193, 194
Slunj, 15
Šmarje, 258
Smederevo, 386
Smičiklas, Tade, 285, 399
Smiljan, 430
Smithers, British Columbia, 491, 503
Smodlaka, Josip, 72, 75, 77
Smokova, Cape (Vis), 137
Smolensk, Soviet Union, 445
Šoban, 283, 285
Sobieski, John, 202
Sofia, 71, 158
Sofi-Pasha, 378
Šojat, Matija, 448
"Sokol" (organization), 387, 414, 488
Sokolović, Mehmed, 377
Soliman, *see* Sulaymān, Suleiman
Solin, 122, 126, 366, 520
Somek, Stepan, 503
Somod, 31
Sonora Valley, 428
Sophocles, 191, 261
Sopron (county), 31
Sopron, Ignjat (Ignac), 277, 280
Soretić, Miho, 263
Sorgo, *see* Sorkočević
Sorić, Dobroslav, 453
Sorkočević or Sorgo, Antonije, 219
Sorkočević or Sorgo, Ivan Franatica, 217, 218
Šoštarko, Dragutin, 443
South America(n), 397, 427, 450
South Bend, Indiana, 400, 433, 435
South Chicago, 457, 461
South Dakota, 429
South(ern)-Slav(ic), Slavism, 44, 77, 82, 83, 157, 158, 192, 313, 317, 419; epics, 307, 308; federation, union, 418, 444; folk poetry, 313; lands, 261, 306; nationalities, 417; and Ottoman period, 303; state, 405; and Venetians, 251
South Porcupine, Ontario, 491
South Wellington, British Columbia, 491
Southern Oregon College, 453
Southwest (American), 462
Spaho, Fehim, 380
Spain, 4, 5, 24, 27, 133, 423, 453; at Lepanto, 130; Ragusan ships in, 134, 394; and Uskoks, 136
Spalatin, Christopher, 453, 511
Spalatum, 122, *see also* Split
Spanish, 428, 450; domination, 196; flu, 482; language, 164, 170, 299, 424; literature, 222; regime, 19; Succession, War of, 24; translation, 206
Spellman, Cardinal, 460
Spencer, Herbert, 285
Spencer County, Indiana, 425
Speyer, Johannes von, *see* Spira, Giovanni da
Spielberg (prison in Moravia), 227
Spiletak, Ilar, 440
Spindleton (Beaumont, Texas), 432
Spira, Giovanni da (Johannes von Speyer), 251
Split, 77, 122, 126, 138, 180, 186, 214, 261, 366, 498, 520; archbishop of, 193; Bernadin of, 253; and Franjo Lučić, 432; and Hektorović, 185; and Marulić, 181; printing presses in, 281; Romanized, 176; shipyards, 150, 152; and Venice, 128, 130
Srbobran, 54, 55
Srebrenica (Bosnia), 179, 207, 520
Sresović, 427
Srijem, 20, 71, 440, 520; county, 28, 30; southeastern, 23, 27; Serbs of, 71; and Turks, 7
Srijemska Mitrovica, 443, 520
Srpska riječ, 280
Srpska sloga, 280
Stadtmüller, Georg, 307
Stanac, 189
Stanford University, 444, 454
Staniša (architect), 339
Stanković, Petar, 487, 488, 498
Starčević, Ante, 63, 86; anti-Serbian, 54; –Frankist, 62, 64; and "Great Croatia," 45; Party of Right, 45, 48, 53; and Trialism, 55
Starčević, Šime, 258
Starcevich, John, 461
Starigrad (Hvar), 427
Starigrad (near Karlobag), 15
Star-Kist Tuna Company, 456
Staroslaveska Akademija (in Krk), 259
State College, Indiana, 453
Stavka, 74
Steed, Henry Wickham, 78, 87
Steelton, Pennsylvania, 408, 409
Stefan Uroš II Milutin, 381
Stellarton, Nova Scotia, 483, 488, 491

Stepinac, Aloysius Cardinal, 434, 460
Stewart, British Columbia, 502
Stipanović, Ivan, 420, 452
Stipković, Nada, 498
Stjepović (Stepovich), Miho, 455
Stjepović (Stepovich), Mike, 456
Stockholm, 497
Stojanović, Mijat, 280, 285
Stojković or Stay, Benedikt, 222
Štokavian or Shtokavian, 39, 158, 159, 160, 195, 204, 205, 206, 208, 211, 213, 229, 236, 239, 367
Stolac, 338
Straka, Ivan Ignatius, 265
Strambotti(sti), 190
Strasbourg, 251
Straussenberg, Arz von, 87
Stražić, Gjuro, 427
Strobach, 283
Štromar, Franjo, 283
Strossmayer, Josip Juraj, 44, 52, 55, 269, 284, 414
Strug, 15
Strzygowski, Josip, 285
Stulac, Jack, 499
Stulli, Joakim, 206, 239, 271
Stupnik, 259
Stürghk, Count, 72
Styduhar, Joe, 454
Styria(n), 8, 9, 10, 12, 16, 18, 25, 26, 193, 261, 520
(Sublime) Porte, 7, 8, 207, 305
Subotica, 281, 520, *see also* Szabadka
Sudbury, Ontario, 487–93 *passim*, 498
Sudetens of Bohemia, 83
Suić, Jerome, 427
Suko of Udbina, 309, 310, 311
Sulaymān ʿĀrif, 331
Sulaymān Bosnawī, 331
Sulaymān Čučak, 331
Sulaymān Mazāḳī, 331, 353
Suleiman (Soliman), 8, 10, 330, 377
Šulek, Bogoslav, 268
Šulentić, Nikola, 457
Šuljaga, Stjepan, 271
Summerland, British Columbia, 491, 503
Supilo, Frano, 55–8, 75, 77, 78, 82, 257, 280
Suppan, *see* Župan
Sušak, 140, 257, 258, 280, 520; printing presses of, 281
Susjedgrad, 264
Sutjeska, 207, 371
Suzanna, 183, 184
Suzzallo, Henry, 444, 463
Svećenski, Louis, 442
Svijet, 270
Svinjar, 230
Sweden, 18, 21
Swedish, 313
Swift Creek, British Columbia, 503
Switzerland, 425, 433, 520; frontier, 87
Sydney, Nova Scotia, 483, 488, 491, 492, 502
Sylvester Patent, 42
Syracuse, New York, 433, 439
Syracuse, Sicily, 120
Syrmium, 302
Szabadka (Subotica), 58
Szabo, Gjuro, 286
Szakmardi, *see* Zakmardi
Széchenyi, Count Stephen, 38
Székely, Luka, 9
Szent Istvan (vessel), 148
Sziget, 10, 191, 193, 201, 210, 262, 521

Taber, Alberta, 483, 487, 488, 491, 503
Table of Magnates (Upper House), 47
Tacoma, 456
Tadich, John V., 429
Tagliamento River, 363
Ṭāhir and Zuhrā, 315
Ṭāhir Ibrāhīm, 331
Tale Ličanin, 308
tambura, tamburica, 318
Tamburitza Day (Michigan), 441
Tamburitza News, 440
Tanasije (architect), 339
Tanasković, Antun, 448
Tanzlinger-Zanotti, Ivan, 206
Tarahumara Indians, 423
Taranto, 147
Tartaglia, Oskar, 72
Tartars, 256
Tashlī Khan, 334
Tasso, 187, 197, 199, 217, 261
Tegethoff, Admiral, 144
teke (monastery), 333
Telesmanich, Bill, 454
Temesvár, 67
Temple University, 454
Tepfer, E., 279
Ternina, Milka, 442
Tesla, Nikola, 430–1, 432, 433, 434, 436
Teuta, Queen, 121
Teutonic, 85, 157
Teutonicus, Guillelmus, 270

Texas, 406, 432, 440; Christian University, 454; Mid-Continent Oil and Gas Association, 432
Thābit Užičewī, *see* ʿAlāʾ-ad-Dīn
Theocritus, 222
Thirty Years War, 18, 19, 20
Thomas (Tomašić), A. D., 458
Thomson, Manitoba, 502
Thoresani, *see* Torresano
Thugut, Count, 34, 35
Timmins, Ontario, 487, 490, 491, 492
Timok, 71
Tipografija (press), 270, 282, 287, 288
Tiskara katoličkog poslaništva, 278
Tiskarski i Litografični Zavod, 273
Tiskarsko poduzeće (Mani and Mlinar), 273
Tisza, Koloman, 51
Tisza, Stephen, 75, 76
Tivat, 151
Tkalec, 283
Tokay, 6
Tolna, 31
Tomašević, Ernest, 288
Tomasevich, Jozo, 453
Tomašić (Thomas), A. D., 458
Tomašić, Dinko (professor), 447
Tomašić, Franjo (general), 37
Tomašić, Nikola (ban), 63
Tomasich, Andy, 454
Tomić or Tomich, Hugo, 457
Tomić or Tomich, J. E., 278
Tomić or Tomich, Peter, 461
Tomiković, Aleksandar, 232
Tominac, John F., 461
Tomislav, king, 124, 125
Topal Osman Pasha, 277, 280
Topić, Ibro, 307
Topolovac, 14
Torbar, Joseph M., 500
Toronto, Ontario, 452, 483, 485, 487, 488, 490–5 *passim*, 498, 499; Maple Leafs (hockey team), 499; University of, 496, 497
Torresano (Thoresani) de Asola, Andrea, 252, 254
trabakuli, trabaccoli, ships, 139
Tradonico, *see* Pietro Tradonico
Tragurium, *see* Trogir
Trail, British Columbia, 491, 496, 503
Transcona, Manitoba, 481, 491
Transylvania(n), 4, 5, 7, 8, 9, 14, 17, 21, 24, 44, 79, 81, 89, 94, 521
Trattner, Johann Thomas, 267, 274
Trattner Press, 267–8
Trattner-Vinković, 258
Travnik, 219, 320, 335, 339, 386
Trbojević, G., 257
Trebinje, 371, 389
Trentino, 74, 79, 80, 87, 90
Trepše, Marijan, 289
Tresić Pavičić, Ante, 398, 412
Trevisano, Andrea, 271
Trevisano, Matteo, *see* Trevižanin, Matija
Trevižanin (Matteo Trevisano), Matija, 255
Trgovačka Tiskara, 280
Trialism, Trialist(ic), "triarchy," 53, 54, 55, 61–5 *passim*, 69, 76, 83, 96, 417
Trieste, 10, 135–9 *passim*, 141, 142, 144, 149, 446, 521; Gymnasium in, 432; non-Croatian businessmen in, 142; Port Authority in, 138; printing in, 258, 259, 273
Triestina, Navigazione Libera, 149
Tripkovich, 149
Triple Alliance, 78, 145
Tripoli, 219
Triune Kingdom (Croatia, Slavonia, Dalmatia), 3–6 *passim*, 10, 12, 14, 15, 17, 18, 19, 21, 29, 35, 41, 42, 55, 61, 62, 89; and Bosnia-Hercegovina, 50, 61, 379; and German language, 31; under Hungarian pressure, 24, 33; (in)dependence vis-à-vis Hungary, 25, 28, 30, 31, 43, 44, 49; and Magyar language, 32; and Military Frontier, 52; and the Monarchy, 63; and Paul Rauch, 59; and Protestants, 39; remnants of, 23; representation of, 27, 47; part of Serbian-Croatian-Slovenian state, 93; and Vienna, 38, 43
Trnava (Slovakia), 263
Trnski, Ivan, 276
Trogir, 122, 206, 263, 521; and boatbuilders, 143, 150; Romanized, 176; and Venice, 128, 130
Trogir, Ivan, bishop of, 202
Trogrančić, Franjo, 511–12
Trol, lithographer, 282
Trpimir, Duke, 125
Trsat, 257
Tršćanski, Lloyd, 259
Truax, Saskatchewan, 503
Trubar, Primož, 193, 194
Truman Administration, 399
Trumbić, Ante, 57, 77, 79, 80, 82, 149

Tubero, Corrinus (Aloysius de Cerva), 179
Tübingen, 261
Tucić, Šime, 426
Tucić, Srdjan, 449
Tudišević, Martin, 218
Tulane University, 454
Tunis, 133
Turan-Altaian, 364
turba (mausoleum), 333
Turčić, Gašpar, 254
Turco-Turanian, 364
Turkalj, Grgo, 448
Turkalj, Josip, 435
Turkalj, Zdenka, 288
Turkey, 90, 135, 137, 138, 302, 305, 362, 372, 378, 389
Turkish: anti- (feeling), 210; aqueducts, 337; arts, 330; attacks, 5, 8, 20, 21, 23, 196; Austrian wars, 228; border, 24; bridges, 337; collossus, 27; conquest, 3, 128, 171, 367; control, rule, 3, 10, 28, 134; Croatia (northwestern Bosnia), 14, 23, 32; "cultureless past," 330; Dalmatia, 15; defeat, 202, 208; domination, period, power, reign, 11, 13, 50, 85, 130, 175, 196, 198, 201, 207, 227, 228, 230, 231, 235, 236, 237, 276, 277, 303, 318–21 *passim*, 323, 329, 339, 368, 373, 375; fleet at Lepanto, 130; forays, 21; forces, 81, 140, 255; government, 368, 373, 386; horse, 3, 20; intervention in Hapsburg-Zápolya struggle, 7; Islamic tribe, 303; losses, retreat, 19, 21, 23, 25, 234; meddah-burlesques, 319; officials, 9; origin, 233, 374; pashalik, 7; pressure, 4, 8; provinces, 8, 175; Republic, 301; sultan, emperor, 132, 382; tyrants, 183; vassal state, 14, 17; -Venetian wars, 224; *see also* Ottoman *and following entry*
Turkish (language): 277, 278, 302, 305, 324, 325, 326, 328, 362, 367, 368, 371, 378; chronicles, 304, 385; -Croatian grammar, 278; expression, words, 203, 231, 301; Latin alphabet used for, 301; literature, 323; poetry, 327; songs, 317; use of words in Croatian, 301–2, 329
Turks, 3, 5, 24, 27, 28, 65, 66, 67, 204, 224, 225, 256, 325, 372; in Albania, 38; "big war" against, 20, 27, 28; in Bosnia, 303, 305, 318, 320, 323, 367, 372, 376, 377, 381, 382, 385; in Bosnia-Hercegovina, 320, 362, 367, 368, 369, 383, 386, 388; in Buda, 7; and the Croatian language, 378; in Dalmatia, 34, 128, 129, 178; and "Friar George," 8; and Holy League, 135; in Hungary, 8; invaders, 15, 19, 191, 256; and Lucić, 184; and Marulić, 182; at St. Gotthard, 20; and Serbs, 373; and Uskoks, 136; and Virovitica, 14; and Venice, 129, 196, 223; and Vlachs, 385, 386, 389; *see also* Ottomans
Tuscan(y), 184, 188
Tuzla, 207, 208, 375
Tvrtko, Bosnian ruler, 367, 387
Twain, Mark, 431
Typografija, 270, *see also* Tipografija
Tyre, William, archbiship of, 177
Tyrol, 10, 36, 363

Učiteljska zora, 280
Udatny, Vladimir, 288
Udbina, 256
Udbina, Suko of, 309, 310
Ukraine, Ukrainian(s), 157, 158, 163, 197, 213, 390, 401
Ukrina River, 375
ʿUmar Efendī, Ḳāḍī of Novi, 328, 346
ʿUmar Muʿallim Nājī, 326
Una River, 8, 9, 13, 14, 23, 27, 30
Ungaro-Croata, 142, 150
Ungnad, Ivan (Hans), 10, 193, 257, 261
Union Army, 427
Unionist (Party), 44, 45, 47, 48, 58, 60, 63, 64
United Printing Company, 457
United States, 77, 79, 82, 85–8 *passim*, 425, 521; Army, 459; Congress, 439, 461; Croatian immigrants to, 394–464 *passim*; 483, 486, 496; Croatian immigrants to Canada from, 479–82 *passim*; Croatian papers in, 475–8, 485, 486; Department of State, 355; Navy, 427; Patent Office, 430; *see also* America, American
U.S.S. *South Dakota*, 461
U.S.S. *Utah*, 461
Upper Austria, 10, 13
Upton, Long Island, 448
Urach (Bavaria), 194, 257, 261, 262
Uremovich, Emil, 454
Ursus Participatius, 124

Uskoks (Italian Scocchi), 134–7
Üsküb, *see* Skopje
Usmiani, Mirko, 453
Ustanak (Mobilization), 10, 24
Ustikolina, 303
Utah, 407
ʿUthmān Bosnawī, 331
ʿUthmān ibn ʿAbd-ar-Rahmān al-Beligrādī, 327, 333, 346
Utišen(ov)ić (Utješenović), Juraj (George), 6, 378
"Utišteonica od Vladanja," 273
Utješenović, *see* Utišenić
Uzovich, John, 427

Vaić, Fedor, 288
Valave, 80
Valdemin, Val de vino or Vinodol, *see* Vinodol
Val d'Or, Quebec, 491, 502
Vallachs, *see* Vlachs
Vallaux, Camille, 120
Valona, 147, 148, 365
Valvasor, Johann Weikhard Freiherr von, 264
Vančik, Vladimir, 452
Vancouver, British Columbia, 480, 486, 487, 488, 490, 492, 494, 495, 498, 501
Vanderbilt University, 454
Vanka, Makso (Maksimilijan), 437–8
Varaždin, 6, 194, 262, 424, 521; Border, 15, 23; "circle," 30; Dicasterium in, 30; Generality, 15, 16, 17, 24; printers, 269, 281; printing presses in, 267, 273, 274, 281; Sabor, 19; and Royal Council, 267; *župa*, 18
Varcar-Vakuf, 335
Vareš, 208
Varešanin, Croatian general, 67
Vasić, Milan, 68
Vasić and Horvat Bookshop, 286
Vasilj, Kvirin, 452
Vasilj, Vendelin, 452
Vasvár, 21
Vatan, 278
Vatican, 257
Večer, 270
Vecki (Djurkovečki), Victor G., 445
Velebit, 15, 412, 521
Velikanović, Ivan, 232, 275
Veliki Tabor, 423
Velimirović, Nicholas, 77
Velzek, A., 287
Venetian Press, 253, 255
Venetian(s), 7, 15, 34, 124, 196, 401; army, 191, 223; claims, 234; in Crete, 129; fleet, shipping, 123–31 *passim*; governor, 378; (and Istrian) cities, 124, 125, 128, 192; and Kotor, 202; losses, 19; navigation, 123; prisons, 227; purchase of Dalmatia, 128; Republic, 34; rule in Dalmatia, 129–31, 176, 186, 203, 206, 225, 255; and South Slavic peoples, 251; tribute, 125; and Trpimir, 125; wars, 223, 224; *see also* Venice
Venice, 21, 134, 135, 139, 144, 147, 182, 183, 519; Arsenale in, 127; book printing and publishing, 210, 251–4, 256, 260, 261, 263, 270, 271, 277, 312; in Dalmatia, 3, 15, 34, 124, 125, 126, 128–37 *passim*, 214, 223, 443; diplomacy of, 7; doge of, 124, 224; and Dubrovnik, 175; and Grabovac, 223; and Grgur of Senj, 255; at Lepanto, 130; and Turks, 196; and Uskoks, 135, 136, 137; and Zvonimir, 126; *see also* Venetian
Venturini, 136
Vera Cruz, Mexico, 423, 424
Verantius, *see* Vrančić
Verböczy, István (Stephen), 4, 194, 262
Verdun, 80, 81, 86
Veress, Blasius, 262
Vergerije, Ivan, 193
Vergerije, Petar, 193
Verona, 223
Veszeli (Wesely or Wesseli), Adalbert Wilhelm, 266
Veszprem, 31
Vetranović (Vetranić) Čavčić or Vetrani, Mavro, 184–5, 191, 203
Veža, Mladen, 288
Victoria, British Columbia, 491
Victorious (British ship), 137
Victory Loan Bonds, 503
Vid, 122
Vida, Girolamo, 180, 200, 211
Vidović, 429
Vidrić, 286, 288
Vidulichs, 480
Vienac, 436
Vienna (Viennese), 7, 9, 10, 12, 27, 28, 34, 35, 38, 75, 83, 87, 91, 262, 263, 264, 380, 384, 423, 425, 521; Archives of, 211; and Ivan Benković, 436; and Berlin, 78; and Borders, 17,

18; casting-house in, 287; Central Parliament in, 45, 46; centralizing tendencies of, 39; Congress of, 38; and Constantinople, 13; and Croatian aristocrats, 32; and Croatian regiments, 89; and Croatians, 57, 64, 73; Council, 23; Court, 14; and Entente Powers, 90, 91; farces, 235; and the French, 35, 36, 38; and Galicia, 90; and General Rukavina, 34; and Glagolitic missal, 252; and Istrian books, 258; journals of, 51; and Kuhačević, 227; Military Academy, 227; Musical Institute, 442; non-Croatian businessmen in, 142; officialdom, 35; and Radić, 61; Reichsrat in, 43, 44; revolution in, 40; and Serbia, 66; siege of, 213; Steed in, 87; and Turkish defeat, 202, 208; Turks advancing to, 40; University of, 445; and Vitezović, 265; warns Zrinski, 20, 22; wars, 373, 376, 379, 389
Vietnam, 462
Vijenac, 269
Vilajetska Štamparija, 277, 278
Vinkovci, 230, 275, 281
Vinodol, 194, 364
Virant, Lina, 288
Virgil(ian), 180, 182, 199, 200, 216, 217, 221
Virginia, 447
Virje, 281
Virovitica, 9, 14; county, 28, 30; old *župa,* 15; printing presses in, 281
Vis (Lissa), 123, 137, 144, 204, 521
Višegrad, 337
Visnic, Larry, 454
Visoko, 320, 321
Vitaliani-Janković Press, 273
Vitaljić, Andrija, 204
Vitezović, Pavao Ritter, 211–13, 223, 225, 234, 238, 239, 264, 265
Vittorio Veneto, 93
Vjesnik (Messenger), 493
Vjesti Press, 273
Vjestnik, 280
Vlach(s) or Vallach(s) (Vlasi), 9, 367, 373, 374, 383, 384, 385, 387; Mauro-, 384, 385, 386, 388, 389; Statute, 15–17
Vlacić-Franković, Matija (M. Flatius Illyricus), 19
Vladislav II Jagellon, 4
Vlahović, J. Marion, 442
Vlahović, Vlaho, 448, 453
Vlasi, *see* Vlachs
Vlaška Street (Zagreb), 264
Voïard, Anne Elisabeth, 313
Voigt, Leopold, 265
Vojna Krajina, *see* Military Frontier
Vojniković-Pezić, Salko, 306
vojvoda (captain, leader): in Military Frontier, 16; of Transylvania, 4, 7
Vojvodić, Viktor, 448, 449
Vojvodina, 54, 373
Volarić, Josip, 259
Volhynia, 80, 86
Volksdeutsche, 403
Volosko, 259, 260, 521
Voltaire, 22
Voralberg, 10
Vorkapić, Slavko, 443
Vošicki, Vinko, 281
Vračan, Josip, 274
Vramec, Antun, 195, 262, 274
Vrančić, Anton, 378
Vrančić or Verantius, Faust, 205, 260
Vranić, Antun, 235
Vranić, Mladen, 496
Vranje, 310
Vrbas River, 14, 27, 32, 337
Vrbnik, 254, 259
Vrhbosna, 279, 280
Vrhovac, Maksimilijan, 268
Vrili (near Kupres), 322
Vrlika, 223
Vrpolje, Slavonia, 433
Vuchich, Steve, 454
Vujica, Stanko, 453
Vukamich, Nick, 455
Vukašinović, Pavao, 270
Vuk Karadžić, *see* Karadžić, Vuk Stefanović
Vukić, I. F. Lupis, 422
Vukovar, 281, 521

"Wacht am Rhein," 319
Wagram, 36
Wahbī Smailkadić, 331
Waine, Alberta, 501
Waite and Savile Ltd., 282
Wake Forest College, 454
Waldstätten, 87
Warasdiner, 74
Washington (D.C.), 79, 84, 410, 418, 432, 446, 448, 449, 452; Capitol Building, 439; and Kreković, 439; Library of Congress, 252; Redskins

(football team), 455; Rock Creek Cemetery, 432; White House, 440
Washington (state), 407, 444, 455
Washington Place (Honolulu), 426
Waterloo, Iowa, 457
Watsonville, California, 427, 456
Wawa, Ontario, 491
Wayne, Alberta, 484, 502, 503
Weasel (British ship), 137
Wedgewood, British Columbia, 502
Weimar, 255
Weiss, Gašpar, 258
Weitz, Gaspar, 275
Weitz, Ivan Krstitelj, 265–6
Weitz, Maria Anna, 266
Wekerle, 59
Welland, Ontario, 481, 488, 490, 491, 492, 503
Wellington, British Columbia, 480, 503
Werthes, Friedrich August Clemens, 313
Wesely or Wesseli, *see* Veszeli
Wesse (Besse), Andrija, 267
Wesselenyi, Ferenc, 264
West Allis, Wisconsin, 409
West(ern): allies, 153; (American), 462, 487; Christianity, 213; civilization, 435; countries, world, 154, 304; culture, 171, 202; -minded, 327; pattern, 316; powers, 379
West Virginia University, 454
Western Reserve University, 316
Westinghouse, George, 430
White, governor, 395
White House, Washington, 440
White Plains, New York, 460
Whiting, Indiana, 409, 416
Widewater, Alberta, 491
Wiener Neustadt, 22, 202, 210, 521
Wilkes College, Pennsylvania, 451, 452
Willard, Wisconsin, 457
Wilson, President, 88, 89, 91, 92, 418, 419, 439, 444
"Windisch" Border, 11, 15
Windsor, Ontario, 439, 483, 485, 488, 490–4 *passim*, 498, 502
Winnipeg, Manitoba, 481, 487, 488, 491, 492, 498, 499; Blue Bombers (football team), 499; Press Club, 498; Royal Ballet in, 496
Wisconsin, 398, 406, 454, 457
Woditzka, Ivan, 273
Würtemberg, 261; Christoph, Duke of, 261
Wuṣlaṭī, ʿAlī-Beg Užičewī al-, 327, 350
Yaḥyā Bosnawī, 331
Youngstown, Ohio, 409, 420, 454, 457
Yugoslav, 37, 52, 73, 77, 78, 380; Academy, 253, 269, 284; -American Navigation Company, 150; Committee,76–82, 84, 417, 418, 449; folklore, 319; idea, 37,77,82,86,89; Kingdom, 412; literature, 320; movement, 50, 76; nation, 78, 489
Yugoslavia, 149, 151, 158, 159, 387, 390, 401, 402, 403, 406, 420, 423, 443, 449, 498; coast, 152, 153; Communist, 420; constitution, 171; Foreign Service, 450; government, 487; languages of, 159; merchant fleet, 150; navy, 151, 153; neutrality in Second World War, 152, 153; ports, 149, 153; refugees from, 404, 405, 433; Royal, 381, 387, 390
Yugoslavism, Yugoslavist, 52, 55
Yukon, Canada, 484, 501
Yūsuf Pasha Mosque, 335

Zabavna biblioteka," 285
Zadar or Zara, 37, 44, 122, 138, 144, 186, 214, 278, 521; and Baraković, 203; bishop of, 209, 255; and book-printing, 272–4; and Budinić, 205; and Krnarutić, 260; and Louis the Great, 127; and Paris Peace Conference, 419; and Pope Alexander III, 176; Resolution, 57; Romanized, 176; Treaty of, 128; and Venice, 127, 128, 130; and Zoranić, 186, 260
Zadrijevac, Marijan, 504
Žagar, Albert, 437
Žager, 283
Zagorje, 11
Zagreb, 9, 11, 26, 44, 46, 49, 54, 63, 70, 79, 144, 159, 194, 195, 234, 235, 256, 285–9 *passim*, 398, 416, 419, 445, 446, 449, 463, 493, 521; Academy of Arts,435, 497,537; Academy of Sciences, 237; (arch)bishop(ric) of,6,209, 234, 371, 410; Atomic Institute, 434; and Ivan Benković, 436; and Bernardin's *Lectionarium*, 253; and book-printing, 263–70, 281, 282; canon of, 211, 262; capital (of a "Great Croatia"), 50, 60; "circle," 30; county, 37; Domobrans, 80; Franciscan monastery, 265; German paper in, 268; and Glagolitic missal, 252; Gradac Hill, 264; graphic artists from,

288; history of, 234; Jesuits, 264, 265, 423; Kaptol, 265, 267, 282; musical institute, 442; "National Council" in, 92; Opera, 443; printing presses in, 281; Radićs in, 60; supreme court in, 433; treason trials, 58; University of, 159, 269, 283, 380, 445, 447; University Library, 262, 283; and Vienna, 93; *župa*, 18
Zagreb (artistic album), 287
Zaharia, Emilia, 496
Zahumlje, 374, 381
Zajc, J., 504
Zaječar, 71
Zajednica, *see* Croatian Fraternal Union
Zajedničar, 421, 423, 486
Zakarīya ibn Ḥusayn ibn Masīḥ, 331
Zakarīya ibn ʿAbdallāh Sukkarī, 331, 354
Zakmardi (Szakmardy) Dianovečki, Ivan, 264
Zaladska county, 30
Zaninović family, 456
Zaostrog, 224
Zápolya, John, 4–7 *passim*, 14; his son, 8
Zara, *see* Zadar
Zarza, Lou, 455
Zaufar, Joseph, 496
Zay, Francis, 378
Zborovčić, Benedikt, 253
Zdelar, Frano, 263
Zec, Miloš, 269
Zeleznak, Mike, 454
Železno (Eisenstadt), 31, 517
Zellick, George, 454
Zellinger, Alojz, 263
Zemaljska tiskara u Zagrebu, 269
Zemun, 277, 280, 521
Zenta, 58, 146
Žepa River, 337
Žerajić, Bogdan, 67
Zerauscheg (Cerauschegg or Cerauscheg), Franjo Zaverije, 267, 283
Zibilić, Luke, 426
Zibilić, Miho, 426
Zigich, Milan, 503
Zindich, Nich., 503
Zitten or Martholosen, 386
Zivich (Živčić), Fritzie, 455
"Živila Hrvatska" (tamburitza orchestra), 440
Život, 285
Zlatarić, Dominko (Dinko), 191, 261
Zlatarić, Jerolim, 371
Zlatarić, Marin, 217
Zmajević, Vicko, 210
Znika, Ivan, 265
Zolović, Josip, 443
"Zora" (singing society), 414, 442
Zoranić, Petar (Albioni or De Albis), 186, 192, 203, 260
Zorich, George, 454
Zorkin, Mladen Giunio, 499, 500, 501
Zotti, Frank, 412, 422, 463
Zrin, 14
Zrinski(s), 9, 11, 18–23 *passim*; Frankapan conspiracy, 19–23, 441, 444; and Montecucculi, 22; properties, 14, 23
Zrinski, Juraj, 262, 273
Zrinski, Katarina, 210, *see also* Katarina-Zrinska
Zrinski, Nikola, 10, 20, 21, 192, 193, 195, 201, 210, 211, 212, 262
Zrinski, Petar, 20, 21, 201, 210
Zrmanja River, 8, 15, 128, 134, 521
Zsitva-Török, Treaty of, 14, 15, 19, 20
Zubak, Ante, 448
Zudenigo, Charles, 453
Žumberak, 15, 480
Žunić, Nicholas: Sr. 500; Jr. 500, 504
župa, 18, 23, 256
Župan or Suppan, Franjo, 268, 269, 283
zurna, 318
Zuzorić, Cvijeta (Fiora Zuzzeri), 190
Zuzzeri, *see* Zuzorić
Zvetina, John A., 447
Zvierkovich, John, 428
Zvizdović, Angjeo, 368
Zvonimir, 126, 414, 493
Zvono–La Cloche, 493
Zvornik, 378, 386